THE
PATIENT SAFETY
HANDBOOK

Edited by

Barbara J. Youngberg, BSN, MSW, JD
University HealthSystem Consortium
Oak Brook, IL

Martin Hatlie, JD
Partnership for Patient Safety
Chicago, IL

JONES AND BARTLETT PUBLISHERS
Sudbury, Massachusetts
BOSTON   TORONTO   LONDON   SINGAPORE

World Headquarters
Jones and Bartlett Publishers
40 Tall Pine Drive
Sudbury, MA 01776
978-443-5000
info@jbpub.com
www.jbpub.com

Jones and Bartlett Publishers Canada
2406 Nikanna Road
Mississauga, ON L5C 2W6
CANADA

Jones and Bartlett Publishers International
Barb House, Barb Mews
London W6 7PA
UK

Library of Congress Cataloging-in-Publication Data

The patient safety handbook / edited by Barbara J. Youngberg and Martin Hatlie.
        p. ; cm.
    ISBN 0-7637-3147-1 (alk. paper)
    1. Medical errors—Handbooks, manuals, etc. 2. Medical care—United States—Quality control—Handbooks, manuals, etc.
        [DNLM: 1. Medical Errors—prevention & control. 2. Patient Care—standards. 3. Safety—standards. WB 100 P298 2003] I. Youngberg, Barbara J. II. Hatlie, Martin J.

    R729.8.P38 2003
    610—dc21

                                                                2003013864

Production Credits
Publisher: Michael Brown
Production Editor: Julie C. Bolduc
Associate Editor: Chambers Moore
Associate Marketing Manager: Joy Stark-Vancs
Manufacturing Buyer: Therese Bräuer
Composition: Interactive Composition Corporation
Cover Design: Kristin E. Ohlin
Printing and Binding: Malloy Lithographing, Inc.
Cover Printing: Malloy Lithographing, Inc.

Printed in the United States of America

07 06 05   10 9 8 7 6 5 4 3 2

CONTENTS

FOREWORD

*In memoriam, Betsy A. Lehman, 39, Boston Globe health
columnist, accidental death by fourfold dose of medication,
Dana Farber Cancer Institute, Boston, Massachusetts,
December 3, 1994.*

In the silent aftermath of personal tragedy, thousands upon thousands of family members struggle over the loss or disablement of loved ones due to slips in the hands of our healers. We appeal now, more boldly than ever before, for modern hospital care to become a safer harbor.

We learn with dismay that today's business-like managed care industry takes a toll of up to 98,000 accidental deaths each year from medical errors in American hospitals, not including outpatient settings. As cited in the Institute of Medicine's report *To Err Is Human,* this tragic and shameful record exceeds U.S. deaths from vehicle accidents, breast cancer, or AIDS.

These unsettling realities are brought home all too vividly to families whose loved ones are gone now due to fatal medical error or who were harmed by a medical system they trusted. This aggrieved mother sees in the grim national numbers the sweet young face of a beautiful and talented daughter who left behind two children suddenly bereft.

Every day, modern medical care saves the lives of sick and hurting people. But patients and caregivers alike know of the need to balance extremely powerful, yet often exquisitely fragile, efforts in the struggle against death and suffering. The challenge is to make it safer for patients who come to have their lives saved or to be healed.

Yet to rely on blaming as a curative for error overlooks the duality of interests in our health care facilities. Unfortunately, my family was made to witness all too closely a long-standing and seemingly stubborn impediment to safety—that is, the tension that exists between the protection of professional reputations on the one hand and the promotion of patient safety on the other.

Furthermore, we see that the very nature of hospital care involves teams of responsible individuals in relay from one to another in the treatment of those whose fate is in their hands. Too often, systemwide accountability and acceptance of responsibility is lacking, although it is obvious that even the care of a single patient invokes a whole system of concern.

The path to greater safety for patients lies strewn with other challenges as well. Among these are the pressures on health care facilities imposed by the widespread adoption of reimbursements under "managed care." If modern-day business-oriented hospitals are turning patients into customers, patients and their families may do well to heed the caution "Customer Beware!"

Indeed, the concept of hospital patient as customer is no longer far-fetched. As new managed care programs have developed, businesses in a position to purchase these plans as employee health benefits are turning a focus on patient safety. Among changes recommended by corporate structured plans is that all prescriptions in hospitals be computerized, and that patients should be guided to the hospitals and clinical teams more likely to produce better outcomes for their particular conditions. The companies aim to reduce avoidable dangers (and thereby costs). Hospitals, as competing health care providers, may do well to heed large purchasers of health care who can recognize and reward hospitals for the safety of patients.

It has been estimated that a program to increase patient safety launched by a coalition of Fortune 500 companies has the potential to save tens of thousands of lives a year and prevent hundreds of thousands of medical errors.

It is ironic, perhaps, that the concern of companies over the rising costs of their employees' health care may help to improve patient safety. Further, at the urging of several major employers, a growing number of health plans nationwide have hired national computer companies to search patients' insurance claims and pharmacy records for those who are not receiving the best medical treatment for their condition. This holds promise also for the reduction of medical errors.

But patients and their families have an essential role in protecting themselves. The passivity of patients and their advocates is outmoded, belonging to another day. We must no longer hesitate to act on our own behalf for safer handling, and must not hesitate to raise questions that may be life saving.

A patient or family who swings open the door to today's complex labyrinth of medical and institutional care senses the hurried, harried beat of the hospital world we trust. We feel it being besieged daily by cost-conscious HMOs and managed care. We sense the strain of the carefully wired receptionist behind the computer at the hospital's admissions desk. We are made anxious in the pressures of a frenetic emergency room, understaffed. We tremble if reporting for precarious life-saving surgery to be magically performed by sanitized, masked human teams.

When we consider the environment we or a loved one has entered, we sense how vital, at every step in our hospital journey, is the safeguarding of a patient's safety. I urge patients, when they are able, or their family advocates, when they accept the responsibility, to ask questions about their care, to be informed as to the procedures they are to undergo, and to pay attention to details involving their care. For example, what are the safeguards against surgery mishaps, against hospital-caused infection, against medical error and improper administration of drugs? A patient's well-placed curiosity regarding his or her own care is not only appropriate, it may be life saving.

This comprehensive handbook on patient safety and risk management reflects the goals of many in the health care industry to advance the reliability of health care systems worldwide. This can be done only through day-to-day recognition that concern for patient safety must be utmost and constant, ingrained both into health care systems and into caring hearts.

Systems devised to maximize patient safety are vital, but so is the responsibility of each individual caretaker. In the awesome drama of conquering disease, death, and disability, many have an important role—the physician, the surgeon, the anesthetist, the nurse and nurse assistant, the pharmacist, and, not least, an informed and wary patient and family advocate.

Mildred K. Lehman

PREFACE

The focus on patient safety has remained constant since the release of the Institute of Medicine's (IOM) report in 1999. Although we are now four years beyond that report, we continue to see dramatic and tragic proof that despite what we have learned, and what we knew before the IOM report became public, we have yet to achieve success in creating a safe and accountable health care system.

This book was created out of the belief that the science of discovery must begin to move more rapidly toward the science of application. As students of health care safety are no doubt aware, the IOM report recommended, among other things, that more learning needed to occur, more research needed to be funded, and more clinicians needed to become engaged in order to understand why health care systems fail. But it is the need to create accountable systems and an infrastructure to support safe and effective care (rather than merely the study of those systems) that is now essential if we are to deliver safe, high-quality health care to our patients. Indeed, since 1999 a great deal of research has been performed and reported. Health care providers and the public have been told, often by researchers not working directly in the clinical setting, what must be done to make our health care systems safe. Yet today, we are still hearing of tragic errors, of inappropriate surgeries done to the wrong patients, of highly lethal medications administered in error, and even of organs transplanted in patients in error, while simple solutions to these types of errors, long since identified, are ignored.

The estimate that 98,000 patients die annually from preventable medical error created consternation in the health care community, with resultant scientific articles criticizing the methodology utilized and the results obtained. Yet there were others who believed then and now that the numbers are actually far higher than researchers first imagined and that indeed medical errors continue to occur at unacceptable and perhaps even increasing rates.

The premise of this book is that the focus on numbers must give way to a commitment to fix the problems. The fact that one beautiful child died because she received the wrong heart during a transplant procedure at a highly recognized and high-quality leader in health care should make us all realize that more must be done in all of our health care facilities—and that it must be done now.

In this handbook, the reader will be provided with some of the background that we believe is necessary to see the context and scope of the problem and to understand the activities and practices associated with the delivery of health care that must be modified if we are truly to create a consistently safe environment for patients. We have included authors not often cited in the safety literature, who we believe add a perspective that supports the conclusion that, ultimately, the creation of a high-reliability organization is about more than just better computers and technology. These authors recognize that interpersonal and ethical imperatives also are essential and must be part of the foundation upon which all of our systems of care are built.

The challenges of providing safe, high-quality, cost-efficient, culturally sensitive health care are significant. Workforce issues, financial pressures, and increasingly complex health conditions requiring increasingly toxic or risky interventions all contribute to the challenge of health care safety. Each of these factors must be considered as we attempt to modify the environment in the pursuit of safety. We are all aware that the costs of health care are rising, in part because of the costs associated with medical errors. The trust that is so important to the therapeutic relationship is eroding. We must begin now to invest in making our organizations safer for patients and providers and in making them economically sustainable.

The current active debate about the need for tort reform must begin with an acceptance of responsibility and recognition that limiting awards in some cases may be appropriate, but not at the expense of diminished accountability and responsibility. We must start to recognize that we cannot hide behind the law or use the threat of litigation as an excuse for not stepping up to our responsibilities.

Many clinicians argue against sharing error data, which might allow others to learn. They are fearful because of our current malpractice crisis. Yet too few appreciate that without an injured patient, few cases would ever reach a courtroom. Similarly, the benefits of recommitting to safety and appreciating its importance can be recognized even in the absence of negligent care. Many malpractice cases are brought against health care providers and organizations due to poor or unanticipated outcomes even when care provided is consistent with the requisite standards. The creation of safer delivery systems and an environment that supports them can enhance a provider's ability to relate to colleagues and to patients in a manner that may indeed reduce litigation.

The argument that safety and the technology to support safe care are impractical at a time when health care is underfunded and many organizations are in dire financial straits seems equally strained, particularly in light of the fact that many organizations find themselves in the financial condition they are in primarily because of their poor-quality, toxic culture and the ever-increasing costs of malpractice coverage.

Despite the many challenges, we remain optimistic that organizations can and will move forward to address issues of patient safety and to transform their current organizations into high-reliability organizations. We are hopeful that this book will assist them throughout that process.

Barbara J. Youngberg

CONTRIBUTORS

Deborah Anderson
President
Respond2, Inc.
St. Paul, MN

George Apostolakis, PhD
Professor of Nuclear Engineering
Massachusetts Institute
    of Technology
Cambridge, MA

John D. Banja, PhD
Medical Ethicist
Emory University Center for Ethics
Atlanta, GA

Paul Barach, MD, MPH
Director of the Center for
    Patient Safety
University of Miami
Miami, FL

Judene Bartley, MS, MPH, CIC
Vice President
Epidemiology Consulting Services
Beverly Hills, MI
Safety Consultant
Premier Safety Institute
Oak Brook, IL

Raj Behal, MD, MBA
Director, Clinical Information
    Management
University HealthSystem Consortium
Oak Brook, IL

Geir Sverre Braut, MD, DPH
Chief County Medical Officer
Rogaland County, Norway

Troyen A. Brennan, MD, JD, MPH
Harvard School of Public Health
President
Brigham & Women's Hospital
Boston, MA

Paul W. Bush, PharmD, MBA
Director of Pharmacy Services
Clinical Assistant Dean and
    Associate Professor
Medical University of South Carolina
Charleston, SC

Christopher Cassirer, ScD, PhD
Chief Executive Officer
Respond2, Inc.
St. Paul, MN

Pamela F. Cipriano, PhD, FAAN
Chief Clinical Officer
University of Virginia Health System
Charlottesville, VA

Michael R. Cohen, RPh, MS, DSc
President
Institute for Safe Medication Practices
Huntingdon Valley, PA

Richard I. Cook, MD
Associate Professor of Clinical
    Anesthesia and Critical Care
University of Chicago
Chicago, IL

Charles R. Denham, MD
Principal, Premier Innovation Institute
President and CEO, Health Care
    Concepts, Inc.
Austin, TX

Yoel Donchin, MD
Professor of Anesthesiology
Department of Anesthesiology and ICU
Hadassah Hebrew University Medical
    Center
Jerusalem, Israel

Erin A. Egan, MD, JD
Senior Associate, Neiswanger Institute
    for Bioethics and Health Policy
Resident Physician, Department of
    Internal Medicine
Loyola University Medical Center
Maywood, IL

David A. Ehlert, PharmD
Director of Clinical Pharmacy Practice
McKesson Medication Management
Milwaukee, WI

Ken Farbstein
Managing Principal
Melior Consulting Group
Needham, MA

Ellen Flynn, BSN, MBA, JD
Director of Quality Services
University HealthSystem Consortium
Oak Brook, IL

John A. Fromson, MD
Vice President for Professional
    Development
Massachusetts Medical Society
Clinical Instructor in Psychiatry
Harvard Medical School
Boston, MA

Pamela K. Gavin
Chief Operating Officer
Safe Care Systems, LLC
Hingham, MA

Roxanne Goeltz
Air Traffic Controller
Minneapolis, MN

Doni Hass
Stuart, FL

Martin J. Hatlie, JD
President and CEO
Partnership for Patient Safety
Chicago, IL

David Hewett, MD
Assistant Medical Director, Litigation
Winchester and Eastleigh Healthcare
NHS Trust
Chairman, Association of Litigation and
    Risk Management
Winchester, England

Lee H. Hilborne, MD, MPH
Professor of Pathology
Director, Quality Management Services
University of California at
    Los Angeles
Los Angeles, CA

Mark Keroack, MD, MPH
Senior Director, Clinical Practice
    Advancement Center
University HealthSystem Consortium
Oak Brook, IL

G. Eric Knox, MD
Professor, Obstetrics and Gynecology
University of Minnesota
    Medical School
Consultant, Perinatal Risk and
    Patient Safety
Minneapolis, MN

Sue Korth, BSN, MPH, PhD
Director, Outcomes and Performance
    Improvement
Nebraska Health Systems
Omaha, NE

Richard Lauve, MD
Vice President
VHA
Irvine, TX

Karin J. Lindgren
General Counsel
University HealthSystem Consortium
Oak Brook, IL

Stephen E. Littlejohn
Executive Vice President/Partner
Kupper Parker Communications
St. Louis, MO

Jerod M. Loeb, PhD
Vice President
Research and Performance Measurement
Joint Commission for Accreditation
    of Healthcare Organizations
Oak Brook Terrace, IL

Tammy Lundstrom, MD
Vice President and Chief Quality and
    Safety Officer
Detroit Medical Center
Detroit, MI

Roy Magnusson, MD, MS, FACEP
Medical Director
Associate Hospital Director
Oregon Health Sciences University
    Hospitals and Clinics
Portland, OR

Arnold Milstein, MD, MPH
Medical Director
Pacific Business Group on Health
Steering Committee Member
The Leapfrog Group
San Francisco, CA

Julianne M. Morath, RN, MS
Chief Operating Officer
The Children's Hospital & Clinics of
    the Twin Cities
Minneapolis, MN

Candice Moore, BSN, JD
Director of Risk Management
University HealthSystem Consortium
Oak Brook, IL

John J. Nance, JD
NPSF Board of Directors
President, John J. Nance Productions
Federal Way, WA

Brock Nelson
Chief Executive Officer
Regions Hospital
St. Paul, MN

Lynne S. Nemeth, MS, RN
Director, Outcomes Management
    Research and Development
Medical University of South Carolina
Charleston, SC

Dennis S. O'Leary, MD
President and CEO
Joint Commission for Accreditation of
    Healthcare Organizations
Oak Brook Terrace, IL

Larry E. Poniatowski, RN
University HealthSystem Consortium
Oak Brook, IL

Carson Porter, JD
e-Health Solutions Group
Board of Directors, National Patient
    Safety Foundation
Vienna, VA

Grena G. Porto
Principal
QRS Healthcare Consulting, LLC
Pocopson, PA

Gina Pugliese, RN, MS
Vice President
Premier Safety Institute
Oak Brook, IL
Associate Faculty
School of Public Health
University of Illinois
Chicago, IL

Marsha Regenstein, PhD, MCP
National Association of Public Hospitals
Washington, DC

David B. Resnick, JD, PhD
Professor, Department of Medical
    Humanities
Associate Director, The Bioethics Center
The Brody School of Medicine
East Carolina University
Greenville, NC

Emily Rhinehart, RN, MPH, CIC, CPHQ
Director, Quality Management Services
AIG
Atlanta, GA

Victoria L. Rich, PhD, RN
Vice President of Patient Services
University Community Hospital
Tampa, FL

Kevin Roberg
Delphi Ventures
Minneapolis, MN

Karlene H. Roberts, PhD
Haas School of Business
University of California, Berkeley
Berkeley, CA

Steven S. Rough, MS
Acting Director of Pharmacy
University of Wisconsin Hospitals
   and Clinics
Madison, WI

Irwin Rubin, BSEE, MS, PhD
President
Tenemos, Inc.
Honolulu, HA

Mary L. Salisbury, RN, MSN
Dynamics Research Corporation
Andover, MA

Peter L. Saltonstall
President and CEO
Safe Care Systems, LLC
Hingham, MA

Robert Simon, EdD, CPE
Center for Medical Simulation
Boston, MA

Kathleen Rice Simpson, PhD, RNC, FAAN
Perinatal Clinical Nurse Specialist
St. John's Mercy Medical Center
Consultant Perinatal Risk and Patient
   Safety
St. Louis, MO

Judy L. Smetzer, RN, BSN
Institute for Safe Medication Practices
Huntingdon Valley, PA

David M. Studdert, LLB, ScD, MPH
Assistant Professor of Health Policy
   and Law

Department of Health Policy
   and Management
Harvard School of Public Health
Boston, MA

K. Bobbi Traber, MD, MBA
Senior Vice President, Medical Affairs
Main Line Health
Radnor, PA

Daved van Stralen, MD
Medical Director for Totally Kids
Assistant Director of Children's Intensive
   Care Unit
Loma Linda University Medical Center
Loma Linda, CA

James E. Vance, MD, MBA
VHA, Inc.
Irvine, TX

Charles Vincent
Professor of Psychology
University College
London, England

Diane R. Weber, RN, BSN, MHA
Senior Director Knowledge Management
University HealthSystem Consortium
Oak Brook, IL

Nancy Wilson, MD, MPH
Vice President and Medical Director
VHA, Inc.
Irvine, TX

David D. Woods, PhD
Ohio State University
Columbus, OH

Barbara J. Youngberg, BSN, MSW, JD
Vice President
Insurance, Risk, Quality &
   Legal Services
University HealthSystem Consortium
Oak Brook, IL

Kuo Yu
Haas School of Business
University of California, Berkeley
Berkeley, CA

CHAPTER ONE

UNDERSTANDING THE FIRST INSTITUTE OF MEDICINE REPORT AND ITS IMPACT ON PATIENT SAFETY

Marsha Regenstein, PhD, MCP

In October 1999, the Institute of Medicine (IOM) released *To Err Is Human: Building a Safer Health Care System,* a report that put the issues of patient safety and medical errors in front of the American public and on the agendas of health care institutions, provider associations, consumer groups, the administration, and the Congress seemingly overnight. The national news networks and other media outlets broadcast the startling finding that up to 98,000 people die in hospitals each year as a result of medical errors and countless more are seriously harmed. And, whereas other industries have worked systematically to improve error rates and adverse outcomes over the past several decades, the health care industry appears to have made woefully few improvements in patient safety and has essentially maintained high medical error rates over the past 15 years.

Despite its shock value and the media attention it received, the IOM report does not include new information about the prevalence of medical errors. It explains the etiology of errors in the health care system and describes ways that other industries have successfully tackled this problem. It also includes detailed analyses of systems failures in the delivery of care to (primarily) hospitalized patients and identifies steps that health care institutions can take to reduce their error rates.

The report is essentially a call to action for policymakers, providers, and the American public to create a groundswell for change. The report's real take-away message is that medical errors are infrequently the result of the lone individual. On the contrary, medical errors are the result of a complex series of system-related problems. In the report's language, the authors call for the health care system to "systematically design safety into processes of care."[1] Thus, error reduction and improved patient safety focus more on designing systems to reduce the likelihood of error and less on identifying the person or persons responsible for the mistake.

This chapter describes the findings in the IOM report and summarizes some of the published literature upon which the findings were based. It also describes public- and private-sector responses to the IOM report and the ways in which various groups have positioned themselves on this issue.

Errors, Adverse Events, and Negligence: Some Common Terminology

With all of the talk about errors coming from a variety of different sources, it is important to designate a set of definitions that can be used to distinguish the types of events that take place within health care environments that apply to patient safety. The IOM report defines *medical error* as "the failure to complete a planned action as intended or the use of a wrong plan to achieve an aim."[2]

Despite the popular appeal of discussing "errors" in health care, most of the literature on this subject, and most of the information in the IOM report, describes *adverse events* or *potential adverse events* rather than *errors*. An adverse event is defined as an injury caused by medical management rather than by the underlying disease or condition of the patient.[3] A potential adverse event carries the potential for injury. Many, but not all, adverse events are preventable. Those that are preventable, or those that are preventable and result only in the potential for harm, are considered errors. Thus, errors may or may not result in adverse events, and adverse events may or may not be the result of errors.[4]

An example commonly used to illustrate the distinction between preventable and nonpreventable events is an adverse event related to the administration of a new antibiotic to a patient who subsequently has a severe allergic reaction. This case could be the result of medical error, or it could be an unavoidable adverse reaction. If the medical record showed a prior allergic reaction to the type of antibiotic, or the health care team failed to ask the patient whether he or she had any allergies to drugs, the adverse event (i.e., the allergic reaction) would have resulted from medical error. If, on the other hand, the patient was asked about allergic reactions and it was clear that there was no history of allergy to this type of medication, the result would be an adverse event that was not the result of medical error.

Medical errors can result from virtually all processes involved in health care delivery. Some of the most common sources are the following:

- Drug-related errors, such as those resulting from prescribing the wrong medication or dosage, misinterpreting the correct prescription or prescribing instructions, and using incorrect routes of administration
- Diagnostic error, such as misdiagnosis leading to an incorrect choice of therapy, failure to use an indicated diagnostic test, misinterpretations of test results, and failure to act on abnormal results
- Equipment failure, such as defibrillators with dead batteries or intravenous pumps whose valves are easily dislodged or bumped, causing increased doses of medication over too short a period of time
- Blood-transfusion-related injuries, such as giving a patient blood of an incorrect type
- Misinterpretation of other medical orders, such as failing to give a patient a salt-free meal as ordered by a physician

Medical Errors and Patient Safety: What Does the Literature Show?

The estimates of deaths of inpatients resulting from medical errors come from two separate studies. The first, published in two parts in 1991 in the *New England Journal of Medicine,* was conducted by Lucien Leape, Troyen Brennan, and colleagues and is referred to as the Harvard Medical Practice Study. It estimates the number of adverse events occurring or discovered in New York hospitals in 1984 and identifies those that resulted from medical negligence. The second, by Eric Thomas and colleagues published in *Inquiry* in 1999, estimates the costs of medical injuries in Utah and Colorado and uses much the same methodology as the Harvard Medical Practice Study.[5] This study also includes an estimate of adverse events occurring or discovered in hospitals and identifies those that are preventable adverse events.

The Harvard Medical Practice Study

Researchers reviewed more than 30,000 randomly selected records from 51 randomly selected acute care, nonpsychiatric hospitals in New York State in 1984. Using data from these records, they developed population estimates of injuries and computed rates according to the age and sex of the patients as well as the specialties of the physicians. Brennan, Leape, and associates found that adverse events occurred in 3.7% of the hospitalizations.[6] More than one quarter of these (27.6%) were due to negligence. Using weighted totals, the authors estimated that among the nearly 2.7 million patients discharged from New York hospitals in 1984, there were more than 98,000 adverse events and approximately 27,000 adverse events involving negligence.[7]

The authors found that more than half of adverse events resulted in minor impairment, with complete recovery in 1 month. About one of seven resulted in disability lasting 1 to 6 months. But about 2.6% of adverse events resulted in permanent, total disability, and 13.6% caused death. Extrapolating to the state of New York in 1984, the authors estimated that 2,550 patients suffered permanent total disability and another 13,451 died at least in part as a result of adverse events.[8]

Although the authors do not identify specifically the percentage of adverse events related to errors (they use the higher standard of negligence), they found that negligence was more frequently associated with more severe adverse events. For example, while about 22% of adverse events leading to temporary disability were caused by negligence, 51% of the deaths associated with adverse events were caused by negligence.

Additional findings from the Harvard Medical Practice Study are as follows:

- Rates of adverse events increased strongly with increasing age of the patient. This could be a result of the fact that older individuals tend to require more complex care with multiple services, drugs, and therapies. Each of these increases the risk of an adverse event.
- The authors found no significant differences in adverse events between patient sexes, although they did find significant differences across diagnosis-related groups (DRGs). For example, the rate of adverse events in vascular surgery DRGs (16%) was about 25 times higher than that for neonatal DRGs (less than 1%). Rates of negligence, however, did not vary across DRGs.
- Approximately 20% of the adverse events caused by negligence occurred during outpatient care before the index hospitalization but were discovered during the index hospitalization.[9]

- Nearly half of the adverse events (48%) resulted from operations. Wound infections were the most common surgical adverse event, accounting for 29% of surgical complications and nearly one seventh of all adverse events identified in the study.[10]
- Drug complications were the most common single type of adverse event (19%).
- There was wide variation in the type of care that resulted in negligence. For example, 17% of the adverse events related to operations were due to negligence, ranging from 13% of the wound infections to 36% of the surgical failures. Negligent care was identified as causing 75% of the adverse events resulting from problems in diagnosis and 77% of those resulting from a therapeutic mishap.
- Drug-related complications were the most common type of adverse event for patients in all age groups except those aged 16 to 44 years, among whom drug complications ranked second to wound infections. Children had the lowest rates in all categories.
- The largest number of adverse events resulted from treatment provided in the operating room. Emergency rooms, intensive care units, and labor and delivery rooms were each the site of about 3% of the adverse events. However, 70% of the adverse events associated with the emergency room were considered to result from negligence, compared with 14% of adverse events in the operating room.
- The most common class of error for physicians, accounting for 35% of all errors, involved the performance of a procedure or operation. Errors in prevention (i.e., failure to take preventive measures) were the next most common (22%). Errors in diagnosis and prevention were the most likely to be considered negligent (75% and 60% involved negligence, respectively).

The Utah and Colorado Study

Eric Thomas and colleagues reviewed medical records of 14,732 randomly selected 1992 discharges for 28 hospitals in Utah and Colorado to estimate the costs of all types of patient injuries. Using methods very similar to those used in the Harvard Medical Practice Study, they found that adverse event rates in Utah and Colorado were similar to those in New York. In addition, they found that the total costs (in discounted 1996 dollars) were $662 million for adverse events, of which $308 million was for preventable adverse events. In the case of preventable adverse events, 46% of the costs were attributable to health care costs. Extrapolating these figures to the 33.6 million admissions in the United States, the authors estimated the national costs of adverse events to be $37.6 billion, of which $17 billion is for preventable adverse events.[11]

Furthermore, the results of the Utah and Colorado study imply that at least 44,000 Americans die each year as a result of medical errors. Even when using this lower estimate (in lieu of the 98,000 estimate from the New York study), deaths caused by medical errors exceed the number attributable to the eighth leading cause of death. More people die in a given year as a result of medical errors than from motor vehicle accidents (43,458), breast cancer (42,297), or AIDS (16,516).

Other Selected Studies

The health services literature is rich with studies that together portray a health care system that abounds with medical errors. Many of these studies address the issue of medication-related errors. For example:

- Each year, medication-related errors, occurring in or out of the hospital, are estimated to account for over 7,000 deaths. This is higher than the number of Americans who die each year from workplace-related injuries.[12]
- In a 1995 study of medication-related problems at a university hospital, an average of three clinical outcomes associated with medication-related problems were detected per patient.[13]
- A 1991 study of iatrogenic cardiac arrests in a university teaching hospital found that during a 1-year period, 28 of 203 arrests in which resuscitation was attempted followed an iatrogenic complication. Seventeen of the 28 patients (61%) died. The authors found that the most common causes of potentially preventable arrest were medication errors and toxic effects, as well as suboptimal response by physicians to clinical signs and symptoms.[14]
- In a study by Cullen and associates that looked at preventable adverse drug events in intensive care units, the authors found that the rate of preventable or potential adverse drug events was twice as high in intensive care units as in general care units. This difference was due to the quantity of drugs prescribed, and not to a high-stress environment.[15]
- David Bates and colleagues evaluated the incidence and preventability of adverse drug events in an urban tertiary care hospital over a 37-day period. The rate of drug-related incidents was 73 in 2,967 patient days, with 27 incidents judged as adverse drug events, 34 as potential adverse drugs events, and 12 as problem orders. Fifty different drugs were involved, and

physicians were primarily responsible for 72% of the incidents. More than half of the events were judged to be preventable.[16]

These studies demonstrate with remarkable consistency the vulnerability of the health care system and the pervasiveness of medical errors. Although they tend to concentrate on hospitalized patients, most of the studies are careful to point out that errors are by no means confined to hospitals. Hospitals tend to provide more accessible records and also demonstrate a longer and more concentrated period of time caring for a patient. They have been a valuable laboratory for research on medical errors.

Hospitals, however, may carry higher error rates than other health care institutions, although this is not determinable in the literature. Most researchers cite the complexity of an institution or health care process as being a risk factor for error. Hospitals are among the most complex health care delivery sites and therefore are likely to carry with them significant risk for error. They also are appropriate sites to begin designing systems for error reduction.

To Err Is Human: The IOM Report and Recommendations

In June 1998, the IOM formed a Quality of Health Care in America Committee[17] to develop a strategy to result in a "threshold" improvement in quality over the next 10 years.[18] The report on patient safety was the first in a series that will address issues of quality in the health care system.

The purpose of the committee's work on patient safety is fourfold:[19]

1. To establish a national focus to create leadership, research, tools, and protocols to enhance the knowledge base about safety.
2. To identify and learn from errors through immediate and strong mandatory reporting efforts, as well as to encourage voluntary efforts, both with the aim of making sure the system continues to be made safe for patients.
3. To raise standards and expectations for improvements in safety through the actions of oversight organizations, group purchasers, and professional groups.
4. To create safety systems inside health care organizations through the implementation of safe practices at the delivery level. This level is the ultimate target of all the recommendations.

The IOM recommendations fall under the four categories just listed and call for a comprehensive effort on the part of all sectors of the health care system and its health care workforce to make patient safety a priority of the industry. The report challenges the health care industry to reduce medical errors by half over a 5-year period. At a minimum, this requires systemwide changes in the way health care is delivered, the relationships among health professionals, and the way health professionals interact with each other and their institutions. It also requires a profound culture shift within health care institutions to identify and root out errors and their underlying systemic causes. It requires an explicit commitment from CEOs, boards of trustees, medical and nursing staff, and a host of other health care participants to view error identification not as the beginning of punitive action, but as an opportunity to learn how to redesign systems so that they are much safer for patients.

The IOM recommends that the federal government establish a new "Center for Patient Safety" that would be housed at the Agency for Healthcare Research and Quality (formerly the Agency for Health Care Policy and Research) to set national goals for patient safety, track efforts, report to the American public, develop a research agenda, and fund projects designed to improve patient safety and reduce medical errors. In what is perhaps its most controversial recommendation, the IOM calls for a mandatory reporting system for the collection of standardized information by state governments about adverse events that result in serious harm or death. (See the chapter appendix for a complete list of the IOM recommendations.) The IOM also recommends setting up voluntary reporting systems to encourage the reporting of less serious adverse events.

The IOM calls for Congressional legislation to extend peer review protections to data related to patient safety and quality improvement that are collected and analyzed for the purposes of designing safer systems. Currently, information developed outside of peer review protections is open to discovery as part of a lawsuit. Thus, calling for mandatory or even voluntary reporting of serious adverse events would require a more protected legal environment to encourage individuals who commit errors (either individually or as part of a system or group process) and those who become aware that errors have occurred to report them without fear of punishment by supervisors or retribution by peers. This appears to be an extremely challenging goal, even in the presence of legal protections, but it is certainly one that could never be achieved without some sort of protection.

It is important to note that these legal protections do not preclude use of information that is "discoverable" through other sources. In other words, the legal protections suggested previously preclude use of information developed through the patient safety reporting process. In the case of negligence or otherwise inappropriate care, information developed pursuant to a legal action outside of the patient safety reporting system would be unaffected by these protections.

The Clinton Administration's Response to the IOM Report

Within days of the IOM report, then-President Clinton publicly under-scored the administration's commitment to improving patient safety and asked a health care quality task force to study the report and make recommendations about how to move forward with a patient safety agenda. The task force, know as the Quality Interagency Coordination (QuIC) Task Force, which originally had been formed in 1998 to focus federal efforts on improving health care quality, was chaired by Department of Health and Human Services Secretary Donna Shalala and Department of Labor Secretary Alexis Herman.[20] In December 1999, it was asked to concentrate on patient safety and medical errors.

The QuIC issued a report in February 2000 that supported virtually all of the IOM's recommendations. QuIC's report included details about ways that federal agencies could assist in the effort to improve patient safety, as well as specific proposals for the Veterans' Administration and the Department of Defense. The most important feature of this report and the president's acceptance of its recommendations was that it supported the original IOM recommendation to create a mandatory reporting system for serious adverse events. It also supported efforts to provide legal protections for reporting for patient safety purposes, while stressing that these protections would not result in the creation of safe harbors for negligent providers.

QuIC's recommendations tended to place the monitoring compo-nents (a mandatory reporting system along with incentives to encour-age voluntary reporting of lesser events) within state systems, and the research, evaluation, and advisory components within federal agencies. Some of the latter efforts would likely involve collaborative efforts be-tween one or more federal agencies and nonprofit organizations that are experienced in the issue of patient safety.

Legislative Proposals on Patient Safety

There appears to be a significant amount of interest in patient safety on Capitol Hill, despite the relatively few bills introduced in Congress as of late 2000 specifically on this issue. Many Hill watchers believed that with so much legislation getting bogged down in election-year politics, Congress might take a "wait and see" attitude and revisit the

health care organizations, and reduce the risk of future sentinel event occurrences. It disseminates the information gathered through these reports through nationwide bulletins known as *Sentinel Event Alerts*.

A sentinel event is "an unexpected occurrence involving death or serious physical or psychological injury, or the risk thereof."[25] The definition was revised in May 1998 and includes a subset of adverse events that signal the need for immediate action. Action is needed if:

1. The event has resulted in an unanticipated death or permanent loss of function, not related to the natural course of the patient's illness or underlying condition.
2. The event is one of the following, even if the outcome was not death or major permanent loss of function:
   - Suicide of a patient in a setting where the patient receives around-the-clock care (e.g., hospital, residential treatment center, crisis stabilization center)
   - Infant abduction or discharge to the wrong family
   - Rape
   - Hemolytic transfusion reaction involving administration of blood or blood products having major blood group incompatibilities
   - Surgery on the wrong patient or wrong body part

Under the policy, these events are subject to review by the JCAHO and may be reported to the JCAHO on a voluntary basis. If the Joint Commission becomes aware that a sentinel event has occurred (either through voluntary reporting or through other means), the health care organization is required to prepare and submit to the JCAHO a root-cause analysis and action plan within 45 calendar days of the event. Thus, though not required to report a sentinel event, organizations that choose to report to the JCAHO are required to meet various reporting deadlines and criteria once the report has been made. Furthermore, following a report, the Joint Commission may decide to conduct a "for cause" survey to determine whether there is a real or potential ongoing threat to patient safety. The JCAHO indicates that these surveys occur infrequently.

The JCAHO has elected to stay out of the debate on mandatory versus voluntary reporting systems. The Joint Commission supports the development of an "effective medical/health care reporting system, whether mandatory or voluntary."[26] It strongly supports the IOM's call for protection of information reported for the purpose of patient safety analyses. In testimony to Congress in 2000, the Joint Commission stated that the sentinel event program had received relatively few reports, in large part because of a lack of statutory protections from disclosure of information. The testimony stated: "We will not be successful in attaining our goals if Congress does not pass federal protections that will encourage the surfacing, evaluating, and sharing of . . . information." The JCAHO also responded to the IOM report.

The Response from the American Hospital Association

The American Hospital Association (AHA) has been very engaged in the issue of medical errors. Shortly after the release of the IOM report, the AHA sent out a Quality Advisory to its full membership, indicating that it was in the process of developing an initiative to improve patient safety. Over the next several months, the AHA contacted hundreds of its members and worked through its regional structure to approve a series of policies on patient safety.

The AHA is working with the Institute for Safe Medication Practices (ISMP) to develop tools for hospitals to improve patient safety, especially regarding the issue of medication safety. ISMP developed a Medication Safety Self-Assessment tool that the AHA sent to all of its members. Hospitals were asked to complete the self-assessment tool and send the results back to the ISMP for analysis purposes. The tool, however, has generated a fair amount of concern among risk managers, who question how the information will be used and whether there are guarantees of confidentiality.

The AHA does not support several of the key recommendations included in the IOM report. First, the AHA supports a voluntary reporting system (except in cases where the state already requires reporting of such events). AHA officials strongly believe that a voluntary system is necessary to foster open communication and error identification and reporting. Second, the AHA does not support the recommendation that the Agency for Healthcare Research and Quality (AHRQ) serve as the appropriate reporting agency. Instead, it recommends that device-related errors continue to be reported to the FDA, that medication errors go to the ISMP, and that other types of errors be reported to other currently existing expert organizations. The AHA does not consider multiple reporting entities to be a drawback.

The Institute for Safe Medication Practices agrees with the AHA in its preference for a voluntary rather than a mandatory reporting system. Its strong belief is that a voluntary system is more likely to produce the culture change necessary for encouraging individuals to come forward and report medical errors.

The AHA supports the IOM's recommendations concerning legal protections for information developed through error reporting. It also supports federal and other efforts to raise awareness about medical errors and provide additional research dollars to study appropriate mechanisms to improve patient safety.

Other Responses

Not surprisingly, several health-related associations and professional groups have issued policy statements or have testified about medical errors. Most often, differences among these parties center on the questions of whether a reporting system should be voluntary or mandatory (or some form of both) and which entity should receive those reports.

A partial list of these organizational responses follows.

- *The American Medical Association (AMA)* supports AHRQ's role in developing information and funding research on patient safety and medical errors. It also supports the extension of peer review liability protections to those involved in patient safety improvement initiatives and confidentiality protections for individually identifiable information reported for health system safety and quality improvement purposes. The AMA does not support a nationwide mandatory error reporting system. The AMA insists that a mandatory reporting system could have unintended consequences and elicit less information than a well-designed, well-run voluntary program. The AMA also believes that Congress should help create a "culture of safety" within health care organizations by allowing medical professionals to convene to discuss patient safety problems and potential solutions without having their discussions, findings, or recommendations become the basis for class action or other lawsuits.

    The AMA established the National Patient Safety Foundation as an independent, nonprofit organization of health care clinicians, consumer advocates, health product manufacturers, public and private employers and payers, researchers, and regulators to develop strategies for improving patient safety. The group has developed an agenda for research, convened several high-level panels to discuss reducing medication errors, and has awarded several research grants to advance patient safety.

- *The American Association of Health Plans (AAHP)* issued a "Statement of Principles" in February 2000 to promote patient safety among its member health plans. Chief among its principles was support for a mandatory, nationally uniform reporting system free from disincentives for reporting life-threatening medical errors and a voluntary system for less serious problems.[27]

This essentially mirrors the recommendation included in the IOM report.

- *The American College of Physicians–American Society of Internal Medicine (ACP-ASIM)* supports the establishment of a nationwide mandatory reporting system for adverse events that result in death or serious harm, adding that reporting requirements should not be overly inclusive or excessively burdensome to institutions or physicians, and should be narrowly defined to include only major errors. The ACP-ASIM also supports a voluntary reporting system of incidents that do not result in fatalities or major injuries.

- *The American Nurses Association (ANA)* supports the creation of a mandatory reporting system but would extend it beyond so-called sentinel events to include a broader range of errors and adverse events. The ANA is particularly concerned about how staffing affects patient safety and would like to see studies that address the extent to which understaffing of nurses is a detriment to patient care.

- *The Anesthesia Patient Safety Foundation (APSF)*[28] urges the nation to move cautiously before instituting the type of mandatory reporting system called for in the IOM report. Instead it urges further study and consultation with expert groups to deliberate the benefits of a mandatory system. The APSF believes that a voluntary system can be set up immediately and, if designed appropriately, can have an enormous impact on patient safety.

Reasons for Optimism: Successful Strategies

Much of the rhetoric about the epidemic of medical errors is accompanied by stories of successful interventions to reduce errors, save lives, and improve patient care. Safety advances in other industries (most notably, the aviation industry) are held up as examples of successful systems redesign that has resulted in vastly improved safety outcomes. Other occupational safety measures also serve as models for health system redesign for safety.

Examples of safety improvements in health care organizations that have resulted in marked (albeit smaller-scale) advances in patient safety also exist. Several quality-related organizations have published *Reducing Medical Errors and Improving Patient Safety: Success Stories from the Front Lines of Medicine,* a glossy report that details eight different approaches to error reduction.[29] Among them are reports about the strides in anesthesiology safety, which has reduced death rates from anesthesiology from roughly 1 in 3,000 to 4,000 in the 1950s, to 1 in

10,000 in the 1970s, and to 1 in 200,000 to 300,000 by 1990. The Anesthesia Patient Safety Foundation attributes this dramatic improvement to the field's attention to identifying safety problems early, promoting research, disseminating information, and promoting an emphasis on patients in clinical practice. According to the APSF, the most important feature of these efforts has been the elevation of patient safety to co-equal status with more traditional concerns, such as determining the molecular mechanisms of anesthesia, developing specialized drugs, or managing critically ill patients.

Also showcased in the report are efforts through the Patient Safety Improvement Initiative at the U.S. Department of Veteran Affairs (VA). The VA set up the National Center for Patient Safety, headquartered in Ann Arbor, Michigan, and run by a physician and former astronaut, James Bagian. The first accomplishment under the new initiative was field-testing a bar-coding system to reduce medication errors at two VA hospitals in Kansas. The results were dramatic, with a 70% reduction in error rates over a 5-year period. The VA planned to have the bar-coding system in place at all VA hospitals by the end of 2000. A similar bar-coding system is planned for blood products used in transfusions. Other initiatives include changes in the way medications are stored and in the use of physical restraints, and improvements in the use of data on medical errors.

Other programs highlighted in the IOM report include the following:

- Efforts at Dana-Farber Cancer Institute in Boston, Massachusetts, to make chemotherapy safer
- Encouraging physicians to use computers to write prescriptions at Brigham and Women's Hospital in Boston, Massachusetts
- Engaging the participation of a pharmaceutical company (Bristol-Myers Squibb) to redesign medication packaging and develop guidelines for naming new pharmaceuticals
- Focusing on managing a few high-risk drugs at Fairview Health Services in Minneapolis, Minnesota
- Using simulation technology at the VA/Stanford Simulation Center in Palo Alto, California, to mimic complex and realistic clinical crisis scenarios

In each of these cases, encouraging results have been shown through the interaction of technology, leadership, and a strong "corporate" commitment to error reduction and patient safety. There have also been efforts across the sites to work with teams of health professionals to stimulate a culture of change and trust—one that welcomes error detection and reporting as an opportunity for improved patient care.

According to the American Hospital Association, the Agency for Healthcare Research and Quality, and other interested organizations, hospitals and other health care institutions can begin a program addressing medical errors with little up-front investment other than commitment to the cause. For example, the AHA suggests that organizations review their policies and procedures for reporting and investigating errors. It also encourages hospitals to access information from organizations such as the Institute for Safe Medication Practices, the Institute for Healthcare Improvement, the Food and Drug Administration, and others who have worked for years on this issue.

The AHRQ has developed helpful lists for improving patient safety from the hospital, health professional, and patient perspective. For example, AHRQ found through its own funded research programs that the following procedures can help reduce medical errors:

- *Computerized adverse drug event monitoring:* Although chart review has been found to be more accurate than computer tracking and voluntary reporting in identifying adverse drug events, it required five times more personnel time. Researchers concluded that the computerized method was the most efficient means of tracking drug errors.
- *Computer-generated reminders for follow-up testing:* Some diagnostic tests require repeat tests to follow up certain conditions. A computerized physician-reminder system for timing of repeat tests was suggested as a useful adjunct to these procedures to prevent patients from being subjected to unnecessary repeat tests.
- *Standardized protocols:* An AHCPR-sponsored study of ICU patients with severe respiratory disease found a fourfold increase in survival rates with computerized treatment protocols.
- *Computer-assisted decision making:* In a study of trauma cases, computerized decision algorithms were tested against physician-generated management plans and evaluated by a panel of trauma surgeons. Overall, the panel rated the computer-supported decisions as more acceptable than those based on judgment alone.

Conclusion

With very few exceptions, the health care industry has been united in its support for a comprehensive effort to reduce medical errors across all sites of care.[30] Nevertheless, as noted earlier in this chapter, there is considerable difference of opinion about the ways that systems of error detection and reporting should be designed. Some of the parties feel strongly that even in the presence of added protections of error-related information, current malpractice law places providers (most often physicians) at risk of legal action. Furthermore, this risk is increased by taking error reporting outside the bounds of the health care institution and placing it in an external repository of information on medical mistakes.

Despite the goodwill that exists on both sides of the debate, the success of future efforts to improve patient safety may rise or fall on issues essentially unrelated to the technical design of safer systems. A redesigned health care delivery system can be successful only with the buy-in from the leadership at the top of health care institutions and from health care professionals at the bedside, both of whom have their reputations on the line when it comes to patient care. Any changes to strengthen patient care by exposing medical errors—albeit for study and redesign purposes only—will have to be balanced by clear and fair protections that encourage full disclosure, regardless of the mandatory or voluntary nature of the reporting system.

Appendix: IOM Recommendations*

1. Congress should create a Center for Patient Safety within the Agency for Health Care Policy and Research. This Center should
   - set the national goals for patient safety, track progress in meeting these goals, and issue an annual report to the President and Congress on patient safety; and
   - develop knowledge and understanding of errors in health care by developing a research agenda, funding Centers of Excellence, evaluating methods for identifying and preventing errors, and funding dissemination and communication activities to improve patient safety.
2. A nationwide mandatory reporting system should be established that provides for the collection of standardized information by state governments about the adverse events that result in death or serious harm. Reporting should initially be required of hospitals and eventually be required of other institutional and ambulatory care delivery settings. Congress should
   - designate the Forum of Health Care Quality Measurement and Reporting as the entity responsible for promulgating and maintaining a core set of reporting standards to be used by states, including a nomenclature and taxonomy for reporting;
   - require all health care organizations to report standardized information on a defined list of adverse events;

- provide funds and technical expertise for state governments to establish or adapt their current error reporting systems to collect the standardized information, analyze it and conduct follow-up action as needed with health care organizations. Should a state choose not to implement the mandatory reporting system, the Department of Health and Human Services should be designated as the responsible entity; and
- designate the Center for Patient Safety to:
  (1) convene states to share information and expertise, and to evaluate alternative approaches taken for implementing reporting programs, identify best practices for implementation, and assess the impact of state programs; and
  (2) receive and analyze aggregate reports from states to identify persistent safety issucs that require more intensive analysis and/or broader-based response (e.g., designing prototype systems or requesting a response by agencies, manufacturers, or others).

3. The development of voluntary reporting efforts should be encouraged. The Center for Patient Safety should
   - describe and disseminate information on external voluntary reporting programs to encourage greater participation in them and track the development of new reporting systems as they form;
   - convene sponsors and users of external reporting systems to evaluate what works and what does not work well in the programs, and ways to make them more effective;
   - periodically assess whether additional efforts are needed to address gaps in information to improve patient safety and to encourage health care organizations to participate in voluntary reporting programs; and
   - fund and evaluate pilot projects for reporting systems, both within individual health care organizations and collaborative efforts among health care organizations.

4. Congress should pass legislation to extend peer review protections to data related to patient safety and quality improvement that are collected and analyzed by health care organizations for internal use or shared with others solely for purposes of improving safety and quality.

5. Performance standards and expectations for health care organizations should focus greater attention on patient safety.
   - Regulators and accreditors should require health care organizations to implement meaningful patient safety programs with defined executive responsibility.

- Public and private purchasers should provide incentives to health care organizations to demonstrate continuous improvement in patient safety.

6. Performance standards and expectations for health professionals should focus greater attention on patient safety.
   - Health professional licensing bodies should
     (1) implement periodic reexaminations and relicensing of doctors, nurses, and other key providers, based on both competence and knowledge of safety practices; and
     (2) work with certifying and credentialing organizations to develop more effective methods to identify unsafe providers and take action.
   - Professional societies should make a visible commitment to patient safety by establishing a permanent committee dedicated to safety improvement. This committee should
     (1) develop a curriculum on patient safety and encourage its adoption into training and certification requirements;
     (2) disseminate information on patient safety to members through special sessions at annual conferences, journal articles and editorials, newsletters, publications and websites on a regular basis;
     (3) recognize patient safety considerations in practice guidelines and in standards related to the introduction and diffusion of new technologies, therapies, and drugs;
     (4) work with the Center for Patient Safety to develop community-based, collaborative initiatives for error reporting and analysis and implementation of patient safety improvements; and
     (5) collaborate with other professional societies and disciplines in a national summit on the professional's role in patient safety.

7. The Food and Drug Administration (FDA) should increase attention to the safe use of drugs in both pre- and postmarketing processes through the following actions:
   - develop and enforce standards for the design of drug packaging and labeling that will maximize safety in use;
   - require pharmaceutical companies to test (using FDA-approved methods) proposed drug names to identify and remedy potential sound-alike and look-alike confusion with existing drug names; and
   - work with physicians, pharmacists, consumers, and others to establish appropriate responses to problems identified through postmarketing surveillance, especially for concerns that are perceived to require immediate response to protect the safety of patients.

8. Health care organizations and the professionals affiliated with them should make continually improved patient safety a declared and serious aim by establishing patient safety programs with defined executive responsibility. Patient safety programs should
   - Provide strong, clear, and visible attention to safety;
   - Implement nonpunitive systems for reporting and analyzing errors within their organizations;
   - Incorporate well-understood safety principles, such as standardizing and simplifying equipment, supplies, and processes; and
   - Establish interdisciplinary team training programs, such as simulation, that incorporate proven methods of team management.
9. Health care organizations should implement proven medication safety practices.

Notes

1. Institute of Medicine (IOM) Committee on Quality of Health Care in America. *To Err Is Human: Building a Safer Health System* [Advance Copy]. Linda T. Kohn, Janet M. Corrigan, and Molla S. Donaldson, editors. Washington, DC: National Academy Press, 2000, p. vii.
2. Ibid.
3. Brennan, T. A., Leape, L. L., Laird, N. M., et al. Incidence of adverse events and negligence in hospitalized patients: Results of the Harvard Medical Practice Study I. *N Engl J Med* 1991;324:370–376.
4. The studies upon which the IOM error estimates are based discuss medical negligence, which is a term generally left out of the IOM study. *Negligence* is a legal term that relates to care that falls below the standard expected of health care professionals (generally physicians) in their community. Some medical errors may not rise to the level of medical negligence.
5. Thomas, E. J., Studdert, D. M., Newhouse, J. P., Zbar, B. I., Howard, K. M., Williams, E. J., Brennan, T. A. Costs of medical injuries in Utah and Colorado. *Inquiry* 1999;36(3):255–264.
6. The authors define *adverse event* as an injury caused by medical management (rather than underlying disease) and that prolonged the hospitalization, produced a disability at the time of discharge, or both.
7. These estimates, along with ones from Thomas and colleagues, were used to form the basis of the national estimates included in the IOM report. The Harvard Medical Practice Study estimates set the higher range in the estimate of 40,000 to 98,000 deaths per year.
8. Brennan et al., p. 371.
9. The Harvard Medical Practice Study identified adverse events and negligence from hospital medical records only. Some of these events

occurred as a result of outpatient treatment or from hospitalization prior to the study period. All of the events occurred or were discovered during the study period hospitalization but could have resulted from prior treatments in or out of the hospital.

10. Leape, L. L., Brennan, T. A., Laird, N., et al. The nature of adverse events in hospitalized patients: Results of the Harvard Medical Practice Study II. *N Engl J Med* 1991;324:377–384.

11. The authors used 1993 data from the American Hospital Association to estimate national admission rates.

12. Phillips, D. P., Christenfeld, N., Glynn, L. M. Increase in US medication-error deaths between 1983 and 1993. *Lancet* 1998;351:643–644.

13. Schneider, P. J., Gift, M. G., Lee, Y., Rothermich, E. A., Sill, B. E. Cost of medication-related problems at a university hospital. *Am J Health-Syst Pharm* 1995;52:2415–2418.

14. Bedell, S. E., Deitz, D. C., Leeman, D., Delbanco, T. L. Incidence and characteristics of preventable iatrogenic cardiac arrest. *JAMA* 1991;265:2815–2820.

15. Cullen et al. Preventable adverse drug events in hospitalized patients: A comparative study of intensive care and general care units. *Crit Care Med* 1997;25:1289–1297.

16. Bates, D. W., Leape, L. L., Petrycki, S. Incidence and preventability of adverse drug events in hospitalized adults. *J Gen Intern Med* 1993;8:289–294.

17. The committee was chaired by William C. Richardson, president and CEO of the W.K. Kellogg Foundation. Members of the committee included representatives from health systems, academics, experts in patient safety and quality of care, major industries, consumer organizations, and medical groups. For a complete list of committee members, see page iii of the IOM report.

18. IOM, *To Err Is Human,* p. ix.

19. Ibid., p. 5.

20. The Clinton administration pointed out, in its public materials on this subject, that its efforts in patient safety and quality predated the IOM report. That may be true, but clearly the impetus for the administration's increased activity specifically on medical errors was the release of the IOM report.

21. In addition, Senators James Jeffords (R-VT), Patrick J. Kennedy (D-RI), Christopher Dodd (D-CT), and William Frist (R-TN) were drafting legislation that would begin to implement the recommendations of the presidential QuIC.

22. See the April 3, 2000, version of the Grassley bill.

23. Rosenthal, J., Riley, T., Booth, M. *State Reporting of Medical Errors and Adverse Events: Results of a 50-State Survey.* Portland, ME: The National Academy for State Health Policy, 2000.

24. Some states require hospitals to report other types of events, such as violence and infectious outbreaks. These do not fall within the IOM's definitions of error and are not included here.

25. See the JCAHO website, www.jcaho.org, for information on the sentinel event policy.

26. Reporting of Medical/Health Care Errors: A Position Statement of the Joint Commission on Accreditation of Healthcare Organizations. http://www.jcaho.org/sentinel/errors.html.

27. The AAHP's stance came as a surprise to some analysts watching this debate unfold. Some of the more skeptical in the group suggested that the AAHP position was advanced to deflect attention from the Patients' Bill of Rights.

28. The Anesthesia Patient Safety Foundation was formed in 1985 to improve the safety of anesthesia administration and reduce adverse effects. The field of anesthesia is the sole area of medicine that can point to dramatic decreases in error rates over the past two decades. These efforts are discussed in a later section of this chapter.

29. The report is the work of Accelerating Change Today (A.C.T.) for America's Health, a collaborative initiative of the National Coalition on Health Care and the Institute for Healthcare Improvement.

30. The July 5, 2000, issue of *JAMA* includes an article under the section called *Controversies* that claims that the data referenced in the IOM report concerning deaths due to medical errors are exaggerated. This claim is refuted by one of the principal authors of the Harvard Medical Practice Study. See McDonald, C. J., Weiner, M., Hui, S. L. Deaths due to medical errors are exaggerated in Institute of Medicine report. *JAMA* 2000;284:93–94; and Leape, L. L. Institute of Medicine medical error figures are not exaggerated. *JAMA* 2000;284:95–97.

CHAPTER TWO

SUMMARY OF *CROSSING THE QUALITY CHASM: A NEW SYSTEM FOR THE 21st CENTURY*

Ellen Flynn, BSN, MBA, JD

Crossing the Quality Chasm is a report prepared by the Institute of Medicine's Committee on Healthcare Quality in America and approved by the National Research Council. It describes the problems in health care today and the changes needed. The report also urges redesign of the system to deliver safe, effective, patient-centered, timely, efficient, and equitable care.[1] These principles or aims are not new to health care. See Table 2-1, where the six aims are cross walked to the JCAHO 10 dimensions of performance that were developed almost 10 years ago. There is little difference between the dimensions of performance and the six aims discussed in this book. The difference is that this book recommends actions needed to reach the six aims and acknowledges that specific goals need to be developed for each aim. The book advocates use of complex adaptive systems theory that says organizations need two things to change: a common purpose and a simple set of rules.[2] The common purpose is the six aims and the simple rules are the 10 rules recommended for implementation discussed in Table 2-1.

Problems in Health Care

A huge chasm exists between the quality of care Americans receive and the quality of care they should receive.[3] JCAHO's promulgation of the

TABLE 2-1

Six Aims for 21st Century	JCAHO Dimensions of Performance
Safe: patients are not injured by care intended to help them	Safety
Effective-Evidence based health care	Efficacy, appropriateness
Patient centered	Respect and caring, continuity
Timely	Availability, timeliness
Efficient	Efficiency, effectiveness
Equitable	

10 dimensions of performance did little if nothing to close this gap over the past 10 years. Times have changed, but the health care system has not changed to respond to the changing needs of patients. Health care workers are not able to make use of the explosion of information that has become available to them in this century. We live in a world where tremendous resources are dedicated to clinical research, but very few clinicians can access this research for clinical decision making. Most health care expenditures are for chronic illness, yet today's health care system was designed to deliver acute care. The current payment system does not support improving the quality of health care, and preventing morbidity and mortality. Teamwork and communication are critical in health care, but little work has been done in that area. The airline industry gained much from the crew resource management work they did with their teams.[4] Finally, these systems are so overwhelmed with problems from staffing, uncompensated care, and payment issues that they do not have the resources to redesign their systems in order to function appropriately today and in the future.

The Institute of Medicines Recommendations

The IOM report calls for all involved in health care to reduce the burden of illness, injury, and disability and to improve health and functioning. It defines the type of health care delivery system needed (safe, effective, patient-centered, timely, efficient, and equitable) through their six aims, and suggests that organizations creatively redesign their systems to meet the six aims, but gives a list of rules (Table 2-2) that organizations must adhere to when striving for their aims. It suggests that Congress should appropriate funds for Department of Health and Human Services (DHHS) to monitor and evaluate progress being made on achieving the aims and provide annually a status report to Congress.[5]

TABLE 2-2[6]

Rules	Description
Accessible	Patients can freely interface with the system when, where, and how it is convenient for them. Traditional face-to-face visits are no longer the sole interaction for the patient and the health care system.
Flexible	Care should be standardized so that the majority of patient needs are met efficiently, but can be customized when individualized care is required to meet the patient's unique needs.
Informed patient decision making	Patients should be given all the information needed to make a decision. Hospitals should share with patients information about their outcomes so that they can choose the organization where they are most likely to have the best outcome. Clinicians and patients should share in decision making.
Free access to information and knowledge	Patients should be given access to their medical records and clinical information. There is a wealth of clinical information available to the patient on the Internet. The clinician's role is to help the patient interpret the information and make sure that the patient has access to the complete information in order to make a sound decision. Patients should have access to their medical records 24 hours a day so that when there is need to use them they can make them available to the clinician who will be caring for them.
Evidence based	Care should be based on the best scientific information available. This is not limited to only the clinical trial–type of research evidence. Physicians and providers should not let their preferences create illogical variances in care. Patients should be able to receive the same standard of care, wherever they go, that is based on the best scientific evidence.
Safe	Patients should not be harmed by the health care they receive, and all health care providers should engage in risk reduction and patient safety.
Transparent	All providers should give patients the information needed to make informed decisions, including information regarding their own performance with regard to safety, evidence-based practice, and satisfaction.
Anticipates needs	Organizations should study scientific evidence and their outcomes. They should standardize care based on the needs of most patients with the ability to customize when necessary.
Decrease waste	Organizations should shift the focus from decreasing cost to decreasing waste of time and resources. The big picture should be considered, including the patient's long-term outcome and resources needed to achieve the best outcome versus short-term cost.
Collaboration	Clinicians and institutions should openly collaborate and communicate to ensure the best patient outcomes.

Crossing the Quality Chasm recommends that the Agency for Health care Policy and Research (AHRQ) should recommend 15 priority conditions based on volume, cost, and risk to target for quality improvement over the next five years.[7] It believes that focusing on illnesses will shift the system to patient-centered care regardless of the specialties involved. The report recommends that AHRQ consider the 15 priority conditions recommended by the Medical Expenditure Panel. They believe that organizations should start implementing the aims in these priority conditions.

1. Cancer
2. Diabetes
3. Emphysema
4. High cholesterol
5. HIV/AIDS
6. Hypertension
7. Ischemic heart disease
8. Stroke
9. Arthritis
10. Asthma
11. Gallbladder disease
12. Stomach ulcers
13. Back problems
14. Alzheimer's disease and other dementia
15. Depression and anxiety

The book recommends that AHRQ coordinate workshops that include health care representatives, other industries, and the research community for the purpose of identifying how health care can learn from others, improve, and implement the following in health care:

- Use of evidence-based best practices
- Information infrastructure to support and improve care
- Coordinated systems
- Effective teams
- Knowledge and skill management
- Use of outcome measurement to improve care and accountability
- Align incentives with improved outcomes[8]

Both Congress and private organizations should fund innovations in achieving the six aims and/or improving quality in the 15 priority conditions. Project funding should support projects with the capability of producing public domain tools that can be shared throughout health care for improvement.[9] The book recommends that AHRQ hold workshops with representatives from health care and other industries and research to find approaches to bring about improvements needed. It believes that too often health care does not involve other disciplines and can lose out on the advances those disciplines have achieved.

There should be core process and outcome indicators to measure quality of care in the 15 priority conditions. The following parties are already involved in measuring these conditions and should be involved in the measurement process:[10] the Foundation for Accountability; Joint Commission on Accreditation of Healthcare Organizations (JCAHO); National Committee for Quality Assurance (NCQA); and Peer Review Organizations (PROs). The Foundation for Accountability has developed quality measures for child and adolescent health, coronary artery disease, end-of-life care, and HIV/AIDS. These include basic management, staying healthy, getting better, living with illness, and changing needs. The JCAHO has developed five areas for indicator development in hospital care: pneumonia, heart failure, acute mi, surgical procedures and complications, and pregnancy and related conditions. The NCQA measures how well care is provided for the following chronic illnesses: cardiovascular disease, cancer, asthma, pneumonia, influenza, and diabetes. PROs are focused on the following areas: acute myocardial infarction, breast cancer, diabetes, heart failure, and stroke.

The Six Aims

The six aims will be the common purpose for change in health care and should be implemented within the framework of the 10 simple rules.

Aim 1

The health care system must deliver safe care to patients and create a safe environment for health care workers to provide care. This report calls on the health care system to build systems where patients are not injured from care intended to help them.[11] It goes on to discuss how the health care organization can achieve this goal.

Patients should receive the same standard of care 24 hours a day, seven days a week.[12] This is going to require health care systems to develop standards and review the care delivered. For example, if the treatment of choice is laproscopic cholecysectomy instead of open cholecystectomy, and Surgeon X does only open cholecystecomy because he is not comfortable with laproscopy, the organization is going to have to find out how it can make laproscopic cholecystectomy available to all patients where the evidence says this is the best treatment option for them. If the organization is going to receive pneumonia patients 24 hours a day, they need to make sure that all patients will receive their first antibiotic within x hours of arrival. This is going to require adequate staffing in multiple areas seven days a week, 24 hours a day to meet the known patient needs at the time. If elective hip surgery patients need physical therapy for three days post op, hospitals will need to evaluate whether to (a) have physical therapists work weekends or (b) perform elective surgery Wednesday through Saturday and have on-call therapists that see emergent surgery patients over the weekend.

Care must be seamless.[13] One of the biggest problems in health care is lack of good communication—more clinicians and care settings involved in a case, the more opportunity for error. Organizations need to create ways for all information to be available to clinicians in a user-friendly format and transferable across care settings, so that critical information such as allergies or DNR orders are not lost because our systems do not communicate with one another. Good communication among the health care team is critical. Health care needs to begin studying the work on crew resource management done in aviation as one way to improve team performance and communication.[14]

Patients need to be informed of treatment, risks, and uncertainty related to treatment.[15] The better informed the patient is, the safer the patient, because he can ask questions and become involved in active recovery of errors. Patients themselves should decide the risks that they are willing to accept for the benefits likely to be achieved.

"When complications occur health care practitioners are required to inform the patient of the event, cause of the complication, assist with recovery and actions necessary to prevent recurrence."[16] This is an excellent goal, but way exceeds any regulatory requirement that exists today. The JCAHO requires health care providers to inform patients of unanticipated outcomes and have said that at minimum a patient needs to be informed of reportable sentinel events.

Some organizations have placed patients and families on their health care organization's patient care review committees because they recognize that patients can help evaluate the quality of care. As the health care system realizes that it is caring for a chronic population, they will begin to realize that many of the patients that they care for know more about their condition and how to manage it than the clinicians who care for them. Organizations will benefit by patient involvement in managing care and spreading the lessons learned to other patients. For example, a long-term asthmatic has tremendous knowledge of how to manage his or her exacerbations and can share a wealth of information with the health care team and other patients on how to improve care for all patients.

The health care system must be capable of identifying errors, making errors visible, and mitigating harm. The reality is that many health care practitioners live in an environment that is fearful of making errors visible. They cannot see the benefit of early recognition and management of problems over hiding events from the injured patient's attorneys. Health care systems cannot wait for changes in the law to begin identifying and preventing errors. Transparent health care systems will go a long way in restoring trust to both patients and caregivers.[17]

This report suggests health care can be made safer through simplification and standardization.[18] Health care organizations must use the human factors research and develop systems that avoid reliance on memory and attend to the effects of human conditions on errors, for example, work hours, work loads, staffing ratios, training, sources of distraction, their relationship to fatigue, reduced alertness, and sleep deprivation.[19]

Aim 2

Health care must be effective. Effective health care services are based on scientific knowledge for those that can benefit and not provided when services are unlikely to provide benefit.[20] There is not evidence on how to best treat all conditions and all types of patients, but where the evidence does exist, health care providers should use the evidence. Scientific evidence is not limited to clinical trial–type of data and must be coupled with clinician judgment to make the best possible decision for the patient. Health care practitioners need to be more thoughtful and systematic in studying their own care and outcomes, so that they can use the information when there is no scientific evidence.

Aim 3

Health care must be patient centered. Patients' preferences, needs, and values guide all decisions. Health care teams should treat patients with compassion, empathy, and responsiveness to the patients' needs, values, and preferences. It recognizes the role and needs of families and other caregivers. Patient centeredness requires mass customization, which combines the uniqueness of customization with the efficiencies of mass production.[21] To achieve mass customization, organizations need to stratify patients and collect information on past needs and preferences. Processes need to be developed based on findings so that the system can meet the needs of most patients, and recognize when customization is needed. Patient-centered care strives at open communication with patients about their illness and how to manage it, and also addresses both physical and emotional comfort, especially at the end of life.

Aim 4

The health care system must be timely. Waiting time has the possibility of causing both physical and emotional harm to patients. Inefficiency in health care is costly and annoying to health care workers. Reducing cycle time in health care could improve quality, reduce cost, and improve both patient and staff satisfaction.[22]

Aim 5

The health care system must be efficient. Efficient care means avoiding waste of supplies, equipment, ideas, and energy.[23] The focus should shift from cost reduction to waste reduction.

Aim 6

The health care system must be equitable. This means providing care regardless of personal characteristics.[24] All Americans should receive the same quality of care.

Even though these six aims are complementary, there will be times when tension among the aims exists. Because unnecessary services serve no purpose and may harm patients, physicians must use ethical principles when there is conflict among aims, such as practicing patient-centered care and practicing effective evidence-based medicine.[25]

Organizations need to have the ability to assess their baseline performance and make changes to improve the system. Organizations need a balanced scorecard that establishes baseline data and measures improvement regarding clinical and financial performance, patient health outcomes, and satisfaction with care. Front-line managers need to use sampling, small-scale rapid cycle testing, modification, and retesting to manage the processes they are improving.[26]

The Secretary of DHHS should be given the responsibility and necessary resources to establish and maintain a comprehensive program aimed at making scientific evidence more useful and accessible to health care practitioners.[27] There should be a renewed national commitment to quality, safe health care that is accountable to the public. The current payment systems need to be examined, impediments to quality improvement removed, and incentives for quality developed.[28] Many health care organizations say that there is little or no incentive to implement preventative programs for diabetes. Many managed care organizations will not pay for these programs because of the cost on the chance that they may not be responsible for the patients' health care years later when the complications are identified and patients require intensive treatment. A research agenda for aligning payment methods with high-quality preventative care is needed.[29]

Clinical education, credentialing, and funding needs to be re-designed to help clinicians prepare for this new environment, but the education should focus on new as well as current clinicians who will be functioning in this new environment. Physicians need to be given incentives to enter specialties that may not be financially rewarding, but for which there is a great demand, based on the growing chronically ill population.

The AHRQ should fund research on how the current regulatory and legal systems facilitate or inhibit achievement of the six aims and how they can be modified for organizations trying to accomplish them.[30]

Challenges in Health Care

The IOM report discusses the work of Wagner and colleagues, which has identified five elements needed to improve chronic care:[31]

1. Evidence-based planned care. Guidelines and protocols are incorporated into practice.
2. Reorganization of the practice to meet the needs of patients who require more time, resources, and closer follow-up.
3. Systematic attention to patients' need for information and behavioral change. There is substantial evidence that counseling, education, and information feedback for patients with chronic conditions improves outcomes.
4. Ready access to clinical expertise. There are many ways to do this: education of patients and physicians, referrals to specialists, consultation processes, collaborative care models in which specialists and providers work together, computer decision support systems, information systems that support care processes, registries issuing reminders, and patient-carried and automated medical records.

Crossing the Quality Chasm explains the challenges of health care today: an aging population; a growing number of complex chronically ill patients; an explosion of new information and technology that is too great for any one health care practitioner to consistently apply to practice; patients without adequate health information to manage their care; misuse, overuse, and underuse of health care services; a payment system that does not encourage or support quality improvement; and many Americans who do not have access to health care.

The problems are significant, but they are not unsolvable. They require fundamental redesign of the health care system. Health care needs to begin investing in information technology to help clinicians take care of the very complex patient populations that are growing more complex every day and to take advantage of all the new research information that is available. Health care organizations need to get started implementing the six aims within the framework of the 10 simple rules. The report recommends using the high-priority conditions to get started on the aims and the rules and using many of the recommendations that have come out of the Institute of Healthcare Quality Improvement over the past five years regarding rapid-cycle change and managing chronic illnesses.

Notes

1. Committee on HealthCare Quality in America, Institute of Medicine, *Crossing the Quality Chasm: A New Health System for the 21st Century* (Washington, DC: National Academy Press, 2001), 5–6.
2. Ibid., 64.
3. Ibid at 1.
4. Ibid., 131.
5. Ibid., 40.
6. Ibid., 61–62.
7. Ibid., 90–91.
8. Ibid., 112.
9. Ibid., 91.
10. Ibid., 102–103.
11. Ibid., 39.
12. Ibid., 45.
13. Ibid., 45.
14. Ibid., 131.
15. Ibid., 45.
16. Ibid., 45.
17. Ibid., 46.
18. Ibid., 122.
19. Ibid., 123.
20. Ibid., 47.
21. Ibid., 49.
22. Ibid., 52.
23. Ibid., 40.
24. Ibid., 40.
25. Ibid., 54.
26. Ibid., 136.
27. Ibid., 146.
28. Ibid., 182.
29. Ibid., 182.
30. Ibid., 208.
31. Ibid., 28.

CHAPTER THREE

INTERPERSONAL RELATIONSHIPS: THE "SOFT STUFF" OF PATIENT SAFETY

Irwin Rubin, BSEE, MS, PhD

> *The most natural division of all offenses is into those of omission and commission.*
>
> —Addison

Imagine picking up your newspaper tomorrow morning and seeing the following headline: Irrefutable Evidence in a Landmark Malpractice Suit Points the Finger of Blame in a Patient's Death at the Heartlessness of the Organization's Senior Executives: The Nationwide Implications Could Be Cataclysmic.

A shiver runs down your spine as your eyes dart to the opening paragraph:

> Unidentified sources reported that Dr. Joshua Caliban, world-renowned surgeon, founding father and CEO of Care Corporation of America (CCA)—the fifth largest health care provider in the nation—called a closed doors meeting late yesterday afternoon. All of the power brokers of Chicago's legal, business, health care, and insurance industries were in attendance.
>
> While the media lined up outside CCA's boardroom door, sounding like vultures cackling in anticipation, a heated discussion was taking place focused on CCA's accountability in the death of a patient. Just before a deathly silence seemed to envelop the boardroom, Dr. Caliban's voice was heard booming above the rising din: "Unless

you all agree to accept my proposal, at 5:30 today, Care Corporation of America will be entering a plea of guilty as charged of managerial malpractice in the death of a patient."[1]

"Interesting hypothetical story," you think, but what has this thing called "managerial malpractice" got to do with the theme of this book on patient safety? Bear with me for a moment. I hope, in this chapter, to convince you that unless your patients are kept safe from interpersonal toxicity anywhere in your organization, the results can be no less lethal than accidentally administering an inappropriate drug. Indeed, accidental administrations of drugs, and other seeming examples of purely medical malpractice, may well have their root causes in managerial malpractice.

Simply put, "staff infections" anywhere in the human culture of your organization, beginning in your boardroom, are as potentially lethal and costly as staph infections in the treatment room.

Defining the Terms

Let us begin with a few critical definitions. When we read on beyond the first definitions of *management* offered in Webster's—handling, controlling, directing—we discover an interesting fact. "Skillfully managing" and "careful treatment" are synonymous. (*Managed care,* like *AC current,* thus becomes a redundant phrase.) Both professions, medicine and management, share a common mission, a special task or purpose. From their unique roles and perspectives, each is responsible for ensuring skillful and careful treatment. Physicians and other providers manage patients. Health care executives and managers manage organizations made up of physicians and other providers. Both professions are striving to ensure their "patients" get skillful and careful treatment.[2] In the process of striving to meet these respective accountabilities, all efforts must be made to eliminate two kinds of errors—those of commission and those of omission.

Consequently, health care organizations have developed a plethora of very detailed patient safety–oriented procedures and protocols. Most of them, like scrubbing down and following other standard sterilization procedures to minimize staph infections, focus on the provision of skillful and careful medical treatment. Passing a Joint Commission on Accreditation of Healthcare Organizations (JCAHO) inspection is dependent on the effective and consistent implementation of such procedures and protocols. They are necessary but insufficient in ensuring total quality management and patient safety.

Why insufficient? Because no comparable set of JCAHO standards exists to cover skillful and careful interpersonal treatment among and between all health care employees. When health care professionals anywhere in the organization do not afford one another "care-full" treatment, interpersonal toxicity begins to breed. When physicians are allowed to verbally abuse nursing colleagues, when residents are humiliated and chastised publicly, when senior executives are put down for disagreeing with the boss, managerial malpractice—not skillful and careful treatment—is taking place. Missing, therefore, from most current safety protocols is an equal focus on protecting patients from the potentially lethal and costly consequences of "staff infections."

So You Want Some Hard Data?

Respected, replicated, hard scientific evidence documents three categories of reasons for paying very careful attention to ensuring that each and every employee is skilled in the careful treatment of their many interpersonal relationships: (1) self-protection, (2) life and death, and (3) economic gain.

Matters of Self-Protection

Let us take self-protection first. Dr. Wendy Levinson and her colleagues at the University of Chicago studied the interactions primary care physicians had with patients during 10 routine office visits.[3] She compared the patterns observed among those who had received no malpractice claims with those who had received two or more claims. She concluded: "Specific and teachable communication behaviors [were] associated with fewer malpractice claims."

Repeated studies in the *Journal of the American Medical Association* have documented this commonsense fact: Patients are less likely to bring malpractice suits against providers who treat them as respected, valued human beings. Rocket science? Quite the opposite. When a frightened, concerned, confused human being—a patient—feels the safety of a respectful, compassionate, empathic, caring human being—a provider—a bond of mutuality is formed between two hearts. This blood, repeated research confirms, is thicker than that which attracts the sharks who seek blood.

The same conclusion is documented in *Leadership for a Healthy 21st Century:* "There has been a startling shift in consumer priorities from price to concerns about treatment. . . . particularly the degree of respect they are afforded."[4] So, if for no other reason, and there are many I will turn to momentarily, it pays—as a self-protective strategy—to learn the "touchy-feely" stuff that makes patients feel safe. Doing so may reduce the likelihood that a patient decides to sue for mal-"treatment."

It is important to note that in self-protection studies, the point of focus, appropriately, is on the quality of the relationship directly between the provider and the patient. The outcome variable is whether the patient decides to sue his or her provider. In the next two categories, the focus shifts to the quality of the relationships between and among providers and staff, and their "infectious" impact on the patient. Specifically, whether the patient lives or dies, and how quickly the patient is discharged from the hospital bed. (Dare I say, how quickly the patient "decides" to heal?)

Because most of the anti-"touchy-feely" arguments seem to be focused on economics, let us deal with the "minor" issue of life and death first.

Matters of Life and Death

Again, we can refer to another medical bible for the hard data we need here. Dr. William Knaus and his colleagues conducted a massive study of over 5,000 patients with acute emergent life-threatening illnesses — the kind referred to in our hypothetical opening newspaper headline. Their results prove that whether or not a patient lives or dies in the emergency department (ED) of an average hospital is significantly correlated to the quality of the average communications that pass between the attending ED physicians and the ED nurses who work at their side in an effort to save a patient's life. After a thorough statistical analysis of a host of variables, Knaus and colleagues conclude that "Differences [from 60% fewer deaths than the national average, in the best of the EDs, to 58% more deaths than the national average, in the worst] appear to relate to the quality of the interaction and communication between physicians and nurses."[5]

If there is bad blood in the relationship between an ED doctor and nurse, or if sharp words pass between them regularly, then the patients they care for are more likely to never speak again. The sworn oath to "first do no harm" speaks to this life and death challenge.

Let us return for a moment to our hypothetical story. Take a hard honest look in the mirror. Are you currently aware of anyone in your organization whose behavior is regularly toxic? Do you know of any physicians who get away with bloody murder behaviorally—behavior you rationalize because they also happen to be high producers? Have you chosen the "politically correct" path instead of confronting your own boss with some constructive criticism. If you can say "yes" to any of these (and it would be quite unusual not to be able to do so), and you have conveniently denied their relevance to patient care, Knaus's research, one hopes, will shake you out of that myth with a jarring jolt. Furthermore, given what we know about the roots of an organization's culture, we cannot help but begin to wonder if this bad blood between the ED doctor and nurse did not start at the top.

Before we turn to the hard data that will eliminate this wonderment and speak to the second axiom upon which the profession of medicine rests, to "first heal thyself," consider the impact on patient safety of a frequent managerial practice these days, downsizing. The following true story is being replicated nationwide daily.

When the Organization Is the Operating Room Patient

One Monday morning, eighteen senior managers of a large metropolitan hospital arrived for work a little earlier than usual, since everyone was under pressure to do more work with shrinking resources. Each was met at the front door by a security guard who walked them to their respective offices. They were given 15 minutes to clean out their desks of all personal belongings. Security entrance cards were taken away as they were escorted out of the building. This phase of a downsizing operation was complete.

When I asked the CEO about the preemptive nature of the strike, he defensively justified his actions by saying, "We knew it was going to be a painful decision. So we felt it would be better to do it quickly and eliminate unnecessary anxiety." My attempt to get him to look at the process used, and not the content—which I am certain was rationally justified in a shrinking economy—fell on deaf ears.

The human organism that is a "patient organization" experienced a most invasive "surgical procedure." Indeed, for those directly cut out, it was truly a death and dying experience. Their lives in that organization had come to an abrupt and crashing halt. And, this entire procedure was performed without benefit of any form of preop preparation. Anything resembling such medical practice in an operating room would violate every known standard of care.

Furthermore, as a result of this "surgical procedure," the entire human organism of the organization had been traumatized.[6] Just imagine, for a moment, being a nurse in the intensive care unit of this hospital. Life and death decisions hang on the singularity of your focus and your split-second decisions. Do you think that for the next several weeks you might just be distracted every time a security guard happened to wander up on the floor? You're darn right you would! And, as a result, you might just make a mistake. In that split second during which you snap your head around, you might just draw a few more cc's of a vital drug that the doctor ordered out of the vial.

Should, heaven forbid, anything disastrous ensue, the suit would be built around charges of medical malpractice, around the hospital's adherence to medical safety procedures and protocols. But we know that in this case these charges are just the symptoms of a deeper issue, namely, managerial malpractice.

The absence of skillful and careful treatment by the health care executives and managers responsible for managing the organization made up of physicians and other providers can, and does, result in lethal accidents.

Let us turn now to the more direct economic costs of a failure to provide a safe hospital culture, one that is free of interpersonal toxicity.

Matters of Economics

The research that follows moves the focus of the importance of the relationship between the "touchy-feely stuff" and patient safety and care from the organization's treatment room to its boardroom. As one astute senior executive put it, "a virus that starts in the board room can and will infect the entire organization." To accord an organization's leadership their rightful role in this conclusion, let us examine a second hypothetical scenario.

Anticipating that an aging loved one who has just come to live with you could, sometime soon, experience a life-threatening illness, you decide to do some research into the quality of care afforded by the two major hospitals in your town. Both hospitals, your research uncovers, surprisingly have the same state-of-the-art high tech equipment. The same number of Board-certified physicians are supported by equally well-trained staffs of nurses, technicians, and the like. Both have received high marks from the JCAHO.

You know better than to buy a book by its cover, so you take your research to another level. Under the cover of a clever disguise, you are able do a random check of an OR in each hospital and, lo and behold, neither has even the slightest trace of any staph infections floating around.

Upon leaving one hospital, however, you do happen to notice two executive-looking types having a heated argument. The only snippet you could hear clearly was the following: "And don't you ever question me again, if you know what's good for you!"

No big deal, you tell yourself. Every organization is subject to personality clashes, backstabbing, and corporate politics. It's the "hard stuff" you've researched that's important, not that soft, "touchy-feely" stuff, so it won't matter which hospital you use. Your loved one will be equally safe in either hospital.

The relationship between these two senior executive types is not healthy. Reading between the lines, which is exactly what any employee who overheard such a conversation would do, the implicit messages would be clear. Conflicts, when they arise, are not resolved as a collaborative effort. Rather, the "golden rule" rules. Furthermore, in this organization, it could be very unhealthy—"if you know what's good for you"—to question a hierarchical superior. Senior executive interactions create unwritten organizational norms, rules of behavior that others follow and thereby pass on.

By inevitable design, persistent interpersonal toxicity in the boardroom of a health care organization of the kind just portrayed sets in motion the creation of an organizational culture. This culture, again by design, will ultimately find its way into the organization's treatment rooms. At best, as we will document shortly, a culture replete with such personality clashes, backbiting, and organizational politics; conflict avoidance or "golden rule" resolution; and fear-creating threats of reprisal significantly increases the likelihood that patients will be kept in their hospital rooms for longer periods. (At worst, as Knaus proved, such "staff infections" are lethal!) And, as every senior health care organization executive is acutely aware in these days of managed care, length of stay in a hospital bed significantly affects the organization's economic health.

What the research drives home is a heretofore overlooked point: If these same senior executives do not begin to become acutely aware that they must do a better job of managing "skillfully and care-fully" the quality of their day-to-day relationships, they are themselves partially accountable for their organization's diseased economic health. They are potentially guilty of managerial malpractice.[7]

The data supporting these commonsense findings are not from an isolated sample of a few hospitals. One database, collected by Dr. George Salmond while he was Director General of Health, involved all of the hospitals in New Zealand.[8] Salmond was replicating an earlier study by Reginald Revans, which involved the major teaching hospitals in almost all of Great Britain.[9] (I emphasize *all* because when you can study the health care systems of entire nations, you have been able to control a large number of potentially confounding variables.)

The results met the most stringent of statistical levels of significance. Lengths of stay for patients in common medical disease categories (asthma, diabetes, cerebral hemorrhage, coronary artery, and gastric and duodenal ulcer) and common surgical categories (varicose veins, hemorrhoids, acute appendicitis, hernia, cholelithiasis, and cholecystitis) significantly varied by hospital. But, in both studies, variations in length of patient stay were unrelated to the size of the hospital, confirming that the results did not reflect the "rich getting richer."

High touch among and between the staff, not high tech, was the explanation. In both cases, patients from common disease categories were discharged more quickly from hospitals where the staff enjoyed trusting, open, respectful (i.e., win–win) relationships with each other.

In a win–win relationship, people feel safe enough to be fully who they are. Their hearts are not filled with the fear, suspicion, and trepidation that characterize interpersonally toxic relationships. When the staff of a hospital gives and receives skillful and careful treatment to one another, they are able to infect patients with this same quality. When patients feel a comparable level of safe, secure human caring, natural healing mechanisms work better and faster.

In both cases, nursing turnover and length of patient stay were significantly correlated.[10] In other words, in those hospitals where nurses couldn't get out fast enough, patients couldn't get out fast. A familiar story about canaries will highlight this truth.

In olden days, before the advent of high technology, miners would carry a canary down into the bowels of the earth with them. When the canary stopped singing and began a frantic effort to get out of its cage, the miners knew that potentially lethal toxic fumes were in the air. Perhaps nurses are performing a similar role. When they sense "poisoned air" in a hospital's culture, they stop singing happily and seek to get out as fast as possible. They know that if they become infected with this toxicity, their ability to continue as the traditional day-to-day dispensers of tender loving care (TLC) will be diminished. And, it is TLC, the absence of "staff infections," that fuels the healing process, not just the absence of staph infections.

Several years ago, I visited a small hospital in Chiba, Japan, that fully understands the vital importance of a nontoxic healing touch. Upon arrival there, we were met at curbside by a woman dressed in a full formal Japanese kimono. Egotist that I am, I falsely assumed it was in honor of my visit. I later found out that this woman was a nurse. Indeed, she had served in that role for over 20 years. In recognition of her long-standing commitment to being a dispenser of TLC, she was awarded the honor of being allowed to be the first hands that touched a patient upon his or her arrival at the hospital.

Imagine! A nurse awarded the honor of being able to greet patients! A far cry from my own health care provider, for example, where the first hand I see is reaching out for a tip to park my car. Or the first voice I hear is a tape recording telling me "how much I am valued." From this perspective, even a cursory glance at where the cutbacks are taking place in health care points not to "fat" but to the "heart." One can only speculate on the impact of such "surgical procedures" on the safety and security of our health care organizations.

What is not a matter for speculation, as the hard data discussed earlier confirm, is that a hospital's human culture (healthy or otherwise), beginning with its senior leadership team, will by definition and design infectiously affect the quality of care a patient receives.

So What Do We Do About It?

If fear, suspicion, mistrust, and the like are the symptoms of an interpersonally toxic organizational culture, what is the antidote? What are the steps needed to make an organization safe so as to increase patient safety, reduce threats to life, reduce malpractice suits, and enhance the normal healing process?

Diagnosis

As would be true in any patient care encounter, the first step is a diagnostic one. An assessment must be made of the current state of health of the organization's human culture, with particular reference to the nature and extent of any interpersonal toxicity. In addressing this question, the first thing we must acknowledge is an inherent and unavoidable conundrum. In a culture filled with suspicion and mistrust, people will be fearful of speaking the truth about the health of their culture. Similarly, when patients do not trust their providers, they will often withhold information vital to an accurate diagnosis, and ultimately to their own healing.

My own approach to handling this diagnostic challenge is to use a tool called the Organizational Excellence Survey (OES). The OES comprises 48 discrete behaviors, qualities known (including via the research cited earlier) to be characteristic of nontoxic healthy human organizational cultures. Representative samples of employees share their anonymous perceptions on two questions: (1) How important is the behavior being treated currently? and (2) How important should the behavior be treated in the future in order to create an excellent healing-oriented organizational culture?

The difference, or delta, of the Should Be score minus the Currently score yields a concrete measure of the degree of interpersonal toxicity in the culture. (The bigger the delta, the more toxicity that exists.) A sampling of the deltas diagnosed in two different health care organizations appears in Table 3-1. (For more information regarding the complete OES, contact the author at temenos@lava.net.)

The lack of interpersonal safety in Organization B, relative to that in Organization A (itself far from being a toxicity-free workplace), is unambiguous. It begins with a relatively innocuous condition of being cut off when trying to make a point, particularly when said point is at odds with someone else's. (Recall the snippet overheard between two senior executives in the hallway of our hypothetical hospital earlier.) The toxicity gets more severe with a marked tendency to avoid both admitting and apologizing for mistakes—a tendency that is fully

**TABLE 3-1   Sample of Organizational Excellence Survey Deltas from Two
                    Health Care Organizations**

Behavior	Organization A	Organization B
Focus on "What can we learn from this mistake?" and not on "Who is to blame?"		
Gracefully accept feedback	47	85
Admit our mistakes	57	81
Apologize for our mistakes	47	77
Pay careful attention without interrupting when people are trying to make a point	28	82
Remain patient and receptive when someone disagrees with or challenges our point of view	47	84

understandable when the typical response to a mistake is to seek someone's head to cut off. It is little wonder that feedback is avoided and
defended, but certainly not accepted gracefully.

Feedback: The Key to Reducing Interpersonal Toxicity

Without feedback, learning is stymied. Without learning, mistakes must
be repeated. Indeed, the entire practice of medicine is built around an
ideal of continuous quality improvement (CQI). Squeezing every last
ounce of learning out of every less-than-ideal outcome—and publicly
sharing this "pain-full" learning with other professionals—is the key to
providing patients with every possible ounce of protection against
medical malpractice. The same principle is the key to protecting patients from interpersonal toxicity anywhere in the organization's culture. A failure to guarantee this outcome has its roots in managerial
malpractice. The same conundrum mentioned earlier rears its challenging head in this area. A poor feedback process both helps to create
an "interpersonally sick" organizational culture and—at the same
time—makes it difficult for the culture to rid itself of its potentially
lethal and costly "disease."

A simple one-minute test will give you a picture of whether or not
the feedback processes at work in your organization can meet this
challenge.

A One-Minute Test: The Health of a Collaborative Relationship

Take a moment and think about someone in your organization. Select
someone with whom it is vital—because of the interdependent nature
of your roles—that you have a truly collaborative relationship.
The quality of your relationship with this person has a direct impact
on the effectiveness and efficiency of your day-to-day efforts. Your
organization's bottom line suffers if you two don't work well together.

Using the following continua, how would you assess the feedback that is exchanged in this relationship?

Focuses on specific behaviors . . Focuses on personality traits

Delivered face-to-face . . . . Delivered indirectly through third parties

Inspiring and empowering . . . . . Deflating and discouraging

Well thought out . . . . Shot from the hip

Delivered with compassion . . . . Delivered "for your own good"

Balanced praise and . . . . Only praise or constructive criticism
constructive criticism

Regular and frequent . . . . Infrequent to nonexistent

Scoring the Test

If you can honestly say the relationship you had in mind is character-ized by the growth-enhancing feedback reflected in the left end of these continua, congratulations are in order. You are a party to Webster's first definition of collaboration. Like two people in the familiar three-legged race, you and your colleague are struggling to move smoothly, in con-cert. Neither one of you can achieve the objective alone. The feedback you exchange with one another allows you, like a finely tuned engine, to stay closely aligned and attuned as you work collaboratively. Little energy is wasted. Unnecessary wear and tear is minimized. Periodic maintenance keeps disruptive friction from occurring. You are a party to what Dr. Tom Campbell and I called in our recent book, *The ABCs of Effective Feedback: A Guide for Caring Professionals* (San Francisco: Jossey-Bass, 1997), a win–win relationship. A win–win relationship— the heart and soul of any truly collaborative relationship—is one in which both parties' task objectives are met while at the same time they feel positive about themselves and each other.

If, on the other hand, the relationship you had in mind is char-acterized by the deflating, self-righteous ("for your own good"), infrequent-type feedback reflected by the right end of these continua, empathy is in order. You are a party to Webster's second definition of collaboration—"cooperating with or willingly assisting an enemy of one's country." You are colluding with another person in eroding one's most valuable asset—the creative resources fueled by one's self-esteem. You are a partner to a lose–lose relationship.

Traditional 360-Degree Feedback: A Lose–Lose versus Win–Win Situation?

Why do we end up in a lose–lose situation and not the win–lose alter-native most of us imagine is possible? In today's complex, rapidly changing health care environment, any interpersonal conflict, mistrust, or misunderstanding that hampers the flow of free, complete, and open communications between key individuals can, as we have documented, prove costly. Learning and feedback go hand in hand—you can't have one without the other. We either learn how to collaborate together or we are colluding to lose together.

Many would like to believe that the traditional 360-degree feedback processes currently in vogue are the answer. They are not! Their value is severely limited by several factors. First, the feedback generally focuses on hard-to-quantify personality traits or aspects of abstract attitudes. Win–win feedback is not about personalities. It is about concrete observable behaviors. Personalities, by and large, are not amenable to short-term change. (Unless, as a manager, you'd like to become a therapist!) Behaviors, however, can be managed.

For example, many traditional 360-degree feedback processes include such "qualities" as "is an effective team player" and "creates an environment of learning." These are what I would call competency domains. They are *not*, like the 48 items in the OES, observable behaviors. They say nothing about how to go about operating successfully within those domains. Whatever behavior a person has exhibited up to this point has led some observers to conclude they are not good team players. But the feedback provides no help regarding what a person needs to do to improve if he or she gets lower than average scores on such dimensions.

If this isn't frustrating enough, the feedback data are anonymous and averaged. What do I do about the fact that there may be wide variance in the ratings several observers provided? Not only don't I know exactly what to do differently, I don't know with whom to do it! Current 360s position the feedback givers as an unfriendly enemy. Many such assessments, for example, include items something like the following: "Provides honest and direct feedback." Imagine! In order to feel that he or she can be completely honest when commenting on someone else's honesty and directness, the rater must be able to provide feedback anonymously!

We are all fallible human beings struggling to use the gift of feedback to improve ourselves. Continuous quality improvement of our many interpersonal relationships is our common challenge. Traditional 360s do little, if anything, to help us learn how to create what the Greeks called a *temenos*—an environment where adults can learn how to seek, give, and receive feedback so they can experience the freedom to learn as children do. A temenos has exactly the environmental qualities that appear to activate and support the natural process of healing.

If the medium is the message, the message of such traditional 360-degree anonymous feedback processes is clear: Direct, honest feedback on specific observable behaviors, exchanged with compassion and sensitivity, is unhealthy. This message will breed lose–lose outcomes instead of the win–win collaborative relationships upon which organizational excellence rests.

Traditional 360s in health care may, in fact, be teaching exactly the opposite of what is needed. They may be "iatrogenic"!

A Case Study

"This sounds fine in theory," you may be thinking, "but can it really work in practice?" The following case example suggests so, with a "big if."

Nighttime Pediatrics Clinics (NPC) in Salt Lake City provides after-hours urgent care to over 50,000 children yearly. As a part of her efforts to create a toxicity-free organizational culture focused on caring, Teresa Lever-Pollary, NPC's CEO, adopted Temenos' Behavior Minder. She noted, "A user-friendly way to get 360-degree feedback 365 days a year was the managerial information system NPC had always lacked. With The Behavior Minder in place, all employees could now be held accountable for managing the quality of their many important day-to-day relationships . . . upon which quality patient care rests."[11]

To demonstrate how the Behavior Minder can be used, Teresa provides us the opportunity to figuratively sit in on a meeting that took place between her and NPC's then newly appointed medical director, Dr. Ken Broadbent. What follows is a snapshot of that meeting in her words.

> Ken's and my relationship was strained, to say the least, in the way that so many relationships were at NPC. Communication between us was becoming stilted, skewed, guarded, and frustrating. Working together felt like more trouble than it was worth. I had serious doubts as to if and how the relationship could continue. I soon learned that Ken was feeling the same way.
>
> Just before I was readying to do the same, Ken initiated the idea that he and I talk out our dynamics. (The integrity and courage it took to do that were among the very qualities that attracted me to him as my medical director in the first place.) To prepare for this meeting, each of us had a few simple tasks to complete. Before we went through the steps involved in entering data into our computers, however, we made an explicit and important emotional agreement. We agreed on how we wanted to feel about one another and ourselves at the end of the interaction. It was critical to both of us that we'd been completely honest and treated one another with respect and integrity. This setting of an "intentional compass" helped us to proceed.
>
> Using The Behavior Minder, we proceeded to enter our individual perceptions of the frequency with which each of us exhibited each

of the 48 win–win behaviors [identical to those used in the OES] in our relationship. (The Behavior Minder is designed to guarantee individual user anonymity. No one but me could see the feedback Ken gave me, and vice versa.) In addition, we had to identify five specific behaviors each wished the other would exhibit more frequently or less frequently to strengthen the quality of the relationship. Then, working separately in the privacy of our own offices, we reviewed the feedback we'd received from the other person before getting together to discuss the results. [Although it is a computerized program, the Behavior Minder does not eliminate or substitute for face-to-face feedback; rather, it facilitates the process.]

Ken and I both approached our meeting with anxiety. As a result, we manufactured a succession of justifiable task-related excuses for having to postpone meeting and looking into the relationship-oriented mirror The Behavior Minder affords. But once we got started, the results were quite extensive. After three hours Ken and I had barely scratched the surface!

The many differences we discovered between our intentions, our awareness of our own behaviors and their consequences, immediately explained the growing sense of loneliness and isolation we'd been experiencing. Instead of confirming our worst fears of mutual uncaring, we found exactly the opposite was true. Each of us, with the best of intentions, had been doing everything possible to show the other how much we cared! But both Ken and I had been acting out of relative ignorance. Assumptions had taken on the air of facts. In particular, we'd each assumed the other's needs were identical to our own. We'd never asked each other which specific behaviors each needed to experience to feel cared for by the other.

With this experience under my belt, I felt a surge of optimism as I planned to integrate The Behavior Minder into NPC's formal appraisal process.[12] [The details of this integration process can be found in the complete case write-up.]

Key Learning Points

Albeit brief, Teresa Lever-Pollary's snapshot highlights several key points about the vital role of feedback in win–win relationships. The avoidance both she and Ken exhibited is perfectly normal and healthy. Feeling as if we are "playing god" should give us a taste of humility and anxiety. Two things about the Behavior Minder quickly bring this anxiety into healthy perspective. First, each of the 48 behaviors is very biased. They are useful as tools only if a win–win outcome is your intention. Second, there can be no "bad scores"! Feedback focuses on frequency of occurrence and desires for more or less. In the sacred space of a temenos, there are no judgments—no good or bad, right or wrong.

Both Ken and Teresa learned very quickly that, because human beings are fallible and imperfect, the best of our intentions often stray from the consequences of our behaviors. "Toxic waste" and the need to clean it up are a fact of life. Furthermore, in the absence of information to the contrary, we have no choice but to do unto others as we would have them do unto us. Teresa used behaviors to reflect her caring for Ken that mirrored the behaviors she would have wanted to receive in order to feel she was cared for—and vice versa with Ken. Win–win relationships require that we do unto others as they would have us do unto them. And, although our needs as human beings are similar, each of us is unique in terms of the specific behaviors we need to receive to meet our needs. Face-to-face, nonanonymous feedback delivered honestly and with compassion is the only way to close these normal human gaps.

The "Big If"

For such win–win feedback to become the heart and soul of a new organizational paradigm, it will have to touch the lives of each and every employee. Independent of the quality of whatever 360-degree tools may be used, how this process of organizational culture change is handled will ultimately determine its success.

As a result, there is an unseen, unrecognized, and unappreciated level of dirty work with respect to the "how" question that leaders of organizational culture change can never delegate. It is non-negotiable. Like Teresa Lever-Pollary, they must be willing to lead by example. Their day-to-day collaborative behavior must serve as a model for others to follow. They cannot make a mockery out of the power of mimicry.

If efforts to reduce interpersonal toxicity from an organization's culture lack this quality, they can have no integrity. Without integrity, feedback must become a lose–lose proposition.

The ultimate losers of both errors of omission and commission are the patients for whom we have taken a two-pronged oath: (1) To first do no harm, and (2) to "first heal ourselves."

Notes

1. *Terminal Care,* forthcoming novel by Irwin M. Rubin, Ph.D.
2. For more on a health care organization as a "patient," see *My Pulse Is Not What It Used to Be: The Leadership Challenges in Health Care,* Irwin M. Rubin, Ph.D. and C. Raymond Fernandez, M.D., The Temenos® Foundation, Honolulu, HI, 1991.

3. Levinson, W., et al. Physician-patient communication. *JAMA* 1997;277(7):553–559.

4. Arthur Andersen and the Health Forum. *Leadership for a Healthy 21st Century: Creating Value Through Relationships. Health Forum Journal* supplement, January/February 1999.

5. Knaus, W., et al. An evaluation of outcome from intensive care in major medical centers. *Ann Intern Med* 1986;104:410–418.

6. "Total Quality Management: Care Dealers vs. Car Dealers," *Physician Executive Journal of Management,* Vol. 18, No. 5, pp. 15–20, September-October 1992.

7. "Behavioral Quality Assurance: The Information Highway's New Lane," Temenos®, Inc., Honolulu, HI, 1996 (Published in *Physician Executive Journal of Management*).

8. Salmond, G. C. A comparative study of disease specific length of stay in New Zealand hospitals. August 1972.

9. Revans, R. W. *Standards for Morale: Cause and Effect in Hospitals* (London: Oxford University Press, 1964).

10. "Nurse Executives as Champions of Caring," *Aspen's Advisor for Nurse Executives,* Vol. 13, No. 7, April 1998.

11. See Rubin, I. M., Campbell, T. J. *The ABCs of Effective Feedback: A Guide for Caring Professionals* (San Francisco: Jossey-Bass, 1998) for a complete description of this case and the Behavior Minder.

12. Rubin, I. M., Campbell, T. J. *The ABCs of Effective Feedback: A Guide for Caring Professionals.* San Francisco: Jossey-Bass, 1998, pp. 90–101.

CHAPTER FOUR

AN ORGANIZATION DEVELOPMENT FRAMEWORK FOR TRANSFORMATIONAL CHANGE IN PATIENT SAFETY: A GUIDE FOR HOSPITAL SENIOR LEADERS

Raj Behal, MD, MBA

Patient safety has emerged as a study of paradoxes in health care: Highly educated and rigorously trained professionals dedicated to patient care are training the future generation of health care professionals, counseling patients and the public in behavior modification, and continually learning—all in a day's work—while at the same time shifting responsibility for patient safety to others, dismissing sobering statistics on harm to patients, resisting reporting of adverse events, and showing reluctance to change their own behaviors or to participate in fixing systems of care. It is like walking into a brightly lit room and flicking off all the lights—suddenly the room that was coherent and reasoned is filled with amorphous shapes and chaos. One must painstakingly find all of the light switches and flick them back on, one at a time.

Senior leaders at hospitals face the enormous challenge of improving patient safety at their respective organizations. The Institute of Medicine (IOM) report *To Err Is Human* suggested that a large number of deaths in the nations' hospitals are attributable to medical errors.[1] The National Quality Forum and other safety experts have recommended creation of a "culture of safety" and a "blame-free culture." A culture of blame, reports suggest, prevails at many health care institutions and acts as a barrier to accurate measurement of adverse events. Health care workers fear blame and reprisal if they report an error occurring on their watch. Some organizations that have historically performed well in traditional quality improvement initiatives may find themselves struggling to get everyone to willfully support the patient safety agenda. According to a Kaiser/Harvard survey, although a third of the responding physicians acknowledged personal experiences with errors in the past year, only a small minority of the physicians surveyed rated medical errors as a top concern.[2] A phenomenon known as "normalization of deviance"—an incremental process by which a system gradually adjusts to safety problems—is considered a barrier to achieving safety goals.[3] A dysfunctional level of collaboration between physicians and nurses is cited as a barrier, and researchers have proposed a model for improving this relationship.[4] The importance of teamwork in organizational learning is well recognized.[5] A shift from the traditional functions of risk management programs to a more proactive role in hospitals is recommended to assure a culture of safety.[6] Reports of early successes in implementation of a model focusing on practitioner frailties and latent system failures[7] and of an approach to using self-assessment tools and formation of oversight committees[8] are encouraging. A framework that collates the aforementioned interventions into a unified approach to improving patient safety is not available.

Little guidance is available to senior leaders at large medical centers regarding a comprehensive and integrated approach to nurturing an organization that supports the agenda of patient safety. How does one go from a culture of blame to a culture of safety? Is a culture of safety both necessary and sufficient to promote patient safety? What are some of the other key components that must be in place to support the safety agenda? In the absence of empirical data on the effect of management strategies on culture and performance in health care, it is suggested that safety practitioners look to a rich literature on this topic from other industries.[9] This chapter presents an organization development framework shown to be successful in other industries for understanding organizational performance and for implementing lasting change. In addition, it provides guidance on how to adapt this framework for improving the state of patient safety within complex health care organizations.

Scenario

Let us begin with a scenario. The CEO of the University Hospital announces a new policy that calls for mandatory reporting of all errors. If errors are reported within 48 hours of occurrence, there will be no punitive action against the reporter. There will be disciplinary consequences for nonreporting once an error is recognized by other means. Reaction of physicians and nurses to this policy is one of the following:

1. Distrust and questioning of the "real reason" the policy is announced
2. Shrugging it off as just another administrative hassle—"safety is someone else's responsibility"
3. Meeting it with enthusiasm as "the right thing to do so we can learn from these adverse events and improve patient care"

What are the organizational conditions that lead to such varied responses? Is the answer to this question "organizational culture"?

What Is Culture?

First, why does one care about the organization's culture? Isn't it organizational performance that leaders should be concerned about? During the following discussion, it should become apparent that culture drives individual and collective behavior, and collective behavior drives organizational performance. It also should become evident that culture is a necessary, but not sufficient, lever for sustainable change. A strong safety culture eventually wilts in the absence of systems support.

An organization's prevailing culture is a set of beliefs and expectations about life within that organization. Culture is deeply rooted in *assumptions,* which are "truths" taken for granted by individuals in the organization. These assumptions are interwoven into the fabric of organizational life to such an extent that they are rarely even thought about or questioned. From assumptions arise *values* and *norms:* what members of the organization consider worthwhile and what is considered to be acceptable behavior in specific situations, respectively. Any change that threatens existing values and assumptions is met with esistance. *Behavior* and tangible products of such behaviors (*artifacts* such as physical buildings, office space layout, policies, etc.) are readily observed and provide an entrée into an organization's culture. Whereas culture describes what the expectations are, *organizational climate* tells us to what extent the expectations are being met. Climate refers to a psychological state that is strongly affected by policies, supervisor behavior, and systems. It is typically perceived at the local work unit level. Organizational climate is amenable to change over a short period of time, whereas culture is more enduring and requires multifaceted interventions over a longer duration in order to change.

Revisiting the Scenario

Let's assume that the intent of the aforementioned policy is to change staff behavior: a shift from nonreporting of adverse events to prompt reporting. Clearly, different cultures will assign very different meanings to the same policy. The concept of "cultural censorship" may be useful to consider here, as applied by Hart and Hazelgrove.[10] They describe the silence produced by cultural censorship—a socially shared silence that is not forced upon others or conspired and only implicitly agreed upon—that can drive adverse events and malpractice even deeper into the "underside of the organization" when mandatory reporting is introduced. As apparent in the first two responses in the scenario, the local effect of the policy may be to create a psychological state of fear or frustration within the work units. Reporting of errors may increase, but it occurs without the staff "buying in." Under these circumstances, nurses may begin to report pharmacist errors, and physicians may start reporting nursing errors. *Self-reporting,* one of the hallmarks of a safe, nonpunitive culture, may never occur. Learning from errors thus never occurs, and a culture of blame persists.

First-Order Versus Second-Order Change

Policies alone do little to promote a culture of safety. They can only effect a first-order, or *transactional,* change without changing the fundamental nature of the organization. If the primary goal is to increase reporting of errors, a first-order intervention may suffice. A change in the organizational structure, new policies and procedures, and a new electronic event-reporting system may be all that is needed. Each new policy must, however, go through the "lens" of culture first. If the new policy does not pose a threat to the values and underlying assumptions held by the staff, it is more likely to be accepted, though not necessarily with any enthusiasm.

If the goal is to improve patient safety and reduce the likelihood of inadvertent harm to patients, a first-order intervention will not be successful. In this case, a second-order, or *transformational,* change is required. Second-order change comes from a combination of multilevel, multidimensional interventions that focus on organizational mission and strategy, leadership style, and the culture of the organization. In a large organization, this type of effort is expended over several years before results are seen.

A conceptual model for understanding the role of reporting errors in the design of a safer health care system is presented in Figure 4-1. Reason has asserted that errors arise from a combination of active

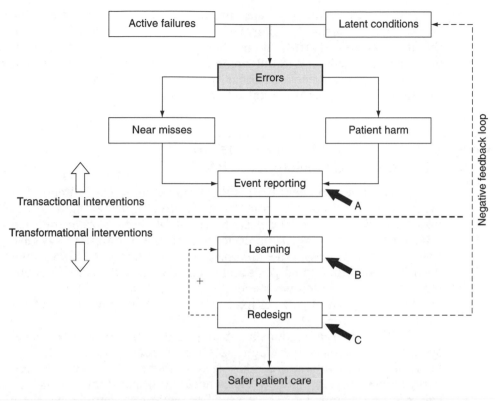

FIGURE 4-1   A conceptual model of the role of event reporting in improving patient safety

human failures and latent system conditions.[11] When holes in various layers of the Swiss-cheese defense system line up just right, errors reach and sometimes harm patients. If an error is intercepted before it reaches the patient, it is referred to as a *near miss*. Once these errors are recognized and reported, they can be further studied so that the staff can learn from what happened and why. More important, this learning can be applied to fix those *latent system conditions* that allowed the error to occur or to propagate. Environmental conditions, such as distractions, and staff fatigue may be the contributory root causes of some of the errors. These conditions can be addressed to reduce the occurrence of *active failures*. Reducing the occurrence of active failures and redesigning systems lead to a safer patient care environment. Learning is incrementally and sometimes exponentially reinforced when staff members observe the outcomes of reporting and making changes.[12] Over time, common latent system conditions are identified and eliminated, incrementally building a safer system for care.

Policies for mandatory reporting and structural changes can increase event reporting (solid arrow A in Figure 4-1). In order to get to the next steps (solid arrows B and C), however, transformational interventions are needed. Without organizational values and norms that motivate learning behaviors, broad participation in development and incorporation of redesign is unlikely to occur.

Creating an Urgency for Change While Providing an Infrastructure for Change to Take Hold

Organization development (OD) is the planned approach to improving organizational capabilities to be more effective in achieving an organization's goals. One of the basic tenets of OD is that organizational effectiveness is contingent upon developing the appropriate systems, structures, and processes. It emphasizes the need to integrate individual needs with organizational goals and to engage individuals in decisions that directly affect their work activities. This approach appears to have validity in the health care setting in the context of improving patient safety.

Health care organizations are examples of complex sociotechnical systems. This perspective emphasizes that technical and human dimensions of work are interrelated.[13] New strategies, structures, policies, performance measurement systems, and training programs are technical solutions adopted to solve specific operational problems. These technical solutions perturb the social system in place, often challenging existing notions of power, autonomy, self-esteem, status, relationships, and security. Failure to consider the social system inevitably leads to resistance and cynicism about "management fads" and eventually erodes organizational trust.[14] Consider what might happen in a tertiary care medical center if a computerized physician order entry system were installed one morning with the expectation that all physicians would use the system and follow the decision rules embedded within.

The Burke–Litwin Model of Organizational Performance and Change

Top-down efforts that are planned and driven by the senior leadership can quickly put in place appropriate structures and policies, whereas bottom-up interventions gradually prepare the front-line staff for effective participation. The latter approach to change relies on OD interventions focusing on culture and brings about "emergent" change.[14,15] A coordinated application of top-down and bottom-up interventions allows the managers and the staff to see results quickly while a "cultural infrastructure" is being erected to sustain long-term performance.

The Burke–Litwin model[16] combines transactional interventions with transformational interventions to bring about sustained improvement in organizational performance (Figure 4-2). Leadership, mission and strategy, and organizational culture are the three key targets for transformational interventions. Transactional interventions are applied to structures, systems, and management practices. The net effect

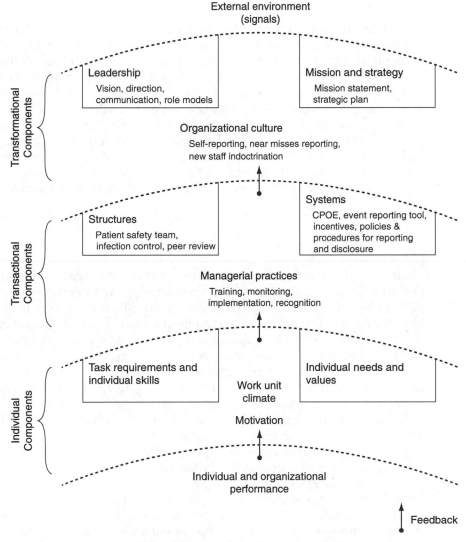

FIGURE 4-2 Translating external demands and internal needs for improving patient safety into organizational performance (adapted from reference 16)

of these interventions is to modify the work unit climate, which in turn contributes to alignment of essential tasks with individual needs and skills. Individuals thus motivated and given appropriate resources improve the organizational performance. Each of the components of the Burke–Litwin framework is described next in the context of patient safety.

External Environment

One of the strongest drivers of organizational change is the external environment. In health care, the external environment is rife with reports on medical errors and the national agenda on patient safety and quality. Several regulatory groups and national organizations, such as the JCAHO, National Quality Forum, and Agency for Healthcare Research and Quality, have promulgated patient safety goals. A few third-party payers have introduced incentives for demonstrable improvements in quality and safety. Television and print media frequently highlight news of medical mishaps as human-interest stories. The environment is sending strong signals to health care professionals and leaders that attending to patient safety issues must be made a higher priority.

Leadership

Leaders need to continually scan the external environment for important trends and signals, and realign their strategy when necessary. The IOM report on medical errors heralded the era of patient safety in the year 2000. Since then the momentum for change has built, albeit slowly. Federal and public agencies as well as the media have embraced this issue and urged action. In the post-Enron era, the call for executive accountability is loud and clear. Although a crisis can be a very effective motivator for change, harm done to organizational morale and reputation may take a very long time to repair.

Senior hospital leaders may find themselves being urged to address two related tasks: creating a culture of safety and learning, and implementing an error reporting system. Without an integrating vision and a structured approach, the outcome may be a few policies that are inconsistently followed and a reporting system that is seldom used. In this undesirable scenario, physicians continue to see safety as someone else's problem, nurses remain silent when unsafe practices are in plain view, and leaders keep pressing for change, while the chief medical officer expresses frustration at being caught in the middle. To break through this impasse, senior leaders have to set direction, align people, and provide motivation.[14,17] They need to consider the following guidelines:

- Develop a vision of safety: what the desired future state of patient safety in the organization looks like.
- Communicate this vision to all staff: what it means to them, and what must change and why.
- Make patient safety an explicit component of the mission.
- Serve as behavioral role models: Adopt transparency in decision making, and hold yourselves accountable to the board of trustees.

In aligning staff around patient safety, the work of the senior leadership begins with a clear and succinct definition of the current problem: what's wrong with the current state of affairs, what is the estimated magnitude of the problem (present or future), what may happen if the problem is not addressed, and what are some of the internal and external drivers for change. This is especially important when the staff does not perceive an imminent problem. If the leadership team cannot answer these questions or communicate their vision with clarity, a call to action to the staff is unlikely to be heard. Storytelling—putting a human face to the safety issue—may prove much more effective in moving staff than precise data on the magnitude of the problem. Statistics on patient falls carefully trended over time are very useful for continuous quality improvement but not for motivating staff. Compare the emotional appeal of a control chart to conversational storytelling such as the following:

> Last month we cared for a 69-year-old grandmother who was admitted for elective hip replacement. She was sedated and anticoagulated. When she got out of bed at 2 AM confused, she tripped over her IV line and landed head first and developed a massive subdural hematoma, which went unrecognized until the morning shift. She required emergency craniotomy followed by repair of a 4-cm tear in her urethra (her Foley catheter bag with balloon inflated was secured to the bedside when she fell). Despite our efforts to resuscitate her, she died the next day. How could this happen here?

The issue and the change must be explained in terms that are meaningful to staff and relevant to their daily work. Outlining what is *not* going to change can be instrumental in alleviating some anxiety. Instead of simply announcing a new policy, the leaders should outline the vision, present an open and transparent leadership style, and ask for commitment. Finally, leaders should accept the ultimate accountability for patient safety and engage the board of trustees' interest and support. Two critical effectors of the leaders' vision that cannot be delegated are mission and strategy, and organizational culture, which are described next.

Mission and Strategy

With the vision of a highly reliable, safe, and effective organization in mind, leaders need to reexamine the organization's stated mission, modify it if necessary, and then communicate it to staff with clarity and resolve. It is important to involve the staff in designing specific tactics that will help create a safer organization. Instead of resigning themselves to the mantra that "culture eats strategy for lunch around here," leaders have to be cognizant of the local culture and anticipate resistance when crafting strategy. Deadlock with the staff is as much a reflection of weakness of the strategy as it is evidence of a stagnant culture. The strategic plan should delineate how the mission is to be carried out. Important elements of the organization's strategy for ensuring patient safety include effective communication of the vision, proactive evaluation and redesign of high-hazard processes, development of appropriate structures and systems, and a focus on shifting the organization's culture.

Organizational Culture

Culture is a set of beliefs and values that allows organizational members to interpret the events they experience and assign meanings to those events.[16] It is "the way we do things here." Changing culture takes sustained effort over time and should not be the sole initial intervention. Cultural change is best pursued in parallel with results-oriented interventions. Capitalizing on small wins over time, leaders can raise awareness among staff and demonstrate that change is possible. More important, improved performance may begin to resonate with individual values of patient care and thereby facilitate incorporation of new behaviors. Senior leaders with a recent tenure may aid their understanding of the organizational culture by examining the practices and values of the founders.

Cultural change is sometimes brought about at the fringes of the organization, often by newcomers. Hiring of new staff members that bring with them a desired set of values in visible positions is an important step. Indoctrination of new staff with a desired set of values and norms relating to a culture of safety may be a useful tactic, with an important caveat: If the newly hired staff members encounter behaviors in the "old culture" that seem to contradict what was just presented to them, they may find it difficult to adhere to the espoused values. Therefore, it is important to work at the same time on changing the old guard. If specific staff members remain irresponsible and unprofessional in their conduct after counseling and confrontation, removal may be the only option. Although difficult, this can be a powerful signal to the remaining staff members that the organization is serious about patient safety. Between the two extremes of hiring and firing lies a middle ground where behavioral change can be attempted.[18] A practical three-stage model for behavioral change is presented later in this discussion.

The role of cultural communications is often underestimated in changing and sustaining cultures: Although explicit modes of communications such as newsletters, announcements, and all-staff meetings are commonly used, implicit cultural messages such as stories, metaphors, and creation of cultural heroes (for example, a surgeon who reported his own error, explained the error, and apologized to the patient, and then helped change the latent conditions so it wouldn't happen again) can be much more powerful in sustaining the new culture.

Management Practices

Management involves planning and budgeting, organizing and staffing, providing control, and solving problems. These activities are distinct from but complementary to what leaders do.[17] Managers reduce complexity and increase predictability in day-to-day activities. Chairs of clinical departments, the chief medical officer, the chief nursing officer, nursing unit managers, the director of quality improvement, and the director of the pharmacy are some of the important stakeholders who manage clinical activities within and across work units. A shared purpose of safe and effective care of patients *within* work units is just as important as it is across the organization, if not more so. After all, it is here, in work units, where patient care, harm, reporting, or blame occurs. Because work units are necessarily multidisciplinary, coordination of functional department-based interventions is crucial for success. Physicians (including house staff in training), nurses, pharmacists, and other front-line workers must hear the leadership and the management team speak in one voice about patient safety. Various management practices such as those related to nurse staffing, house staff training, attending physician accountability, and implementation of computerized physician order entry are effective in improving patient safety when they are woven into the organizational strategy toward this goal.

Whether the management should use incentives to encourage behavior change remains an open question. Use of incentives assumes that individual behavior is the main constraint that limits performance. Faced with financial incentives, individuals attempting to work harder soon reach a performance plateau. To break through this plateau, support from systems and structures must be present. Incentives may be more effective if directed at the organization or at least at the department level. Incentives may be more effective in reinforcing desired behaviors than in creating new behaviors.

Structures and Systems

Structure refers to an arrangement of human resources required for execution of a strategy. Organizing staff into specific functions and roles, bestowing decision-making authority, and facilitating relationships are examples of structural interventions. Creation of a Patient Safety Team or appointment of a Patient Safety Officer is a structural change for the specific purpose of advancing patient safety. This entity or individual should report to the senior leadership and have decision-making authority. Members of this team should be carefully selected, keeping in mind that personal relationships can often accomplish more than a policy directive. The infection control and epidemiology staff should work closely with this team. The existing physician peer-review and recredentialing arrangements may not be effective in inculcating physician accountability for patient safety; some organizations will need to reexamine these relationships in this new context.

Systems interventions involve policies and procedures for facilitating the daily work; examples include policies for reporting adverse events, for full disclosure to patients who are harmed, and for disciplining malicious practitioners. Computerized physician order entry systems with decision support, electronic event-reporting tools, ICU alarms, incentive mechanisms, and the use of various forcing functions are examples of systems. There is a well-established role for process and systems redesign in eliminating latent conditions that allow errors to propagate. Making it difficult to use hazardous equipment incorrectly is a simple yet powerful example of system constraints. As a reminder, structural and systems interventions can only bring about first-order change. Used in isolation, they do nothing to change the fundamental nature of the organization. They do nothing to change a "blame culture" into a "safety culture" when other aspects of organizational life are left unattended.

Task Requirements and Individual Skills

Some staff members may resist change because they lack the skills required for participation. What is required of individuals and the skills they possess must match. Training in communication, use of electronic reporting systems, analysis of data, and use of specific tools such as failure mode analysis and root cause analysis can provide essential skills for the required tasks.

Work Unit Climate, Individual Needs, and Motivation

When individuals possess the right skills for the required tasks, are working under a resourceful work unit climate in a supportive and open culture, have their professional needs and values fulfilled, are hearing a clear and consistent message from the senior leaders, and know without a doubt what is required of them, they are motivated to achieve organizational goals of improving patient safety. Incentives, which may be monetary or in the form of professional recognition, can help sustain new behaviors that are consistent with a safety culture.

Changing Behavior

Three-Stage Change Model

Staff behavior is an overt manifestation of the organizational culture. A model for approaching behavior change includes the following three stages:[19,20]

1. Unfreeze old behavior.
2. Introduce new behavior.
3. Refreeze new behavior.

Each stage requires a specific intervention. In the first stage, motivation and readiness for change are introduced by (1) creation of discomfort with the current situation, (2) introduction of anxiety or guilt, and (3) provision of psychological safety. Old behaviors can be unfrozen by providing reasons why the status quo is undesirable; this may include presentation of data, trends, and stories to make the case for change. Availability of data in itself does not guarantee that the information will be assimilated or even perceived by the staff. Organizational behavior experts have long established that disconfirming information must connect to what individuals deeply care about before they will take any action.[20] Not meeting important professional goals creates anxiety, whereas violation of personal ideals generates guilt. This type of communication does not have to be negative as long as the triad of disconfirming information, important goals, and personal ideals is recognized in planning change. Finally, recipients of disconfirming information must feel safe in accepting it. If acceptance means losing face or credibility or feeling worthless, defense mechanisms will rise and information will be discarded. One way to provide psychological safety is by reassuring staff that the problem is not unique: Others have faced it and succeeded in implementing change.

Once individuals are motivated to discard old behaviors, the next step is to identify role models, peers, or other respected members of the professional network who already have incorporated new behaviors in their work. When this is not sufficient or role models are not available, a scan of the external environment may reveal individuals or organizations in other industries that are operating under the values espoused. A frequently used example of an external entity exemplifying a culture of safety is the airline industry.

In the third stage, new behaviors are reinforced to ensure that change is not transient. The work environment and significant relationships with peers, superiors, and other team members should provide positive feedback. The positive impact on patient outcomes should resonate with professional values.

Summing Up

Culture is an important lever for introducing and sustaining change in an organization. Nurturing a culture of safety is necessary but not sufficient for improving the state of patient safety within organizations. Transactional interventions that focus on organizational structure, systems, and policies are unlikely to produce lasting new behaviors. Measurement of near misses and patient harm is an important component of a patient safety program. In order to bridge the chasm in safety, however, these changes must be reinforced by a fundamental shift in the organizational life. Leaders must set a new direction, align people, and provide motivation. Organization development interventions that have long been used in other industries can now be used to diagnose an ailing patient safety program or, better yet, to design a highly reliable and safe health care organization.

References

1. Institute of Medicine. *To Err Is Human: Building a Safer Health System.* Washington, DC: National Academy Press, 2000.
2. Blendon, R., DesRoches, C., Brodie, M., et al. Views of practicing physicians and the public on medical errors. *N Engl J Med* 347:1933–1967, 2002.
3. Gaba, D. Structural and organizational issues in patient safety: A comparison of health care to other high-hazard industries. *California Management Review* 43:83–102, 2000.
4. Zwarenstein, M., Reeves, S. Working together but apart: Barriers and routes to nurse-physician collaboration. *Jt Comm Qual Improv* 28:242–247, 2002.
5. Firth-Cozens, J. Cultures for improving patient safety through learning: The role of teamwork. *Quality in Health Care* 10(Suppl II):26–31, 2001.

6. Kuhn, A., Youngberg, B. The need for risk management to evolve to assure a culture of safety. *Qual Saf Health Care* 11:158–162, 2002.

7. Ketring, S., White, J. Developing a systemwide approach to patient safety: The first year. *Jt Comm Qual Improv* 28:287–295, 2002.

8. Wong, P., Helsinger, D., Petry, J. Providing the right infrastructure to lead the culture change for patient safety. *Jt Comm Qual Improv* 28:363–372, 2002.

9. Davies, H., Nutley, S., Mannion, R. Organizational culture and quality of health care. *Qual Saf Health Care* 9:111–119, 2000.

10. Hart, E., Hazelgrove, J. Understanding the organizational context for adverse events in the health services: The role of cultural censorship. *Qual Saf Health Care* 10:257–262, 2001.

11. Reason, J. Human error: Models and management. *BMJ* 320:768–770, 2000.

12. Carroll, J., Edmondson, A. Leading organizational learning in health care. *Qual Saf Health Care* 11:51–56, 2002.

13. "Organization Development and Change," in Bowditch, J., Buono, A., *A Primer on Organizational Behavior* (New York: John Wiley & Sons, 2001), 312–338.

14. Beer, M. How to develop an organization capable of sustained high performance: Embrace the drive for results-capability development paradox. *Org Dynamics* 29:233–247, 2001.

15. Beer, M., Nohria, N. Cracking the code of change. *Harvard Business Review* 133–141, May–June 2000.

16. Burke, W., Litwin, G. A causal model of organizational performance and change. *Journal of Management* 18:523–545, 1992.

17. Kotter, J. What leaders really do. *Harvard Business Review* 103–111, May–June 1990.

18. "Organization Culture and Effectiveness," in Bowditch, J., Buono, A., *A Primer on Organizational Behavior* (New York: John Wiley & Sons, 2001), 285–311.

19. Lewin, K. *Field Theory in Social Science* (New York: Harper & Row, 1951), 228–229.

20. Schein, E. *Process Consultation, Volume 2: Lessons for Managers and Consultants* (New York: Addison-Wesley, 1987).

CHAPTER FIVE

TOWARD A PHILOSOPHY OF PATIENT SAFETY: EXPANDING THE SYSTEMS APPROACH TO MEDICAL ERROR

David Resnick, JD, PhD

The Problem of Medical Error

The publication in 1999 of the report from the Institute of Medicine (IOM) entitled *To Err Is Human* has sparked considerable discussion about the incidence and etiology of errors in medicine, as well as policies and procedures for minimizing errors.[1] The IOM report estimated the annual deaths from medical errors to be between 44,000 and 98,000, or more than the annual deaths from motor vehicle accidents (43,458) or breast cancer (42,297).[2] The IOM arrived at this number by extrapolating from error rates from three different studies of medical error. Studies of hospital errors conducted in Colorado and in Utah in 1992 placed the death rate from errors at 44,000 annually.[3] The third study, which was conducted in hospitals in New York, placed the death rate at 98,000 annually.[4] The IOM estimated that the total national costs resulting from medical errors, which included health care costs, lost income and productivity, and disability costs, was between $37.6 billion and $50 billion per year.[5]

The IOM report also analyzed some of the probable causes of medical errors. It drew a distinction between two types of causes of error in medicine: *individuals* and *systems*.[6] For example, if a patient in a hospital receives the wrong dose of medication, one might look for an individual to blame for this mistake, such as the doctor who wrote the prescription, the pharmacist who filled it, or the nurse who administered it. Medical malpractice lawsuits encourage this type of thinking because plaintiffs often name individuals as defendants. For example, a hospital patient who is harmed as a result of receiving the wrong dose of a medication might sue the doctor, the nurse, and the pharmacist, as well as the hospital. Health care institutions have also accepted this individualistic framework because a hospital, nursing home, or managed care organization may discipline or fire a member of its staff who makes errors. Medical licensing boards reinforce this approach to error because they frequently discipline practitioners who make mistakes. For example, a pharmacist who makes too many errors could have his or her license suspended.

The IOM report redirects the analysis of medical error from individuals to systems: "the emphasis . . . is about how to make systems safer; its primary focus is not on 'getting rid of bad apples,' or individuals with poor records of performance. The underlying assumption is that lasting and broad-based safety improvements in industry can be brought about through a systems approach."[7] The IOM reports draws on the work of Charles Perrow and James Reason, who studied the role of systems and individuals in causing accidents, such as the space shuttle *Challenger* disaster.[8]

The IOM report defines a system as a "set of interdependent elements interacting to achieve a common aim."[9] For example, a system relating to the administration of medications in a hospital would include the media used to communicate prescription orders, such as paper, phone, or email; methods for verifying communications; computer programs to record medication orders and to check for drug interactions; protocols for checking prescriptions; terminology for referring to different medications, dosages, and means of administration; and procedures for identifying patients and storing and marking medications on the ward.[10] There are many different ways that the system for administering a medication may break down. For example, there might be a miscommunication between the doctor and the nurse or pharmacist; the hospital might use similar names to refer to different medications, which may result in confusion at times; the patient may receive the wrong medication because of unclear labeling, and so on.

The important point to glean from the IOM report is that when errors happen, it may be more useful to focus on systems rather than on individuals as sources of error. Indeed, since human beings are far from perfect, we should expect that they will make mistakes. The best way to improve safety in an industry is to design systems that eliminate or minimize errors.

The IOM report is a key milestone in the development of patient safety, and it has helped to stimulate other agencies to focus on patient safety, such as the Department of Health and Human Services, the American Hospital Association, and the Joint Commission on Accreditation of Healthcare Organizations (JCAHO). This chapter will go one step beyond the general tenor of the IOM report and argue that those who are concerned with patient safety should rethink and critique some of the foundational ideas and assumptions that play a key role in reducing error and improving safety. Although it is important to address health care systems, it is also important to address the basic ideas and assumptions—the philosophies (or worldviews)—that people use to implement and design systems. The IOM report addresses some philosophical issues related to patient safety without referring to them as philosophical issues. For example, the IOM report recommends that "health care organizations and the professionals affiliated with them should make continually improved patient safety a declared and serious aim by establishing patient safety programs."[11] The report also recommends that "performance standards and expectations for health professionals should focus greater attention on patient safety."[12]

This chapter identifies and describes several different ideas and assumptions that play an important role in medical error and explains why the health care industry should address the foundational issues related to medical error. The key components of a patient safety philosophy that this chapter examines include the definition of "medical error," the degree of commitment to error reduction, and the acceptance of error.

From Systems to Philosophies

To get a better understanding of the difference between a system and a philosophy or worldview, it is useful to refine the distinction between an individual and a system. For the purpose of this chapter, an individual could be any individual thing that can be uniquely identified. For example, cars, marbles, trees, and planets are "individuals" in this sense of the word. Human beings can also be individuals, of course. If we have a group of individuals, then this group could be called a collection or assortment, if it is not organized in any particular way. For example, a pile of books on the floor might be a collection. The difference between a collection of individuals and a system of individuals is that a system involves some method for organizing the individuals and assigning them different roles (or places) within the system.[13] All of the individuals are organized (or controlled or regulated) for the sake of some common aim or goal. For example, the Dewey Decimal System is a method for arranging books in a library according to a particular organization based on numbers and letters assigned to different types of books. Our solar system organizes the planets, asteroids, moons, and comets around a common focal point, the sun.

If we think of systems as types of organizations, it follows that there can be systems of different sizes, depending on the level of the organization. Nowhere is this more evident than in the biological world, where there are levels of organization ranging from molecules, organelles, and membranes at the lowest level; to cells, tissues, and organs at the intermediate level; to organisms, populations, and ecosystems at the highest level. The IOM report recognizes this point: "Systems can be very large and far-reaching, or they can be more localized."[14] However, the report does not expand on this idea and focuses on particular, localized systems in health care.

What would be a "large and far-reaching" system relating to medical error? How would this system differ from more localized systems? If we think of systems relating to human beings, lower-level systems might include families, businesses, professional associations, community associations, and volunteer organizations. Intermediate-level systems might include social institutions, such as marriage, sports, or medicine, as well as governments. At the very highest level of organization, we would find those systems that we can regard as philosophies in society. These might include political ideologies, such as democracy, communism, and fascism; economic systems, such as capitalism and socialism; religious traditions, such as Christianity, Islam, and Buddhism; and even scientific ideas and assumptions, such as determinism, the uniformity of nature, and Darwinism.

A philosophy (or worldview) consists of a set of basic ideas and assumptions that address fundamental questions in a discipline or human activity. The academic discipline known as "philosophy" studies these basic ideas and assumptions. Philosophies are much more abstract than intermediate- or lower-level systems. A dollar bill is a concrete thing that is part of the United States' monetary system. But capitalism is an abstract idea (or theory) that consists of a set of beliefs and assumptions about the organization of production, the generation of wealth, and the distribution of goods and services in society. As we shall soon see, abstract ideas also define the health care industry's approach to medical error.

It follows from this analysis that it is very important to understand these philosophies if one wants to understand human behavior, since higher-level principles and goals may explain and justify behavior at lower levels. For example, no explanation of marriage in the United States would be complete without some reference to the particular marital arrangements and rituals adopted by various religious practices as well as their religious beliefs. No explanation of voting behavior in the United States would be complete without some reference to particular political races as well as the idea of democracy. Also, a justification of a particular policy or procedure may refer to some higher-level goal or principle. For example, one might justify the rules of the patent system by arguing that they promote the advancement of science and the practical arts by giving incentives to inventors and entrepreneurs.

While it is important to understand philosophical ideas and assumptions in order to explain events that occur at lower organizational levels, it may be more difficult to change these ideas than it is to change lower-level systems. For example, it is much easier to change a particular regulation designed to promote good working conditions for employees than it is to change capitalism. It is much easier to change the time that a church offers its worship services than it is to change Christianity or Hinduism. This does not mean that it is impossible to change philosophies or worldviews. However, attempts to change a worldview may meet with a great deal of resistance for the simple reason that a worldview affects so many different lower-level systems. A change in a worldview is like a political or scientific revolution because it results in a new way of thinking about the world—new ideas, new beliefs, and new values.[15] We will return to this point when we examine the health care industry.

Philosophical Ideas and Assumptions and Medical Error

Having laid some groundwork for the significance of philosophical ideas and assumptions in understanding human behavior, we can now apply this framework to the analysis and etiology of medical error. As noted earlier, the IOM report has provided an excellent discussion of the systems approach to medical error. To develop a philosophical approach, we should try to understand the basic ideas and assumptions that can reduce medical error and enhance patient safety. These ideas could be held by different individuals in the health care industry, including practitioners, managers, and patients. To identify some of these different ideas, it will be useful to ask the following key questions: What ideas are likely to improve patient safety and minimize error? and, conversely, What ideas are likely to worsen patient safety and increase error? This chapter identifies some fundamental ideas that play a key role in patient safety.

Idea 1: The Definition of Medical Error

The definition of error itself plays a very important role in reducing errors, since one cannot reduce something if one does not know what it is. Ever since the time of Socrates, philosophers have attempted to answer definitional ("what is it?") questions. What is a medical error? Let's start with the prior question, What is an error? This question seems easy to answer, but it is not. A great deal hinges on the type of system we are analyzing. For example, if our system is a mechanical measuring device, such as a thermometer, we could say that the thermometer makes an error when the temperature it indicates is not the same as the actual temperature.[16] Thus, an *incorrect* measurement is one type of error. The measurement is incorrect because it does not accurately represent the state of the world.

In scientific research, errors occur when we unintentionally hold beliefs that are incorrect (i.e., not true). A false belief (or epistemological error) is a belief that does not correspond to the facts. For instance, if we accept the hypothesis that a particular drug is safe and effective, when in fact it is not, then we have committed what is known as a type I error (false positive). If we accept the hypothesis that the drug is not safe and effective, when in fact it is, then we have committed a type II error (false negative).[17] Scientists confront errors constantly in research and have developed methods and procedures for reducing and eliminating them. Hence, the scientific method is often said to be "self-correcting." Some scholars have argued that the only way that science can move toward the truth is by eliminating errors.[18]

If we move away from science and consider the practical arts, then we may view errors as mistaken (or incorrect) actions (i.e., practical errors) rather than as mistaken beliefs. Since actions are not true or false, we must measure actions against some type of standard other than correspondence with the facts. We could say that an action is correct if it corresponds to the rules and norms that govern that action, and an action is incorrect if it does not correspond to the rules and norms that govern it. For example, various rules and norms govern the game of baseball. An error could occur when someone performs an action that fails to conform to those rules and norms, such as dropping a ball or making a poor throw.

We might consider some incorrect actions to be unethical or illegal rather than erroneous. For example, if a person accidentally takes someone else's umbrella, we would consider this to be a mistake. If a person *intentionally* takes someone else's umbrella, we would consider that to be theft. The same point also applies to erroneous beliefs: A person who intentionally publishes erroneous data might be guilty of fraud or misconduct, but a person who unintentionally publishes erroneous data might be guilty only of error or negligence.[19]

Thus, whether we are considering epistemological or practical errors, some elements of the definition of error are the same: (1) Errors are *deviations* from the correct belief or conduct, and (2) Errors are *unintentional*. The major difference between erroneous beliefs and erroneous actions is that the former are beliefs that do not agree with the facts, whereas the latter are actions that do not conform to the appropriate norms. If there is a situation in which there are no facts or norms (i.e., a "gray" area), it follows that there can be no errors but only disagreements or differences of opinion.

How should one define "error" in medicine? If we construe medicine as a science, then its errors should be understood as epistemological errors. If, on the other hand, we view medicine as a practical art, then its errors should be practical errors. So is the aim of medicine to obtain correct beliefs or to perform correct actions? Is it a science or a practical art? This is a complex question that will not be addressed in detail here. For the purposes of this chapter, we will assume that medicine is both an art and a science: It is concerned with forming correct beliefs as well performing correct actions.[20] Thus, errors in medicine could be epistemological or practical.

Moreover, in medicine, incorrect beliefs may lead to incorrect actions. For example, suppose that an emergency room doctor examines a 32-year-old patient with chest pain and determines that he has not had a heart attack, when, in fact, he has had a heart attack. The doctor diagnoses the chest pain incorrectly and sends the man home with a prescription for a tranquilizer. The man subsequently has a heart attack and dies. In this case, the doctor formed an erroneous belief as a result of poor clinical judgment. She acted on that erroneous belief by performing an incorrect action: She sent the man home when she should have kept him in the hospital for more medical tests and supervision. The belief was erroneous because it did not agree with facts, and the action was erroneous because it did not conform to the rules and norms of medicine, that is, the standard of care.

The IOM report adopts a definition of error that encompasses incorrect actions and beliefs: "An error is defined as a failure of a planned action to be completed as intended (i.e., error of execution) or the use of the wrong plan to achieve an aim (i.e., error of planning)."[21] In this definition, a "failure of a planned action" could be viewed as an incorrect action, and a "use of the wrong plan" could be viewed as an incorrect belief.

Although this definition of error seems clear enough, it requires some interpretation to apply it to actual cases. What is a "failure of a planned action"? If a nurse gives a patient a dose of a drug 1 hour too late, would this be a failure of a planned action? What if the dose is given only 5 minutes late? Perhaps the only planned action is that the patient should receive the dose of the medication at an appropriate time, left to the discretion of the nurse. Thus, it might not be an error if the dose is given 5 minutes or even 1 hour too late. Also, what is the "use of the wrong plan"? If a doctor writes a prescription for the wrong drug, would this be "the wrong plan"? Suppose that the drug is not the "wrong drug" but is simply a drug that is not as effective as a different drug; would this be the "wrong plan"? If one thinks long and hard about medical error, it would appear that each practitioner may make dozens of minor mistakes on a daily basis, because each practitioner will deviate from the proper beliefs or actions. Should we count all of these deviations as errors?

Thus, while the IOM's definition offers some useful guidance, one must interpret the definition in order to apply it to particular cases. In interpreting and applying the definition of error, one confronts problems relating to the scope of the definition: Should it have a broad scope or a narrow scope? If one adopts a very narrow and limited interpretation of the definition of error, then one is less likely to report errors or make serious attempts to improve safety. If one adopts a broader and more comprehensive interpretation, then one is more likely to report errors and make serious attempts to improve safety. On the other hand, an interpretation of a definition could be too broad to be useful. If one sees errors everywhere, it is practically impossible to report all of them or do anything about them.

So what is the proper way to interpret the scope of the definition of error? One useful way of restricting the scope of the definition is to distinguish between *harmful* and *harmless* errors. A harmful error is one that *has caused or could cause* harm; a harmless error is an error that has not caused harm and is not likely to cause harm. For example, giving a dose of a drug 5 minutes late would probably be a harmless error; failing to give the dose at all would probably be a harmful error.

Suppose that a nurse is about to give a patient the wrong drug, due to a labeling problem, but another member of the health care team catches him before he makes this error. Although many people might be tempted to not report this error because it did not result in harm to the patient—"no harm, no foul"—health care professionals should avoid this temptation. They should report these near misses because these are events that could have caused harm and might cause harm the next time they occur. To promote patient safety, health care professionals should learn from their near misses and make changes to prevent "direct hits."

Another way of restricting the scope of the definition would be to distinguish between *preventable* and *unpreventable* errors. It would seem to be pointless to spend time and effort trying to identify or analyze errors that are not preventable. An error is preventable if there is something that someone could have realistically done to stop the error from occurring. For example, if a doctor has a heart attack while operating on a patient, this is an error that is probably not preventable. Amputating the wrong foot is an error that is probably preventable.

The IOM report recognizes the relationship between errors and preventable adverse events. The IOM report defines an adverse event as an "injury caused by medical management rather than the underlying condition of the patient. An adverse event attributable to error is a preventable adverse event."[22] Thus, it appears that the IOM report would recommend that the health care industry focus its efforts on errors that led to or could lead to preventable adverse events.

To summarize this section, the definition of error is a basic idea that plays a key role in the prevention of error. Because health care providers and industry leaders must know how to recognize errors in order to report them, a comprehensive and useful definition of error is essential. Because medical errors may involve incorrect beliefs as well as incorrect actions, the definition should encompass a wide range of activities in health care, ranging from diagnosis and decision making to the administration of medications and the preparation of patients for surgery. Furthermore, the scope of the definition should not be too narrow or too broad. It should focus on errors that are harmful (or potentially harmful) and preventable, that is, errors that have caused or could cause preventable adverse events.[23]

Idea 2: The Priority of Patient Safety

The second idea is self-explanatory: The health care industry will not make significant progress toward reducing errors unless health care industry leaders, practitioners, and even patients have a strong commitment to error reduction. As noted earlier, the IOM report recognizes the importance of a strong commitment to error reduction and patient safety. The report makes several recommendations that speak to a national commitment to patient safety, including the creation of a national center for patient safety, mandatory reporting of adverse events,[24] peer review protections for patient safety inquiries,[25] and performance standards for patient safety.[26] The IOM report also recommends that health care institutions take several steps to demonstrate their commitment to patient safety, including developing patient safety programs, implementing systems for reporting and analyzing errors, and implementing well-understood safety principles, such as standardization of equipment and processes.[27] Many organizations have already begun to implement these recommendations.

Although these recommendations make a great deal of sense and suggest a strong commitment to patient safety, they still do not answer some of the fundamental questions about the priority of patient safety, such as, How important is error reduction? Does it have a high priority or a low priority? and Is it viewed as valuable for its own sake or only as valuable for the sake of some other goal, such as patient satisfaction? These questions are important to answer, because a patient safety program is doomed to failure if people in the health care industry have only a superficial commitment to patient safety. To succeed in reducing medical errors, industry leaders, practitioners, and patients must have a sincere commitment to safety and error avoidance. They must back up their public endorsements of patient safety with time, money, and resources.

One simple way to determine how much a person (or organization) values something is to determine whether he or she values it for its own sake (i.e., intrinsically) or only for the sake of something else (i.e., extrinsically). A person who values something intrinsically will continue to value that thing even when his or her circumstances change, whereas a person who values something only extrinsically will value that thing only as long as it is necessary to achieve some other goal. For example, a person who values exercise for its own sake will continue to exercise when he does not need to exercise to lose weight, control his diabetes, attract a mate, or achieve some other goal. A person who does not value exercising intrinsically will stop exercising regularly whenever the occasion permits. Likewise, an organization that values patient safety intrinsically will continue to value patient safety even when the organization does not need to emphasize patient safety to achieve some other goal, such as patient satisfaction or profitability. On the other hand, an organization that does not value patient safety for its own sake will cut corners on patient safety whenever the occasion permits.

One way of restating this point is to say that patient safety should be one of the core values of the health care industry. It should receive equal billing with other core values, such as quality improvement, patient satisfaction, health promotion, medical education, and medical research and development. Health care organizations can demonstrate their commitment to patient safety by touting the importance of patient safety in their brochures, policies, Web pages, and public communications; by developing patient safety programs; by hiring patient safety officers; and by collecting, analyzing, and interpreting patient safety data. Health care practitioners can demonstrate their commitment to patient safety by talking to other professionals about safety issues, by following patient safety guidelines, by reporting errors, and by helping to develop systems that are designed to improve safety. Last but not least, patients can play a key role in the patient safety movement by helping to prevent errors. Patients should be more than mere passive recipients of health care; they should be active participants. For example, a patient could ask a nurse if he or she has double-checked a medication order, and could ask a pharmacist about dangerous drug interactions and precautions for use. A patient should also discuss issues related to her own safety with her doctor, such as potential risks and steps that she can take to minimize those risks.

In other words, everyone in the health care industry—from doctor to patient to CEO—needs to think "safety first." This may sound like an obvious or even trivial point, but if it is, then why is error such a big problem in health care? Somehow, somewhere, many people have forgotten this simple point. There is nothing wrong with reemphasizing this point time and again, if this is what it takes to improve patient safety.

Although it is important to emphasize the intrinsic value of patient safety, it may be strategically wise to argue for the importance of patient safety by providing evidence that it tends to promote other worthwhile goals, such as quality improvement, customer satisfaction, and even profitability. Health care industry leaders will be hesitant to invest in patient safety programs unless they can see how these programs are likely to affect the bottom line. Although it seems rather obvious that reducing and preventing medical errors would increase patient satisfaction, quality improvement, and profitability, it would still be useful to study the relationship between patient safety and these other values in order to build the case for patient safety and to understand how it affects different aspects of health care. Is a hospital with a good safety program less likely to be sued than one without a good safety program? This would be a question worth investigating. Thus, it may be useful to invest some time, money, and effort in conducting research on the relationship between patient safety and other goals.

Idea 3: The Acceptance of Error

Another idea that can play an important role in patient safety is the acceptance of errors (or lack thereof). It sounds a bit paradoxical that one should accept errors in order to prevent them, but it is true. Although errors should be avoided, people and systems are not perfect. Health care practitioners who do not acknowledge and accept this important fact may deny, rationalize, and refuse to report errors. The most effective way of dealing with errors is to acknowledge that they happen and are likely to happen, again and again. Indeed, one might argue that errors are necessary in order to improve human conduct and to design better systems, since one can learn from one's mistakes. Experience is the best teacher. It is unfortunate that patients and health care professionals must suffer the consequences of error, but this is unavoidable. The only way to completely avoid errors in medicine would be to never practice medicine.

There is considerable evidence that doctors have a hard time dealing with their own mistakes.[28,29] Doctors tend to not talk about their mistakes, or, when they do, they may try to rationalize or deny them.[30] Evidence also indicates that doctors suffer from stress, anxiety, guilt, and depression when they make mistakes.[31] Albert Wu relates his personal experience of a medical error he encountered:

> When I was a house officer another resident failed to identify the electrocardiographic signs of the pericardial tamponade that would rush the patient to the operating room that night. The news spread rapidly, the case was tried repeatedly before an incredulous jury of peers, who returned a summary judgment of incompetence. I was dismayed by the lack of sympathy and wondered secretly if I could have made the same mistake—and, like the hapless resident, become the second victim of medical error.[32]

Wu then diagnoses the problem that is affecting the profession of medicine:

> Strangely, there is no place for mistakes in modern medicine. Society has entrusted physicians with the burden of understanding and dealing with illness. Although it is often said that "doctors are only human," technological wonders, the apparent precision of laboratory tests, and innovations that present tangible images of illness have in fact created an expectation of perfection. Patients, who have an understandable need to consider their doctors infallible, have colluded with doctors to deny the existence of error. Hospitals react to every error as an anomaly, for which the solution is to ferret out and blame the individual.[33]

According to Wu, doctors have a difficult time dealing with medical error because they and their patients have come to expect perfection, and because hospitals also expect perfection and blame individuals instead of examining systems. Other doctors have expressed similar sentiments. Some argue that medical culture and the myth of infallibility prevent doctors from facing their mistakes.[34]

Atul Gawande, a surgical resident, argues that the threat of medical malpractice liability plays an important role in the problems that doctors have in responding to error:

> The deeper problem with medical malpractice suits is that by demonizing errors they prevent doctors from acknowledging them and discussing them publicly. The tort system makes adversaries of patient and physician, and pushes each to offer a heavily slanted version of events. When things go wrong, it's almost impossible for a physician to talk to a patient honestly about mistakes.[35]

Risk managers and hospital attorneys have had a change of heart in recent years about disclosing errors to patients. At one time, hospital risk managers and attorneys would strongly discourage health care professionals from disclosing errors to patients. This policy was based on the idea that the patient would be likely to sue the practitioner or the hospital if he or she discovered the error. However, a growing body of evidence indicates that the consequences of nondisclosure are worse than the consequences of disclosure, since a patient who discovers an undisclosed error may become angry and vindictive. He may think that the hospital has tried to cover up the error, and he may sue the hospital out of spite or just to acquire information.[36] Today, most risk managers recommend that physicians communicate honestly and openly with patients and their families about medical errors that result in adverse events.[37]

However, there is a legal and ethical dilemma in communicating to patients honestly about medical errors, because what practitioners say to patients may be admitted into evidence in court as an admission of guilt.[38] But how can one communicate "honestly" with a patient without admitting that one has made a mistake or is at fault? This is a difficult ethical and legal issue, which this chapter will not attempt to solve.[39] On the other hand, it is important to develop an appropriate response to this issue in order to promote the acceptance of medical errors and effective communication about medical errors.

How can the health care industry increase the acceptance of medical errors? The first place to begin would be to implement programs that offer psychological counseling and support to practitioners who make mistakes. This program should go beyond the peer review activities that occur in health care, which usually focus only on particular episodes and tend to involve finger pointing. A support program should address the long-term consequences of medical errors for practitioners and should not be an exercise in finger pointing. Such a program should offer doctors, pharmacists, and nurses sympathy and empathy. An ideal model would be a support group similar to the groups that offer support to cancer patients, grieving families, and alcoholics and drug addicts. As Wu notes, "the kind of unconditional sympathy and support that are really needed are rarely forthcoming."[40] He also observes that there can be some very drastic consequences for doctors when they have trouble dealing with mistakes: "some physicians are deeply wounded, lose their nerve, burn out, or seek solace in alcohol and drugs."[41]

However, the inability of health care professionals to deal effectively with medical error has roots that extend deep into the heart of medicine. Thus, to increase acceptance of error, one must do more than just offer counseling and support, one must also change medical education and training, since it is likely that health care professionals learn how to respond to error while they are students and interns. Pilpel, Schor, and Benbasset argue that the medical curriculum should include discussions of medical error so that students may learn how to cope with error and come to understand that it is inevitable but also preventable.[42]

Speaking from his own experience as a surgical intern, Gawande claims that doctors need to acknowledge their fallibility but that medical education and practice teach the opposite lesson.[43] *Fallibilism* is simply the idea that one could be mistaken. In the 19th century, the prominent American philosopher Charles Peirce argued that science is fallible because today's scientific theories and hypotheses may be refuted some day. Nevertheless, science can make progress toward a more complete understanding of nature, even though it will make many mistakes along the way.[44] Almost 30 years ago, two other philosophers argued that medicine is fallible.[45] If doctors adopted this philosophy, they would be more scientific because they would strive to recognize and correct their mistakes, and they would also be, ironically, more humanistic because they would accept their mistakes as an inevitable part of the advancement of medical knowledge and practice.

It is also important to develop programs that help patients come to understand and accept errors in medicine. Patient educational materials in hospitals should include information on medical errors. Hospitals and health care organizations should also provide counseling and support for patients and families who are the victims of medical error. Finally, there should also be programs for health care administrators.

Conclusion

This chapter has expanded on the systems approach to medical error and considered how philosophies (or worldviews) can play a role in patient safety and error prevention. It has identified, described, and discussed three foundational ideas that play a key role in patient safety.

The first idea is the definition of "medical error." The definition should include errors related to incorrect actions as well as errors related to incorrect beliefs, and it should focus on errors that are preventable and cause harm or are likely to cause harm.

The second idea is the commitment to patient safety. Health care professionals, health care administrators, and patients should make patient safety one of the core values in health care. They should value safety for its own sake, not just for the sake of its effect on other values, such as quality improvement, patient satisfaction, or profitability.

The third idea is the acceptance of medical error. Health care professionals, health care administrators, and patients should learn to accept medical error so they may deal with it effectively. Health care organizations should provide support and counseling for practitioners who make mistakes, and medical, pharmacy, nursing, and other health care schools should include a discussion of medical error in their curricula. Risk managers and hospital attorneys should also develop policies for dealing with the dilemmas involved in honest and open communication about medical errors with patients.

Notes

1. Institute of Medicine, *To Err Is Human: Building a Safer Health System* (Washington, DC: National Academy Press, 1999).
2. Ibid., 22.
3. Ibid.
4. Troy Brennan et al., "Incidence of Adverse Events and Negligence in Hospitalized Patients: Results of the Harvard Medical Practice Study," *New England Journal of Medicine* 1991;324:370–376.
5. IOM, *To Err Is Human*, 22.
6. Ibid., 44–45.
7. Ibid., 42.
8. Charles Perrow, *Normal Accidents* (New York: Basic Books, 1984); James Reason, *Human Error* (New York: Cambridge University Press, 1990).
9. IOM, *To Err Is Human*, 44.
10. Ibid., 31–33.
11. Ibid., 12.
12. Ibid., 10.
13. These distinctions between "individuals," "groups," and "systems" are part of the standard vocabulary of the branch of philosophy known as ontology, which studies the basic constituents of the universe. For further discussion, see W. V. Quine, *Word and Object* (Cambridge, MA: MIT Press, 1964); and Nelson Goodman, *The Structure of Appearance* (Indianapolis: Bobbs-Merrill, 1966).
14. IOM, *To Err Is Human*, 44.
15. This observation is based on the work of Thomas Kuhn, who argued that scientific revolutions involve changes in worldviews. Kuhn also held that scientists tend to resist changes of belief that threaten their worldviews. See his *The Structure of Scientific Revolutions*, 2nd ed. (Chicago: University of Chicago Press, 1970).
16. Alvin Goldman, *Epistemology and Cognition* (Cambridge, MA: Harvard University Press, 1988).
17. Donald Brown, Kenneth Michels, and Benjamin Winer, *Statistical Principles and Experimental Design* (New York: McGraw-Hill, 1991).
18. Karl Popper, *Conjectures and Refutations* (New York: Basic Books, 1962).
19. The definition of "misconduct" in research does not include error. "Misconduct" is intentionally fabricating or falsifying data, or intentionally plagiarizing research. See Panel on Scientific Responsibility and the Conduct of Research, *Responsible Science*, Vol. 1 (Washington, DC: National Academy Press, 1992).
20. Daniel Albert, Ronald Munson, and Michael Resnik, *Reasoning in Medicine*, 2nd ed. (Baltimore: Johns Hopkins University Press, 1999).
21. IOM, *To Err Is Human*, 28.
22. Ibid., 24.
23. The risk management department at University Health Systems of Eastern Carolina has developed a comprehensive event reporting form that distinguishes among nine different categories of reportable events, ranging from "Category I: An event occurred that may have contributed

to or resulted in the patient's death" to "Category A: Circumstances or events that have the capacity to cause error, harm, loss." The form also has a category for reporting errors that occur but do not reach the patient. University Health Systems of Eastern Carolina, Event Reporting form, 0289-RM/Rev.12-01/Event Report, 2001.

24. IOM, *To Err Is Human*, 7.
25. Ibid., 9.
26. Ibid.,10–11.
27. Ibid., 12.
28. David Hilfiker, "Facing Our Mistakes," *New England Journal of Medicine* 1984;310:118–122.
29. John Christensen, William Levinson, and Paul Dunn, "The Heart of Darkness: The Impact of Perceived Mistakes on Physicians," *Journal of General Internal Medicine* 1992;7:424–431.
30. Theo Mizrahi, "Managing Medical Mistakes: Ideology, Insularity, and Accountability Among Internists in Training," *Social Science and Medicine* 1984;19:135–146.
31. Albert Wu, "Medical Error: The Second Victim: The Doctor Who Makes the Mistake Needs Help Too," *British Medical Journal* 2000;320:726–727.
32. Ibid., 726.
33. Ibid.
34. Paul McNeill and Merrilyn Walton, "Medical Harm and the Consequences of Error for Doctors," *Medical Journal of Australia* 2000;176:222–225.
35. Atul Gawande, *Complications: A Surgeon's Notes on an Imperfect Science* (New York: Metropolitan Books, 2002).
36. Gerald Hickson et al., "Patient Complaints and Malpractice Risk," *Journal of the American Medical Association* 2000;287:2951–2957.
37. See, for example, Vanderbilt University Medical Center, Guide to Risk Management. <http://www.vanderbilt.edu/RiskMgmt/quality.htm#report>. Accessed December 4, 2002.
38. John Strong et al., *McCormick on Evidence*, 5th ed. (St. Paul, MN: West Publishing, 1999), 372–393.
39. McNeill and Walton, "Medical Harm."
40. Wu, "Medical Error," 727.
41. Ibid.
42. David Pilpel, Robert Schor, and John Benbasset, "Barriers to Acceptance of Medical Error: The Case for a Teaching Program," *Medical Education* 1998;32:3–7.
43. Gawande, *Complications*, 187–201.
44. Charles Peirce, "The Scientific Attitude and Fallibilism." In: J. Buchler (ed.), *Philosophical Writings of Peirce* (New York: Dover Publications, 1955), 42–60.
45. Samuel Gorovitz and Alisdare MacIntyre, "Toward a Theory of Medical Fallibility," *Journal of Medicine and Philosophy* 1976;1:51–71.

CHAPTER SIX

THE FALLACY OF THE BODY COUNT: WHY THE INTEREST IN PATIENT SAFETY AND WHY NOW?

Jerod M. Loeb, PhD and Dennis S. O'Leary, MD

It is often assumed that medical errors represent the antithesis of health care quality. Yet over the last few years, some of this nation's most prominent—and consistently highly rated—health care facilities have faced very public scrutiny for major medical errors. Even with considerable organizational emphasis on contemporary quality management processes—including compliance with accreditation requirements—errors in medicine occur every day. And there is clearly a perception that medical errors are increasing in number and in severity. In essence, health care quality, in the negative form of medical errors, has never before been so prominent on the radar screens of key stakeholders, including public policymakers, health professionals, health care organizations, the media, and patients themselves. The 1999 report of the Institute of Medicine (IOM), *To Err Is Human,* galvanized significant public and professional interest in medical errors; however, much of the research base upon which the Institute's report was built was gathered years earlier. Indeed, the highly publicized annual mortality figures of 44,000 to 98,000 deaths per year caused by medical errors were extrapolated from medical records studies dating back to 1984.

Although there is still considerable controversy surrounding the accuracy of the extrapolated numbers of deaths and injuries associated with medical errors, it is clear that the problem is pervasive. Unfortunately, an accurate count of the numbers of deaths or injuries that are attributable directly or indirectly to medical errors is impossible today. Even within a given health care facility, accurate counting is difficult—and in some cases, impossible—because of the legal, cultural, and administrative barriers to the reporting of errors. This leads to the inevitable conclusion that whatever the number, it is underreported and, at the same time, too high. Worse yet, absent a salutary mechanism whereby errors can be consistently reported and analyzed, and the lessons learned disseminated, the very same errors are likely to occur repeatedly within the same institution and across institutions.

Since the mid-1960s, a plethora of medical and scientific literature has been published that is pertinent to understanding and preventing medical errors. This includes case reports describing adverse events, observational and epidemiological studies, sociological works, studies in cognitive psychology, human factors and engineering analyses, and other types of scientific investigations. Even in the face of this mounting knowledge base, the annual toll of deaths and serious injuries attributable to medical errors seemingly continues to rise unabated.

Patient safety as a loosely defined public policy issue first arose in association with the considerable public and professional attention paid to the "malpractice crisis" of the 1970s. During that era, the American College of Surgeons published the first-ever patient safety manual. In the 1980s, anesthesiologists began a formal effort to improve outcomes associated with anesthesia administration. This dedicated research effort, supported in large part by the American Society of Anesthesiologists under the aegis of the Anesthesia Patient Safety Foundation, spawned significant improvements in perioperative care. In fact, mortality from anesthesia-related complications has improved from about 1 death per 15,000 surgical cases in the 1980s to less than 1 death per 200,000 cases today, a remarkable achievement in patient safety.

The Harvard Medical Practice Study, originally published in 1991, provided a large population-based examination of the incidence of adverse events in hospitals and is the source of the high-end annual error-related mortality estimates cited in the 1999 IOM report. By the mid-1990s, it appeared that the nation's hospitals were facing an epidemic of wrong-sided surgery, medication misadventures, and other frightening and tragic types of errors. In late 1994, Lucian Leape, one of the coauthors of the Harvard Medical Practice Study, published an important essay on error in medicine in the *Journal of the American Medical Association*. Leape compared medicine with other types of high-risk industries—most notably, aviation and nuclear power—and concluded that poorly designed systems were responsible for the majority of deaths and avoidable injuries associated with errors in medicine. In fact, health care incorporates many of the same attributes of other high-risk industries, including exquisitely complex procedures, multiple-step processes, tight coupling, time pressures, and substantial human engagement. Yet, health care organizations and many individual health care practitioners have remained unaware of, or have been reticent to embrace, the tools and techniques used by engineers in other fields of endeavor to enhance safety and reduce risks.

Recognizing the importance of learning from other high-risk industries that have grappled with safety-related concerns (e.g., nuclear power, the chemical industry, aviation), the American Medical Association, the American Association for the Advancement of Science, the Joint Commission on Accreditation of Healthcare Organizations, and the Annenberg Center for Health Sciences at Eisenhower Medical Center convened in 1996 the first in a series of national, multidisciplinary conferences designed specifically to bring together representatives from disparate industries to learn from each other about reducing and preventing medical errors. The first conference drew nearly 300 attendees. One of the most compelling sessions focused on a tragic medication error at a Florida hospital that resulted in the death of an 8-year-old boy during a relatively minor surgical procedure. The discussants included the patient's anesthesiologist, the hospital's nurse risk manager, the hospital's CEO, the plaintiff's attorney, and a representative from the media. Although there was discussion about what had happened and the response of the organization to the error, the emphasis on identifying and learning from the underlying root causes of the error was the session's principal take-home lesson. This session was subsequently featured in a front-page story in *USA Today*.

At this conference, the Joint Commission announced a new policy respecting the reporting of sentinel events.* Also at the conference, the American Medical Association announced the imminent formation of a patient safety foundation, modeled after the Anesthesia Patient Safety Foundation. One of the most important insights to come out of this first Annenberg conference was an appreciation of the extent of the cultural, legal, and organizational barriers standing in the way of the changes necessary to create an environment in health care conducive

---

*A sentinel event is defined by the Joint Commission as any unexpected occurrence involving death or serious physical or psychological injury, or the risk thereof. Serious injuries specifically include a loss of limb or function; the phrase "or the risk thereof" includes any process variation for which a recurrence would carry a significant chance of a serious adverse outcome.

to reporting on, and learning from, errors. Perhaps the most crucial change needed—and still absent today—is federal confidentiality protections for reported events and their associated root cause analyses.

A second Annenberg conference, convened 2 years later, drew a significantly larger audience, but little progress was evident with respect to changing the extant cultures within health care or improving global understanding of the underlying epidemiology and demographics of medical errors. Although root cause analyses submitted to the Joint Commission in association with voluntary sentinel event reporting were providing important new information about the causes—and thus future prevention—of sentinel events, only a relatively small number of accredited health care organizations were contributing cases to the database. What was clear by 1998 was that any substantive solutions would require strong commitment by the executive leadership of health care organizations. Unfortunately, this conference and multiple subsequent discussions on health care errors and patient safety have attracted very small numbers of these leaders.

The Social Context: Alignment Versus Nonalignment

It is helpful to assess the intense scrutiny being given to the issue of medical errors by the general public and by health care professionals in the context of the countervailing social and political forces at play. The desire to identify an individual to blame and punish in the aftermath of a medical error is an instinctive and understandable response to what, in many cases, has resulted in irreparable harm to a patient. Such a response is structured to find the guilty party, punish him or her, and provide damages or relief to the victim, or both. These instincts are driven in large part by a society that seems to believe that legal redresses exist and are appropriate for any and all problems. However, such responses—with the possible exception of those situations in which an individual practitioner is found to be practicing negligently—have little demonstrated effect on preventing future occurrences of the same or similar events, even within the same institution.

The subculture of health care reflects and amplifies these pervasive attitudes and behaviors. Indeed, physicians, nurses, and other health care professionals are educated and trained in a model that emphasizes the ability of the individual to control and determine clinical outcomes and the accountability of the individual in the face of adverse occurrences. By contrast, no health care professionals—nor, for that matter, any health care executives—are schooled in systems engineering and its potential applications to providing safe care for patients. Thus, when an adverse event does occur within a health care setting, the health care professional at the proximal ("sharp") end of the occurrence is humiliated and has no reason or incentive to report it internally. If the occurrence does become known internally, blame and punishment *of individuals* are, in most organizations, sure to follow.

It is perhaps ironic that most errors in medicine do not result from individual carelessness but are rather almost always the result of systems-related flaws in design or implementation. Lack of awareness of this reality and lack of knowledge about how systems problems can be effectively addressed are in fact even more serious problems. For instance, tested mechanisms for reducing the incidence of errors already exist, such as unit dosing for medications, computerized physician order entry systems, prominent preoperative marking of the correct surgical site, and removal of concentrated potassium chloride from floor stocks. Yet, remarkably, not all health care facilities have implemented even the simplest of these system fixes.

Meanwhile, solutions are regularly proposed that represent "swat the mosquito" reactions to the problem rather than draining the swamp. For example, the mandatory public reporting of medical errors by health care organizations is often promoted as a definitive solution to error commission. However, there is no evidence to suggest that such public reporting—especially absent confidentiality for the investigatory findings—will have the salutary effect of reducing the incidence of errors. Rather, it is a virtual certainty that forcing public reporting will drive further underground any error reports that can be hidden. This will have a clearly deleterious effect on the ability of the affected health care organization—and other health care organizations—to learn from adverse occurrences. The seemingly simple solution—voluntary, confidential error reporting—may go against the grain of societal instincts; however, the preponderance of evidence respecting nonpunitive, confidential reporting systems suggests that they can be quite effective in generating useful information regarding errors, their frequencies, and their underlying causes.

To illustrate, the Safe Medical Devices Act of 1990 requires reporting to the Food and Drug Administration any serious injuries or illnesses related to the failure or misuse of specified medical devices. However, there is little evidence that such mandatory reporting has resulted in any significant improvements in patient safety. Similarly, although some individual states have mandatory reporting requirements for certain serious medical errors that result in patient harm, these data have generally only accumulated over time. In some cases, the reports have been used to punish individuals and organizations. Substantial underreporting is a known characteristic of these systems, and there are neither incentives—positive or negative—to report nor any ability to identify cases that were not reported. Finally, there are no instances in which these state databases have been used to disseminate lessons learned and to suggest measures for preventing future errors.

By contrast, the Joint Commission's voluntary, confidential reporting system has produced a database rich with lessons learned and progressively shared. Whenever a sentinel event occurs, the accredited organization is expected to complete a thorough and credible root cause analysis, identify and implement systems improvements to reduce risk, and monitor the effectiveness of those improvements. Although the immediate causes of most sentinel events are almost always linked to human fallibility, the root cause analysis is expected to reach well beyond this level to underlying organizational systems and processes that can be redesigned to create protections against future human error and to protect patients from harm when human error does occur. The admittedly selective voluntary reporting of sentinel events has nevertheless progressively expanded the Joint Commission's database of such events and their underlying causes. The database categorizes the most common underlying causes of these events and the strategies that accredited organizations have used to reduce risk to patients. This has permitted the Joint Commission to regularly distribute to health care organizations information about sentinel events and how they can be prevented through its quarterly newsletter, *Sentinel Event Alert.*

Under the Joint Commission's sentinel event policy, a defined subset of sentinel events are subject to review and may be reported to the Joint Commission on a *voluntary* basis. The policy provides for the reporting of only those sentinel events that affect recipients of care (patients, clients, residents) and have resulted in unanticipated death or major permanent loss of function not related to the natural course of the patient's illness or underlying condition. Also subject to voluntary reporting are suicide of a patient in a setting where the patient receives around-the-clock care (e.g., hospital, residential treatment center, crisis stabilization center); infant abduction or discharge to the wrong family; rape; hemolytic transfusion reaction involving administration of blood or blood products having major blood group incompatibilities; and surgery on the wrong patient or wrong body part. An organization that experiences an adverse event that it defines as a sentinel event but which does *not* meet the criteria for review by the Joint Commission under its sentinel event policy is still required to complete a root cause analysis and act upon its results. However, the root cause analysis need not be made available to the Joint Commission.

Since January 1995, the Joint Commission has reviewed approximately 1,000 sentinel events. The majority of the reported sentinel events in the Joint Commission's database involve inpatient suicide ($\approx$19%), serious medication error ($\approx$13%), operative or postoperative complication ($\approx$12%), wrong-site surgery ($\approx$9%), and delays in treatment ($\approx$5%). More than 78% of the reported cases have resulted in patient death. It is difficult to extrapolate from these data to estimate the actual incidence of various types of errors because the database contains only those events reported, not all events that have occurred. The data are likely to be skewed toward those specific events less likely to be hidden within the health care organization or from the patient, family, or media. The widespread dissemination of lessons learned and preventive strategies appears to have had some impact. Although more anecdotal than statistically significant, there appear to have been dramatic reductions in deaths attributable to the administration of floor stocks of undiluted potassium chloride and to the use of patient restraints. By contrast, there appears to be no diminution in the frequencies of patient suicide and wrong-site surgery.

In essence, the accreditation process is itself a risk reduction activity. When recently analyzed, 43% of existing Joint Commission standards were found to relate directly to patient safety. In July 2001, the Joint Commission implemented additional consensus standards that address specific issues identified in the expanding knowledge base respecting medical errors and adverse events. These standards underscore the responsibility for organizational leadership to create a blame-free environment that encourages error identification and remedial steps to reduce the risk of future occurrences. Additional standards require organizational engagement in proactive systems analysis as an error prevention strategy and training at all levels that focuses both on new patient care technologies and methods and on teamwork and error identification, analysis, and prevention. Finally, the new standards address the importance of effective communication in the care delivery process, the use of knowledge-based information, and the need to inform the patient, and when appropriate, the patient's family, of unanticipated outcomes of care.

Disparate Approaches of Key Stakeholders

What was clearly distinctive about the release of the IOM report (as opposed to the myriad individual reports on medical errors published over the years) was the tremendous national and international attention the report garnered. As often happens in the face of intense media attention, public policymakers faced this "wake-up call" by declaring a "crisis" and promoting a series of legislative remedies, only a few of which were soundly designed or responsive to the educational challenges inherent in better understanding and preventing errors in medicine.

Meanwhile, disparate entities in both the public and private sectors have sought to be responsive to the recommendations contained in the IOM report. The report recommended prominent roles for the National Quality Forum and the Agency for Healthcare Research and Quality to set standards for adverse event reporting and to analyze and disseminate best practice information. The Agency for Healthcare Research and Quality is devoting approximately $50 million to projects addressing specific issues in patient safety. The Veterans Health Administration, long a leader in patient safety, is focusing on developing a nonpunitive reporting mechanism modeled after the Aviation Safety Reporting System, which uses the National Aeronautics and Space Administration as the third party to which reports are sent. A comprehensive federal government response—through the President's Quality Interagency Coordinating Task Force—was formulated less than 3 months after the release of the IOM report. That response envisions a mandatory reporting system in which both states and peer review organizations (PROs) would have prominent roles. The Health Care Financing Administration is also said to be developing a new Medicare condition of participation that will require hospitals to have medical error reduction programs. Purchasers have also begun to address the challenges framed by the IOM report. For example, the Leapfrog Group, a coalition of large corporate purchasers, is promoting an agenda that contemplates the shifting of purchases of medical care to those hospitals that have incorporated computerized physician order entry, use intensivists in critical care settings, and meet certain volume thresholds for specified surgical procedures.

However, the core unresolved issue—whether confidentiality protections should be afforded to reported adverse events and their associated root cause analyses—lies in the lap of the United States Congress. Here, public policymakers have come to a definitive fork in the road, where one pathway would respond to demands for holding providers accountable to the public, while the other would respond to demands for improved patient safety. Unfortunately, Yogi Berra's situational advice—"When you come to the fork in the road, take it"—is not an option in this instance.

Down the accountability pathway lies "mandatory" reporting and public reporting of adverse event frequencies on at least an organization-specific basis. Although these "body counts" would un-questionably place the harsh spotlight of accountability on the guilty organizations (which will eventually be virtually all health care orga-nizations), such a public policy position would lie in stark contrast to the increasingly broad-based efforts to create "blame-free" environ-ments within health care organizations.

In reality, most adverse events in health care remain hidden from view, even within health care organizations themselves. The Joint Com-mission both accepts voluntary reports of adverse events from organi-zations and aggressively scans media reports across the nation on a daily basis in search of such occurrences. The number of identified cases in a given year has never exceeded 350, and of these, approxi-mately three quarters are self-reported. Contrasting this number with the figures cited in the IOM report provides a dramatic illustration of the extent to which adverse events can be concealed. A public policy position that provides incentives for even greater concealment would not only fall well short of its basic objective but would also undermine efforts to surface, study, and learn from adverse events with the objec-tive of redesigning safety into organizational systems to prevent future occurrences.

Down the patient safety improvement pathway lies opportunities to make health care safer in the multiple settings in which it is provided. This pathway would provide confidentiality protections both for re-ported events and their associated root cause analyses. Although it might provide for voluntary or required adverse event reporting, it would do so for constructive purposes, such as trending for epidemi-ological purposes, identifying broadly applicable system redesign applications, and sharing lessons learned and recommendations with provider organizations and practitioners. The entity or entities to which such reports would be provided could lie in either the public or private sectors, with the expectation that such information would be shared among the entities on a "need to know" basis. The ultimate accounta-bility for health care organizations would be (and is) to design safety into their internal systems using information gleaned from their own analy-ses and recommendations from external data-based sources.

The public policy pathway chosen by lawmakers will have profound implications for patient safety for decades to come.

Identifying and Learning from the Root Causes of Error

Professions outside of medicine have learned a great deal about the importance of thorough analyses of the root causes of errors and, from those analyses, have learned how to build safer systems. This is true in aviation, nuclear power, the chemical industry, air traffic control systems, and others. This engineering emphasis has brought safety to the fore and, in so doing, has driven the design of safer systems. Systems designed for safety provide tolerance for errors by building in appropriate redundancies. Indeed, the engineering approach has progressed from managing errors to preventing errors from occurring in the first place. In this design effort, particular emphasis has been placed on the impact of human factors. This has included attention to potential adverse events whose occurrence may result from either active failures or by latent conditions that predispose to failure. Although the general language and concepts of systems analysis (e.g., root cause analysis, failure mode and effects analysis) and the basic principles of human factors analysis are relatively new to medicine and health care, they have been well known in other high-risk industries for decades.

From such studies have emerged important concepts such as the notion that most errors arise not from the aberrant behavior of an individual, but rather from systematic—and oftentimes predictable— organizational factors. Unless and until health care embraces such analytical tools, it is unlikely that significant and sustained improvements in patient safety will be realized. It is abundantly clear that organizations themselves are almost always in the best position to assess what went wrong with internal systems and processes following an adverse event. Although some basic education in the conduct of thorough root cause analyses is often necessary, the necessary drill-down to identify the proximate and distal cause or causes of the error, and, more important, assess the process breakdown or breakdowns that might have occurred, is best handled locally. Such internal investigations are designed to repetitively ask the question "Why? Why? Why?" as each step in a sequence of complex processes is analyzed.

High-reliability organizations create safer operating environments by limiting the potential for errors within the system. A variety of models are being promulgated for use in health care organizations to reduce risk and enhance patient safety. Among the most common are those approaches that focus exclusively on human factors (e.g., design of new programming modules for infusion pumps), those that espouse the basic principles of quality improvement (e.g., programs to increase the use of beta blocker medications after myocardial infarctions), those that focus exclusively on technical improvements (e.g., computerized physician order entry systems), and those that concentrate on lessons from cognitive psychology (e.g., limiting residents' work hours). Each of these separate approaches has positive characteristics that will eventually be part of the solution. What is lacking, however, is an amalgamation of these models and alignment of the various approaches to enhancing patient safety and reducing risk. Standardized, agreed-upon methodologies that capitalize on the positive attributes of each model are essential to the achievement of further progress.

Patient safety solutions invariably appear to be counterintuitive. Blaming individual practitioners or even organizations when errors occur does not improve patient safety. Counting and publicly reporting errors does not improve patient safety. Malpractice claims against individual practitioners and organizations have not improved patient safety. Creating health care organizational cultures where staff feel safe in reporting errors and confident that action will be taken to address these errors—indeed, where staff themselves are integral to the solutions—will create environments where patients themselves can justifiably feel safe as well. However, only with professional, organizational, and societal cultural change, the complete and unabashed support of health care organizational executive leaders, and the design and redesign of safety into health care organization systems and processes will significant advances in patient safety actually be experienced.

CHAPTER SEVEN

MISTAKING ERROR

David D. Woods, PhD and Richard I. Cook, MD

Introduction

Throughout the brief history of the patient safety movement (Hatlie, 1996), stakeholder groups have asked the authors for definitions and taxonomies of human error grounded in science. The questions are of the same form: Each group feels that their progress on safety depends on having a firm definition of human error. Each group seems to believe that this definition will enable creation of a scorecard that will allow them to gauge where their organization stands in terms of being "safe."

Each group's search for the definition, first in the medical literature and then in the general scientific literature, becomes mired in complexity and terms of reference. As definitions appear in the medical literature about patient safety, they seem too specific to particular areas of health care or too vague if broad enough to cover health care in general. The definitions offered are often the product of committee consensus processes and thus too ad hoc to have scientific standing. The definitions offered involve arbitrary and subjective methods of assigning events to categories (e.g., "definitions" that propose to include as errors those events that "could have led to harm"). The resulting counts and extrapolations seem open to endless reassessment and debate (Leape et al., 1991; Kohn et al., 1999; Brennan, 2000; McDonald et al., 2000; Leape, 2000). The definition of error becomes more elusive.

Some within the stakeholder groups turn to social and behavioral science researchers who have grappled with the "human error problem" that has dogged progress on safety in other high-risk industries. Nuclear power, aviation, manufacturing, and the military have invested heavily in basic and applied research on human error over the past 20 years. Although some of this research—and some outspoken researchers—rely on human error being a discrete, well circumscribed, static entity, progress on safety in these industries has come, in large part, from abandoning efforts to attack error.

Driven partly by spectacular failures—the reactor failure at Three Mile Island in 1979 is the archetype—researchers have developed new means for looking into how systems fail and how people in their various roles contributed to *both* success and failure. The research, collectively known as the "New Look" (Rasmussen, 1986; Woods et al., 1994; Reason, 1997), drew on many different disciplines including cognitive science, organizational theory, and cognitive engineering, but it has consistently focused on empirical studies of people at work. The results of these efforts challenge the conventional "folk" assumptions about the relationship between "error" and failure.

To researchers, beginning with the question "What is error?" misleads stakeholders into a thicket of difficulties where answers seem always just around the corner but never actually come into view. The efforts to answer this seemingly simple question—efforts that inevitably become entangled with social factors and lose sight of the research base—actually block progress on safety (Cook, Woods, Miller, 1998). The New Look offers an alternative to "error" as the target of efforts to improve safety (Woods and Cook, 2002).

The need to redirect effort away from error seems counterintuitive when health care is so obviously confronted by a "human error problem." But this is precisely the situation that confronted researchers at the beginning of the development of the New Look (Hollnagel, 1983). At that time, the folk model of accident causation was firmly in place among researchers and error seemed a plausible target for work on safety. It was only after a long period of empirical research on human performance and accidents that it became apparent that answering the question of what is error was neither the first step nor a useful step, but only a dead end.

How are we to respond to those who seek definitions and taxonomies in their efforts to improve safety? Faced with an equally difficult problem in 1897, Frank Church replied to a letter from an 8-year-old girl named Virginia who asked if there really was a Santa Claus. As a way of summarizing what the New Look has revealed about error and safety, we propose our own version of both Virginia's letter and Church's response.

Dear David and Richard,

Our professional group just sponsored a consensus meeting on patient safety and medical error. We were all shocked by the Institute of Medicine reports. As highly motivated professionals committed to serve our patients, we decided to take proactive steps to improve patient safety in our area of medicine.

In our consensus meeting we developed an agenda for progress and strategic action. At the top of our list, we put the need for agreement on definitions of medical errors. Until we reach agreement on this we will be unable to create the error-tracking programs we need to measure the size of the problem and to evaluate the effectiveness of new interventions. However, despite much struggle, we have been unable to achieve consensus on a set of acceptable and workable definitions.

We are soliciting input from different experts on human error outside health care to help us develop these definitions. *What is human error?*

Thank you for your help.

Virginia

Here is our reply:

Dear Virginia,

You are not the first to ask us about "human error." When researchers began studying the role of human performance in system failure, they asked the same questions, thinking that they would find the answers if only they worked hard enough and long enough.[1]

There were good reasons for them to look for the answer. Accidents, sometimes very big ones, seemed to involve human error, and the costs of these accidents were such that getting a clear idea of what human error is seemed essential for progress on safety. The researchers did not have much success however. Instead, they found a different sort of way of looking at accidents and failures, a way we now call the New Look. This is a way of understanding how systems fail and how people in their various roles contribute to both success and failure.[2]

To answer the question as you have posed it would require us to accept a set of conventional assumptions about error. We now

---

[1]Cook (1999) traces how individuals and organizations recapitulate the learning steps that gave rise to the current understanding of the relationship between safety, systems, and human performance.

[2]The core of the New Look results can be seen in the work of Jens Rasmussen (1986; 1990a; 1990b; 1994; 1999); Erik Hollnagel (1983; 1993; 1998; 1999; Hollnagel and Amalberti, 2001); and Woods et al. (1994). Parallel work on high reliability organizations can be found in Rochlin (1999) and Weick et al. (1999).

understand that these assumptions are incorrect. The focus on defining and counting error has distracted other industries from productive work on safety. The research results can help you find more useful questions to ask.

First off, we want you to understand that the term "error" is used inconsistently in our everyday conversations about safety and accidents.[3] There are at least three ways that the term is used:

- Sense #1. Error as the *cause* of failure: "This event was due to human error." The assumption is that error is some basic category or type of human behavior that precedes and generates a failure. It leads to variations on the myth that safety is protecting the system and stakeholders from erratic, unreliable people.
- Sense #2. Error as the *failure itself,* i.e., the consequences that flow from an event: "The transplant mixup was an error." In this sense the term "error" simply asserts that the outcome was bad and produced negative consequences (e.g., injury to a patient).
- Sense #3. Error as a *process,* or more precisely, *departure from the "good" process.* Here, the sense of error is of deviation from a standard, that is a model of what is good practice, but the difficulty is there are different models of what is the process that should be followed: e.g., what standard is applicable, how standards should be described, and what it means when deviations from the standards do not result in bad outcomes. Depending on the model adopted, very different views of error result.

While you might think that it would always be clear from the context which of these senses people mean when they talk about error, in practice the senses are often confused with each other. Even worse, people sometimes slip from one sense to another without being aware that they are doing so.

Of course, what people are interested in is "error" in the second sense of bad outcomes and how to prevent them. You can see this yourself by this simple thought experiment. Imagine that we have managed to eliminate all accidents from health care but that many errors remain (third sense). Would anyone be interested in error? Probably not. Now suppose instead that we somehow eliminated all the *errors* from health care but that accidents continued to occur. Would anyone be interested in error? Again, probably not.

The motivation to explore error comes from accidents. The research that forms the New Look has two main sources: (1) the base of behavioral science about how individuals and groups cope with complexity and conflict in real world settings and (2) a growing set

---

[3]The work of Jens Rasmussen and Erik Hollnagel have led the way. See in particular: Rasmussen (1999), Hollnagel (1983; 1993; 1998), and Hollnagel and Amalberti (2001). The description of the first 3 senses is drawn from Hollnagel's work (1993).

of empirical studies on accidents, near-accidents, and real-world work, sometimes called "technical work" studies. The research view of "error" derived from the New Look has produced five conclusions pertaining to "error":

Conclusion #1: *Defining error-as-cause (Sense #1) blocks learning by hiding the lawful factors that affect human and system performance.*

The critical observation that gave rise to the New Look was that errors were *heterogeneous* and not directly comparable events that could be counted and tabulated. The standard way we say this today is that the label error should be the starting point of study and investigation, not the ending point.

It is tempting to stop the analysis of an adverse event when we encounter a person in the chain of events. Continuing the analysis *through* individuals requires workable model cognition of individuals and of coordinated activity between individuals. It turns out to be quite hard to decide where to halt the causal analysis of a surprising event. Although there are theoretical issues involved in this *stopping rule problem*[4] the decision about when to stop most often reflects our roles as stakeholders and as participants in the system. We stop when we think we have a good enough understanding, and this understanding is, not surprisingly, when we have identified human error as the source of the failure.

The idea of error-as-cause also fails because it trivializes expert human performance. Error-as-cause leaves us with human performance divided in two: acts that are errors and acts that are non-errors. But this distinction evaporates in the face of any serious look at human performance.[5] What we find is that the sources of successful operation of systems under one set of conditions can be what we label errors after failure occurs. Jens Rasmussen likes to quote Mach (1905) on this point: "Knowledge and error flow from the same mental sources, only success can tell one from the other."

Instead of finding error and non-error, when we look deeply into human work we find that the behaviors there closely match the incentives, opportunities, and demands that are present in the workplace. Rather than being a distinct class of behavior, we find the natural laws that influence human cognition and performance are *always at work,* sometimes producing good outcomes and sometimes producing bad ones. Trying to separate error from non-error makes it to harder to see these factors.

---

[4]Rasmussen (1990b) is the standard statement of the difficulty. For an approach to deal with the problem see Rasmussen (1994). For examples of the difficulty in health care see Cook et al., *A Tale of Two Stories* (1999).

[5]The best introduction to the complexity of expert performance is found in Gary Klein's book *Sources of Power: How People Make Decisions* (MIT Press, Cambridge MA, 1998).

Conclusion #2: *Defining error-as-consequences (Sense #2) is redundant and confusing.*

Much of the time in health care, the word "error" is used to refer to harm—generally *preventable* harm—to patients. This sort of definition is almost a tautology: it simply involves renaming preventable harm as error. But there are a host of assumptions that are packed into "preventable" and these are almost never made explicit. We are not interested in harm itself but, rather, *how harm comes to be.* The idea that something is preventable incorporates a complete (albeit fuzzy) model of how accidents happen, what factors contribute to them, and what sorts of countermeasures would be productive. But closer examination of "preventable" events shows that their preventability is largely a matter of wishing that things were other than they were.

To use "error" as a synonym for harm gives the appearance of progress where there is none. It would be better if we simply were clear in our use of language and referred to these cases in terms of the kind of harm or patient injuries. Confounding the label error with harm simply adds a huge amount of noise to the communication and learning process.

Conclusion #3: *Defining error-as-deviation from a model of "good" process (Sense #3) collides with the problem of multiple standards.*

The critical aspect of error-as-process-deviation is deciding how to determine what constitutes a deviation. Some have proposed normative models, e.g., Bayes Theorem, but these are rarely applicable to complex settings like health care domains, and efforts to use this approach to assess human performance are misleading.[6]

Some have argued that strict compliance with standard operating practices and procedures can be used to define deviation. In other fields, however, it was quickly discovered that standard operating practices capture only a few elements of work and often prescribe practices that cannot actually be sustained in work worlds. In transportation systems, for example, where striking may be illegal, labor strife has sometimes led workers to adopt a "work-to-rule" strategy. By working exactly to rule, workers can readily make complex systems stop working. Attempts to make complete, exhaustive policies that apply to all cases creates or exacerbates double binds or to make it easy to attribute adverse events to "human error" and stop.[7]

---

[6]Humans are not Bayesian machines and their success in the world is not the result of Bayesian statistics so comparing their performance to Bayesian models necessarily misrepresents the nature of work, cf. Gigerenzer F., Simple Heuristics: Things that make us smart (Oxford University Press, 1999) and Klein's Sources of Power.

[7]Lucy Suchman's (1987) book illustrates how expert practice is more than just following standard policies and procedures; *Behind Human Error* captures the double binds that can arise; and Woods and Shattuck (2000) summarize the basic tradeoff and forms of failure from this point of view.

Choosing among the many candidates for a standard changes what is seen as an error in fundamental ways. Using finer or coarser grain standards can give you a very wide range of error rates. In other words, by varying the standard seen as relevant, one can estimate hugely divergent "error" rates. Some of the "standards" used in specific applications have been changed because too many errors were occurring or to prove that a new program was working. To describe something as a "standard" when it is capable of being changed in this way suggests that there is little that is standard about "standards."

This slipperiness in what counts as a deviation can lead to a complete inversion of standardizing on good process: rather than describing what it is that people need to do to accomplish work successfully, we find ourselves relying on bad outcomes to specify what it is that we want workers not to do. Although often couched in positive language, policies and procedures are often written and revised in just this way after accidents. Unfortunately, hindsight bias plays a major role in such activities.

Working toward meaningful standards as a means for assessing performance and defining error as deviations might be a long-term goal but it is fraught with hazard. To make standards work requires not only clear statements about how to accomplish work but clear guidance about how conflicts are to be handled. Specifying standards for performance for only *part of the work* to be done creates double binds that undermine expert performance creating conditions for failure. To use standards as a basis for evaluating performance deviations requires the continuous evaluation of performance against the standard rather than (as is often the case) simply after bad outcomes become apparent. One practical test of this is whether or not deviations from standards are actually detected and treated in the same way independent of the actual outcome.

To limit the damage from the multiple standards problem, all must carry forward in any tabulation the standard used to define deviations. *This is absolutely essential!* Saying some behavior was an error-as-process-deviation has no meaning without also specifying the standard used to define the deviation.

There are three things to remember about the multiple standards problem. First, the standard chosen is a kind of *model* of what it means to practice before outcome is known. A scientific analysis of human performance makes those models explicit and debatable. Without that background, any count is arbitrary.

Second, a judgment of error is not a piece of data which then can be tabulated with other like data; instead it is the end result of an *analysis*. Its interpretation rests on others being able to decompose and critique that analysis. The base data is the *story* of the particular episode—how multiple factors came together to produce that outcome. Effective systems of inquiry about safety begin with and continually refer back to these base stories of failure and of success in the learning process.

Third, being explicit about the standard used is also essential to be able to critique, contrast, and combine results across events, studies, or settings. When these standards are dropped or hidden in the belief that error is an objective thing in the world, communication and learning collapse.

In the final analysis, the science has shown that "error" is an example of an *essentially contestable* concept. In fact, any benefit to the search for error only comes from the chronic struggle to define how different standards capture and fail to capture our current sense of what is expertise and our current model of the factors that make the difference between success and failure.

Gradually, the research activities that comprise the New Look have led to recognition of a fourth sense of "error."[8]

Conclusion #4: *Labeling an act as "error" marks the end of the social and psychological process of causal attribution.*

If you really want a definition of error, Virginia, we suggest you use this one.

Taken together, the research on how people actually apply the term "error" shows that "error" is a piece of data about reactions to failure that serves as a placeholder for a set of *socially derived beliefs* about how things happen. As stakeholders, our judgments after the fact about causality are used to explain surprising events. *Thus, in practice, the study of error is the nothing more or less than study of the psychology and sociology of causal attribution.* There are many regularities and biases—e.g., the hindsight bias—that determine how people judge causality. The heterogeneity and complexity of real-world work make these regularities and biases especially important: because the field of possible contributors includes so many items, biases may play an especially important role in determining which factors are deemed relevant.

These results are deeply unsettling for stakeholders because they tell us that the use of the term "error" is less revealing about the performance of workers than it is about ourselves as evaluators. As researchers, advocates, managers, and regulators, we are at least as vulnerable to failure, susceptible to biases and oversimplifications, and prone to err as *those other people*. Fallibility has no bounds in a universe of multiple pressures, uncertainty, and finite resources.

Error is not a fixed category of scientific analysis. It is not an objective, stable state of the world. Instead, it arises from the interaction between the world and the people who create, run, and benefit (or suffer) from human systems for human purposes—a relationship between hazards in the world and our knowledge, our perceptions, and even our dread of the *potential* paths toward and forms of failure.

---

[8]This sense of error was first articulated in Woods et al. (1994) and Cook and Woods (1996).

What is the consequence of error being the result of processes of attribution?

Although you did not say so explicitly, the question of what is error was predicated on the notion that we can and should treat error as an objective property of the world and that we can search for errors, tabulate them, count them. This searching and counting is futile.

The relationship between error and safety is mirage-like. We find ourselves in a desert, seeing safety glimmering somewhere in the far distance. To begin the journey, we feel we must gauge the distance to our goal in units of "error." This presumption about the location of safety is illusory. Efforts to measure the distance to it are little more than measuring our distance from a mirage. The belief that estimates of this number are a necessary or even useful method of beginning an effort to improve safety are predicated on the apparent location of the mirage.

The psychology of causal attribution, however, tells us that it is our beliefs and misconceptions about failure and error that have combined to make the mirage appear where it does. The New Look research tells us that progress toward safety has more to do with the metaphorical sand underneath our feet than it does with the tantalizing image off in the distance. When we look closely, we see how health care workers are struggling to anticipate forms of/paths toward failure, actively adapting to create and sustain failure-sensitive strategies, and working to maintain margins in the face of pressures to do more and do it quickly. Looking closely under our feet we see:

1. How workers and organizations are continually revising their approach to work in an effort to remain sensitive to the possibility for failure;
2. How we and the workers are necessarily only partially aware of the current potential for failure;
3. How change is creating new paths to failure and new demands on workers and how revising their understanding of these paths is an important aspect of work on safety;
4. How the strategies for coping with these potential paths can be either strong and resilient or weak and mistaken;
5. How dependent the culture of safety is on remaining dynamically engaged in new assessments and avoiding stale, narrow, or static representations of risk and hazard;
6. How overconfident nearly everyone is that they have already anticipated the types and mechanisms of failure, and how overconfident nearly everyone is that the strategies they have devised are effective and will remain so;
7. How missing the side effects of change is the most common form of failure for organizations and individuals; and
8. How continual effort after success in a world of changing pressures and hazards is fundamental to create safety.

In the final analysis, safety is not a commodity to be tabulated, it is a chronic value "under our feet" that infuses all aspects of practice. *People create safety under resource and performance pressure* at all levels of the sociotechnical system. They continually learn and adapt their activities in response to information about failure. Progress on safety ultimately comes from helping workers and managers create safety.

The folk models about human error are pervasive and seem self-evident. Challenging those folk models calls into question not only closely held beliefs, but also policy and investment decisions. The dissonance between belief and results is uncomfortable at best. Yet, Virginia, the need to make real progress on safety leaves us no choice but to point out how easy it is for all of us to fall back into fallacies and myths about human error. We must make the contrast very stark:

> The misconceptions and controversies about error and safety are rooted in the collision of two mutually exclusive paradigms or world views. One view is that erratic people degrade an otherwise safe system. Thus, work on safety is protecting the system (us as managers, regulators, and consumers) from unreliable people. This is a Ptolemaeic world view (the sun goes around the earth). To defend this world view in the face of the data on human performance and how complex systems fail takes ever greater effort (more and more epicycles by analogy).
>
> The other paradigm or world view is that *people create safety under resource and performance pressure* at all levels of the sociotechnical system by learning and adapting to information about how we all can contribute to failure (this is the basic lesson from New Look research about human performance, success and failure). This is a Copernican world view (the earth goes around the sun). Progress comes from helping people create safety. This is what the science says, despite how odd it sounds: *help people cope with complexity under pressure to achieve success.*
>
> We can blame and punish under whatever labels are in fashion but that will not change the natural laws that govern human performance, nor will it make the sun go round the earth. The paradigm shift demanded if real progress is to be made on safety it is, not surprisingly, extraordinarily difficult. We have windows of opportunity for improving safety, but only if all of us are up to the sacrifices involved in building, extending, and deepening the ways we can help people create safety.
>
> So are people sinners or are they saints? An old debate, but neither view leads anywhere near to improving safety. Making safety begins with recognizing the paradox that, simultaneously, we are both the source of success and of failure. How could it be otherwise?—as we create, operate, and modify human systems for human purposes.[9]

---

[9]From Woods (2000b).

Virginia, you wanted a simple, pragmatic answer and did not expect to walk into this onslaught of complexities. But accidents arise from the complexities of the domain, not from its apparent simplicity. The attraction of error as a target for work on safety is illusory. No progress or success is possible if we remain trapped in a Ptolemaeic search for erratic other people or if we try to straddle the two paradigms. Either you are working in the Ptolemaeic paradigm, or you throw it off *completely* and move onto the fascinating and productive challenges of deepening the Copernican paradigm of observing, modeling, and enhancing how we cope with complexity and create safety under pressure.

Virginia, adopt the new paradigm and begin by looking for ways to understand the changing vulnerabilities and pathways that expose patients to risks of injury as a result of care. Investigate how people cope with complexity—usually successfully. Search out the sources of resilience that allow them to produce success when failure threatens.[10] In combination, these efforts will allow you to *create foresight,* to recognize, anticipate, and defend against paths to failure that arise as health care organizations and technology change, and to do so *before any patient is injured.*

David Woods and Richard Cook

Summary of the New Look Research Findings

Doing things safely, in the course of meeting other goals, is and has always been part of operational practice. As people in their different roles are aware of potential paths to failure, they develop failure-sensitive strategies to forestall these possibilities. Failures occurred against this background when multiple contributors—each necessary but only jointly sufficient—combine. Work processes do not choose failure but *drift toward it* as production pressures and change erode the defenses that normally keep failure at a distance. This drift is the result of systematic, predictable organizational factors at work, not simply erratic individuals. To understand how failure sometimes happens one must first understand how success is obtained—how people learn and adapt to create safety in a world fraught with hazards, tradeoffs, and multiple goals (Cook et al., 2000).

---

[10]Many resources are beginning to emerge on the new paradigm and how it can lead to a new set of methods and means to improve safety. A sampler includes Hollnagel (1999) and Svenson (2001) exploring barrier analysis; Carthy et al. (2000) and Reason (2001) looking at the resilience in surgical services; Woods and Shattuck (2000) in analyzing an accident; Weick et al. (1999) in characterizing how high reliability organizations show high resilience.

It is clear that high levels of performance are achievable. For example, researchers have studied organizations that have been remarkably successful in managing potentially hazardous technical operations, and the empirical results match the New Look (Rochlin, 1999). Achieving such high levels of performance does not flow from rooting out error, but rather through anticipating and planning for unexpected events and future surprises. Past success is not a reason for confidence, instead, continued investment in anticipating the changing potential for failure is energized by the deeply held understanding that our knowledge base is fragile in the face of the hazards inherent in work and the changes omnipresent in the environment.

The theme that leaps out from the New Look results is that failure represents *breakdowns in adaptations* directed at coping with complexity. Success relates to organizations, groups, and individuals who produce resilient systems that recognize and adapt to change and surprise. The measure of success for groups and organizations is the ability to "create foresight—anticipate the changing shape of iatrogenic risk, *before* patients are injured" (Woods, 2000).

References

Amalberti, R. (2001). The paradoxes of almost totally safe transportation systems. *Safety Science, 37,* 109–126.

Brennan, T. A. The Institute of Medicine Report on Medical Error—Could It Do Harm? *N Engl J Med* 2000;342:1123–1125.

Carthey, J., de Leval, M. R., and Reason, J. (2000). Understanding Excellence in Complex, Dynamic Medical Systems. In Proceedings of the 44th Annual Meeting of the Human Factors and Ergonomics Society/IEA2000, July, 2000.

Cook, R. I. (1999). Two Years Before the Mast: Learning How to Learn About Patient Safety. In Hendee, W. (ed.), Proceedings of *Enhancing Patient Safety and Reducing Errors in Health Care.* National Patient Safety Foundation, Chicago IL (held at Annenberg Center for Health Sciences, Rancho Mirage, CA, Nov. 8–10, 1998).

Cook, R. I., Woods, D. D., and Miller, C. (1998). *A Tale of Two Stories: Contrasting Views on Patient Safety.* National Patient Safety Foundation, Chicago IL, April 1998 (www.npsf.org/exec/report.html).

Cook, R. I., Render, M. L., and Woods, D. D. (2000). Gaps in the continuity of care and progress on patient safety. *British Medical Journal, 320,* 791–794, March 18, 2000.

Hatlie, M. *Examining Errors in Health Care: Developing a Prevention, Education and Research Agenda, October 13–15, 1996* (Annenberg Center for Health Sciences at Eisenhower, Rancho Mirage, CA, 1996).

Hollnagel, E. (1983). *Human Error.* Position paper for NATO Conference on Human Error, Bellagio, Italy (available at http://www.ida.liu.se/~eriho/Publications_0.htm).

Hollnagel, E. (1993). *Human Reliability Analysis: Context and Control.* London: Academic Press.

Hollnagel, E. (1998). *Cognitive reliability and error analysis method—CREAM.* Oxford: Elsevier Science.

Hollnagel, E. (1999). Accidents and barriers. In J.-M. Hoc, P. Millot, E. Hollnagel and P. C. Cacciabue (Eds.), Proceedings of Lez Valenciennes, 28, 175–182 (Presses Universitaires de Valenciennes).

Hollnagel, E., and Amalberti, R. (2001). The Emperor's New Clothes or Whatever Happened to "Human Error"? Proceedings of the Fourth International Workshop on Human Error, Safety, and Systems Development (HESSD-01), Linköping, Sweden, June 11–12, 2001.

Klein, G. A. (1998). *Sources of Power: How People Make Decisions.* Cambridge, MA: MIT Press.

Kohn, L. T., Corrigan, J. M., and Donaldson, M., eds. (1998). *To Err is Human: Building a Safer Health System.* Washington D.C.: Institute of Medicine.

Leape, L. L. Institute of Medicine medical error figures are not exaggerated. *JAMA,* 2000;284:95–97.

Leape, L. L., Brennan, T. A., and Laird, N. M. Incidence of adverse events and negligence in hospitalized patients: Results of the Harvard Medical Practice Study II. *N Engl J Med,* 1991;324:377–384.

Mach, E. (1905). *Knowledge and Error.* Dordrecht: Reidel Publishing Company.

McDonald, C. J., Weiner, M., and Hui, S. L. Deaths due to medical errors are exaggerated in Institute of Medicine report. *JAMA,* 2000;284:93–95.

Rasmussen, J. (1986). *Information Processing and Human-Machine Interaction.* New York: North Holland.

Rasmussen, J. (1990a). The role of error in organizing behavior. *Ergonomics,* 33:1185–1199.

Rasmussen, J. (1990b). Human Error and the Problem of Causality in Analysis of Accidents. *Phil Trans R Soc Lond.* B 327, 449–462.

Rasmussen, J. (1994). Risk Management, Adaptation, and Design for Safety. In B. Brehmer and N.-E. Sahlin (Eds.) *Future Risks and Risk Management.* Dordrecht: Kluwer Academic.

Rasmussen, J. (1999). The concept of human error: Is it useful for the design of safe systems in health care? In C. Vincent and B. deMoll (Eds.), *Risk and Safety in Medicine.* London: Elsevier.

Reason, J. (1997). *Managing the Risks of Organizational Accidents.* Brookfield, VT: Ashgate Publishing.

Reason, J. (2001). *Assessing the Resilience of Health Care Systems to the Risk of Patient Mishaps.*

Rochlin, G. I. (1999). Safe operation as a social construct. *Ergonomics,* 42(11):1549–1560.

Suchman, L. (1987). *Plans and situated actions. The problem of human machine communication.* Cambridge: Cambridge University Press.

Svenson, O. (2001). Accident and incident analysis based on the accident evolution and barrier function model. *Cognition, Technology, and Work,* 3, 42–52.

Weick, K. E., Sutcliffe, K. M., and Obstfeld, D. (1999). Organizing for high reliability: Processes of collective mindfulness. *Res Organizational Behavior,* 21:23–81.

Woods, D. D. (2000a). Behind Human Error: Human Factors Research to Improve Patient Safety. *National Summit on Medical Errors and Patient Safety Research,* Quality Interagency Coordination Task Force and Agency for Healthcare Research and Quality, September 11, 2000.

Woods, D. D. (2000b). Patient Safety and Human Factors Opportunities. *Human Factors and Ergonomics Society Bulletin,* 43(5).

Woods, D. D., and Cook, R. I. (2001). From Counting Failures to Anticipating Risks: Possible Futures for Patient Safety. In L. Zipperer and S. Cushman, Editors, *Lessons on Patient Safety,* National Patient Safety Foundation.

Woods, D. D., and Cook, R. I. (2002). Nine Steps to Move Forward from Error. *Cognition, Technology, and Work,* 4(2):137–144.

Woods, D. D., and Shattuck, L. G. (2000). Distance supervision–local action given the potential for surprise. *Cognition, Technology, and Work,* 2, 86–96.

Woods, D. D., Johannesen, L., Cook, R. I., and Sarter, N. B. (1994). *Behind Human Error: Cognitive Systems, Computers and Hindsight.* Human Systems Ergonomic Information and Analysis Center, Wright Patterson Air Force Base, Dayton OH (available at http://iac.dtic.mil/hsiac/ productBEHIND.htm).

CHAPTER EIGHT

THE INVESTIGATION AND ANALYSIS OF CLINICAL INCIDENTS

Charles Vincent and David Hewett, MD

Why do things go wrong? Human error is routinely blamed for disasters in the air, on the railways, in complex surgery, and in health care generally. However, quick judgments and routine assignment of blame obscure a more complex truth. The identification of an obvious departure from good practice is usually only the very first step of an investigation. Although a particular action or omission may be the immediate cause of an incident, closer analysis usually reveals a series of events and departures from safe practice, each influenced by the working environment and the wider organizational context. Presently, this more complex picture is gaining acceptance in health care,[1-3] but still is seldom put into practice in the investigation of actual incidents.

In a series of papers, the Clinical Risk Unit, University College London, has developed a process of investigation and analysis of adverse events for use by researchers.[4-8] Two years ago a collaborative research group was formed between the Clinical Risk Unit and members of the United Kingdom Association of Litigation and Risk Management (ALARM). This group has adapted the research methods to produce a protocol for the investigation and analysis of serious incidents for use by risk managers and others trained in incident analysis. The full protocol gives a detailed account of the theoretical background, process of investigation, and analysis, with detailed case examples and standard forms for use in the investigation process.[9]

We are, of course, well aware of the pioneering work carried out by the Joint Commission on Accreditation of Healthcare Organizations (JCAHO) on sentinel event analysis in the United States,[10] and we share a similar perspective. Other formal approaches have also been developed.[11] There are a number of other types of investigation both within medicine and in other high-risk environments, which we are currently reviewing. Our aim is not to compete directly with the Joint Commission approach, but rather to suggest that incident analysis and investigation in health care is at a very early stage of development, and that a substantial research program is needed. Moreover, it is not clear what concepts in the investigation of error are appropriate in health care, what methods are most appropriate for different settings, or what the ultimate value of each approach may be. Very probably, several different approaches could be of value, as other settings have demonstrated.[12]

Our own approach diverges from that of the JCAHO in a number of significant respects. First, we draw directly on Reason's organizational accident model.[13,14] Although the JCAHO refers to it, and their approach has clearly been influenced by "systems" thinking, it does not seem to be based on a specific model. Second, our approach is very much investigator-led, in comparison with the JCAHO's team-based, reflective, and brainstorming approach. It seems likely to us that, on this score at least, different approaches will be preferred in different contexts. Third, our approach is deliberately formal and may lend itself to greater precision. This feature might be useful in a research context, or indeed any setting where a more rigorous method is required. Equally, one might imagine the JCAHO's approach to be more appropriate when an open process is required to maximize team involvement. Fourth, the JCAHO method relies on a wide variety of techniques and offers a number of ways to conceptualize the causes of an incident. This suggests to us that neither we nor the JCAHO are yet confident of how best to conceptualize accidents or represent the findings. We believe that this remains a matter for further research and investigation. It cannot, in the long run, be acceptable to rely on the personal preferences of the investigator, whoever that may be.

In summary, therefore, we believe that the investigation and analysis of clinical incidents is still at a very early stage, both in terms of practical experience and especially in terms of research. There is much to be gained by exploring and researching different approaches, with the long-term aim of a greater common understanding of this important topic. In this chapter we introduce the main ideas and methods of our own approach and present sections of a case analysis to illustrate the methods in practice.

Research Foundations

The basic theory underlying our protocol and its application derives mainly from research previously undertaken in settings outside health care. In the aviation, oil, and nuclear industries, for instance, the formal investigation of incidents is well-established procedure.[13,14] Studies in these areas have led to a much broader understanding of accident causation, with less focus on the individual who makes the error and more on preexisting organizational factors. Such studies have also illustrated the complexity of the chain of events that may lead to an adverse outcome.[1,2,5,6] The root causes of adverse clinical events may lie in factors such as the use of locum doctors and agency nurses, communication and supervision problems, excessive workload, and educational and training deficiencies as well as resource allocation decisions made in isolation from their practical consequences.

In health care, the development of preventive strategies from such analyses has not yet been fully exploited. However, the potential for these approaches is apparent in other domains. For instance, the inquiry into the Piper Alpha oil disaster led to a host of recommendations and the implementation of a number of risk reduction strategies, which covered the whole industry and addressed a wide range of issues. These included the setting up of a single regulatory body for offshore safety, relocation of pipeline emergency shutdown valves, the provision of temporary safe refuges for oil workers, new evacuation procedures, and requirements for emergency safety training. Most interestingly, oil companies had henceforth to actively demonstrate that hazards had been minimized and had been reduced to levels that are as low as could reasonably be expected.[15-17]

Incidents are opportunities to learn about the gaps and shortcomings in the way organizations manage processes or technologies within which accidents occur. This "organizational learning" paradigm is very different from the more traditional approaches, which are often more judicial in character,[18] a fact also emphasized by the Joint Commission.

Reason's Organizational Accident Model

The protocol and the methods described in this chapter are firmly rooted in Reason's organizational accident model.[13,14] Reason's model was originally developed for use in complex industrial systems as a means of understanding the relationships among the various factors involved in the genesis of accidents and, by extension, of identifying methods of accident prevention. The method of investigation implied by the model is first to recognize the institutional context within which an accident has occurred, and then to examine the chain of events that led to an adverse outcome and consider the actions of those involved. Finally, the investigator, crucially, looks further back through the organizational hierarchy at the conditions in which staff were working and the general context in which the incident occurred.[7,8]

The first step in any analysis is to identify active failures—unsafe acts or omissions committed by those at the "sharp end" of the system (pilots, air traffic controllers, anesthetists, surgeons, nurses, etc.) whose actions can have immediate adverse consequences. These may be slips (such as picking up the wrong syringe), lapses of judgment, forgetting to carry out a procedure, or, rarely, deliberate departures from safe operating practices, procedures, or standards. In our work we have substituted the term *care management problems* (CMPs) for *active failures*. In practice, care management problems may encompass a series of active failures, such as failure to monitor over a period of time. Having identified the CMPs, however, the investigator then considers the conditions in which errors occur and the wider organizational context. These are the significant factors that influence staff performance and that may precipitate errors and affect patient outcomes.

A Framework for the Analysis of Risk and Safety in Medicine

We have extended Reason's model and adapted it for use in a health care setting, classifying the error-producing conditions and organizational factors in a single broad framework of factors affecting clinical practice.[7]

At the bottom of the framework are patient factors. In any clinical situation, the patient's condition will have the most direct influence on practice and outcome. Other patient factors, such as personality, language, and any disability, may also be important because they can influence communication with staff, and hence the probability of an incident.

Higher up in the framework are individual (staff) and team factors. Individual factors include the knowledge, skills, and experience of each member of staff, which will obviously affect their clinical practice. Each staff member is part of a team within the inpatient or community unit, and part of the wider organization of the health service. The way an individual practices, and his or her individual impact on the patient, is both constrained and influenced by other members of the team in the way they communicate, support, and supervise each other. In turn the team is influenced by line management actions and by more distant decisions made at a higher level in the organization. These decisions are likely to include policies regarding the use of agency staff, continuing education, training, and supervision, as well as the availability of equipment and supplies. Management decisions also affect the conditions in which the team works, including staffing levels, workload, and the physical conditions of the building together with the environment at large. The organization itself is affected by the institutional context, including politically imposed financial constraints, external regulatory bodies, and the broader economic and social climate. Each level of analysis can be expanded to provide a more detailed specification of the components that make up each major factor. For example, "team factors" includes items on verbal communication between junior and senior staff as well as between different health care professions; the quality of written communication, such as the completeness and legibility of notes; and also the availability of supervision and support.

Definitions and Essential Concepts

Reason's model and our framework provide the conceptual foundations for the investigation process. Before describing the procedural steps contained within the investigation process, we will define some basic terms. These are explained in greater detail in what follows, and examples are given in the case analyses.

The Incident

Essentially an incident is something that happened to a patient, a clinical outcome with harmful or potentially harmful effects. The criteria for selecting an incident for investigation are discussed further later in the chapter.

Care Management Problems

Care management problems are actions or omissions by staff in the process of care. They have two essential features, both of which are required to be present if a particular CMP is to be selected for detailed investigation and analysis:

1. Care deviated beyond safe limits of practice.
2. The deviation had a direct or indirect effect on the eventual adverse outcome for the patient. (In cases in which the impact on the patient is not immediately apparent, it is sufficient that the CMP had a potentially adverse effect.)

Note that each CMP is to be identified individually and each will be analyzed separately to determine the reasons for its occurrence.

Clinical Context and Patient Factors

For each CMP identified, the investigator records salient clinical events relating to the condition of the patient at the relevant time (for example, bleeding heavily, blood pressure falling). Other patient-related factors affecting the process of care (for example, patient very distressed, patient unable to understand instructions) are also recorded.

Specific Contributory Factors

For each CMP, the investigator uses a process, both during interviews and afterward, to identify the factors that led to that particular CMP. For example:

- Individual factors may include a lack of knowledge or experience in either a member of staff or a group.
- Task factors might include the nonavailability of test results or specific treatment protocols.
- Team factors might include poor communication between staff.
- Work environment factors might include high workload or inadequate staffing.

All or any of these might contribute to the occurrence of a single CMP.

General Contributory Factors

A further distinction needs to be drawn between specific contributory factors and general conditions in the unit. The investigator will differentiate between those contributory factors that are only relevant on that particular occasion and those that are long-standing or permanent features of the unit or, perhaps, of a member of staff. For instance, a failure of communication between two midwives may have contributed to a care management problem. If this is unusual and seldom occurs, then it is a specific contributory factor and not a general factor with wider implications. If, on the other hand, this problem is quite frequent, then the investigator would note a general contributory factor of "poor communication," something that would have clear implications for the safe and effective running of that unit.

Similarly, the investigator might ask:

- Does the lack of knowledge shown on this occasion imply that this member of staff requires additional training?
- Does this particular problem with this guideline mean that the whole guideline needs to be revised?
- Is the high workload due to a temporary and unusual set of circumstances, or is it a more general problem affecting patient safety?

The Investigation Process

Reviewing the Case Records

Accounts may be taken from written reports of staff members, case notes, or interviews with staff. Analysis may be limited if only written reports are considered, because it may not be possible to explore the full range of conditions that allowed the event to occur, as can be done in an interview.

The first task, from the necessarily incomplete and sometimes incorrect information immediately available when an incident is first reported, is to make an initial summary of the event and record it. Next, identify the most obvious CMPs. In some instances there may only be one, but nearly always with a serious incident several problems conspire to create the event. At this point we recommend assigning a preliminary grading to the incident. This will be based on factors such as the seriousness of the outcome for the patient, the likelihood of recurrence, the threats to the organization that are posed by it, and the costs that may be incurred in both compensation and system recovery. The grading will indicate the depth and completeness of investigation and analysis that may be required. Before starting the interviews, the key staff involved are listed and decisions are made about who should be interviewed and in what order they should be seen.

Framing the Problem

The next task is to decide which section of the process of care to examine. This is not always a straightforward task. It depends less on the condition of the patient at any particular time and more on when and where problems first arose, something that may only become apparent during the investigation. For instance, a hemorrhage may have been badly managed, leading ultimately to the patient's death 2 weeks later. The chronology may summarize 3 weeks of care, most of which may be of high standard. However, the analysis must concentrate on those aspects where problems were apparent, for example, in the preparation for surgery, conduct of the surgery, and postoperative monitoring, in order that appropriate lessons may be learnt.

Undertaking the Interviews

Interviews should be undertaken in private and, if at all possible, away from the immediate place of work in a relaxed setting. The purpose of the interview is simply to find out what happened, a fact that must be clearly explained at the outset. The style adopted should be supportive and understanding, not judgmental or confrontational. Where it becomes clear that a professional shortcoming has occurred, it is best that this should be allowed to emerge naturally from the conversation, and should definitely not be extracted by cross-examination. Most staff members are genuinely disturbed when it becomes clear that something they have done has contributed to an incident. Normally, additional support is essential at this point, and the staff member should be allowed, through supportive discussion, to start to come to terms with what has happened.

There are several distinct phases to the interview, and it will generally be more effective to move through these in order. Each interview should take between 20 and 30 minutes, depending on the degree of involvement. Ideally two interviewers are used, one leading the interview and the other taking notes and asking more detailed supplementary questions. The phases are detailed in the following subsections.

What Happened? Establishing the Chronology and Outcome

The investigator should first establish the role of the member of staff in relation to the incident as a whole, and record the limits of his or her involvement. Next the chronology of events is established as the staff member recalls them.

How Did It Happen? Identifying the Care Management Problems

In the second phase, the investigator should first explain the concept of a care management problem. Next, the member of staff is asked to identify the main CMPs as he or she sees them, without worrying about whether or not anyone is or is not to blame for any of them. The task is to identify all important acts or omissions, or other breakdowns in the clinical process, that were (with hindsight) important points in the chain of events leading to the adverse outcome. Subsequent questions may elicit the reasons behind specific actions (for example, Why did you not call for help at that stage?) and explore references to strong emotions, such as anxiety or anger, which sometimes highlight crucial points.

Why Did It Happen? Identifying the Contributory Factors

In the third phase, the investigator goes back and asks separately about each of the care management problems that the staff member may have information about or direct experience of. Questions should cover contributory factors at all levels of the framework. Each care management problem may be associated with several factors at different levels of the framework that were implicated in its occurrence. These might include, for example, poor motivation (Individual), lack of supervision (Team) and inadequate training policy (Organization and Management). Although the framework has higher-level, organizational factors at the top, it may be more natural in clinical terms to begin by inquiring about patient factors, then moving up the table through task factors, individual factors, and so on. The full protocol contains a much more detailed framework of factors that may be helpful when formulating questions.

Distinguishing Specific and General Contributory Factors

When a member of staff identifies a clearly important contributory factor, the investigator should be sure to ask a follow-up question. Was this factor specific to this occasion or would you regard this as a more general problem on the unit? The prevention of future incidents relies on identifying general, systemic problems, rather than isolated difficulties that are unlikely to recur.

Finally, the investigator should ask the staff member if he or she has any other comments to make or questions to ask. The approach is quite structured, and, although encouraging staff contributions, it is still important to allow time for more open reflection and comment.

Analysis of the Case

The core of the process is to ask: What happened? How did it happen? Why did it happen? What can we learn from this and what changes should we make, if any? In the analysis the same basic format is followed, this time drawing together the material from the case records, interviews, and the investigator's own observations.

The first step in the analysis is to produce an agreed-upon chronology of events, identifying any important areas of disagreement between accounts or between the case notes and the memories of the staff. The starting point for the chronology will generally be the point at which the patient entered the hospital, though relevant events before the patient's arrival (for example, previous treatment, a misleading referral letter) may also need to be recorded. However, it is important to identify and focus on the most important part of the chronology (see "Framing the Problem").

The next stage is to identify the key care management problems. These will normally have been provided by the staff themselves during the interviews, as well as from the investigator's own clinical knowledge and expertise. The investigator should look back over the list and ensure that all the care management problems are specific actions or omissions rather than more general observations on the quality of care, which should be recorded elsewhere. It is easy to note down "poor teamwork" as a care management problem, which may be a correct description of the team, but it should properly be recorded as a contributory factor within specific CMPs.

The next step is to attempt to specify the conditions associated with each of the care management problems, using the framework as a guide and as a way of reflecting on the many factors that may affect the clinical process. Interviews with staff will already have provided lists of both specific and general contributory factors. Where these conflict, it may be necessary to make a judgment as to the most important causes of the events.

A separate analysis should be carried out for each care management problem, though the depth and detail of the contributory factors identified may vary for each one. It is particularly important to distinguish *specific contributory factors,* which describe the reasons for the care management problem on that particular occasion, from *general contributory factors* that the investigator judges to be more long-standing features of the individual, team, or working conditions. Factors that are specific to the occasion and that do not reflect more general problems will usually have no long-term implications for the quality and safety of practice. They do not normally require action or changes of any kind. The final list of general contributory factors for each care management problem is examined, and those that have implications for action are identified. The protocol contains blank forms with appropriate headings to facilitate both the interview and analysis.

Preparation of the Report

Once the interviews and analysis are completed, make a composite of all of them, detailing the whole incident from start to finish. If the protocol is followed systematically and the interviews and analysis conducted thoroughly, the report and implications of the incident should emerge from the analysis in a relatively straightforward fashion. When the composite is complete, there should be a clear view of the problem and the circumstances that led up to it. The flaws in the care process will be readily apparent. The final report can be drawn up using the documentation, which by now will include the following:

- A summary of the chronology
- A list of the care management problems with their contributory causes, giving most emphasis to general contributory factors and emphasizing any positive features of the care given
- Recommended action and time scales for each one of the general factors requiring attention

Case Examples

Attempted Suicide in an Inpatient Psychiatric Unit

This case example is based on real clinical events but has been altered in various respects to preserve the anonymity of those involved.

Eight members of staff were interviewed, six nurses and two junior doctors. Three of these people were closely involved in the incident reported. The other five staff members had been peripherally involved but had also been disturbed by the incident and approached the interviewer directly because they wanted to discuss it.

- There was no formal risk assessment in the ward round, confirmed by the medical notes, which are very sketchy in this respect. The junior doctor (MR) stated that B (the patient) was not specifically asked about urges to self-harm or suicidal ideation.
- When the junior doctor saw B the day before the incident, he recorded that B was not depressed and not suicidal.
- B subsequently attempted to harm or kill herself by cutting her wrists. When found by the nurses, attempts to care for this patients' needs were chaotic and unsupervised, contributing to greater patient harm.
- To avoid the risk of fainting, B should have been taken to the clinical room in a wheelchair. In addition, she should have been put on oxygen and had her pulse and BP taken before the duty doctor reached the ward. B's wrist had not been bandaged properly.
- When B was first taken to the clinical room, the nurses did not lie her down as a precaution against fainting. When the doctor arrived, B was sitting with her arms hanging down. The nurses should have had her hold her arms up above her head to prevent further bleeding.
- The second junior doctor could not insert a cannula for an IV infusion.
- Staff had to look for supplies to clean B's neck and wrist. Although this did not take long, any delay could have severe consequences with more serious cases.
- There was no formal, structured, and supportive discussion of the incident focusing on how staff felt and whether the incident could have been dealt with better or even prevented. Some staff talked about it briefly with one or two colleagues when they had time, while others went home still disturbed and discussed it with friends.

Whether or not this incident is regarded as preventable, lessons can certainly be learned from it. B was seen by several doctors at different times, many of whom were inexperienced or unsupervised, or coming to grips with a new job. Actions of some of the staff could have been questioned, but when the broader picture is considered and the contributory causes are examined, more general, and perhaps more worrying, problems can be identified. The junior doctors, through no fault of their own, were acting beyond their competence on several occasions. Clear training needs are apparent in regard to the induction of new staff and the medical abilities of psychiatric nurses. Equipment and supplies were poorly maintained, and no one appeared to have had overall responsibility for this important task. The poor design of the ward also appears to have been a contributing factor in that B was able to harm herself without fear of being observed and without much chance of being discovered quickly.

The lack of support and supervision involved in the incident is perhaps the most glaring problem, at least in the view of the junior doctors. On his first day, another patient had a medical problem that MR had never encountered before. He had not been told how to contact the consultant for help, and the consultant's secretary did not know how to contact him either. MR eventually managed to get help from another junior doctor. He tried subsequently to discuss the issue with the consultant, who was very dismissive. MR was quite disturbed by his unhelpful and unsupportive attitude. MR felt very strongly that he did not have enough experience to deal with a patient like B, and was keen to discuss the difficulties he had encountered because he considered them to have had profound implications for the safe functioning of the unit.

It is sometimes too easy to concentrate only on what went wrong or what could have been done better in relation to a case. This analysis also revealed several positive features in the management of the incident. Pointing these out explicitly is important for staff morale and helps present a more balanced picture of the functioning of the team and the system in general. For instance, staff had correctly advised B to stay in the hospital when she had wanted to return home; there were no delays or difficulties in summoning and getting help, either from other nurses on the ward, the junior doctor, or the emergency services; once B had been discovered, the staff worked efficiently, calmly, and effectively as a team; and staff recognized the seriousness of the incident and subsequently put B on total observation.

Implementation of the Protocol in a British Hospital

The implementation of clinical risk management throughout the hospital has been an evolutionary process that has spanned four years since 1995. There was already in place a reasonable infrastructure for dealing with nonclinical risks, but it was not capable of processing clinical incidents. (It is important to note that in Britain, clinical risk management encompasses active patient safety programs and is not restricted to medico-legal and insurance matters.)[19]

From the outset it was obvious that the maternity department posed the greatest risks to the organization as a whole. This could be inferred from data about complaints and litigation (85% of the costs of claims). Although there was no evidence that the quality of care was of a particularly low standard, the consequences of clinical problems were potentially very severe. Thus it made sense to start in that department. The approach adopted was to build on the existing well-established arrangements for perinatal death reviews.

First of all a small group designed an incident reporting form with help from a large firm of defendant lawyers who had experience of designing these. The notion that the form had to collect all possible incidents no matter how trivial was rapidly rejected in favor of a targeted approach concentrating on a list of indications for reporting. These included stillbirth, suspected birth asphyxia, postpartum hemorrhage, third-degree tears, delayed caesarean section, and so forth. At the same time, one of the senior midwives was given protected time to investigate incidents and to prepare reports for the senior obstetrician and gynecologist to review. The latter individual then proposed service changes to the managers and his clinical colleagues when this was indicated. The lawyers also made a presentation to the medical and midwifery staff to explain why the system should be introduced.

This system started well, largely because of the enthusiasm of the senior obstetrician. It became clear, however, that the senior midwife needed support and further training, which was not readily available. Fortunately, the protocol research had just been proposed, and she joined with the authors and others to participate in the work of the research team. This experience helped to fill the gap in formal training as the methodology evolved.

As experience with collecting information about incidents grew, it became clear that the role of the midwife was crucial. Not only did she investigate incidents, but staff started to tell her a great deal more about matters that concerned them. As a well-known staff member who had worked in the department for many years, she was able to tactfully identify incidents that might otherwise not have been reported. Slowly the culture began to change. After the senior obstetrician retired, impetus faltered for a while, but with the arrival of a new head of midwifery, it was reestablished. The process became formalized, with a monthly risk management meeting being established. Also, the need to formally grade incidents for severity was recognized. The monthly meeting was set up to ensure that recommendations were followed through into practice. The protocol for investigation, described previously, became an important tool for collecting information about the most serious incidents that were being reported.

At around this time the entire National Health Service in the United Kingdom was required to implement a new process of clinical quality management referred to as "clinical governance."[20] In order to implement this, a central clinical governance committee was set up supported by committees based on the clinical directorates in the hospital. Risk management became one of the four main areas of activity for these committees. The structure and processes that had evolved in the maternity department now became applicable to the rest of the hospital. By this stage, the scale of the risk management undertaking meant that structures had to become even more formalized. A risk management strategy for the whole hospital was in place, with a clinical risk policy subordinate to it. The policy statement made specific reference to the relationship between investigation and discipline:

> We consider that a clear statement which indicates that a blame culture will not be encouraged is a crucial requirement before sufficient trust can be established to create an open climate in which reporting and investigation will flourish.

The severity grading system relies on assessments relating to the severity of outcome for the patient, the probability of recurrence, the magnitude of any public relations problems, and the potential for litigation. These, applied to a matrix, produce one of four colored grades: green, yellow, amber, or red. The color then indicates the correct administrative pathway for investigating and reporting the incident.

- Green incidents are simply counted and noted. The counts are then regularly reported to the directorate managers. Examples of green-coded incidents would include mislabeled specimens, simple drug administration errors, and lost documents. Action follows not on the basis of a single event, but on the identification of a rising trend.
- Yellow incidents require a straightforward commonsense investigation with a minimum of documentation. Recommendations are usually clear and need to be monitored by local managers to ensure implementation. Some of these incidents will require reporting to external agencies for follow-up. Examples might include prescription errors identified by the ward pharmacist, equipment malfunctions (with minimal harm to patients), imaging the wrong body part, patients falling out of bed and sustaining fractures, and detained patients leaving without proper authorization. These incidents are reported to the directorate-based governance committees.

- Amber incidents require a less detailed investigation using the protocol, usually at the level of the main headings and principal factors. Often there are only one or two CMPs, but the impact is such that the most senior levels of management need to be aware of the problem. Examples might include issuing erroneous pathology test results that caused an incorrect line of treatment to be followed, serious drug administration errors, incorrect minor operations, missed fractures, and inappropriate discharges followed by immediate readmission.
- Red incidents are very serious and require a full and detailed report, followed by recommendations. These incidents are reported at the central clinical governance committee and may also be reported to the main hospital board. Such incidents might include inappropriate interpretation of a cardiotocograph tracing leading to birth asphyxia and death or brain damage, inappropriate discharge from the Accident and Emergency Department followed by death due to a cause present but not recognized when seen in the ER, and a major diagnostic equipment failure leading to inaccurate reports in a screening program.

Discussion

The protocol has been found to be of considerable assistance in investigating and writing up reports on serious events. It is time consuming, but so is any other form of detailed investigation. An important advantage is that it encourages investigators to be systematic and to review the incident as a whole rather than becoming fixated on one aspect. Clinicians faced with reviewing an incident often concentrate exclusively on the medical process and will overlook obvious systemic failures and totally ignore environmental factors. Similarly, those who are trained to interpret health and safety legislation will often fail to see clear-cut clinical failures. The protocol, both by its structure and content, avoids bias and forces a comprehensive review.

A structured and systematic approach means that the ground to be covered in any investigation is, to a significant extent, already mapped out. The protocol helps to ensure a comprehensive investigation and facilitate the production of formal reports. Although the procedure may initially appear complicated and time consuming, our experience is that using the protocol actually speeds up complex investigations by focusing the investigators on the key issues and bringing out the systemic factors that must ultimately be the target of the investigation.

These systemic features are addressed when long-term risk reduction strategies are implemented. Once the general contributory factors are identified, these lead automatically to the implications and action points. The final report almost writes itself.

We have noted that even very experienced clinicians find that following a systematic protocol brings additional benefits in terms of comprehensiveness and investigation expertise. Clinicians are accustomed to identifying the problematic features in the management of a case, and so can easily identify the care management problems. However, the identification of contributory factors and the realization that each care management problem may have a different constellation of contributory factors are less familiar tasks. A systematic approach pays dividends when exploring these. The protocol does not attempt to supplant clinical expertise. Rather, the aim is to utilize clinical experience and expertise to the fullest extent.

A formal, systematic approach also brings benefit to the staff involved. The methods used are designed to promote a greater climate of openness and to move away from finger pointing and the routine assignment of blame. This is quite different from the quasi-judicial approach that can be brought to bear in formal inquiries. If a consistent approach to investigation is used, members of staff who are interviewed tend to find the process less threatening than traditional unstructured approaches, especially when the same procedure is being followed with everyone involved.

We have found that formal training and practice with the protocol is needed before it can be used to its full effectiveness. Presentations and training sessions have suggested that the basic ideas can be grasped relatively quickly, but that the full method must be absorbed relatively slowly. Guided practice on the investigation of incidents, preferably in a local context, is essential to become familiar with the methods. Investigators who can carry out an investigation with agreed-upon guidelines can then be designated in each clinical area. Each of these investigators requires specific training, time, and support to carry out detailed investigations using this protocol. The provision of these resources is a test of management resolve in dealing effectively with major incidents and learning from them.

Although we believe that the protocol is an effective and valuable tool, we consider that it is still at a relatively early stage of development, both conceptually and practically. Formal evaluation is needed, and a great deal more practical testing is required. We plan to revise and develop the protocol in the light of experience and formal evaluation. We also believe that the protocol has potential as a research instrument, in that analyses of case series of incidents will be considerably more powerful if a common method is applied to all. In the meantime, however, it is already proving a powerful means of investigating and analyzing clinical incidents and drawing out the lessons these incidents have for enhancing patient safety.

Acknowledgements and Further Information

Members of the ALARM research group, who developed the protocol with the two authors, are Jane Chapman, Sue Prior, Pam Strange, and Ann Tizzard.

Copies of the full protocol are available from the Association of Litigation and Risk Management, Royal Society of Medicine, 1 Wimpole Street, London W1, United Kingdom.

References

1. Eagle, C. J. et al., "Accident Analysis of Large-Scale Technological Disasters: Applied to Anaesthetic Complications," *Canadian Journal of Anaesthesia* 39 (1992):118–122.
2. Cook, R. I., and Woods, D. D. "Operating at the Sharp End: The Complexity of Human Error," *Human Error in Medicine,* ed. M. S. Bogner (Hillsdale, NJ: Lawrence Erlbaum Associates, 1994).
3. Reason, J. T. "Human Error: Models and Management" *British Medical Journal* 320 (2000):768–770.
4. Vincent, C. A., and Bark, P. "Accident Analysis," in *Clinical Risk Management,* ed. C. A. Vincent (London: BMJ Publications, 1995).
5. Stanhope, N. et al., "Applying Human Factors Methods to Clinical Risk Management in Obstetrics," *British Journal of Obstetrics and Gynaecology* 104 (1997):1225–1232.
6. Taylor-Adams, S. E. et al., "Applying Human Factors Methods to the Investigation and Analysis of Clinical Adverse Events," *Safety Science* 31 (1999):143–159.
7. Vincent, C. A., Adams, S., and Stanhope, N. "A Framework for the Analysis of Risk and Safety in Medicine." *British Medical Journal* 316 (1998):1154–1157.
8. Vincent, C. A., Taylor-Adams, S., Chapman, E. J. et al., "How to Investigate and Analyse Clinical Incidents: Clinical Risk Unit and Association of Litigation and Risk Management Protocol." *British Medical Journal* 320 (2000):777–781.
9. Vincent, C. A. et al., *The Investigation and Analysis of Clinical Incidents: A Protocol* (London: Royal Society of Medicine Press, 1999).
10. Joint Commission on Accreditation in Healthcare Organizations, *Root cause analysis in healthcare* (Oakbrook Terrace, CA: JCAHO, 2000).
11. van Vuuran, W. et al., *The Development of an Incident Analysis Tool for the Medical Field,* Report EUT/BDK/85 (The Netherlands: Eindhoven University of Technology, Faculty of Technology Management, 1997).

12. Fahlbruch, B. et al., "Event Analysis as Problem Solving Process," in *After the Event: From Accident to Organizational Learning,* eds. A. Hale and B. Wilpert (Oxford: Pergamon, 1997).

13. Reason, J. T. *Human Error* (New York: Cambridge University Press, 1990).

14. Reason, J. T. *Managing the Risk of Organizational Accidents* (Aldershot: Ashgate, 1997).

15. Cullen, W. D. *The Public Inquiry into the Piper Alpha Disaster* (London: Department of Energy, HMSO, 1990).

16. Hughes, H. "The Offshore Industry's Response to Lord Cullen's Recommendations," *Petroleum Rev* Jan (1991):5–8.

17. Ferrow, M. "Offshore Safety: Formal Safety Assessments," *Petroleum Review* Jan. (1991):9–11.

18. Hale, A. R. et al., eds., *After the Event: From Accident to Organizational Learning* (Oxford: Pergamon, 1997).

19. Vincent, C. A. ed., *Clinical Risk Management Enhancing Patient Safety* (London: BMJ Publications, 2001).

20. Secker-Walker, J., and Donaldson, L. "Clinical Governance: The Context of Risk Management," in *Clinical Risk Management Enhancing Patient Safety,* ed. C. A. Vincent (London: BMJ Publications, 2001).

CHAPTER NINE

PATIENT SAFETY AND ERROR REDUCTION STANDARDS: THE JCAHO RESPONSE TO THE IOM REPORT

Larry E. Poniatowski, RN

The Joint Commission on Accreditation of Healthcare Organizations (JCAHO) evaluates and accredits nearly 18,000 health care organizations and programs in the United States. An independent, not-for-profit organization, the Joint Commission has been accrediting the majority of the over 5,000 hospitals in the United States since 1951.[1] The standards that are used to survey hospitals address an organization's level of performance in key functional areas and set forth performance activities that affect the safety and quality of patient care.

In November 1999, the Institute of Medicine (IOM) released the groundbreaking patient safety report *To Err Is Human: Building a Safer Health System.*[2] The recommendations for the health care industry from that report included the following:

- Establish a Center for Patient Safety within the Department of Health and Human Services (DHHS).
- Require mandatory reporting of errors to state agencies.
- Engage consumers, purchasers, accreditors, and regulators.
- Affect a culture shift to make safety a top priority.

The report went on to make recommendations at the hospital level. These recommendations were an effort to make hospitals a safer place for patients. They included the following:

- Establish patient safety programs with defined executive responsibilities that are clearly focused on patient safety.
- Implement nonpunitive systems for reporting and analyzing medical errors.
- Incorporate well-understood safety principles.
- Establish interdisciplinary team training for providers of patient care that incorporates proven methods of team training.

Since 1996, two years prior to the release of the Institute of Medicine's report, the Joint Commission has had in place a sentinel event reporting requirement. Quite a few revisions have occurred in these requirements since then; the Joint Commission published the newest policy and procedures in July 2002. The definition of a sentinel event in the policy was revised in November 1997.

The Joint Commission defines a sentinel event as an unexpected occurrence involving death or serious physical or psychological injury, or the risk thereof. Serious injury specifically includes loss of limb or function. The phrase "or the risk thereof" includes any process variation for which a recurrence would carry a significant chance of a serious adverse outcome.[3]

Such events are called *sentinel* because they signal the need for immediate investigation and response. Accredited organizations are expected to identify and respond appropriately to all sentinel events occurring in the organization or associated with services that the organization provides or provides for. Appropriate response includes a thorough and credible root cause analysis, implementation of improvements to reduce risk, and monitoring of the effectiveness of those improvements. Organizations' activities in response to sentinel events are routinely assessed as part of all triennial and random unannounced surveys.

On February 27, 1997, after reviewing over 200 sentinel events, the Joint Commission published the first *Sentinel Event Alert,* entitled "Medication Error Prevention–Potassium Chloride." This began an effort by the Joint Commission to periodically publish alerts describing trends in sentinel events and providing health care organizations with information relating to the occurrence and management of sentinel events in Joint Commission–accredited health care organizations. *Sentinel Event Alerts* were published when appropriate as suggested by trended data received by the Joint Commission through the investigation of sentinel events occurring in accredited organizations. It was believed that in sharing information regarding the occurrence of sentinel events, a reduction in the frequency of medical errors and other adverse events would occur.

Organizations were expected to review each Sentinel Event Alert and, if relevant to the services it provided, implement the accompanying expert prevention recommendations published with the alert. If an organization felt that the recommendation would not be effective in its organization, it was to implement a workable alternative preventative strategy and explain this alternative at the time of its next survey by the Joint Commission.

After publication of the Institute of Medicine's report, the Joint Commission on Accreditation of Healthcare Organization's first response to the issues it raised was to revise its own organizational mission. The old mission had emphasized continuously improving the quality of care provided to the public in health care organizations in the United States. The revised mission includes a safety emphasis, and now reads, "to continuously improve *both the safety* and quality of care provided to the public through the provision of health care accreditation and related services that support performance improvement in health care organizations."[4]

A next step for the Joint Commission was to define its public policy position on reporting and managing medical errors. To measurably improve patient safety, the Joint Commission supports the creation of an effective national reporting system, voluntary or mandatory in nature. If mandatory reporting were to be required, only well-defined "serious adverse events" should be reported. A nationally accepted standard definition of "reportable sentinel event" would be promulgated. Organizations that experienced such an event would be required to do an in-depth analysis of each event, with the guarantee of federal protection from disclosure. Following this level of analysis, the organization would then develop both an action and follow-up plan. The analysis, action plan, and follow-up would be shared with the appropriate oversight bodies.

When the Joint Commission developed new and revised standards specific to the support of patient safety and medical/health care error reduction, it took a further step to improve the safety of patient care and reduce medical/health care errors. These standards were finalized and included in the hospitals standards manual, with an effective date of July 1, 2001.[5] Sets of patient safety standards were developed and field-tested for inclusion in most of the other standards manuals that are published by the Joint Commission.

These standards recognize the critical role that hospital leaders play in ensuring the integration, support, and acceptance of patient safety efforts in the hospital. Although these standards do not require any new organizational structure or position, they do require a high level of integration and coordination of an organization-wide safety program that encompasses such safety-related activities as performance improvement, environmental safety, and risk management. Further, these standards challenge leaders to create an environment that encourages recognition and acknowledgement of risk to patient safety and of medical/health care errors and that focuses on processes and systems while minimizing individual blame. The focus is both proactive and reactive, requiring mechanisms that predict risk as well as requiring that safety be engineered into the design of new processes, functions, and services in the hospital.

The Standards

Leadership

LD.5 *The leaders insure the implementation of an integrated safety program throughout the organization.*

LD.5 is the key new leadership standard, describing in detail what senior hospital leaders are accountable for in complying with these new safety standards. The eight items that constitute the intent of LD.5 describe the minimal components of an integrated and organization-wide patient safety program. Further, these items can serve as a template for developing an organization's patient safety program structure and the documentation necessary for standards compliance.

1. The designation of one or more qualified individuals or even an interdisciplinary group to manage the organization-wide patient safety program. This does not require that the hospital create a new department or new position.
2. Definition of the scope of the safety program activities, that is, the type of occurrences to be addressed. Typically, these would range from "no harm," frequently occurring slips all the way to sentinel events with serious outcomes.
3. A description of the mechanism that ensures that all components of the health care organization are integrated into and participate in the organization-wide program.
4. Procedures for the immediate response to medical/health care error, including care of the affected patient(s), containment of risk to others, and preservation of factual information for subsequent analysis.
5. Clear systems for internal and external reporting of information relating to medical/health care errors.
6. Defined mechanisms for responding to the various types of occurrences, such as root cause analysis in response to a sentinel event, or conducting proactive risk reduction activities.

7. Defined mechanisms for support staff who have been involved in a sentinel event.
8. At least annually, a report to the governing body on the occurrence of medical/health care errors and actions taken to improve patient safety, both in response to actual occurrences and proactively.

This standard clearly requires that the organization develop written plans that address who, when, and how issues relating to patient safety and medical/health care errors throughout the hospital. This includes clear lines of defined authority for the management of the organization-wide safety function, as well as policies or procedures that describe the scope, integration, and steps for predicting and responding to various patient safety and medical/health care error situations being monitored throughout the organization. This standard recognizes that there is a very real human emotional cost to staff who are involved in at least a sentinel event situation. Organizations are thus to develop staff support mechanisms. The organization is finally to report at least annually to its board on organizational efforts to track and respond to these issues.

LD.5.1 *Leaders ensure that the processes for identifying and managing sentinel events are defined and implemented.*

LD.5.1 was a simple revision to an existing hospital standard. Besides changing the standard number, an additional requirement was that the organization determine a definition for near misses that was related to the organization's approved definition for a sentinel event. The Joint Commission's definition of near miss is "any process variation which did not affect the outcome, but for which a recurrence carries a significant chance of serious adverse outcome. Such a near miss falls within the scope of the definition of a sentinel event, but outside the scope of those sentinel events that are subject to review by the Joint Commission under its Sentinel Event Policy."

A near miss is a significant event that is invaluable in assisting an organization to focus on patient safety and medical/health care error measurement and prevention efforts. It is much better for all involved to investigate the potential of an adverse outcome than to react to an actual sentinel event. The theme of prevention and proactive risk management begins to be emphasized with this standards revision.

LD.5.2 *Leaders ensure that an ongoing, proactive program for identifying risks to patient safety and reducing medical/health care errors is defined and implemented.*

The intent of this new standard requires that organizations direct attention to the proactive assessment of risk as a major hospital strategy to improve patient safety through the reduction of the potential for medical or health care errors to occur. Hospitals are to use data that already exist on the occurrence of sentinel events throughout the hospital industry to assist in focusing their efforts. Of all the new safety standards, LD.5.2 may cause the most compliance effort for an organization.

At least annually, organizations are required to select at least one high-risk process for proactive risk assessment using failure mode, effects, and criticality analysis (FMEA); however, this approach does not preclude other approaches.[6] The process selection should be based in part on information published periodically by the Joint Commission. Organizations will need to show surveyors some form of documentation of the process selection process. If an organization does not choose to base a process selection on *Sentinel Event Alerts* or other patient safety information and alerts published by the Joint Commission, a clear rationale will have to be presented to the surveyors for this selection.

These standards became effective July 1, 2001. An associate director in JCAHO's Division of Research stated, "in order to demonstrate full compliance with this standard, organizations have an entire year to compile and aggregate data." However, he went on to state, "By the end of July 2002, organizations are expected to show process improvement results."[7]

Two issues in this standard's intent statement will prove to be problematic. The first is that an organization is required to measure the improvement; that is, did improvement actually occur? Essentially, FMEA could go on indefinitely. If measures show that the process was not improved, then a new failure mode process and process redesign are required until an organization is satisfied that patient safety risk is either eliminated or minimized to an acceptable extent.

Second, once the organization has an acceptable process redesign in place, there must be a strategy to maintain the gain, to use an old quality improvement term. The last item in this intent statement requires that an organization develop a strategy to insure that once risk is minimized or eliminated, this effect is maintained over time. Proving compliance with this standard during a survey could be problematic without concrete documentation.

Failure mode, effects, and criticality analysis (FMECA or simply FMEA) is a disciplined design review technique for identifying potential design and process failures before they occur, with the intent of eliminating them or minimizing the risk associated with them. Although new to health care, FMEA as a discipline or concept has been around for a number of years, originally having been developed in the United States military in 1949. Used in conjunction with more traditional "reactive" methods of performance improvement, a much more effective patient safety approach would result.

FMEA has been in worldwide use in the aviation, nuclear, aerospace, chemical, auto, and food processing industries. In 1988, the ISO 9000 series of business management standards were issued. The requirements of ISO 9000 pushed organizations to refocus quality efforts on the needs, wants, and expectations of customers.[8] With the Institute of Medicine report,[9] health care providers were challenged to find ways to make medicine safer for patients in American health care.

In health care, the quality focus has typically been retrospective in nature. Measurement concentrated on looking for errors after they had already happened: Why did an event occur? Improvement efforts then were aimed at preventing the error from occurring in the future. American industry has established that quality improvement involves both retrospective measurement and proactive risk assessment and reduction. Incorporating the proactive FMEA approach in health care and applying this approach to patient safety is a natural progression encouraged by the IOM report recommendations.

"If it ain't broke, don't fix it" becomes "If it ain't broke, try to break it (at least theoretically)." When you can find potential for failure (breakage) of a process, then redesign it to make it less prone to failure or breaking.

LD.5.3 *Leaders ensure that patient safety issues are given high priority and addressed when process, functions or services are designed or redesigned.*

Standard LD.5.3 is new, but is actually scored in the Performance Improvement chapter of the hospital standards manual, specifically at PI.2. When a standard appears in italicized text in the standards manual, it indicates that either the standard is not scored, or, as in this case, the actual score is given at a different standard. Language was added to the intent statement of PI.2 that mirrors the requirements addressed in the intent of LD.5.3. This new language requires that when processes, functions, or services are designed or redesigned, information from within the organization and from other organizations about potential risks to patient safety, including the occurrence of sentinel events, be considered and, when appropriate, used to minimize the risk to patients affected by the new or redesigned process, function, or service. Again, organizations are being required to act proactively.

Other minor revisions and additions were made in the Leadership chapter of the Joint Commission hospital standards manuals. These revisions and additions made improving patient safety a leadership responsibility and priority. Of note in these more minor revisions is a requirement that leaders create and foster a culture that emphasizes cooperation and communication that will lead to improvement in patient safety (LD.3.2). There is also a recognition that even the best-designed process can lead to patient safety problems and increased medical/health care error if there is variation in the manner in which the process is executed by staff. Leaders are charged with a responsibility for measuring error-prone and high-risk processes and taking appropriate action when significant variation is noted (LD.3.4.1).

Closing out the revisions and additions to the Leadership chapter are standards that require leaders to support activities that support the improvement of patient safety at the same level as improving organizational performance. Hospital leaders provide adequate human resources for these activities and give these staff sufficient time and support to be effective. Appropriate staff members are assigned in sufficient numbers to ensure programs in the pursuit of improvement and risk reduction priorities. Leaders allow enough time for performance improvement activities and activities to improve patient safety, and provide needed information and technical assistance. Each department determines what resources are sufficient for its improvement efforts and activities to improve patient safety.

LD.4.5.5, a new standard, requires leaders to objectively assess the adequacy of their resource support to both performance improvement (PI) and patient safety efforts. This needs to be documented in such a manner that it can be presented to Joint Commission surveyors. As usual, there are no concrete recommendations in the standard or intent statement that structure the assessment or even hint at how often leaders need to look at this issue. This is a standard issue that might be missed by some organizations.

As had been required with performance improvement, leaders now must measure the effectiveness of their contributions to improving patient safety in the organization. Surveyors will be assessing how leaders

- Set measurable goals for improving patients safety
- Gather information to assess their effectiveness in improving patient safety
- Draw conclusions on their findings, and implement improvement in these activities
- Evaluate their performance in supporting sustained patient safety improvement

Patient Rights and Organizational Ethics

RI.1.2.2 *Patients and, when appropriate, their families are informed about the outcomes of care, including unanticipated outcomes.*

Included in the new patient safety standards was one standard added to the Patient Rights and Organizational Ethics chapter of the manual.

Released with little fanfare or explanation, RI.1.2.2 has stimulated more confusion and discussion than all other patient safety standards. The intent of this standard is that the responsible licensed independent practitioner (LIP), or someone designated by this individual, explains the outcomes of any treatments or procedures to the patient whenever these outcomes differ significantly from those that had been anticipated. The family is to be included if and when appropriate.

To clearly understand what this standard requires, one should understand what is *not* required.[10] This standard does *not* require an organization to have a policy for full disclosure, as many appear to believe. Merely telling a patient what the results of treatment or procedure were in no way relates to the accepted definition of full disclosure.

Since much confusion seems to exist over what this standard actually requires an organization to do, it is important to understand first, what this standard does not require. You are not required by Joint Commissions standards to inform patients about the following:

- Errors that did not affect the patient's outcome
- How and why the error occurred
- Who committed the error

At the current time, surveyors have been instructed to determine the organization's process for informing patients about outcomes of care or treatments, especially when those outcomes differ significantly from outcomes that were anticipated. However, there is no requirement for any specific documentation of the process, especially any requirement that this conversation be an entry in the patient's medical record.

Organizations should proceed cautiously when developing any policy on disclosure. Although the Joint Commission has not made specific requirements, it will hold an organization responsible for complying with self-defined policies. Do not create a policy with which acceptable compliance is difficult at best.

Excellent guidelines exist to assist in developing a credible and ethical disclosure policy. A paper by the American Society for Healthcare Risk Management of the American Hospital Association entitled "Perspectives on Disclosure of Unanticipated Outcome Information," is a thorough and extremely credible treatment of the subject.[11] The University HealthSystem Consortium has published a white paper entitled *Shining the Light on Errors: How Open Should We Be?* for its member hospitals, which addresses disclosure, including the legal ramifications of both disclosure and nondisclosure.[12]

The Joint Commission also added references to patient safety in both the Improving Organizational Performance and the Management of Information chapters of the accreditation manual for hospitals. PI.2 and its link to the new leadership standard LD.5.3 has already been discussed.

Improving Organizational Performance

PI.3.1 *The organization collects data to monitor its performance.*

This standard includes both items that an organization should consider for possible collection as well as data that an organization is required to collect. In the category of "consider for collection" are the following two new items:

- Patient, family, and staff opinions, needs, perceptions of risks to patients, and suggestions for improving patient safety
- Staff willingness to report medical/health care errors

Data required for collection regard the needs, expectations, and satisfaction of individuals. The organization asks them about how the organization can improve patient safety. Remember that both the new and revised patient safety standards were effective July 1, 2001. In relation to patient safety suggestions, there will need to be a track record that coincides with the effective date of the new requirement in PI.3.1.

PI.4.3 *Undesirable patterns or trends in performance and sentinel events are intensively analyzed.*

Because of the revision of the standard, organizations are now required to perform intense analysis regarding hazardous conditions. The Joint Commission's definition of hazardous conditions is "any set of circumstances (exclusive of the diseases or condition for which the patient is being treated) that significantly increases the likelihood of a serious adverse event." This will require that organizations create an operational definition for "hazardous condition" and, based on this definition, create a threshold for determining when a clinical process meets the requirement for an intense analysis.

Further, an intense analysis is required for those topics selected by leaders for proactive risk assessment and reduction (see LD.1.4 and LD.5.2). Intense analysis involves studying in great detail how a process is performed or how it operates, how it can malfunction, and how errors can occur (FMEA).

PI.4.4 *The organization identifies changes that will lead to improved performance and improve patient safety.*

This revised standard requires that once a change in a system or process is identified, organizations perform a pilot test of the improvement. This test requires the development of measures of system or process improvement that clearly show that change resulted in improvement to performance and/or patient safety. Testing of planned improvements has proven to be problematic to many organizations. A typical approach has been to find an opportunity for improvement, design the improvement strategy, implement a change, and then go right on to the next project. Many times an organization never looked back, taking a leap of faith that the improvement would always work as designed and never need to be tweaked for full effectiveness.

Management of Information

IM.1 *The hospital plans and designs information management processes to meet internal and external information needs.*

IM.1 is an old standard but has a revised intent. The intent statement now requires an organization to further assess its information management needs based on an additional criterion, its identification of barriers to effective communication among caregivers. These barriers are to be identified through both retrospective performance improvement activities and predicted when proactive risk identification activities are applied to systems and processes in the organization. Planning for improvement would then also require a change to the organization's information management plan.

IM.5 *Transmission of data is timely and accurate.*

Organizations are required to pay particular attention to processes for ensuring accurate, timely, and complete verbal and written communication among caregivers and all other involved in the utilization of data. This revision requires that organizations consider communication among caregivers when conducting either retrospective performance improvement activities or proactive risk identification activities.

IM.7.2 *The medical record contains sufficient information to identify the patient, support the diagnosis, justify the treatment, document the course and results, and promote continuity of care among health care providers.*

A minor additional requirement has been added to the intent requiring that test results relevant to the management of the patient's condition be included in the medical record.

IM.8 *The hospital collects and aggregates data and information to support care and service delivery and operations.*

An addition to the intent statement requires that the organization's information management function have the ability to support reduction in risks to patients.

IM.9 *Knowledge-based information systems, resources, and services meet the hospital's needs.*

A final revision to the information management standards requires organizations to acquire, assemble, and transmit knowledge-based data to support activities to reduce risk to patients. Also, print and nonprint information resources now need to include successful practices. These successful practices provide a source of reference to patient safety and medical/health care error reduction efforts.

Patient and Family Education

PF.3.7 *Education includes information about patient responsibilities in the patient's care.*

The intent of this revised standard adds the dimension of describing the patient as a partner in the health care process. The patient must accept certain responsibilities. While specific attention is directed at educating patients and families about their role in helping to facilitate the safe delivery of care, the intent describes the responsibilities of the patient and family to actively participate.

Continuum of Care

A very minor addition was made to the intent statement of CC.4 and CC.5. The statement that "communication and transfer of information between and among health care professionals [is] essential to a seamless and safe and effective process" was added.

Human Resources

HR.4 *An orientation process provides initial job training and information and assesses the staff's ability to fulfill specified responsibilities.*

The revision to this staff orientation standard is the added requirement that the orientation process emphasize specific job-related aspects of patient safety. This job-related patient safety orientation should be easily pointed out to the surveyor. The requirement is for orientation to specific job-related aspects of safety, so an overall orientation to the general principles and organizational philosophy of patient safety really does not comply with this standard's intent. The orientation to safety needs to get to the on-the-job level to insure true compliance.

HR.4.2 *Ongoing in-service and other education and training maintain and improve staff competence and support an interdisciplinary approach to patient care.*

The additional language in the intent of this standard includes a requirement for the inclusion of safety-oriented material in ongoing training conducted within the organization. Further language emphasizes team training and familiarization with reporting mechanisms for medical/health care reporting as a means to create a blame-free culture in the organization.

Definitions

This section provides the Joint Commission's definitions for terms used throughout the revised and new standards.[13] Since these definitions are in the Glossary section of the *Accreditation Manual for Hospitals,* they are official, and as such it is strongly recommended that organizations use them when defining systems or processes that promote patient safety. It is extremely important when you or other organizational staff are dealing with surveyors or survey processes to define your terms or data elements carefully and to speak the same language as the Joint Commission's surveyors.

- *Error.* An unintended act, either of omission or commission, or any act that does not achieve its intended outcome.
- *Sentinel event.* An unexpected occurrence involving death or serious physical or psychological injury or the risk thereof. Serious injury specifically includes loss of limb or function. The phrase "or risk thereof" includes any process variation for which a recurrence would carry a significant chance of a serious adverse outcome.
- *Near miss.* Used to describe any process variation which did not affect the outcome, but for which a recurrence carries a significant chance of serious adverse outcome. Such a near miss falls within the definition of a sentinel event, but outside the scope of those sentinel events that are subject to review by the Joint Commission under its Sentinel Event Policy.
- *Hazardous condition.* Any set of circumstances (exclusive of the diseases or condition for which the patient is being treated) that significantly increases the likelihood of a serious adverse outcome.

Goals of the Standards

This set of new and revised standards constitutes one of the most extensive and thorough additions to the Joint Commission hospital standards since the manual was rewritten in 1994 to recast standards to emphasize a functional, system, and process orientation rather than the departmental focus of traditional Joint Commission hospital standards prior to that year. The Joint Commission has integrated these new and revised patient safety and medical/health care error standards throughout the major functional chapters of the manual, just as hospitals are expected to integrate patient safety and medical/health care error reduction throughout the hospital.

These standards require that organizations create an open culture where mistakes and errors are reported without fear of retribution. Even through the era of continuous quality improvement and the newer performance improvement concepts of Joint Commission standards, hospitals have stubbornly clung to the "bad apple" approach when responding to negative outcomes of patient safety and medical/health care errors. The Joint Commission recognizes that fear of retribution and a culture steeped in a blame-placing mentality propagate the reactive approach to error. Staff members are unwilling to come forward and may even hide both small and large errors that negatively affect patients.

Another significant concept woven through these standards is a prospective rather than a reactive approach to patient safety. In an environment of open communication where health care professionals work together across professional and departmental lines, errors and negative patient outcomes become the focus of preventative strategies, rather than the blame placing and excuses that have become so much a part of modern health care. Providers of patient care can seek to do no harm through an open and honest exploration of processes that prevent harm before it reaches the patient.

At the same time as the new safety standards were first published, the Joint Commission also changed the requirements for how organizations were to respond to the *Sentinel Event Alerts,* which had been published since 1998. During the two years of their publication by the Joint Commission, a number of issues regarding the alerts had been raised. First, the almost monthly publication of sentinel event alerts puts an unfair burden on hospitals. Since hospitals were expected to discuss each alert as well as examine the recommendations for risk reduction accompanying these alerts, monthly publication overtaxed most organization's quality structures. Second, how issues were chosen to become sentinel event alerts was called into question. The alert on Creutzfeldt-Jakob disease, published in June 2001, contained information based on only two related sentinel events. Organizations questioned the true "expertness" of the recommendations made in many of the *Sentinel Event Alerts.* Finally, organizations complained that surveyors questioned their choice of alternatives to the official risk reduction sentinel event recommendations based on opinion and not evidence-based clinical data.

The Joint Commission convened a task force of clinical and measurement experts in late 2001 and early 2002 to study and recommend changes to its process of producing sentinel event alerts and risk management recommendations and how these issues were surveyed. On July 1, 2002, the Joint Commission announced the launch of the annual National Patient Safety Goals with six safety goals for 2003. The process involved an expert task force of clinicians external to the Joint Commission who examined the existing sentinel event alerts and recommendations and selected six goals and eleven recommendations that all organizations surveyed beginning on January 1, 2003, would be required to implement. Every year on July, more goals and recommendations will be announced for the coming calendar year.

Organizations can implement alternatives to the recommendations if those alternatives are determined, upon review by the Sentinel Event Alert Advisory Group, to be at least as effective as the published recommendations in achieving the goals. The process for reviewing alternative recommendations will be communicated to accredited organizations in a future issue of *Joint Commission Perspectives* and will be posted on JCAHO's website. Failure by an organization to implement all of the recommendations or acceptable alternatives will result in a single special Type I recommendation.

The six safety goals for 2003 were as follows:

1. *Goal:* Improve the accuracy of patient identification.
   A. *Recommendation:* Use at least two patient identifiers (neither to be the patient's room number) whenever taking blood samples or administering medications or blood products.
   B. *Recommendation:* Prior to the start of any surgical or invasive procedure, conduct a final verification process, such as a "time out," to confirm the correct patient, procedure, and site, using active—not passive—communication techniques.
2. *Goal:* Improve the effectiveness of communication among caregivers.
   A. *Recommendation:* Implement a process for taking verbal or telephone orders that requires a verification "read-back" of the complete order by the person receiving the order.
   B. *Recommendation:* Standardize the abbreviations, acronyms, and symbols used throughout the organization, including a list of abbreviations, acronyms, and symbols not to use.
3. *Goal:* Improve the safety of using high-alert medications.
   A. *Recommendation:* Remove concentrated electrolytes (including, but not limited to, potassium chloride, potassium phosphate, sodium chloride >0.9%) from patient care units.
   B. *Recommendation:* Standardize and limit the number of drug concentrations available in the organization.

4. *Goal:* Eliminate wrong-site, wrong-patient, wrong-procedure surgery.
   A. *Recommendation:* Create and use a preoperative verification process, such as a checklist, to confirm that appropriate documents (e.g., medical records, imaging studies) are available.
   B. *Recommendation:* Implement a process to mark the surgical site, and involve the patient in the marking process.
5. *Goal:* Improve the safety of using infusion pumps.
   A. *Recommendation:* Ensure free-flow protection on all general-use and PCA intravenous infusion pumps used in the organization.
6. *Goal:* Improve the effectiveness of clinical alarm systems.
   A. *Recommendation:* Implement regular preventive maintenance and testing of alarm systems.
   B. *Recommendation:* Assure that alarms are activated with appropriate settings and are sufficiently audible with respect to distances and competing noise within the unit.

A final step in the Joint Commission's efforts to improve patient safety and reduce medical/health care errors came on March 14, 2002, when it announced sponsorship of a national campaign aimed at making patients active partners in efforts to prevent medical/health care errors. The campaign, called Speak Up, urges patients to actively involve themselves in their own clinical care.[14] Efforts to increase consumer awareness and involvement are supported by the Centers for Medicare and Medicaid Services.

To help prevent errors, patients are encouraged to SPEAK UP:

Speak up if you have questions or concerns, and if you don't understand, ask again. It's your body and you have a right to know.

Pay attention to the care you are receiving. Make sure you're getting the right treatments and medications by the right health care professionals. Don't assume anything.

Educate yourself about your diagnosis, the medical tests you are undergoing, and your treatment plan.

Ask a trusted family member or friend to be your advocate.

Know the medications you take and why you take them. Medication errors are the most common health care errors.

Use a hospital, clinic, surgery center, or other type of health care organization that has undergone a rigorous on-site evaluation against established state-of-the-art quality and safety standards, such as that provided by JCAHO.

Participate in all decisions about your treatment. You are the center of the health care team.

Patients are instructed to download a "Speak Up" brochure from the Joint Commission's website. The brochure contains simple advice about actions that patients can take to protect themselves while in a health care organization and make their health care experience positive. The advice is organized under each of the headings that compose the acronym *Speak Up*.

The Joint Commission thus has responded to an increasing public awareness that patient care is not safe and is fraught with the potential for both minor and major mistakes—oversights and errors that negatively affect patient care outcomes. Recognizing a responsibility to the public, the Joint Commission has revised its organizational mission statement and created new as well as revised standards for hospitals that focus on the reduction of medical and health care errors to improve the safety of care provided in organizations it accredits. By then defining the role that health care consumers play in ensuring their own safety, the Joint Commission has joined all the major participants of health care—providers, accreditors, regulators, and the public—to reduce health care and medical errors for a safer health care environment.

Notes

1. Joint Commission on Accreditation of Healthcare Organizations. Facts About the Joint Commission on Accreditation of Healthcare Organizations. http://www.jcaho.org/whatwedo_frm.html.
2. Institute of Medicine, Committee on Quality of Health Care in America. *To Err Is Human: Building a Safer Health System.* Washington, DC: National Academy Press, 1999.
3. Joint Commission on Accreditation of Healthcare Organizations. Sentinel Event Alerts. http://www.jcaho.org/whatwedo_frm.html.
4. Joint Commission on Accreditation of Healthcare Organizations. Facts About the Joint Commission on Accreditation of Healthcare Organizations. http://www.jcaho.org/whatwedo_frm.html.
5. Joint Commission on Accreditation of Healthcare Organizations. *Comprehensive Accreditation Manual for Hospitals: The Official Handbook.* CAMH Update 1, February 2001. Oakbrook Terrace, CA: Joint Commission on Accreditation of Healthcare Organizations, 2001.
6. "Using FMEA to Assess and Reduce Risk." *Joint Commission Perspectives on Patient Safety,* November 2001:1–3.
7. "Get Ready for Survey: Incorporating Patient Safety into the Survey Process." *Joint Commission Perspectives on Patient Safety,* December 2001:1–3.
8. McDermott, Robin E., et al. *The Basics of FMEA.* Portland: Productivity, Inc., 1996.
9. Institute of Medicine, *To Err Is Human.*

10. "Talking with Individuals and Their Families at the Sharp End of an Error." *Joint Commission Perspectives on Patient Safety,* August 2001: 1–2.
11. "Perspectives on Disclosure of Unanticipated Outcome Information." American Society for Hospital Risk Management, April 2001. http://www.ashrm.org.
12. *Shining the Light on Errors: How Open Should We Be?* Oak Brook, IL: University HealthSystem Consortium, 2002.
13. Joint Commission on Accreditation of Healthcare Organizations. *Comprehensive Accreditation Manual for Hospitals: The Official Handbook.* Oakbrook Terrace, CA: Joint Commission on Accreditation of Healthcare Organizations, 2002.
14. Joint Commission on Accreditation of Healthcare Organizations. Speak Up: Help Prevent Errors in Your Care. http://www.jcaho.org/speakup_bro.html.

CHAPTER TEN

APPLYING EPIDEMIOLOGY
TO PATIENT SAFETY

Mark Keroack, MD, MPH and
Emily Rhinehart, RN, MPH, CIC, CPHQ

Epidemiology is a relative newcomer among the medical sciences. Although its roots go back to Snow's studies of cholera in 19th-century London, its widespread application to the explanation of disease causation dates back only to the 1950s. Since that time, there has been a rapid growth of studies that have clarified the causes and risk factors of disease through careful observations of affected populations by methods that account for confounding clinical factors. Epidemiologic approaches have led to major breakthroughs in our understanding of cardiovascular diseases, cancer, and emerging infectious diseases, and their application to nosocomial infection control has led to systematic advances in prevention. However, epidemiologic tools have received little attention in advancing patient safety, largely because of concerns that underreporting of medical errors by clinicians will yield invalid data regarding the incidence of events that lead to patient harm.

The seminal chart review studies of Brennan and others that raised the consciousness of the medical community regarding medical error were epidemiologic in design, using surveillance by standardized chart review to estimate the incidence of errors and the deaths they caused.[1,2] The findings were highlighted in the Institute of Medicine report *To Err Is Human,* causing a national outcry for improvement and a renewed interest by governmental funding agencies in understanding and controlling medical error.[3] Although the report has called for a 50%

reduction in deaths from medical error by 2005, more than a decade after those original epidemiologic studies there has been little activity devoted to estimating the current rate using epidemiologic methods. Current approaches to understanding medical error have focused instead on intensive case reviews called root cause analyses, patterned after industries such as aviation and nuclear power, in which errors are relatively less common than in health care and much more dramatic in their manifestations. This method has proved its value for isolated events; however, approaches also are needed that enable quality and risk managers to learn from the numerous, more minor events that occur daily in modern hospitals and other health care settings. This chapter explores the ways in which the tools of epidemiology can answer this need, augmenting our understanding of medical error and complementing traditional case investigation approaches.

Epidemiology Versus Case-Based Analysis: The Forest and the Trees

There is a long history of individual case analyses in medicine, evidenced by the tradition of clinicopathological conferences and morbidity and mortality rounds. Although some have dismissed these approaches as less than scientific when measured against the exacting standards of the controlled clinical trial, it is now clear that much progress has been made in advancing patient safety by in-depth analyses of isolated catastrophic events. The merits and shortcomings of this sort of "qualitative research" were well described by Runciman[4] nearly a decade ago and recently reviewed by Kaplan and Barach.[5] Over the years, root cause investigations have advanced by borrowing from the lessons learned by the aviation and nuclear power industries, shifting their focus from finding and blaming culprits to identifying systematic flaws in the processes of care that predispose clinicians to commit errors.[6]

The advantages of this approach are several. Root cause analysis can identify plausible causes of catastrophic events without requiring the standard of proof of a clinical trial. This means that an organization does not have to wait for recurrences of rare events, such as wrong-sided surgeries or infant abductions, in order to take corrective action. It allows the adoption of self-evident solutions, such as the removal of concentrated potassium chloride solutions from clinical wards to prevent fatal overdoses or the redesign of anesthesia tubing to prevent incorrect connections. When coupled with insight into human factors issues, it allows for a detailed, open-ended narrative that can lead to solutions not initially contemplated by the investigators. Lastly, by recounting a compelling story of care gone bad, case-based analysis can move the culture of an organization to face the existence of flaws in its systems. Because of these advantages, as well as its strong track record of accomplishment in disciplines such as anesthesia, root cause analysis will remain the preferred method for rare and catastrophic events.

However, the very elements that make the case-based investigative approach the methodology of choice for rare events make it a weaker method for events that occur commonly. Incident reports are usually selected for root cause analyses when there was considerable harm to the patient or the potential for considerable harm, but analysis of more minor events, such as missing laboratory tests or missed medication doses, may uncover system flaws every bit as serious as those uncovered through the investigation of rare, catastrophic events. In fact, reports of near misses have been shown to be valuable in improving safety in other industries.[6] If overall improvement of patient safety is the goal, one cannot afford to overlook the potential information from numerous event reports of common errors. However, if only the most serious events are selected for in-depth analysis, reporting of minor events will be discouraged and their potential importance discounted by staff.

An analysis focused on selected cases also will lead to conclusions that are weaker and narrower than cases analyzed as groups. The role of clinical or other contributing factors that would make the event more likely to occur is largely conjectural in an individual root cause analysis, because comparisons between the case being analyzed and other, similar cases are not performed. The potential contributions of such factors as age, comorbid conditions, site of care, and time of day cannot be discerned from an analysis focusing on a single case. A classic epidemiologic example will help illustrate this point.

Modern infection control traces its roots to the pioneering studies of Semmelweis on puerperal fever in the mid-1800s. His critical contribution was in discovering differences in rates of maternal death due to this common infection between different wards of the Allegemaines Krankenhaus in Vienna.[7] Although the disease occurred both in divisions attended by midwives and medical students, rates on the latter divisions were threefold higher. Semmelweis established the key risk factor of care by a medical student in the infection and hypothesized that the performance of autopsies by medical students led to cross-contamination of patients with contaminated materials. Institution of handwashing policies for the medical students led to a reduction of rates similar to those observed in the wards attended by midwives. It is unlikely that a detailed investigation of a single case of disease would have led to this insight; rather, noting differences in rates in clearly defined subpopulations at differential risk for disease led to a testable hypothesis regarding a key causal factor.

Surveillance Systems Past and Present

The current management of patient safety in most health care organizations begins with incident reporting by front-line clinical staff. However, risk managers acknowledge that they are informed of most significant events not through incident reports, but via pages or urgent telephone calls from the staff. They may or may not eventually record the event on an incident report. Thus, incident reports are not actually used for their primary purpose—notifying the risk manager and triggering an investigation. Most are used for a secondary purpose—as a tool to document that proper procedures were followed after the occurrence of an adverse event.

Incident reports have been revised to capture more detailed data on a variety of events. This has resulted in several problems that hinder their use as a surveillance tool. For example, it is common to see forms that are lengthy and detailed, sometimes containing dozens of variables on a single page printed in a very small font. Alternatively, separate forms may exist for medication events, falls, behavioral events, and so forth. In addition, since the reports have evolved primarily to a documentation tool, several sign-offs may be required before a report reaches the desk of the risk or quality manager. This often leads to weeks of delay while the report moves from one manager's desk to another, reducing the value of interviews based on recall for those events deserving further investigation. While the problem of underreporting of errors and adverse events is often ascribed to a culture of blame that exists in many organizations regarding error reporting,[8,9] the problem is made worse by tools and processes that are cumbersome and confusing.

Because of concerns regarding unreported events, many organizations have implemented changes in traditional incident reporting tools and processes. A few organizations have developed electronic event reporting systems that have the advantage of collapsing numerous paper forms into a single reporting tool and reducing the time lost in transferring paper between departments. Locally developed tools include the system at the University of Missouri at Columbia.[10] Systems that focus on a single type of error include the MedmaRx system developed by US Pharmacopoeia and the Medical Error Reporting System for Transfusion Medicine (MERS-TM) developed at Columbia University.[11,12] More broad-based tools include the products developed by Doctorquality.com and the University HealthSystem Consortium.[13,14] Experience with implementation of these latter products shows that lowering the barriers to reporting, when coupled with efforts to reduce blame and focus on system improvements, can lead to severalfold increases in reporting.[15,16] As numbers of reports increase, the average severity of a report tends to decrease. Indeed, a significant fraction of reports are of "close calls" or "near misses" in which chance or an active intervention prevented the error from reaching the patient. Encouraging this sort of reporting broadens the view of staff regarding the prevalence of human error in health care and its potential consequences.

If all event and near miss reports represent opportunities for learning about system flaws, how does a quality or risk manager come to grips with a growing number of reports in an organization that has made a commitment to patient safety? Prioritization methods have been suggested, including the VA Severity Assessment Matrix,[17] in which events that are most severe or most likely to recur receive priority for intensive investigation. This approach still tends to discard the majority of reports, however, some of which may herald future catastrophe. For example, the administration of a vitamin pill to the wrong patient may be dismissed as having no consequences, but it may provide clues to systematic flaws in the medication administration process that could lead to administering a far more toxic agent to the wrong patient in the future. Furthermore, the greatest disincentive to reporting for a front-line clinician is the message that nothing was done with the report filed. If one's only analytic tool is intensive case investigation, then a majority of reported events will be discarded in the current environment of limited analytic resources.

Developing Surveillance Systems for Errors and Adverse Events

An effective surveillance system should accomplish four main objectives. Monitoring the occurrence rate of a specific adverse event will allow the organization to (1) determine the overall magnitude of the problem relative to others, (2) decide whether it is increasing or decreasing in incidence, (3) identify which patient groups or care areas are most affected and therefore most in need of resources, and (4) decide whether efforts to improve are being effective. The term *surveillance* conjures up the image of a highly trained professional reviewing patient charts using strict case definitions or interviewing at-risk individuals using highly structured questionnaires. However, many forms of surveillance are far less exact. Aggregation of death certificate information was the first example of disease surveillance and is still used to track national trends in disease, in spite of its well-publicized shortcomings.[18,19] When legionnaire's disease and AIDS first came to attention, case definitions were rudimentary and inexact, but they nonetheless focused national attention on the emerging threats and allowed estimates of their magnitude and spread.[20,21] In each case, inferences made from tracking imperfect measures enabled the identification of specific risk factors that allowed investigators to focus more rigorous observation efforts in the areas where they would be the most fruitful. Such will likely be the case with the data sets on adverse events now being developed by pioneering organizations committed to a better understanding of patient safety.

Baylor Grapevine Hospital has implemented the Doctorquality.com computerized event reporting system and has coupled it with a senior leadership initiative to encourage reporting.[15] The leaders of the quality program found that simple trending of rates of adverse events could be accomplished by unit managers, allowing quality and risk staff to focus on priority areas. At the University of Wisconsin, hospital-wide implementation of the UHC Patient Safety Net, coupled with policies to encourage open reporting, has increased event reporting over the previous paper system by 260%.[16] The ability to select areas for more intensive review from these data is analogous to infection control programs in which routine infections are trended and interventions focused on areas of high severity or strategic importance, or instances when rates increase beyond preset limits. Note that in the individual case approach, cases merit investigation by virtue of the impact or potential impact on a single patient, whereas in the epidemiologic approach, groups of cases merit investigation by increases in overall rates or clustering in specific areas or patient groups.

The passive collection of adverse event reports must be augmented by a more structured and targeted approach to problem areas led by quality and risk managers. This may entail direct data collection through chart review, direct observation of clinical processes, or efforts to encourage front-line clinicians to focus their reporting on specific areas of interest. As these managers reevaluate and redesign their systems to focus on specific process errors and adverse events, they should first examine the basic principles of epidemiology and methods of disease surveillance. Surveillance is defined by the Centers for Disease Control and Prevention (CDC) as "the ongoing, systematic collection, analysis, and interpretation of health data essential to the planning, implementation, and evaluation of public health practice, closely integrated with the timely dissemination of these data to those who need to know."[20]

Going forward, systems for ongoing surveillance must be developed to focus on specific patients at risk, process errors, and adverse events and outcomes. Just as infection control abandoned the practice of total surveillance and the calculation of hospital-wide infection rates a number of years ago, risk management needs to hone its measurement approach and recognize, for example, that a hospital-wide medication error rate is not valid or useful in risk analysis or risk reduction. In approaching the collection and analysis of risk data, risk managers can successfully follow the recommended steps for developing a population-based surveillance system outlined in Table 10-1.[21]

TABLE 10-1   Steps in Developing a Surveillance Program

1. Assess the population at risk.
2. Select the process(s) and/or outcome(s) for surveillance.
3. Develop definitions.
4. Develop data collection methods and tools.
5. Calculate and analyze rates.
6. Apply risk stratification.
7. Report results on a regular schedule and use the data for the development of risk reduction strategies.

Assessing the Population at Risk

First, the patient population should be assessed for the risk of specific errors or adverse events and outcomes. If the population at risk is defined too broadly, the resulting data will be crude and will not lead to identification of specific risks or contributing factors that can be remedied. Reporting should focus on those populations with the greatest risks, targeting either frequent errors or severe events. This will facilitate the use of the data for further, more detailed study or the development of process improvements. Choosing the patient population on which to focus may be prompted by many considerations, including patients with high-mortality conditions or procedures, patients in strategically important programs (e.g., trauma patients in the region's only Level I trauma center), patients in new clinical programs, or patients in areas where baseline trends seem to indicate opportunities for improvement.

Selecting the Processes and Outcomes for Surveillance

As incident report forms have evolved, risk managers have included long lists of errors and events in very complex, difficult-to-read forms. Redesigning the incident reporting system provides an opportunity to focus on more specific errors and events. This may be accomplished by simplifying forms to allow for more free text, limiting the scope of the form to concentrate only on the most common or significant errors, or utilizing computer technology to tailor the questions being displayed to the event being reported. Limiting the list of events meriting the focus of risk and quality management staff will allow these professionals to (1) select more valid indicators of risk and related variables, (2) develop stable and accurate rates of incidence of the selected error or event, and (3) further refine the definitions of groups at risk and other risk factors. This will result in the development of more focused risk analysis studies that will more likely lead to valid conclusions and specific risk reduction strategies.

As part of a renewed approach to data collection, it is useful to determine which errors or adverse events should be captured and analyzed by considering the following factors:[20]

- Frequency of the event or error
- Negative impact (e.g., likelihood to lead to a claim or more serious outcome)
- Potential for prevention
- Specific risks within a patient population (e.g., obstetrics)
- Relationship of the adverse event to the process of care
- Resources available for reporting/surveillance

For the reasons mentioned earlier, most paper-based systems are not reliable guides for determining the incidence of adverse events. Computerized systems have shown promise in augmenting reporting substantially, often revealing potential areas of focus. Previous projects in which intensive measurement of specific processes or outcomes were conducted also may help guide the prioritization process. Lastly, the risk or quality manager's own experience in the organization may often serve as an accurate guide for those types of events most frequently associated with patient harm or liability risk exposure.

Because most areas of opportunity in systems of care require a team effort in order to improve them, it is advantageous to decide on priority areas in collaboration with other interested and involved individuals. This may include the participation of quality management staff as well as selected representatives from the nursing and medical staff. Input from clinicians who care for specific high-risk populations (e.g., obstetricians, emergency room staff) is valuable both in designing valid and relevant reporting tools and in gaining buy-in from those who will be involved in reporting and improvement initiatives.

Developing Definitions

Any surveillance system must include specific definitions for the data elements being collected. Taking the time to identify or develop definitions will contribute to more consistent, accurate, and reliable data. The first step in developing definitions is to search for existing definitions. For specific populations, definitions may have already been developed by professional organizations such as the American College of Obstetrics and Gynecology (e.g., delayed cesarean section), the American College of Surgeons (e.g., surgical wound classification), or the American Society for Anesthesiology (e.g., ASA score). Participation of clinicians from these specialty groups, as discussed earlier, will facilitate the identification of already existing definitions. For process errors or adverse events that may occur across multiple patient populations, such as medication errors or falls, a literature search should be conducted to find definitions already developed by others. Adoption of an existing definition may allow for external comparisons or benchmarking in the future. The Agency for Healthcare Research and Quality has funded research into the development of a national consensus classification system for medical errors and adverse events.

The proper criteria for determining the occurrence or category of events should be made available to those being encouraged to report, but because most events are observed by professionals trained in clinical care rather than data analysis, first-hand reports will have inaccuracies related to a misunderstanding of definitions. Areas of concern, determined by passive surveillance by untrained reporters, will require review by personnel well versed in the agreed-upon definitions. Ongoing staff education will sharpen the accuracy of reports by front-line clinicians with time, and it should be borne in mind that the first, crucial step in surveillance is the willingness of a clinician to come forward to share that an adverse event has occurred at all. Given the bias toward underreporting of errors and adverse events, inaccurate data are far better than no data at all.

Developing Data Collection Methods and Tools

Surveillance can be performed in a variety of ways. Incident reporting systems are usually passive surveillance systems that rely on staff members to recognize, report, and record events. In some cases, reports may be stimulated by making it clear that the organization is interested in specific types of events as part of a focused quality improvement project. Nosocomial infection surveillance, on the other hand, is a form of active surveillance focused on specific outcomes. This type of surveillance is easier to conduct than surveillance of other adverse events and errors because of the existence of objective corroborating microbiologic data. Active surveillance of error has been conducted in a few studies of medication errors in which trained observers scored errors as they occurred in clinical settings; however, this approach has not been adopted beyond research settings.[22] Given the long tradition of incident reporting, coupled with the difficulties of active surveillance by trained observers, it is likely that broad-based passive surveillance that relies on front-line staff reporting will remain the norm, with more active surveillance undertaken only in areas of focus suggested by the passive reports or mandated by regulatory and accrediting agencies.

In addition to being active or passive, surveillance may be concurrent or retrospective. Occurrence screening is a form of retrospective surveillance, with quality staff reviewing charts of patients at risk for a particular type of event. Surveillance of nosocomial infections, on the other hand, is concurrent in most cases, with infection control personnel reviewing microbiologic data on a daily basis to detect infections as they are diagnosed. The timeliness of reporting for errors and adverse events is determined largely by policies, procedures, and tools. Events associated with serious patient harm or serious error (e.g., maternal death or wrong-site surgery) tend to be reported by telephone to quality and risk personnel, whereas more routine events, such as minor falls or medication errors, may take weeks or months to come to the attention of quality and risk staff due to delays in processing paper reporting forms. Computer-based event reporting systems avoid these delays, but their adoption is just beginning.

Although they rely upon others to identify and report events, risk managers must determine what elements should be included on an incident report to characterize or describe the epidemiology of events in their organizations. Descriptive data for most incident reports should include the information listed in Table 10-2. In addition, some authors and risk management programs have categorized errors and adverse events by various types to allow for aggregate reporting.[23-26] The major categories for adverse events utilized in the UHC Patient Safety Net reporting tool are listed in Table 10-3. It is also customary to categorize the extent of harm to the patient, using a system such as that developed by the National Coordinating Council for Medication Error and Prevention (NCC-MERP),[26] given in Table 10-4. The National Center for Patient Safety of the Veterans Administration has advocated a system in which severity is scored along with the observer's estimate of the likelihood of the recurrence of the event.[17] In addition to systems for categorizing types of events, there are emerging systems that seek to characterize medical error based on human factors analysis. These systems seek to provide a framework for understanding the underlying causes of error according to broad general types applicable to all complex organizations. Another suggested taxonomy for the underlying

---

TABLE 10-2   Basic Data Elements for Event Reporting

Date and time of event
Patient identifier (i.e., name and/or record number if event involved a
    specific patient)
If patient involved, age and gender
Individual(s) involved in the event (if different from the one reporting)
Location where event occurred
Type of event (by category)
Harm to patient (by category)
Brief narrative description of circumstances that led to event
Suggestions for avoiding future occurrences of the event
Individual reporting the event (anonymous reporting optional)

TABLE 10-3 Categories for Description of Errors and Events

Medication error
Adverse drug reaction
Fall
Equipment problem
Error related to procedure, treatment, or test
Complication related to procedure, treatment, or test
Transfusion event
Skin integrity problem
Behavioral problem (e.g., assault, elopement, etc.)
Other patient events
Visitor events
Staff events
Unsafe conditions with potential for harm

TABLE 10-4 Harm Scoring System for the National Coordinating Council for Medication Error Reporting and Prevention

No Error

Category A: Circumstances or events that have the capacity to cause error

Error, No Harm

Category B: An error occurred but the error did not reach the patient
(An "error of omission" does reach the patient.)
Category C: An error occurred that reached the patient, but did not cause patient harm
Category D: An error occurred that reached the patient and required monitoring to confirm that it resulted in no harm to the patient and/or required intervention to preclude harm

Error, Harm

Category E: An error occurred that may have contributed to or resulted in temporary harm to the patient and required intervention
Category F: An error occurred that may have contributed to or resulted in temporary harm to the patient and required initial or prolonged hospitalization
Category G: An error occurred that may have contributed to or resulted in permanent patient harm
Category H: An error occurred that required intervention necessary to sustain life

Error, Death

Category I: An error occurred that may have contributed to or resulted in the patient's death.

causes of error is the Einthoven classification system adapted for health care from error analysis in the nuclear power industry. Whatever classification system is used, one should be careful to distinguish the categories for actual events (the "what") from categories for factors that contributed to those events (the "why").

The goal of any classification system is to separate clearly distinct types of events, determine the frequency of each, and develop a common language for describing events that will allow comparisons between like organizations. Beyond providing meaningful rates, the data also must be informative enough for the risk manager to decide when to do additional analyses of an event through chart review or interviews. Because of this, incident reports also may include sections of free text in which the reporter gives contributing detail regarding the event, an interpretation of why the event occurred, or suggestions for preventing recurrences. This additional detail allows a triage function by managers, with some events meriting additional investigation through chart review or interview and others simply being aggregated in graphs or tables. This prioritization function has become critical in systems that have encouraged increased reporting through broad organizational initiatives to reduce blame and through implementation of electronic reporting tools.

Calculating Rates and Analyzing Data

As risk managers strive to improve event data for tracking, trending, benchmarking, and demonstrating risk reduction, they must employ rate-based measures. Although sentinel events should be counted one at a time, more common events should never be reported or counted using the number of events only. They should always be put into a rate in order to allow for trending or comparison between units or among organizations.

Incidence rates are the most commonly used and are very simple to apply to risk management data. The numerator of the rate is the number of times the specific event or error occurred in the observed population. The denominator includes the population at risk for the event of interest multiplied by the time the population was at risk (e.g., 50 patients at risk for 2 days each yields 100 patient-days of risk). A constant often is used to transform the result into a uniform quantity to allow for easier comparisons. Constants are usually multiples of 10 to ensure that the rate includes at least one integer (whole number) to the left of the decimal point. This avoids the need to manipulate awkward numbers: 4.3 errors per 1,000 patient-days is a preferable convention to 0.0043 medication errors per patient-day. When calculating incidence rates, it is important to remember the following:

1. Cases in the numerator must be taken from the population at risk, represented in the denominator.
2. Counts in the numerator and the denominator must be taken from the same period of observation.
3. Persons included in the denominator should be at risk for the event of interest in the numerator.[27]

TABLE 10-5   Patient Falls by Inpatient Unit for April

Nursing Unit	Number of Falls	Patient-Days	Incidence
4 West	6	182	33 per 1,000 pt-days
4 North	12	720	16 per 1,000 pt-days
5 West	7	460	15 per 1,000 pt-days
5 North	2	900	2.2 per 1,000 pt-days
6 East	4	62	64 per 1,000 pt-days

The more one can narrow the population to those at actual risk, the more accurate the estimated frequency (i.e., incidence) and risk of the adverse event will be. For example, the use of the number of hospital admissions as a denominator to calculate medication error rates is crude and inaccurate. Patient-days would be an improvement as a denominator, since a patient with a 4-day admission would have on average twice the risk of exposure as one with a 2-day admission. Focusing measurement on a specific population receiving numerous medications (e.g., cardiology or oncology patients) will yield more meaningful data. The use of incidence rates allows for valid comparisons and identification of real differences in frequency, whereas the raw numerators alone may not. In the example in Table 10-5, focusing attention on the ward with the most falls (4 North) would divert attention from the ward with the highest rate of falls (6 East).

Rates also may be determined for the frequency with which a given procedure or trial results in the event of interest (because time is not specified, it is technically not an incidence rate). Examples would include 4 medication errors per 1,000 doses administered or 6 complications of anesthesia per 1,000 operative cases. Note that medication errors may be expressed either as an incidence rate (e.g., 4 errors per 100 patient-days) or as a rate per procedure (e.g., 4 errors per 1,000 doses).

Applying Risk Stratification and Subgroup Analysis

Calculating an overall incidence rate presumes that the rate remains constant over the time period of observation and across the population; however, that does not always reflect clinical realities. For example, adverse drug events are more common among neonates and among all patients in intensive care settings.[28,29] Heterogeneity of risk within the patient population or across the period of observation calls for risk stratification. Although this may sound like a complicated statistical approach, it is not. Stratification simply puts data into various categories to compare rates for one group or time period within the population to others.

For example, risk stratification may involve sorting the population at risk by a common variable, such as age, gender, or admitting diagnosis. More precise stratification can help to identify the groups within

TABLE 10-6   Risk Stratification by Wound Class

Wound Class	Number of Infections	Number of Surgeries	Rate of Infection (%)
I. Clean	3	160	1.8
II. Clean contaminated	11	240	4.6
III. Contaminated	13	56	23.2
IV. Dirty	5	12	41.6

a population at greatest risk (e.g., patients on opiates, who are at greater risk for falls). The point of the analysis is to discern differences in rates for the subgroups in question that will further the understanding of the cause of the event being studied, in much the same way that Semmelweis advanced the understanding of handwashing by choosing to analyze rates among different types of caregivers. Whenever possible, one should use established clinical classification systems known to discriminate between populations at differential risk, such as the ASA score for anesthesia risk, or the American College of Surgery scoring system for risk of surgical site infection,[30] used to stratify risk of infection as shown in Table 10-6. The crude surgical site infection rate for this population is 6.8%, but because the population is heterogeneous in its risk, it is more meaningful to show the rate for each risk category. This would allow comparisons between institutions that cared for different proportions of patients in each category.

When stratification systems have not been established for the event being studied, selection of subpopulations for analysis represents a sort of hypothesis testing based on understanding of the event in question. For example, one might analyze medication errors in medical patients boarding on surgical floors compared with those on medical floors to see if meaningful differences in rates emerged. Even a homogeneous population may be stratified if different periods during the time of observation are associated with different risks. For example, the time spent in intensive care versus a regular ward could be analyzed for differences in rates of medication error or pressure sore development in order to decide upon the design and scope of improvement initiatives.

Basic risk stratification as just described will improve risk analysis in most organizations, but as the measurement of patient safety data matures, more sophisticated methods will undoubtedly be applied. Statistical techniques to determine the statistical significance of one rate versus another can be applied (e.g., chi squared or Student's *t* tests). Logistic regression can be applied to a data set to analyze the circumstances where more than one stratification variable affects the rate. This would be used to calculate the relative contributions of variables such as age and opiate use on the rate of falls, for example. These more sophisticated strategies

TABLE 10-7   Errors While Administering Oral Medication, by Subgroup of Error

Type of Error	Number of Errors	Number of Doses	Prevalence
Wrong medication given	14	14,284	9.8 per 10,000 doses
Wrong dose	32	14,284	22.1 per 10,000 doses
Wrong patient	12	14,284	8.4 per 10,000 doses
Patient allergic	4	14,284	2.8 per 10,000 doses

are more likely to be applied to clinical research studies seeking to understand the true causative factors for a given type of event in an environment where more active surveillance is performed.

In a stratified analysis, a single event is analyzed for different segments of the population at risk. This is different from an analysis of multiple endpoints, in which different types of events are analyzed for the same population. For example, analyzing the risk of stroke for patients with and without hypertension is an example of a stratified analysis. Analyzing the risk of stroke versus myocardial infarction in a group of patients with hypertension is an example of analysis of multiple endpoints. The distinction is an important one as we develop our understanding of distinct types of errors and adverse events. For example, rather than reporting a crude rate of medication administration errors, the errors may be sorted by the step in the medication administration process: prescribing, transcribing, dispensing, administration, and monitoring. These are not strata of risk for error, but rather different types of errors grouped under the broad heading of medication error. Reducing the overall medication error rate is impossible without understanding the relative frequency and causes of the relevant types. Even for a single type of error (administration), it is possible to perform a subtype analysis, as shown in Table 10-7.

Whether a given type of event deserves to be separated into a distinct category is more than a semantic exercise. The precision of a classification system, and the learning that can be gained by using it, is directly related to the extent to which it is free from redundancy (multiple names for the same type of event) and degeneracy (single name for different types of events).

Reporting Results and Using the Data for the Development of Risk Reduction Strategies

By applying epidemiologically sound techniques to define, collect, and analyze selected event data, the quality or risk manager should realize a number of benefits. First, application of more rigorous measurement methods will allow a focus on the appropriate areas for risk reduction. It will also facilitate internal comparison across units and patient populations and demonstrate the impact of improvement initiatives. Valid benchmarking between organizations has come of age in areas such as nosocomial infection rates and adherence to national guidelines. This requires standardization of definitions and methods of measurement. Although this is not yet possible in the realm of medical error, it will become possible as national reporting systems and standards develop, as recommended by the IOM, and as the value of eliminating blame for error reporting becomes more widely appreciated. Even though meaningful cross-organizational comparisons are a thing of the future, organizations that begin a disciplined approach to measurement and data analysis will have a better understanding of their own risk epidemiology, allowing them to focus resources and evaluate the impact of interventions.

Reporting results of risk measurement and analysis is critical to the success of the patient safety program. Results should be presented to quality and safety oversight committees using visual methods such as tables, graphs, charts, and other displays. The type of display should be suitable to the data and the intended message. For example, a table is usually quite effective in demonstrating the characteristics of a population, a bar chart may demonstrate incidence within various strata of the population, and a line graph can show improvement over time. When presenting the same set of risk data over time to a committee or board, it is preferable to use the same type and format of charts and graphs each time. The group responsible for interpretation and risk management will be able to recognize significant changes more quickly. A suggested format for reports to the board or quality improvement committee is shown in Figure 10-1.

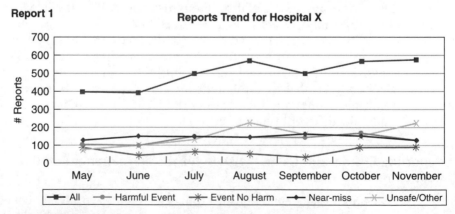

FIGURE 10-1   Four sample reports from the UHC Patient Safety Net
Source: University Health Consortium, 2003, Oak Brook, Illinois. Used with permission. (*Continued*)

Report 2   **Harm Score Distribution for Hospital X**

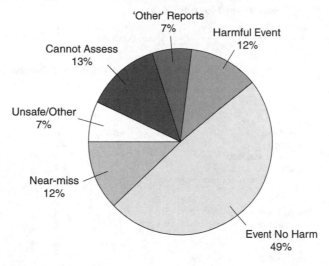

Report 3

Medication Error Subcategories	Count	%
Dose Omission	492	27%
Extra Dose	84	5%
Improper Dose/Overdosage	229	12%
Improper Dose/Underdosage	102	6%
Wrong Drug	160	9%
Wrong Dosage Form	44	2%
Wrong Duration	22	1%
Wrong Rate (IV)	57	3%
Wrong Route	22	1%
Wrong Strength/Concentration	61	3%
Wrong Technique	8	0%
Wrong Time	80	4%
Wrong Patient	66	4%
Monitoring Error	46	3%
Unauthorized Drug	13	1%
Narcotics Discrepancy	3	0%
Inadequate Pain Management	1	0%
Other Medication Error	222	12%
Blank	124	7%
Total	1,836	100%

FIGURE 10-1   (*Continued*)

Report 4

Contributing Factors Report for Hospital X

Organization Name: Hospital X
Time period: Jan-Dec 2002

	Manager score	Pharmacist score	Quality/Risk score	Unique Reports With Factor
Team Factors				
Communication Problems	218	253	101	496
Change of Service	10	10	4	22
Cross-coverage	8	14	5	26
Shift Change	28	79	19	113
Unplanned workload	93	55	10	157
Holiday	1	4	0	5
Subtotal Team Factors	**358**	**415**	**139**	**819**
Work Environment				
Distractions/Interruptions	213	173	46	414
Limited access to Patient Info	17	7	4	27
Poor Lighting	4	2	4	8
High Noise Level	64	3	2	69
Equip Malfunction				0
Equip Availability				0
Subtotal Work Environment	**298**	**185**	**56**	**518**
Task Factors				
Training issue	126	110	60	263
Emergency	38	1	7	46
Inexperienced staff	69	94	18	170
Inadequate resident supervision	14	10	4	26
Cardiac/respiratory arrest	4	0	4	6
Order entry system problem				0
Subtotal Task Factors	**251**	**215**	**93**	**511**
Staff Factors				
Float staff	16	13	1	30
Agency, temp or traveler	49	22	8	74
Staff scheduling				0
System for covering patient care	43	28	15	79
Insufficient Staffing	15	11	9	34
Subtotal Staff Factors	**123**	**74**	**33**	**217**
Patient Characteristics				
Patient compliance/adherence		3		3
Patient understanding		1		1
Language barrier				0
Family member cooperation		8		8
Subtotal Patient Characteristics	**0**	**12**	**0**	**12**
Organizational/Management				
No 24h pharmacy	6	1	0	7
Bed Availability				0
Boarder pt/Different service	5	2	2	9
Observation patient				0
Policies/Procedures lacking	25	38	7	68
Policies/Procedures unclear				0
Subtotal Org/Mgmt	**36**	**41**	**9**	**84**

FIGURE 10-1   (*Continued*)

Concerns Regarding an Epidemiologic Approach to Patient Safety

Numerous criticisms and caveats regarding a measurement-driven approach to patient safety management have been advanced, and most can be grouped into the following categories:

- Most events are underreported because of caregivers' fear, denial, or time constraints, so that conclusions based on rates cannot be meaningful.
- Systems that rely on voluntary passive reporting by caregivers do not conform to standard definitions either of the events or the potential populations at risk, leading to misclassifications that invalidate the potential data set.
- The simple enumeration and aggregation of events fail to capture the richness of narrative detail from those involved in the process, detail that is essential to our learning about the events.

Each of these issues has been encountered in other disease surveillance systems, and there are lessons to be learned for the patient safety movement.

The bias of underreporting and underdetection has plagued the surveillance of newly recognized or emerging diseases for decades. In some instances, breakthroughs depended on technologic advances such as specialized culture media (e.g., legionnaire's disease) or specialized diagnostic techniques (e.g., hepatitis B). In other instances, when relying on reports from caregivers themselves, some underreporting continues to be a problem. The reluctance of operating surgeons to report delayed surgical wound infections may lead to underestimates of true wound infection rates, but it does not invalidate tracking established trends. Fear and shame are other potential causes of underreporting, which have affected the reporting of cases of AIDS or, in another era, of cancer. When biases remain constant over time, however, meaningful conclusions may still be drawn from imperfect data—conclusions that allow decision making in the allocation of resources to address specific problems.

When events occur to alter biases, dramatic changes in incidence may be seen, as in the implementation of anonymous reporting systems for AIDS or in the more scientific view of cancer that emerged in the 1960s. In the realm of patient safety, the rate at which reports are offered will depend greatly on how protected workers feel from repercussions for honest mistakes, the ease of the process of reporting, and the perceived role of reporting in making positive changes in the system of care. It has been observed that management initiatives to foster a blame-free approach to event reporting, sometimes coupled with

novel electronic reporting tools, may lead to dramatic increases in reported events.[31,32] Efforts to improve the ease of reporting in a system
of surveillance typically lead to a temporary inflection of the incidence
rate, followed by a new trend line more accurate than the previous one.
The lessons from other disease surveillance systems are that the growing pains associated with the attempts to bring systematic measurement to a new or newly appreciated disease or condition should not
lead away from measurement; rather, patience and persistence are what
reap ultimate rewards. Based on the lessons from these other surveillance systems, scientists and managers in the field of safety should
remain open about the potential usefulness of trended rate data in advancing our learning.

   An additional reservation regarding the epidemiologic approach to
patient safety concerns the inaccuracy of events reported by front-line
clinicians. The need for precision in interpreting definitions of nosocomial infections has given rise to the role of the modern infection
control practitioner. Is a similar level of precision needed in patient
safety? Clearly, many slips and lapses in everyday practice do not require specialized training to recognize or report. Thus, reports on falls,
equipment failures, and most medication errors are more likely than
not to be accurate with regard to the fact that an event has occurred.
Furthermore, in the case of reporting near misses, it would be difficult
to design a useful system for collecting data on events that do not require documentation in the medical record without relying on the willing and enthusiastic participation of those actually doing the work.
Because of all of these reasons, improving accuracy in event reporting
for patient safety will more likely require broad-based educational
efforts than the establishment of a new class of professionals.

   Although the risk or quality manager usually can place trust in the
accurate reporting of the objective details of an event or near miss,
interpretations of why it happened need to be approached with the
skepticism of a skilled investigator. The input from those involved in
the event is considered crucial, but it also should be borne in mind that
causal theories abound during the initial recognition of breaches of
safe care. A disciplined approach to the collection of data on putative
causal or contributing factors will help the investigator avoid jumping
to easy conclusions regarding root causes. The effective investigator
will use aggregate reports of common events to help focus attention
on those areas needing more intensive epidemiologic study, as detailed
earlier in this chapter.

   The last objection to epidemiologic approaches to patient safety is
the fear that narrative detail will be lost, preventing investigators from
thinking "outside the box" of a rigid classification system. Utilizing
epidemiologic methods to trend adverse events and identify areas of

high risk does not mean that one should abandon the tested method of detailed narrative and root cause investigation for selected cases. The latter approach has its greatest usefulness in events where one is inclined to ask "How could this happen?" Examples would include hundredfold overdoses, surgery on a wrong body part, or switching of one newborn for another. In each of these cases, the event occurs in spite of policies and procedures designed to prevent it. On the other hand, epidemiologic data analysis is a preferred approach for events that are subtler, frequent, and often accepted as part of the normal events in the care of patients, such as missed medication doses, minor falls, or delayed test results. While a single instance of the latter type of event may be considered to be within the bounds of acceptable practice, only an aggregate analysis demonstrating a high rate of event occurrence would suggest the need for more intensive scrutiny. In addition, a high rate or a rate at variance from an accepted standard may not be perceived or acknowledged by clinicians until careful analysis is performed. The iterative application of measurement and feedback serves to heighten awareness of the problem and strengthen the resolve to improve. This approach has also proved its value in the reduction of rates of nosocomial infection and surgical complications. In short, epidemiologic approaches and intensive reviews of individual cases should be seen as complementary, not antagonistic.

Summary and Conclusions

Major advances have been achieved in patient safety through attention to analysis of human factors and reduction of cultural barriers to reporting of events. As we succeed in learning more about the numerous everyday events that threaten patient safety, traditional methods for selecting certain cases for review (and ignoring the rest) will limit an organization's ability to achieve its goals for building safer systems of care.

Epidemiologic methods show promise in helping risk and quality managers to deal with the growing number of event reports by tracking rates and identifying groups at greater risks for events. The approach can add understanding to underlying causes of the events and allows for selection of those problems requiring focused review and intensive investigation. The bias inherent in passive reporting of errors and adverse events will make these initial determinations crude at best and will make comparisons between organizations uninformative. However, the history of disease surveillance provides us with several examples of the usefulness of aggregating and analyzing data on events that are only partially captured or incompletely understood. As the value of reporting becomes more widely appreciated and as systems for classifying events become standardized, comparing rates regionally and nationally will allow identification of innovative strategies that have successfully improved patient safety. Systematic measurement and epidemiologic analysis of events will then become the foundation of efforts to monitor trends, understand causes, and demonstrate improvements in patient safety.

References

1. Brennan, T. A., Leape, L. L., Laird, N. M. et al. Incidence of Adverse Events and Negligence in Hospitalized. New Engl J Medicine 1991; 324:370–376.
2. Thomas, E. J., Studdert, D. M., Newhouse, J. P. et al. Costs of Medical Injuries in Utah and Colorado. Inquiry 1999;36:255–264.
3. Institute of Medicine. *To Err Is Human*. National Academy Press. 2000.
4. Runcinman, W. B. Qualitative versus quantitative research–balancing cost, yield and feasibility. Anaesthesia and Intensive Care 1993;21:502–505.
5. Kaplan, H., and Barach, P. Incident reporting: science or protoscience? Ten years later. Quality and Safety in Health Care 2002;11: 144–145.
6. Barach, P., and Small, S. D. Reporting and preventing medical mishaps: lessons from non-medical near miss reporting systems. British Medical J 2000;320:759–763.
7. LaForce, F. M. The control of infections in hospitals: 1750–1950. In Wenzel, R. P., *Prevention and Control of Nosocomial Infections*. Baltimore: Williams and Wilkins, 1997, pp 3–18.
8. Antonow, J. A., Smith, A. B., and Silver, M. P. Medication error reporting: a survey of nursing staff. J Nursing Care Quality 2000: 15:42–48.
9. Brewer, T., and Coldis, G. A. Postmarketing surveillance and adverse drug reactions: current perspectives and future needs. JAMA 1999; 281:824–829.
10. Kivlahan, C., Sangster, W., Nelson, K. et al. Developing a comprehensive electronic adverse event reporting system in an academic medical center. Joint Commission J Qual. Improvement 2002;28:583–594.
11. MedMarx by US Pharmacopeia. www.medmarx.com.
12. Marx, D. The just culture. Published at www.mers-tm.net.
13. Adverse Event Reporting System. www.doctorquality.com.
14. University HealthSystem Consortium. UHC Patient Safety Net. www.uhc.edu.
15. The Quality Letter. November 2001, pp. 10–11.
16. Donna Sollenberger, CEO, University of Wisconsin Health System, personal communication.

17. Bagian, J. P., Lee, C., Gosbee, J. et al. Developing and deploying a patient safety program in a large health care delivery system. Joint Commission J Qual. Improvement 2001;27:522–532.

18. Buehler, J. W. Surveillance. In R. P. Wenzel, *Prevention and Control of Nosocomial Infections.* Baltimore: Williams and Wilkins, 1997, pp. 435–458.

19. Feinstein, A. R. *Clinical Epidemiology.* Philadelphia: Saunders 1985, pp. 581–587.

20. Fraser, D. W., Tsai, T., Orenstein, W. et al. Legionnaire's Disease: description of an epidemic of pneumonia. New Engl J Medicine 1977;297:89–97.

21. Centers for Disease Control and Prevention. Kaposi's sarcoma and *Pneumocystis* pneumonia among homosexual men—New York City and California. Morbidity and Mortality Weekly Report 1982;30:305–308.

22. Barker, K. N., Flynn, E. A., Pepper, G. A. et al. Medication error observed in 36 health care facilities. Archives Int Med 2002;162:1897–1903.

23. Frey, B., Kehrer, B., Losa, M. et al. Comprehensive critical incident monitoring in a neonatal-pediatric intensive care unit: experience with the system approach. Intensive Care Med 1999;26:69–74.

24. Dovey, S. M., Meyers, D. S., Phillips, R. L. et al. A preliminary taxonomy of medical errors in family practice. Quality and Safety in Health Care 2002;11:233–238.

25. Lesar, T. S., Briceland, L., and Stein, D. S. Factors related to errors in medication prescribing. JAMA 1997;277:312–317.

26. National Coordinating Council for Medication Error Reporting and Prevention. www.nccmerp.org.

27. Checko, P. J. Use of statistics for epidemiology. In R. Olmsted, *Infection control and applied epidemiology: principles and practice.* St. Louis, MO: Mosby-Year Book, Inc. 1996, pp. 11-1–11-5.

28. Kaushal, R., Bates, D. W., Landrigan, C. et al. Medication errors and adverse drug events in pediatric inpatients. JAMA 2001;285:2114–2120.

29. Cullen, D. J., Sweitzer, B. J., Bates, D. W. et al. Preventable adverse drug events in hospitalized patients: a comparative study of intensive care and general care units. Critical Care Medicine 1997;25:1289–1297.

30. Kluytmans, J. Surgical infections including burns. In R. P. Wenzel, *Prevention and Control of Nosocomial Infections.* Baltimore: Williams and Wilkins, 1997, pp. 841–865.

31. Davidoff, F. Shame: the elephant in the room. Quality and Safety in Health Care 2002;11:2–3.

32. Lawton, R., and Packer, D. Barriers to incident reporting in a healthcare system. Quality and Safety in Health Care 2002;11: 15–18.

CHAPTER ELEVEN

PATIENT SAFETY IS AN ORGANIZATIONAL SYSTEMS ISSUE: LESSONS FROM A VARIETY OF INDUSTRIES

Karlene H. Roberts, PhD, Kuo Yu, and Daved van Stralen, MD

The 1999 Institute of Medicine publication of *To Err Is Human: Building a Safer Health System* directed national attention to the issue of patient safety. Although its content is laudable in nailing the culprit behind the accident scene as being the organization or the system of organizations that together provide health care, its title is misleading. For years accident investigations and industrial psychological and human factors research on worker safety identified the worker/operator as the person behind the industrial accident. This perspective results in name-and-blame, then train-or-fire, cultures in industries concerned with safety.

For example, until quite recently investigations of U.S. Navy aviation accidents didn't look beyond the skin of the airplane for perpetrators. Once mechanical failure was ruled out, the investigation went on to look for operator failure, while failing to recognize that even when operators do fail, there is usually an organizational or systemic reason for failure. One might, for example, observe that the pilot was poorly trained. Is that the pilot's fault? Amount and kind of training are usually dictated by organizational policy. One might ask about the role of the commanding officer in the failure. Did he or she have a need to push his or her squadron beyond its capacity? Was the commanding officer under orders to deliver firepower to inaccessible places? How much pressure was brought to bear on him or her by his or her superior officers? One might also ask about the culture of the organization or system. Had the organization built a John Wayne–type individualistic macho culture when teamwork was required?

Over the last few decades, there has been a major shift in our social conception of the function of medical care.[1] Medicine has shifted from a disease-oriented to a health-oriented enterprise. That is, outcomes that are indicative of health care quality and safety have begun to include not only mortality and morbidity, but also the quality of life associated with illness and treatment. Physical functioning (e.g., pain, energy levels, sleep quality), cognitive functioning (e.g., memory, concentration), and emotional well-being (e.g., affective responses, suffering, anxiety, vitality) have all become part of the assessment of health-related quality of life.

This patient-centered ethic underscores the provider's obligation to inform the patient of potential adverse outcomes and solicit and take seriously the patient's self-report regarding unacceptable risks. In addition, such an ethic requires providers to be responsive to the patient's subjective experiences of the downside of care. Patient-centered care reminds us that health care excellence and safety not only concerns itself with technical excellence but also with the patient's experience of care. Patient-centered care encourages patients to communicate valuable information to their caretakers as well as mandates caretakers to take proactive approaches to elicit nuanced but valuable information that can improve patient safety. Patient-centered care parallels the shift from regarding patient safety as a human factors issue to a systems and organizational issue because, although it might take a single doctor to treat a disease, it takes a team of doctors, nurses, and other health care providers and administrators as well as an organization of safety culture and reliable operations to treat a person.

Foundations of Research That Can Inform Safety Issues

If the traditional industrial and human factors research on safety is largely unhelpful to us in teasing out the etiologies of medical error, is there any work that is more helpful? Engineers and statisticians, human factors researchers, psychologists, and sociologists have made forays into research issues concerned with reliability enhancement or risk reduction. The engineering perspective has, not surprisingly, centered on physical aspects of systems. Human factors researchers and psychologists are largely interested in individuals and groups, and sociologists take a more macro view of the social context in which people work. Here we will draw on both the psychological and sociological approaches.

Sociologists preceded psychologists in developing interests in risk mitigation through a side door, the study of catastrophe. At first these researchers were only interested in disaster aftermath, how the social fabric of a community regenerates itself after destruction.[2,3] In addition, what were originally viewed as individual-level constructs, such as panic, soon came to be seen more as socially driven.[4] In 1978 Barry Turner noted that until that time the only interest in disasters was in responses to them. He provided the first social psychological approach to accidents, looking at the socially driven components of causes.

Human factors and social psychological threads of activity regarding reduction of error merged in the aviation industry. The introduction of reliable jet transports in the airline industry and in the military in the 1950s brought with it a dramatic reduction in aircraft accidents. It became apparent that the remaining accident contributors had more to do with people than with technology. As in many other industries (for example, medicine and the commercial marine industry) it was often noted that 70% to 80% of the problems involved operator error.

Much of the social psychological research on crew resource management came from Robert Helmreich's laboratory at the University of Texas. One of his contributions is the Cockpit Management Attitudes Questionnaire (CMAQ), a 25-item Likert scale assessment of attitudes regarding crew coordination, flight deck management, and personal capabilities under conditions of fatigue and stress.[5] Helmreich adapted this questionnaire for operating room use in the medical industry. Dr. David Gaba at Stanford and the Veteran's Administration, Palo Alto, borrowed heavily from it in the development of his Survey of Patient Safety Cultures in Healthcare Organizations.[6] This is an example of applying research results obtained in one industry to the needs of another.

In 1984, Charles Perrow's seminal book *Normal Accidents: Living with High-Risk Technologies* was published (it was recently republished). Based on his experience as one of the few social scientists asked to contribute to the Three Mile Island investigation, Perrow analyzed a large number of industrial accidents. He concluded that some technologies, like commercial nuclear power plants and modern militaries, are so dangerous they should be shut down altogether because their technologies are both tightly coupled (one event follows immediately after another without mediation) and complexly coupled (events are so complexly linked that their causal relations cannot be deciphered).

High-Reliability Organizations Research

Simultaneously with the publication of Perrow's book, a group of researchers came together at the University of California, Berkeley. They were interested in the ways organizations achieve risk reduction and highly reliable operations in spite of the great odds against it as hypothesized by Charles Perrow. They focused their interests on what they called high-reliability organizations (HROs). Their contention was that while some technologies are indeed worrisome enough that in an ideal world they shouldn't exist, calling for their overthrow is unrealistic. Thus, we need to do the best we can to insure nearly error-free operation of these technologies. They also demonstrated that relatively low-technology organizations, such as banks, can cause similar degrees of devastation.[7]

Although the original researchers have dispersed, their concerns with risk mitigation were picked up by organizational scholars at other universities. These researchers have studied a diverse group of organizations, including those that should have avoided catastrophe and didn't and those that did. They work in parallel with people coming from the other traditions previously discussed. Thus, today there is considerable interest in risk mitigation that can be and is translated into patient safety issues in the medical industry. Although some of the HRO research is directly cited in *To Err Is Human,* a number of additional findings from it are alluded to without direct citation because of the nature of the testimony behind these kinds of reports.

Findings from HRO Research

Here we summarize some major findings from HRO research. We then discuss reliability-enhancing features that were missing in a failed organization and illustrate how a finely tuned HRO operated to avoid catastrophe. We then discuss an application of HRO findings in a health care setting and conclude with suggestions about the kind of research on reliability enhancement and patient safety that should be done in medical settings. HRO findings are divided into two sets: those having to do with major organizational processes, and those more appropriate to a category we call command and control. Some of these processes are more tractable than others. Managers may want to address the easy issues first.

Seven of the HRO research findings are organizational processes. First, HROs are flexibly *structured* so they can move rapidly from bureaucratic tight coupling to more flexible, malleable forms as conditions change. Thus, when an aircraft carrier is in port with little to do, its command can afford to be top-down bureaucratic. But when it is in air operations at sea, its command has to be far more flexible to meet the changing conditions or "fog of war."[8,9] Second, HROs must emphasize *reliability* over efficiency. In fact, reliability rivals productivity as the bottom line.[10] The *cultures* of HROs are heavily imbued with reliability and safety "musts."

Rewards are appropriately used in HROs.[7] They reward the behavior that is desired and avoid rewarding behavior A while hoping for behavior B.[11] HROs are characterized by the perception that *risk exists* and that strategies also exist to deal appropriately with it. Both appropriate attention and strategies must be in place.[7] In HROs, individuals must engage in valid and reliable *sense making.*[12] That is, they must come to the correct conclusions about the meaning of things that are happening around them.[13] Finally, the different senses or meanings people draw from their situation must be meaningfully worked together and integrated across the organization through the *heedfulness* of individual players. Managers try to maximize this integration when they talk about "making sure we're all on the same page." One doesn't have to see the totality of the situation (unless one is at the top of the organization), but should recognize how one's role fits into the roles of the rest of the people in the organization.[14,15] People do not, for example, attend just to the physiology of the situation, but rather to the integration of physiology with the teamwork to deal with it, the state of the patient's family, and so forth.

Although the next five findings are also concerned with organizational processes, we highlight them here as command-and-control issues. HROs are characterized by *migrating decision making.*[9,16] That is, decisions migrate to the part of the organization in which the expertise exists to make them. The highest-ranking person is not always the appropriate person to make a decision. Migrating decision making would be impossible in rigid organizational structures. In addition, in HROs the top management always has *the big picture,* or an overall sense of what is going on. HROs are characterized by *redundancy.* There needs to be sufficient slack so if one party doesn't catch a mistake, another will. In addition, there must be *formal rules and procedures* that are spelled out to and followed by all organizational participants. Finally, HROs are characterized by enormous amounts of *training.*

Departure from Safety

During the 1970s and early 1980s the two major shipping groups in the Baltic Sea began to lower prices, cut costs, and transform their ferries into floating hotels with casinos, night clubs, and shopping malls. Transforming ferries into palaces of entertainment doesn't remind passengers and crewmembers of the potential risks involved in sea travel. The crews were structured to focus on achieving high efficiency and economies of scale through standardization, specialization, and routinized decentralization.

Early one spring evening in 1994, the passenger ferry *Estonia* left its home port and steamed toward its next port, Stockholm, into the teeth of a Baltic Sea storm. Noises from the front of the ship were ignored. The captain headed the ship directly into the waves (3 to 4 meters high) and into an increasingly strong wind. The ship left port at 1915 hours and sailed normally until about 0100 hours. On the bridge the master noted that she was rolling and that they were 1 hour behind schedule despite having all engines running. Shortly before 0100, during his scheduled rounds on the car deck, the seaman on watch heard a metallic bang. The master attempted to find the sound, but none of the orders given or actions taken by him or the crew was out of the ordinary.

Further observations of the noise were made at about 0105 by passengers and off-duty crewmembers. When a seaman reported water on the deck, it was news to the bridge. At 0115 the third engineer saw an enormous inflow on his monitor. He didn't report this to the bridge because he assumed the bridge had the same picture. And he didn't slow the ship down because he was waiting for orders from the bridge. In fact, the engines automatically shut down, and he tried to restart them. The officers on the bridge probably didn't look at the monitor.

The visor (top half of the double doors) separated from the bow at about 0115. As a result, the ramp was pulled fully open, allowing water to rush in. The distress message traffic from *Estonia* began at 0122 hours; the last one was at 01:29:27. The ship disappeared from the radar screens of other ships in the area at about 0150 hours.

The *Estonia* was one of a class of ferries with very large bows, and experience with similar designs was limited. The crew work schedule was 2 weeks on and 2 weeks off. This crew was in the 13th day of a 14-day cycle. It was relatively inexperienced. That night, except for the short time the captain was on the bridge and during the time the storm was increasing, the ship's responsibility was in the hands of the first through the fourth mates. The shift from 0100 to 0600 was in the hands of the second and fourth mates, with respectively 2.5 and 1.5 years of experience. These men were not trained to deal with heavy weather. The life boat orders were not given until 5 minutes after the list developed, and the time available for evacuation was between 10 and 20 minutes.

In this case the organizational structural problem is clear. Although standardization, specialization, and routinization are good strategies for operating organizations faced with benign and unchanging circumstances, they are very poor strategies if the organizations must face new, unexpected contingencies. This is well illustrated by the fact that the engineer failed to report the water on the deck to the bridge and failed to turn the engines off. Under routinization, it was appropriate for him to think the captain would tell him what to do. The industry's decision to change their ships into travel playgrounds was a system characteristic within which ships had to operate with no increased attention to structural safety enhancements.

The emphasis on efficiency over reliability is also clear. The new structure, with its focus on such things as shopping malls, directed attention away from reliability as a primary goal. It also changed the culture from one of seagoing wariness to one of having fun. That the reward system was out of kilter is clear. The master was concerned about schedules and therefore pushed his ship into rough seas. There was no reward system for other crewmembers to report activities that could put the ship in harm's way. It is unclear from evidence available to us whether the ship saw itself as experiencing risky situations. What is clear is that if the crew did so, they did nothing about it.

Sense making was not done in an appropriate way. Vigilance was entirely lacking on the bridge. It is probable that a bridge monitor showed exactly what was happening, but the crew failed to see it. The master had exactly the wrong picture of what was transpiring. Even when evidence of danger was clearly on the bridge's monitors, he and his crew failed to perceive it. The situation with the engineer shows even more clearly the absence of appropriate sense making. He *had pictures* of water. Despite that information, he tried to override an automatic engine shutdown. In every case, representation of the situation was incorrect. The decisions made on the bridge appear to have been rational responses to a situation that didn't exist. Without appropriate sense making, it was impossible to engage in heedful interaction.

Migrating decision making failed to occur, as in the case of the engineer failing to make a decision he was supposedly qualified to make, and waiting for the captain to give him orders. Clearly, the captain failed to have the big picture. Redundancy didn't exist, or someone would have said "why are we doing this?" Although we have no evidence of this, it appears that formal rules of safety didn't exist, weren't practiced, or weren't considered important. The case includes several references to lack of experience or training.

A Safe Landing

Following is an incident that could have turned into a disaster. In fact, it started as a disaster. One night in the summer of 1999, an F/A 18 Hornet (fighter/attack aircraft) was first in the launch cycle aboard the U.S.S. *Constellation,* awaiting launch from catapult 1. Upon launch the aircraft ingested rubber catapult covers that someone failed to remove from the catapult. The pilot (call sign "Oyster") could only manage his plane in full afterburner and at low altitude. He needed to land by trapping with the hook of the aircraft one of the wires at the rear end of the ship, preferably number 3. A number of people are involved in the story, including the landing signal officer, called Paddles. (Paddles he was in World War II movies, and Paddles he is today.) During flight operations the carrier is always followed by an escort (picket) ship and flies its helicopter as safety precautions. Here's the incident, as told by the pilot:

There I was. Manned up in the hot seat for the 2030 launch about 500 miles north of Hawaii (insert visions of "The Shore Bird" and many mai tais here). I was positioned to be first off of cat one (insert foreboding music here) in the launch cycle. As the cat fires, I stage the blowers and am along for the ride. Just prior to the end of the stroke there's a huge flash and a simultaneous boom! and my world is in turmoil. My little pink body is doing 145 knots or so and is 100 feet above the Black Pacific. And there it stays—except for the knot package, which decreases to 140 knots. The throttles aren't going any farther forward despite my Schwarzzenegerian efforts to make them do so.

From out of the ether I hear a voice say one word: "Jettison." Roger that! A nanosecond later my two drop tanks are Black Pacific bound. The airplane leapt up a bit but not enough. I'm now about a mile in front of the boat at 160 feet and fluctuating from 135 to 140 knots. The next comment that comes out of the ether is another one worder: "Eject!" I'm still flying so I respond, "Not yet, I've still got it." Finally, at 4 miles from the ship I take a peek at my engine instruments and notice my left engine doesn't match the right (funny how quick glimpses at instruments get burned into your brain). About now I get another "Eject!" call. "Nope, still flying." At $5\frac{1}{2}$ miles I asked the tower to please get the helo headed my way as I truly thought I was going to be shelling out. At some point I thought it would probably be a good idea to start dumping some gas. At 7 miles I eventually started a (very slight) climb. A little breathing room.

Air Traffic Control chimes in with a downwind heading and I'm like: "Ooh. Good idea and throw down my hook." Eventually I get headed downwind at 900 feet and ask for a squadron representative on the radio. While waiting I shut down the left engine. In short order I hear his voice. I tell him the following: "OK, my gear's up, my left motor's off and I'm only able to stay level with minimum blower." At ten miles or so I'm down to 5000 pounds of gas and start a turn back toward the ship. Don't intend to land but don't want to get too far away. Of course as soon as I start in an angle of bank I start dropping like a stone so I end up doing a five mile circle around the ship. Air Traffic Control is reading me the single engine rate of climb numbers based on temperature, etc. It doesn't take us long to figure out that things aren't adding up. One of the things I learned in the training group was that the Hornet is a perfectly good single engine aircraft. It flies great on one motor. So why do I need blower to stay level!?

By this time I'm talking to air traffic control, the Deputy Air Group Commander (who's on the flight deck) and the Air Group Commander (who's on the bridge with the Captain). We decide that the thing to do is climb to three thousand feet to see if I'm going to have any excess power and will be able to shoot an approach. I get headed downwind, go full burner on my remaining motor and eventually make it to 2000 feet before leveling out. Start a turn back toward the ship and when I get pointed in the right direction I throw the gear down and pull the throttle out of AB. Remember that flash/boom! that started this little tale? Repeat it here.

I jam it back into after burner and after three or four huge compressor stalls and accompanying deceleration the right motor comes back. I'm thinking my blood pressure was probably up there about now and for the first time I notice that my mouth feels like a San Joaquin summer. (That would be hot and dusty.)

This next part is great. You know those stories about guys who deadstick crippled airplanes away from orphanages and puppy stores and stuff and get all this great media attention? Well, at this point I'm looking at the picket ship at my left at about two miles and I say on departure freq to no one in particular, "You need to have the picket ship hang a left right now. I think I'm gonna be outta here in a second." I said it very calmly but with meaning. Paddles said the picket immediately started pitching out of the fight. Ha! I scored major points with the heavies afterwards for this. Anyway, it's funny how your mind works in these situations.

OK, so I get it back level and pass a couple miles up the starboard side of the ship. I'm still in min blower and my (fuel) state is now about 2500 pounds. Hmmm. I hadn't really thought about running out of gas. I pull it out of blower again and sure enough . . . flash, BOOM! I'm thinking that I'm gonna end up punching out.

Eventually discover that even the tiniest throttle movements cause the flash/boom thing to happen so I'm trying to be as smooth as I can. I'm downwind a couple miles when the Air Group Commander comes up and says "Oyster, we're going to rig the barricade." Remember, he's up on the bridge watching me fly around and he's thinking I'm gonna run outta fuel too. By now I've told everyone who's listening that there is a better than average chance that I'm going to be ejecting—the helo bubbas, god bless 'em, have been following me around this entire time. I continue downwind and again, sounding calmer than I probably was, call Paddles. "Paddles, you up?" "Go ahead," he replied. "I probably know most of it but you wanna shoot me the barricade brief?" (He was awesome on the radio, just the kind of voice you'd want to hear in this situation.) He gives me the brief and at nine miles I say, "If I turn now will it be up when I get there? I don't want to have to go around again." "It's going up now Oyster, go ahead and turn." "Turning in, say final bearing." "063" replies the voice in air traffic control (another number I remember—go figure).

I intercept glideslope at about a mile and three quarters and pull power. Flash/boom. Add power out of fear. Going high. Pull power. Flash/boom. Add power out of fear. Going higher. (Flashback to LSO school. . . . "All right class, today's lecture will be on the single engine barricade approach. Remember, the one place you really, really don't want to be is high. Are there any questions? Yes, you can go play golf now.")

Another landing signal officer is backing up Paddles and as I start to set up a higher than desired sink rate he hits the abort light. Very timely too. No worries. I cleared the deck by at least ten feet. As I slowly climb out I say, again to no one in particular, "I can do this." I'm in blower still and the Air Group Commander says, "Turn downwind." Again, good idea. After I get turned around he says, "Oyster, this is gonna be your last look so turn in again as soon as you're comfortable."

I lose about 200 feet in the turn and like a total dumbshit I look out as I get on centerline and that night thing about feeling high gets me and I descend further to 400 feet. Flash/boom every several seconds all the way down. Last look at my gas was 600-and-some pounds at mile and a half. "Where am I on the glideslope?" I ask Paddles and hear a calm "Roger Ball." Now the ball's shooting up from the depths. I start flying it and before I get a chance to spot the deck, I hear "Cut, cut, cut!" I'm really glad I was a Paddles for so long because my mind said to me "Do what he says Oyster" and I pulled it back to idle. (My hook hit 11 Oyster paces from the ramp.) The rest is pretty tame. I hit the deck, skipped the one, the two and snagged the three wire [and] rolled into the barricade about a foot right of the centerline. Once stopped my vocal chords involuntarily yelled "Victory!" on the radio. (The 14 guys who were listening in air traffic control said it was pretty cool. After the fact I wish I had done the Austin Powers' "Yeah Baby!" thing.) The lights came up and off to my right there must have been a gazillion people. Paddles said that with my shutdown you could hear a huge cheer across the flight deck.

I open the canopy and start putting my stuff in my helmet bag. I climb down and people are gathering around patting me on the back when one of the boat's crusty yellow-shirt Chiefs interrupts and says, "Gentlemen, great job but fourteen of your good buddies are still up there and we need to get them aboard." Here I sit with my little pink body in a ready room chair on the same ship I did my first cruise in 10 years and 7 months ago. And I thought it was exciting back then. By the way, I had 380 pounds of fuel when I shut down. Again, remember this number as in ten years it will surely be *fumes man, fumes I tell you!**

---

*This account has been widely discussed in the Navy, and is in the public domain. There is no known published source.

Although militaries are hierarchically structured, notice how in this case the structure was sufficiently elastic to allow many parts of the ship to help Oyster: the captain and air group commander on the bridge, the deputy air group commander and Paddles on the flight deck, the squadron representative in the tower, and the air traffic controller in the air traffic control center on the third deck. If efficiency had ruled over reliability, many things might have occurred differently. Perhaps the order to eject would not have gone out as soon as it did or the drop tanks would have not have been dropped as early as they were. The culture of reliability is illustrated by the several "must do's" Oyster engaged in that clearly came from his training.

The rewards for Oyster were clearly in the right place. In the first place, it was assumed by his superiors on the ship that he knew what he was doing, particularly when he refused to eject. Second, he was rewarded for getting the picket ship out of harm's way. Everyone perceived that risk existed, and appropriate strategies were in place to handle the risk. Valid and reliable sense making was surely characteristic of Oyster, and information from air traffic control and the squadron representative helped him to make appropriate sense of his situation. He needed the heedfulness of the air group commander, the deputy commander, Paddles, the squadron representative, and air traffic control, each of whom saw his own role in the situation and helped keep it knit together.

Migrating decision making was also apparent. Oyster, not his superiors, made the decision about what to do. When he landed, a lower-level chief (aviators are officers) ordered him from the deck. Although we don't know this from the case, it is likely the captain of the ship had the big picture. We have some evidence that the air group commander did. We certainly know that redundancy was at work when Oyster and the air group commander simultaneously thought about the plane's fuel state. Formal rules and procedures guided Oyster's activities and were clearly evident when Paddles gave Oyster the barricade brief. Training was evident throughout (Oyster had over 10 years' experience flying off ships), and he mentions it with regard to the characteristics of the Hornet and the class on barricade approaches. Hopefully, every evolution a ship does is a training evolution.

A Broader Story

A number of researchers have confirmed that these and other organizational processes are necessary for reliability enhancement, which broadly includes safety. The information was obtained through analyses of accidents as well as systematic research in HROs. Work was done in the commercial nuclear power industry,[17] the commercial airlines,[18,19] primary school education,[20] wildland fire authorities,[12] community fire authorities,[9] the U.S. Navy,[8,21] offshore oil and gas platforms,[22] offshore pipeline operations,[23] commercial shipping,[24] and other aspects of the commercial marine industry.[25]

A number of organizations have applied some of the findings of the work in a variety of different ways. It was used to develop training programs in community policing.[26] The U.S. Coast Guard used it as a basis for their comprehensive Prevention Through People program, the only management program the Coast Guard developed to reduce mishaps and errors. The Society for Worldwide Interbank Financial Telecommunications (SWIFT) used various aspects of the work to develop what it calls its Failure Is Not an Option program. SWIFT moves 97% of the money that is moved worldwide and very successfully progressed through both the European move to the euro and Y2K.

Findings from this research are behind a recently conceived program for the U.S. Navy. After the fatal crashes of three F-14 aircraft in 1996, the Navy developed a Human Factors Quality Management Board to review its safety-related activities in carrier aviation. At the request of the board, the Navy developed what is now called the aviation Command Safety Assessment. This is a device to help aircraft squadron commanding officers assess the safety readiness of their squadrons in comparison with all squadrons in the database, squadrons of the same type, squadrons at sea or on land, and so forth. The program is on the Web at safetyclimatesurveys.org. To date it has been used by about a third of the naval aviation squadrons and some aviation maintenance squadrons.[6] The Marine Corps ground forces are beginning a special project to adapt the instrument to their specific needs. The commercial aviation community is showing considerable interest in this approach.

Some aspects of the approach, including specific items, were borrowed by David Gaba at the Palo Alto Veteran's Administration Hospital for use in the Patient Safety Center of Inquiry's development of a safety assessment for the Veteran's Administration.[6]

An Application in the Health Industry

Loma Linda University Children's Hospital (LLUCH) is the tertiary children's hospital for a geographic area more than three times the size of the state of Vermont. The population is 2.5 million people, with 500,000 younger than 15 years. The catchment area includes urban, rural, and wilderness areas, with a large number of desert and mountain communities. The LLUCH pediatric intensive care unit (PICU) has 25 beds with an average daily census of 21 patients, 9 on ventilators. One hundred five registered nurses are assigned to the PICU, with 14 on duty at any one time. There are 20 respiratory care practitioners, with 4 working at any one time. Four residents rotate through the PICU for 1 month at a time, one from emergency medicine and three from pediatrics. Pollack, Cuerdon, and Getson report mortality rates of 7.8 ± 0.8% for PICUs with more than 18 beds.[27] The PICU at LLUCH had a 5.2% mortality rate in 1996. About half of the admissions come through LLUCH's pediatric critical care transport system, now one of the larger transport services in the country.[28]

In an environment that has numerous social and psychological hazards, particularly for the nurses, the PICU philosophy is to support the bedside caregiver with an organizational culture of safety that encourages learning from mistakes in collaborative teams. Teamwork and team formation are fostered. Shaming, naming, and blaming, particularly after a bad outcome, are not accepted. There are many ways to approach care in the PICU; no one method is touted above the rest. The center of care is the team and support for the team leader and bedside caregiver. During rounds the patient is presented to the group for discussion of the diagnosis, general treatment plan, potential problems that may develop, and the family's response to the situation. All participants have an opportunity to present their perceptions, and ideas and questions are solicited. As a general rule, the team doesn't move on until all caregivers feel comfortable with the plan. Doctors, pharmacists, respiratory care practitioners, nurses, and a clinical dietitian make rounds presentations.

The Loma Linda University PICU can be described in the context of the good organizational processes and command-and-control mechanisms identified in HROs. The HRO concepts adopted by Drs. Daved van Stralen and Ronald Perkin include risk awareness, process auditing, quality review, appropriate rewards, and command and control.

Risk awareness increased over the first several years, with the goal of identifying a child who is in a state of covert compensated physiologic dysfunction. Van Stralen and Perkin began a program of in-service lectures specific to the various disciplines (nursing, respiratory care, resident physicians). They also developed two regularly scheduled conferences, one directed to emergency medical service providers and the other directed to nurses in emergency departments and intensive care units. Today it is rare for a patient to unexpectedly deteriorate in the PICU.

Process auditing in the PICU includes systematic checks and formal audits to inspect for problems in the "process." For LLUCH, the process is providing critical care medicine in an environment of physiologic uncertainty and instability. The unit constantly entertains the thought that it has missed something. It encourages questioning and the presentation of data that support or refute the working hypothesis. Quality review is performed to ensure that the PICU has the lowest rate of potentially pre-ventable mortalities and morbidities. Quality improvement reviews are made by formal standing committees of the institution. Referent levels for quality improvement are adopted from nationally accepted norms and the medical, respiratory care, and nursing literature.

Appropriate rewards are made to encourage participation in patient care. Through participation of all disciplines, the PICU seeks to reduce accidents and the level of stress on caregivers while improving morale. The team is composed of members who respond quite well to symbolic rewards. As members demonstrate knowledge, insight, and discretion in care of patients, they tend to play a larger role in tactical and strate-gic management. Their opinions are more frequently sought and in-corporated into care plans.

Command and control plays a major part of care and has given the unit its greatest successes. In the PICU this concept includes decision migration, authority gradient, situational awareness, redundancy, rules and procedures, and training.

The PICU fosters decision migration to the best-qualified caregiver (recognizing the limits to caregiver decision making). At the interface with a patient emergency, the most qualified person to make or guide decisions is the bedside caregiver. Frequently, team members can't pre-dict what will work in a specific situation. However, quick decisions can bring stability to a rapidly changing situation during crisis situa-tions. The authority difference that can occur between the physician or surgeon and other team members can lead to tragedy; this is especially likely if authority differences inhibit low-status members from offering valuable information that disagrees with the judgments of high-status members. In the past few years, nursing staff has made use of a form for professional interactions. These forms follow up the chain of com-mand from the nurse to administration. It then moves downward to the physician involved through his or her chain of command. This insu-lates the nurse from reprisal.

Situational awareness comes both with experience in the PICU and experience as a supervisor. Experienced staff almost always teaches new staff. This is of major importance because residents come to the unit with limited experience in critical care. Van Stralen and Perkin rely on experienced nurses and respiratory therapists to teach the residents. Redundancy ensures thoroughness in evaluating the patient and in choosing a therapy. Many of the signs they monitor are measured by two methods; furthermore, during resuscitations, several team mem-bers will monitor the same vital sign.

Rules and procedures have allowed respiratory therapists and nurses to influence medical care to a greater degree and with a quicker response to change. As a teaching institution and one that develops new therapies, the PICU has the goal of always considering itself in training. Consequently, its members watch each other's performance and give assistance through mutual teaching and learning.

Conclusions

While van Stralen and Perkins have demonstrated at Loma Linda the effective application of HRO research findings to reduce errors in the PICU, much research remains to be done. Researchers must view health care from a systems perspective as well as from the perspective of a single unit. Errors are made in units and errors are made across units. Policies and procedures developed in one unit influence errors that develop in adjacent or distant units.

As complexity theory suggests, systems that consist of independent actors whose interactions are governed by a system of recursively applied rules naturally generate stable structure.[29] Here, we suggest that some good HRO practices or potentially good "rules," once applied to organizational systems, might generate increasingly safer and stable structures because the output of one application of rules becomes the input for the next round. That is, positive feedback loops that result from the interactions of a large number of components eventually simplify structures and give clarity to operations that enhance safety, crowding out irregular or nonstandard microscopic behavior and structures.

Research into how health care systems structure themselves would help us develop concepts of adaptability and flexibility useful in the medical industry. Medical practitioners need to know the conditions under which complex, tightly tied medical units and systems must incorporate flexibility. We also need to examine closely how roles should be interrelated in and across health care units. The imbalance of power held by physicians is probably dysfunctional to the delivery of safe health care. Once we know what appears to be appropriate role interrelationship, we need to address the issue of how training institutions should deal with this knowledge. We need also to develop ideas about training mechanisms to disseminate such research findings and encourage their application. Last, we need to observe empirically how intervention of any kind affects the interdependence of the system, as well as how interventions of several kinds can combine and integrate to create larger systematic changes. These are tough nuts to crack!

Although David Gaba has begun to develop a culture assessment along HRO lines for the Veteran's Administration, more work needs to be done on this issue. The concept development work is far from complete and needs to be carried on in medical settings. Although constructs such as command and control seem useful, these constructs have not been sufficiently fleshed out. Nor does the instrument derived from these constructs have adequate psychometric properties. We need a good way to assess culture in medical settings that clearly follows from theoretical development. The cultures of various continuous medical units need to be examined together to see how one influences the other. Training needs can be identified from cultural phenomena.

As we saw from our examples, reward systems are extremely important to the adequate management of HROs. However, appropriate rewards are often specific to their situations. We need to develop a taxonomy of appropriate rewards for medical systems. We suspect that current policies in many medical units foster the use of the wrong rewards, if for no other reason than the requirements of managed care.

One of the most difficult research issues will be the investigation of sense making within and across units. Understanding the cognitive functioning of a single individual is difficult. But the characteristics of HRO operations require the integration of cognitions across many individuals. Mapping this integration to develop a picture of the heedfulness of a unit is challenging. Mapping the integration of units constituting a system is even more challenging.

References

1. Sharp, V., and Faden, A. *Medical Harm: Historical, Conceptual, and Ethical Dimensions of Iatrogenic Illness* (New York: Cambridge University Press, 1998).
2. Quarentelli, E. L. ed., *What Is a Disaster?* (London: Routledge, 1998).
3. Turner, B. M. *Man Made Disasters* (London: Wykeham Press, 1978).
4. Quarentelli, E. L. "The Nature and Conditions of Panic," *American Journal of Sociology* 60 (1954):267–275.
5. Helmreich, R. L. et al., *Revised Versions of the Cockpit Management Attitudes Questionnaire (CMAQ) and CRM Seminar Evaluation Form,* NASA University of Texas Technical Report 88–3 (Austin, TX: University of Texas, 1991).
6. Singer, S. J., Gaba, D. M., Geppert, J. J., Sinaiko, J. D., Howard, S. K., and Park, K. C. (2003). "The culture of safety: Results of an organization-wide survey in 15 California hospitals." *Qual Saf Health Care* 12(2003): 112–118.
7. Libuser, C. "Organizational Structure and Risk Mitigation," PhD diss., University of California, Los Angeles, 1994.
8. Roberts, K. H. "Some Characteristics of One Type of High Reliability Organization," *Organizational Science* 1 (1990):160–176.

9. Bigley, G. A., and Roberts, K. H. "Structuring Temporary Systems for High Reliability," *Academy of Management Journal* (in press).
10. La Porte, T. R., and Consolini, P. "Working in Theory but Not in Practice: Theoretical Challenges in High Reliability Organizations," *Journal of Public Administration Research and Theory* 1 (1991):19–47.
11. Kerr, S. "On the Folly of Rewarding A While Hoping for B," *Academy of Management Journal* 47 (1975):469–483.
12. Weick, K. E. "South Canyon Revisited: Lessons from High Reliability Organizations," working paper, University of Michigan, 1995.
13. Weick, K. E. *Sense Making in Organizations* (Thousand Oaks, CA: Sage, 1995).
14. Weick, K. E., and Roberts, K. H. "Collective Mind and Organizational Reliability: The Case of Flight Operations on an Aircraft Carrier Deck," *Administrative Science Quarterly* 38 (1993):357–381.
15. Roberts, K. H., and Bea, R. "When Systems Fail," *Organizational Dynamics* (2001).
16. Roberts, K. H. et al., "Decision Dynamics in Two High Reliability Military Organizations," *Management Science* 40 (1994):614–624.
17. Schulman, P. "The Analysis of High Reliability Organizations," in *New Challenges to Understanding Organizations*, ed. K. H. Roberts (New York: Macmillan, 1993), 33–54.
18. Tamuz, M. "Developing Organizational Safety Information Systems for Monitoring Potential Dangers," in *Proceedings of PSAM II* 2, eds. G. E. Apostolakis and T. S. Win (Los Angeles: University of California, 1994), 7–12.
19. Weick, K. E. "The Vulnerable System: An Analysis of the Tenerife Air Disaster," *Journal of Management* 16 (1990):571–593.
20. Stringfield, S. "Attempting to Enhance Students' Learning Through Innovative Programs: The Case for Schools Evolving into High Reliability Organizations," *School Effectiveness and School Improvement* 6 (1995):67–90.
21. Bierly, P. E., and Spender, J. C. "Culture and High Reliability Organizations: The Case of the Nuclear Submarine," *Journal of Management* 21 (1995):639–656.
22. Hee, D. D. et al., "Safety Management Assessment System (SMAS): A Process for Identifying and Evaluating Human and Organization Factors in Marine System Operations with Field Test Results," *Reliability Engineering and System Safety* 65 (1999):125–140.
23. Bea, R. G. "Risk Based Engineering Design of Marine Systems: The Human and Organizational Factors (HOF)," Paper presented at the State of the Art Pipeline Risk Management Conference, Perth, Western Australia, November 11, 1999.
24. Boniface, D., and Bea, R. G. "A Decision Analysis Framework for Assessing Human and Organizational Error in the Marine Industries," Paper presented at the Symposium on Human and Organizational Error in Marine Structures, Ship Structure Committee, Society of Naval Architects and Marine Engineers, Arlington, VA, November 1996.

25. Grabowski, M. et al., "Decision Support and Organizational Forms in a High Velocity Environment: Responses to Catastrophic Oil Spills," in *Advances in Expert Systems for Management: Evaluation and Value in Knowledge Based Systems*, eds. M. Grabowski and W. A. Wallace (Greenwich, CT: JAI Press, 1997).

26. Sarna, P. C. "Sense Making in the Incident Command: Developing and Maintaining the 'Big Picture,'" Paper presented at IDER/IEPC Conference, The Hague, October 12–14, 1999.

27. Pollack, M. et al., "Pediatric Intensive Care Units: Results of a National Study," *Critical Care Medicine* 21 (1993):607–611.

28. McCloskey, K. A., and Johnston, C. "Critical Care Interhospital Transports: Predictability of the Need for a Pediatrician," *Pediatric Emergency Care* 6 (1990):89–92.

29. Drazin, R., and Sandelands, L. "Autogenesis: A Perspective on the Process of Organizing," *Organization Science* 19, no. 3 (1992).

CHAPTER TWELVE

ADMITTING IMPERFECTION: REVELATIONS FROM THE COCKPIT FOR THE WORLD OF MEDICINE

John J. Nance, JD

The proverbial hush falls over the crowd as the Olympic athlete pauses at the starting point, focusing his mind and preparing to do battle with gravity, the record book, his fellow competitors, and himself. At last the seminal moment arrives and the contestant explodes into motion. Thousands of spectators watch in person along with millions more before TV sets around the world, each of the spectators drawn onto the razor edge of the moment as the uncertain outcome unfolds.

The task before the athlete is nothing less than to push hard at the envelope of human endurance and dexterity, forcing his body to perform better, faster, with greater accuracy, and closer to the ideal of flawlessness than anyone who has dared this competition before.

But as we watch him struggle, the element that rivets us so—the element that suspends time and space with unbearable suspense—is the absolute knowledge that failure is not only a possibility, it is, in fact, a distinct likelihood.

This we understand as a species: The possibility of human failure makes success all the sweeter, and not just in sports. Philosophers and poets alike have long extolled the incalculable value of the struggle against the possibility or probability of failure as an element that defines us and elevates us to achieve more than what we are. "A man's reach should exceed his grasp," wrote Robert Browning, "or what's a heaven for?"

Moreover, we understand that little if anything in human existence is guaranteed, including our own continued existence. "Civilization," wrote Will and Ariel Durant, "exists by geological consent, subject to change without notice," and as we live with uncertain geology and uncertain physiology, we face on a daily basis the evidence that life can end in a heartbeat.

Yet, whether by operation of an eternal optimism inextricably inherent in the human species or by a need for institutional denial, we humans not only reach routinely beyond our grasp, but we also elevate certain members and *classes* within our own species to an eternally unachievable status: infallibility. We assume that with enough years of practice and instruction, we can perform perfectly all of the time. This is nothing less than a classic contradiction, a dichotomy of immense proportions. The same race of beings, in other words, that can fully understand the propensity for human imperfection in one class of human endeavors refuses to accept that propensity in others. Yet the propensity for human failure is not a variable characteristic. It is universal.

Throughout the ages, humans have invested those trained to fulfill higher callings with the presumption of omnipotence and perfection. Kings and prelates, for instance—both presumed to be the invested representatives of God—not only dominated Western humanity from the first century after Christ through the Middle Ages, but were presumed *by definition* to be incapable of error. With a great and staggering gulf between the common man and those in control (based on education and position), that primal investiture of assumed perfection was one that served the convenience and comfort of the people as much as it sprang from faith or the actual perceived performance of the nobility. One *wanted* one's king to be infallible, since life and prosperity in whatever form depended on his protection, his judgment, and his performance as leader and defender of the state. Correspondingly, the head of a church *needed* to be presumed infallible in order to be given the authority to translate for the common man the will of the deity. So, too, the rising class of masters of various crafts and professions were afforded the presumption of perfection by those of lesser position, experience, and ability, and to such ranks were added the presumed intellectual infallibility of senior scientists and professors of the nobility, especially as we rounded the end of the eighteenth century and built a foundation of technological achievements on which would be raised the industrial revolution.

The late nineteenth century brought with it a further expansion of this expectation of human perfection, but this version—inasmuch as it encompassed the practitioners of professions and trades without reference to station of birth, royalty, or inherited position—was testimony to the need of society to *depend* on the performance of these venerated practitioners (of whatever profession) precisely because their performance had become so critical to society.

A captain of the British navy or any other great navy, for instance, was charged with the responsibility and presumption of possessing perfect judgment by the time he had acceded to that rank. After all, Britain, for one, granted its captains godlike authority over their human charges, including the power to order any crew member executed at any time for any reason. Although the Lords of the Admiralty passed judgment on just how perfect their captains' performance might be, no one else was afforded the right to question a commander. There was an enforced presumption, held dear by ordinary seamen and junior officers alike, that the captain was, in fact, incapable of error. Yet, in the last moments of his life, many a seaman must have flailed as much against the reality that his captain had been wrong as against the waters of a shipwreck that were about to engulf him. And, of course, for a seaman to *question* the judgment of his captain was a capital offense punishable by death in whatever gruesome form the captain chose.

So, too, in the nineteenth century was the physician raised from the status of benevolent medicine man and healer to the practitioner of a profession that, insofar as it incorporated ways and means mysterious to the average citizen, required the presumption of perfection. One had to trust that a physician knew what to do and how to do it, and that trust came hard in the ages before anesthesia, microbiology, antibiotics, and the abilities to heal and soothe granted by modern pharmacology became available. One has only to examine the history of the field physicians of the Union and Confederate armies during the American Civil War to understand the required level of blind trust. It was the physician who pronounced the need to saw off damaged limbs, inflict horrible pain in attempts to reassemble broken bodies, or consign the wounded to death. To the recipients of such emergency/trauma medicine, trust was enabled by the comforting belief that the process of medical training had transformed these healers from mere mortals to something more, and that added element was infallibility. The dead could be mourned more easily, the broken and sick resigned more benevolently on the advice of a medical man whose word could be trusted absolutely. We, as a species, wanted and needed the inherent comfort of that presumption, despite its terrible predations on the very practitioners it sought to sanctify.

Now, in the third millennium of Western time-keeping, the ranks of those who must be presumed infallible have expanded yet again. At their core, they still encompass the healer, the physician, and all those arrayed with the physician in providing professional health care. But they also encompass those whose fingers hover over nuclear triggers and those in control of various machines and systems on which our lives periodically depend, such as airline pilots, civilian ship captains, and even railroad engineers. Whenever we place our lives and physical well-being (or those of our loved ones) in the skilled hands of other humans, we try hard to convince ourselves that those so trusted have been trained to a standard that allows them to perform without flaw and without error. We make these presumptions, yet react with institutional fury when someone so anointed has the temerity to prove less than perfect. We have as humans, in other words, created a systemic presumption of the possibility of human perfection and assigned that presumption to mere mortals engaged in a wide array of pursuits, the expertise for which has been granted by training and experience, not birth. It is an endemic expectation, and it is a myth. But the most dastardly element of the expectation of professional perfection is that *we professionals* have been trained to believe it!

Although a major point of this chapter is transference to health care of some of the revolutionary lessons recently learned by aviation about dealing with human failures and human nature, the inescapable truth is that the very same challenges of human imperfection causing injuries and deaths are faced by medical professionals every day. What's new is the perspective developed by aviation, the unique approach to handling fallible humans in a human system demanding critical performance at near-perfection levels. Yet there are basics that apply to all of us in any human endeavor, and before taking you into aviation's revelatory experiences, this bedrock element of commonality should be discussed.

Pilots, military commanders, operators of nuclear power plants, and tens of thousands of other highly trained, highly skilled, highly motivated people learn their professions with the understanding that they will be expected to rise to the level of operational perfection and will be dealt with harshly if they fail. Indeed, the security of their job, they are told (by word and by deed), depends on making no mistakes (or at least on making no large, costly mistakes that must be explained). So, too, are physicians and nurses trained to believe they can become infallible, and those who train them browbeat that expectation into their students with such effectiveness that the majority of medical practitioners are launched with a severely dysfunctional contradiction ticking away inside their psyches like a bomb: "I must be perfect. My teachers and my peers are perfect. People will think much less of me if I'm not perfect. Yet, I see increasing evidence that I am not perfect and may never achieve that status, and I must hide that possibility at all costs."

The Myth of Medical Infallibility

The practice of medicine and the very operation of the health care industry have been built on the foundation of the mythological assumption that professionals can achieve perfection. Aviation built its citadel of operational safety on the very same assumption. Using that precept eliminates the need to build safety systems to absorb human mistakes, because there should *be* no human mistakes to absorb. Yet, medical mistakes are, by definition, human mistakes, and that fact becomes immediately offensive to the system and all within it. Thus, a human practitioner who commits an imperfect act by making a mistake does nothing less than offend and assault the belief system upon which health care as an industry and a profession has been built.

There are only two major pathways to use in dealing with human mistakes. One is to get rid of (or sanction and retrain) the flawed human. The other is to massively alter the expectations and structure of the system to accept and anticipate the existence of human imperfection. Historically, both health care and aviation have always chosen the former.

Traditionally, firing the person or persons who are determined to have committed a medical error enabled the system to maintain the facade of normalcy. The system could thus proclaim that the *expectation* of human perfection was still valid, but that the *system's* only mistake was picking the wrong human.

Yet human mistakes—medical mistakes—never occur in a vacuum as a singular, unsupported event. It is axiomatic that there is always a chain of acts or omissions that surrounds the triggering human mistake and enables it, just as it is axiomatic that there is never a single, isolated cause for an airline accident.

Take the classic example of a nurse who accidentally prepares a solution of undiluted potassium chloride for IV infusion instead of the heavily diluted solution ordered by the attending physician. When the patient's heart stops in chemical obedience to the expected physiologic reaction, there is no question that the nurse's mistake was the triggering element. But what of the *enabling* elements that were undisputedly under the control of the *system?* Why was undiluted potassium chloride available outside the confines of the pharmacy? Where was the special training to warn the nurse of the dangers of any potassium chloride infusion? Where were the established procedures or forcing functions that would have made such a mistake impossible?

When we proceed from the assumption that nurses, doctors, and pharmacists (and all other health care professionals) will never be able to completely expunge mistakes from their professional performance, it becomes obvious that simply firing or disciplining (or even retraining) the nurse who makes a medical mistake does absolutely nothing to repair the safety gaps in the delivery system itself. Only by building safety buffers—emergency backups, if you will—can the system safely and routinely absorb future human mistakes short of patient impact. Certainly, firing a nurse assures that *that* nurse will never make *that* mistake in *that* facility again, but the next nurse hired to replace him or her may, especially if the surrounding environment is not restructured. Clearly, simply firing or eliminating flawed humans and replacing them with others does virtually nothing to correct the system's vulnerability. The system itself must be changed.

That is precisely where we are in American health care at the dawn of the third millennium: possessed of a system that, despite its stunning successes in delivering the best health care in history to the largest number of people, nevertheless enables and sometimes facilitates a staggering number of patient injuries and deaths each year.* This happens not because the system employs "bad" humans who should never have been trusted to be perfect. It happens because the system employs humans who are generically incapable of absolute perfection, yet wrongly expects precisely what they generically can never provide: continuous flawless performance. In so doing, it reflects not just the self-generated expectations of medical professionals, but the misguided expectations of an entire population who dearly wants to believe that their physicians, nurses, and health care providers have been somehow elevated to a status of perfect judgment, knowledge, and performance.

That popular expectation of perfection has been a part of the airline industry for the past 40 years. As startling as it may seem, one of the first major steps in improving airline safety was to lower the expectations of airline customers, urging them to accept the reality that pilots, as humans, are not perfect, but that integrated safety systems that fully anticipate human fallibility can and do approach perfection.

When any of us approach an airline's ticket counter these days with the intent to fly, we are well aware of several realities: (1) Commercial aviation is not 100% safe and sometimes does end in crashes and tragedy, and (2) the safety record of commercial aviation has not only continued to improve, but flying is without question the safest method of travel.

But if airlines and their personnel are not perfect, why do we climb aboard? Because the airline industry and the media have done an effective job of educating the population about the methods the airlines use to achieve such incredible safety records: simulators, intensive training, checkrides, high standards, checklists, backup systems backing up backup systems, and within the last decade, increasing public exposure to the seismic change in the culture of the airline cockpits.

---

*Dr. Lucian Leape in February 2001 prepared a graphic comparing health care to numerous other publicly trusted professions, trades, and activities, showing that those admitted to hospitals were taking only a slightly lesser risk than bungee jumping from a bridge or other high precipice, and a slightly *more* hazardous one than mountain climbing, with mortality rates from medical accidents (medical mistakes) at approximately 1 per 1,000 patients.

Aiding this process have been the open and continuously visible investigations of the National Transportation Safety Board (NTSB). Although much of the public still mistakenly views the process of accident investigation as a process designed to lay blame, an increasing number of Americans understand that the NTSB is not interested in blame, but in uncovering all the contributing causes to an accident so that the system may be adjusted appropriately in time to prevent a new accident from similar causal factors. This constant public exposure of the process has slowly but profoundly changed the role of airline pilots from that of an arcane priesthood whose ways were too mysterious to know to that of a cadre of highly trained professionals who, though imperfect and thoroughly human, utilize advanced methods of teamwork and technical ability to achieve what few thought possible a half century ago: almost perfect systemic performance.

Aviation as a Cautionary Example for Health Care

The road to this status, however, has been rough. Since 1977, aviation has lived through a revolution that health care is now entering, a painful redefining of reasonable expectations of human performance in a human system and how to minimize the effects of human failure. The scope of the changes has been vast, and it has taken fully 20 years to reach the threshold of maturity. In short, aviation as a community has embraced the reality of human imperfection and altered its training courses and its systemic structures to do two things: work to minimize human errors, and prepare aviation systems to safely absorb those errors that cannot be fully eliminated. The results have been demonstrable and impressive gains in flight safety through the process of building systems that are redundant enough to safely absorb not only mechanical failures, but human failures as well.

Why is this a process health care should study closely? Because the lessons that aviation purchased with the blood of lost passengers and crew members have direct applicability to the medical community.

Airline pilots, and pilots in general who fly for compensation or for the military, are traditionally charged with the same expectation of perfect performance as doctors, nurses, pharmacists, and other health care professionals. Historically, aviation has built its systems and organizations on the very same myth that there will be no dangerous human errors that the system from time to time must be able to safely absorb. Unlike health care, however, the aviation industry has been forced by the very public nature of its mistakes to come to grips with human failure at a much earlier time. Specifically, aviation safety leaders were forced by the terrible drumbeat of accidents in the 1970s to face four

major systemic flaws that were preventing the aviation safety system
from improving further:

1. Aviation's historic refusal to fully accept the inevitability of
   human failure and readjust the safety system to both minimize
   their causes (such as fatigue, distraction, anger, and lack of
   standardization) while safely absorbing those human mistakes
   that remain
2. The presence of massive barriers to communication among crew
   members and associated members of the operational team (such
   as dispatchers, mechanics, pilots, and flight attendants), which
   too often prevented the passage of vital information at critical
   times
3. The traditional method of grading the worth of cockpit leadership
   based on omnipotence and infallibility rather than on the most
   interactive and effective use of human resources
4. The inability to appropriately utilize teams and teamwork

Similarities between Aviation and Health Care

Aviation and health care share a staggering commonality, which means
that each can learn from the other. Both fit the description coined by
Dr. James Reason of Britain of a "sharp end" industry, in which the extensive infrastructure of knowledge, investment, performance history,
and invested capital (the so-called blunt end of the organization) can
be instantly imperiled by the human mistake of someone working at
the so-called sharp end. The sharp end is the place where the entire collective professional capabilities of the organization rest in the hands of
one or more practitioners working in a highly dynamic and changeable
environment in which successful outcomes may be routine, but cannot
be assured.

In other words, one slip in aviation, and an airliner may be lost.
One slip in the operating room, and a patient may be lost. In fact, the
following definition fits both professions:

> Highly trained, highly motivated professionals working in a real-time,
> high-pressure environment, using very sophisticated implements and
> tools under great public and regulatory scrutiny, where the penalties
> for failure are potentially very great in both human and monetary
> terms.

Certainly, the penalties for crashing an airliner are very great in
"both human and monetary terms," just as the potential penalties for losing a patient to a medical mistake include not only the nightmare of lawsuits and diminished stature, but also the specter of intense professional

self-doubt, deep remorse, and, typically, the weight of undeserved shame and blame exacerbated by an archaic system of disciplining humans for the offense of being human.

This, too, is an element of historic commonality—the propensity when something goes wrong to ask the question "Who's wrong?" versus the correct systemic question, "What's wrong?"

Aviation is replete with stories of pilots and mechanics fired for making a mistake that, in fact, would have been impossible without extensive "help" from the system in which that professional worked. Although professionals in health care and aviation must have professional performance standards and disciplinary systems to enforce them, using discipline to address a purely human failure is a useless, counter-productive exercise rooted more in tradition than logic.

Take the example of a Delta Airlines Boeing 727 crew of three highly trained and experienced pilots who crashed on takeoff in 1985 at Dallas–Fort Worth airport because they forgot to position the flaps correctly. All three men not only responded to the checklist, but looked in the direction of the gauges that would have told them the true position of the flaps (extendable panels on the back of the wing that enable a jet to take off and land at slow airspeeds). As heard on the cockpit voice recorder, all three responded "Fifteen, fifteen, green," meaning the flaps were in the correct position for takeoff. The flaps, however, were in the zero position, as clearly indicated on the gauges that all three men looked at and all three men misinterpreted.

How could that happen? Because, as human beings, we sometimes see and hear what we expect to see and hear, even though that may be at variance from what's actually there. This was, in other words, a mistake that resulted simply from the status of being human. There were no rules about how to look at the forward panel that were violated, no missed checklists, and no intent by any of the pilots to ignore procedures. All three simply failed as human beings.

The pilots all survived the crash, though some of their passengers did not. Delta, acting in accordance with the tradition of aviation and health care (a tradition that dictates that the responsible parties pay an appropriate price for failure), fired the pilots. They did so in part to send a message to all other Delta pilots: "If you fail like these men did, you, too, will be terminated."

But the failure was a *human* failure, a *human* vulnerability. So the actual message sent by Delta was utter nonsense: "If you make a human mistake that you neither intended to make nor had any control over, we will fire you. Therefore, don't you dare be human."

It is impossible to find any corrective value in that message, other than to let the rest of the pilot force know that their jobs depended precariously on the fickle element of fate. Such a misuse of discipline does violence to the goal of understanding our human failure potentials so that we can design better systems to prevent those human potentials from resulting in dangerous situations like inadvertent no-flap takeoffs.

In other words, firing a pilot or a nurse to address an inadvertent human error and thus leaving the important systemic questions of what nurtured the error into a disaster unanswered and unaddressed becomes a form of organizational narcotic: It makes the system feel good at the same time as it guarantees addiction to more repetitions of that and other mistakes.

The Safety Hazards of the Isolated Omnipotent Leader: Firing Captain Kirk

The four major mistakes aviation was making, listed earlier, are all facets of the same basic malady: the presumption of human infallibility. But once airlines began institutionally admitting that its crews could make mistakes, a renaissance was triggered in method and outlook that began leading to the elimination of the most serious barriers to communication among crew members. At the same time, aviation began redefining what constituted a good leader and working to invigorate true teamwork in the cockpit and the cabin.

The vast majority of health care professionals recognize the name James T. Kirk as the fictional captain of the United Federation Starship *Enterprise* from the 1966–1969 vintage NBC/Paramount science-fiction television series *Star Trek*. Kirk (played by actor William Shatner) was largely representative of the way leaders were supposed to think and act, whether in health care, aviation, the military, or business in general. They were expected to be strong-willed, technically competent, highly innovative individuals who needed no one's advice and who were extremely careful to maintain the image of command.

Specifically, Jim Kirk was ready to fire off orders at any time with a firm air of infallibility in reaction to any problem. Other than the reports and responses he requested from his crew, Kirk neither needed nor wanted anyone's advice, because (1) he already had the perfect answers, and (2) the act of requesting or accepting a subordinate's recommendation might somehow suggest to the crew that he was less than omnipotent.

Kirk, in other words, embodied the accepted model of a modern physician, and too often the resultant model of a leader in nursing, pharmacy, and any other position of management in medical practice. And, of course, the Kirk method was the very essence of what airline captains and military commanders alike were supposed to be: omnipotent, perfect, and endlessly effective.

The problem, of course, was not that health care professionals or airline professionals had begun spending time studying the *Star Trek* school of command as portrayed by Kirk and then emulating him, but rather that the writers of the show had effectively captured our model of leadership without a corresponding portrayal of the fact that the Kirk command style was demonstrably hazardous to human health.

Kirk, like health care professionals and pilots alike, was surrounded by subordinates, the vast majority of whom fit the definition of being "highly trained, highly motivated professionals." Those professionals were there to contribute their intellect, training, and human compassion to the job at hand, which was always to serve the best interests of the common goal. So, too, are subordinate pilots paid salaries and given expensive training to provide something more than companionship and blind obedience in an airliner cockpit. Yet in health care, aviation, and the USS *Enterprise,* subordinates were not free to contribute their professional abilities without severe constraints.

In the case of the airline industry, a long string of galvanizing disasters in the 1970s served to force a seminal change in attitude and culture. It was impossible, for instance, to ignore the fact that the information that could have saved 583 lives on a foggy runway in the Canary Islands in 1977 resided in the minds of two subordinate pilots. The chief pilot of KLM Royal Dutch Airlines had begun a hurried takeoff without the proper clearance, but that information could not be passed to the captain simply because the copilot and flight engineer could not bring themselves to question or override a man in whom they had such confidence and held in such respect.

The location was the airport at Tenerife in the Canaries, and the problem was the sudden arrival of several jumbo jets diverting into the normally sleepy airport because the main island airport of Las Palmas had been temporarily closed by a bomb threat. The KLM flight carried a charter group inbound from Amsterdam, and the crew was supposed to pick up an outbound charter group and return to Amsterdam on schedule. After a frustrating several hours trying to get refueled and get under way, the KLM captain was in a state of agitation by the time he turned his huge aircraft into position at the end of the foggy runway and began pushing the throttles forward to go.

"Wait a minute, sir," the first officer/copilot had said, "We don't have the clearance yet."

Captain Jacob Van Zanten had pulled the throttles back in embarrassment, yet, like all senior leaders, admitting embarrassment or mistake was not an option. "I knew that," the captain said. "Get the clearance." Time was passing, and Van Zanten had only a few minutes left to get off the ground before running past his maximum projected crew duty time limits. Were he to exceed those limits, the entire charter flight would have to be stopped for 12 hours of crew rest, costing the airline over $30,000 dollars and costing Jacob Van Zanten considerable embarrassment. This captain, in other words, wanted to get airborne as fast as possible.

The tower controller issued the first of the two required clearances, but Van Zanten, mistakenly believing that both the air traffic control clearance *and* the takeoff clearance had been issued, pushed the throttles up again to start the takeoff roll.

Suddenly, the experienced copilot was thrown into an incredible diplomatic dilemma. He had already corrected—and embarrassed—his senior commander once. He did not want to do it again! Unable to force himself to point out that the captain was, for a second time, attempting takeoff without a clearance, he tried clearing them for takeoff by simply announcing the fact to the tower, hoping the tower controller would order them to hold position, and thus solve the problem.

This was, after all, his boss in the left seat, and one of the most beloved men at KLM. Van Zanten was the chief pilot. He was the director of safety, an important post. He was also the man whose face was all over the world in a two-page slick magazine ad for KLM, the very spokesman for the safety and performance excellence of Dutch aviation. The bright halo over Van Zanten's head—his assumed status of infallibility and omnipotence—was too powerful to allow the other two officers in the cockpit unfettered communication of the extremely vital fact that the takeoff clearance had not yet been issued and other aircraft were moving around in unknown locations on the airport surface in the foggy conditions.

The copilot's garbled statement to the unseen tower controller that "We are . . . at . . . takeoff, KLM," a puzzling nonstandard transmission, led to a mistaken reply by the tower controller: "Okay. . . . stand by, I will call you."

Unfortunately, another aircraft, puzzled at the meaning of the strange phrase uttered by the copilot, pressed its transmit button milliseconds after the tower controller had spoken the word "Okay." The new transmission blocked the tower controller's following order to stand by, and suddenly the KLM first officer was left with the impression that the tower had approved the self-announced takeoff roll.

"Set power," ordered Captain Van Zanten. "We go."

Approximately 30 seconds later, at 112 knots, which was well below flying speed, the huge Boeing 747-200 rolled out of the clouds that had been obscuring ground visibility and slammed into a Pan American 747 that had missed a turn and was sitting sideways on the runway. The ensuing fireball led to the worst loss of life in airline history to that date.

Similarly, a United Airlines crew ran a huge four-engine DC-8 out of fuel and crashed 7 miles short of the Portland, Oregon, airport one December night in 1978 because the two experienced subordinate pilots were so used to being overruled by an autocratic captain that they'd given up trying to communicate with him. They couldn't even tell him that they were about to flame out after an hour and twelve minutes of preparations for a relatively routine emergency landing.

In 1982, a situationally disconnected Boeing 737 captain disregarded four warnings from his vastly more qualified young copilot and tried to haul their ice-encrusted Air Florida jet into the air with only three quarters normal power. Instead of sustaining flight, they thundered into the nearby 14th Street Bridge over the Potomac River in Washington, DC, killing all but five, and most Americans watched the amazing helicopter rescue of those five from the icy river on live TV.

Blockages of critical cockpit communication were occurring for many reasons and causing crash after crash, but the ultimate cause of this lack of communication was the dysfunctional cockpit culture. More specifically, it was the utter absence of *teamwork*.

Aviation professionals had collectively thought of airline cockpit crews as exemplifying the best aspects of teamwork. But teamwork requires a team, and a team does not consist merely of one giving orders and others carrying out those orders—which was essentially the way airliners were flown. By the early 1980s, it had become obvious that somehow in the maturation of the airline business, airline cockpits had been allowed to develop a culture that was essentially and dangerously dependent on the captain's skill and judgment to the exclusion of all other influence. Although there were certainly large numbers of captains who sought the advice and participation of their subordinate pilots, the model—the norm—was the autocratic captain essentially flying solo in a multiplace aircraft with other qualified pilots who were very careful about countering him, making suggestions, or ever attempting to override his decision. In other words, the Captain Kirk model of leadership was the norm.

The word *culture* is important here, because when a dysfunctional human culture develops, the culture itself often does not recognize its own dysfunctionality. Thus, even subordinate pilots who were well aware of their inability to influence a headstrong captain would adopt the same autocratic methods when they became captains, thus perpetuating the problem. The phrase "This is the way we've always done it" was too often used to justify the continuation of a demonstrably dangerous environment, just as tradition and training too often serve to perpetuate the same sort of autocratic, noncommunicative environment among physicians, nurses, and health care workers.

Although a surgical operating room (OR) provides a close parallel to the crucible of an airline cockpit in many ways, there are numerous dissimilarities. For example, the OR involves numerous variances in professional training and people working for different entities coming together to practice under the same roof, whereas an airline crew works for the same entity and is trained to the same standards. Nevertheless, in terms of whether vital information can flow in unfettered fashion between members of a true team, the OR, the intensive care unit (ICU), and the emergency department (ED) present high-pressure parallels to the cockpit. In all cases, blocked communication, excessive hierarchies, poor leadership techniques, and the absence of a common vision (i.e., patient safety) involve the same principles.

But these principles apply far beyond the ED, the ICU, and the OR. These principles apply wherever two or more medical professionals are engaged in a common purpose and need to cooperate and communicate for the good of the patient and the good of the mission.

The leadership style traditionally taught by example in most medical and nursing schools matches the leadership style traditionally expected of pilots in command in that we were all essentially trained to emulate the command style of Captain Kirk.

In medical practice as well as in aviation, the concurrent need to keep up the *appearance* of infallibility, firm control, absolute knowledge, and self-sufficiency is beyond well established—it's endemic. Newer nurses are careful about questioning or challenging more experienced nurses or management nurses, who in turn are often loathe to question or challenge strong-willed doctors, who in turn are careful about challenging or countering stronger-willed, better-established doctors. Senior people are afforded such high levels of respect that subordinates will routinely question their own judgment or professional knowledge rather than quickly accept the idea that a respected leader might be making a mistake. In addition, even when a senior leader invites full participatory critique and open communication, the subordinates—in the absence of specific training and tangible cultural change—are too often unwilling to speak up.

The airline cockpit held precisely the same problems: captains whose mere level of experience or status as a captain retarded or eliminated critique, questioning, or even professional oversight by the other pilots in the same cockpit; and subordinate pilots who felt constrained and refused to speak up, even when invited to do so by a fully participatory captain. These are serious barriers to communication that prevent those with critical knowledge from passing that knowledge to a leader in timely fashion. In airline cockpits this communication malady was regularly permitting the failure of a single human being—the captain—to metastasize into a fatal accident even though one or more of his or her crewmembers had timely knowledge that the captain's chosen course of action was dangerous. So, too, have countless patients been injured or killed by medical mistakes made by experienced practitioners in the presence of other health care professionals who knew something was wrong, but could not or would not speak up.

How Aviation Addressed Teamwork Problems

It took more than 5 years after the Tenerife disaster before the beginnings of a solution surfaced to address the problem of retraining or firing the Captain Kirks in airline cockpits. United Airlines, which had suffered the embarrassment of the Portland crash and one other near Salt Lake City resulting from poor to no cockpit communication and coordination, identified the problem not as a need for democracy in the cockpit (an oft-heard criticism), but as a need to invest the leader—the captain—with a new charge: the responsibility to appropriately utilize all the resources entrusted to him, *inclusive* of the human crewmembers. In order to train United's pilots how to discharge this strange new responsibility, United created a new FAA-approved course called CLRM, cockpit leadership resource management, later shortened to cockpit resource management (CRM), and finally changed to *crew* resource management to reflect the growing realization that the crew—the team—included the flight attendants, the mechanics, the dispatchers, and everyone else operationally involved.

In principle, CRM is a fairly simple process of training captains to accept their fallibility as humans and accept the concept that their worth as leaders is measured by how well they can consistently invite, extract, and utilize the full intellectual and professional capabilities of the other pilots and crewmembers—their "resources"—by invigorating and perpetuating an atmosphere of unfettered communication.

At the same time, it became vitally important to train the copilots and flight engineers as well as flight attendants (in later versions of the courses) that they had an unshakable responsibility to speak up assertively and not keep silent when something needed to be said. Certain additional procedures were coined, such as the "two challenge" rule, which dictated that when a subordinate pilot realized professionally that something had to be done, he or she was to challenge the captain and the copilot twice, and even if not listened to, was to make it happen.

In February 1989, United Airlines Flight 811 was on climbout some 60 miles from Honolulu, southbound for New Zealand, when the incompletely closed forward cargo door blew out, killing nine passengers and seriously damaging the fully loaded 747. Using the newly trained principles of CRM and full communication, the three pilots successfully returned the jet to Honolulu International during a harried emergency in which the flight engineer twice saved the aircraft: first, by dumping fuel before being directed to do so, and second, by speaking up when the captain was about to mistakenly ditch the aircraft, an act that would have killed all aboard given the extensive damage to the airframe.

CRM, even though never mandated by the Federal Aviation Administration, has become the gold standard in crew training in aviation. By the mid-1990s no U.S.-based airline could qualify for decent insurance rates without adopting both the CRM course and the CRM philosophy. There are many versions and variations of CRM courses, but they all have in common the basic philosophy of "leadership with participation, and [subordinate] assertiveness with respect."

CRM courses are not adaptable to health care without significant modification. Airlines learned by trial and error that psychologists teaching pilots didn't work, but that when pilots and flight attendants were trained as facilitators and became the teachers to their own people, the effectiveness of the CRM courses soared.

So, too, CRM must not only be adapted in health care, but equivalent teaching of the concepts of teamwork must be taught by medical professionals to medical professionals. This is an evolving science, but the benefits from altering the way the community looks at communication, teamwork, leadership, and the willingness to ask for advice and assistance with no hesitation or shame are critical to improving patient safety and significantly decreasing the opportunity for human mistake to metastasize into patient impact.

The Picard Method

The citing of *Star Trek* in a serious work may seem strange, but in fact the writers of all versions of the show have given both health care and aviation some highly useful examples of the extremes of leadership style and have crystallized those styles in the command personalities of Captain Kirk (of the original series) and Captain Jean-Luc Picard (of *Star Trek Next Generation,* which appeared some 25 years later).

Consider, for instance, the remarkable difference between those command styles. Where Kirk, under fire, would rattle off orders and ignore contrary advice (as well as belittle the would-be adviser), Picard would almost immediately call his senior officers into an emergency staff meeting, a move that enabled him to extract in the shortest period of time the maximum intellect from his highly trained, highly motivated crew. Thus equipped with a better array of advice and options than he could have generated by himself, Picard would then use his cognitive intellect and command abilities to come up with better decisions. Picard made sure his crew understood that, while he was an excellent commander, he was also an imperfect human and thus needed to utilize all his people to improve the effectiveness of his leadership. That command style, as ably portrayed by Shakespearean actor Patrick Stewart, was never one of weakness. Picard retained virtually all of his crew's respect and his leadership and command authority. But by utilizing all the human resources at his command, he was a far better commander and the very model of what the airline industry has come to expect of its airline captains.

The Picard method is the correct one for health care as well. Dr. Picard, Nurse Picard, pharmacist Picard, administrator Picard—the list of positions for which this method of interactive leadership is the correct one is endless. The best leaders must be redefined as men and women who are virtually unafraid of asking for the advice and counsel of the professionals and subordinates around them, and who are skillful in extracting the last ounce of intellect and participation from such people in order to facilitate better decisions. That takes a substantial change in the way leaders view themselves. It takes self-confidence, development of new communication skills and techniques, the virtual abandonment of the traditional tendency to compete with one's eager subordinates, and the comfortable willingness to say in word and deed, "I am human, I am imperfect, and that very recognition makes me a strong and reliable leader who knows how to work safely within my own limitations."

Conclusion

The worth of the airline experience to health care is quite simple: The new definition of what it takes to lead has been forged in the fires of airline disasters and the extensive renaissance in teamwork and communication methods that resulted from those accident investigations. No longer are dangerously impossible claims of human infallibility acceptable. No longer is autocratic, noncommunicative leadership tolerable. No longer are health care participants given the false luxury of silence, or the challenge of using excessive diplomacy as a license to remain silent.

From the smallest clinic to the largest hospital, this massive change in the way we view teamwork, communication, leadership, and human fallibility is the basic formula needed to change the structure of health care's approach to the very real patient safety issues before it. The vast majority of human errors that metastasize into patient injury or death, whether involving medication errors or otherwise, can be prevented by attacking and improving bad systems, not assuming the presence of bad people. And the necessary changes in health care are the very same ones made over the last 20 years in aviation.

CHAPTER THIRTEEN

REPORTING AND PREVENTING MEDICAL MISHAPS: SAFETY LESSONS LEARNED FROM NUCLEAR POWER

George Apostolakis, PhD and Paul Barach, MD, MPH

High-hazard or high-reliability organization (HRO) production systems (LaPorte and Consolini, 1991; Roberts, 1990) face unusual demands for error-free operation because of the potentially catastrophic outcomes associated with mistakes and the intense attention directed to their performance by regulators and the public. These HROs operate essentially without errors over long periods of times. Because safety requires chronic vigilance, HROs are characterized by a chronic state of unease. HROs share the following common operational and organizational characteristics: Safety is a hallmark of their organizational culture, operation of the systems is considered to be a team rather than an individual function, communication and reporting adverse events and near misses are highly valued and rewarded, emergencies are rehearsed and the unexpected practiced, and feedback is essential. The prototypic high-hazard industry is nuclear power generation because of the potential for catastrophic accident and the complex interdependencies among systems (Perrow, 1984), the public scrutiny associated with the Three Mile Island incident and the Chernobyl disaster, and the intense public fear of radiation (Weart, 1988). Other such organizations include chemical processing plants, air traffic control, aircraft carriers, and (more recently) blood banks. Traditionally, health care has not been thought of as a high-hazard industry, despite the high level of risk of injury and death faced by patients. This is because the injuries do not occur in large numbers as a result of catastrophic accidents.

The nuclear power industry has been safety conscious from its beginning in the 1950s. The sensitivity of the public to nuclear power has led to the expenditure of large amounts of resources both by the industry and the Nuclear Regulatory Commission (NRC) on the development of tools for the analysis of potential accidents. It is probably the most heavily regulated industry. The regulations that the NRC has promulgated have fostered the creation of a safety culture that is continually improving. For example, the number of "significant events" fell from 2.38 events per year for the average plant in 1985 to 0.07 events per year in 1996 (NRC, 1997).

The insights gained by analyzing operational experience in a variety of ways have been a major contributor to this improvement process. The early safety philosophy focused on hardware failures and was based on the principle of "defense in depth." This principle "employs successive compensatory measures to prevent accidents or mitigate damage if a malfunction, accident, or naturally caused event occurs at a nuclear facility" (NRC, 1999). The nuclear industry was the first to perform probabilistic risk assessments (PRAs) for whole plants and to embrace the insights that such integrated studies produced. The first PRAs (in the 1970s) demonstrated that even though the application of defense in depth resulted in low public risk, human errors were significant contributors to hypothetical accidents and could, in fact, defeat defense-in-depth measures. Operational experience, including Three Mile Island and Chernobyl, confirmed this finding.

The efforts to understand the role of human error in the 1970s and early 1980s led to the development of models for errors during routine operations, such as during maintenance (Swain and Guttmann, 1983) and during recovery actions that take place in the course of an accident (Apostolakis, Bier, and Mosleh, 1988). The former models have withstood the test of time and are still being used. It was soon realized, however, that recovery errors were modeled in a simplistic way that did not account for the insights that human error theorists were developing. The emphasis was on the "sharp" end of human performance. These models are now referred to as first-generation models (Dougherty, 1990). Second-generation models have been in development since the mid-1980s.

The emphasis of second-generation models is on the *context* within which the plant operators function (Barriere et al., 1998). The assumption is that the operators, like health care practitioners, are experienced and dedicated people who will take the best course of action given a particular context. The context is shaped by the design of the plant, the information reaching the operators regarding the plant conditions, the organizational structure of the facility, the policies of senior management, and other relevant "performance-shaping factors." This structure is based on the work of human error theorists (Rasmussen, 1986; Reason, 1990, 1997; Hollnagel, 1993). The emphasis on context is a major paradigm shift. The first-generation models referred to "human error," with its connotation of blame. The second-generation models search for conditions that create an "error-forcing context" and do not assign blame.

Most health care organizations attack these problems in what is fundamentally a qualitative approach. In the nuclear power industry, however, perhaps because of its engineering roots, it was realized early that if an issue could not be quantified, cost-effective solutions would be difficult to develop. The tools for monitoring and improving safety developed for nuclear power plants provide a technical foundation for and integrate into an organization's quality and performance improvement programs.

This chapter discusses the evolution of the safety philosophy in the nuclear power industry, especially as it pertains to human performance and safety culture. Methods for the analysis of operational experience (root cause analysis and accident sequence precursor analysis) are presented and their applicability to health care organizations is explored. Finally, the organizational differences between nuclear power plants and health care organizations are investigated.

Safety Culture

A major milestone in the evolution of nuclear safety was the introduction of the concept of *safety culture* by the International Nuclear Safety Advisory Group (INSAG) of the International Atomic Energy Agency in Vienna (IAEA, 1991). INSAG defines safety culture as "that assembly of characteristics and attitudes in organizations and individuals which establishes that, as an overriding priority, nuclear plant safety issues receive the attention warranted by their significance." It further states that "safety culture has two major components: the framework determined by organizational policy and by management action, and the response of individuals in working within and benefiting by the framework. Success depends, however, on the commitment and competence provided both in the policy and managerial context by individuals themselves." The identification of organizational policy and management action as major components of safety culture is consistent with Reason's model, in which "unsafe acts" are influenced by both fallible management decisions and line management deficiencies (Reason, 1990).

The INSAG work has had a significant impact on how plant safety is viewed. The plant is now viewed as a *sociotechnical* system in which human performance and organizational issues are as important as hardware performance. The organizational structure, including the coordinating mechanisms (e.g., work processes and programs) and organizational factors (e.g., communication and formalization), plays a central role in determining this context. Research work on organizational factors has been intensified in both the nuclear industry (Davoudian, Wu, and Apostolakis, 1994a, 1994b; Jacobs and Haber, 1994; Becker, 1997; Apostolakis, 1999; Sträter and Bubb, 1999) and other high-hazard industries (Paté-Cornell, 1990; Hurst et al., 1991; Paté-Cornell and Fischbeck, 1993; Bea, 1998; Papazoglou and Aneziris, 1999).

INSAG pointed out that an important component of a good safety culture is the ability of the plant organization to collect and analyze data from operational experience and to learn from it (IAEA, 1991, 1994). The new risk-informed reactor oversight process that the NRC has promulgated also identifies these activities as being key to a well-run facility and calls them the "corrective action program."

The Work Process Analysis Model

Nuclear power plants, like many other industrial facilities, exhibit the characteristics of what is known in organizational theory as a machine bureaucracy (Mintzberg, 1979). As a result of this organizational structure, nuclear power plants rely on work processes to conduct activities. Recognizing that work processes are the prime coordinating mechanisms at plants, the work process analysis model (WPAM) has been developed (Davoudian, Wu, and Apostolakis, 1994a, 1994b; Apostolakis and Wu, 1995; Apostolakis, 1999).

One of the goals of WPAM is to understand how the organization works and what can go wrong. In answering that question, a task analysis is performed. The output of the task analysis is a flow diagram for the work process, accompanied by a cross-reference table and an organizational factors matrix. Each box on the flow diagram is an individual task (Figure 13-1). The top portion shows the action performed, and the bottom portion shows the defenses used to catch any errors that may have occurred. For example, in the corrective maintenance work process, looking at the task of prioritization, we see that the action is prioritization and the defenses are multiple reviews. The cross-reference table provides an easy way to see who performs an action or defense and which department they are in. Finally, the organizational factors matrix maps the organizational factors to specific tasks.

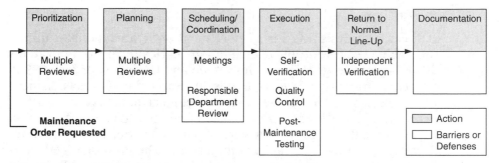

FIGURE 13-1 The flow diagram for the corrective maintenance work process
Reprinted from *Reliability Engineering and System Safety,* vol. 45, Davoudian et al.,
pp. 107–125, copyright 1994, with permission from Elsevier.

As shown in Figure 13-1, the corrective maintenance work process
is made up of several tasks. The majority of maintenance errors cited
in incident investigations occur in the execution task. However, many
times contributing factors, committed in other parts of this or other
work processes, contribute to the commission of the unsafe act in the
execution task. For example, if procedures referenced in a work package are not appropriate for a specific task, resulting in a maintenance
error, a contributing cause is an error that occurred in the planning
task. Another example is when procedures referenced in work packages
are deficient. In this case, a contributing cause is the deficient procedure. This indicates an error somewhere within the procedure-writing
work process.

The strength of WPAM is that it models the way in which plants
actually conduct work. It can be used to link organizational factors to
these activities. As part of the development of WPAM, Jacobs and
Haber (1994) identified 20 organizational factors related to nuclear
power plant safety. Examples are goal prioritization, resource allocation, technical knowledge, and communications.

Data Analysis

The nuclear power industry has developed several techniques for data
analysis that are used to analyze operational experience for common
causes or common characteristics. These tools are used to identify underlying organizational and programmatic (O&P) issues responsible for
many past events or conditions—that is, local or global O&P issues.

Root Cause Analysis

Root cause analysis (RCA) is a key element of organizational learning. The Joint Commission on Accreditation of Healthcare Organizations (JCAHO) provides guidance on how to do an RCA in health care (1996). It focuses on "sentinel" events, that is, unexpected variations in a medical process. It acknowledges that "all clinical processes are part of larger systems in the organization. Therefore, special cause variation in performance that occurs in the care of patients is frequently the result of common causes in organization systems." The proposed methodology answers the standard questions of RCA: What happened? Why did it happen? What was the proximate cause? What processes were involved? Methods recommended for answering these questions are Pareto charts; scatter diagrams; failure mode, effect, and criticality analysis; fault tree analysis; barrier analysis; and change analysis.

However, as is the case even in some high-hazard industries, the recent developments in human error theory have not been incorporated into these root cause analyses in health care. The emphasis is on identifying the immediate proximate causes, for example, an individual's error or equipment malfunction. As Leape (1994) observes, this results in punishment "through opprobrium or peer disapproval." Several researchers have pointed out that blaming individuals is not the right response to incidents and near misses because human errors have their roots in the organization itself (Leape, 1994; Staender, Kaufmann, and Scheidegger, 2000).

The practice in the nuclear industry follows the general approach that the JCAHO describes. The difference is highlighted by recent work by a research team at MIT (Weil and Apostolakis, 1999). A systematic methodology has been developed for searching for organizational deficiencies utilizing the concept of work processes and Reason's (1990, 1997) model for human performance. The five major steps of this methodology are described in the following subsections.

Step 1: Description of the Incident

In this step, the investigator recreates the incident, determines the conditions prior to the incident, and maps out its progression. A case example from health care could be as follows. An anesthesiologist is in charge of the anesthesia for an elderly patient about to undergo a prostatectomy. It is going to be a long case, and the patient has expressed preference for general anesthesia. The patient is very anxious, so in the operating room prior to induction, the anesthesiologist begins to sedate him intravenously with a combination of diazepam and fentanyl. During preoxygenation with 100% oxygen, the patient's face suddenly flushes and he appears to seize, jerking about in an uncoordinated fashion. He is not breathing very well, and the anesthesiologist is unable to communicate with him. After ventilating him with 100% oxygen, the anesthesiologist discovers that the syringe of fentanyl, a narcotic, is still full, but the syringe of succinylcholine, a muscle relaxant (paralyzing agent) is not. The anesthesiologist quickly realizes he has switched one drug for the other. Drug switches are common, with potentially disastrous consequences if not recognized and appropriately treated.

Step 2: Identification of Hardware and Operator Contributions

After completing the description of the incident, the investigator begins analyzing it. At this point, the investigator should have a clear idea of the circumstances surrounding the incident, and the failures that caused it. The investigator begins organizing the incident by separating it into its constituent parts. The number of different constituents depends on the complexity of the incident. In simple incidents such as individual equipment failures (e.g., a valve failing to respond because of a short circuit), there may be only one constituent part (in this case, the short circuit). However, in severe incidents, operator errors, and hardware failures hindering recovery actions, there may be several constituent parts. Each constituent of the incident represents either a piece of hardware or an operator action that contributed to the incident. For the purpose of this methodology, hardware constituents are referred to as *contributors,* whereas human constituents are referred to as *contributions.*

In our health care example, there is only a human contribution, the drug switch, but there are potential latent hardware factors.

Step 3: Classification of Event Constituents as Preinitiator or Postinitiator

Having identified the constituent parts of the incident, they are further separated into preinitiator and postinitiator. The term *initiator* denotes the start of the incident under investigation. This distinction is more appropriate for operator contributions than hardware contributors. Operator contributions would be analogous to, for example, a surgeon or an anesthesiologist performing a certain task. In our example, the operator contribution would be the switching of the drugs.

Subsequent to the initiation of an incident, if necessary, operators begin recovery actions. During recovery, the context surrounding their actions is markedly different from their actions before the start of the incident. For one, there is usually a higher degree of stress and increased time pressure. Additionally, their behavior could be more error-prone knowledge-based behavior, as opposed to the rule-based behavior found in preinitiator operating conditions (Rasmussen, 1986). Therefore, we would clearly expect to find a much different set of circumstances surrounding the actions of operators in the two different time frames. As a result, the investigator would analyze the two different classes of operator actions from a different vantage point. Hardware contributors, on the other hand, are not as sensitive to preinitiator and postinitiator states. Hardware is not affected by time pressure and stress like its human counterparts.

In the health care example, the analyst would recognize that the unsafe act of unintentionally swapping the drugs was the initiating event. The recovery actions necessary by the anesthesiologist would be noted; namely, the patient would be ventilated until the muscle relaxant wore off, and then the patient would be nurtured to safety.

Step 4: Identification and Analysis of Human Contributions

The next step in the methodology is to determine what, if any, organizational deficiencies contributed to the human contributions. Using the hardware contributors as starting points, the investigator traces them back to their organizational roots, if any, as shown in Figure 13-2. The investigator analyzes both human contributions and hardware contributors.

After identifying a human contribution, its place in the organization—defined by which program it occurred in, which work process, and which task within the work process—is identified. Once the investigator identifies where a human contribution occurred, this suggests additional places to look for other human contributions and contributing factors.

Although Figure 13-2 shows a clear distinction among programs, work processes, and tasks and implies a hierarchical relationship among them, in actuality the lines between different programs and even between programs and work processes are blurred. For example, it is not uncommon for a work process to belong to more than one program. In any case, following the determination of where in the organization the human contribution belongs, organizational deficiencies that facilitated its occurrence are sought.

Human contributions are classified according to Reason's terminology because, depending on the classification, the terminology suggests where to look for organizational deficiencies. For example, if an investigator classifies a human contribution as a psychological precursor, then the investigator may want to look for line management deficiencies and, subsequently, the fallible decisions contributing to them. Alternatively, if an investigator classifies a human contribution as a

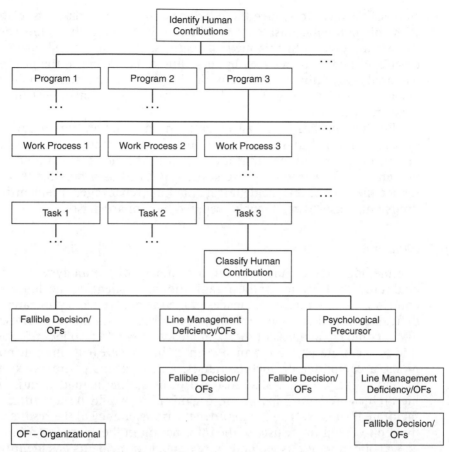

FIGURE 13-2   Identification and analysis of human contributions to an incident (Weil and Apostolakis, 1999)

senior management fallible decision, he may want to look for other fallible decisions contributing to its occurrence. In this fashion, the investigator will trace human contributions back to their organizational roots.

For our health care example, we would recognize that the counterpart work process would be the delivery of the anesthesia. A work process is generally a sequence of tasks, each task handled by a different team. The delivery of the anesthesia is performed primarily by the anesthesiologist. This would be identified as a weakness in the work process in that checks and balances are not provided as a safety measure. For example, in the United Kingdom, for other reasons, technicians give the narcotics and also help out the anesthesiologist. The investigation of this event would lead to consideration of existing safeguards as possible ways to reduce the overload of tasks and risks associated with this particular unsafe act. Additionally, building the database of events analyzed with this method might show that the risk of other unsafe acts could be reduced by including a technician in the process. An analysis of the cost benefit of this recommendation would be needed to decide if it was less than the total accumulated cost of adverse events.

Further analysis would also identify needed elaboration in how the drugs are labeled and packaged. Both drugs are transparent and are drawn in 10-cc syringes that are identical and not preidentified. Involvement of other work processes is suggested as a possible way to reduce the risks of this incident (e.g., having prepackaged, preidentified drugs with easy-to-read labels prepared by a pharmacist).

Step 5: Output

The methodology culminates with a summary of the analysis that includes the identification of the organizational deficiencies, the dominant contributors, and the consequences of the incident. Each organizational deficiency is tied to a specific human contribution via the work process.

A complete analysis of the example event would also identify such things as counterpart line management in health care (e.g., in some hospitals, a committee of doctors, nurses, and surgeons performs as line management; a floor walker also performs as line management). The hierarchical relationships in the organization would be identified to facilitate the analysis and to improve the transparency of the results delivered to the ultimate user of the information in the operating room.

Application of this methodology to nuclear incidents has identified six organizational factors that have influenced human performance in the majority of near misses, as well as the specific tasks in the work process in which they have had an impact (see Table 13-1).

Accident Sequence Precursor Analysis

The nuclear power industry calls near misses "accident precursors" (Minarick, 1990; NRC, 1992; Sattison et al., 1995; Budnitz et al., 1998). Feedback from a strong precursor analysis program has assisted the industry in having a continually improving safety record over the last 15 years (Poloski et al., 1999). This analysis proceeds prospectively, in a direction opposite to that of root cause analysis. Given the precursor, the analysis identifies the events that prevented the precursor from leading to an undesirable consequence (typically, damage to the reactor core). This is achieved by "mapping" the event onto the event and fault trees of the plant's probabilistic risk assessment (PRA) model.

TABLE 13-1   Important Organizational Factors

Communication	Refers to the exchange of information, both formal and informal	Pervasive—most important between different units and departments
Formalization	Refers to the extent to which there are well-identified rules, procedures, and/or standardized methods for routine activities and unusual occurrences	Execution
Goal prioritization	Refers to the extent to which plant personnel acknowledge and follow the stated goals of the organization and the appropriateness of those goals	Prioritization
Problem identification	Refers to the extent to which plant personnel use their knowledge to identify potential problems	Planning, scheduling, and return to normal line-up
Roles and responsibilities	Refers to the degree to which work activities are clearly defined and the degree to which plant personnel carry out those work activities	Execution
Technical knowledge	Refers to the depth and breadth of requisite understanding that plant personnel have regarding plant design and systems, and the phenomena and events that bear on their safe and reliable operation	Job-specific knowledge—execution; broad-based knowledge—prioritization, planning, scheduling, and other tasks

Source: Weil and Apostolakis (1999).

The purpose of the accident sequence precursor (ASP) analysis is to determine how close the precursor came to being an accident with undesirable consequences. Human recovery—the ability of operators to detect, localize, and correct system faults caused by either human error or technical failure—is critical to understanding how to improve both systems and training perspectives.

The three primary steps of precursor analysis are as follows. After a precursor event occurs, the first step is to gather relevant information about the event. The information that is gathered includes items such as what components failed, which human actions were in error, what was the chronology of events, and what were the complicating factors. Then, after the information-gathering step, one maps the event onto the PRA model, that is, onto the event and fault trees that depict the potential accident sequences. This step entails setting up the risk model conditional on the precursor event. The last step represents the numerical calculation of the relevant risk metrics, for example, the probability of damaging the

Initiating Event	Safety System 1:	Safety System 2:	Consequences
Doctor calculates the wrong dosage, resulting in under- or overdosing of the patient.	Pharmacist declines to prescribe miscalculated dose until doctor reviews medical chart or doctor is called back or prescription is sent back noting needed modifications; doctor reissues a correct prescription.	Nurse questions suitability of drug knowing condition of patient (e.g., approximate weight and severity of illness), bringing these to attention of doctor, who then adjusts prescription.	

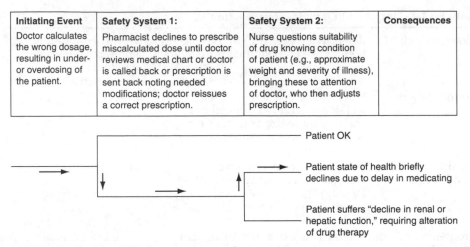

Patient OK

Patient state of health briefly declines due to delay in medicating

Patient suffers "decline in renal or hepatic function," requiring alteration of drug therapy

FIGURE 13-3   Example of a precursor analysis

reactor core, conditional on the occurrence of the precursor. A systematic analysis of near misses similar to the precursor analysis found in the nuclear industry does not exist in the health care industry.

As an example of this analysis, we look at a near miss in which a doctor prescribes the wrong drug dosage, the pharmacist fails to notice it, but a nurse questions the prescribed dosage and brings it to the attention of the doctor. The event tree of Figure 13-3 shows the possible scenarios. The scenario with the arrows shows what actually happened. It also shows that the only event that prevented a more serious consequence was the nurse bringing her observation to the attention of the doctor. One can proceed and estimate the probability that the nurse would have failed to do this. This is the conditional probability of a serious consequence for this near miss. From the risk management perspective, one may consider adding additional safeguards so that the probability of preventing the recurrence of this scenario will be smaller. This analysis requires event and fault trees, that is, a PRA-like risk model for the organization.

Efforts are now being taken to create medical near miss incident reporting systems (NMIRS) (Gambino and Mallon, 1991; van der Schaff, 1998) to supplement the limited data available through mandatory reporting systems focused on preventable deaths and serious injuries. Analysis of near misses versus adverse outcomes offers several advantages (Barach and Small, 2000):

1. Near misses occur two to three hundred times more frequently, enabling quantitative analysis.
2. Fewer barriers to data collection exist, allowing analysis of interrelationships of small failures.

3. Recovery strategies can be studied to enhance proactive interventions and de-emphasize the culture of blame.
4. Hindsight bias is more effectively reduced.

A Perspective on Data Analysis

The "facts" for the analysis are obtained by reviewing completed investigations (root cause or apparent cause) and "bucketing" the information in several key dimensions. The distribution of the inappropriate actions in the various dimensions identifies common causes or characteristics of an organization. Therefore, the standard process for analysis can be summarized as follows:

1. The results of completed investigations are reviewed from problem-reporting documentation.
2. Inappropriate actions identified in these investigations are recategorized into multiple key dimensions. The following primary dimensions are utilized:
   a. Organization (e.g., professional group)
   b. Work process
   c. Key activity
   d. Organizational/programmatic failure mode
   e. Human error failure mode
   f. Human error type (skill based, rule based, knowledge based)
   Other dimensions may be used to facilitate the common-cause effort (e.g., task performance frequency, task complexity).
3. The distribution of the inappropriate actions in the listed dimensions may be analyzed using a number of methods, such as Pareto charts and statistical analysis.
4. Dominant areas of "common characteristic" are identified, validated with the management team, and then investigated using sophisticated root cause analysis techniques.
5. Corrective actions identified are then implemented and monitored for effectiveness during the next common-cause analysis.

It is important to emphasize that the goal of RCA and ASP analysis is increased understanding of processes and systems, not identification of blame. It does not help patients merely to shift blame from front-line workers (doctors, nurses, and pharmacists) to middle and upper managers. Managers (even CEOs) are also embedded in complex systems that give them inadequate information and feedback and reward them for behaviors that appear beneficial in the short run but have hidden long-term consequences. RCA and ASP analysis help to expose systemic problems. These methods help sensitize people at all levels to defects and traps hidden in equipment, routines, and so forth, including the broader consequences of their intentional and unintentional acts (Carroll, 1998). Such participation also generates support for change among stakeholder groups whose work will be affected.

Assessment of Safety Culture

The IAEA has developed guidelines for use by Assessment of Safety Culture in Organizations Teams (ASCOT) (IAEA, 1994). The objective is to biopsy and assess the effectiveness of safety culture in a nuclear facility. The review is not an audit against set standards, but rather an opportunity to share experiences or good practices. The part that deals with organizational learning uses indicators such as the existence of clear instructions for incident reporting and the existence of formal means for learning from operating experience. Adapting the ASCOT guidelines to health care, focusing on organizational learning and the identification of relevant performance indicators for health care, could offer major insights into adverse events and near misses in health care.

In the health care industry, the JCAHO has provided guidelines for the assessment of the environment of care (JCAHO, 1998). The JCAHO requires health care organizations to design and implement a safety management plan that provides processes for the "ongoing monitoring of performance regarding actual or potential risk related to one or more of the following: staff knowledge and skills; level of staff participation; monitoring and inspection activities; emergency and incident reporting; or inspection, preventive maintenance, and testing of equipment." In other words, incident reporting does not necessarily have to be monitored by the hospital in order for the hospital to be accredited. However, the JCAHO recognizes the unique operating conditions that must exist at different health care organizations (e.g., due to specialization of care at some facilities, the effects of parent HMOs, and the restrictions imposed by insurance) and therefore the limitations of designing an assessment method for surveying "the 5,000 member hospitals in the nation every three years" (Gerlin, 1999). The ASCOT approach is a more formal approach than what the JCAHO has recommended and can be adapted to health care organizations.

Differences and Similarities Between Nuclear Power and Health Care Organizations

As mentioned earlier, nuclear power plants are heavily regulated. This has important implications for their organizational structure. Nuclear plants divide and subdivide labor to allow for specialization. As a consequence of these divisions, work must be coordinated to ensure that each unit receives the necessary input to meet its objective and that the different unit objectives are compatible with the overall objective of the organization. The prime coordinating mechanisms at plants are work processes. Other coordinating mechanisms include programs and procedures. A *work process* is a sequence of tasks designed to achieve a specific goal. A work process is carried out by a number of teams at different times. A *program* (e.g., the corrective action program) is a term used by plants to organize groups of work processes. It reflects a high-level policy. A *procedure* can be defined as a sequence of steps designed to perform a specific task, usually implemented by one team.

We have cited Mintzberg's (1979) definitions of machine and professional bureaucracies. A health care organization can be modeled as a professional bureaucracy that includes aspects of a machine bureaucracy, namely, work processes. Work processes are found to be a coordinating mechanism in several key areas of a health care organization (e.g., the drug delivery system can be modeled as a sequence of tasks). The work of nurses is very prescriptive and regulated and can benefit from the identification and analysis of the underlying processes of a machine bureaucracy. The prescriptive approach to nursing is evident in their increased rate of reporting of incidents (Taylor-Adams et al., 1999). When nurses were asked why they report incidents, the response was that this was the way it was done, that this was the protocol. This prototypical infrastructure could allow the development of models that could guide decision makers in developing more effective contexts of operation. For example, a model of the tasks of intensive care unit nurses can help management understand and communicate the risks associated with changing staffing levels of specific departments. A specific use of the model of the infrastructure would be for the rational allocation of resources by management and other health care providers. The risk associated with short-staffing the operating rooms, for example, can be addressed with respect to costs and the impact of this type of organizational change on the sharp end of the organization. In other words, administrators would now be able to more concretely address whether this change in management would create error-forcing contexts associated with high risks of adverse events.

The standardization of skills for professionals is an ongoing process throughout their careers. It is done through training processes that can also be modeled as sequences of tasks similar to work processes. However, for physicians, standardization is rarely the case, providing significant variations that contribute to error-forcing contexts. For example, a large hospital has 26 orthopedic surgeons, and insists on having eight different equipment kits to replace a hip. Maintaining the different types of kits is costly, requires costly additional training, and provides opportunities for mix-ups and misapplied maintenance.

Modeling this type of standardization emphasizes the need to ask whether we can reduce the number of kits that deal with one type of operation. The identification and further development of organizational learning mechanisms that use the adapted nuclear methods can affect the safety culture of the organization (as well as the institutionalized safety culture of the medical industry) by raising the issue and initiating investigations into simplifications of certain techniques.

Both the organizational differences and similarities between nuclear power and the health care industry affect the whole cycle of organizational learning in health care. For example, root cause analysis should identify the work processes involved and the particular tasks in which errors occurred. In a purely professional bureaucracy (e.g., the anesthesiologist independently prepares and delivers the necessary drugs), such a step is not required but can be beneficial in identifying weaknesses such as a lack of checks and balances found in the autonomous delivery of the drug by the anesthesiologist. The dissemination of lessons learned is also facilitated by the existence of work processes; the work process ensures that the protocols of specific tasks (as well as individual training) are modified to address these organizational deficiencies.

In a purely professional bureaucracy, one has to rely on the training of individuals to a much larger extent. However, because of the high rate of change in the health care industry's technical core (both the procedures performed by health care practitioners and the machines used for performing procedures) and the economic constraints of today's health care market, the training of individuals necessitates additional safeguards for continued maintenance and improvements to the level of care provided. Brennan (2000) leaves the "creativity and commitment" of reducing medical errors to doctors and nurses, an operating core already burdened by trying to keep pace with new procedures and machines while meeting the increasing demands for a cost-effective industry. Hospital administrators and even accreditation commissions should play a more proactive role in designing an organization that can (1) learn from near misses (as well as adverse events) and (2) provide a framework and the necessary tools for the organization to learn.

The regulatory environment in the nuclear industry fosters openness and the public disclosure of equipment malfunctions and near misses. The utilities must report to the NRC all "abnormal" events by submitting Licensee Event Reports (this system is currently being revised with industry cooperation; the new system is Equipment Performance and Information Exchange [Baranowsky et al., 1999]). For more significant occurrences, the NRC forms augmented inspection teams that investigate the incident and issue detailed reports. Similar mandatory reporting systems do not exist in health care (Barach and Small, 2000). Thus, some of the information needed for meaningful analysis is lacking. Of course, the litigious environment in the health care industry is a real concern, whereas in the nuclear industry it is nonexistent.

Conclusions

Nuclear power, like many other high-risk industries, exists in a highly charged political, financial, and legal environment. Despite the high-risk milieu of the nuclear power industry, no penalties are associated with reporting close calls or safety challenges. The Three Mile Island accident led to the emergence of industry-wide norms that supported additional regulation. The dread of even a single potential catastrophe and its implications for all industry members outweighed any objection to widespread safety changes. Backed by communal pressure, local proactive safety methods became institutionalized and effective across the industry. The most important lessons include the following:

- Poorly designed processes and cultural weaknesses cause the majority of human errors.
- Prevention of human errors costs less than dealing with the consequences.
- Performance monitoring and trending are essential to human error reduction.
- A good corrective action program is essential.
- Integrated efforts in error prevention, detection, and correction, ranging from the senior management levels to the individual contributors, are critical to sustained performance improvement.

Finally, we note that the intensified approach to process improvement through a focus on safety in the nuclear power industry has led to financial gains through power production enhancement (fewer outages, shutdowns, and reduction of capacity).

References

Apostolakis, G. E. (1999). "Organizational Factors and Nuclear Power Plant Safety." In: *Nuclear Safety: A Human Factors Perspective,* J. Misumi, B. Wilpert, and R. Miller (eds.). Padstow, UK: T.J. International, 145–159.

Apostolakis, G., Bier, V. M., and Mosleh, A. (1988). "A Critique of Recent Models for Human Error Rate Assessment." *Reliability Engineering and System Safety,* 22, 201–217.

Apostolakis, G., and Wu, J-S. (1995). "A Structured Approach to the Assessment of the Quality Culture in Nuclear Installations." In:

Proceedings of the International Topical Meeting on Safety Culture in Nuclear Installations. La Grange Park, IL: American Nuclear Society.

Barach, P., and Small, S. D. (2000). "Reporting and Preventing Medical Mishaps: Lessons from Non-medical Near Miss Reporting Systems." *British Journal of Medicine,* 320, 759–763.

Baranowsky, P., Mays, S., et al. (1999). "Operating Experience Risk Analysis Branch Program Overview." NRC staff presentation to the Advisory Committee on Reactor Safeguards, meeting of the Joint Subcommittee on Reliability and Probabilistic Risk Assessment, Rockville, MD, December 15–16.

Barriere, M., Bley, D., Cooper, S., et al. (1998). *Technical Basis and Implementation Guidelines for a Technique for Human Event Analysis (ATHEANA).* Report NUREG-1624. Washington, DC: Nuclear Regulatory Commission.

Bea, R. G. (1998). "Human and Organizational Factors: Engineering Operating Safety into Offshore Structures." *Reliability Engineering and System Safety,* 61, 109–126.

Becker, G. (1997). "Event Analysis and Regulation: Are We Able to Discover Organizational Factors?" In: *After the Event,* A. Hale, B. Wilpert, and M. Freitag (eds.). New York: Pergamon Press, 197–214.

Brennan, T. A. (2000). "Sounding Board." *New England Journal of Medicine,* 342, no. 15, 1123–1125.

Budnitz, R. J., Lambert, H. E., Apostolakis, G., et al. (1998). *A Methodology for Analyzing Precursors to Earthquake-Initiated and Fire-Initiated Accident Sequences.* Report NUREG/CR-6544. Washington, DC: Nuclear Regulatory Commission.

Carroll, J. S. (1998). "Organizational Learning Activities in High-Hazard Industries: The Logics Underlying Self-Analysis." *Journal of Management Studies,* 35, 699–717.

Davoudian, K., Wu, J-S., and Apostolakis, G. (1994a). "The Work Process Analysis Model." *Reliability Engineering and System Safety,* 45, 107–125.

Davoudian, K., Wu, J-S., and Apostolakis, G. (1994b). "Incorporating Organizational Factors into Risk Assessment Through the Analysis of Work Processes." *Reliability Engineering and System Safety,* 45, 85–105.

Dougherty, E. M. (1990). "Human Reliability Analysis — Where Shouldst Thou Turn?" *Reliability Engineering and System Safety,* 29, 283–299.

Gambino, R., and Mallon, O. (1991). "Near Misses — An Untapped Database to Find Root Causes." *Lab Report,* 13, 41–44.

Gerlin, A. (1999). "Curing a Culture of Its Denial, Part 4." *Philadelphia Inquirer,* 15 September, A1.

Hollnagel, E. (1993). *Human Reliability Analysis: Context and Control.* London: Academic Press.

Hurst, N. W., Bellamy, L. J., Geyer, T. A. W., and Astley, J. A. A. (1991). "A Classification Scheme for Pipework Failures to Include Human and Sociotechnical Errors and Their Contribution to Pipework Failure Frequencies." *Journal of Hazardous Materials,* 26, 159–186.

International Atomic Energy Agency (IAEA). (1991). *Safety Culture.* Safety Series no. 75-INSAG-5. Vienna: International Nuclear Safety Advisory Group.

International Atomic Energy Agency (IAEA). (1994). *ASCOT Guidelines.* Vienna: International Nuclear Safety Advisory Group.

Jacobs, R., and Haber, S. (1994). "Organizational Processes and Nuclear Power Plant Safety." *Reliability Engineering and System Safety,* 45, 75–83.

Joint Commission on Accreditation of Healthcare Organizations (JCAHO). (1996). *Conducting a Root Cause Analysis in Response to a Sentinel Event.* Oakbrook Terrace, CA: Joint Commission on Accreditation of Healthcare Organizations.

Joint Commission on Accreditation of Healthcare Organizations (JCAHO). (1998). "Management of the Environment of Care." *CAMH Refreshed Core,* Section 2. Oakbrook Terrace, CA: Joint Commission on Accreditation of Healthcare Organizations.

LaPorte, T. R., and Consolini, P. M. (1991). "Working in Practice but Not Theory: Theoretical Challenges of 'High-Reliability Organizations.'" *Journal of Public Administration and Research,* 1, no. 1, 19–47.

Leape, L. L. (1994). "Error in Medicine." *Journal of the American Medical Association,* 272, no. 23, 1851–1857.

Minarick, J. W. (1990). "The US NRC Accident Sequence Precursor Program: Present Methods and Findings." *Reliability Engineering and System Safety,* 27, 23–51.

Mintzberg, H. (1979). *The Structuring of Organizations.* Englewood Cliffs, NJ: Prentice-Hall.

Nuclear Regulatory Commission (NRC). (1992). *Proceedings of an NRC Workshop on the Use of PRA Methodology for the Analysis of Reactor Events and Operational Data.* Report NUREG/CP-0124. Washington, DC: Nuclear Regulatory Commission.

Nuclear Regulatory Commission (NRC). (1997). *NRC Information Digest.* Report NUREG-1350, vol. 9. Washington, DC: Nuclear Regulatory Commission.

Nuclear Regulatory Commission (NRC). (1999). *White Paper.* Washington, DC: Nuclear Regulatory Commission.

Nuclear Regulatory Commission (NRC). (2000). *Strategic Plan, Appendix: Fiscal Year 2000–Fiscal Year 2005.* Draft Report NUREG-1614, vol. 2, part 2. Washington, DC: Nuclear Regulatory Commission.

Papazoglou, I. A., and Aneziris, O. (1999). "On the Quantification of the Effects of Organizational and Management Factors in Chemical Installations." *Reliability Engineering and System Safety,* 63, 33–45.

Paté-Cornell, M. E. (1990). "Organizational Aspects of Engineering System Safety: The Case of Offshore Platforms." *Science,* 250, 1210–1217.

Paté-Cornell, M. E., and Fischbeck, P. S. (1993). "PRA as a Management Tool: Organizational Factors and Risk-Based Priorities for the Maintenance of the Tiles of the Space Shuttle Orbiter." *Reliability Engineering and System Safety,* 40, 239–257.

Perrow, C. (1984). *Normal Accidents.* New York: Basic Books.

Poloski, J. P., Marksberry, D. G., Atwood, C. L., and Galyean, W. J. (1999). *Rates of Initiating Events at U.S. Nuclear Power Plants: 1987–1995.* Report NUREG/CR-5750. Washington, DC: Nuclear Regulatory Commission.

Rasmussen, J. (1986). *Information Processing and Human-Machine Interaction: An Approach to Cognitive Engineering.* New York: North-Holland.

Reason, J. T. (1990). *Human Error.* New York: Cambridge University Press.

Reason, J. T. (1997). *Managing the Risks of Organizational Accidents.* Aldershot, UK: Ashgate.

Roberts, K. H. (1990). "Some Characteristics of One Type of High Reliability Organization." *Organizational Science,* 2, 160–176.

Sattison, M. B., Thatcher, T. A., Knudsen, J. K., Schroeder, J. A., and Siu, N. O. (1995). "Advanced Accident Sequence Precursor Analysis, Level 1 Models." Paper presented at the Twenty-Third U.S. NRC Water Reactor Safety Information meeting, Bethesda, MD, October.

Staender, S., Kaufmann, M., and Scheidegger, D. (2000). "Critical Incident Reporting. Approaches in Anaesthesiology." In: *Safety in Medicine.* Oxford, UK: Elsevier Science, 65–81.

Sträter, O., and Bubb, H. (1999). "Assessment of Human Reliability Based on Evaluation of Plant Experience: Requirements and Implementation." *Reliability Engineering and System Safety,* 63, 199–219.

Swain, A. D., and Guttmann, H. E. (1983). *Handbook of Human Reliability Analysis with Emphasis on Nuclear Power Plant Applications.* Report NUREG/CR-1278. Washington, DC: Nuclear Regulatory Commission.

Taylor-Adams, S. E., Vincent, C., and Stanhope, N. (1999). "Applying Human Factors Methods to the Investigation and Analysis of Clinical Adverse Events." *Safety Science,* 31, 143–159.

Van der Schaff, T. W. (1998). "Hospital-wide Versus Nationwide Event Reporting: An Empirical Framework Based on Single-Department Studies in Hospitals." In: *Proceedings of Enhancing Patient Safety and Reducing Errors in Health Care.* Rancho Mirage, CA: Annenberg Center, 190–192.

Weart, S. R. (1988). *Nuclear Fear: A History of Images.* Cambridge, MA: Harvard University Press.

Weil, R., and Apostolakis, G. (1999). "Identification of Important Organizational Factors Using Operating Experience." Paper presented at the Third International Conference on Human Factor Research in Nuclear Power Operations, Mihama, Japan, September 8–10.

CHAPTER FOURTEEN

TRIAL AND ERROR IN MY QUEST TO BE A PARTNER IN MY HEALTH CARE: A PATIENT'S STORY*

Roxanne Goeltz and Martin J. Hatlie, JD

Authors' Note

Presented here is the personal narrative of a cancer patient named Roxanne Goeltz who has become quietly—but firmly—determined to be an actual, functioning, decision-making partner in the treatment of her disease, a thymoma that was first discovered in her chest cavity in July 2000. Keep in mind two factors as you read her story. First, Ms. Goeltz's brother, Mike, died in a hospital from what the health care literature would call an "unexpected adverse outcome" about 6 months before her journey into health care with her cancer diagnosis. The family suspects medical error in that case, but has not sued. Second, Ms. Goeltz is an air traffic controller by profession and, as such, a seasoned professional player in a complex, dynamic system that is constantly managing the risk of failure.

Ms. Goeltz's experiences are presented with commentary by Martin J. Hatlie, JD, a lawyer who also is the president of Partnership for Patient Safety, an initiative that works with consumers and health care systems to advance the safety and reliability of health care services worldwide.

Goeltz

Having looked over notes I've taken in the last 2 years, I realize the journey I have been on to be a partner in my care is not over and probably never will be. To get where I am now has been a struggle of self-education, since there are no resources readily available to teach me how to be an effective patient partner. In the health care arena of today, the very notion of clinician–patient partnering is only a small seed. Consumers who are trying to be partners with their health care providers are not likely to speak or think in terms of being a partner. What motivated me was my brother's death and the realization we—the patient and/or family members and friends—have our part to play in increasing our safety in the health care system. From that idea grew the belief that I had to be an effective partner with the people treating me.

You can tell if you're dealing with a person like me, because I'm the one asking pointed questions and pushing when I have to for direct and honest answers. I'm also the one doing my own research and bringing in data to back up my concerns. I think you often see patients like me as "difficult" because we may not easily fit into the way your office works or maybe the way you work. The health care worker in today's system does not have time to establish the connection that is needed for a meaningful encounter with a partnering patient. Patients like me are not likely to fall in line with the time frame allotted for the appointment. We have learned to understand that your work is time-pressured and driven by economics. However, we can't accept it because to do so would be irresponsible to our families and ourselves. When you establish a "one-way" communication relationship, when you dictate the care you think we need or the circumstances in which we have to fit, when you state your medical opinion and send us out the door, we think you're taking the easy way out. If I'm going to be your partner, yes, I need to be fully informed and I want all the information and advice you have to give. I also need to be heard and to have my thoughts and feelings—including my fears—considered. I also want input into the strategy for what my care will be.

Hatlie Commentary

Recent pronouncements on patient safety from the National Institute of Medicine and others have called for a redesign of the health care system to be patient or family centered (National Institute of Medicine, 1999, 2001). Yet too often, an invisible wall separates patients and their clinicians that undermines both information exchange and empathic understanding between them. It is at least partially fair to say that this wall was built and is continually reinforced by a legal system that encourages patients and clinicians to become adversaries when something goes wrong. The adversarial system was championed by our forefathers as the best way to see that all factors in an event alleged to cause injury are reasonably brought out and presented to an impartial judge and/or peer jury. As medical malpractice litigation has evolved, however, it's become increasingly angry and sensational. The adversarial process of today more often presents juries with two or more distorted pictures of the facts, as opposed to different perspectives on what really happened. More important, it has undermined the free flow of communication and empathy between clinicians and patients that is crucial to producing optimal outcomes.

Ms. Goeltz works professionally in an industry that respects and relies on the contributions to safety of every team member and culturally strives to keep each person managing risk fully informed. She found herself being treated for cancer in a very different environment, where she wasn't made to feel like a member of the team and where her own sense of responsibility as a patient wasn't always acknowledged.

Goeltz

My brother died in September 1999. The first time I visited my clinic after his death was in February of 2000, for stuffiness and earaches that I couldn't shake. It was a very scary experience for me, and I went with my teenaged son, who had similar symptoms. When I think back on it, I wonder if my sickness was a sympathetic reaction to his, motivated by an unconscious decision that I was not going to let him go into a system I didn't trust by himself. I also wonder if I was so scared of the doctor that I needed another reason to get me there.

That visit did nothing to reassure me. There was no real interaction with the doctor. We sat; he listened to our symptoms, prescribed some pills to dry up our congestion, and then sent us on our way. Nothing made me feel like a partner. I took the prescriptions, had them filled, and started taking them without really paying any attention to what it was we were taking or why.

I went to the clinic again in May, for dizziness and various other rather vague symptoms, and remember sitting there, telling myself that I was going to talk to whoever saw me about what happened with my brother, because maybe what I was suffering from was depression. I chickened out, even though the health care worker was responsive and seemed interested in me. She listened attentively to the symptoms I gave her, but she also conveyed in her body language and manner that she did not have a lot of time. I did not want to impose, so I gave her a hurried and clipped explanation of how I felt. Why is it that when we go into the health care system we have come to feel that it is normal to have to hurry? I think we've learned that from our health care workers' example, because what's normal now is to get hurried, incomplete information from our clinicians. I left with a feeling I can only call resignation and instructions to "give it three more weeks" for my dizziness and other symptoms to go away.

I couldn't wait. Internally I was in sheer panic that there was something horribly wrong with me. I'd done some research on the Internet and came up with several possibilities. I had to find someone who would listen, so I called the nurse line that is available through my insurance. She was patient, listened to my symptoms, and suggested that I make an appointment with my doctor to be examined. When I told her my only doctor was a gynecologist, she recommended that I give that office a call. When I did so, the person who answered the telephone chastised me. To quote, "Doctor does not see patients for headaches. Call another department." She then ended the call, without any referrals or suggestions about where to find a different doctor. My response was to cry, telling myself that it was obvious why Mike died and feeling very sorry for myself because no one cared. But after a day of wallowing in self-pity, I realized that I had to take the initiative. It was my health and well-being at stake and I had a responsibility to take care of myself.

I went back to the clinic the next day. As I sat in the waiting room, I gave myself a pep talk about how I was going to speak up and talk until I was satisfied that someone heard what I had to say. But I chickened out again! It's amazing to me how I let the system intimidate me into being quiet. The doctor gave me an antibiotic for a slight ear infection and sent me home. I left with my tail between my legs beating myself up for being so weak!

Hatlie Commentary

Ms. Goeltz would agree that at this stage in her interaction with the health care system, she was not being an effective player. A defensive reader could argue with some legitimacy that she had no one to blame but herself—a sentiment that Ms. Goeltz would agree with as well. But as we dig deeper, a richer lesson can be learned.

What was going on with Ms. Goeltz? Many things, in fact. She had nonspecific symptoms that clearly were very worrisome but which she did not have the resources to self-diagnose. She also was grieving for her deceased brother and afraid of health care because that's where he died.* She also was angry and very confused about who to be angry with—herself or her health care providers.

From a systems point of view, all of these were risk factors contributing to Ms. Goeltz not getting—or even being able to effectively ask for—the care she needed. But, while her life circumstances were uniquely hers, many others in the patient population have stories, fears, and communication skill deficits of equal intensity.† These individualized risk factors are what make the challenge of achieving safety in health care exponentially harder than any other sector of human activity. Establishing reliable service models would be much easier if patients were standardized or their roles more contained.

Much has been made about transferring safety lessons learned in the commercial airline industry to health care. For health care providers, the analogies and extrapolations from airline crew risk management to clinician teams are relatively clear and instructive. Looking at the metaphor from a service recipient's point of view, however, reveals the increased magnitude of the safety challenge in health care. Airline passengers are rather fungible in terms of the risk factors they contribute to the safety equation. With the exception of intentional acts of terrorism, passengers have a much smaller role to play in creating risk and, accordingly, much less responsibility in managing risk than patients have.‡

If our social goal is to effectively manage risk in health care, we are called upon as a community to meet this challenge. Looking at Ms. Goeltz's account from a systems perspective, it is notable that she did manage to access the system on several occasions. There were, then,

---

*Mike's treatment did not occur in the same health care organization providing Ms. Goeltz's care.

†Public opinion polling indicates that more than 40% of the U.S. population believe that they themselves, a family member, or a close friend has been the victim of medical error (National Patient Safety Foundation, 1997). The collective fear about health system safety was palpable after the release of the IOM's first report on safety in November 1999. More than 50% of Americans followed that story for over a week, evincing its strong relevance to people's everyday concerns.

‡An interesting model, not explored extensively yet as a lesson for the health care system, is the measurably successful efforts in this country to change the cultural normalcy of getting behind the wheel of a car while intoxicated. The very public campaign of Mothers Against Drunk Drivers was successful in transforming social understanding as to who is accountable for managing this risk, essentially creating a model of shared responsibility among drivers who drink, their friends, those selling alcohol, the press, lawmakers, educators, and others. Arguably, in the effort to advance public safety, drunk drivers and patients "who don't do what they are supposed to do" have more in common than patients and airline passengers do.

several opportunities for the system to probe further into this patient's nonspecific complaints and generate trust. Rather than doing so, it conveyed the impression that the system and the people in it were too busy to care about patients' worries and fears.

Goeltz

I was so upset that when I got home I called the clinic again and made an appointment with an internal medicine specialist, asking for the first one who had an opening! The appointment was 3 weeks out and happened in June 2000. I will never forget this doctor for as long as I live. When I talked to him, I felt like I was stepping off a steep cliff. He not only caught me, but also in his words and manner encouraged me to keep jumping off each cliff I came to; I believed he would be there to support me. I shared all my symptoms, Mike's story, my fear of being written off as depressed, and my worry that depression was masking real physical problems. He listened without rushing me, calmly writing notes. He thought about what I had to say, and encouraged me to say more. I felt like he was pulling out of me the information I so wanted to discuss with someone who had expertise to help me decipher what was going on. We parted that day with a series of tests set up and a plan to look at the possibility of depression if the tests indicated I was sound physically. He asked me if I was in agreement with the route he had mapped out! I left there feeling much better about the health care system in general and remember thinking that maybe some of them did care and could be trusted. Although I didn't put it together at that moment, it was the beginning of partnering with my doctor!

One of the tests—a chest x-ray—identified a problem. The doctor had ordered it because I reported being short of breath, a symptom I was initially hesitant to reveal because I thought it was related to the weight I had gained and I was embarrassed! It was the doctor's respect for me and my resulting trust in him that encouraged me to share this vital piece of information. The x-ray came back showing a small shadow by my lungs, which prompted a CT scan identifying a mass in my chest.

Ever since Mike died I had preached to friends, family, coworkers—basically anyone who would listen—about how our family accepted part of the responsibility for his death. Mike was not aware of his own family medical history, which made him more vulnerable to a bad outcome than he should have been. Because the hospital was an unfamiliar environment, we should have been with him to support him. If we had been there, perhaps we could have answered questions or spoken up if he was too sick or intimidated to do so, supplying information to his doctors and nurses that might have made a difference. Instead we left him alone; he passed away without anyone knowing it. No one teaches us that mistakes can be made in hospitals—if anything, we are led to believe the opposite—but we should have known it and not been complacent. We also should have done our part in ensuring his safety.

I learned from my brother's death the importance of having someone with you 24 hours a day, 7 days a week while you are in the hospital. Based on my own experience, I also knew or should have known that it's also important to have someone accompany a patient to significant appointments as well. Once again, however, I didn't follow my own advice, and was alone when I learned of my test results. I ran from the doctor's office after being told I had the mass, wishing someone had been with me for the news yet simultaneously determined that I wasn't going to tell anyone. I would handle this by myself! I soon realized that would not be possible and asked God to give me the strength and dignity to deal with this part of my life.

My next appointment was with the cardiothoracic surgeon, during which I thought he was to do a biopsy of the mass to determine if it was cancer. I went to this appointment with a small infantry of supporters: my husband, son, stepson, and best friend. My husband went with me into the exam room. The first impression made by the surgeon was one of a gentle confidence, and our communication was an extraordinary example of what it means to be partners.

I was anxious to know whether the mass was cancer, and really wanted the biopsy that I was expecting done. He disagreed. But, rather than discounting my wishes or telling me what to do, he fully explained his rationale. The location and size of the mass next to my vital organs required it to be removed in his opinion, whether or not it was cancer. He advised that doing a biopsy and a subsequent surgery would put me through an unnecessary procedure, but he left it up to me to decide what I wanted to do. In that one episode of communication, I knew he was a person who respected and was listening to me. I felt I could share all my feelings and concerns with him, and I did. I made the decision to follow his advice before our appointment was over, and said "Let's take it out, I am ready. I have not eaten since before midnight, so let's do it now!"

He laughed and told me that things do not happen that quickly. He was going on vacation for 2 weeks and we could schedule it after that. I shook my head and told him I had a personal reason for wanting to have it happen this week; my son was in town from school and I wanted him to be here. He acknowledged that personal reason and suggested that one of his colleagues could do the surgery. I shook my head again, looked him in the eye and said, "No, I have just shared my most personal feelings and fears with you. I trust and want you to do the surgery." He looked at me for a few seconds. I felt just as confident as he seemed to be. Then he smiled and invited me to go with him to see his scheduler. I had surgery 2 days later, before he went on vacation!

While I was satisfied with myself for how I dealt with this surgeon, I must say that it only happened because he allowed it to happen. He partnered with me at the level I wanted and was capable of handling. He also invited me to call him if I had further concerns. I did so, the night before surgery as I was experiencing very cold feet. He responded to my page quickly, listened to my being nervous, and was very reassuring. I relaxed and thanked him, confident that the decision he helped me reach was the right one for me.

Hatlie Commentary

As Ms. Goeltz's story eloquently expresses, respect is an attitude. It's communicated and received in several ways, through words, tone of voice, body language, and responsiveness. Patients seeking medical attention are—virtually by definition—sick, injured, or, at least, worried. As such, they are intrinsically vulnerable and often react irrationally. Ms. Goeltz, like many patients, knew she should be doing things differently but, controlled by fear, she behaved in ways that made no sense even to her. When an intimidated patient can manage to communicate despite his or her fear or embarrassment, a truly existential moment in the relationship between healer and patient is created. If the doctor or nurse responds in a manner that acknowledges the dignity of the patient despite the patient's dependency, as well as acknowledging the patient's role as ultimate decision maker about what will be done to him or her, a much more functional relationship is created. If the "healer" responds with an attitude that is dismissive, that opportunity for a rich partnership relationship is squandered, and cynicism or anger eventually takes its place.

Goeltz's surgeon not only responded to her concerns respectfully, but in her view made the partnership "happen" by giving her the permission she needed to express her fears and embarrassing thoughts. As a group, surgeons are not renowned for their people skills, but from Goeltz's perspective the communication was direct and clear. Her surgeon gave her information and medical advice in language that she could understand and made it clear that the decision about treatment was hers to make. He then listened for her decision and responded to it. He did not underestimate her ability to deal with the information he provided. That interchange is what led her to trust and feel empowered and, in a very real way, responsible for her own treatment decisions. Her surgeon should bottle the formula and sell it. He'd make a fortune.

For nearly 13 years, I was the American Medical Association's strategist on tort reform. During that tenure, time and again I heard physicians lament the deterioration of the trusting relationship between patient and physician, more often than not blamed on the interference of the tort system. True, the tort system does position patients and clinicians as potential adversaries, and I agree that this is a disservice to both. The economics of reimbursement are perhaps an even more powerful disincentive to the establishment of a functional healer–patient relationship because of the pressure created for "efficient" use of time.

But the fact remains that clinicians continue to have the opportunity day to day, encounter by encounter, to establish trusting relationships with their patients. I believe that patients who feel like partners in their own treatment are also more likely to join with their health care providers in advocating for reimbursement reform and legal policies that support a strong physician–patient relationship. Conversely, clinicians who convey the message that they are too busy to listen or too distant to care about their patients' fears diminish the goodwill their patients historically have had toward their healers.

Goeltz

The first day after the surgery to remove the mass in my chest cavity, I suffered a pulmonary embolism. I had not been up or out of my bed for 32 hours after my surgery, in part because the nurses on my unit were clearly overworked. I had to urinate, and finally a nurse had time to help me. As I sat up at the edge of my bed, I became short of breath. But I had to pee! So, I did not say anything, and the nurse helped me to the bathroom. As I sat in the bathroom, I tried to concentrate on the task at hand but the breathing problems worsened. Telling the nurse that I could not breathe is the last thing I remember before realizing I was back in bed with my nurse putting an oxygen mask on me. As the nurse left to summon a doctor, I could see through my mask my 24/7 team member mouthing words of encouragement, "Stay calm, breathe slowly." I was really glad she was there.

Several people tried to convince me to "blame the nurse" for my embolism—especially other nurses!—but I don't think the fault is hers. She was the only nurse on duty that morning. She was covering two wings of patients, and every time she would get ready to help me she was called away to something more urgent. The system failed her and me. I also heard later that the surgeon had blamed himself. How ridiculous. I know embolisms are a risk of surgery and are not always preventable.

In the hospital, now recovering from both chest surgery and an embolism, the oncologist assigned to me saw me for the first time. By that time I must have had some kind of reputation, because he greeted me by saying "I was elected to come talk to you." He then told me I had a malignant thymoma. Unfortunately for me, he caught me in a gap of my 24/7 coverage and I was alone.* When I heard the word *malignant,* I shut out everything that came after it and began crying. The oncologist was impatient and asked what I was crying about. I told him I was upset because he had just told me I had cancer. He said he had not. What ensued could only be described as an argument. Shortly into it, the oncologist threw up his hands, said he would have someone else talk to me in the morning, and walked out.

I still can't believe he handled me so poorly. Essentially we were arguing over a technicality. My tumor was considered a malignant thymoma because of its location near vital organs (heart and lungs), but the cells making up the tumor did not appear to be cancer cells. I wanted to hear I did not have cancer, but even more than that I wanted the truth. I accepted the oncologist's explanation, but didn't really know if I should trust him because we had not established an interactive rapport, as I had with my other doctors. After my discharge from the hospital and during my first visit with my cardiothoracic surgeon, he made a statement that added to my confusion about the oncologist's explanation. "Now Roxanne, you know you have cancer," he told me. I believed him and was attempting to deal emotionally with that diagnosis, yet the statement by the oncologist that I didn't have cancer was something I desperately wanted to be the truth. It was a confusing situation at best, and it took over a year to sort out my feelings and the facts. In the end, the oncologist turned out to be the one who was technically wrong. My stage III thymoma had two "fingers" that had penetrated the sac that contained the tumor and penetrated my phrenic nerve. Technically, cancer is any type of cell that is able to infiltrate other cells or organs in your body. The fact that my rampant thymus cells had infiltrated my phrenic nerve made it cancer.

The difficult interchange between the oncologist and myself raises another argument for the importance of a 24/7 team. Cancer patients are going to be emotional, especially as they are wrestling with a new diagnosis. If the clinician can't deal with that, a good option is to talk to a supportive person, who can then work with the patient in a

---

*Going into this surgery I had organized among my friends and family 5 days of continuous 24/7 presence of someone in my room. The goal of this team is to ensure that someone is always there, asking the kinds of questions I would ask when I can't because I'm sleeping, drugged, or groggy. My hospital stay was longer than anticipated because of the pulmonary embolism, and the oncologist visited me on day 6, after the 24/7 coverage I organized was over.

supportive way to give them the information they need. I did want the truth and found other ways to get it when we were unable to respectfully communicate with each other.

Hatlie Commentary

Seasoned systems people understand how successful teams function. What do they do when confronted with a system that isn't effectively including the patient as a member of the team? Goeltz's solution was to organize an alternate team of her own that she could rely on to support and protect her in an environment she had the expertise to recognize was not very patient centered. Her attitude toward the postsurgical nurse also reflects an understanding of a basic safety principle: Blaming individuals for bad outcomes frequently masks underlying systems deficiencies that set workers like that nurse up to fail. As an air traffic controller, Goeltz works in an environment where teams share accountability and support one another when a bad outcome occurs. Individuals who blame each other or take complete responsibility themselves for a bad outcome sound wrong to her. It's everybody's job to manage risk.

Goeltz

In November 2000 I faced a second surgery for suspected ovarian cancer. I had cysts that appeared to be growing. Given that I had rampantly growing cells in my thymus, both my gynecologist and I were worried this could be serious. In consultation with my doctor, I decided to have an elective hysterectomy, which was done 3 months after the removal of my thymoma. Fortunately, tests showed it was not cancer.

The gynecologist reminded me of my cardiothoracic surgeon. She was very willing to give me all the information I requested and encouraged my active participation during appointments and in setting up the surgery, which was for suspected ovarian cancer. I wish I could say the same about all the people who worked with and around her. I know it is necessary for doctors to manage their time well and to keep from being overwhelmed with calls from patients. We both must rely on nurses and office personnel to be part of the treatment team. But my family has experienced office staff making statements about treatment issues that exceed their expertise, and we've experienced them editing information we think is important so that the doctor doesn't hear it. I am highly sensitive about this because it was a factor in my brother's death. My family has a history of aneurysms, which we shared with a nurse, who made the judgment that it wasn't relevant to what was going on with Mike. He died and I wonder to this day if he would have had a chance if that information we gave the nurse had been passed effectively to his doctors.

To determine if my radiation treatment needed to be interrupted or if we could wait until its completion before doing surgery, my oncologist ordered a CA-125 blood test. She explained that if the levels were high, ovarian cancer was very likely and we would want to do surgery right away. When I got home I got on the Internet and got all the particulars. Although my doctor had said the results would take a couple of days, when I called about them the nurse could not find any results, and she told me that it could take up to 2 weeks or longer. I waited instead of pushing back. I think I was tired of bucking the system at that moment and emotionally overwhelmed that I could be facing more cancer. I think the nurse was also overwhelmed when I called and said what she did basically to get me off the telephone. When I called 2 weeks later, the nurse said the same thing: She could not find the results. Clearly something about the process was wrong, and I was determined to do whatever had to be done to figure out what was going on. I began telling her what I knew, that I had the test taken at the hospital with my other labs for radiation treatment and coumadin monitoring. This prompted her to realize she needed to look in a different computer, because tests taken in the hospital are on a different computer system than those done at the clinic. In fact, the test results were probably available the first time I called. The nurse knew about the second computer system, and she had access to it. She just hadn't stopped to consider that they might be there.

Nothing bad happened to me as a result of this mix-up, since my CA-125 test results showed in the normal range. But, if it had not, 2 weeks would have been lost in dealing with ovarian cancer. The doctor was going to terminate my radiation to get me into surgery if the levels had been high, so I really believe those weeks would have been important if I had had cancer.

The health care system could have done two things to prevent this kind of thing from falling between the cracks. First, nurses could be trained to be more directly factual about what they do or do not know. During that first phone call, the nurse told me what she did either because she didn't know how long blood tests take or because she didn't have time to deal with me. Second, at the time the sample was taken from me, I could have been given more specific instructions about where to call or what to say about where the test was taken when I did call. Something as simple as "Your doctor will need to refer to the hospital computer to get these results" would have done it. Either of these steps would have given the nurse and I the opportunity to problem solve during the first conversation, instead of 2 weeks later.

What did I learn from this experience? It is that one cannot count on everyone in the health care system being trained well enough to ask the right questions or to be thorough enough to find answers. I was able to help my gynecologist's nurse do her job better, but I had to take the initiative. I suspect she didn't see me as a partner at all in achieving the goal of keeping me healthy. As I now advise everyone I talk to, if you're going to be a partner in your health care decisions, you have to drive the conversation until you get your questions answered. If you do not get an answer you are happy with, keep asking and pushing to get what you need to be informed.

Hatlie Commentary

Goeltz the air traffic controller knows a dangerous system when she sees or smells one. Although the mix-up she describes may have been "small" and no bad outcome was produced, systems people realize that these small failures too often combine with other small failures to cascade into full-blown disasters. Systems people are also trained to know that the most reliable teams are those that try hard to share information fully and accurately. Hurried conversations or statements asserted as fact when the speaker doesn't really know all the facts undermine effective team communication. They are a sign of unreliable system/team performance. And they lead to things like airplane accidents and patient injuries.

Goeltz

After my surgeries and radiation treatments, I had two follow-up appointments with the oncologist I'd clashed with earlier. I wanted to work with him and hoped that if we met under less stressful circumstances we could communicate. I brought information to our appointments I'd gathered through my own research to help establish my follow-up care plan. I truly believe I gave him a chance to work with me, but after two appointments I knew I had to trade him in. He would not discuss the studies I brought with me or address any of my concerns, pooh-poohing them as unimportant. His treatment plan was vague and he relayed it to me in a condescending manner. I had no say in what kind of protocol would be used for follow-up monitoring and care.

I wasn't interested in another confrontation with him, so I went to my primary care doctor and told her I wanted to see a different oncologist. Her back was turned to me when I said this, and I remember noticing her visibly tense up. I continued, saying I needed someone who was willing to consider my input and respond to my concerns. She listened and she agreed, giving me a referral and an appointment slip to see a new oncologist.

However, changing doctors was easier said than done. When I took the appointment slip to the front desk, the scheduler tried to set me up with my original oncologist. I calmly but firmly said no. She wouldn't accept my answer initially, and strongly advised me that doctors did not like it when other doctors saw their patients. I informed the scheduler it was a decision made with my primary care doctor and suggested she talk to her if she needed an explanation but that I wanted the referral I had been given. And by being firm and calm, she then became very helpful in setting up the appointment.

I went into that first appointment with the new oncologist with the conviction that I was going to lay out at the beginning how I wanted our relationship to be, then see if he was willing and able to be that kind of doctor for me. He was! He acknowledged my concerns and reviewed with me the data I had brought in on thymoma. Admitting he had only seen one other thymoma years ago in an elderly woman, he said he was willing to learn with me. Since there was not an established protocol for follow-up treatment on thymomas, we came up with one together with which we were both comfortable.

During a second appointment with him 6 months later, we went over the results of the CT scan done in early November 2001. This was the fourth scan I had done since my surgery, and they all appeared to show a soft tissue mass in my chest that could have been several things. The possibilities included scar tissue following my first surgery, a shift in the position of my internal tissue following the first surgery, or regrowth of the thymoma. While we were in agreement that the best thing to do was continue to watch, I noticed that each time a new scan was taken it was only compared with the one taken immediately before it. Although there was variation from scan to scan that could have been indications of tumor growth, the results were still inconclusive. I also learned that each interpretation of a scan was somewhat subjective, given that my position in the scanner or small movements that I might make in the process could account for the variation from scan to scan. For these reasons, I asked whether it would make sense to compare the most recent exam with the earliest, taken in October 2000. My doctor agreed and said he would request it and let me know the results.

I didn't hear from him, but waited from early November through the holidays before becoming a pest. When I left a phone message with his office the first week of January 2002, it was not returned. I called again the next week, and got a response saying that the results between the July 2001 and November 2001 scans were such and such. This was not the comparison the oncologist and I had agreed upon doing, so I called back leaving another message to this effect. They acknowledged the misunderstanding and did the comparison. When the oncologist finally got the results, he called and explained them to my husband because I was not available. He then mailed the written report to me with a note to call him if I had any questions. The comparison of scans did show more definitively that there had been no real change in the mass in the year preceding November 2001. From a patient's point of view, this was much more reassuring than being told after each scan that it was unclear whether there was new growth and we'd just keep watching.

I appreciate the way my current oncologist is working with me and considering my suggestions. I don't think my original oncologist would have been as forthcoming. He wouldn't have explained things, probably rationalizing that he knew best and that there is no reason to worry the patient about things he or she won't understand. I have outgrown that kind of doctor, and I am educating others to outgrow them as well. The safety of their health care depends on it.

Hatlie Commentary

While the little mix-ups in the exchange of messages about the CT scan comparisons are troubling, what's notable is how patient and providers worked together to recover from these system failures. Mistakes do happen in complex, dynamic, time-stressed environments, and the ability to recover before an injury occurs is a huge part of effective risk management. Goeltz's pestering has actually become a part of the safety net. She and her 24/7 teams track what is supposed to happen according to the treatment plan, and she communicates with the system when it doesn't. The goal is not to nail the system or people who work within it or to build a record for a lawsuit; it's to help that system perform better by becoming part of it.

Concluding Summary

Hatlie

A fearful stranger to the health care sector when she became a frequent user 2 years ago, Goeltz clearly is now a sophisticated and creative partner. She is fully engaged in decision making and holds the decisions made as her own. Physicians often worry that their patients don't fully consent to the treatment given them, because they don't fully understand the risks. This is often a factor in malpractice litigation. Goeltz's healers don't have that worry.

When it comes to the complicated process of treatment, Goeltz doesn't take for granted that the system will operate optimally, and holds herself accountable for doing what she can to deliver good outcomes for herself and her loved ones. She knows her active participation keeps the system safer. She challenges those she meets who want to discount her role and refuses to be treated by those who can't meet and adapt to those challenges. She has a lot to teach us all.

Goeltz

The circumstances of my brother's death are what taught me the crucial importance of active participation in my own health care. The best tribute I can pay to him is to continue trying to show consumers and those in health care how they can partner with each other to truly improve safety.

To those health care workers who are willing to work with me, and put up with my challenging them from time to time, please accept my deepest gratitude. I would not be as healthy as I am today without you and maybe I wouldn't even be alive. I know your jobs aren't easy, and you have earned my greatest respect.

References

National Institute of Medicine, Committee on Quality Care in America. (1999). *To Err Is Human: Building a Safer Health System.* Washington, DC: Institute of Medicine.

National Institute of Medicine, Committee on Quality Care in America. (2001). *Crossing the Quality Chasm: A New Health System for the 21st Century.* Washington, DC: National Academy Press.

National Patient Safety Foundation. (1997). *Public Opinion Study on Patient Safety Issues.* Chicago, IL: National Patient Safety Foundation.

Wilson, N., and Hatlie, M. (2001). Advancing patient safety: A framework for accountability and practical action. *Journal of Healthcare Quality,* 23, no.1, 30–34.

CHAPTER FIFTEEN

HEALTH CARE LITERACY AND PATIENT SAFETY: THE NEW PARADOX

Candice Moore, BSN, JD

Literacy in the United States has been defined as "an individual's ability to read, write, and speak in English, and compute and solve problems at levels of proficiency necessary to function on the job and in society, to achieve one's goals, and develop one's knowledge and potential.[1] At the dawn of the 21st century, in one of the wealthiest and freest societies on earth, illiteracy has become one of the greatest barriers to effective, safe health care.[2]

Although no study has directly measured the general literacy of the U.S. population, the National Adult Literacy Survey (NALS) taken in 1992 allowed an accurate estimation to be made.[3] According to the survey, 40 to 44 million adult Americans, or approximately one quarter of the U.S. population, are functionally illiterate, meaning that they may lack the skills to function adequately in society. Another 50 million have marginal literacy skills. Another 32 million people, or 13.8% of the population, speak a language other than English at home. These people come from all backgrounds; however, functionally illiterate adults are more likely to be older, poorer, and less educated and to have more health concerns. Limited English proficiency (LEP) is also a recognized barrier to functional literacy and will be covered in a later section of this chapter.

Unfortunately, the population's health literacy, or functional literacy, "the degree to which individuals have the capacity to obtain, process, and understand basic health information and services needed to make appropriate health decisions," may be significantly worse than general literacy because functional literacy is context specific and therefore less familiar to most of the population.[4]

Functional health literacy has been described as an individual's ability to read and comprehend prescription bottles, appointment slips, informed consent documents, insurance forms, and patient education materials, often while in a stress-filled state or with physically and mentally reduced capacity. An individual may be able to understand materials with which he or she is familiar, such as work-related forms or documents, but struggle with documents that have unfamiliar vocabulary and concepts.[5]

Functional illiterates may read at or below a fifth-grade level, or may not be able to read at all. The 50 million people who are marginally illiterate may be able to locate and generally understand information in a simple text, but are unable to perform tasks that require them to acquire or assimilate information from complex and lengthy texts. Because of the literacy demands placed upon patients in the increasingly complex health care system, adults who are functionally illiterate or marginally literate are likely to have low health literacy skills.[6]

Compounding the problem of health literacy is the language of medicine, which is highly technical and complex. The link between health and literacy has been previously researched, but the studies primarily assessed the reading level of written health education materials. Physicians trying to develop an easy-to-use tool to measure and document the reading level of patients in order to study the health-related differences between levels of literacy skills devised a literacy assessment tool called the Rapid Estimate of Adult Literacy in Medicine (REALM).[7]

The REALM tool enabled the research physicians to examine health behavior differences between people with high and low scores for literacy. Later, these same colleagues noted that women with limited literacy skills did not understand the purpose of a mammogram and therefore did not seek screening. The REALM tool tests a person's ability to read through a list of medical terms and adjust from short and easy words to more difficult, multisyllabic words. This correlated well with reading tests and was a good marker for literacy level.

The need for this type of testing was indicated by the first national assessment of functional literacy skills. The National Adult Literacy Survey in 1992 found that half of the U.S. adult population had limited literacy skills. The NALS focused on functional literacy and became the critical element in publicizing the issue of health literacy. Other studies have reported low comprehension in other critical areas, such as understanding written directions regarding medication, understanding clinical appointment slips, and understanding informed consent forms. Of the Medicare patients in one study, the authors found that[8]

- 48% did not understand the written instructions "take medicine every 6 hours."
- 68% did not know the significance of a stated blood sugar value.
- 27% could not identify their next appointment.
- 27% did not understand "take medicine on an empty stomach."
- 100% could not understand a statement of Medicaid rights written at a 10th-grade level.

A study of 3,260 new Medicare enrollees in a national managed care organization found that inadequate health literacy increased steadily with age, from 16% of those aged 65 to 69 to 58% of those older than 85.[9]

Poor health literacy has profound economic consequences. The estimated additional health care expenditures due to low health literacy skills are estimated to be about $73 billion in 1998 health care dollars.[10] This number includes an estimated $30 billion for the population that is functionally illiterate, plus $43 billion for the marginally literate.[11] To put this number in perspective, the amount is about what Medicare is expected to pay to finance physician services, dental services, home health care, prescription drugs, and nursing home care combined. A study of Medicaid participants found that those reading at the lowest grade levels (0–2) had average annual health care costs of $13,000, compared with the average of $3,000 for the population studied. Health care literacy costs affect not only the patient with the low skill level but also the health care providers and insurance carriers.[12]

Low health literacy skills also contribute to higher utilization of health care services. Using data from a nationally representative sample of the U.S. population aged 16 and older, the National Academy on an Aging Society examined the impact of literacy on the use of health care services. The study found the following:[13]

- Among adults who stayed overnight in a hospital in 1994, those with low health literacy skills averaged 6% more hospital visits and stayed in the hospital nearly 2 days longer than adults with higher health literacy skills.
- Among adults with at least one doctor visit in 1994, those with low health literacy skills had on average one more doctor visit than adults with higher health literacy skills.
- When self-reported health status is taken into account, patients with low health literacy skills had fewer doctor visits but used substantially more hospital resources.

Literacy and Safety

Many patient safety initiatives depend on effective communication between the health care professional and the patient. In the past, a patient and his or her family physician may have had a close relationship that allowed the physician more opportunity to determine the patient's ability to understand and assimilate the care and treatment prescribed. Given the current complexity of health care, the fragmentation of care among many specialties, and the sophistication of procedures and treatments, there is little doubt that patient–physician communication may be suffering. Health care providers have a very narrow window of opportunity to communicate effectively with patients. If 40 million American adults are functionally illiterate, and 99 million Americans have chronic illnesses, there are countless examples every day of the health care system failing those most in need.[14]

Furthermore, 30 years ago there were only about 650 prescription drugs, and the average hospital stay for an acute myocardial infarction (MI) was 4 to 6 weeks. Today, there are more than 10,000 prescription drugs, and a hospital stay for an acute MI is only 1 to 2 days.[15] The patient is sent home without skilled care and advised to change his lifestyle and diet, stop smoking, get his cholesterol and blood pressure under control, begin a new medication regimen, return for a follow-up appointment in 4 weeks, and reduce stress. Years ago, patients with newly diagnosed asthma were instructed to take theophylline and encouraged to be diligent about compliance. Today, asthma patients are asked to self-monitor their disease with a peak flow meter, select and correctly use the appropriate inhalers, augment therapy with tapering doses of oral steroids, and avoid all asthma triggers, including changing their home to reduce environmental hazards. Also, patients are asked to use but not overuse the emergency department, the primary physician, and subspecialists.[16] Patients are inundated with massive amounts of information about their diagnosis, sent home with powerful and potentially dangerous medications, and offered little in the way of follow-up. In response to this shockingly ineffective communication, if the patient is "noncompliant" in any form we blame her, her family, or the HMO. But we never look to see if we failed the patient by not communicating with her on her level and in a way that ensured her understanding of her illness. We have built an entire system based on the assumption that patients can read and understand complex materials.

The increase in chronic conditions such as diabetes, high blood pressure, and congestive heart failure now requires patients to know more about their health care and take an active part in disease management. Inadequate functional health literacy places an even greater barrier to educating patients with chronic diseases. These diseases require education related to achieving control of their behaviors and lifestyles, as well as education to help them avoid adverse health outcomes and to self-manage their condition.

These same functionally illiterate adults may also have difficulties simply encountering the health delivery system. They are less likely to use screening procedures, follow medical regimens, keep appointments, or seek help during the course of a disease. They are also less likely to utilize mainstream health care information from sources such as the Internet, magazine articles on disease prevention, or newspaper notices regarding vaccination schedules or flu shot opportunities.

Inadequate health literacy may also adversely affect a patient's health in a more direct way. Patients with prostate cancer who also had low literacy skills tended to be diagnosed later in the course of the disease, regardless of race. Low literacy has also been correlated with excessive hospitalization, which may indicate poor compliance with self-care management, inability to comprehend medication administration, and confusion over symptoms experienced.[17]

Treatment compliance has also been affected by literacy skills. A study that looked at the importance of health literacy among other predictors of compliance with treatment for HIV found that education and health literacy were significant predictors of the patient's ability to follow the ordered treatment.

Patients who cannot understand or follow basic health information are menacing quality improvement efforts. Although many provider groups are becoming aware of the problem of health literacy, they may be reluctant to address it for fear of being accused of deflecting criticism.

Assessing Health Literacy

Americans are reportedly more educated than at any time in our history, with the average educational attainment of U.S. adults being above the 12th-grade level.[18] A physician or nurse may not be aware of a patient's low literacy level. Although most patient assessment forms ask the patient how many school grades were completed, this is not an accurate indicator of a person's ability to read. One study showed that 27% of patients with a high school diploma and 17% of those with some college education had inadequate or marginal health literacy.[19] Another study of five family practice clinics showed that over 60% of the patients tested had a reading skill that was at least three grade levels lower than the grade they had completed.[20] Reading ability also cannot be predicted by occupation, physical appearance, or socioeconomic status.

Many patients with low literacy are extremely articulate and highly functional otherwise. They have successfully hidden their reading or comprehension deficiencies to the point where even their families are unaware of their limitations. Often these patients have developed elaborate strategies to conceal and compensate for reading difficulties.[21] An additional problem with identifying low-literate adults is that many people with limited reading skills do not realize they have a problem with reading.[22]

As a means to help identify patients with low literacy skills, the Test of Functional Health Literacy in Adults (TOFHLA) was developed by physicians at Emory University, modeled on the NALS. Available in English and Spanish, the test simulates items in the health setting that require reading skills (e.g., pill bottles, standardized appointment slips, instructions for procedures) and grades the patient's comprehension on a scale of 0 to 100. Patients scoring less than 60 are considered to have inadequate health literacy.[23]

The first step in addressing this widespread problem is to have the tools necessary to identify those patients with low health literacy. Warning signs of low health literacy include the following:[24]

- Patients who appear disinterested or incurious about new information provided to them, or who agree to a treatment plan too readily without asking questions.
- Patients who frequently miss appointments or appear on the wrong date.
- Patients who seem confused about when their prescriptions are due to be refilled or call for refills weeks after they should have run out.
- Patients who appear for testing or procedures without having completed the necessary preparation, such as not eating or drinking, or taking premedication.

Health care practitioners can use other means to detect low health literacy levels as well. For example, if the patient always brings someone with him or her to appointments or asks to discuss written materials with family members, this may signal a literacy problem. Continually forgetting reading glasses or not filling out forms completely may also indicate some problems with comprehension or legibility. Although it would never be advisable to give a patient a test to ascertain his or her level of literacy, many other means may be used to assess a person's literacy level.

Another area of confusion may come from the fact that patients who are not familiar with scientific concepts may not understand language that is frequently used by clinicians, such as "normal range," "signs of shock," or "take this medication until your symptoms subside." Antibiotics that have been prescribed to be taken for a full 10-day course may be stopped when the patient begins to feel better. Physicians often fail to tell the patient the reasoning for taking the entire course, believing instead that it is "common sense" or, at the very least, something that every adult knows. In addition, practitioners would be wise to consider the terms they use for certain conditions or concepts. Many people with low literacy tend to interpret words literally. *Hypertension* may indicate to a patient that they are "hyper." Patients also vary widely in their ability to comprehend commonly used medical terms. Only 13% of the 125 participating patients understood the meaning of *terminal,* 35% understood *orally,* and 18% understood *malignant.*[25]

Regulations Addressing Health Literacy

Title VI of the Civil Rights Act of 1964 and Medicare/Medicaid regulations prohibit discrimination against individuals seeking health care services.[26] Title VI states, "No person in the United States shall, on ground of race, color, or national origin, be excluded from participation in, be denied the benefits of, or be subjected to discrimination under any program or activity receiving Federal financial assistance." Because federal funding of health care is pervasive, nearly every health care provider is bound by Title VI.

The Department of Health and Human Services (DHHS) has long recognized that Title VI requires linguistic accessibility to health care. In addition, the Office for Civil Rights (OCR), along with DHHS, has consistently interpreted Title VI to require the provision of qualified interpreter services and translated material at no cost to patients.

Various provisions of Medicare and Medicaid also prohibit discrimination by health care organizations that receive federal aid.[27] Since Medicaid regulations also require that state programs be designed to operate in compliance with Title VI, these regulations have been applied in a manner that ensures that speaking a language other than English does not constitute a barrier for covered services.

The Hill–Burton Act, enacted by Congress in 1946, encouraged the construction and modernization of public and nonprofit community hospitals and health centers. In return for funds, hospitals agreed to comply with a "community service obligation," which lasts in perpetuity. OCR has consistently taken the position that this obligation requires Hill–Burton fund recipients to address the needs of LEP patients.

Private accrediting agencies such as the Joint Commission on Accreditation of Healthcare Organizations (JCAHO) and the National Committee for Quality Assurance (NCQA) have also established standards involving the issue of health literacy. The JCAHO requires that health care information be communicated to patients and their families in a manner that they can understand, considering their individual literacy levels.[28]

The NCQA, the agency that accredits managed care organizations, has adopted similar standards to ensure that documents are readable and available in languages that reflect the membership populations of these institutions. The U.S. Congress and the Food and Drug Administration have recognized for years the need to improve patients' understanding of prescription medication.[29]

In addition, the Omnibus Reconciliation Act of 1990 requires that pharmacists offer counseling to Medicaid patients to ensure that they understand how to take their medication safely and effectively. This education must occur every time a patient goes to the pharmacy to have a prescription filled or refilled. In a hospital, where someone other than a pharmacist is interacting with the patient, that professional (e.g., the physician or the nurse) must provide the necessary medication information. Whoever does the education must provide the information in a way that is understandable to the patient. In 1998, the American Medical Association (AMA) adopted policies that recognized limited literacy as a barrier to effective medical diagnosis and treatment. The AMA Foundation has undertaken a multiyear initiative to increase awareness of health literacy issues.

Informed Consent

Informed consent has long been a critical component of effective physician–patient communication and patient safety initiatives. Much has been written over the years about such issues as what constitutes valid consent, the written consent form as being only one part of the consent process, how the failure to give proper consent can lead to medical malpractice, and who in the health care chain has the burden of providing the information necessary for a valid informed consent.

Informed consent issues take on new meaning when the patient has low literacy or limited English skills. A signed consent form may not be adequate proof of consent if the patient did not possess the capacity to understand the information included in the consent form. Even if the consent form is considered "easy to read," the patient still may not have understood the information regarding the risks, benefits, and alternatives to the proposed treatment. Inadequate communication with patients may result in liability under tort principles if damages result from treatment administered in the absence of informed consent. Also, the provider's violation of language access laws may raise the presumption of negligence in some states.[30]

The treating physician has the responsibility to verbally inform the patient about the procedure in a language or manner that can be understood, and then to ascertain whether the patient has actually understood the information being conveyed. If this individual has inadequate English to demonstrate understanding of the information to give an informed consent, the physician may be required to provide an interpreter to ensure that a written form is properly executed and that the patient's consent is informed and valid.

One study assessed the readability of informed consent documents through application of the Fry Readability Scale. Researchers found that 66% of the forms were at a level considered to be "scientific/technical." Researchers recommend that to ensure a patient's understanding of the information in the consent form, medical personnel need to pay closer attention to the average reading level when approving forms for distribution.[31] Another study recommended assessing the "readability of the clinic's printed materials including a surgical consent form using the simple measure of Gobbledygook (SMOG) formula."[32]

The following are examples from hospital informed consent documents:

I am aware that, in addition to the risks specifically referred to in Item 2 above, there are other risks that attend the performance of any surgical or other procedure. I am also aware that the practice of medicine and surgery is not an exact science, and I acknowledge that no guarantees have been made to me concerning the results of the proposed treatment. (Flesch-Kincaid reading level 12.0)

In consideration of those hospital/physician and medical services rendered by ABC Medical, I hereby assign to ABC Medical all of my right to medical reimbursement, including but not limited to, the right to designate a beneficiary, add dependent eligibility and to have an individual policy continued or issued in accordance with the terms and benefits under any insurance policy, subscription certificate or other health benefit indemnification agreement otherwise payable to me for those services rendered by ABC Medicine and its physicians. (Flesch Reading Ease, 0%; Flesch-Kincaid reading level 12.0)

Consent to Treatment: The undersigned voluntarily consents to the rendering of such care, including diagnostic procedures and medical treatment, by authorized agents and employees of the XYZ Hospital, and by its Medical staff, or their designees, as may in their professional judgment be deemed necessary or beneficial. The undersigned acknowledges that no guarantees have been made as to the effect of such examination or treatment on his/her condition. If a health care worker is accidentally exposed to this patient's blood or body fluids, the XYZ Hospital may perform appropriate tests on this patient's blood to determine if the worker has contracted a transmissible agent (such as HIV, Hepatitis). The testing will be at no cost to the patient and the tests will be confidential. (Flesch-Kincaid reading level 12.0)

Clearly, much thought has gone into providing complete information for patients to understand and follow. The bigger question is, "We're sending the message, but is anyone receiving?" For patients to fully participate in their own care, they need to be able to understand both formal and informal communication. The health care practitioner should view communication as interactive, a give-and-take exchange of information with the ability to adapt the message to fit the listener.

To improve the understanding of information by patients with low health literacy, the practitioner should (1) slow down and take the time to assess the patient's health literacy skills, (2) use "common language" rather than medical terminology, (3) use visual aids to enhance understanding and subsequent recall, (4) limit the information given at each interaction and repeat as needed, and (5) use a "teach-back" or "show-me" approach to confirm understanding.

Limited English Proficiency

English is the predominant language of the United States. According to the 1990 census, English is spoken by 95% of its residents. The United States, however, is also home to millions of national-origin minority individuals who are limited English proficient (LEP). That is, they cannot speak, read, write, or understand the English language at a level that permits them to interact effectively with health care providers.[33]

The very nature of the relationship between the patient and physicians, nurses, and other health care professionals requires mutual trust, which flows from communication between the professional and the patient. When the languages spoken are not common to both, communication will be severely impeded.

Different approaches have been taken to bridge language gaps. One approach has been to encourage minority patients to bring family members along during visits or hospitalizations to interpret for the patient. Adults with limited English proficiency often rely upon their minor children to interpret for them, with occasional disastrous results.

In a New York Times article entitled "For Immigrant's Children, an Adult Role," an immigrant mother from Puerto Rico blamed her daughter's partial paralysis on her inability to speak English. According to the woman, her lack of English-speaking skills prevented her from communicating a symptom that might have helped physicians accurately diagnose her daughter. The young daughter was relied upon to convey her symptoms instead; based on that account, the physician diagnosed the flu. Her illness was not the flu, however, and her symptoms worsened, leading to permanent nerve damage in both legs.[34]

The practice of using family members or minor children as translators, while seemingly convenient and cost-efficient, has severe problems associated with it and may be in violation of Title VI of the Civil Rights Act of 1964. The use of untrained interpreters may result in a misunderstanding of the necessary concepts to ensure a proper translation. The other problem is that even if concepts are understood, the presence of a family member may obstruct the flow of confidential information. It is not difficult to imagine a situation in which a patient would be reluctant to disclose personal details necessary to make a diagnosis or report a symptom.

The Office for Civil Rights has enforcement authority that derives from Title VI. This enforcement encompasses the duty of health and human service providers to ensure that LEP persons can meaningfully access programs and services. Title VI promised equal access to federally assisted programs and activities. Unequal access encountered by an LEP person results in a poorer quality of health and social services; in the case of health care, services that are denied, delayed, or misdelivered can have devastating consequences. There is no part of the health care experience—from admission history to informed consent to discharge instructions—that does not rely on accurate levels of communication. All entities that receive federal financial assistance from DHHS, either directly or indirectly, are covered by the policy guidelines of Title VI.[35]

Extensive case law affirms the obligation of recipients of federal financial assistance to ensure that LEP persons can meaningfully access federal-assisted programs. In *Lau v. Nichols,* 414 U.S. 563 (1974), the U.S. Supreme Court recognized that recipients of federal financial assistance have an affirmative responsibility to provide LEP persons with meaningful opportunity to participate in public programs.[36]

Title VI regulations prohibit both intentional discrimination and policies and practices that appear neutral but have a discriminatory effect. Therefore, a hospital's policy related to the availability of interpreters does not have to be intentional to be discriminatory, but may be a violation of Title VI if there is an adverse effect on the ability of an LEP person to access health care services.

The next question to ask is, How can Title VI compliance be achieved? The key to compliance is to ensure that the language assistance provided results in accurate and effective communication between the patient with limited English proficiency and the health care provider.

There are no set guidelines that must be implemented to ensure compliance, but certain actions may assist in ensuring meaningful access to LEP persons:

- *Assess the population served by the health care organization.* The health care entity should do a thorough assessment of the language

needs of the population that will be served by them, including
identifying non-English languages likely to be encountered. This
can be done by census data, patient data, or a market survey of the
community. It is also advisable to keep accurate documentation of
patient's individual language needs and how the patient's language
needs were met.

- *Develop a written policy.* A written policy should be in place and
  easily accessible, and relate to language access by identifying and
  assessing the individual language needs of the LEP patient. The
  policy should also include the right of LEP patients to receive free
  language assistance and notices of their rights in language they
  can understand.

- *Identify resources to utilize to provide effective language
  assistance.* This includes making arrangements that provide
  language assistance in a timely fashion and that are centrally
  located and available.[37]

- *Hire bilingual staff who are trained and competent in the skill of
  interpreting.* Hiring trained interpreters can avoid many of the
  hurdles associated with LEP patients. Although this is costly,
  depending on the patient population served, it may be worth the
  effort in the long run. Contracting with an outside interpreter
  service is also an option that allows for flexibility and response.
  Some health care organizations are also turning to community
  volunteers to fulfill the need for interpreters. Any community
  approach should be made with formal arrangements between the
  hospital and volunteer that emphasize the obligation of
  communication and confidentiality. Community-based
  organizations or volunteers may also be used to ensure that
  accurate, readable translations have been made. Telephone
  interpreter services may also be utilized effectively when a quick
  response is needed.

- *Translate written materials that are routinely given to patients in
  English.* According to Title VI, vital documents must be provided
  in other languages. Although specific "vital documents" to be
  translated have not been spelled out by DHHS's policy guidance,
  a document "should be considered vital if it contains information
  that is critical for assessing the federal fund recipient's services
  and/or benefits, or is required by law."[38] Hospital patients are
  often given standard forms, documents, instructions, and other
  papers upon admission or discharge to the hospital. Many of
  these can be easily translated into other languages for ease of
  communication and to provide equal access to services.

The OCR considers a health care organization to be in compliance
with the Title VI requirement to provide written materials in non-English

languages if the following guidelines have been followed:

- The recipient/covered entity must provide translated written materials for each LEP language group that constitutes 10% or 3,000, whichever is less, of the population of persons eligible to be served or likely to be directly affected.
- If the LEP group does not fall within the above parameters, but constitutes 5% or 1,000, whichever is less, at a minimum vital documents must be translated into the appropriate non-English languages of such LEP persons, and other documents may be translated orally.
- For all LEP groups consisting of fewer than 100 persons of the population served, written notice of the right to receive language assistance must be provided.

Addressing Health Literacy

Many challenges face the health care industry as the result of documented evidence that up to half of U.S. adults may be unable to sufficiently understand written and verbal communication to fully participate in their own health care.

Proper communication is vital in any patient–caregiver relationship, but much more so for patients with low health literacy. The following suggestions are offered for communicating with these patients:

- Simplify your language whenever possible. Speak slowly and pause between sentences or information that is complex. It is not talking down to someone to use terms they can understand. Fear of "dumbing down" the language has been widely used as a reason for not addressing communication issues. Proper, well-crafted plain language will not, however, be construed as condescending by the patient.
- Define words that are medical related or new to the patient. When large amounts of information are to be given, break it into smaller chunks and stop in between to assess the patient's understanding.
- Whenever possible utilize visual aids, pictures, diagrams, or videos for clarification or better understanding. Many people respond better to visual cues than to auditory ones, and the combination will enhance learning for any population.
- Read over all written materials with patients. It may help health care professionals to ask themselves what areas (e.g., computers, car engines) are confusing to them and to put themselves in the context of their own nonexpert status. This allows a more objective view of the information given to patients to ascertain its readability.

Health care marketing brochures, instruction sheets, forms, letters, and surveys are widely used by health care organizations for such purposes as teaching, disease prevention, and health promotion, appointment reminders, and billing. The problem is that typical health materials have an information overload, with too many long words and complex sentences, technical jargon, and an uninviting tone. The core message is often not clear, and the desired behaviors are not emphasized.

The following compliance document from a billing company serves as an example of text that is too complex to be readily understood:

> Company Employees are not authorized to alter billing/encounter documents received from a provider. Incomplete documents or documents containing errors will be returned to the provider for completion/correction. The Company recognizes that it shares the responsibility with its clients for ensuring that all requests for payment submitted to third party payers and other responsible parties contain only true and accurate data and that all claims for payment for services are fully justified by appropriate documentation. Therefore, the Company will adopt policies and procedures that include periodic training of all Employees in proper documentation of services and billing rules, and the Company will periodically monitor its performance.[39]

This passage includes multisyllabic words, jargon, long sentences, and complex ideas. Words longer than three syllables are more difficult to understand than words with only one or two syllables. In this example, some of the words can be changed without changing the meaning. For example, *authorized* can be rewritten as *approved,* and *ensuring* as *making sure.*[40]

Jargon is also used in health care brochures and can be especially difficult for the reader to understand. Jargon is industry-specific language—a type of professional shorthand—and assumes that the reader has prior knowledge of these terms. Jargon is appropriate between professionals, but should not be used with patients. Long sentences are also difficult, because they require the reader to understand and remember all the words from the beginning of the sentence to the end. Only 15 words and one concept per sentence are easier to understand.

The Maine Health Literacy Program demonstrated how health information could be simplified with the following example:[41]

Before

A positive HIV test indicates that you are infected with HIV and that you can pass the virus to other people. Inaccurate positive and negative test results occur occasionally. For this reason, a negative test result does not guarantee that you are not infected. Rarely, a positive test result is inaccurate and indicates that you are carrying HIV even if you are not.

After

A positive HIV test most likely means that you have the HIV virus and can pass it on to others. Sometimes the test results are wrong. If your test is positive, there's a very small chance you don't really have the virus. If your test is negative, there's still a chance you may have the virus.

Next Steps

The recent publicity surrounding medical error and the government and private sector's emphasis on error reduction on a large scale have added new importance to the issue of literacy and how it affects patient safety efforts. A recent emphasis of the patient safety movement has been patient empowerment, an escalating initiative to get patients/consumers actively involved in their own and their families' care.

The JCAHO has launched a new Speak Up campaign, which urges patients to become active, informed, and involved participants in their care.[42] According to the JCAHO, research has shown that patients who actively take part in their health care decisions are more likely to have better outcomes. This has also been supported by the Centers for Medicare and Medicaid Services.

The JCAHO specifically encourages patients to "speak up if there are questions or concerns, and if you still don't understand, ask again." Other suggestions by the JCAHO include paying attention to the care being received, making sure that the right treatment or medication is being administered, becoming educated about the diagnosis, and participating in all treatment decisions.

For organizations that have experienced the results of inappropriate or unnecessary testing, clinical inefficiency, misdiagnosis, negative outcomes, and malpractice due to cultural and literacy issues, risk management has become an active part of communication. The Mutual Insurance Corporation of America felt strongly enough about the connection between communication and liability to discount the malpractice insurance premiums for physicians who participate in cultural competency training.[43]

Many barriers stand in the way of achieving a public movement for addressing health literacy issues. The biggest barrier is the tremendous stigma attached to illiteracy, so that many patients hide the fact that they have difficulty reading or writing. Whereas other populations in need of assistance—whether minorities, the physically disabled, or mentally challenged individuals—have large constituencies, there is no constituency that rallies around the issue of health literacy. There is nothing to readily identify an individual who has trouble navigating the health care maze. A patient's silence is often interpreted as consent, understanding, and compliance. Very often though, nothing could be further from the truth. In fact, the entire issue of literacy is often characterized as an education issue, not a health issue, and therefore not worthy of significant attention.

There is not much litigation surrounding improper interpreter services, as of yet. However, the American Civil Liberties Union has filed suit against the University of San Francisco based on its failure to provide sufficient interpreter services for its LEP populations.[44] Organizational inertia also exists as a barrier to effectively assessing and implementing health literacy initiatives. Many organizations may be reluctant to change patient information materials, fearing that to do so would be to dumb things down. Also, individual groups or professionals may see their specialized language as part of the power they can wield over others. Although this is in no means a conscious effort to disenfranchise any patient, years of professional study and indoctrination make it difficult to change communication styles, or to even recognize the disconnect between what is being said by the practitioner and what is being understood by the patient.

Communicating with patients is a challenge even when the playing field is level. But communicating effectively when patients lack the literacy and language skills needed to understand complex concepts and multisyllabic words is essential in the quest to improve patient safety. Miscommunicating with patients and families who do not understand can be expensive in terms of health care over- and underutilization, misdiagnosis, medical error, and satisfaction. It is incumbent upon those at the forefront of the patient safety movement to recognize the seriousness of health literacy and to begin to seek ways to change our essential communication practices. No initiative will be as effective in promoting patient safety as the recognition of literacy issues and the diligent application of sound and effective communication practices.

Notes

1. National Literacy Act, 20 U.S.C. Section 1201 (1991).
2. Joanne G. Schwartzberg, "Health Literacy: Can Your Patient Read, Understand, and Act Upon Your Instruction?" Available: http://www.rmf. harvard.edu/publications/forum/v20n6/article5/body.html. Accessed 5 April 2002.
3. American Medical Association, "Health Literacy: Facts About Health Literacy." Available: http:www/ama-assn.org/ama/pub/print/ article 3125.3308.html. Accessed 4 April 2002.
4. Mark V. Williams, "Recognizing and Overcoming Inadequate Health Literacy, a Barrier to Care." *Cleveland Clinic Journal of Medicine,* vol. 69, no. 5 (May 2002):415–418.

5. Ronald M. Davis, "Health Literacy Report of the Council on Scientific Affairs of the American Medical Association." Available: http://email.americanmedicalassociation.org/servlet/webacc/kjvnmbmlcmOu/GWAP/AREI. Accessed 10 April 2002.

6. Center for Health Care Strategies and the National Academy on an Aging Society, "Low Health Literacy Skills Increase Annual Health Care Expenditures by $73 Billion. Health Literacy Fact Sheet." Available: http://222.agingsociety.org/healthlit.htm. Accessed 10 April 2002.

7. Rima E. Rudd, "A Maturing Partnership." *Focus on Basics,* vol. 5, issue C (February 2002). Available: http://ncsall.gse.harvard.edu/fob/2002/rudd.html. Accessed 5 April 2002.

8. Williams, "Recognizing and Overcoming Inadequate Health Literacy," 416.

9. Schwartzberg, "Health Literacy."

10. Center for Health Care Strategies and the National Academy on an Aging Society, "Low Health Literacy Skills."

11. Ibid.

12. Ibid.

13. Ibid.

14. American Medical Association, "Health Literacy."

15. Williams, "Recognizing and Overcoming Inadequate Health Literacy," 416.

16. Davis, "Health Literacy Report."

17. Williams, "Recognizing and Overcoming Inadequate Health Literacy," 416.

18. Davis, "Health Literacy Report."

19. Williams, "Recognizing and Overcoming Inadequate Health Literacy," 416.

20. Ibid.

21. Rachel Y. Moon, Tina L. Cheng, Kantilal M. Patel, Lalanit Baumhaft, and Peter C. Scheidt, "Parental Literacy Level and Understanding of Medical Information." *Pediatrics,* vol. 2, no. 2 (August 1998):1–6.

22. Ibid., 1.

23. Williams, "Recognizing and Overcoming Inadequate Health Literacy."

24. Risk Management Foundation, "Tips for Effects of Health Literacy on Treatment Adherence." Available: http://www.rmf.harvard.edu/patientsafety/resources/healthlit/tips/body.html. Accessed 5 April 2002.

25. Williams, "Recognizing and Overcoming Inadequate Health Literacy," 416.

26. Linda McIntosh, comp., "An Overview of Regulations Addressing Health Literacy: Health Literacy Toolbox 2000." Available: http://www.prenataled.com/healthlit/default.asp. Accessed 5 April 2002.

27. Ibid.

28. Ibid.

29. Davis, "Health Literacy Report."

30. Jane Perkins et al. "Ensuring Linguistic Access in Health Care Settings: Legal Rights and Responsibilities." Available: http://www.healthlaw.org/pubs/19980131lingaccess.html. Accessed 5 April 2002.

31. Raich, P. C., Plomer, K. D., and Coyne, C. A., "Literacy, Comprehension and Informed Consent in Clinical Research." *Cancer Investigation,* vol. 19, no. 4 (2001):437–445.

32. Emily Zobel, "An Updated Overview of Medical and Public Health Literature Addressing Literacy Issues: An Annotated Bibliography of Articles Published in 2001." Available: http://www.hsph.harvard. edu/healthliteracy/literature4.htm. Accessed 5 April 2002.

33. Office for Civil Rights, "Policy Guidance: Title VI Prohibition Against National Origin Discrimination as It Affects Persons with Limited English Proficiency." Available: http://www.hhs.gov/ocr/lep/guide.html. Accessed 14 May 2002.

34. "For Immigrant's Children, an Adult Role," *New York Times,* 15 August 1991.

35. Office for Civil Rights, "Policy Guidance."

36. *Lau v. Nichols,* 414 U.S. 563 (1974).

37. Office for Civil Rights, "Policy Guidance."

38. U.S. Department of Health and Human Services, Office of Minority Health, "National Standards for Culturally and Linguistically Appropriate Services in Health Care [Executive Summary]." 65 *Federal Register* 52762, 52764 (30 August 2000).

39. Helen Osborne and William Katz, "Simplicity Is the Best Medicine for Compliance Information." *Journal of Health Care Compliance,* vol. 3, no. 3 (May–June 2001):79–80.

40. Ibid.

41. Plimpton, S., and Root, J. "Materials and Strategies That Work in Low Literacy Health Communication." *Public Health Reports,* vol. 109, no. 1 (January 1994):86–92.

42. JCAHO Speak Up campaign. See http://www.jcaho.org/ general+public/patient+safety/speak+up/speak+up.htm.

43. U.S. Department of Health and Human Services, "National Standards."

44. Duffy and Alexander. 26 ANNA 507. Lexis Science and Technology Laboratory.

CHAPTER SIXTEEN

USING A ROOT CAUSE ANALYSIS PROCESS TO ANALYZE ISSUES OF SAFETY

Sue Korth, BSN, MPH, PhD

Health care accidents within the confines of a hospital typically happen one at a time. Therefore, they do not get media attention comparable to that of an airline crash killing hundreds of people.[1] However, eventually the total number of lives lost may be the same over the course of time, with multiple errors occurring. Who is paying attention to the total numbers? Are they getting reported to one responsible person or are they scattered across the abyss of hospital departments? Current process analysis in risk management suggests that accidents result from multiple complex problems and are not the fault of one person.[2]

Processes, often called policies and procedures, take place throughout the confinement of any given patient, on multiple occasions, by multiple people. Because of all the hands in the pot, many errors can occur. The error may occur because of any one of multiple reasons. It might be because staff are not trained correctly, or because the policy or procedure is outdated and does not apply to the current equipment being utilized. Perhaps the training was inadequate, and staff did not feel free to ask questions. Maybe this was the first time through the procedure for the caregiver, and he or she would have liked to have had some help but there was no one to ask. Some other emergency may have come up, and the caregiver did not have time to return to check on the patient. Whatever the cause of the problem, it is the current practice of most hospitals to assign blame to the ones most closely related to the problem—that is, the bedside caregivers.

The structure of the identification system for medical errors needs to be evaluated. Multiple forms usually exist for various incidents, which are sent to multiple departments within the organization for reporting and evaluation. A less than adequate reporting system may be in place, with little or no oversight of the entire process. Managers of departments may receive little or no feedback regarding the overall incidents in their departments; therefore, the "individual" who "committed" the error receives little or no feedback either. The system seems to point fingers at the caregivers, slap a few hands, and wait for the next report to arrive. How can improvements be made in a process that has no ownership or oversight?

Perhaps these complex systems, known as hospitals, need to look at the overall process before assigning blame and fix the problem before it gets bigger and much more expensive for the hospital, the caregiver, and the patient. Many hospitals are turning to their risk management department and to a process called root cause analysis. Root cause analysis is a tool that has long been used in engineering[3] and is now being utilized in health care as well to examine the underlying (root) causes of adverse events.[4]

The Analysis Process

According to Mary K. Wakefield, the director of the Center for Health Policy, Research and Ethics at George Mason University, in a lecture entitled "Quality Improvement and Public Policy: Focus on Medical Errors," most errors don't lead to injury. It's just that the quality of care is not as safe or as good as it could be. Many of these errors can be avoided and may lead to potential injury if not corrected. She further notes that the error systems are becoming increasingly complex, with a mix of players (doctors, nurses, and other health care providers). Even with instruction on the front end, there are many times when an inadequate system is unable to compensate for errors. Systems must have excellent players, who collaborate to become excellent team members. Our goal is to educate staff so they can be the best. We want them to be equipped to provide the best care to promote the best outcomes for our customers.

To help with the process of retrospective analysis of medical mistakes, a variation of a process known as man-technique-organization (MTO) analysis can be utilized. This is an accident investigation method that was originally developed by NASA and has been adopted by many other industries. MTO analysis helps investigators identify the human and system problems that may have contributed to an accident, find the underlying causes of the accident, and develop preventive actions.[5]

TABLE 16-1　Root Cause Analysis Process

Action	Actor(s)
To be completed within 5 working days of notification of the event:	
1. Case identification	All personnel throughout the hospital
2. Development of event timeline	Risk management/SMPC
3. Discussion of event timeline (additions/deletions)	RCA team,* and others as needed
4. Revisions of event timeline	Risk management/SMPC
5. Initial conclusions (enabling factors, latent errors, situational factors, flawed safety barriers, active failures)	RCA team
To be completed within 2 weeks of notification of event:	
6. Action plan, including development of and steps for monitoring	Involved department; leadership/ RCA team
To be initiated within 2 weeks of notification of event:	
7. Action plan implementation and monitoring	Involved department/PICC
8. Educational review of plan	RCA team, and others as needed
To be completed within 4 weeks of notification of event:	
9. Final report to PICC	SMPC
To be completed, if necessary, within 1 week following PICC:	
10. Report to credentialing/med. exec. if indicated	PICC
Initial monitoring is to be completed no later than 3 months postimplementation on all plans. Further monitoring will be determined as needed by the involved department and RCA team.	
11. Follow-up/review of case for completion of action plan implementation	PICC

SMPC, system medical performance coordinator; RCA, root cause analysis; PICC, performance improvement coordinating committee.

*RCA team: Performance improvement director, chief medical officer, system medical performance coordinator, and physician/staff/director/manager from involved area.

We began the development of a root cause analysis process (Table 16-1), in combination with the MTO process, by developing a timeline and obtaining approval through our committee structure. Each health care organization will need to determine and develop, with legal counsel, what constitutes a root cause analysis evaluation. (All sentinel events are an automatic trigger for a root cause analysis.) This information should then be placed into a department policy, and the policy must be consistently followed.

Participants in each root cause analysis include the basic root cause analysis (RCA) team (the medical director, performance improvement director, and a nurse called a system medical performance coordinator). Other members of the team include variations of other staff, including individuals directly involved in the event, along with the medical staff, managers, relevant service line staff, and the director if needed. The nurse facilitates the group. The team focuses on systems and processes rather than individual performance. It is difficult, at times, not to want to place blame, but it is the job of the facilitator to lead the group away from this blame and to focus on process improvement.

The process begins by identification of an issue that meets the criteria for a root cause analysis to be done. The risk management nurse reviews the chart and develops a timeline to the best of his or her ability. The summary is then sent to our performance improvement coordinating committee (PICC) for a vote to determine if a formal RCA should be completed. If the PICC, with the information presented, feels an RCA needs to be completed, the entire RCA team is then gathered. The timeline is refined and revised according to the recollection of the participants and the documentation on the record.

The basic RCA team then categorizes the events into enabling factors, latent errors, situational factors, flawed safety barriers, and active failures. An *enabling factor* could be the result of lack of education for the caregiver. *Latent errors* can lead to the first active failure because of a flawed procedure (e.g., the medication was checked but not the patient's name). *Situational factors* may be uncontrolled by the problem that occurs (e.g., two patients on the same unit have the same name). If the entire process or procedure is not followed, the system has broken down and a safety barrier that should have prevented the error did not do so. This is referred to as a *flawed safety barrier* (e.g., if both the patient's name and identification number should have been compared and only the name was checked). An *active failure* can occur when a process is done incorrectly (e.g., not going through an assigned process, like checking a patient's identification against a medication label for the same patient prior to administration).[6]

It may be necessary and easier to map out or flowchart the process to identify issues or processes that are not working. Several methods can accomplish this. One method, an Ishikawa diagram,[7] more commonly known as the fish bone, can be used to diagram the process. A cross-functional diagram can be utilized, and titles assigned to each category. A complex flowchart can also be utilized. We found that putting together a simple table with the events across the top horizontally and the names of the barriers listed to the side or vertically was most efficient for our purposes. This was an easy method for us to identify all of the issues.

Upon completion of these steps, the involved department leadership and the RCA team come together to develop and agree upon an action plan for improvement. This action plan may include review of a policy and procedure to make it more understandable, or perhaps development of a new policy. It may involve changing a process, educating staff, or changing a form. The steps that are agreed upon need to have a responsible person accountable for implementation and follow-up, and commitment to a timeline must be made. Again, we used a table for identification, assignment, and completion dates.

The entire team is brought back together one more time to provide closure. This final meeting of the team allows the staff to understand the flaws that were identified in the process and what has been done to correct them. It also helps staff to understand that the "blame" has been placed on the process, which will be fixed, and not the individual. Many errors are delicate because they may make or break a very good employee. If the employee understands that there was more than one person involved in the process, the load of the error may be lightened. Knowing the process will be corrected so that others will not face the same issues will help as well. Although we are changing the philosophy to be "blame free," caregivers still feel a certain amount of guilt. This is a step in the educational process that is often left out. To prevent a mistake from happening again, it is best to educate the staff involved and help them have an understanding of why it happened. You can bet they will not forget the incident or what changed in the process. Involved staff will more than likely be placed in the situation time and time again; thus, you have just prevented a recurring error.

To complete the loop, a summation report should be sent to the hospital performance or quality improvement committee. This committee should review the root cause analysis and the action plan to ensure all the necessary steps have been taken to promote change and prevent the error from occurring again. A member of this committee should be assigned the task of following up to make sure all of the action plan steps have been taken and accomplished within the appropriate timeframe. The quality committee should identify issues that need to be taken to other committees in the hospital. Medical staff issues may be passed on to the credentialing committee or to the medical executive board when indicated. The entire root cause analysis process is not closed until the action plan is complete. Copies of the policies, procedures, or changed processes should be kept with the completed file. A reaudit process is completed in 6 months to ensure implementation of the action plan.

Regulatory Issues

Each organization will need to review state laws as they relate to discovery. In some states, projects related to performance or quality improvement are protected from discovery. If this is true for your state, then the working group for each root cause analysis should be convened at the direction of the hospital's performance or quality improvement review committee. It is extremely important that the participants in a root cause analysis have this understanding prior to beginning the process. It is also important that any notes they have made for themselves become part of the analysis file. They must also be instructed that the issues related to a case should not be discussed outside the meeting, as that conversation would then become discoverable because it was not part of the root cause analysis process.[8]

Error Reporting Initiatives

Who reports errors and how do they get reported? How do we know that we are receiving all the necessary reports we need for both retrospectively and proactively reviewing processes? We don't! We need to be able to change the atmosphere in our organizations to a "nonblame" reporting process. Until this happens, we won't change what needs to be changed. So how can this be accomplished? With the help of our planning department, we put together a campaign regarding medical errors. Through the initiatives of our Critical Success Factors (hospital-wide improvement ideas), we put together a plan.

We completed a system analysis. The analysis enables individuals to identify opportunities to improve heath care provider performance by modifying the system or by modifying the behavior of individuals in the system. System analysis has successfully been applied in multiple other industries.[9] Deming and Juran pioneered these methods. Deming emphasized statistical quality control, whereas Juran emphasized group process and utilizing the suggestions of employees.[10] Our system analysis reviewed the process of reporting the error and then of looking at the root cause analysis of why the error occurred.

Originally, probably like most health care facilities, we asked our staff to fill out several forms for reporting errors. We had one for medication errors, one for falls, one for visitors, one for this, and one for that. Not many staff were accustomed to filling out the reports, and they were unfamiliar with which report to fill out when, much less with how to find the report to fill out in the first place. Once the form was found and filled out, staff weren't sure where to send it. The bottom of the form may have said (in small print) "send yellow copy to the infection control department and keep the original" or something to that effect. Maybe staff followed those instructions last time, but didn't hear anything back, so figured it didn't go to the right person. Then when evaluations came, and staff were "dinged" because they "had a medication error" during the past year, they wondered why they ever reported the error in the first place. Nothing changed! Maybe they knew

10 other people who had errors and didn't fill out a form and got a better raise. You can be sure they won't fill the form out the next time. Sound like a familiar scenario to you?

Initially, we put together a presentation for the management staff of the hospital to help them understand the new blame-free system. The delivery of a consistent message by all leadership was critical to the acceptance of this process by all employees and customers of the hospital.[11] We used other mechanisms, such as the hospital newsletters, employee forums, and department meetings, to explain the system. Although this systemwide culture change was not readily believed, much less accepted, the word spread on the general topics of the root cause analysis process and the educational opportunities it offered. Eventually, the new method was gradually seen as a process improvement initiative and accepted by the staff.

In the system review, we identified not only a cumbersome number of events, but also lack of any follow-through. We determined the reporting form was too hard to find, so we decided to develop an online form. Because of access problems with computers, this idea was ineffective as well. We determined to leave some type of printed form in place, and to combine the forms into one. We also established a phone line for reporting errors.

The error reporting data needed to go to one source to be put into a tracking system. We developed a job description for a new position, a system medical performance coordinator (SMPC), who would be responsible for keeping track of all the errors in the system, sending them to the appropriate department for follow-up, and trending the errors. Through the trending, the SMPC would determine the need for root cause analysis. Summary reports to the directors of the departments were established on a monthly basis. RCA was utilized for education purposes for departments across the health care organization.

The SMPC reports to the performance/quality committee of the hospital on a monthly basis and was made a member of the committee. The committee has identified the performance improvement coordinating committee (PICC) as the core structure for quality reporting for the hospital. All quality information feeds into this committee for review and trending, and reports are provided on a quarterly basis back to the standing committees. Quality issues needing further analysis can be forwarded to the appropriate hierarchy of the committee structure.

Proactive Analysis

One final suggestion is to be proactive in your analysis. We picked our top five risk departments, as agreed upon by consensus, to begin a proactive risk analysis process. We utilized the tool developed by the

University Hospital Consortium (UHC). This tool is modified by department to look at identified specific risk areas (e.g., monitoring, equipment, documentation needs). It is divided into two parts. The first helps to identify the level of risk and the opportunities for improvement; the second focuses on the specific risk entities. Each risk area is ranked from 0 to 3 (0 = no risk, 1 = low, 2 = medium, and 3 = high). Utilizing a provided formula and a scoring key, a risk is established, which will help identify possible areas of greatest exposure to risk. You can now begin to proactively manage the risks identified.[12]

The goal is to complete a proactive risk assessment of each of the identified areas on an annual basis. Measure your progress on an internal basis from established benchmarks using the UHC tool. Utilize the department procedures and processes that have shown improvement and decrease in risk to educate other departments. Share the information and the procedures. The ultimate goal is to decrease the risk to patients and minimize the exposure to untoward events.

Notes

1. Ternov, S. "The Human Side of Medical Mistakes." In P. Spath, ed., *Error Reduction in Health Care.* San Francisco: Jossey-Bass, 2000.
2. Van Cott, H. "Human Errors: Their Causes and Reduction." In S. Bogner, ed., *Human Error in Medicine.* Hillsdale, NJ: Lawrence Erlbaum Associates, 1994.
3. Reason, J. *Human Error.* New York: Cambridge University Press, 1990.
4. Beardsley, D. *First Do No Harm: A Practical Guide to Medication Safety and JCAHO Compliance.* Marblehead, MA: Opus Communications, 1999.
5. Ternov, "Error Reduction."
6. Ibid.
7. Ishikawa, K. *What Is Total Quality Control? The Japanese Way.* Englewood Cliffs, NJ: Prentice Hall, 1985.
8. Rex, J. H., Turnbull, J. E., Allen, S. J., et al. "Systematic Root Cause Analysis of Adverse Drug Events in a Referral Hospital." *The Joint Commission Journal of Quality Improvement,* vol. 26, no. 10, October 2000.
9. Adair, C. B., Murray, B. A. *Breakthrough in Process Redesign.* New York: American Management Association, 1994.
10. Lawler, E. E. *High Involvement Management.* San Francisco: Jossey-Bass, 1986.
11. Rex, Turnbull, Allen, et al. "Systematic Root Cause Analysis."
12. University Health Consortium. *Comprehensive Risk Assessment Tool: A Workbook for Assessing Risk in Hospitals and Integrated Delivery Networks.* Available from University Health Services Consortium Services Corporation, 2001 Spring Road, Suite 700, Oak Brook, IL 60521.

CHAPTER SEVENTEEN

THE LEADERSHIP ROLE OF THE CHIEF OPERATING OFFICER IN ALIGNING STRATEGY AND OPERATIONS TO CREATE PATIENT SAFETY

Julianne M. Morath, RN, MS

Patient safety will be a way of life for the chief operating officer (COO), given a more informed view of safety as a system, increased government regulation and oversight, specific accreditation standards through the Joint Commission on Accreditation of Healthcare Organizations and other organizations, payer requirements and incentives such as those proposed by the Leapfrog Group, and consumer demands for information and accountability. But most important, patient safety must be the fundamental aim or promise of the health care system to those who need and depend on us. As such, the COO role must be dedicated to unwavering and continuous attention, learning, and actions to design and operate systems that do no harm. This is what operations is all about. The other requirements in operations will follow when the design and operations for safety are done well.

Safety in health care is critical. Catastrophes can destroy an organization's reputation and profitability. The elements that form professional, national, and organizational cultures can come together to define and advance a safety culture or can create an unsafe operating environment.[1] A safety culture extends beyond a single organization's quest for world-class safety. Patient safety must become a value. Patient safety requires a joint belief in the importance of safety and a shared understanding of what it will take to create the culture of safety. The COO role is pivotal in initiating and continuing the dialogue and work strategies needed to accomplish this. The starting place is the operating environment, for which the COO has a direct responsibility.

The role of the COO in patient safety is to align and engage the energy of the organization to provide the highest quality of care and service, based on the most current professional knowledge and knowledge of patient and family needs and preferences. This includes the design and operation of systems in which this level of care and service delivery is not only possible but actively facilitated. The work of operations begins with building systems that do no harm. Although the focus of this chapter is patient safety, it is important to note that employee and environmental safety are inextricably linked to patient safety. In summary, the COO role is to engage others to

- Design and operate systems based on evidence in safety science
- Develop and support people who provide care and services to develop greater capacity in teamwork, risk awareness, risk mitigation, and resiliency
- Build a culture of safety and continuous learning in which care and services are delivered
- Focus and align resources to create greater safety
- Assure evidence-based, patient-centered, and system-centered work is being done

This chapter describes how this role can be operationalized.

Building systems that reduce the probability of accident and harm requires recognition and understanding of four basic concepts. These are as follows:[2]

1. Health care is a complex system, and complex systems are inherently risk prone, particularly operating rooms, intensive care units, and emergency rooms, where teamwork is essential and crises are common.
2. People, no matter how competent and vigilant, are fallible because they are human and hence physically and psychologically limited in memory capacity and the ability to deal with simultaneous multiple cognitive demands.
3. People create safety by defending against risk, intercepting error before it reaches the patient. They are also perpetrators of risk due to their being human, and are therefore subject to stressors such as fear, fatigue, and social factors that impair cognitive and motor function.
4. Safety is a system and can pose threats of failure from inadequate or clumsy equipment, fatigue-inducing schedules, flawed or incomplete procedures, excessive incentives for production, and risk-prone professional and organizational cultures often associated with faulty communications.

Accepting these concepts, the responsibility of the chief operating officer is to recognize the nature of emerging risks and operate a system of safety in the design and engineering of processes and in the management of processes to eliminate or mitigate risk. The foundation for this work is nurturing a culture, or people system, to see, live, and breathe safety. This is not about cautioning people to be more careful. It is rather about improving the systems in which people operate, and increasing their ability to perceive, identify, and close the gaps to eliminate or mitigate latent failures and vulnerabilities in those systems. Through an "alert field" in which people see and report risk, prediction and prevention of accidents can occur. A question that should be top of mind for the COO and actively pursued is: "Is this a safe place to give and receive care?"

A Call to Action

The work of patient safety is a challenge culturally, strategically, and technically. A starting place to examine these challenges is via a patient safety manifesto, or declaration of intent to act. Such a declaration was first organized by the Harvard Executive Session on Reducing Medical Error and Increasing Patient Safety.[3] The outline of the manifesto was an outcome of the sessions conducted semiannually over the course of three years, 1997 to 2000. The manifesto is a helpful organizing framework for the chief operating officer to examine, align, and mobilize the work to be done.

The elements of the patient safety manifesto are as follows:

1. Declare patient safety urgent and a priority.
2. Accept executive responsibility.
3. Import and apply new knowledge and skills.
4. Establish blameless reporting.
5. Assure accountability.
6. Align external controls.
7. Accelerate change.

These elements will be described to explore the role of the COO.

Declare Patient Safety Urgent and a Priority

Declaring patient safety urgent and a priority must be done in a manner that is relevant, credible, and taps into attributes of the organization's culture that serve to inspire. The promise "we will do no harm" is a powerful change lever to engage the organization. However, despite the Institute of Medicine (IOM) report[4] and multiple studies of medical accident, most notably the Harvard Practice Study,[5] many health care leaders, clinicians, and consumers remain unaware of patient safety issues. They are also unaware that most adverse events and medical accidents that cause harm are recurrent, and therefore predictable and preventable. There are many reasons for this. Among the reasons are the belief that medical accidents and errors are an inevitable part of health care; gross underreporting; denial and fear of shame and punishment; or the belief that current performance is an acceptable standard of care. Communication of an urgent priority needs to reside in the belief that we can and must do better. This message needs to be coupled with an accurate understanding of the current reality of the safety experience within the organization.

From a practical perspective, arguments regarding the validity of research are futile. The question is: "What is your experience?" Bringing the stories of patient safety to life and relevance is part of the COO's role of knowing and defining current reality as the platform for change. This can be accomplished through multiple strategies. Following are two suggested strategies that not only bring forward local experience but also engage clinicians.

Patient Safety Dialogues

The first strategy is to convene thought-leaders or key influential people in the clinical environment. They are readily identifiable. They are the individuals who peers seek out to learn what is new, ask their opinions, and request consultations. Bringing them together to explore the questions "Is this a safe place to receive and give care?" "How do you know?" and "What is your experience?" invites and legitimizes conversations about events, near misses, barriers, and sources of safety. These stories are typically not shared, but rather individually experienced. In this dialogue, a collective consciousness regarding safety in the organization is raised. Such recognition of experience quickly leads to conversations regarding actions to prevent errors and accidents from occurring. It creates a safe place or architecture to expand such dialogue throughout the organization in pursuit of improvement.

Focus Groups

Another strategy is to conduct focus groups of key stakeholders by discipline, department, and patient and family consumer groups. A tool such as the one designed by Nancy Wilson at the VHA-Inc., a Texas-based health care alliance, can be adopted and used in all care environments to understand the culture of safety.[6] The strength of the focus group approach is that the data collection is in itself an intervention to build a safe, confidential, blameless environment in which to talk and learn about safety. Focus groups can provide specific information about perceived barriers to safety and processes that need to change.

These focus groups' data, rich in detail, create a portrait of the organization that can be reflected back and used to define its current state and serve as a baseline to measure change. Although the IOM report and studies reported in the literature are helpful to frame the issue and initiate a national conversation, it is the actual experience of the organization that provides traction for change.

Naming Safety as a Priority

Returning to the fundamental promise or pledge "do no harm" amplifies the characteristic of the health care culture that can be called upon to align its members to explicitly identify patient safety as a priority. This is not without risk. Explicitly and publicly addressing patient safety creates exposure for the organization and its members. It is therefore essential to engage the governing board, professional and medical staff, insurance carriers, and legal counsel in understanding the ethical imperative, issues, and strategy.

As risk perception and reporting are increased, historical methods of tracking safety, such as medication error rate, will dramatically increase. The need to understand what will occur and why is essential. Initially, such reporting can be experienced as a decline in safety or an increase in events. A more informed view will realize that risks and events are now becoming visible, and so may be addressed. Manipulating and chasing rates will not improve safety. At this time in the evolution of understanding safety in health care, the story of how the systems are operating is what is important. This assertion will be examined more closely in the section about establishing a blameless reporting system.

Accept Executive Responsibility

The role of leadership requires personal commitment, strategy, and the use of tools. There are some critical "culture carriers," powerful messages usable to amplify aspects of the existing culture to build greater safety. The first such message is to publicly accept executive responsibility for patient safety. There can be no question of the priority of patient safety. The message must be clear, consistent, and concrete. The COO, as operations leader, provides a steady drumbeat of messages, measures, and feedback to the organization about patient safety. The COO also incorporates known practices to enhance safety in his or her work and requires the same of others. At the same time, the COO must incorporate strategies to remove barriers to safety as they are identified.

The COO role is to hardwire patient safety into the daily life and operations of the organization. Embracing and applying lessons learned from leaders in other industries, such as aviation, nuclear power, fire fighting, and manufacturing, can inform and accelerate action. Known safety principles from industry that can be incorporated into daily work include the following:[7]

- Train staff in effective teamwork, decision making, risk awareness, and error management as well as technical aspects of the job.
- Simplify and standardize work processes and products, such as the use of a consistent monitoring system.
- Design self-correcting systems or redundant systems that make it difficult to do the wrong thing, such as verifying messages about who will take what action when, or using technical monitors to complement judgment.
- Reduce reliance on human memory through protocols, checklists, and automated systems, checking with colleagues.
- Use automation carefully through the meticulous design of manual processes that can be converted well to automation, such as the medication record documentation process.
- Learn how each function of the organization works by studying it as a flow process. This requires a comprehensive audit of each step in a sequence.
- Drive out fear of blame in error reporting and set up systems so that data can be collected to learn about error and near misses. The risk should be in failing to report, not in the act of bringing bad news.
- Find out what is going on by developing sources, asking questions, and walking around. This is accomplished by being visible and actually reviewing in person the work activity.
- Do what obviously needs to be done one by one, step by step. When processes need correction, take action.
- Do not tolerate violation of standards or failure of staff to take available countermeasures against error (such as input from colleagues and use of checklists), and hold people accountable for their actions.

Another principle to incorporate into daily work is making implicit knowledge explicit.[8] Implicit knowledge is the information and know-how that individuals uniquely possess. In health care, a great deal of the work in developing care paths, clinical protocols, and best-of-practice models concerns making explicit each provider's knowledge about how a care process works. Working to define the knowledge that people have and don't know they have is a critical step in understanding workflow and seeing the whole picture. It also helps focus on these questions: Who in the system has knowledge and who gets to ask the questions?

The aviation industry would suggest that everyone has knowledge about different things and everyone can ask questions. The COO has a responsibility to both model and set the expectations for team-based communication, explicit sharing of information and knowledge, and tools to transfer knowledge and information such as those referenced earlier.

Leadership Exemplar: The Alcoa Story

An important example of leadership in safety is Paul O'Neill, former CEO of Alcoa. A Harvard case study describes O'Neill's leadership at Alcoa.[9]

> Paul O'Neill became CEO of Alcoa in June 1987 and was reported to have "immediately stunned corporate directors, industry analysts, and competitors when he announced his top priority: safety." He believed that the names of employees killed or injured should not be turned into numbers and rates. He didn't believe productivity necessitated increased risk or that accidents and injuries were the inevitable costs of doing business. He rather believed that to focus on safety required understanding of processes and systems in exquisite detail, and that understanding would lead to better and more productive operations. While Alcoa had an industry record for safety, O'Neill raised the bar and demanded management to zero defect. To eradicate accidents and injuries, he required recalibrating an operational approach from measuring what caused accidents to learning how to prevent them from occurring in the first place. For example, if a worker fell off a machine, he asked: "What was he doing on the machine anyway?" "Was the machine designed with control mechanisms that actually increased risk?"

The Alcoa story is an example of leadership's explicit focus on the basics of safety. O'Neill recognized that safety could be a rallying focus for the workforce. By focusing on safety and pursuing the root causes of accidents, the company prioritized improving process flow, which led to increased productivity and reduced the cost of accidents and errors. This is the boldness of approach required by the COO in operating a care delivery system of high reliability. The results at Alcoa are legendary. The same focus, discipline, and commitment can be executed in health care.

High Reliability

To fulfill the vision of creating a safety culture, one that consistently demonstrates the characteristics of high reliability, operational leadership tools must be learned and used. Before describing leadership tools, a brief reference to aspects of high reliability may be helpful. Martin Hatlie, president of the National Partnership for Patient Safety, summarizes these characteristics as being the following:[10]

- Trust and transparency
- Reporting
- Flexibility in hierarchy
- Perceived to be just and accountable
- Engaged and dedicated to continuous learning

An illustration of the characteristics of high reliability is provided in the article "When Failure Is Not an Option," by Robert Pool.[11] Berkeley researchers ask you to imagine the following:

> Shrink your airport to only one short runway and one ramp and gate. Make planes take off and land at the same time, at half the present time interval, rock the runway from side to side, and require everybody to leave in the morning and return the same day. Turn off the radar to avoid detection, impose strict controls on radios, fuel the aircraft in place with their engines running, wet the whole thing down with salt water and oil, and man it with 20-year-olds, half of whom have never seen a plane.

This is a depiction of the operating conditions of *Nimitz*-class naval aircraft carriers, an environment operated by an organization that is highly reliable in its ability to avoid error. There are lessons in this example for health care and the COO. The U.S. Navy requires command rules and manuals of operating procedures to govern the flight deck processes, making explicit lessons learned from years of experience. Navy training is designed so that these procedures are second nature to the individuals who serve.

The article also describes another dimension of this highly structured hierarchical organization. The organizational structure shifts as pressures and risk increase during the launch and recovery of planes. The crew interact as colleagues, not superiors and subordinates. Cooperation and continual communication is part of the operation. With planes taking off and landing once a minute, things happen too quickly for instruction, delegation, and authorization to occur. The crew works as a team by watching each other and by communicating constantly and repeatedly. Each member of the team understands his or her role and that of the other members of the team. The constant flow of observation and communication identifies mistakes, the latent errors, before they cause damage or an accident. Experienced personnel continually monitor the flow, listening for everything that doesn't fit and correcting mistakes before they cause error.

In an emergency, such as a deck fire, a third organizational structure emerges. If any emergency occurs, the crew reacts immediately and without direction. Each crew member assumes a preassigned role and fulfills the role according to carefully rehearsed procedures. The safety of the ship and crew is everyone's responsibility. Even the lowest-ranking crewmember has not only the authority but the obligation to halt operations immediately under proper circumstances. The researchers report, "Although his judgment may later be reviewed or even criticized, he will not be penalized for being wrong and will often be publicly congratulated if right."[12]

Apply this description to the operations of a health care organization, division, or department where the safety of patients, staff, and families is a paramount concern. This is the COO's challenge in orchestrating high reliability. High-reliability organizations are both centralized and decentralized, hierarchical and collegial, rule bound and learning centered.[13] They also emphasize constant communication directed toward avoiding mistakes. Constant watching and interacting are used to advise, detect, and act on any sign of trouble. In addition, high-reliability organizations look for ways to constantly improve and never take success or safety for granted.

Import and Apply New Knowledge and Skills

Researchers Carolyn B. Libuser and Karlene Roberts identified common factors in safety from studying high-reliability organizations.[14] These factors define skill sets and tools that the COO can import and apply from other industries. Among the most relevant tools that need to be applied in health care to create safety are the following.

Process Auditing

Process auditing involves establishing a system for ongoing checks and formal audits to spot unexpected safety problems. Questions for the COO include the following:

- Is there an objective process to inquire about, review, and measure critical areas of performance for the organization and its parts?

- Is there an internal audit function outside of defined workgroups, departments, or care units to conduct such audits and report?
- Are critical indicators systematically measured, reported, and reviewed with frequency and regularity?
- Is a formalized framework for safety self-assessment used, such as the ones now becoming available through the National Patient Safety Foundation and other professional organizations?
- Are accrediting and regulatory surveys used as an opportunity for rigorous self-assessment?

Reward Systems

Questions concerning incentives or rewards for the COO include the following:

- How are reward systems used to drive the attention and behavior of the organization?
- Are reward systems aligned consistently with promoting safe practices and behavior?
- Are shortcuts being made and rewarded to reduce costs?
- How are disclosures of risk- and failure-prone practices managed?

Pursual of Safety Standards

In studies of catastrophic accidents such as the *Exxon Valdez* oil spill, the Chernobyl nuclear power plant explosion, and the chemical gas spill in Bhophal, India, standards for safety and quality were found to be subordinated to cost. Industry standards of basic safety were not met. Questions concerning safety standards for the COO are as follows:

- Do clear standards exist that differentiate safe, high-quality practices from substandard practices?
- Are monitors of performance against relevant best-in-class standards in place and rigorously applied?
- Is performance improvement required and monitored to achieve best-in-class performance standards?

Perception of Risk

Perception of risk has two aspects: whether the organization or its members are aware of risks that exist and, if awareness of risk exists, what measures are being taken to minimize risk. This relates to what data are collected, monitored, and acted on. In high-reliability organizations, there are effective monitoring systems and the organization acknowledges and confronts existing reality. Questions for the COO include the following:

- Do you require and regularly use effective monitors?
- Are the measures used the right measures, and of sufficient sensitivity, to detect early signals of declining performance?
- Are actions to improve required, along with an ongoing follow-up to ensure improvement is sustained?

Command and Control

Formal rules and procedures are necessary. These are not meant to create bureaucratic complexity, but rather to ensure adherence to the standards and shared knowledge of best practices. This implies intelligent and thoughtful application of rules and procedures, not routinized compliance. The rules and procedures should foster knowledge-based decisions, in which experts can determine when a variation or innovation is required because of a unique condition. This factor is expanded by Roberts and Libuser, who outline the following command-and-control elements.[15]

- *Migrating decision making:* The person with the most expertise makes the decision.
- *Having redundancy:* Back-up systems are in place, whether consisting of people or technology support.
- *Seeing the big picture:* Senior managers see the big picture, and therefore do not micromanage, but attend to patterns and systems.
- *Establishing formal rules and procedures:* There is hierarchy, with procedure and protocol based on evidence.
- *Conducting ongoing training:* Investment is made in the knowledge and skills of workers at the front line. This includes training in teamwork, such as crew resource management technologies.

A self-assessment against these criteria or characteristics of high-reliability organizations is a helpful step in determining the status of an organization and provides a baseline for action. The COO must have ongoing rigorous assessment in place to continually understand the status of safety in the organization, starting with the highest-risk procedures or processes. This is a different process from that of investigating errors and failures after they occur. Partnering content experts with outside human factors and engineering expertise can proactively detect latent failure and system vulnerabilities, allowing preventive actions to close gaps in safety. Although health care is probably more complex than any other industry and has unique features, it has much to learn and apply from other industries and domains of science, such as the common factors that humans bring to all fields. The COO should seek these lessons out and calibrate the expectations of risk and quality professionals to increase their skill portfolios to include patient safety.

Apply New Tools and Build Infrastructure

Because the domain of patient safety is vast, a considerable armamentarium of tools is required. Establishing clear expectations, policies, and mechanisms to engage the patient and family as partners in creating safety is a responsibility of the chief operating officer. The tools described in this chapter are instrumental for the COO role.

Knowledge Base

Numerous tools in education and training are required to build a knowledge base for patient safety. Three concepts are of particular utility. They are as follows:[16]

- *The Swiss cheese model.* This represents the nature of emerging risks in complex systems, with defenses and vulnerabilities.
- *The blunt and sharp end.* This illustrates how expertise is applied and error or accident is experienced at the point where provider and patient exist in exquisite vulnerability, at the sharp end. The table is set, however, for that encounter at the blunt end, or the governance and management end, where decisions regarding such things as policy, production, and resource allocation are made. The high influence of these two disparate but interrelated parts of health care is a powerful reminder of the need to close the distance between front office and front line to understand the complexity of technical work in health care.
- *Hindsight bias.*[17] This concept, from the field of human factors, illustrates that it is human nature for people in hindsight to simplify conditions and underestimate the complexity that people involved in an error or accident were dealing with at the time of the event. The most common result of hindsight bias is to attribute the cause of a medical accident to "human error." Having thus found a scapegoat, all learning stops and the conditions that were present lay in wait to realign to produce another accident in the future.

Rapid-Cycle Change

Rapid-change technologies, such as PDSA cycles[18] and rapid replication,[19] are proven best practices to accelerate change and improvement. The COO's urgency, focus, and skills in this area are critical in requiring and mentoring the changes needed to improve patient safety. For example, specific best practices to adopt and implement include the best medication practices identified by the Massachusetts Hospital Association and the National Patient Safety Partnership, the surgical site identification advanced by the professional association for orthopedic surgeons, and others reported in the literature.[20] Attention should be given to lessons from the aviation industry in applying crew resource management training for care teams in high-risk areas, such as operating rooms, labor and delivery suites, and intensive care suites. It is essential to build an arm of the organization to assist managers and front-line staff in acting on reported information of risk.

Language

Accepting that language shapes culture, thoughtful and deliberate use of a new vocabulary to reflect the new look of safety is required. Consider using the following replacement of terms and deliberately building new language into the COO and management vocabulary:[21]

- *System* versus *isolated event.* An accident results from latent failures or weaknesses in a system. These failures or weaknesses are cumulative and interactive. Research has revealed that at least four errors must align to produce an accident. A recent analysis of a catastrophic medical accident revealed 82 errors or system failures contributing to the event. An isolated single cause is rare.
- *Analysis* or *study* versus *investigation.* A process of analysis or study is used to learn how systems work and how the pieces fit together to create the whole. The learning from rigorous analysis can be applied to predict and inform interventions to prevent future failures. An investigation carries the connotation of a process to assign blame. It is typically a linear search to determine a single cause or "bad apple."
- *Accountable* versus *blame.* Health care professionals are accountable for their work. They have a responsibility to ensure they possess current knowledge and demonstrate competence in the work they perform, as well as the interdependence they have in that performance. In addition, they must appreciate how systems work and how people are the human components of systems that sometimes contribute to failure as well as create

safety. Blame fixes on a scapegoat, rather than a pursuit of a deeper understanding of failure. Historical methods of blame, train, and punish have not worked to improve safety.

- *Blameless* versus *punitive* or *retaliatory*. A blameless environment is one where health care personnel feel comfortable and compelled to report failures and near misses so they can be studied. Punitive or retaliatory environments create an atmosphere where health care staff are afraid to disclose failures and near misses, thus eliminating the opportunity to learn from mistakes.
- *Heedful procedure* versus *routine procedure*. Heedful procedures are designed so that they cannot be performed without thinking. Rather, they include steps that demand attention before action can take place. Routine procedures are those that are performed so many times they can become automatic, and as such introduce greater risk.
- *Hierarchy* versus *bureaucracy*. Hierarchy is a system of formal rules, procedures, training, and decision making based on evidence. Senior managers see the big picture and therefore do not micromanage, but attend to patterns and systems. Decisions are made by the person with the most expertise. Bureaucracy is a system of administration marked by adherence to fixed rules; authority by position, not expertise; red tape; specialized and isolated silos; and the politics of control.
- *What happened?* versus *Whose fault is it?* The question "What happened?" invites analysis of the conditions surrounding an error or accident. Asking "Whose fault is it?" immediately seeks to place blame and resorts to the social attribution of human error as cause.
- *Accident of failure* versus *human error as cause*. Accident describes a breakdown in a system, which is complex and needs analysis. Error suggests that only one factor, usually noted as human error, is the cause. If human error is assigned as the cause, all learning stops.
- *Multicausal* versus *root cause*. Studies of accidents reveal that at least four failures must occur and line up to create the conditions for an accident to occur. The Swiss cheese model illustrates the multicausal concept, suggesting that multiple failures or errors align to produce an accident versus a single source. Understanding this and pursuing the deeper story of an accident discloses the contributing conditions, latent vulnerabilities, or trajectories that lead to accidents. Analysis of the deeper story in turn allows for systemic actions to reduce the probability that a similar accident will occur in the future.

- *Learning* versus *judgment.* To build safer systems to prevent failures from happening again, an organization must be committed to learning from mistakes. A noted archeologist was quoted as saying, "Dig where you stumble, for that is where the treasure is." Such a mind-set directs a passionate curiosity to dig deeply into understanding sources of failure, where we stumbled, and also the sources of success, where error was averted. Judgment closes down inquiry.

Process Auditing Tools and Methods

This area was addressed under the section on high reliability. Process auditing tools and methods move safety into a proactive role.

Architecture for Learning

Minicourses with national experts, attended by interdisciplinary members of the organization; dialogues to invite informal exploration of safety; self-learning packets; orientation and training modules; and ongoing publications in the communication vehicles of the organization serve to teach, reinforce, and stimulate learning among all members of the health care delivery system.

Policies to Advance Partnerships with Patients and Their Families

- *"Nothing about me without me."* This policy embraces practices and tools to involve the patient and family in decision making and participation in the care process. It includes providing information to patient and family through multiple media such as print, Internet, video, courses, counseling, and conferencing, in a timely manner and in a way that can be understood. This includes ensuring translators and translated materials for the multicultural communities served. Informational content focused on what patient's families need to know, ask, and do to create safety with their providers is empowering and an essential part of care.
- *"If it looks wrong, it is wrong."* This is a policy that not only legitimizes but requires anyone who perceives a risk to safety to stop the process. This includes the patient and family. All participants in the care process have the responsibility to stop until the question of risk has been thoroughly examined and safety established. This policy, fashioned after the "Andon Cord" in industry, empowers all participants in the health care system to act to establish safety without regard to hierarchy.

- *Disclosure and truth telling.* This policy is one that provides guidance in working with patients and families in the face of an error or medical accident. It consists in establishing and guiding the practice of communication and is a powerful culture carrier. The National Patient Safety Foundation has published a statement of principle to talk to patients about health care accidents and adverse events. Elements of disclosure include a prompt and compassionate explanation of what is understood about what happened and the probable effects, what is being done to ensure safety, the assurance that a full analysis will take place to reduce the likelihood of a similar event happening to another patient, what changes are being made based on the findings of the analyses as they are known, and an acknowledgment of accountability.[22] Skills training in critical communication is needed, and the COO has the responsibility to ensure the necessary resources.

Response to Medical Accidents

It is the responsibility of the COO and other designated senior managers to be immediately notified and to respond to medical accidents, significant near misses, and sentinel events. Clear policies and operating procedures are required to set expectations and guide action. The response to medical accidents both defines and shapes a safety culture. The direct involvement of senior leadership with patient, family, and affected staff is an important statement of commitment and accountability.

Measures

An essential tool for the COO is measurement. Measures serve as the gauges to determine whether desired changes are taking place and desired effects are being achieved. Increasing the frequency of measures and providing feedback to front-line workers can accelerate and sustain change. Although measuring medical error is complicated, a starting point is to measure increased reporting. Measures also need to be built for public accountability as well as for internal and industry-specific learning and improvement.

Assign Accountability

A specific work plan with ambitious aims, goals, assigned accountabilities, and measures is an essential tool. Defined and focused resources to execute the plan are also needed. The work plan provides a road map to achieve the aims, as well as a method for the organization to align contributions and gauge effectiveness. Serious consideration should be given to the designation of a technical leader for patient safety to help execute the patient safety work plan. A patient safety leader or director is a role that complements the COO as content expert, consultative resource to managers and front line providers, and catalyst for the organization to develop greater capacity at the sharp end or front line of care.

Assigning accountability also carries with it the requirement to actively engage employees and professional staff in the design and execution of the safety agenda. Providing care that is free of defect is a shared interest among those who have committed their careers to health care. Actively engaging all stakeholders, however, starts with an inspiring aim, goals, and associated measures that are directly relevant to patient care. As mentioned throughout this chapter, the leadership strives to create a confidential and safe space, ask questions, and consistently follow through, eliminating the skepticism that patient safety is a fad, a buzzword, or shallow rhetoric. Such action emphasizes the work of patient safety as a long-term and never-ending disciplined pursuit.

Mentoring an Accountability System

The COO mentors the required accountability system by holding managers directly responsible for taking action to eliminate or mitigate known risks, urgently responding to near misses, and engaging in continual dialogue and learning about creating ever-increasing levels of safety. Every conversation becomes curriculum content of accountability in the management system of the organization.

Engaging the Organization

There are many examples of engagement strategies. A specific engagement strategy is to work with managers to establish a safety log in each unit for staff to enter safety information. Managers and medical leadership should meet regularly with an interdisciplinary team to review the content of the log, prioritize, and plan resolving actions to eliminate or mitigate risks identified.

A safety action team can be assembled at each local unit, populated by interdisciplinary and interdepartmental staff who are empowered to take the necessary actions to implement changes that increase safety and reduce the probability that accidents will occur. They can develop and use data sources, such as logs, safety reports, provider insights, and patient and family feedback. They can also scan relevant literature for ideas from the experience of others.

At a broad organizational level, a patient safety steering committee with membership from across the organization, including professional staff, clinical front-line staff, consumers, and board members, can be appointed to advise on strategy, formulate policy, and monitor results. They may also act as resources and emissaries of patient safety to the organization. The role of the COO in chartering and chairing such a forum is a powerful and visible message about the commitment to and priority of patient safety in the organization. It also provides a forum for practicing clinicians, clinical leaders, administrators, communication experts, consumers, and governing directors to engage in promoting safety and the changes that must be made to achieve ever-increasing levels of safety in care delivery.

Further areas of engagement include leveraging information technology and clinical staff expertise to design the necessary decision supports, alerts, documentation processes, information migration, and reports to enhance patient safety. Direct order entry, dose-range checking, bar coding, and alerts for incompatibilities and allergies in the medication use system are a starting point. The use of information technology is just beginning to be a fully realized domain of patient safety. Although not a technical expert, the COO's role involves gaining a working knowledge of what is possible, and engaging cross-functional experts to anticipate and build what is necessary.

Establish Blameless Reporting

Reporting for accountability, reporting for learning, and reporting for intervention are important COO considerations. The discussion of this facet of the patient safety manifesto will focus on reporting for learning and intervention, while noting that public accountability, by reporting medical accidents to the appropriate agencies and authorities, is an obligation and is addressed in the section "Align External Controls."

The reporting system is not only a tool, but a deep cultural intervention to nurture an "alert field" and empower front-line technical and clinical providers. Characteristics of the system include a blameless and confidential reporting system, robust analysis and pattern detection, feedback, and communication of lessons learned. The system should encourage and reward increased risk perception and reporting of near misses, vulnerabilities, and "accidents waiting to happen." A reporting format with limited fixed fields and greater room for text allows the story of existing conditions that contributed to error and accident to be identified, explored, and better understood. This requires greater analytical investment but yields richer intelligence about how systems and processes are actually operating. Transparency is a characteristic of the reporting process that enables everyone to learn from failures, accidents, and acts of prevention.

Reporting and tracking data for purposes of learning and improvement require an environment of confidentiality and privilege of protection. The health care workplace must be free of blame, punishment, and liability exposure so that full disclosure and learning can take place. This, however, does not apply to circumstances of gross negligence, intention to harm, unethical behavior, impairment due to drugs or alcohol, or failure to learn over time. These circumstances, although rare, pose a threat to patient safety and must be dealt with swiftly, fairly, and professionally from an administrative perspective.

Recognition and celebration of risk identification and reporting, through providing timely feedback, telegraphing lessons learned, taking action, and saying "thank you," reinforce a culture that is alert, critical, and heedful in its work. Rather than normalizing deviance through routine or through resignation and acceptance of the status quo as the standard, this environment critically examines everything it does and engages in learning and improvement. Changing the frame of reference from "incident reporting" to "safety reporting" removes historic connotations of performance judgment and expands reporting to a productive stance in identifying near misses and risks. Importing lessons from the aviation industry is one of the best practices for developing a reporting model for health care.

Align External Controls

Safety cultures are created through trust, knowledge, and well-designed interventions to produce desired effects. The role of the COO is to actively foster these characteristics inside the organization and in the societal context in which the organization operates.

The broad view of patient safety encompasses three domains: how society understands and talks about safety, how the legislative and legal system acts, and what we do inside and across health care organizations and systems.

The emphasis of this chapter has been on what to do inside health care organizations and systems. However, the role of the COO must encompass influencing the public discourse on patient safety. The legal system and media are very challenging. The societal call for "heads to roll" when something goes wrong in medical care must be respected and met with accountability and open dialogue to appreciate the paradox of contemporary health care. This paradox is that with dramatic increases in the ability to cure and treat injury and disease and perform "miracles" of medicine comes the expectation of perfect outcomes and infallible providers. The very technology that introduces breakthroughs in science also introduces new and unprecedented risk that leads to medical accident. The COO role is one that must actively seek avenues to influence, interpret, and create forums to explore the complexities of patient safety. The exquisite tension between public accountability and the public's right to know versus provider confidentiality and privilege of protection in pursuit of improvement must be managed. These notions are not mutually exclusive, but require a balance-seeking dialogue.

The active involvement of the COO with regulatory and accrediting bodies is increasing. The need to align external controls to promote, rather than undermine, efforts to improve safety is critical. This involves mutually exploring messages and behaviors that create partnership, while also eliminating messages and conduct that create barriers. Working with professional organizations to promote patient safety through educational offerings, skills development, care competencies, and expanded research efforts is another leadership activity.

The COO role includes working with government and with professional organizations, especially those with purchasing power, to require pharmaceutical and device industries to submit products to human factors testing, engineer safety features into product design, and use labeling practices that elevate safety above marketing considerations. Engaging the media is increasingly important to encourage responsible reporting of the issues in medical accidents rather than sensationalizion of specific cases, which may cause internal safety reporting and analysis to go underground for fear of reprisals. Working toward tort reform is another COO consideration in preparing an environment for patient safety.

The Business Case

The COO is required to operate the organization cost-effectively in order to provide affordable care and services, allow for financial resources to reinvest in the growth and capability of the organization, and help ensure long-term viability. This chapter would be incomplete without explicitly addressing the business case for patient safety. Beyond the ethical imperative to improve safety, there is a compelling business case.

The business case for patient safety is reducing cost through improving care and eliminating the costs of poor quality. This serves as a more compelling rallying point for efficiency and productivity than the cost-cutting messages that plague the health care industry and may have had the effect of increasing risk and undermining safety. The original Harvard Practice Study concluded that 6.7% of all hospital admissions experience a medical error; of these, 3.4% result in an adverse event, and 14% of those events are fatal.[23] It was this study, extrapolated to national demographics, that created the compelling comparison that the number of annual hospital deaths is equivalent to the death toll that would result from the crash of two jumbo jet carriers each week. Studies are now suggesting that deaths from medical accident, currently reported as the number eight public health problem in the United States, are grossly underestimated. Applying these early findings allows an organization to model the predicted number of patients expected to experience an adverse event.

The studies further noted that each adverse event added $4,700 in costs of care.[24] A simple economic model can be constructed to estimate the increased cost to the burden of illness due to adverse events. Analyzing actual adverse events in an organization to determine the cost is a worthwhile initiative. Engaging the chief financial officer in this exercise is an important strategy to develop awareness and appreciation of the issue. It is important to note that few errors and adverse events are caused by unusual or rare circumstances.[25] Rather, these adverse events constitute a familiar list: wound infection, drug overdose, wrong drug, bleeding from anticoagulation, insulin reaction, missed diagnosis, and falls. Because these risks and events are known and predictable, they are also preventable. It is estimated that these preventable events represent over 72% of medical accidents and errors.[26]

Studies further found that the setting of care was not significant in preventability, thereby focusing attention systemwide to hospital, clinic, emergency department, free-standing ambulatory care, and diagnostic settings.[27] The work of patient safety is not isolated to the highest-risk clinical inpatient environments but is the work of the entire system of care, with particular attention to the handoffs and transitions between areas and functions.

The business case for patient safety involves reducing the costs of poor quality through the development of aligned and effective systems of care delivery in every part of the continuum from suppliers of products to care encounters. When patient safety, or the reduction of error and accident, becomes an explicit business strategy, then errors and accidents must be examined in enormous detail. The organization, not the individual, must be examined from a process flow perspective. Efficient and effective systems are safe systems.[28]

In most health care organizations, people have learned to work around unnecessary complexity, process failure, and other system issues. When people adapt their practices around faulty systems, waste is usually produced. Waste in processes adds additional cost burden and frustration to the work of patient care. This "normalization of deviance" is not only costly but adds risk of error and accident to the care system.

An engaged and stable workforce is a contribution to safety and reduces the cost of turnover and declining productivity. A safe organization builds confidence and a reputation that can translate to loyalty and market share. However, an investment is required. Designating an operating budget to support patient safety and sponsoring applied research funding are COO responsibilities. The business case, through economic modeling of preventable errors and adverse events, refocusing resources to the safety agenda, and integrating safety into the core expectations of all managers, allows providers to begin to identify sources of funding.

Summary

The COO plays a pivotal role in defining, inspiring, and developing an aligned organization that consistently demonstrates the characteristics of high reliability. Ensuring effective human resources systems and management practices in recruitment, training, and ongoing ensurance of competence is essential. Setting and communicating clear expectations that risk perception, reporting, and error prevention are the responsibility of each individual and the collective obligation of everyone is essential. Dedicating the resources to educate about and advance patient safety underlies COO and organizational commitment. Hardwiring patient safety into the strategy, management and measurement system, and reward system of the organization integrates patient safety as part of the organization, not an initiative grafted onto it. Nurturing patient and family partnerships through policy, protocol, and practices is foundational. The willingness and enthusiasm to do the heavy lifting of the work in patient safety, and the courage to stay the course and model the way, is the COO's role in aligning operations to build systems that do no harm.

A final note: The more you know and do in patient safety, the more you will see to do. The stages in increasing patient safety create a clearer line of sight to the evolving knowledge of the topic and the greater depth of application and action that is called for. As our industry effectively tackles the known risks of today's environment, new knowledge, technology, pharmaceutical agents, and challenges, such as changes in workforce demographics, will be continually introduced, with new emerging risks. By aggressively learning the lessons of today, there will be greater intelligence and capacity to address the challenges of the future. This challenge is one of the worthy pursuits of the COO role that adds value to health care delivery.

Notes

1. Helmreich, R., and Merritt, A. *Culture at Work in Medicine and Aviation: National, Organizational and Professional Influences* (Aldershot, UK: Ashgate, 1998).
2. Helmreich, R. et al., "Applying Aviation Safety Initiatives to Medicine," *Focus on Patient Safety* 4, no. 1 (2001):1–2.
3. Weingart, S. "Patient Safety Manifesto," notes from the Executive Session on Medical Error and Patient Safety, Division of Health Policy Research and Education, Harvard University, Harvard Medical School, Malcolm Wiener Center for Social Policy, John F. Kennedy School of Government, January 29, 2000.
4. Institute of Medicine Committee of Healthcare in America, L. Kohn et al., eds., *To Err Is Human: Building a Safer Health System* (Washington, DC: National Academy Press, 1999).
5. Leape, L. L. et al., "The Nature of Adverse Events in Hospitalized Patients: Results from the Harvard Medical Practice Study II," *New England Journal of Medicine* 324 (1991):377–384.
6. Wilson, N., and Study Team, "Patient Safety: Listening to Healthcare Employees," Cooperative Study of Veterans Health Administration, Care Group, Kaiser Permanente, and National Patient Safety Foundation, sponsored by Department of Veterans Affairs, 1998.
7. Nance, J. D. "Managing Human Error in Aviation," *Scientific American* May (1997):62–70.
8. Norman, D. *The Psychology of Everyday Things* (New York: Basic Books, 1988).
9. Clark, K. B., and Margolis, J. D. "Workplace Safety at Alcoa," Case 9-692-042 (Boston: Harvard Business School Publishing, 1991), 1–2.
10. Hatlie, M. Patient Safety Collaborative Lecture Series, Voluntary Hospitals of American Regional Collaboratives, 2000.
11. Pool, R. "When Failure Is Not an Option," *Technology Review* 100 (1997):38–45.
12. Ibid.
13. Libuser, C. B., and Roberts, K. "Risk Mitigation Through Organizational Structure," paper to be submitted, 1998.
14. Ibid.
15. Ibid.
16. Reason, J. *Managing the Risks of Organizational Accidents* (Brookfield, NY: Ashgate, 1997).
17. Cook, R. for the Cognitive Technologies Laboratory, *How Systems Fail* (Chicago: Cognitive Technologies Laboratory, 2002).
18. Langley, G. J. et al., *The Improvement Guide: A Practical Approach to Enhancing Organizational Performance* (San Francisco: Jossey-Bass, 1996).
19. Cauldwell, C. *Mentoring Strategic Change in Health Care: An Action Guide* (Milwaukee, WI: ASQC Quality Press, 1995).
20. Joint Commission on Accreditation of Healthcare Organizations. *Sentinel Event Alert* 6 (Oakbrook Terrace, IL: JCAHO, 1998).

21. Minnesota Hospital and Healthcare Partnership and Minnesota Medical Association, "Redefining the Culture for Patient Safety [brochure]" (St. Paul, MN: Author, 2000).

22. National Patient Safety Foundation, "NPSF Statement Principle: Talk to Patients About Health Care Injury," *Focus on Patient Safety* 4, no. 1 (2000):3.

23. Brennan, T. A. et al., "Incidence of Adverse Events and Negligence in Hospitalized Patients: Results from the Harvard Medical Practice Study I," *New England Journal of Medicine* 324 (1991):370–376.

24. Leape et al., "The Nature of Adverse Events in Hospitalized Patients."

25. Johnson, J. A., and Bootman, J. L. "Drug-Related Morbidity and Mortality and the Economic Impact on Pharmaceutical Care," *American Journal of Hospital-System Pharmacy* 54 (1997).

26. Leape, L. L. et al., "Preventing Medical Injury," *Quality Review Bulletin* May (1993):144–149.

27. Ibid.

28. Massmann, J. as quoted in "Taking the Mistakes Out of Medicine," feature of the Children's Hospitals and Clinics of Minnesota, J. Shapiro, *U.S. News and World Report* July (2000):50–66.

CHAPTER EIGHTEEN

THE SUCCESSFUL QUALITY PROFESSIONAL: FRAMEWORK, ATTRIBUTES, AND ROLES

K. Bobbi Traber, MD, MBA

The role of the quality professional has rapidly changed in the last decade as the science of continuous quality improvement (CQI) and total quality management (TQM) has taken hold in the health care industry. As health care leadership has embraced this new philosophy of systemwide continuous quality improvement, the role of the health care quality professional has expanded. No longer are quality managers simply responsible for the auditing and reporting of quality standards or events after they occur. Modern health care quality professionals must be proactive facilitators of multidisciplinary groups and have the knowledge, tools, and skills to effect change throughout a health care organization. This chapter examines the historical context, discusses the organizational framework required, and describes the leadership attributes and skills necessary for the quality professional to be successful in the rapidly changing health care environment that focuses on patient safety.

Background

During the early twentieth century, efforts to improve the quality of care focused on the development of professional licensure standards for physicians and nurses. In 1912, the Joint Commission of the

Standardization of Visiting Nursing developed criteria for community health nursing that delineated age, education, and licensing
requirements. During the same period, the American Medical Association pushed for reforms in medical education, which culminated in
the publishing of the Flexner report. Similar to the nursing proposal,
the Flexner report proposed standards for the education and licensure
of physicians. During this time, quality managers focused on issues
of licensure; consumers of health care did not question the quality of
patient care. Poor outcomes were deemed beyond human control.

The focus on licensure standards evolved to a focus on improving
the quality of the operational delivery of care in the 1940 to 1960 era.
The quality literature published during this time examined the adequacy of medical and nursing practice as compared with accepted
standards. In 1952, the Joint Commission on Accreditation of Hospitals
(now the Joint Commission on Accreditation of Healthcare Organizations, JCAHO) was formed. The design of this newly created organization was to send a team of experts to evaluate the quality of the
organization against a set of minimum standards.

Societal focus on consumer protection and the right to health care
largely influenced quality evaluation in the 1960s. Social Security
amendments created Medicare and Medicaid. The role of the quality
professional was largely one of utilization review, which was required
by the federal government. Also during this era, Donabedian (1966)
proposed a model for evaluating quality of care through assessment
of structure, process, and outcome. Outcome, however, received little
attention until much later.

Quality and *quality assurance* were common terms in the 1970s.
There was rapid growth in the literature on issues of quality, along with
concerns about the rising cost of care. Regulatory agencies, including
the federal government and the JCAHO, played significant roles in the
evolution of quality at this time. In 1972, the Bennett Amendment
established the Professional Standards Review Organization (PSRO)
to ensure that services rendered were medically necessary and that the
quality of the services met professionally recognized standards of care.
The JCAHO began to require hospitals to continually evaluate patient
care against explicit measurable criteria focused on patient outcomes.
However, despite the application of measurement systems to the auditing of care, these measurements were generally retrospective. The quality professional was rarely required to design and implement change.

By the 1980s, the JCAHO standards had evolved from isolated problem identification and reporting to mandating a coordinated hospital-
wide approach to clinical problem solving. The quality assurance staff
were required to transition from simple data collection tasks to problem identification and assessment and the development of action plans

TABLE 18-1   Comparison of Quality Strategies

	Traditional Quality Assurance	Continuous Quality Improvement
Purpose	Improve the quality of patient care	Improve the quality of all services to patients and families
Scope	Problem oriented	Process oriented
Focus	Departmental-based examination	Interdepartmental relationships
	Individual care evaluation	Integrated care process examination
Accountability	Departmental leadership and accountability	Organizational leadership and accountability

for improvement. This change required the quality professional to begin interacting with multiple key organizational leaders. The quality officer was expected to gather and analyze clinical and administrative data, support change implementation, and measure the impact. The focus in the 1980s, however, was still on the *individual* as the cause of a problem; rarely were integrated processes evaluated and identified as causative factors.

In 1985, JCAHO changed its philosophy from a problem-focused one to one that required organizations to monitor all important care processes. This transition further broadened the role of quality professionals, requiring them to develop and use information system tools to ensure comprehensive monitoring programs. The quality professional was for the first time required to analyze, integrate, and report quality information from multiple sources, including infection control, utilization review, and risk management. By the 1990s, JCAHO had made a full transition from a quality assurance strategy to one of continuous quality improvement. Highlights of this transition are summarized in Table 18-1.

In 1997, JCAHO mandated the institutional reporting of four (later six) clinical outcomes with their ORYX program and began incorporating this requirement in the survey process. The Joint Commission's board of commissioners in February 2000 approved an enhancement to their measurement program by developing standardized *core measures*. These measures were developed in five disease process areas by multidisciplinary expert panels and had the following goals (JCAHO, 2000):

- Providing a mechanism for monitoring health care organization performance on a continuous basis between triennial surveys
- Focusing surveys on areas within an organization that represent the greatest opportunities for improvement

- Helping organizations identify issues that require attention
- Establishing a national comparative database to support benchmarking, health services research, and internal quality improvement activities
- Providing the content for future public release of performance information relating to the provision of health care services
- Fostering standardization of performance measurement
- Encouraging the use of evidence-based treatment protocols
- Focusing on core measures that have proven to have a positive impact on clinical outcomes

The core measure reporting process enables interinstitutional quality comparisons and has been incorporated into hospital surveys.

This brief survey of the history of quality has demonstrated the evolution of the quality professional's role from a data gatherer and regulatory expert to that of an information manager and leader of institutional change. The quality professional must be positioned in the organizational framework and empowered by senior leadership to have the freedom to examine hospital-wide processes. He or she must be able to gather and analyze data from multiple sources and demonstrate the leadership skills to facilitate interdisciplinary groups to develop solutions and implement change.

Required Organizational Framework

Driven by external regulatory changes and demands for quality outcomes by patients and payers, the quality assurance department evolved in the last decade from a centralized supportive role for a few clinical leaders to one that communicates and coordinates initiatives among multiple departments. Success as a quality professional is dependent not only on the personal attributes of the employee but also on the institutional quality culture, organizational quality infrastructure design, and the programmatic resources allotted.

Institutional Culture

The philosophy of continually improving the quality of care and service does not take hold instantaneously within an organization through a leadership mandate but takes several years to evolve. An organizational cultural change often requires the transformation of institutional beliefs and values from a philosophy that believes that quality is the responsibility of a specific department to one that believes that quality is the responsibility of everyone who works in a hospital or system and should be part of everyday practice. CQI requires a shift from a focus on individual blame to one of team effort for continual evaluation and change.

To achieve the degree of organizational penetration and philosophical shift required, CQI principles and practices must be adopted in the core foundation of the organization through their incorporation into the institutional mission, vision, and strategic priorities. Top leaders must establish quality organizational values and set forth a clear vision for continuous quality improvement and a work plan to achieve that vision. Senior leaders must "walk the talk" and incorporate the CQI philosophy in all aspects of evaluation of clinical care and services. Leaders must support the organizational change by removing barriers as they arise and allocating the resources necessary to ensure success.

Organizational Infrastructure Design

Integration of continuous quality improvement hospital-wide or health system-wide requires an organizational structural design that will facilitate quality evaluation across entities (hospitals) and disciplines (nurses, physicians, and hospital-based departments). This integration is facilitated through the positioning of quality leaders within an organization as well as the design of the working committees. The CQI departmental leader should report directly to the highest levels of an organization, either directly to a chief operating officer in a hospital or a senior vice president in a health system, thereby empowering the person to effect change. The CQI departmental leader does not necessarily have to have direct accountability for all quality-supporting departments (for example, infection control, risk management, and clinical resource management), but he or she must act as a facilitator of information exchange and support implementation of change.

At the University of Pennsylvania Health System (UPHS), the quality reporting structure is representative of a coordinated decentralized structure (Figure 18-1). CQI, termed clinical effectiveness and quality improvement (CEQI) at our institution, is implemented by the directors of quality at each entity, with coordination at the health-system level through the UPHS CEQI committee. An academic organization such as ours, with clinical departmental chairs, adds another layer of complexity in organizational modeling. Physicians at two of our four hospitals (HUP and PMC) are part of the academic practice organization and report directly to the clinical chairs. To integrate the hospital leadership with the academic structure in this segment of our health system, a subcommittee of the clinical chairs was formed to oversee quality, with representation from physician, nursing, and hospital administration leadership. This committee reports to the medical board (executive committee) at the individual institutions. At the hospital level, each clinical

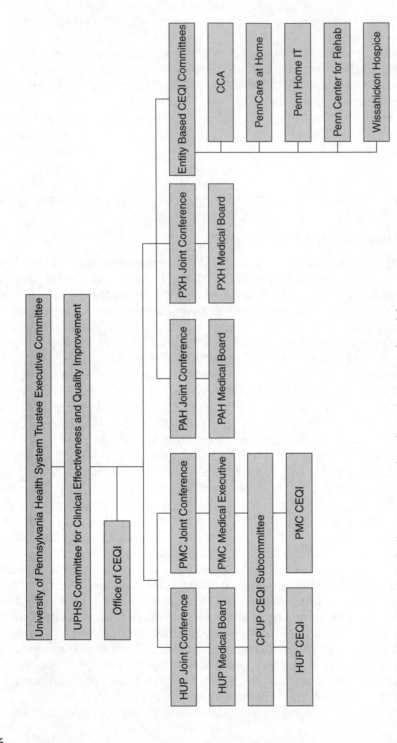

FIGURE 18-1 UPHS clinical effectiveness and quality organizational model.
Source: University of Pennsylvania Health System. Used with permission.

chair identified a physician leader in his or her department accountable for departmental clinical effectiveness and quality improvement initiatives. These physicians lead multidisciplinary quality teams that report to the entity CEQI committees, along with the traditional quality committees of infection control, safety, and so forth. Table 18-2 delineates the roles of the various committees. Ultimately, all measurement and results of quality initiatives must be reported to the trustees of the hospital or health system as required by the JCAHO.

The success of a CQI program leader depends not only on the organizational model but also on the organizational understanding of accountability, alignment of incentives, and the monitoring and reporting of outcomes. Prior to the organizational redesign at UPHS and the integration of the academic structure with the quality infrastructure, quality accountability was diffuse in our organization, with the clinical chairs viewing quality as primarily a hospital responsibility. With the development of the subcommittee of clinical chairs and the designation of departmental lead physicians, quality accountability returned to the physician community. To support this change, the incentive program for clinical chairs and CEQI physician team leaders included CEQI outcomes.

Defined accountability and aligned incentives are important but not sufficient to enable success for a CQI program leader. Development of a monitoring and feedback process after change is implemented is critical to ensure and sustain organizational change. At the University of Pennsylvania Health System, we chose to implement a "balanced" performance report with department-specific measures in patient satisfaction, clinical effectiveness, quality, and operational effectiveness. These performance reports are updated monthly and distributed to the clinical chairs, team leaders, and administrative leadership. We have extended this process to the development of physician-specific performance reports to support the health system initiative as well as the credentialing process.

Quality Resources

In addition to facilitating a culture change and designing a supportive organizational model, senior leadership must support the quality professional leader with access to data analysts and team-support coordinators as well as the most current information technology tools to ensure success. At the University of Pennsylvania Health System, the Office of Clinical Effectiveness and Quality Improvement was created, which reports to the senior quality leader in our organization (see Figure 18-1). This is a small department of highly skilled data analysts and team-support coordinators. The department is responsible for developing and

TABLE 18-2   Roles of the UPHS CEQI Committees

Committee	Roles
UPHS CEQI Committee	• Coordinate and monitor all UPHS initiatives and programs in the areas of clinical resource management and quality • Identify and disseminate "best practices" among entities • Identify areas of opportunities and develop supporting programs for improvement
Entity Joint Conference	• Monitor and report progress on CEQI initiatives to the entity trustees • Ensure compliance with regulatory, accrediting, and managed care requirements
Entity Medical Board (Executive Committee)	• Monitor and coordinate all initiatives pertaining to CEQI and quality (CEQI, incidence and occurrence, credentialing, and legal review committees) • Ensure compliance with regulatory, accrediting, and managed care requirements
UPMC CEQI Subcommittee of the Clinical Chairs (CPUP, HUP, and PMC only)	• Develop strategy and monitor progress of CEQI initiatives • Approve annual goals and targets • Ensure coordination of all UPMC initiatives for improvement of clinical resource management and quality (best practices, CVAC, payer denial task force, IS enhancements, etc.) • Oversee access to confidential quality and financial information • Ensure compliance with regulatory, accrediting, and managed care requirements
Entity CEQI Committee	• Support target development and monitor CEQI team progress utilizing the performance report format (patient satisfaction, clinical effectiveness, quality, and operational effectiveness) • Ensure compliance with regulatory, accrediting, and managed care requirements • Maintain written reports of conclusions, recommendations, actions taken, and results of actions

UPHS, University of Pennsylvania Health System; CEQI, clinical effectiveness and quality improvement; UPMC, University of Pennsylvania Medical Center; CPUP, Clinical Practices of the University of Pennsylvania; HUP, Hospital of the University of Pennsylvania; PMC, Presbyterian Medical Center; IS, information systems.

maintaining databases, analyzing and distributing the outcomes of change through the mechanism of performance reports, and supporting the physician team leaders in their quality improvement efforts as required.

As the complexity of regulatory-required outcome reporting increases and the demands by clinicians for detailed clinical data accelerate, the need for more frequent, complex outcome reports from sophisticated information management tools becomes paramount. Large databases with user-friendly query tools are necessary. Web-enabled, point-of-service data-gathering tools are needed to feed the traditional financial databases. Senior leadership must support funding, and the quality professional must be able to oversee the acquisition or development of these information management tools.

The Quality Professional: Attributes

Given the right organizational framework, support personnel, and tools, successful implementation and management of a continuous quality improvement process is then highly dependent on selection of the *right* quality professional leader. Unlike in the days of quality assurance, the modern quality professional must possess leadership skills and have significant multifaceted knowledge to ensure organization-wide involvement and success.

Leadership

"Leadership is different from management" (Harvard Business School, 1998). Health care quality professionals need not only to possess management skills but also to be effective change agents. Quality professionals must be leaders.

> Management is about coping with complexity. . . . Without good management, complex enterprises tend to become chaotic in ways that threaten their existence. Good management brings a degree of order and consistency to key dimensions like the quality and profitability of products.
>
> Leadership, by contrast, is about coping with change. Part of the reason it has become so important in recent years is that the business world has become more competitive and volatile. . . . Major changes are more and more necessary to survive and compete effectively in this environment. More change always demands more leadership. (Kotter, in Harvard Business School, 1998)

As delineated by Kotter, leaders need to produce change; to do so, they need to *set direction, align and motivate people*, and *create a culture of leadership.* Setting direction, according to Kotter, is a fundamental skill of a leader. Quality professionals need not only to manage the process of change in an organization, but also to utilize their expertise to develop the strategy for change. Quality managers need to be visionary and innovative. There is no road map for quality that is successful in every organization; the quality professional needs to understand his or her own organization's complexity and culture and then design solutions that will work in that environment.

Quality professionals also need to align disparate groups and motivate people. Often the culture of health care organizations is a silo-based "ownership" of processes. The quality professional needs to be able to facilitate interdepartmental meetings, keeping them focused on the end game of quality, not turf struggles. The quality professional needs to motivate, not control, these disparate groups. He or she needs to generate highly energized behavior that can cope with the inevitable barriers to change. The quality professional needs to motivate people through a clearly articulated vision of quality and to recognize and reward participants for even small successes.

Lastly, quality professionals need to create a culture of leadership. Continuous quality improvement is not the work of one, but is the compilation of the work of many. Quality professionals need to identify and support leaders throughout the organization. They need to set the vision and direction and then facilitate the multiple organizational leaders as they effect change. At the University of Pennsylvania Health System, we believe this to be the main reason for our recent success. Historically we identified only a single quality officer. Now, we have created an associate vice president position whose role is not to manage but to cultivate the clinical quality leaders throughout the organization.

Knowledge

As external and internal demands increase, the quality professional must bring to the position a significant amount of knowledge in multiple areas.

- *Regulatory and accreditation requirements:* Although quality improvement must be viewed as having internal benefits, the quality professional must have extensive knowledge of the external regulatory and accreditation demands on quality. Often, the quality professional either leads or is actively involved in the organizational JCAHO process.
- *Payer regulations:* Payers, whether governmental (Medicare and Medicaid) or private (managed care), are focused on quality. Quality outcomes both improve patient satisfaction and reduce

costs (length of stay and readmissions) for the payers. Many experts feel that competition among payers and providers will be heavily dependent on quality outcome reporting in the future.

- *Hospital processes:* With the transition from quality assurance with the individual as the focus to continuous quality improvement with process as the focus, detailed knowledge of the workings of the hospital is important as a foundation for redesign and change implementation. The quality professional needs to understand the access (admission, discharge, and transfer), patient care (diagnostic and therapeutic), and hospital billing processes, which often have gaps leading to quality issues.

- *Basic financial understanding of the costs of care:* The mandate for improved quality has been partially driven by the rising costs of care and the worsening financial margins of providers. The quality professional needs to understand the primary drivers of cost in his or her organization so that when quality improvement is measured, its impact on the cost of care is assessed.

- *Measurements and clinical outcomes:* Knowledge of what to measure and the location of data sources is important for the quality professional. Outcome measurement is important not only for internal stakeholders but is mandated by the external environment as well (JCAHO, HCFA, and managed care).

- *Statistics:* An important corollary of measurement is the ability to determine whether the impact is statistically significant or not. Therefore, the quality professional must have working knowledge or access to experts in statistical methods.

- *Clinical care:* Although not absolutely mandatory, clinical knowledge is a very beneficial asset for a quality professional. The ability to interpret quality events independently and critique clinical solutions will aid in the ability of the quality professional to understand severity and implement change.

- *Information management and systems:* Last but not least is the requirement of knowledge of information systems. The quality professional needs to have general knowledge of the major applications in the hospital (admission, hospital billing, operating room scheduling, order entry, clinical documentation, results repository) so that as change is examined, information system solutions may be considered. In addition, the quality professional needs to have knowledge of database structure and be able to use data query tools. He or she needs to know what external comparative databases exist and where to access them.

Unlike any other time in the evolution of health care quality, the quality professional must have knowledge of a broad array of topics.

Since no coordinated educational programs exist (to the best of my knowledge) to train quality professionals, senior people in the organization are usually selected. More and more, the chief quality officer is a physician leader in the organization, often in administrative partnership with a nursing leader. Physician leaders add tremendous value in their ability to engage in peer dialogue and understand the complexity of the decision-making process. Because the physician directs 80% of the cost of care, a physician quality leader is an asset to the organization as it merges clinical cost-effectiveness with quality.

The Quality Professional: Organizational Roles

Given the high demands of the external environment and the complexity of health care organizations today, the managing roles of the quality professional may vary among organizations. The quality professional leader may be asked to manage clinical resource and risk management. He or she may be responsible for other traditional quality committees, such as infection control, ethics, and safety. The quality professional may be asked to lead the JCAHO and state survey efforts. Management roles outside those of quality data analysts and coordinators are not necessary but may ease the complexity of the position and the need for multiple people in the same area in an organization.

The leadership roles of the quality professional are necessary regardless of the organization's size or complexity. As previously discussed, he or she will be required to function as a "consultant, motivator, educator, and systems designer" (Bleich, in Schmele, 1996). Given the degree of knowledge and skill required, the quality professional is probably well served by possessing a graduate degree in health care administration or the like. Professional organizations that provide "best practice" education sessions are an important source of learning for the quality professional because they are often without peers within an organization.

Conclusion

The role of the quality professional has dramatically changed over the last decade. Leadership skills along with traditional management savvy are now required to facilitate multidisciplinary groups, often with divergent issues. The quality professional is also required to possess significant knowledge in regulatory, financial, and information systems areas. He or she must possess significant organizational cultural and process knowledge in order to identify root causes and effect change. Selection of the right person can transform an organization from a problem-driven quality organization to one that is continually proactively examining all services to ensure maximum health care quality for both the internal and external stakeholders. Success for the quality professional is achieved when every member of an organization is engaged in continuous quality improvement as an integrated part of his or her daily work.

References

Donabedian, A. (1966). Evaluating the quality of care. *Milbank Memorial Fund Quarterly,* 44, 194–96.

Harvard Business School. (1998). *Harvard Business Review on Leadership.* Boston: Harvard Business School Publishing.

Joint Commission on Accreditation of Healthcare Organizations. (2000). http://www.jcaho.org/perfmeas/coremeas/cm_ovrw.html.

Kimberly, J. R., and Minvielle, E. (2000). *The Quality Imperative: Measurement and Management of Quality in Healthcare.* London: Imperial College Press.

Schmele, J. A., ed. (1995). *Quality Management in Nursing and Health Care.* Albany, NY: Delmar Publishers.

CHAPTER NINETEEN

THE ROLE OF THE RISK MANAGER IN CREATING PATIENT SAFETY

Grena G. Porto

The goal of health care risk management is to create and maintain a safe and effective health care environment for patients, visitors, and employees, thereby preventing or reducing loss to the organization.[1] This goal has remained constant since the birth of the profession 30 years ago, but the methods used to accomplish it have changed and evolved to accommodate evolution and innovation in the profession. The emergence of patient safety as a national priority following the release of the Institute of Medicine's report on medical error[2] has changed the way providers view risk and safety. Acceptance and complacency about the inevitability of patient injury is evaporating rapidly as providers confront increasing demands from patients, regulators, and payers for safer care.

There is some evidence that a safety culture is emerging in health care. High-reliability intensive care units have been identified by some authors.[3,4] However, more work is needed to make entire health care organizations high-reliability organizations. Risk managers can and must play a key role in this process if the transformation of health care into a high-reliability industry is to succeed. This chapter discusses the strategies and tactics that risk managers must employ to make health care safer in their organizations.

What Is a High-Reliability Organization?

Comparisons of error rates between health care and other industries have shown that the health care industry tolerates a rate of error that would be considered unacceptable by NASA, aviation, the nuclear power industry, and even the postal service.[5] In light of this, health care has begun to study these other industries to identify strategies that may be adapted to health care to help reduce error.

High-reliability organizations are highly complex and hazardous systems that are fraught with risk of error and injury, yet which operate over long periods of time without errors or injury. Examples of high-reliability organizations include aircraft carriers, NASA, and nuclear power. Studies of high-reliability organizations[6,7] have shown that they share common features:

- *Auditing of risk:* An ongoing system of checks designed to detect both expected and unexpected risk and safety problems.
- *Appropriate reward system:* A mechanism for rewarding both the organization and the people in it for safety-oriented behavior.
- *System quality standards:* An acknowledged system that is the "gold standard" in safety.
- *Acknowledgment of risk:* These organizations acknowledge that risk exists and address the risk by adopting strategies to mitigate it.
- *Command and control:* A management model that balances authority and teamwork and is characterized by migrating decision making, built-in redundancies in systems and people, senior managers with "big picture" orientation who do not micromanage, formal rules and procedures, and training.

Safety in high-reliability organizations is not left to chance; it is the result of careful planning and design. The challenge for health care risk managers is to find ways to design these features into their own organizations. Some parallels already exist; however, modification is needed to make these features more effective in creating safety. What follows is a discussion of each of the features of high-reliability organizations, the existing counterparts in health care, and the changes that are needed to enhance the features to create safety.

Auditing of Risk

Health care risk managers use a number of tools to audit risk, including incident reports, referrals from other departments such as quality improvement (QI), informal reports from staff, medical record reviews, and regular rounds of patient care units. Each of these methods of auditing risk has strengths and weaknesses. As cost pressures have escalated in health care organizations and resources have become scarce, there has been an increased reliance on voluntary reporting systems to identify risk, since they consume the least amount of resources. The information generated by these reports is analyzed, categorized, quantified, and often used to compare the organization's performance with respect to either its own past experience or the experience of other organizations.

There are several problems with this approach to auditing of risk. First, incident reporting systems are often burdensome, requiring the front-line worker, already pressed to attend to multiple competing priorities, to complete a written form. Second, the form itself tends to limit the information to that which can be described by a series of checkboxes. Narratives are discouraged, as is speculation about possible causes of events. Instead, emphasis is placed on aggregation of data; thus, much valuable information about the causes of events is lost. Third, incident reporting systems are punitive in nature because the reporter's identity is attached to the report and the information contained in the report often forms the basis for disciplinary action against the reporter or another party. This creates a disincentive for reporting. Finally, there are few incentives for reporting, because reporting is rarely rewarded and the reporter seldom receives feedback about the report or the outcome of the analysis.

One of the most successful risk auditing programs in existence is the Aviation Safety Reporting System (ASRS).[8] The system was implemented in 1975 with the goal of creating a safer aviation system by collecting information from the acknowledged safety experts in the field—front-line workers such as mechanics, pilots, and air traffic controllers. Today, it receives and processes approximately 35,000 reports annually. Some of the key characteristics that make ASRS successful are as follows:

- *Nonpunitive reporting structure.* The reporting system is operated by NASA rather than by the aviation industry or its regulators, thereby removing the threat of punitive or regulatory consequences for reporters. In addition, the name of the reporter is removed from the report after a brief evaluation period, ensuring that his or her identity will not be revealed. The ASRS has found that eliminating fear by safeguarding the identity of the reporter is key to encouraging reporting.
- *Emphasis on detailed narratives rather than on aggregate or frequency data.* The reporting system solicits detailed narratives from reporters, including their theories about what happened and why. The ASRS has learned that truly useful information about

how accidents occur comes from the observations of those involved in the event, not from trending aggregate data.

- *Nonburdensome reporting.* The forms are simple and easy to use. Follow-up to the initial report occurs through telephone conversations with expert analysts who staff the reporting center. The reporter is not inconvenienced in any way by the reporting process; this also serves to encourage reporting.
- *Feedback to reporters.* Information about identified hazards is provided to front-line aviation workers in the form of alerts, newsletters, and other publications, which reinforces the importance of reporting. Currently, ASRS issues approximately 20 safety alerts per month.

Voluntary reporting systems currently in use in health care share few of the critical success factors of the ASRS model. However, health care risk managers, as custodians of voluntary reporting systems, can play a critical role in transforming these systems into successful risk auditing systems by emulating the ASRS model. This can be achieved by doing the following:

- Eliminate confusing and restrictive definitions about what is reportable, which creates barriers to reporting. Instead, encourage widespread and automatic reporting of all potential safety problems, including close calls, screening out information that is not useful after it is received.
- Eliminate duplicative reporting and standardize the reporting process to avoid confusion. Use the same system for reporting of all potential safety problems.
- Create multiple methods of accessing the reporting system, including oral, written, and electronic reporting options, to accommodate the needs and preferences of reporters.
- Offer anonymity in exchange for information when needed. Even in a nonpunitive reporting culture, some health care workers will feel threatened by reporting and will need the security of anonymity in order to participate in the reporting system.
- Press for a nonpunitive reporting policy that does not tie disciplinary action to reports. The risk manager must be prepared to educate the entire organization, including senior management, about the deleterious effects of tying discipline to voluntary reporting.
- Implement an amnesty policy that offers freedom from disciplinary action in exchange for timely good-faith reporting. Most errors are due to system defects rather than individual failure. An amnesty policy makes a convincing case for the organization's commitment to building a culture of safety while

still allowing for disciplinary actions against those who intentionally harm patients.

- Encourage narratives that provide detail about how the event occurred and possible contributing factors. These narratives are the richest source of information about how accidents truly occur and therefore provide the best hope for designing system changes to prevent future accidents.
- Provide for a mechanism for immediate response to a serious hazard. This not only prevents recurrence of a problem, but also provides important feedback about the organization's commitment to the safety program and reinforces reporting.
- Discontinue counting, trending, and other quantitative analysis that provides little useful information. This activity consumes valuable resources that could be better devoted to analyzing narratives and disseminating important information about lessons learned.
- Create incentives for reporting, such as rewards for safety reports that lead to improvements. Adopt the strategies used by other industries, including commemorative plaques, small gifts, and other tokens to acknowledge the contribution of the "safety hero."
- Provide feedback about lessons learned from reporting to the front-line health care worker. This will reinforce the importance and utility of the reporting system. Feedback should take the form of stories about events reported, the causes identified, and actions taken to improve safety as a result. This type of feedback is more likely to be remembered and used by the health care worker than quantitative data on the frequency of events reported.
- Train staff on the importance and role of reporting in creating safety, and on their own role in patient safety.

Appropriate Reward System

High-reliability organizations recognize that reward is more important than punishment in motivating and changing behavior. They know that in order for a specific behavior to take hold and become routine practice, it must be rewarded. At the same time, disincentives that might discourage the behavior must be removed. Health care organizations rarely reward employees for safety-related behavior, though this practice is commonplace in other settings, such as aerospace engineering and even the military. Experience from these industries has shown that even small rewards can have a profound effect on culture and morale.[9]

Health care risk managers are uniquely positioned to lead the development of a reward system that encourages safety-related behavior because of their access to a wide variety of identified problems and solutions. They can do this by

- *Identifying the safety-related behaviors the organization wishes to encourage.* This can be done in consultation with other members of the management team, as part of the development of an organization-wide safety plan. These behaviors might include timely reporting of actual or potential safety problems, questioning of decisions by others that seem to compromise patient safety, effective teamwork, and involvement in work process redesign to enhance safety.

- *Identifying and removing disincentives caused by undue burdens associated with the safety-related behaviors.* For example, if the organization wants to discourage a practice it deems unsafe, such as multiple-dose medication vials, but fails to provide a safe alternative that is convenient, such as timely delivery of unit doses, it has created a disincentive for the safety-related behavior it wishes to encourage. Until the disincentive is identified and removed, the safety-related behavior will not be widely adopted.

- *Identifying and removing disincentives caused by fear.* If a safety-related behavior, such as reporting actual or potential patient injury, is accompanied by a negative consequence for the reporter, such as reprimand from a superior or hostility from a coworker, the desired behavior will be avoided. Likewise, if the safety-related behavior is rewarded only when it is without negative consequences for the organization, a disincentive is created. For example, if employees are encouraged to halt a procedure when they have safety-related concerns, but are rewarded only when their concerns are well founded and punished when they are not, a disincentive is created. It is important that all disincentives be removed and rewards applied consistently, even when safety-related behaviors prove unnecessary.

- *Identifying and removing disincentives caused by lack of knowledge or interest.* For a patient safety program to succeed, it must have the commitment and participation of all levels of the organization. Health care workers are not likely to support a program that is imposed on them with little opportunity for their input. By implementing training and outreach programs that enhance the knowledge of the health care worker and increase opportunities for involvement, the health care risk manager can promote the success of the safety program. As mentioned in the previous section, feedback and responsiveness are also important components that reinforce participation in the safety program and maintain commitment and interest.

- *Creating rewards for safety-related behaviors.* Rewards need not be costly or elaborate to have the desired effect. Even financially challenged organizations can implement a system of rewards that can greatly enhance employee commitment to and involvement in the safety program. For example, recognition at a meeting, perhaps accompanied by a plaque or other token, is a powerful reward that can greatly motivate not only the recipient but others in the organization to continue to support the safety program. This is especially true if the reward and recognition comes from a member of senior management, such as the CEO.
- *Publicizing rewards and success stories.* Rewards are most effective when they are well known and celebrated within the organization. Not every success story must be celebrated and not every safety-related behavior must be rewarded. But rewards, recognition, and celebrations should occur frequently enough to demonstrate the organization's commitment to the safety program. Newsletters can be an effective means of publicizing rewards and success stories.

System Quality Standards

In high-reliability industries, there is consensus regarding what constitutes safety, and standards exist against which organizations can measure themselves. Often there is an industry leader that is recognized as having achieved the highest standards of safety and that others try to emulate.

In health care, patient safety standards are still evolving. The Institute of Medicine (IOM) report[10] released in 1999 helped to accelerate this process and contained a number of recommendations that are becoming accepted as standards. The Joint Commission on Accreditation of Healthcare Organizations has also published standards on patient safety,[11] incorporating many components of the IOM's recommendations. In addition, the Leapfrog Group, a coalition of large national corporations representing their interests as purchasers of health care, has begun setting standards in patient safety.[12] They have identified three strategies—computerized physician order entry, evidence-based referrals, and intensive care unit (ICU) physician staffing—that have been shown to improve patient safety and have announced their intention to use these as selection criteria for the contracting of health care services on behalf of employees. Finally, the Institute for Safe Medication

Practices (ISMP)[13] has been instrumental in developing and disseminating medication safety standards.

Patient safety leaders are beginning to emerge, and there have been well-recognized efforts by some organizations, such as Children's Hospital in Minneapolis, to create a high-reliability organization based on established principles.[14] The Veteran's Health Administration has also demonstrated leadership in patient safety for its work in developing nonpunitive reporting systems.[15]

Although the health care risk manager is not in a position to propel the organization to a position of industry leadership, he or she can play an important role in helping the organization meet emerging standards in patients safety. This can be done by

- Assisting in the development and implementation of an organization-wide patient safety plan that identifies patient safety as a top priority.
- Ensuring that there is a mechanism for prompt identification and analysis of patient safety problems, including identification of root causes and themes across events and root causes.
- Ensuring that corrective actions planned as a result of incident analysis incorporate principles of human factors engineering, cognitive bias, and adult learning so that risk of error can be minimized. This includes decreased reliance on memory and vigilance, use of constraints and forcing functions, and standardization and simplification of work processes when possible.
- Recognizing the importance of teamwork in error prevention and lobbying for organizational support and commitment of resources to teamwork training in high-risk areas, such as the emergency department, operating room, and ICU.
- Promoting a culture of safety in which all health care workers are empowered to make decisions that support patient safety without fear of retribution.
- Promoting inclusion of patients in the design of the systems and processes of care.
- Ensuring that patients who suffer a harm-causing adverse event are provided with all known information about what happened, why it happened, and what consequences they should expect as a result.
- Working to identify system failures prospectively, practicing failures, and designing for recovery from failure.
- Working to create a learning environment that encourages reporting of errors and close calls and focuses on learning from these rather than on blame and reprisal.

- Helping the organization to prepare for the installation of computerized order entry systems.
- Helping prepare the organization to meet evolving requirements in the area of evidence-based referrals and ICU physician staffing.
- Identifying and introducing emerging standards in the area of medication safety.
- Monitoring developments of technological solutions, such as bar coding, that help to prevent error.
- Monitoring and maintaining current knowledge about the development of other patient safety solutions that the organization may wish to consider adopting.

Acknowledgment of Risk

High-reliability organizations acknowledge that risk exists rather than create unrealistic expectations about performance and outcomes. In addition to acknowledging risk, these organizations take steps to reduce or mitigate risk, designing a system focused on detection and recovery from error, rather than simply accepting that errors are inevitable.

To acknowledge risk, it is first necessary to talk openly about it. In health care organizations, discussion about risks or errors has been traditionally discouraged because of fears of liability and regulatory consequences. This tendency to avoid discussion of risk and error precludes mitigation of risk, because it is not possible to discuss potential solutions to a problem without discussing the problem.

However, health care providers' fears about discussing risk and errors are not well founded. Disclosure of medical errors, even to patients, does not lead to increased liability, and in fact has been shown to decrease the risk of a lawsuit. Further, discussion of errors with colleagues and patients has been shown to have benefits for both patients and providers, enabling patients to forgive, providers to be forgiven, and the organization to learn from the error and make plans to mitigate future risk of error.

Health care risk managers are in a unique position to lead an organization's journey to acknowledgment of risk. Because risk managers have traditionally been the guardians of information about errors and risk, they can begin to educate senior management and other levels of the organization about the benefits of information sharing as a means to acknowledge, demystify, and ultimately reduce risk of error. This can be done by

- Developing a policy that permits and rewards reporting of error and close calls, as outlined previously

- Encouraging health care workers to share information about errors and close calls, permitting them to learn from one another's experiences
- Promoting a shift toward a blame-free culture that recognizes that failure is a property of the system rather than the individual
- Emphasizing the importance of error as an opportunity to learn how to prevent future errors
- Focusing on rapid recognition and recovery from error
- Developing a program that addresses identified risk proactively, with system redesign and appropriate allocation of resources

Command and Control

In high-reliability organizations, command-and-control functions are management processes designed to balance authority and teamwork and enable rapid and easy transition between these two models as needed to create safety. Command-and-control functions in high-reliability organizations have five characteristics:

- Migrating decision making that enables the person with the most expertise to make decisions, regardless of rank
- Redundancy in people and equipment so that backups are always available when needed
- Senior managers with strategic vision who don't micromanage, allowing experienced subordinates with more direct knowledge to make decisions as needed
- Formal rules and procedures that provide true guidance and are followed
- Training, so that expertise is planned for and developed, not left to chance

In health care, there exists a rigid hierarchy in which the physician is viewed as the "captain of the ship" to whom other members of the team must be subservient. This rigid management style does not change as circumstances change. Yet we know that this management model is not the best one for preventing error.

Making changes in the command-and-control model of a health care organization requires the commitment and leadership of senior management as well as a change in culture and thinking throughout the organization. However, as an organization evolves toward high reliability, the risk manager can assist in the transition to the new management model by

- Encouraging front-line workers to become involved in problem solving and encouraging managers to involve them

- Analyzing work processes and identifying gaps that require strategic redundancies to prevent errors, especially when the risk of error or the severity of the consequences is high
- Developing policies, procedures, and guidance documents that are clear, easy to use, and serve as useful resources for the front-line worker rather than as evidence of compliance for regulators and accreditation agencies
- Becoming a strong champion for training programs as a means to reduce risk of error, especially when budget pressures dictate otherwise.

Conclusion

Health care risk managers can play an important role in helping their organizations make a transition to high-reliability organizations. This involves not only changes in processes but also a shift in culture and thinking. The risk manager's own long-held views about the practice of risk management may be challenged by the changes necessary to achieve high reliability as an organization. Long-standing practices involving reporting of errors and sharing of information may have to be abandoned in favor of more progressive concepts that allow the organization and everyone in it to truly understand error, thereby learning how to prevent it. Although daunting, this shift provides the health care risk manager with a welcome opportunity to emerge as the organization's safety leader.

Notes

1. Carroll, R., ed. *Risk Management Handbook for Healthcare Organizations,* 3rd ed. San Francisco: Jossey-Bass, 2001.
2. Kohn, L. T., Corrigan, J. M., Donaldson, M. S., eds. *To Err Is Human: Building a Safer Health System.* Washington, DC: National Academy Press, 1999.
3. Roberts, K. H. Organizational change and a culture of safety. Paper presented at Enhancing Patient Safety and Reducing Errors in Health Care, Rancho Mirage, November 1998.
4. Knox, G. E., Simpson, K. R., Garite, T. J. High reliability perinatal units: an approach to the prevention of patient injury and medical malpractice claims. *Journal of Healthcare Risk Management,* Spring 1999:24–32.
5. Leape, L. L. Error in medicine. *JAMA,* 1994;272:1851–1857.
6. Roberts, K. H. Some characteristics of high reliability organizations. *Organization Science,* 1990;1(2):160–177.
7. Roberts, 1998.

8. Reynard, W. D., Billings, C. E., Cheaney, E. S., et al. *The Development of the NASA Aviation Safety Reporting System.* NASA Reference Publication 1114. Washington, DC: NASA, 1986.

9. Roberts, 1998.

10. Kohn, 1999.

11. Available at www.jcaho.org.

12. Available at www.leapfroggroup.org/safety3.htm.

13. See www.ismp.org.

14. Shapiro, J. P. Taking the mistakes out of medicine. *US News & World Report,* 2000;129(3):50–66.

15. Adelson, R., Bieber, J., Blum, L., et al. *Patient Safety: Listening to Healthcare Employees.* Chicago: National Patient Safety Foundation, 1998.

CHAPTER TWENTY

REDUCING MEDICAL ERRORS: THE ROLE OF THE PHYSICIAN

Roy Magnusson, MD, MS, FACEP

The Changing Landscape

The practice of medicine changed drastically over the past century. The discovery of hundreds of new medications, techniques, and technologies significantly expanded our ability to deliver care that improved the duration and quality of our lives. To support this tremendous expansion in knowledge and clinical practice, training programs grew longer and medical specialization became essential. Medical care was gradually transferred to an ever more complex health system environment. In today's hospital, a single patient may undergo several potentially dangerous procedures and treatments while interacting with dozens of people, including physicians, nurses, technologists, and other staff.

As care became more complex, the number of patients receiving medical services grew. Larger health systems now coordinate hundreds of thousands of patient visits, admissions, operations, or outpatient procedures each year. All of this occurs in a health care system in which the economic pressures are to provide medical services as rapidly and inexpensively as possible. Although health systems have spent large sums during the past decade developing information systems, the efforts were often focused on financial systems to either manage capitated contracts or bill efficiently and accurately to avoid being accused of fraud and abuse as the government changed payment guidelines.

Although the trends toward team management, aggressive therapeutic protocols, and large, efficient institutions were essential to progress, there was definitely a downside to these changes. The potential for a medical mishap or serious complication grew as well. Is it any wonder that there is growing concern about serious or even fatal mistakes being made?

The Institute of Medicine (IOM) report issued in late 1999 estimated that between 44,000 and 98,000 unnecessary deaths occur each year in the United States alone.[1] The IOM committee pointed out that although recent medical research and technological advances permit one set of ideal outcomes, the overall health system lags behind this standard in its ability to deliver an ideal level of care consistently to the population as a whole. The result is a frustrating gap between what we know to be the best care and what we provide on a daily basis.

In its follow-up report in March 2001 entitled *Crossing the Quality Chasm,* the Institute of Medicine outlined a strategy to close the gap between known best practice and the overall care delivered.[2] The committee called for a national commitment to improve the quality of care to new levels, with an emphasis on making medical services safe, effective, patient centered, timely, efficient, and equitable.

> To this end, the committee proposes the following agenda for redesigning the 21st century health care system ... that purchasers, regulators, health professions, educational institutions, and the Department of Health and Human Services create an environment that fosters and rewards improvement by
>
> 1. Creating an infrastructure to support evidence-based medicine,
> 2. Facilitating the use of information technology to redesign safer and more efficient systems,
> 3. Aligning payment and financial incentives with clinical quality outcomes, and
> 4. Preparing the workforce to better service patients in a world of expanding knowledge and rapid change.[3]

If completely implemented, these recommendations will bring sweeping change once again to our health systems and the practice of medicine.

Central Role of the Physician

In simpler times, physicians played the absolute leadership role in health care. As the expert and decision maker, the physician was the central figure in coordinating the care of patients by supervising small groups of support staff. In today's health care setting, physicians have less direct control over many of the decisions that affect their patients, often working in collaboration with scores of people in support of the clinical effort. Paradoxically, coordinating medical care under these complex circumstances requires even stronger physician leadership at all levels in the organization if consistently excellent clinical outcomes are to be achieved.

Physicians can assure quality in many concrete ways. Whether you are an active front-line clinician or the medical director of a large facility, your contributions toward the safe, effective delivery of care can be substantial. For any system, large or small, the delivery of excellent medical services really boils down to the ability of that system's providers to make the right clinical decisions and then execute the diagnostic and treatment plans without delay or mishap. Efforts to guarantee good care must therefore focus on the quality of the providers involved, the information available to them, the redesign of systems that support the effort, and the ability of the organization to evolve rapidly along with medical knowledge and technology.

Selecting the Medical Staff

The most important element in providing quality care is the caliber of the people making decisions and performing procedures. Traditional quality efforts recognized the central role of the physician; as a result, many of the early quality efforts focused on the selection and initial assessment of providers applying for medical staff privileges. Establishing training standards, verifying credentials, and carefully matching the physician's experience with the privileges given are all required practices in today's health systems. None of these activities can be done effectively without physician involvement. In recognition of this, these processes are a primary function of the medical staff organization.

Although the credentialing and privileging process is conducted routinely in all hospitals, the challenge of selecting good providers is far from routine. Many issues need careful consideration as reasonable new standards are set. How much additional training is required before a surgeon may independently perform a new technique such as laparoscopic surgery? How will allied health professionals such as nurse practitioners and physician's assistants be integrated into our health care system? Do we have the right mix of talent in our medical staff to meet the medical needs of our community? Physicians must be engaged in these medical staff discussions in order to avoid situations in which providers and level of care are not appropriately matched. Although some of these decisions may be controversial and therefore difficult, to ignore training standards is to invite serious potential for medical errors and a reduced overall quality of care.

The Value of Peer Review and Ongoing Assessment of Clinical Performance

Periodic review of the care provided is another basic building block of any quality effort. Quality committees, chart review, and morbidity and mortality conferences are all established methods of such review. Newer methods of collecting information electronically may reduce the time required to collect this information and help direct attention to serious issues. Peer review can only be done by physicians and must be done in a fair and confidential setting. For our residents and medical staff, honest review of cases is at times difficult but is always rewarding. These are the lessons we never forget. It is an essential part of our ongoing education.

It is essential that the medical staff leadership create a culture that discourages disparaging clinical anecdotes in the hallway and promotes honest, confidential, evidence-based dialogue among providers. Patients will benefit, physicians will benefit, and fewer medical errors will occur in the long run.

Collecting and Using Outcomes Data

More and more often the results of our work are measured at the program or institutional level. For example, transplant programs monitor the survival rates of transplant patients and the rejection rates of transplanted organs. This information is helpful in comparing institutional performance with that of other programs or evaluating the effect of newly implemented clinical practice changes.

As care becomes more complex and is performed by teams, this aggregate data can be used to direct discussion and problem solving within the team. This presents yet another leadership opportunity for physicians. Design of appropriate outcomes measures and collection methods will make the information credible. Regular review of outcome results, coupled with evidence-based medical decision making, is a very effective way to improve the outcomes of care over time. The strongest programs have in common one essential element: a physician leader who is committed to the program, works effectively with a team of providers, and uses information to continually improve clinical outcomes and reduce the potential for medical error.

Identifying and Assisting the Impaired Physician

The 1999 Institute of Medicine report, *To Err Is Human,* emphasized the importance of creating a "no blame" atmosphere in which systems issues can be identified and addressed. This approach is very important in the peer review, case review, and outcomes data approach outlined earlier. Still, on occasion we must turn our attention to the performance of an individual. We are human beings, with all the strengths and frailties that make us human. Alcohol use, drug dependence, depression, or physical changes can directly affect the performance of a physician and result in medical errors. It is the responsibility of the medical staff to encourage confidential reporting and evaluation of these delicate problems. A timely, complete assessment of the situation followed by treatment and monitoring recommendations can save the life of a patient and the career of an otherwise excellent physician.

Many medical staff organizations have a physician's committee that performs this function. Members of this committee must be both firm and compassionate in their approach. This is yet another opportunity for the medical community to assist in making health care safe and to gain credibility with the public at large. A further satisfaction is that of assisting a colleague by directing him or her to needed treatment.

Dealing with Disaster

Regardless of the quality of the people involved, the unexpected occurs in medicine. The 1999 IOM report estimated that somewhere between 44,000 and 98,000 patients die unnecessarily in the United States each year as a result of less than optimal care. Anyone who has been in medicine for even a short time has been witness to a clinical event that has caused him or her to pause and ask some fairly disturbing questions. Should I have predicted this bad outcome? Would another approach have been better? Was this my fault?

Because physicians are on the front lines where clinical care takes place, they are often the first to realize that an unexpected outcome has occurred. Unfortunately, the physician is also likely to be seen as the individual most responsible by the patient or family. Emotions can run high at moments like this. The patient and family may experience pain, loss, fear, and anger. They often vent these emotions with aggressive questioning and even allegations of wrongdoing. Physicians and other health care staff also experience intense reactions of disappointment, fear, and anger. In the back of everyone's mind is the concern over possible litigation. Communication among the parties can become strained or may even be avoided altogether. This can result in further misunderstanding and inconsistent care. Errors can be perpetuated or compounded because routine clinical interactions are disrupted.

When things are not going well, it is human nature to look for someone or something to blame. Patients, families, and providers can jump to less than logical conclusions or superficial solutions, missing the opportunity to really study what happened, identify the root cause, and correct the circumstances that led to the incident. If we are to reduce the frequency of serious medical errors, physicians must be willing to participate and lead discussions about care not only in the peer review setting but also in the multidisciplinary setting of a team trying to find out what went wrong. Problems with quality are not isolated to decisions alone. Errors lurk in the handoffs between providers and in the assumptions we make about what happens in other parts of the hospital. The only way to sort out what really happened is to get all involved parties together and search for the root cause. This means opening up the discussion to pharmacists, nurses, technicians, managers, and other involved staff. This is the only way to fix system issues.

Consider the following example. In order to provide a much more modern and comfortable facility, a hospital elects to build a new wing in the medical center to care specifically for children. Planning is extensive, and the process of building and moving into the facility is very smooth. One year later, surgery is being performed on a 2-year-old with a tumor in his liver. The anesthesiologist has 4 units of blood on hand since the tumor is known to be quite vascular. During the surgery, bleeding escalates. The surgeon cannot control the hemorrhage, and a call for more blood goes out. The blood bank, located some distance from this new wing, immediately begins routine cross matching, not knowing that this blood is needed emergently. A second call is made, upgrading this request to an emergency, and type-specific blood is matched and sent. The combined preparation and transport time, however, is too long. The child exsanguinates in the operating room despite all efforts of the surgical team to control the bleeding.

Very soon thereafter, the anger within the team becomes counterproductive. In their defensiveness, each group begins blaming the other. Positive working relations that took years to build are in jeopardy. To make matters worse, the team has no clear way to prevent what happened from recurring. Something needs to be done.

The team is called together 2 days after the incident, and a detailed root cause analysis is done. This has many positive effects. First, it gives each person a chance to express his or her feelings about the system that had let this happen. Second, care processes are diagrammed in step-by-step detail. As a result, several potential improvements are identified. Suggestions include having type O blood in the operating suite at all times, using the mass transfusion protocol that had been developed for trauma patients, and setting standards for clear communication between operating rooms and the blood bank. The case is also reviewed in the online journal *Mortality and Morbidity* to share the experience with other surgeons and residents and to discuss care options and alternatives that can be used in the future. Participants feel somewhat better knowing that some good came from the case, in that the system was improved. No similar episodes occured in two additional years of operation.

Taking an emotionally charged disaster like this and creating something positive is not easy. Without strong physician leadership and the participation of all parties, it is impossible. Make sure that your facility has a process for reporting and investigating critical events. Encourage physicians to participate and work with nursing and administration to learn from these experiences and improve the systems supporting the clinical effort.

Systems Redesign

In the Institute of Medicine's follow-up report, *Crossing the Quality Chasm,* the importance of redesigning systems to compensate for the volume and complexity of today's health system was highlighted:

> The committee believes information technology must play a central role in the redesign of the health care system if a substantial improvement in quality is to be achieved over the coming decade. Automation of clinical, financial, and administrative transactions is essential to improving quality, preventing errors, enhancing consumer confidence in the health system and improving efficiency. . . .
>
> Sizable benefits can be derived in the near future from automating certain types of data, such as medication orders.[4]

The impact of computers on hospital workflow has been incredible. Sometimes helpful, sometimes frustrating, computers have become so plentiful in clinics that it is difficult to find enough counter space to write a simple note in the chart. This is not a trend that is likely to abate, as is evidenced by the IOM comments just quoted.

Over the next decade, physicians will see the automation and redesign of every aspect of their work. Office management systems, patient management systems, digital radiographs, electronic medical records, email communication with patients, Web-based software and physician access pages, physician order entry, and bar coding drugs are but a sampling of the information technology systems that administrators are considering right now. So many systems are being developed and piloted that the rate-limiting factor in this change is no longer technology—it is our ability to finance and deploy these new systems and then train people to use them.

I recently had the personal and painful experience of leading the implementation of a digital radiography system at a university health system that included both hospital and clinic use. This yearlong endeavor taught me several important lessons with respect to implementing new systems to be used by physicians. Here are just a few.

- Implementing systemwide change requires early involvement of key stakeholders, especially physicians who use that system extensively.

- There must be a clear and compelling advantage for physicians or they will not support the effort.
- Electronic systems are not necessarily an improvement, and issues of patient safety can develop as a result of the new technology.
- A clear understanding of how the physician uses the information and how the new system will affect the physician's workflow is required to plan a successful system.
- Training busy providers on new systems requires tremendous effort, creativity, and flexibility.

Assuming that the IOM report is correct and that these systems will be critical in our effort to become more efficient and error free, what is the role of the physician in system redesign? The answer is simple: early involvement of front-line practitioners in all major systems projects. This planning takes a considerable amount of time, but both the health system and the physicians have much to lose if it is done poorly. A willingness to work with information technologists and administrators to revise and redesign workflow has the potential for creating effective systems that make the practice of medicine easier and less error prone. Shortcuts in this initial planning stage prior to the selection of hardware and software options will result in a very expensive system that interferes with patient care and makes efficient practice impossible. If new systems are being planned at your institution, you must get in on the ground floor and have a clinician on the team.

Many larger organizations have taken this concept a step further by assigning one or two physicians with computer experience to the information technology (IT) planning team. The chief medical informatics officer can be very helpful in long-range strategic planning for clinical IT systems.

Matching Resources to Needs: Physicians as Senior Administrators

Medical errors increase when the system designed to provide care is overwhelmed. In this era of managed care, many health systems are forced to make difficult resource allocation decisions that may affect the quality of patient care. Tighter and tighter control of costs must be balanced with outcomes and safety considerations. This can only be done if the providers who see the effects of administrative choices are actively involved in health system administration.

Physicians can contribute to this effort in many ways. Cooperating with reasonable cost containment efforts is a great first step. Set aside favorites and use less expensive implants, devices, or medications if the clinical results will be the same. Physicians can also set high expectations and quality standards while advocating for safe patient care in their own clinic or hospital.

Ideally, in your community, physicians are in leadership positions and participate regularly when both financial performance and clinical outcomes are measured and discussed. Make sure that physicians are actively participating in the highest levels of your organization.

Establishing Standards and Policy

Certain aspects of care are high risk and therefore deserve focused discussion and guidelines. Examples of these include medication order writing, conscious sedation, and the restraint or seclusion of patients. Physicians can help reduce the potential for medical mishaps and prevent patient injury by authoring practical policies and then by enforcing safety guidelines.

We recently created an electronic medication administration record (MAR) at our institution in an effort to clean up the handwritten MAR and reduce the likelihood of error. In doing so, we discovered many nonspecific orders being used by medical staff. "Hold drug X" was one such common order. We became concerned when we realized that this order was interpreted differently depending on the nurse and the setting. Some nurses held a single dose, whereas others thought this order was equivalent to stopping the drug until a restart order was written.

The potential for error with vague orders like this is obvious, but let's face it, old habits are hard to break. The point here is a simple one. Physicians today are not working with a small group of people who "know what I mean when I say hold drug X." Physicians must be as clear as possible in their communication and order writing. Stricter guidelines will be required, and we must support that concept. The same is true of other policies directed at high-risk aspects of care. In the future, cooperation and understanding of the importance of making care safe will be expected of all health care professionals.

Evidence-Based Medicine

"In the current health care system, scientific knowledge about best practice is not applied systematically or expediently to clinical practice. An average of about 17 years is required for new knowledge generated by randomized controlled trials to be incorporated into practice, and even then application is highly uneven."[5]

Practice guidelines for the optimal care of many disease states have been created, but consistent application of these is still not a reality.

According to the 2001 IOM report, "Patients should receive care that is based on the best available scientific knowledge. Care should not vary illogically from clinician to clinician or from place to place."[6]

This assessment prompted the IOM to recommend that the Department of Health and Human Services be given the responsibility and necessary resources to establish and maintain a comprehensive program aimed at making scientific evidence more useful and accessible to clinicians and patients.

Physician leadership in the development of these standards will be important. The acceptance and use of such guidelines will depend on the extent to which practicing physicians are involved and educated on the science behind the guidelines. Bringing best practices into an organization and implementing advances in medical science should be rapid and consistent. Physician leaders will be called upon to make it so.

Conclusion

All things considered, these are very exciting times to be a physician. The unbalanced emphasis on cost cutting and reduced reimbursement for medical care that defined the 1990s is being challenged by those interested in the results of what physicians do. Improved outcomes and preventing unnecessary complications are excellent goals that we can all support. The basic principles have been laid out in this chapter. They are easy to describe but difficult to implement. It will be well worth the effort, however, because each of these topics could contribute something positive to your patients if implemented well. Make sure your organization carefully selects and evaluates its providers. Offer your expertise in the development of more efficient systems of care. Set and meet standards that will make the hospital or clinic a safer place. Your patients will be better off, and it may even bring the joy back into the practice of medicine.

Notes

1. Kohn, L. T., Corrigan, J. M., Donaldson, M. S., eds. *To Err Is Human: Building a Safer Health System*. Washington, DC: National Academy Press, 1999.
2. Institute of Medicine. *Crossing the Quality Chasm*. Washington, DC: National Academy Press, 2001.
3. Ibid.
4. Ibid.
5. Ibid.
6. Ibid.

CHAPTER TWENTY-ONE

ENGAGING GENERAL COUNSEL IN THE PURSUIT OF SAFETY

Barbara J. Youngberg, BSN, MSW, JD

A critical stumbling block impeding many organizations from fully engaging in practices associated with the creation of high-reliability organizations may be the advice of counsel. Although it is easy to understand why counsel representing health care organizations are skittish, given the dramatic escalations in malpractice verdicts and settlements over the past few years,[1] perhaps in their zeal to protect the organization they are actually inhibiting the organization's ability to protect its patients. Health care professionals' concern over unwanted, at times nonmeritorious, and increasingly costly litigation is understandable, but they are often urged to consider these problems as a failure of the legal system. Although that may at times be the case, organizations and providers must recognize that it could also be related to failures of the health care system's peer review processes and quality improvement or risk management processes, which should be structured to identify and prevent adverse patient outcomes or medical complications and negligent care. Because the fear of litigation often discourages open discussion of error and methods of reducing those errors, it might be prudent for health care attorneys to assist their organizations in designing a more structured performance improvement system and peer review process so that care outcomes can be studied, rather than litigation outcomes. Because the escalating costs of malpractice frequently fuel discussions associated with the need for tort reform, health care organizations should also recognize that quality improvement opportunities hold the promise not only of significant improvement in patient outcomes, but also of significant reductions in health care costs.

In-house counsel often characterize their job as being the protection of the organization's assets—of course, meaning its financial assets. These costs are typically viewed as the costs traditionally associated with malpractice litigation (including indemnity payments made to injured patients and defense and legal expenses paid to those involved in developing and advancing a legal defense). Providing counsel with an understanding of the costs of poor quality might help them see their job more broadly and could allow them to focus on the importance of their role as it relates to assisting the organization to create an enhanced system for performing peer review that insulates the committee from antitrust claims when they actually invoke disciplinary actions and that holds all providers, leaders, and managers accountable. In addition, if patients (rather than money) were viewed as the primary asset of the organization, perhaps the role of in-house counsel could change its focus. Counsel could and should serve as an essential partner in the pursuit of a safe and error-free organization and should recognize their essential role in promoting and designing structures that identify practices, practitioners, and systems that are at the root of the cases they later must defend on behalf of their clients.

Equally important in this dialogue is the recognition that the damage component of our tort system is flawed and in need of reform, but that, more often than not, plaintiffs have sustained some type of injury at the hands of a health care provider or organization. It is the injury that generally fuels both the patient's need for information and the demand for retribution. Only by creating a structure that helps the organization understand and respond to the problems associated with error will the organization truly ever be able to get ahead of the problems inherent in the tort system.

The science surrounding the study of error and the factors contributing to it is advancing and can provide assistance to organizations seeking to get ahead of the problem, but it may require a different way of thinking for all of those who are part of the team. And for the first time, it might require that the organization's counsel see themselves as part of the team that not only contains errors but also proactively assists the organization in addressing the causes of them. This might include enhancing the nature of the peer review process and ensuring that all state requirements are met, thereby creating a process that ensures maximum likelihood of protection of all who participate.

What is clear from reading the literature about the safety practices of health care is that for many years very well-intentioned professionals have tried to make their environments safe, using a variety of new techniques and philosophies. What is equally clear is that in almost any organization, there are a number of individuals who know why errors occur and who is often involved and what needs to be done to make the system more safe. It would seem, then, that having identified the problem, it would be relatively easy to fix it. But for many reasons, this has not been the case.

For years, the literature has been quick to blame many of the problems being faced by the health care system on a damaged legal system. The cost of defensive medicine, the rising costs of malpractice coverage, the plaintiff's bar eager to make millions by wrongfully suing the competent provider—some of these problems and characterizations may be true, but what is equally true is that preventable errors continue to occur and they often result in injury to the very individuals our systems are supposed to protect. Only by truly reducing preventable medical errors can we hope to get in front of the malpractice problems.

You can't get ahead of the problem of medical error by hiding behind the law. The law of negligence, particularly medical malpractice, evolved in response to a need. It is equally compelling to note that you cannot change behavior if you design a system that continually looks the other way when it becomes aware of systemic and personal failures. A different system of learning and accountability must be established.

I have heard in-house attorneys and defense counsel advise against the sharing of error data for the purpose of learning, stating that they don't want to provide a road map for a plaintiff's attorney. My response has generally been, Better a road map than a client!

Many in health care today would state that the reason they cannot get their organizations behind the creation of an accountable system of quality is the fear of what might be discovered that will place the organization in an unfavorable light. Of equal concern is that many physicians fear legal retribution by their colleagues if indeed they institute actions that limit another physician's practice, and thus they are unwilling to truly assist in the disciplinary activities necessary to create an accountable health care system.

Protection of Medical Error Data

Three general rules of evidence could potentially protect medical error data in an online or paper-based reporting tool from disclosure: the remedial action privilege, attorney–client privilege, and the work product doctrine.[2] The IOM report says all three have major limitations. The remedial action privilege applies solely to information submitted to prove negligence or a product defect. Attorney–client privilege is limited to communication between an attorney and a client either seeking or providing advice or in anticipation of litigation: Disclosure of information to a third party under this protection destroys the privilege. Work product doctrine protects the thoughts and mental impressions of an attorney, data that are not typically found in paper or online medical error reports.

The remedial action privilege prevents admission of actions taken after an adverse event occurs to prove negligence or a defective product. The purpose of the privilege is to encourage defendants and potential defendants to take action to improve safety without the fear that the information will be used against them. It recognizes that remedial actions are not necessarily related to negligence. All states except Rhode Island have adopted this rule.[3] Some courts have extended this privilege to include self-evaluative reports or other postinjury analyses and reports. A California court ruled that hospital peer review activities were protected from discovery on the theory of remedial action privilege.[4] This privilege does not prevent admission of these reports to prove issues other than negligence or product defect.

In response to a poor benchmarking showing, plaintiffs would argue that a hospital's efforts to remediate the process or system that led to the poor performance are evidence that the prior system was defective. There is a strong public policy argument to be made that subsequent remedial measures, as in a product liability case, should not be admissible to prove negligence by the hospital for the medical error. For the same reason, a plaintiff suing a widget manufacturer cannot use evidence of a later design change as evidence the widget was previously defective or caused the injury.[5]

In Illinois, courts have made clear that the nature and content of the internal peer review process itself are privileged and confidential under the Medical Studies Act.[6] Because subsequent remediation is clearly part of the internal peer review process, it follows that such activities should be protected from disclosure in Illinois. Many states in addition to Illinois have created specific protections for health care facilities and providers in an effort to facilitate the creation of a process in health care settings or between peer providers that truly allows for the identification and correction of problems associated with providing health care. These statutes should be examined carefully and utilized fully to afford the organization the highest level of protection possible under each individual state's laws.

Attorney–client privilege protects communication between attorneys and clients, although a client may waive this privilege. In medical institutions, the client is usually limited to the "control group," or senior management, of the organization. The privilege will rarely protect data sent to an external entity and may not be useful in protecting reports that are prepared by those other than senior management. In *Chicago Trust Company v. Cook County Hospital,* the court found that incident reports submitted by a nurse and respiratory therapist were not protected under attorney–client privilege because the nurse and respiratory therapist were not part of the hospital control group;[7] that is, they were not clients of the attorney who received the reports. The reports were not addressed to an attorney or prepared by an attorney, they were not memoranda or communication to or advice from an attorney, and they contained only factual information. The court said that even if these documents were privileged, the privilege was waived when the documents were sent to the hospital quality committee.[8]

Attorney work product doctrine protects materials created by or on behalf of a lawyer in anticipation of litigation. It protects the thoughts and ideas of the attorney, and only the attorney can waive the privilege. Many states have found that this doctrine does not apply to incident reports because they are completed in the ordinary course of business and seldom contain the thoughts and ideas of attorneys. In addition, many current incident reporting systems are now designed to collect data on near miss events and data related to other types of situations in the organization that will never be the subject of legal action. In *Columbia/HCA Healthcare Corporation v. Eighth Judicial District Court,* the court found that incident reports are filled out in the ordinary course of business because Columbia requires hospital personnel to fill out preprinted forms when an unusual event occurs.[9] They are not completed in anticipation of litigation. Even if they were, if the plaintiffs can show that they have a substantial need for the information and cannot get the information in any other way, access to incident reports may be granted.

Peer Review Protection

The peer review privilege is one statutory protection that may provide legal protection for medical error data. It differs from state to state but is the most promising source of protection.[10] One common element of state peer review privileges is that they protect peer review or quality improvement committee activities if performed in a manner designed to ensure consistency and quality of purpose. Some states protect data collected at the direction of a quality improvement committee or the findings of quality improvement committees that are made in the interest of reducing morbidity and mortality and improving the quality of care. These privileges vary considerably in their reach and strength and typically do not protect documents that are prepared in the course of rendering services to patients or conducting business for an organization. Therefore, the peer review privilege does not typically protect medical records or accident reports that are a routine part of business, but will protect documents prepared as an organization identifies quality problems, discusses possible solutions, and modifies the environment to bring about desired change.

Most statutes require that all information collected remain confidential within the peer review or quality improvement committee and not be disclosed to others. Many statutes do not address interhospital collaboration, even when the hospitals are within an integrated delivery system.[11] In *Of the Estate of Stanley W. Howard,* the court found that the applicability of the medical peer review privilege relates to the way in which the document was created and the purpose for which it was used, not its content.[12] This case found that incident reports in the peer review system created by the Massachusetts legislature are a core component of peer review because they begin the process and are necessary to the committees' work product.[13] Many states only protect the case analysis by the quality improvement or peer review committee, not the information that was sent to the committee or the actions taken by the committee.

In a well-publicized case arising in the state of New York, *Zion v. New York Hospital,*[14] the plaintiffs sought production of documents from the Joint Commission on Accreditation of Healthcare Organizations (JCAHO) that they believed would support their claims of negligence against the hospital. The hospital denied the release of these documents, citing the New York education law that allows for protection of privileged information. The hospital prevailed in its argument in a strong opinion of the court, which wrote: "Affording such a privilege to the records of the JCAHO furthers the goal of improving the quality of hospital care, a goal which both the statute (see, *Matter of Albany Medical Center Hospital v. Denis,* 161 AD 2d 1030: *Lilly v. Turecki,* 112 AD 2d 788) and JCAHO seek to achieve."

Confidentiality of these records encourages the surveyed hospital to engage in open and candid discussion of hospital conditions, thereby enabling the hospital to learn from mistakes. Stripping the records of the confidentiality the Joint Commission guarantees to the hospitals that seek its services would frustrate this purpose. Although "the exemption from disclosure for the JCAHO records, may, on occasion, hamper a malpractice plaintiff's ability to ascertain relevant information, the legislature has made a determination that, on balance, this consideration is outweighed by the benefit the privilege confers on the general public."[15]

Plaintiffs' attorneys have tried to get access to peer review–protected materials when bringing suits against a hospital for corporate negligence in credentialing physicians. They have argued that the data must be available in these cases because it is the only way to judge if the hospital is fulfilling its responsibility to assess the competence of providers. In California, Colorado, and New York, the courts have held that peer review activity is protected from discovery and is not available even when the issue is the adequacy of the hospital in carrying out its role of assessing the competence of its medical staff.[16] In Texas, however, the court found that there was no legislative intent in the peer review statute to protect hospitals from negligent credentialing claims.[17]

The Health Care Quality Improvement Act[18] provides federal protection for peer review activities and those who participate in the process in good faith. The act protects the participants from antitrust or libel allegations, but it was not crafted to protect the information reviewed by the quality improvement or peer review committees. It is unclear whether this act would be useful in protecting online reporting activity or information shared to facilitate discussions about improving quality or promoting safety from discovery, so legislation at the federal level would be helpful to protect these data. Legislation has been enacted by Congress to protect some medical quality assurance records, but it limited the scope to federally operated health care facilities. These examples demonstrate that Congress is at least aware of the need for federal protection of peer review information.

With the focus now on patient safety, multiple bills have been advanced in the House and the Senate to protect information gathered to study and improve patient safety. Bills by Nancy Johnson (D-CT),[19] Jim Jeffords (D-VT),[20] and Ted Kennedy (D-MA)[21] provide definitions of the term *patient safety data* and create protections for organizations that share such data to study error reduction. Each bill also creates a role for the Department of Health and Human Services as its relates to furthering the study and science of error.

Web-based error collection tools are relatively new to health care, and protection of these data is untested in most states. There are several reasons, however, why sending medical error data to a Web-based error collection system may not waive the hospital's peer review privilege. As the recipient of medical error data from a hospital, any collecting or aggregating agency could be deemed to be acting as an agent or designee of that hospital's peer review committee; those activities, therefore, including the data collected, could be protected. The Illinois Medical Studies Act (MSA) specifically provides protection for the peer review activities of "Patient Care Audit Committees, Medical Care Evaluation Committees, Utilization Review Committees, Credential Committees and Executive Committees, or their designees."[22] Current protection afforded under the Health Insurance Portability and Accountability Act for business associates may also serve to provide protection for these types of data.

The Value of Error Data to Plaintiff Attorneys

There are three types of data that may be of interest to plaintiff attorneys: (1) patient-identifiable data about the specific event, (2) aggregate data about the involved institution's performance in similar events, and (3) similar-occurrence data that relate to a specific aspect of the case where the plaintiff's attorney is attempting to prove negligence.[23]

The last two categories of data are available to plaintiff attorneys without a medical error report, online reporting tool, or collaborative data project. Hospital-identifiable aggregate data regarding complications and mortalities are publicly available and can easily be used to infer negligence or to support or impute an organization's mismanagement of specific diseases or diagnoses. Examples of aggregate data are the coronary artery bypass graft mortality rates and total joint replacement complication rates available through Internet sites such as www.healthgrades.com. Plaintiff attorneys have not used these data frequently, but they could use the data to show that the organization had prior notice of an issue that it had not addressed. Similarly, many states (Pennsylvania and New York among them) have mandatory reporting requirements for specific groups of patients or specific types of adverse events and periodically make this data public to show practice variations (and possibly quality variations) among organizations or providers. Participation in data-sharing projects, coupled with a strong safety or performance improvement program, could be used to offset data that may one day present an organization unfavorably in a public format; participation also may be used to argue that the organization has a strong commitment to quality improvement and the prevention of harm to patients.

In a Florida medical malpractice case, similar-occurrence data were used when an obese plaintiff alleged that the defendant obstetrician injured her child by delivering her on a standard bed versus a drop-down bed.[24] The court held that the records of other obese women who the obstetrician had delivered were relevant and discoverable to show whether other infants of obese women sustained injuries when delivered on a standard bed. The defendant had to provide the records of obese patients, with their names redacted.[25] An internal or external reporting system coupled with a safety management program would have alerted the organization and provider if there were newborn complications when obese women delivered on standard beds or would have provided the organization with data to refute the allegation.

The first category of data of interest to plaintiff attorneys, patient-identifiable data about the specific event, is mainly of interest to fortify one or more elements in a malpractice action against an individual or health care facility. The elements of a negligence suit include duty owed by the provider to the plaintiff, a breach of that duty, the breach of duty being the proximate cause of injury to the plaintiff, and damages suffered related to the injury. Incident reports are highly sought after by plaintiff attorneys because they are viewed as the "real story" behind the event. Whereas the medical record contains (mostly) objective information and data, the incident report fills out the story with details that may definitively show provider error or negligence.

Each organization must determine if the risk of possible discovery outweighs the benefits of collecting and analyzing information from an incident report. The major benefit of having knowledge of a medical error is that the mishap can be fully investigated, with a root cause or criticality analysis performed as necessary. Early claims processing can begin also, if warranted. The benefits of tracking and trending all reported errors include the ability to identify systems issues, detect individual practitioner or practice issues, and focus on clinical risk areas in need of support and education. Instructing staff on the importance of objective nonretaliatory reporting of incidents can go a long way toward reducing the value of these reports for plaintiff's counsel, and a policy of open disclosure to patients when errors do occur could certainly alleviate the need for a plaintiff's attorney to find value in these reports.

A Defense Attorney's Strategy

As more sophisticated error data collection becomes prevalent and hospitals look to enhance their reporting structures, defense attorneys are increasingly being asked whether this information is legally protected from disclosure in litigation. The answer is a qualified "yes," with the following caveats: Data can be protected from disclosure if they are limited, there is limited distribution of the data collected, there is a limited purpose for collecting the data, and the structure of the committees and processes designed by the organization comports with the requirements of the law.

Every state has enacted legislation protecting peer review activities in hospitals, to some extent. Certain states have very strong protections for data generated by those activities, whereas other states have weaker protections that might allow for disclosure.

The Joint Commission states that "performance monitoring and improvements are data driven. Every organization must choose which processes and outcomes (and thus which types of data) are important to monitor based on its mission and the scope of care and services it provides."[26]

The challenge to hospitals is to comply with this Joint Commission standard while protecting the collected data under state peer review legislation, such as the Illinois MSA.[27] Like many state peer review statutes, the MSA outlines what data and peer review activities are protected, whose data and activities are protected, and when they are protected. On its face, the MSA protects computer-based medical error data as "reports . . . or other data." The MSA protects "All information, interviews, reports, statements, memoranda, recommendations . . . or other data . . . of accredited hospitals or their medical staffs . . . used in the course of internal quality control or . . . for improving patient care."[28]

The court in *Chicago Trust v. Cook County Hospital*[29] ("Cook County") said that the Illinois MSA does not protect the following:

- Material created in the ordinary course of business
- Material created for the purpose of rendering a legal opinion
- Material created to weigh potential liability risk
- Material created for later corrective action by the hospital staff
- Pre-committee material used by a peer review committee

The Cook County case instructs Illinois hospitals that they must establish how, when, and why certain material is privileged before it is collected.

Various ways to protect data before they are collected are as follows:

- *Refer to medical error data collection in your hospital's peer review policy:* All hospital peer review committee policies and procedures should specifically incorporate medical error data collection as part of the information gathering, tracking, trending, monitoring, and deliberation process that is used in medical staff peer review.
- *Encourage anonymous reporting:* The MSA is premised on the belief that without statutory peer review privilege, the medical staff would hesitate to frankly evaluate their colleagues.[30] Allowing anonymous medical error reporting advances this policy of encouraging an open flow of information through the peer review process.
- *Stress performance improvement rather than peer review:* The Joint Commission's new patient safety initiative speaks primarily of performance improvement and patient safety activities. Since successful performance improvement will reduce the need for peer review activities, because of fewer errors, review committee policies with an eye toward tying performance improvement, patient safety, and peer review together more closely.

Although Illinois law obviously is not controlling outside of Illinois, some of the logic behind it might be helpful for all health care organizations to consider. The best approach for hospitals still concerned about discoverability is to consider error data collection as a minimalist incident report, which simply serves as a trigger for further detailed peer review. Unfortunately, many paper-based incident reporting systems allow for health care providers to enter an unlimited amount of subjective information, often pointing fingers of blame at specific parties.

Another consideration: The data in a medical error reporting system or paper tool do not provide plaintiff attorneys with any information that is not available through other discoverable tools such as the medical record, personnel files, or depositions. At deposition, a plaintiff's attorney will gather far more, and more detailed, information from the involved health care professionals than he or she will get from the medical error report. Therefore, data protection through peer review statutes is only temporary until the litigation discovery process begins.

Another area of concern is what effect benchmarking of data has on legal protection of the information collected. The Joint Commission states that "Certain types of data and information need to be accumulated over time to support the hospital's clinical and management functions . . . [including] analysis of trends over time . . . [and] performance comparisons over time within the hospital and with other hospitals."[31] Accordingly, the Joint Commission clearly supports an organization that benchmarks or shares medical error data "to effect behavioral changes in itself and other health care organizations to improve patient safety."[32]

What a hospital does when faced with the bad news that it has scored poorly when benchmarked against other hospitals for a given indicator is critically important. This is true whether the benchmarking project is related to reported medical errors or complication rates developed from public information. If hospital leadership dismisses the poor benchmarking performance, forbids future benchmark study participation, builds obstacles to error improvement efforts, or otherwise does nothing, consider the ramifications:

- A plaintiff's attorney could argue that the hospital does not place a high priority on patient safety and high-quality medical care—a public relations problem.
- Quitting a benchmarking program after poor performance results, if even a possibility, will not be well received by any jury—a legal problem.
- Increased claims arise from medical errors—an economic problem.

- Ignoring benchmarking data allows a known, documented potential danger to patients to continue—a moral and ethical problem that could become a serious legal problem in those states allowing punitive damages against hospitals and health care providers.

The appropriate response is for the hospital risk or quality manager to launch an investigation and assessment of the root causes of that poor performance, determine whether it is a true systemic problem or a data problem, then implement an action plan to improve performance, and monitor progress to ensure the effectiveness of the solution. This response will reduce future claims. In the event of a claim, such preventive and remedial activity may be useful to mitigate damages by showing that the hospital had instituted an aggressive program to identify and correct systemic problems and had acted reasonably to prevent the occurrence.

If hospitals share benchmarking data with other organizations that are outside the scope of the peer review process, will that action waive the privilege? If the Joint Commission mandates hospitals to conduct ongoing monitoring of patient safety, the public policy behind state peer review statutes should protect data generated by that monitoring. To encourage frank and open information gathering during this "monitoring process," all data gathered by these systems should be protected.

The Joint Commission has effectively expanded the scope of the performance improvement or peer review process outside the hospital by expressly encouraging the ongoing proactive reduction of medical errors. In fact, the Intent section of Standard PI.2 specifically states that performance review processes, when they are designed well, draw on a variety of information sources, including sources external to the hospital: Such a process "incorporates available information from within the organization and from other organizations, about potential risks to patients."[33]

Similarly, the Joint Commission contemplates that a hospital will "link with external databases and information networks."[34] The cited Joint Commission language demonstrates the intent to expand the current idea of performance review to include data from external databases and information from other hospitals. Therefore, protections for such data must likewise expand. Hospitals are well advised to carefully limit their data to the dictates of the relevant state peer review statute. The biggest patient safety problem is not bad people but good people working in bad systems. Fostering open communication and disclosure of errors and encouraging systemic fixes throughout the health care industry are parts of an important new public policy that has yet to be adopted by state courts or incorporated into state or federal data and peer review protection legislation. In the meantime, hospitals are advised to limit the data reported, limit who has access to those data, and limit the use of those data to ensure greatest protection for those data.

In-house attorneys, external defense counsel, and any lawyers working with health care organizations and providers have many opportunities to use their knowledge and skills to assist in creating high-reliability organizations. Providing excuses related to the ineffectiveness of current laws, the lack of predictability of the current tort system, or the current antagonism felt by the public toward the health care system may not be the most effective way for their value to be realized.

Notes

1. *Addressing the New Health Care Crisis: Reforming the Medical Litigation System to Improve the Quality of Health Care.* U.S. Department of Health and Human Services, Office of the Assistant Secretary for Planning and Evaluation, Washington, DC, March 3, 2003.
2. Kohn, L. T., Corrigan, J. M., Donaldson, M. S., eds. *To Err Is Human: Building a Safer Health System.* Washington, DC: National Academy Press, 2000, 117.
3. Ibid.
4. *Fox v Kramer,* 22 Cal. 4th 531, 994 P2d 343, 2000 Cal LEXIS 1566, 93 Cal Rptr 2d 497, 2000 Cal Daily Op Service 2082, 2000 DAR 2805 (2000).
5. Restatement of Torts.
6. *Zajac v St. Mary of Nazareth Hospital,* 212 Ill App 3d 779, 571 NE2d 840 (1st District 1991).
7. *Chicago Trust Company v Cook County Hospital,* 298 Ill App 3d 396, 698 NE2d 641 (1st Dist 1998).
8. Ibid.
9. *Columbia/HCA Healthcare Corporation v Eighth Judicial District Court,* 113 Nev 521, 1997, 5–6.
10. Kohn, Corrigan, Donaldson, eds. *To Err Is Human,* 119.
11. Ibid., 120.
12. *Carr v Howard, administratrix of the Estate of Stanley W. Howard,* 426 Mass 514, 689 NE2d 1304, 1998 Mass Lexis 24.
13. Ibid.
14. *Sidney E. Zion, as administrator of the Estate of Libby Zion, Deceased v New York Hospital, et al.,* 183 AD2d 386, 590 NYS2d 188, 1992 NY App Div.
15. Ibid.
16. *Posey v Supreme Court of Colorado,* 196 Colo 396, 1978; *West Covian Hospital v Superior Court of Los Angeles County,* 153 Cal App3d 134, 1984; *Parker v St. Clare's Hospital et al.,* 159 AD2d 919.

17. *AGBOR v St. Luke's Episcopal Hospital,* 912 SW2d 354; 1995 Tex App LEXIS 3007.
18. Health Care Quality Improvement Act of 1986, 38 USC 5705; 38 CFR 17.501; 10 USC 1102.
19. Patient Safety Improvement Act of 2002 (HR 4889). House Ways and Means Committee, September 10, 2002.
20. Patient Safety and Quality Improvement Act (SR 2590), June 5, 2002.
21. Patient Safety Improvement and Medical Injury Reduction Act (SR 3029), September 24, 2002.
22. Illinois Medical Studies Act, 735 ILCS 5/8-2101 (1997).
23. Kohn, Corrigan, Donaldson, eds. *To Err Is Human,* 114–115.
24. *Amente v Newman,* 653 So2d 1030, 20 FLW S172 (1995, Fla).
25. Ibid.
26. *Comprehensive Accreditation Manual for Hospitals: The Official Handbook.* Oakbrook Terrace, IL: Joint Commission on Accreditation of Healthcare Organizations, 2002, Intent of Standard PI.3.1.
27. Illinois Medical Studies Act.
28. Ibid.
29. *Chicago Trust Company v Cook County Hospital.*
30. *Stricklin v Becan,* 293 Ill App 3d 866, 689 NE2d 328 (4th Dist 1997).
31. *Comprehensive Accreditation Manual,* Intent of Standard IM.8.
32. *Comprehensive Accreditation Manual,* LD.39.
33. Ibid.
34. *Comprehensive Accreditation Manual,* Intent of Standard IM.1.

CHAPTER TWENTY-TWO

GROWING NURSING LEADERSHIP IN THE FIELD OF PATIENT SAFETY

Mary L. Salisbury, RN, MSN and Robert Simon, EdD, CPE

We have had the privilege and the opportunity of traveling to health care organizations across the country. Maintaining a practice that spans the continent broadens the spectrum of professional input beyond that of the institution-based provider. In our travels, we find that professionals easily discuss and eagerly entertain the considered perspective of others. Beyond engaging discussion, our responsibility as researchers is to listen and log conditions, observe, and postulate solutions. We find that whenever we visit a health care organization, we are confronted by caregivers characterizing the condition of patient safety with an identical exclamation and inquiry:

- "It is awful out there; we are working in the worst of times and the best of times."
- "Beyond the issue of staffing, why is the voice of nursing seemingly silent regarding patient safety and the development of comprehensive solutions?"

The exclamation is intensely expressed and appears omnipresent. Caregivers state that a gulf exists between the standards of health care delivery and actual outcomes. Our investigation, direct observations, and patient interviews serve to confirm their perspective. The specific aim of this chapter, therefore, is to sort this out and do the following:

1. Describe what is happening relative to health care, nursing, and patient safety; summarize the history, duty, and current perspective of nursing
2. Establish the key characteristics of a comprehensive solution to the problem of patient safety
3. Explicate the form and function of patient safety (form as it exists in the concept of *vision*; function as it exists in the concept of *teamwork*)
4. Present a comprehensive patient safety solution that can move health care from the worst of times toward the best of times

The Worst of Times

The health care arena is a battlefield rife with the cratered remains of the repeated and haphazard bombs of change. Within a period of 4 years, two-thirds of the nation's health care organizations merged (Danzon, 1994). Of these conglomerations, undeterminable numbers have disaffiliated and remerged, giving rise to tidal crashes of cultures. So ravaged, the health care geography little resembles the healing arenas where once we received and delivered the fruits of our education.

Displaced from health care homelands by the ongoing maneuvers of organizational mergers, joint ventures, and managed care affiliations, nurses and physicians alike are separated from the work they once knew and understood. Stunned caregivers tell stories regarding their professional alienation and that of their equally stunned leaders, who stagger about like mapless captains on rudderless ships. One of our client hospitals characterized changes in the health care arena this way, "First we downsized; then we right sized; now we capsize." To further the alienation, jargons du jour constantly emerge to create a new and unrecognizable language of health care. Unable to interpret the landscape or the language of these newly merged worlds, caregivers fail to anticipate the lurking patient care dangers and for these reasons fail to establish safe arenas of care. Isolated, caregivers believe that they are left to respond, or react, alone.

The Best of Times

Professionals are seeking solutions. We care. The vehicle that will carry many of these solutions is this simple yet profound handbook. This particular handbook's topic is patient safety, and the book carries with it the acknowledgment that any solution addressing patient safety would be incomplete without the perspective of nursing. This fact and opportunity provide a segue to the interrogative regarding the absent voice of nursing and the subsequent perception that nursing problem solves in isolation, along the lines of the discipline. Perhaps the two most compelling perspectives are summarized by the following:

- With nursing absent from the table, no patient safety solution can be considered comprehensive. The term *comprehensive* prescribes a solution that is inclusive and therefore mandates an outcome-based solution that includes all disciplines and aspects of care that affect patient experience. The issue of proper and appropriate staffing, although central to the concept, does not provide the single link to safety. Staffing is a necessary condition, but proper staffing alone is not sufficient to prevent the occurrence of error.
- With nursing absent from the table, any solution developed along a discipline's line fails to recognize the agenda for national patient safety and a central tenet of the National Patient Safety Foundation (1998), namely, that safety does not reside in an individual. Rather, patient safety is a condition that emerges from the collective interactivities of caregivers working in systems designed to produce desired outcomes.

Background: History and Duty of Nursing in Comprehensive Patient Safety

Patient safety, for nursing, is encapsulated in the term *advocacy*. Advocacy is the intent of the profession. Despite that fact, the concept grows vague as organizations fail to respond to the wisdom of its providers and as the term disappears into the riptides and undertow caused by the breaking waves of new language. Corporate mergers, cultural collisions, changing professional perspectives, and emerging patient safety collaboratives all serve as sweeping reasons why the language of advocacy has been pulled into the sea of patient safety rhetoric. Although nursing is rooted in patient safety under the term advocacy, the changes have been too many and caregivers have grown weary. Unable to make sense of these changes, many caregivers have shut down (Clemmer, 1992). Still, the historic and current vision of the discipline embodies the concept of patient advocacy. Nurses believe that they are advocates and are quick to attest the same. An emergency department (ED) nurse of greater than 30 years' experience contributes the following exemplar that illustrates this point:

> As a nurse of many years, I speak to a time when my colleagues and I were educated to commit our lives and organize our care around a

simple philosophy: "to do for the patient the things that they could not do for themselves." We were the conscience for the unconscious, the voice for the voiceless, the mobility for the immobile, the courage for the disheartened, and the anticipator of danger for those rendered unable to anticipate. This philosophy was core to each provider and created a vertical snap to our ranks that resulted in the delivery of care through and towards a common ideal. This philosophy of advocacy was integrated deep into the culture of caring; a fact that served to further buffer us against the frailty of our humanness, that of the potential to err. Despite its brevity, the statement was comprehensive, easily assimilated, and continues to organize my care yet today.

To respond to this philosophy fully is to fully advocate, and to plead in favor of the patient's best interest necessitates comprehensive patient safety. The two concepts are inextricably linked, and for nursing the concept of patient advocacy is integrated deep into the action of caring.

When informally surveyed, nurses do not see patient safety as some new and late-breaking insight; rather, it is their belief that it has always been and continues to be a part of what they do. Line-level nurses are clear that they are not absent from the patient safety movement; rather, their impact has been limited. They believe that their voices are not heard within their organizations, and that this perspective is further reinforced by the constant presence of consultants du jour. Caregivers are clear that although the rhetoric of organizations spins along the line of patient safety, corporate decisions follow the line of economics.

Characteristics of a Comprehensive Patient Safety Solution

The first set of characteristics of a comprehensive patient safety solution must be as follows: one vision, one language, but all disciplines.

Awareness, always the first characteristic to arrive, is not enough. Despite growing efforts and approaches to patient safety education, knowledgeable caregivers with excellent clinical skills do not ensure the success of a safety program. Millensen (1997) unequivocally stated that knowledge does not equal action. The question remains, "If everyone agrees that patient safety is desired and is a worthy aim of providers, why then don't all health care professionals provide safe care?" The answer is complex, but considerable observations indicate the following:

- *Leaders are lost to their staff.* Daily, leaders are reassigned, cross-assigned, or overassigned and are, therefore, rarely present to observe the nature of staff work or to mentor actions of safety.
- *Staff are lost to their leaders.* Visionless, staff work without a corporate meaning; they determine and decide for themselves what needs to be done and then defer performance to the skills installed by their primary discipline.

- *Vision is meaningless.* The health care merger experiences have created foreign corporate entities with unknown climates. Unsettled and alienated from the organizations they once knew, caregivers are suspicious of the overnight appearance and disappearance of visions. As the universe of patient safety becomes further stratified within a national agenda, there is neither universal vision nor understanding among disciplines regarding the language and the symbols of comprehensive safety. We have not been able to agree on what it should look like and what it should do.

A call to duty is one means to reduce the disconnect between knowledge and action and to ensure outcomes. The judicial perspective regarding the standards of clinical duty is well defined (American Nurses Association [ANA], 1995), but less delineated are the standards and the language necessary to assess patient safety solutions. Although the disciplines are seeking support from the professional organizations, in lieu of forthcoming standards and language, patient safety advocates preliminarily state that comprehensive patient safety solutions must provide three core outcomes:

1. *Unity.* One vision ensures safety by demonstrating an understanding that safety is a condition that emerges from the collective interactivities of caregivers working in systems designed to prevent inadvertent outcomes (National Patient Safety Foundation [NPSF], 1998). Therefore, a comprehensive patient safety solution must be unifying, establishing a common work with a common language and providing the initiative that organizes multilevel caregivers around a common goal. That goal is to ensure patients' access to safe, cost-effective, high-quality care that is composed of repeatable processes with predictable and positive outcomes.
2. *Error reduction.* High-reliability theories support the conclusions that errors are reduced in systems with repeatable processes producing predictable and positive outcomes (Sagan, 1993). These processes assume stable and appropriate staffing patterns at the unit of delivery.
3. *Patient and staff satisfaction.* Satisfaction is one outcome of fulfilling expectations, and patient and provider safety are often linked (Institute of Medicine [IOM], 2000). Moreover, when health care systems are designed to ensure that caregivers are safe and can deliver safe care, patients benefit.

The second set of characteristics of a comprehensive patient safety solution must therefore be as follows: unity of vision, error management and reduction, and patient and staff satisfaction.

If the original premise is true and nursing is absent from the discussion table, how then does nursing leverage its collective knowledge and considerable lessons learned to ensure its presence in the face of the emerging body of patient safety literature and findings and ensuing actions (IOM, 2000)? When examined,

- *The solution in form is vision.* Staff are caught in the aftermath of the daily health care eruptions; blinded, they roam alone. A meaningful vision from leaders is essential to restore their sight. Although a thorough examination of vision exceeds the scope of this chapter, a short discussion is provided.
- *The solution in function is teamwork.* Teamwork offers the practical skills required to assist caregivers in understanding their work by establishing clear roles, a common and meaningful language, and unity through shared vision, goals, and outcomes. A case study later in this chapter provides an example for exploring teamwork as a solution to ensure the three core outcomes of unity of vision, error management and reduction, and patient and staff satisfaction.

The Form of Patient Safety Is Embodied in Vision

Vision is important to the actions of creating meaning and providing a clear sense of direction to the work that individuals do; organizations cannot survive without vision. The literature indicates that individuals delivering care within an organization that has a clearly established vision and leadership skilled in the translation of that vision have a higher level of commitment, productivity, and job satisfaction than individuals who do not (Senge, 1990; Pritchett and Pound, 1991). Both the vision and the language must be shared within an organization. The language used within an organization and the staff's recognition and understanding of that language are vitally important to the leader's ability to translate statements of vision into something meaningful. Caregivers, connected and engaged in meaningful work, translate statements of vision into outcomes for patients (Westrope, Vaughn, Bott, and Taunton, 1995). Absent a clear organizational vision and outspoken, decisive leaders, caregivers and their patients will be troubled.

The Function of Comprehensive Patient Safety Is Embodied in Teamwork

Teamwork provides a concrete set of practical skills that everyone can learn and use. Teamwork organizes caregivers around a common operational language that is used to articulate patient safety. Individuals organized around a specific goal influence the behaviors of others to work and achieve together (Cannon-Bowers, Oser, and Flannagan, 1992). In health care, individuals are challenged to work within and across department lines; at times they form teams (e.g., code teams), but in general they are trained, evaluated, and socialized to succeed as individuals (Morey et al., 2001; Risser, Simon, Rice, and Salisbury, 1999; Swezey and Salas, 1992). So, how does teamwork achieve the effect of comprehensive patient safety? Our experience has shown that teamwork helps to ensure the three core outcomes of patient safety: unity, reduction in errors, and improved patient and staff satisfaction.

Caregivers organized into health care teams deliver improved outcomes (Morey et al., 2001). Teamwork is multidimensional: Individuals bring to bear their individual skill sets, exercise those skills while functioning within their team role, and coordinate activities with their teammates to achieve the expected work outcomes (Swezey and Salas, 1992, p. 13). Additionally, teamwork mitigates three key issues that undermine patient safety: unclear roles, lack of accountability, and humans providing care in poorly designed and organized complex systems.

Error, the type of error (whether active or latent), and the subsequent development of safeguards against that type of error are really at the heart of what safety is all about. A large factor in active and latent medical error is that humans traditionally function as individuals working in poorly organized groups to deliver care in poorly designed and organized, complex health care systems. These systems provide little support regarding stable climates and established structure, and often fail to provide the necessary resources to caregivers. In this context caregivers must make complex decisions that are tightly coupled to emerging and unstable conditions of high-acuity care delivery (Cook and Woods, 1994; IOM, 2000). To support this discourse, and develop a common understanding, three terms must be defined: coupling, active error, and latent error.

- *Coupling,* a mechanical term, refers to the degree to which an environment is forgiving or unforgiving of certain actions. The provision of health care is often in the context of time-compressed multidimensional events wherein decisions must be made in an environment that is not tolerant of errors (IOM, 2000). The tightly coupled nature of health care defines an added dimension of urgency; lives are at stake.
- *Active errors* are inadvertent events that occur during the delivery of care and whose effects are immediate (IOM, 2000).
- *Latent errors* are embedded into the environment, are a part of operations, and may be termed "precursors or preconditions" to error (IOM, 2000).

Unrecognized and therefore unaddressed latent errors lead to provider errors (Reason, 1990). Latent errors may plague caregivers repeatedly but become normalized into a climate of deviance and lie dormant in the environment until a tightly coupled event emerges, catalyzing the latent system error into an active error. Examples are chronic understaffing; similar names or packaging of medications; breach of standards, such as improper monitoring during conscious sedation procedures; and improper use of equipment. The following is an example of the improper use of equipment: In many places it has become a standard practice to use one monitor to serve two cubicles. The monitor viewed in cubicle A is connected to the patient in cubicle B. A tightly coupled event results and catalyzes the latent error into an emerging event when an overloaded attending physician views the worrisome vitals and EKG and, not recognizing that the vital signs belong to the patient in the adjacent cubicle, prescribes an intervention on the wrong patient's chart.

Principle 3 of the Institute of Medicine's principles for the design of safety systems in health care organizations (IOM, 2000) recommends the following: "Train in teams those who are expected to work in teams." The danger of a latent error manifesting itself is reduced when the precursors and preconditions of care are optimized, that is, when the structure and climate for teamwork are secured: Processes and procedures are standardized, resources are optimal, and individuals know and understand their roles. The chances for active error are reduced when information is maximized by sharing situation awareness factors; plans and decisions are made, communicated, and updated as necessary; a common mental model of the expected outcomes is established; caregivers cross-monitor the activities of others; workload is balanced; and timely individual and team feedback is provided constantly and consistently, thereby informing the team processes (IOM, 2000).

Teamwork Case Study: MedTeams

When designing comprehensive patient safety solutions, teamwork provides a compelling multidisciplinary model of health care delivery. The following is a case study of the MedTeams research project and provides a concrete demonstration of teamwork's power to unify staff and improve performance; reduce error by trapping, managing, and mitigating the outcome of active and latent errors embedded in the reality of our humanity and in health care systems; and provide patient and staff satisfaction.

History

Aviation has been examining safety issues and actively seeking and engaging solutions for decades. Safety in aviation is something that all the stakeholders (i.e., government officials, management, pilots, and passengers) want. Previous research performed for U.S. army aviation showed that aircrew coordination training developed by Dynamics Research Corporation (DRC) improved mission performance by at least 20%, reduced safety-related task errors by over 40%, and resulted in estimated annual savings (from accident avoidance) in excess of $30 million. Based on these results, DRC and government researchers began to look for other high-stress, high-stakes environments that would benefit from team training.

Strong parallels were observed between the fields of tactical aviation and emergency health care (Simon et al., 1997; Weiner et al., 1993; Westrope, Vaughn, Bott, and Taunton, 1993). It was noted that the delivery of emergency care, like aviation, is composed of events where individuals undertake time-compressed, critical decisions and actions often based on incomplete information; demand effective coordination of interdisciplinary professionals; and understand that poor decision making and performance can lead to costly or deadly results.

Although teamwork is not a substitute for an excellent operational or clinical skill set, the initial advantages of teamwork are intuitive to participants. When applied to the domains of aviation and emergency care, those benefits became apparent to all stakeholders. Safety is something that aviators and caregivers want, passengers and patients need, and that managers and leaders can support by creating climates that actively promote teamwork behaviors (Clemmer, 1992; IOM, 2000; Morey et al., 2001; Risser et al., 1999; Simon et al., 1997).

Despite the strong parallels, it was important that the teamwork principles and the lessons learned in aviation undergo review, adaptation, and adoption by the caregivers who deliver emergency care (IOM, 2000). To execute the MedTeams project, a national panel was formed, composed of emergency care physicians and nurses from around the country, a cadre of knowledgeable consultants, emergency care professional societies, and clinical and behavioral experts from DRC. This MedTeams Project Subject Matter Expert Panel worked to adapt aviation-oriented teamwork training to the field of emergency care delivery, evaluate the effectiveness of MedTeams in operational settings, and ensure that the final MedTeams system could be sustained after the research dollars had been spent.

Needs Assessment: Teamwork in Emergency Health Care

To determine need, the initial MedTeams work focused on a closed-case review. Using a Teamwork Failure tool, closed cases were reviewed and assessed for teamwork failures (Risser et al., 1999). Physician and nurse pairs systematically reviewed 68 medical malpractice claims that arose through 4.7 million patient visits from eight emergency departments (EDs) across the country. A total of 476 teamwork failures were identified within the closed cases, for an average of about seven failures per case. These findings led to the conclusion that in each case effective teamwork could have prevented patient harm or injury, avoided over half the documented deaths, and avoided expensive litigation. Using actual costs and applying a national index, researchers calculated the cost of the teamwork failures as $350,000 in malpractice costs (indemnity and expenses) per 100,000 ED patient visits. Translated into practical terms, this means that the conservative amount added to each ED patient's visit to cover the litigated cost of teamwork failures is $3.50.

The behaviors that frequently led to teamwork failures were documented and subsequently integrated into a core curriculum. Central to that curriculum development was a fourfold premise:

1. Teamwork behaviors that improve caregiver coordination and prevent errors are a learnable set of skills (Morey et al., 2001).
2. Individuals trained and skilled in the behaviors of teamwork are equipped to work together to deliver more reliable, high-quality patient-focused care with improved outcomes as well as enhanced patient and staff satisfaction (Morey et al., 2001).
3. Each member of the team remains responsible and accountable to maintain an awareness of the patient's assessment and plan of care and to advocate and assert a position on behalf of the patient. This action of asserting a position and advocating on behalf of the patient is key to breaking the chain of errors (Cook and Woods, 1994, pp. 273–277; Morey et al., 2001; Risser et al., 1999).
4. Most errors unfold over an extended period of time and are observable and recognizable; therefore, they are interruptible (Cook and Woods, 1994, p. 274).

The MedTeams Teamwork Training System

MedTeams is an outcome-based patient safety solution initially delivered to the department as a teamwork training course. MedTeams is a behaviorally oriented, theory-grounded, scientifically based, comprehensive solution to the problem of patient safety.

MedTeams delivers the adapted aviation-based teamwork training to ED staffs, with specific attention paid to team operating rules and the use of a set of standardized teamwork behaviors. The start-up training course, entitled Emergency Team Coordination Course (ETCC), addresses how teams form, the principles of teamwork, the essential operational issues, and the reinforcements required to promote the effective delivery of emergency care. The MedTeams behaviors and course are organized around the five dimensions of teamwork principles common to highly effective teams: (1) maintaining team structure and climate, (2) planning and problem solving, (3) communication, (4) workload management, and (5) improving teamwork skills.

The MedTeams teamwork training system equips clinically expert caregivers to work as a team organized around the goal of the right care delivered in the right way. MedTeams training equips team members with the skills to identify, capture, and manage or mitigate the active or latent errors that unfold or lie dormant within their system. The details of each MedTeams teamwork dimension are discussed next.

Team Dimension 1: Team Structure and Climate

The care delivery unit of a MedTeams organization is its team. As an organizational model, MedTeams divides an ED into functional units called *core teams*. These core teams are composed of 4 to 10 staff members, including physicians, nurses, technical caregivers, and administrative assistants. Each team member clearly knows which team he or she belongs to and which patients are assigned to the team. An ED maintains from one to four core teams during any given shift, depending on the expected patient volume and the actual staffing level. During the course of emerging events, such as incoming trauma or medical resuscitations, team members peel off from the core team and join with others to form an ad hoc team that delivers care until patients are handed off or members are relieved to return to their core team function and role. Leadership is trained to become skilled in the duties and responsibilities relative to creating and maintaining the climate and structuring the supports that are required to implement and sustain teamwork behaviors.

Team dimension 1 safeguards against latent error by ensuring that the proper climate and system structures for the delivery of care are in place, that team members are knowledgeable of their roles, and that upon arrival each new team meets to discuss resource and patient flow issues and takes the necessary actions to correct any existing issues.

Team Dimension 2: Plan and Problem Solve

Failure to advocate and assert a position on behalf of the patient was recognized in the needs assessment by the MedTeams physician–nurse pairs as core to teamwork failures that too often resulted in patient harm or injury. Team dimension 2 is designed specifically to safeguard against that failure. The action of advocating and asserting a position on behalf of the patient is key to interrupting active and unfolding errors. In traditional care, individuals assess their patients and develop and hold a mental model of the patient's problems, needs, and expected outcomes. A working diagnosis is developed, plans are designed, and all actions prescribed proceed along nursing and along medical discipline lines. In MedTeams, the essential act of communicating across the disciplines moves information from the mental model of an individual to a shared mental model within a team. The patient's plan is shared and agreement held by all members, who in return effectively cross-monitor the actions of each other against the established plan.

When the actions of a provider differ from the expected actions, any team member recognizing that difference is responsible for advocating and asserting a position on behalf of the patient. This expectation is not a license to mutiny. Rather, the asserting individual assumes a difference in information between caregivers. That is, the unstated assumption is "I have information that you do not. If you had the additional information that I have it would alter the patient's plan of care." Therefore, this action effectively traps the active error and manages or mitigates its outcome.

Team Dimension 3: Communicate with the Team

Effective communication is essential to timely and accurate information exchange, ensuring proper plans of care, and creating the team's shared mental model for each patient. Team dimension 3 establishes the common language necessary for understanding the actions of team members. The practical skills of communication and conflict resolution are taught and practiced. Effective communication ensures that caregivers maintain a shared mental model for each patient; moves information forward to the key decision maker, who in return acts on the patient's plan of care; and maintains situation awareness across the team.

Team Dimension 4: Manage Workload

MedTeams is not a substitute for appropriate staffing; without the proper staffing level, no patient safety solution is effective. Research indicates that caregivers are at risk when workload is too high (Serig, 1994). Team dimension 4 equips caregivers with the skills necessary to monitor and balance workload within and across teams.

Team Dimension 5: Improve Team Skills

Team dimension 5 establishes the formal and informal means for teams to share their information, improve processes, and enhance the safe delivery of care.

Improving the Delivery of Emergency Care: MedTeams Validation

The statistics representing validation of MedTeams are pending publication (Morey et al., 2001). The data demonstrate the effectiveness of MedTeams in improving patient outcomes, caregiver effectiveness, patient and staff satisfaction, and patient safety. Additionally, an analysis of the savings attributed to reduced litigation costs and improved outcomes has been completed and demonstrates a savings that substantially exceeds the $3.50 per patient figure initially estimated in the project needs assessment.

The MedTeams Research Project results show conclusively that when staff are trained and MedTeams is implemented, the quality of care delivery improves, as evidenced by the following:

- Error rates drop significantly. Additionally, patients admitted to the hospital are "packaged" more completely (i.e., patients and their families know why they are being admitted, patients have their ID bands on, and intravenous and intravenous medications are run or given as prescribed).
- Performance improves. Data indicated that despite increases in acuity and volume, the length of stay remained steady and several specific quality indices improved.
- Patients' perception of care is more positive. The number of patients reporting a high level of satisfaction and an improvement in their sense of well-being is greater for the sites with MedTeams implementation.

A MedTeams organization with individuals properly engaged and exercising their MedTeams teamwork training skill set can ensure the reliable delivery of high-quality care to the communities it serves. The leaders of a MedTeams organization can measure the impact: Staff can reduce errors and improve the effectiveness of their performance, and patients can sense and communicate the difference.

Leadership Considerations

Leaders must establish the infrastructure that ensures principle 3 of the Institute of Medicine's principles for the design of safety systems in health care organizations: "training in teams those who are expected to work in teams" (IOM, 2000). Latent, embedded error is reduced when the optimal precursors and preconditions to the successful delivery of care are in place, the structure and climate for teamwork are secured, processes and procedures are standardized, resources are optimal, and individuals who recognize and understand their roles are free to focus on the delivery of care. However, leading a human behavior change process requires education and support, careful planning and preparation, concrete and decisive actions, and great consideration afforded to the details of department operations and care delivery (Locke, 2000). Although these essential leadership actions begin to cull the latent errors embedded within systems, they take time to learn.

MedTeams addresses this issue and is designed to move departments from the single dimension of quality initiatives to the multiple dimensionality of true culture change by providing training and support over time (Clemmer, 1992; Locke, 2000). The following describes each delivery phase of the MedTeams System.

- Delivery phase I engages leadership in preparing the climate and structuring the environment for the transition to a team-based care delivery system, including planning the details of the change initiative (Locke, 2000).
- Delivery phase II provides training to physician and nurse pairs and their leadership in the practical steps for undertaking a cultural change and installing MedTeams in their department (Locke, 2000).
- Delivery phase III provides a forward focus on obtaining a change in culture. If unattended, the good effects of MedTeams will disappear. Fostering MedTeams behaviors within and across departments through sustainment and integration methods is essential. Leadership receives education specific to coaching and mentoring these skills. Our ongoing research in sustainment indicates that the active involvement of leadership is essential to optimal MedTeams implementation.

For the purpose of this discourse, *leaders* are those who have the power to formally influence caregivers. The following discussion contains the seeds of action that are relevant and applicable for both formal and informal leaders. MedTeams establishes a structure and climate of care delivery through concrete actions and environmental improvements to install and sustain teamwork behaviors. Leaders engage in the following actions:

1. *Assess the organization's readiness to change.* Leaders are assisted in performing a readiness-to-change assessment. The department assesses its operations or resources for positive and negative resources. Leadership reviews the department against specific criteria (e.g., whether there be a change of leadership in the next 12 months, whether leadership is willing to organize staff as small teams, whether leadership is willing to incorporate MedTeams standard procedures and techniques into routine or daily activities). Additionally, leaders assess for stability relative to organizational structure, leadership, and staffing. These actions further identify and mitigate some of the preconditions to errors.
2. *Establish the vision.* Leaders must establish and communicate the vision and the purpose for change. They train to develop and communicate the strategic implementation plan; determine and communicate the expected performance accountabilities; and develop and communicate which outcomes are important. When these determinations are made, the staff can be engaged to unify around common goals.
3. *Plan for MedTeams success and prepare the climate.* During this aspect of implementation, leaders clarify the purpose of change

and gain the commitment of key stakeholders. Leaders enlist the ongoing commitment and support of the organization by establishing MedTeams as an infrastructure that adds a vertical snap to operations and ensures the strategic plan. Additionally, this commitment ensures the necessary resources of money, staff replacement, classroom and audiovisual support, training time, and sustainment activities. Leaders and their staff must determine the necessary team structure for their department and then coordinate and communicate the structure to all staff. Planning and coordinating the decision-making process is essential.

4. *Implement behaviors.* Leaders and certified ETCC instructors train the staff and provide ongoing coaching and mentoring. Leaders continue to monitor the growth of their staff into MedTeams behaviors. A multidisciplinary MedTeams patient safety committee is established and provides the methodology for reviewing active errors and identifying and resolving the preconditions for latent error.

5. *Sustain behaviors.* This is a critical component. It is an area where management initiatives traditionally have stumbled. Leaders and their staff evaluate and formalize structures and processes essential to MedTeams performance. Leaders continue their focus on teams by coaching and role modeling, and the instructors continue to teach new staff and refresh current staff on the behaviors and updates of MedTeams.

6. *Integrate the behaviors into a comprehensive cultural change.* Individuals serving on the MedTeams patient safety committee add to their problem-solving methodology by creating methods for fostering MedTeams behaviors into staff performance over time. A new culture of patient safety is obtained when vision moves from an external existence displayed in the form of slogans and initiatives to an internal initiative that emerges as an outcome of professionals engaged in the collective process of purposeful and cooperative care delivery.

7. *Evaluate outcomes.* The processes of leadership are informed by a data-driven evaluation system. Leadership determines and defines the state of excellence at their organization and is supported in their ongoing processes with a suite of measures that enhances their current process improvement efforts and that is sensitive to teamwork.

Teamwork Summary

Teamwork is a powerful tool. It provides the medium for leaders and staff to communicate with each other and to provide information to their patients. Teamwork ensures (1) the hearing and understanding of patient safety in multidisciplinary multidirectional ways, (2) the creation of outcome-based solutions, and (3) leadership and caregiver accountability.

Teamwork cannot solve everything. The profession must be educated about the national patient safety agenda. It is undeniable that staffing shortages threaten to undercut patient care initiatives, but nursing cannot abdicate its obligation to patient safety. It is clear that patient safety in the form of advocacy is deeply rooted in the profession of nursing, but this fact is of little use in responding to the national agenda of patient safety unless nursing leverages its extensive knowledge of this advocacy. To achieve comprehensive change, a concerted effort by providers is required to research, adapt, and adopt solutions that are multifaceted and multidisciplinary. Synergy will develop between the disciplines and, over time, outcomes will result that bring us full cycle, from the worst to the best of times.

The MedTeams teamwork training system achieves and ensures lasting comprehensive patient safety. It establishes the characteristics of a comprehensive patient safety solution:

- *Unity.* Safety emerges from the collective interactivities of caregivers working in a system designed to prevent inadvertent outcomes. MedTeams establishes the proper and appropriate climate and structure for care provision; clear vision and roles that organize multiple levels of caregivers around the common goal of safe, efficient, and effective patient care; and a common language for providers. In so doing, patients are ensured access to safe and effective care that is composed of repeatable processes with predictable and positive outcomes.
- *Error reduction.* Individuals trained in the MedTeams behaviors develop responses and repeatable processes to deliver predictable outcomes that in return ensure high-reliability health care promulgated at the unit of delivery.
- *Patient and staff satisfaction.* The high-reliability outcomes achieved by MedTeams-trained caregivers are evidenced by improved delivery of effective care and reduced active and latent errors. As a result, patients and staff are more satisfied. MedTeams is designed to ensure that caregivers are safe and can safely deliver care. Patients and staff both benefit.

MedTeams responds to and ensures the IOM recommendation in principle 3. Caregivers trained in MedTeams teamwork behaviors

- Work to manage and mitigate active and latent errors.
- Ensure that team climate, structures, and processes are in place that identify and address the precursors and preconditions of error and in return ensure proper outcomes.

- Ensure against normalizing system deviance.
- Ensure maximal flow of information to decision makers. That information translates into the right patient receiving the right plan accompanied by the right prescriptives and procedures to result in the right outcome.
- Ensure clear roles, standardize terms and processes, and simplify procedures.

Conclusion

Health care is spinning out of control. It is time to sort things out. As it relates to patient safety, control and meaning are established through a common language and lexicon of error. To move from the static condition of control into the dynamics of progress, patient safety research must build on its emerging knowledge base to provide unity of vision, reduction of error, and patient and staff satisfaction. To ensure the construction of this research framework, the disciplines must hold a common vision, speak a common language of patient safety, and research aspects of comprehensive patient safety. Research development must proceed to theory that will give rise to form and function. Form is embedded in vision, and function manifests in teamwork. Without that vision and a language that is understood and accepted by all disciplines, knowledge will not equal action, and patient safety will not happen.

Teamwork brings us full circle. Teamwork provides form and function for comprehensive patient safety, teamwork assesses for and ensures the presence of nursing, and teamwork is a multidisciplinary vehicle to move us from the worst to the best of times.

References

American Nurses Association. (1995). *Scope and Standards for Nurse Administrators.* Washington, DC: American Nurses Publishing.

Cannon-Bowers, J. A., Oser, F., and Flanagan, D. L. (1992). "Work Teams in Industry: A Selected Review and Proposed Framework." In R. Swezy and E. Salas (Eds.), *Teams: Their Training and Performance* (pp. 355–377). Norwood, NJ: Ablex.

Clemmer, J. (1992). *Firing on all Cylinders: The Service/Quality System for High-Powered Corporate Performance.* Homewood, IL: Business One Irwin.

Cook, R. I., and Woods, D. D. (1994). "Operating at the Sharp End: The Complexity of Human Error." In M. S. Bogner (Ed.), *Human Error in Medicine* (pp. 255–310). Hinsdale, NJ: Lawrence Erlbaum.

Danzon, P. M. (1994). "Merger Mania: An Analysis." *Health Systems Rev* 27 (6), 18–28.

Institute for Healthcare Improvement. (1997). "The Quest for Error-Proof Medicine." *Drug Benefit Trends* 9 (6), 27–29.

Institute of Medicine. Kohn, L. T., Corrigan, J. M., and Donaldson, M. S. (Eds.). (2000). *To Err Is Human: Building a Safer Health System.* Washington, DC: National Academy Press.

Leape, L. (1994). "Error in Medicine." *JAMA* 272 (23), 4.

Locke, A. (2000). *MedTeams Teamwork System Implementation Guide.* (Training materials: Available from Dynamics Research Corporation, 60 Frontage Road, Andover, MA 01810.)

Millensen, M. (1997). *Demanding Medical Excellence: Doctors and Accountability in the Information Age.* Chicago: University of Chicago Press.

Morey, J., Simon, R., Jay, G., Wears, R., Salisbury, M., Dukes, K., and Berns, S. (2002). "Error Reduction and Performance Improvement in the Emergency Department through Formal Teamwork Training: Evaluation Results of the MedTeams Project." *Health Science Research,* December 2002, 1553–1581.

National Patient Safety Foundation. (1998). *A Tale of Two Stories: Contrasting Views of Patient Safety.* Chicago: NPSF, p. 1. Available: http://www.npsf.org/exec.front.html.

Pritchett, P. L., and Pound, R. (1991). *Business as Usual: The Handbook for Managing and Supervising Organizational Change.* Dallas: Pritchett Publishing.

Reason, J. (1990). *Human Error.* New York: Cambridge University Press.

Risser, D., Simon, R., Rice, M., and Salisbury, M. (1999). "The Potential for Improved Teamwork to Reduce Medical Errors in the Emergency Department." *Annals of Emergency Medicine* 34, 373–383.

Sagan, S. (1993). *The Limits of Safety.* Princeton, NJ: Princeton University Press.

Senge, P. (1990). *The Fifth Discipline.* New York: Doubleday-Currency.

Serig, D. I. (1994). "Radiopharmaceutical Misadministrations: What's Wrong." In M. S. Bogner (Ed.). *Human Error in Medicine* (pp. 179–195). Hinsdale, NJ: Lawrence Erlbaum.

Simon, R., Morey, J., and Locke, A. (1997). *Full Scale Development of the Emergency Team Coordination Course and Evaluation Measures.* (Available from Dynamics Research Corporation, 60 Frontage Road, Andover, MA 01810.)

Swezey, R. W., and Salas, E. (Eds.). (1992). *Teams: Their Training and Performance.* Norwood, NJ: Ablex.

Weiner, E. L., Kanki, B. G., and Helmreich, R. L. (Eds.). (1993). *Cockpit Resource Management.* San Diego: Academic Press.

Westrope, R. A., Vaughn, L., Bott, M., and Taunton, R. L. (1995). "Shared Governance: From Vision to Reality." *JONA* 25 (12), 45–54.

CHAPTER TWENTY-THREE

ENGAGING THE BOARD OF DIRECTORS AND CREATING A GOVERNANCE STRUCTURE

Kevin Roberg and Brock Nelson

Background on Children's Hospitals and Clinics of Minnesota

Children's Hospitals and Clinics was created in 1994 by the merger of the Children's Hospital of St. Paul and Minneapolis Children's Medical Center. Children's–St. Paul was opened in January of 1924, and Children's–Minneapolis in 1973.

Today Children's is the largest children's health care organization in the upper Midwest, with 268 staffed beds at its two hospitals in St. Paul and Minneapolis. Children's offers comprehensive, integrated medical and surgical pediatric care, with more than half its beds dedicated to critical care services. Children's board of directors consists of 12 members, each serving a 3-year term.

Creating a Patient Safety Agenda

The place we always start is with this question: Why did Children's decide to embark on a safety agenda in 1999? It was a matter of many pieces coalescing, from many directions, to form a very clear and ultimately simple picture.

First, we had a new chief operating officer, who came to us in June 1999. Julie Morath had been part of patient safety efforts in her position at Allina Hospitals and Clinics, and had taken part in the Harvard executive session on patient safety earlier that year. Julie brought to Children's not only a passion for patient safety but also, importantly, a vision on how to align and organize operations around it.

Children's also had recently gone through a sentinel event with a family that in many ways was a model for the need for disclosure, authenticity, and timeliness. We received many lessons from that event—painful but clarifying—which we'll talk more about later in this chapter.

Finally, we saw an opportunity to build on the safe, high-quality health care that had always been a Children's Hospitals and Clinics hallmark. Our philosophy puts the family at the center of care, and we come to work every day knowing that we cannot do our job well without them.

Putting all these factors together, we concluded that it was time to make patient safety not only our priority, but our highest priority. Simply put, it was the right thing to do. It was right for our families to always feel they were bringing their children into a safe environment—one that will "do no harm." It was right to assume that even one sentinel event per year is one too many. And it was right for Children's to live our philosophy, fully and completely.

Considerations

We began in the summer of 1999 to do the groundwork with Children's board of directors. In preparation for passing an official resolution to begin the journey, we needed to explore answers to some pretty complicated issues. We asked ourselves:

- Would this substantially affect our medical and legal exposure?
- How would this affect the trust and confidence of families in us and our ability to care for their children?
- How would this play in the community—what was the possible public relations impact?
- How would private and referring physicians react? With fewer than 10% of physicians at Children's being employees, would an aggressive safety agenda engage or chill our relationship with them?

We received input from Children's staff, from national safety experts, and from our legal counsel. Any hospital board that does the same sort of inquiry won't—as we did not—receive absolutely conclusive answers to any of these questions. There are many shades of gray, and many aspects of these issues have not yet been played out. Nevertheless, our board decided that a focus on patient safety was important enough that we shouldn't wait until everyone felt perfectly comfortable with every issue.

We concluded, even in our brief examination of the topic, that there was both an ethical imperative and a business case for doing this work:

- First and foremost, we needed to maintain trust with the consumer. Every year, hundreds of families place their most precious possession—their child—in our care. We needed to emphasize to them in no uncertain terms that patient safety is our highest priority.
- We recognized that our reputation was on the line, in the broadest sense. We enjoy a tremendous amount of credibility in our community, strengthened by the fact that we are seen not only as a care provider but also as an ethical institution.
- We needed to visibly keep the promise "to do no harm." This is at the core of our being as a health care provider.
- Beyond the obvious human benefits, the fact is that patient safety saves money. A culture of safety reduces the cost of poor quality (the cost of accidents).
- Finally, we recognized that committing to a safety culture could become a focal point to create alignment and focus for operations.

In September 1999, the Children's board of directors formally adopted a resolution that placed our paramount and ethical obligation for patient safety at the forefront of the organization. Then, in November 1999, the Institute of Medicine (IOM) released its provocative report on medical errors. That report reinforced that we were on the right track. The public's reaction to the report demonstrated that their trust and confidence in health care were threatened and that work needed to be done for them to be regained.

Gathering Data

We had embarked on the journey, but we needed to know more about the road ahead. From October through November 1999, Children's conducted a series of focus groups with staff members and selected patient families. We conducted 18 groups, comprising 101 people in total. The stakeholders we listened to included nurses (front-line staff as well as nursing managers); pharmacy staff; medical directors; residents and medical students; respiratory care providers; chaplaincy and social work staff; and most important of all, parents of our patients.

We gained two huge lessons from those focus groups. First, and perhaps most surprising: The parents we talked to already knew everything about risk and accidents. The people who participated in the focus groups were longtime Children's families—parents of children who had

TABLE 23-1   What the Internal Focus Groups Told Us

- Patient safety is job number 1.
- Children's is a safe place, but we can do better.
- Everyone believes that reporting risks and accidents will improve the care we provide.
- Getting past blame needs to be balanced with personal responsibility.
- Patient safety gives us a focus for the future direction of our organization.

chronic needs. These were the people who knew us best. And they knew *everything.* They wanted, even yearned for, a legitimate partnership with us to help create safety for their children.

Second, we learned from our clinical staff (nurses, physicians, and others) that patient safety is an issue that would connect front office (administrators) and front line (providers) in purpose, values, and mission of the organization: Cost and productivity would follow doing the right thing clinically. Providers always want to do the right thing for their patients, and were eager to do more. This was an issue that would bring all disciplines and departments together. Table 23-1 summarizes the insights gained from the focus groups.

Building a Culture of Safety

After digesting the information from the focus groups, we devised some implementation steps to put an aggressive patient safety agenda into practice at Children's. We decided that our first step was to literally create a new organizational culture, one that has patient safety as its focus. That would take raising awareness and deepening our staff's knowledge of the subject. Ways in which we did this included the following:

- We invested in education and training regarding "the new look of safety." An important feature of creating a safety culture is education for our staff. One of the key pieces is giving everyone access to a new vocabulary. We literally give all staff and board a glossary of terms (see Table 23-2).
- We devised a series of mini-courses for staff. These take place twice a year, in the spring and fall, and featured nationally recognized safety experts. The half-day sessions also feature presentations by Children's staff, who talk about their safety efforts.
- We instituted "patient safety dialogues" in our hospitals. These are one-hour sessions facilitated by members of Children's patient safety steering committee. They take place every couple of months, at a variety of locations.

TABLE 23-2   Words to Work By: A New Vocabulary for Staff About Safety

Use	Do Not Use	Why?
Accident or *failure*	*Error*	*Accident* describes a breakdown in a system. They are complex and need analysis. *Error* suggests that only one factor, usually noted as human error, was the cause (which is rarely the case). Error is a social attribution and a result of the need to attribute blame or find a simple and single cause.
Multicausal	*Root cause*	Studies show that at least four failures must occur and line up (multicausal) for an accident to happen. Therefore, there is no such thing as a root cause or single source of an accident.
Learning	*Judgment*	When we are open to learning from mistakes or failures, we understand how multiple factors work together and we can be proactive in preventing them from happening again. If we are judgmental about situations, we instead are blaming a particular person or event. Learning stops and we are not helping prevent the failure from occurring again.
Accountable	*Blame*	Professionals are accountable for their work, meaning that they have a responsibility to be actively involved in ensuring their knowledge and competence to perform their work and to understand how systems work. It also means understanding how they are the human components of systems that sometimes contribute to failure as well as create safety. Blame is used to find an excuse or bad apple rather than a greater understanding.
Examination or *study*	*Investigation*	An *examination* is what we do to learn how systems work and how the pieces fit together to create the whole. We learn from the results and use them to predict and shape our actions to prevent failure. An *investigation* assigns blame to someone or something. It is typically a very linear search to determine a single cause.
System	*Isolated event*	An accident results from latent errors or weaknesses in a system. These errors or weaknesses are cumulative and interactive. Therefore, an accident is not an isolated event.

- We created self-learning packets. Recognizing that our workforce has little downtime, we created packets filled with basic background information about patient safety. Some of these basics include the glossary of patient safety terms and models explaining the system approach to safety, such as the Swiss cheese and the blunt-end/sharp-end models.

Clinical Focus

Simultaneous with increasing education and awareness, we also began our clinical quality improvement by focusing on our medication-use system. This was a strategic choice, as it was an aspect of patient safety that touched every discipline. In addition, we knew medication use had the greatest opportunity for improvement and therefore the greatest opportunity for success. We organized our emphasis around the implementation of best practices in medication use.

We recognized that we needed (and still need) to enhance the infrastructure of patient safety. We have divided this task into three key strategies: increasing the number of safety reports, improving timely analysis of the reports, and sharing the "lessons learned" throughout the organization. To help create an *alert field*—employees constantly thinking about improvements—we encourage our employees to report everything: accidents, accidents waiting to happen, system breakdowns, and near misses. We also want to hear about good catches, improvement ideas, and lessons learned.

Hardwiring Patient Safety into the Organization

To effect a long-term change in culture, we know that patient safety needs to be at our core. We are integrating it into official policies and procedures and visible leadership by the board and administration at the highest levels.

The patient safety agenda has been built into Children's strategic plan, approved and monitored by the board. A regular report of key performance indicators is compiled and presented quarterly to the management staff of Children's by either the CEO or the COO, as well as to the board of directors. The CEO also sees individual sentinel event reports within 24 hours. The CEO presents a segment on patient safety at every new employee orientation at Children's.

Hardwiring safety into the organization reached into the quality committee of Children's board. Every month, progress on our safety plan is reported to this group as a standing item. In addition, those monthly quality committee reports are shared at our bimonthly board meetings.

Children's annual management incentives are organized around achieving, among other things, increased reporting of safety risks and accidents. Patient safety leadership is integrated into all job descriptions of management.

Finally, we created a patient safety steering committee to provide ongoing direction. The membership of the committee brings together physicians, pharmacists, bedside nurses, and at least one parent. We want to use the wisdom and experience of those at the sharp end of creating safety because they are the people who can best direct our effort to reshape our culture.

Results

Our commitment to a patient safety agenda has made a good start. In 2000, Children's increased the number of safety reports by 40%. Two pilot safety action teams began operating to make local changes at the department level. (In 2001, this strategy went organization-wide: All clinical units created their own safety action teams.) Our medication use safety plan is 85% implemented. Chemotherapy administration is at zero defect.

In addition, in 2000, Children's Hospitals and Clinics of Minnesota received awards from the National Patient Safety Foundation and was featured in the July issue of *US News and World Report,* recognizing our efforts. Everyone in the organization understands that safety is our priority—all departmental and program operational plans align with this ongoing strategic focus.

We know we aren't there yet. In fact, we know we'll never be done with this work. And we know there will be plenty of bumps along the way.

Full Disclosure to Families

The extent of Children's legal risk regarding full disclosure to families is one of those bumps. But it's also at the core of why this work is so very important. Let Brock tell the story about a turning point for him and for Children's patient safety agenda:

> There are many pieces of information that would supply context for this story (as usual in these cases), but let me tell the story bluntly, because this is the way the family experienced the event: their child died while under our care. A misdiagnosis had been made and that delayed appropriate cancer treatment by one year. The family threatened a lawsuit, but it was dismissed, because the child's probability

of survival was less than 50%. Children's lawyer and risk manager, prior to a meeting between me [the CEO] and the family, advised me to not volunteer information and to not admit that the hospital made a mistake.

It was the worst meeting I had ever participated in. The family wanted the truth, which the hospital had, and they were stonewalled. I will never do that again. However bad the truth is, the only thing worse is not knowing the truth.

After this experience, we knew in our hearts why full disclosure to families was the right thing to do. It made sense intellectually, too. Here's why:

- *We would maintain the integrity of disclosure.* We are already encouraging staff to disclose everything to the organization, whether it's accidents or near misses or accidents waiting to happen. This tactic creates an alert field to keep ourselves constantly aware and to prevent future accidents. Being open and alert with each other, then, creates a natural extension to model the same behavior with families.
- *We would abide by the principle of family-centered care.* "Nothing about me without me" translates into full participation in decision making by the families of our patients. We also support the primacy of families' knowledge of their children and their children's health: "It if looks wrong, it is wrong" gives a family permission to question us and to stop a procedure if they think something differs from their understanding or previous experience of their child's care. If we are truly family centered, then, how can we not share information about an accident?
- *Disclosure is fundamental to rebuilding trust and confidence.* The patient–caregiver relationship is intimate, complex, and highly charged. In the case of children, the relationship is even more complicated. At Children's, we recognize that every day parents place the lives of their children into our care. They *have* to trust us and be confident that we will do our very best in every way to help their most precious possessions. When an accident occurs, that trust is shaken to the core. Talking to the family and answering their questions as honestly as possible—even under highly upsetting conditions—is the first step to repairing the relationship. Families want to hear the answers to the questions "What happened?" and "What is being done to prevent future accidents or errors?"; they also want to hear us say we're sorry and acknowledge our accountability. We think that giving them those answers, those words, is the least we can do.

TABLE 23-3   Conditions Required for a Safety Agenda to Be Effective

- Leadership and accountability from the board
- Technical knowledge and expertise in operational leadership
- Organizational culture focused on the care of patients and knowledgeable of current reality (i.e., that there are accidents in health care)
- Ability to align external influences — legislative, legal, regulatory — to support and create incentives to follow known best practices to promote patient safety, especially blameless reporting

In the End: Some Advice

Be prepared to be strong in the execution of a patient safety agenda, because once you announce it, you *will* be scrutinized. The scrutiny comes from the public, your patients and their families, and the media—and also from the inside. At the start, your own staff will be wary: Is this a passing fancy or is someone finally going to listen to those of us on the front lines? That's why the commitment has to be unwavering and it has to start at the top (see Table 23-3).

Once you announce your commitment and start acting on it, everyone is united. Very simply, there can be no higher purpose than patient safety in the minds of doctors, nurses, other employees, administrators, or board members. Many organizations struggle with integration questions these days. Here's what we're discovering: A vigorous commitment to a patient safety agenda is the best model for integration you can have.

Accidents take an incalculable toll on both families and the staff involved. More mundanely, accidents cost money and organizational energy. A focus on patient safety is the ethical, right thing to do, any way you look at it. We wish we had done it a long time ago.

CHAPTER TWENTY-FOUR

TEAMWORK COMMUNICATIONS AND TRAINING

Richard Lauve, MD

There is no limit to what one man can achieve so long as he does not require getting credit for it all.

—Henry Grady

It's easy gettin' good players. The hard part is gettin' them to play with each other.

—Casey Stengel

Definitions and Initial Thoughts

Teamwork is by definition the work done by groups of individuals greater than one. While this may seem obvious, what is not so obvious is what is required for groups of individuals to work together. Many of us have not been trained in the intricacies of working together with other individuals. Indeed, a great many of us have been trained in organizations or professions where individual work is highly valued and rewarded, and the only communication required is orders given to others. The central command-and-control management style may be highly effective for organizations such as an army, where rote obedience and an established hierarchical chain of command best maintain order and safety, but is inadequate for organizations that deal with constant variation and rapid change and must rely on individuals, each with a particular set of knowledge, skills, or perspectives.

If individuals are to come together and collaborate (i.e., work as a team in intellectual endeavors for a common purpose), attention must be given to training these individuals in the expected collaborative behaviors and the communication styles necessary for collaboration to succeed.

Reducing the Barriers to Collaboration

The Need for a Team

The more complex the system to be improved, the more complex the team that must be brought together and the more difficult will be true collaboration. Having a clear vision and common goal for the group certainly provides motivation, but even the highly motivated group runs the risk of achieving little, if attention is not paid to the barriers to collaboration. Therefore, the first task for you, as the leader, is to instill in each individual on the newly formed team an awareness that the group has a purpose. This involves more than simply establishing a mission and a vision; instead, the need for the team itself must be established. I am referring now to the realization that no individual can achieve what the team is required to achieve.

This concept will be foreign to the culture of many health care organizations, because individualistic work and organization have been the historical standards and ideals of health care. This reality is probably best demonstrated by the mandate from the Joint Commission on Accreditation of Healthcare Organizations (JCAHO) in recent years that performance improvement initiatives in its accredited organizations should involve "cross silo" efforts by several components of the organization. This revealing requirement demonstrates years of JCAHO observation of the fragmented nature of quality improvement in hospitals, where quality departments rarely coordinated with medical staffs or other operational areas within the hospital. This often resulted in simultaneous but disjointed efforts to address similar opportunities by the quality department, operating room nursing leadership, materials management, the medical staff, and others, without significant collaboration or communication between the silos. The JCAHO observed not only inefficient duplicative efforts within the organization, but also movements by the various parties at cross-purposes to the other components of the organization.

With a mission as significant and complex as improving the environment of safety that our patients experience, it becomes difficult to imagine how any single individual or, for that matter, any focused silo could possibly achieve improvement without involvement of other components of the hospital. If we are to seize the full potential of possible gains in reducing medication errors, as a specific example, not only will product acquisition/materials management departments and pharmacies need to be involved, but nurses, physicians, group purchasing organizations, and ultimately product manufacturers will need to be components of the improvement effort.

If your organization is having difficulty understanding why performance improvement or quality can't handle patient safety alone, try emphasizing the benefits of collaboration. The concept is relatively simple, yet escapes those not familiar with it. Collaboration allows for the possibility of *synthesis,* a product by definition not possible without the input of at least two individuals. Many will be confused by this concept, and believe that *collaboration* is a euphemism for *compromise.* Synthesis is far from compromise. Synthesis is the product of two or more distinct perspectives, separate and apart before coming together, combining to make something not possible without the joining of the two (or more). The process of synthesis produces something new, never before realized or imagined prior to the joining. Compromise is more akin to a reduction or an overlap, usually involving areas of commonality and agreement.

Try this example to stimulate the proper vision of collaborative synthesis: children. Who can view a child as a compromise between the genetic materials of their parents? The bringing together of two separate influences has the potential for creating something totally new, never before imagined, and not possible without the joining of the two.

One more hint on breaking through the barrier of understanding the need for a team: I find that many times one party to the potential collaboration (a new team member, for example) will believe that his or her perspective is the correct one and will not value the richness of potential possible through synthesis with others. The following exercise can be done with two people, or mini-teams of two formed solely for the exercise. Show one person, or one half of the teams, a square with an X through it. Show the other person, or other half of the teams, a right triangle. The two views look something like Figure 24-1. Now

FIGURE 24-1   Two views of the same object

tell the two individuals, or both members of the mini-teams, that they have seen two views of the same thing. What is it?

The dynamics that emerge are phenomenal. Some groups won't show each other what they have seen. Some will converse and conclude that you are lying to them, that it can't possibly be the same thing. But eventually, two people will think, using full input from both groups, and realize that these simple figures can only represent two views of a pyramid—one from close up at ground level, and the other from directly above. It is nearly impossible for anyone to conclude with accuracy the true nature of the object from a single view. Combining the information from both observations almost always leads to the correct conclusion. After this exercise, I once had the CEO of a 750-bed hospital, a retired general and decidedly a central command-and-control authoritarian manager, approach me. "You know," he said, "its never bothered me before that other people have different points of view than mine. They have every right to be wrong. But that pyramid thing, that really got to me."

Individual Domination

Very commonly, when groups are formed from a pool of individuals who have not previously collaborated, certain persons or a person within the group tends to dominate over others. This is particularly true when the group members come from an organization that fosters and supports individualism, and whenever people of disparate rank come together on a team. The challenge for the group leader is then to give the more shy, docile, subordinate, or quiet individuals a structured environment that promotes their participation.

The solution to the dominating individual, in most cases, lies with the team leader's knowledge and execution of the nominal group technique combined occasionally with a small dose of parliamentary procedure. In the nominal group technique, the team is posed a question, problem, idea, challenge, or opportunity followed by the request that each member of the group work silently for a few moments to record his or her own ideas. For example, the group might be considering the high incidence of drug administration error during code blue or resuscitation efforts. The group might be told, after some discussion of the facts known about the problem, "Take a few moments to write down what you feel should be done about this problem. Writing just one idea is acceptable, but if you have several, please record them all." Asked openly, this is the ideal invitation for the dominating individual to climb aboard the soapbox and espouse his or her views, solutions, and implementation plans to secure a 100% cure. The input of the group might easily be lost. With each member working silently alone, the individuals gain the opportunity to think without contamination of others' ideas.

Next, the leader asks each individual to report to the group one idea from his or her list. One member of the group is asked to record the reported ideas on a flip chart. This job is ideally given to the dominating member. Not only does it give that individual an important job that distracts him from feeling the need to dominate the conversation, but it materially takes him out of immediate participation mode and forces him to listen in order to record correctly. After each person has reported one idea, the leader goes around the room again, and again if necessary, until all ideas have been recorded. Only then is a discussion allowed about the ideas. Grouping and splitting ideas is allowed and will promote the discussion.

After all the ideas are grouped, related, split out, and discussed, the group votes on prioritization. Sequential multivote ballots have the greatest probability of building consensus. For example, if the group has identified eleven possible actions, force each member to vote for three. After tallying the votes—notice that your group's previously dominating individual is being kept very busy—make a cut where the votes fall off abruptly. If five ideas each got more than seven votes, but the next-highest vote getter only got four votes, consider the five ideas your "top five." More discussion is often needed at this point, but if no consensus emerges, vote again. This time each member gets two votes. If two or three ideas are separated from the others, then vote again, eventually getting to one vote per member and identifying a single top-priority action item. With a little practice, this technique can be used very rapidly to focus even a medium-sized group of seven to nine individuals.

Another way to deal with dominating individuals, particularly when they are repeating the same speech about their preferences, is to "call the question." This parliamentary maneuver of calling for a vote is best performed by a member of the group, and not the leader; however, the group's leader can promote the maneuver with questions such as "Can I take that as a motion?" or "Would you like to make that in the form of a motion?" This is very powerful when immediately following the dominating individual's speech. Either the dominator's idea will be adopted, or the group can move on to other ideas. Whichever course the group takes, progress will be made, and the group will avoid a paralysis of analysis and the domination of a single member.

Resources

I often hear complaints about not having enough resources to carry out actions, and sometimes even enough resources to have meetings.

People not being able to give their time to sit and think about a new approach, a new set of ideas, or a new problem is often the greatest barrier to a new team. There is no doubt that time is our greatest resource, and few health care organizations have slack time when it comes to the skilled problem solvers you will want on your team.

Conflicting agendas of team members and frank turf protection frequently manifest as inadequate time to attend meetings. It is possible that individuals have been asked to do more than humanly possible. If so, top management must resolve this situation, as will be discussed in a moment. On the other hand, the individual that "simply does not have the time for another meeting" may be engaged in turf-protecting behavior. The team leader's job is to search for the possibility that a team member may be threatened by the formation of the new team. Candidates for this behavior include all of the members important to the function of the new team and for whom a similar function was previously under their purview. For a patient safety initiative, this could be the head of pharmacy, materials management, quality, performance improvement, risk management, corporate compliance, or any other silo of the hospital that previously dealt with safety issues.

The team leader's job is to reduce turf as a barrier to progress for the new team. Recall Henry Grady's quote from the beginning of this chapter. The truly inspired, and safety-motivated, leader will have no difficulty approaching a turf protector. The withdrawn individual needs reassurance that her participation is critical, and that by definition she is under no particular threat from the new group. In fact, the participation of the corporate compliance officer (substitute whatever title is appropriate) is so critical that the individual's job is in jeopardy only if she does not participate. Appeal to her ego: "We need your perspective on this issue," or "We cannot get this done without you." Emphasize that the job is bigger than any single department, and that this effort is an attempt to work across departments, not replace any one. It's a team effort. The job requires more than a corporate compliance perspective (to continue with the previous example), but that perspective is a critical part that the team cannot be without.

Inadequate prioritization from top management can kill any endeavor, but especially one that requires bridging previously recognized silos. Only the CEO and board can make it clear to recalcitrant participants that their position's involvement is critical and that their involvement is an important part of their job description.

It is the job of any given individual's superior to require his or her participation in the organization and to assist with prioritizing the many issues before that individual. Above the supervisor lies the workings of the board's strategy process. Ultimately, the board must make it clear that the proper resources are to be made available to succeed in a patient safety initiative. Conversely, confusion over which task or unpriority items on your full plate to tackle first is the difficult but primary task of the midlevel manager to sort out. Few CEOs will long tolerate the middle manager who constantly complains about "too much to do." Resolving this conundrum is a daunting task for many middle managers. I suggest always approaching your superior with a suggested course of action to resolve these issues. "I can do that. Will it be acceptable for Project B to take a back seat to this?" is always preferable to "I just have too much to do."

For any manager who is "on board" with patient safety as a high-priority item but is having trouble securing resources from the CEO or others above, I suggest the following strategies. First, find ways to communicate that patient safety is an investment, not an expense. For medication error interventions, this is already done for you. Get, and distribute, the following: *Pharmacotherapy* vol. 16, no. 6 (1996), which shows a 16.7 to 1 return on investment in certain pharmacy error reduction efforts, and *JAMA* vol. 280, no. 15 (October 21, 1998), which demonstrates a 5 to 1 return on computer-assisted programs for drug selection.

Second, show how you can quickly measure and report the results of your intervention. For example, measure the difference between the pharmacy time needed to clarify orders using preprinted order forms and handwritten forms for a focused intervention—say, chemotherapy orders. Give the feedback the following month (e.g., 123 minutes of pharmacy and nursing time for handwritten orders versus 27 minutes for preprinted orders over a one-month period).

Third, realize that the top leadership is not your enemy in this. They—your board, CEO, and CFO—have distinct and valid obligations to the financial well-being of the organization. Nothing will secure the support of the top leadership faster than showing them the aligned incentives of what's best for the patient and what's best for the bottom line. Remind them that "best performers" all over the country are doing this, with decidedly positive effects on their public relations image, and positive financial results.

Training

The team leader is the only individual who needs team dynamics training. Such training is ideal for all members, but not necessary, and impractical in our budget-constrained environment. One aspect of training, however, is very difficult to do without everyone at least having a taste, and that is systems thinking. If your team has never thought in an interdisciplinary manner before, you will have difficulty accomplishing collaborative synthesis. Ideally, your team should attend a team collaboration workshop. This experience not only teaches the fundamentals but also, if properly done, provides the opportunity for the team to practice under the guidance of experts in team systems thinking as applied to evidence-based medicine.

If the budget allows for additional training, seek out an experienced trainer in chaos theory as it applies to groups and management of organizations. (Of course, if you are lucky enough to find a collaborative-team workshop that includes chaos theory concepts, grab it.) Chaos, or emergent control as it is sometimes called, is (among many other things) a dynamic way of viewing what happens in a group of people. It uses organic models that are inherently meaningful to health care workers. Metaphors such as the immune system understood as a hive of bees or a forest are very easy for most health care professionals to relate to. The further elucidation of these concepts is far beyond the scope of this chapter, but one of the underlying constructs encourages a team to celebrate its self-determined direction. This is particularly useful for the team leader. Your ideas about how to begin addressing patient safety may be very different from the risk manager's ideas. If the team identifies with his or her ideas, celebrate that direction for the team. Remember that part of the "getting credit for it" thing that Henry Grady referred to includes not having to always "do it your way." Be happy that you have a team that wants to do something, whatever it is!

Allowing the team to determine its own direction is intimately connected to the modern concepts of power, or authority, within an organization. When we think of authority in an organization, we often think of the formal authority. This is also referred to as the legitimate, official, or titled authority. As a team leader or committee chair, such authority rests in you. It also rests in the CEO of your organization. By virtue of title, job description, designation by a higher authority, or sometimes just history, these figures have responsibility. They may or may not actually have authority to act, not act, choose a course of action, secure resources, allocate those resources, prioritize, and so forth. These are the classic measures of "real" authority. The individual with the formal authority is, however, always the one held responsible or rewarded for action, lack of actions, and so forth. Unfortunately, we have all seen the designation of formal authority with responsibility, but without the true ability to take action.

The ability to take action always lies with what is referred to as the *informal authority.* Sometimes, this informal authority resides with a superior, who has the real power to allow or not allow action. For a discussion of the need to manage a superior who constrains results by restricting resources, refer to the Resources section earlier in this chapter. If you are lucky, you have both, and this is certainly possible. For now, consider the ability to take action as residing within the group itself, as it ultimately does—always.

Just as commonly as informal authority resides with a superior, so too the real control of results actually lies with the members of the team. Remember that we started this whole discussion with the premise that "it takes a team." One person can't get the job done. So without the cooperation, at a minimum, of the team members, no action will be taken. Even with all the resources in the world, a leader will accomplish nothing without followers. It is their "ownership" of the plan of action that is critical to accomplishments. Therefore, it is the realization by the team leader that the team has the true authority to act or not act that frees him or her to celebrate the emergent control seen within a well-functioning group.

To paraphrase Harlan Cleveland in *The Knowledge Executive,* authority is always delegated upward within any educated group. The instant the group ceases to delegate authority to the leadership (whether it be the formal or informal authority figure), that individual loses all power to accomplish anything. Remember Casey Stengel. You could in theory be the best team leader in the world, with great ideas, but you will accomplish nothing if you can't get the team to "play together."

Communications

The most important aspect of communications in a group, indeed the sine qua non, is to value input from every member. The lowest-ranking participant can provide the group with a unique insight that inspires breakthrough change in your organization. This is diametrically opposed to the central command-and-control mind-set. As the team leader, you must truly believe and have as a contagious attitude that it is the line troops who really know what the problem is and have the unique perspective on how to fix it.

In the culture of the Ritz Carlton organization, whomever the guest approaches is the right person. If that individual can't help the guest, he or she won't leave the guest until someone who can has been found. Once I was participating in a group effort to cut the time from call to answer when a patient rings the call button. A night housekeeping employee on the team listened attentively to the discussion and finally said, "I don't know why they think I can't help with this. They don't want me talking to patients. I can tell if they need a spill cleaned up or something else. I can't help with chest pain, but if they really need a nurse I'll bet I can make that clearer than any call button!" The comment hit most of us like a ton of bricks, and initiated a culture change in the organization. Everyone responded to calls for help. What a novel idea in a hospital. Clerks and housekeeping staff were trained in the recognition of medical emergencies, and patient satisfaction scores skyrocketed.

As a team leader, you will have to be sensitive to the group's dynamics. If conflict or simple inattention to a member emerges, try

Rogers' Rule. Carl Rogers, in *On Becoming A Person,* recommends this simple tool: Every speaker must repeat the message of the previous speaker, to the satisfaction of the previous speaker, before being allowed to voice his or her own opinion or ideas. You don't have to actually announce this rule. I find if you simply begin using it, others will follow. Everyone will listen more attentively. Emotional reaction will dissipate. "Positions" will be replaced by concepts, ideas, clarified understandings, and synthesis of ideas. Leaders will hear themselves and others saying, "So if I understand you correctly . . ." and "Did you mean this or that?" We cannot synthesize new ideas from the input of others if we cannot listen to them and understand their meaning. Real listening and clearly presented ideas are the basis of true communication and are required for collaborative synthesis to take place.

Some Final Advice

You're changing the culture of your organization, not your shorts. Don't be discouraged with slow progress and the persistence of the smell of dirty laundry. Team collaboration, synthesis of new ideas, and investment in performance improvement that has demonstrated financial returns are all new ideas for many health care organizations.

Celebrate your victories. You don't need the entire medical staff to adopt the new standard order set for sliding-scale insulin. Just one physician will do. With one, you have the opportunity to measure the difference between his or her performance and the others. Now measure the right thing and demonstrate the differences. Physicians are highly competitive individuals. Show them a better way and they will follow. And now, your one physician will become your champion to get the word out to his or her peers. In the words of a Native American proverb, "You don't have to turn the whole herd, just the buffalo in front."

CHAPTER TWENTY-FIVE

TEAMWORK: THE FUNDAMENTAL BUILDING BLOCK OF HIGH-RELIABILITY ORGANIZATIONS AND PATIENT SAFETY

G. Eric Knox, MD and
Kathleen Rice Simpson, PhD, RNC, FAAN

In today's health care environment, *teams, teamwork,* and *team building* are words often said, seldom heard, and only rarely considered operational reality.[1] This is true in spite of the relentless cost, production, and efficiency pressures operating to diminish patient safety in all contemporary health care organizations. Understanding how multiple diverse professionals can most efficiently and effectively work together on clinical units (the "sharp end") remains a clear organizational imperative.[2]

Unfortunately, most clinical units responsible for delivering safe patient care continue to function as discrete and separate collections of nurses, physicians, and other patient care professionals rather than as a single team with mutually agreed-upon goals, tactics, and incentives. In extreme examples, the critical relationship between nurses and physicians (which heavily influences the professional relationships of all other team members) has been described as "strained or barely tolerable."[3] The result is a demanding, complex, and fragmented system in which both patients and clinicians must heroically—often unsuccessfully—struggle to reach the elusive goal of providing safe patient care.[4]

By contrast, successful organizations in a wide variety of other professional and technical industries facing similar or more difficult challenges have come to recognize multidisciplinary teams as the unifying principle for creating operational excellence and success.[5]

Recently, similar thoughts applied to health care have begun to be reported. Morey and colleagues have suggested that increased patient safety and operational efficiency in emergency departments can result from formalized team-based training and operational structure.[6] Team simulation in the domain of anesthesia or surgery is being proposed as a means to increase human performance.[7]

In addition, characteristics of safe obstetrical units with a decreased likelihood of system error or medical accident occurring have been described.[8] These clinical units function in a manner similar to what has been defined as *high-reliability organizations*.[9] High-reliability organizations are those that operate highly complex and hazardous technological systems essentially without mistakes over long periods of time.[10] Examples of this type of organization are nuclear power plants, airline in-flight and traffic control operations, and the technical side of the banking industry.[11]

In high-reliability organizations, safety is the hallmark of organizational culture and professional behavior. In addition, teamwork is the key operating principle, with both production and safety thought to be created by teams (rather than individuals). Safety is spoken and thought about and has at least as high a priority as does production in all operational decisions. Team interaction is collegial rather than hierarchical, and each team member has an obligation to speak up if a question of safety arises.[12] Communication (including reporting of accidents and near misses) is highly valued and rewarded. It is understood that when team members fail to engage in respectful interactions, errors can occur.[13] Emergencies are rehearsed, and the unexpected is practiced. Successful operations are viewed as potentially dangerous because success leads to system simplification and shortcuts.[14] Preparation, practice, and evaluation of team decision making and the resulting consequences are a constant feature of day-to-day operations.

It is hypothesized that increased patient safety would result if the principles of teamwork and high reliability could be more widely introduced and applied in sharp-end clinical units.[15] This chapter explores three questions regarding why wider adoption of teamwork has not occurred in the health care domain:

1. What are the factors that prevent key clinical leaders (i.e., nurses and physicians) from realizing what other service groups assume to be self-evident?
2. What needs to be done by health system and organizational leadership to create teamwork and high reliability at the clinical sharp-end point of care?
3. What behaviors and attributes distinguish a team-based model of delivering safe care from the current silo-based model of coexisting individual professionals?

The Why, What, and Why Not of Teamwork

Why Teams Are Superior

In virtually every performance domain studied, teams perform better than collections of individuals operating within confined job roles and responsibilities.[16] Whether it is customer service, innovation, product development, health care quality, safety in high-risk technically complex domains, health care resource utilization, or decision-making competence, the conclusion is invariably the same.[17-21] In any situation requiring a real-time combination of multiple skills, experiences, and judgment, teams—as opposed to individuals—create superior performance.

Katzenbach and Smith[22] have summarized the factors that explain the superior performance inherent in teams.

- No single individual can possess the complementary skills and experience required to respond efficiently to operational challenges such as innovation, quality, customer service, or patient care emergencies.
- Communication established between professionals during team formation creates the basis for efficient real-time problem solving.
- Teams build trust and confidence in each member's information, intellectual challenges, and differing adaptability to change.
- Importantly, working in teams that achieve significant performance goals provides personal satisfaction and fun. Given the inherent external stress existing in health care, maintaining a pleasant, nonhostile work environment is a key component in every organization's attempt to survive.

What Is a Team?

One of the most difficult tasks in creating an effective team is understanding what it is and, importantly, what it is not.[23] Although the chemistry of personalities, "getting along," and team building are important components in the creation of teams, they do not, individually or collectively, define or describe a team in a functional or operational sense. Rather, a team is a *discrete unit of performance,* not a positive set of values. True teams (as opposed to simple work groups or social interaction) can be identified by the following operational principles:

- *Consensus (agreeing to agree):* The primary purpose of any clinical unit can be defined very differently from different professional vantages. Physicians, nurses, and other professionals simply see the world differently. To be successful, each clinical management team needs to articulate and reach consensus on mission, vision, goals, and objectives.[24] Although different professionals are indeed different, it is necessary to acknowledge and respect the unique contributions that each can make toward reaching team goals and objectives. Ultimately, if increased and increasing patient safety is the stated and desired goal, it will be necessary to develop a common methodology for creating that reality.

It is important to note that it may not be possible or desirable to gain complete consensus for each decision.[25] The concept of consensus is sometimes used by those who refuse to agree to anything, as a barrier to stop the group from moving forward. They suggest that consensus means each and every team member must agree to all points of any initiative. Consensus in that model actually means minority rule and can effectively halt any progress toward articulating and reaching common goals. As an alternative, the use of consensus to indicate that the majority of the team *agrees to agree* and to acknowledge that complete consensus may not always be possible and therefore not necessary for the group to go forward is a critical first step toward successful teamwork.

- *Mutual accountability:* Each member of a team-based operational unit must be willing to hold the team rather than himself, herself, or other individuals accountable for success or failure.
- *Organizational discipline:* Teams will only succeed in an organization that recognizes the team rather than the individual as the operating unit, has strong overall performance standards, pushes for ever larger achievement goals, and has sufficient discipline to adhere to these principles.
- *Task:* The more demanding the performance challenge, the better the resulting team. Creating "the safest hospital" works much better as a catalyst for teamwork than simply "doing pathways" in an effort to "enhance collaboration."
- *Time:* A specific time limit within which ultimate or temporary goals must be achieved keeps teams on task and focused.

Behaviors and Attributes of Effective Teams

Effective teams exhibit the following behaviors and attributes:[26]

- *Clear purpose:* The vision, mission, goal, or task of the team has been defined and is now accepted by everyone. There is an action plan that supports and gives definition to the stated organizational purpose.
- *Informality:* The climate tends to be informal, comfortable, and relaxed. There are no obvious tensions or signs of boredom.

- *Participation:* There is much discussion, and everyone is encouraged to participate.
- *Listening:* The members use effective listening techniques such as questioning, paraphrasing, and summarizing to get multiple ideas and perspectives into all discussions.
- *Civilized disagreements:* There is disagreement, but the team is comfortable with this and shows no signs of avoiding, smoothing over, or suppressing conflict.
- *Consensus decisions:* For important decisions, the goal is substantial, but not necessarily unanimous, agreement through open discussion of everyone's ideas, and avoidance of voting or easy compromises.
- *Open communication:* Team members feel free to express their feelings on the tasks as well as on the group's operation. There are few hidden agendas. Ongoing communication takes place outside of meetings.
- *Clear roles and work assignments:* There are clear expectations about the roles played by each team member. When action is taken, clear assignments are made, accepted, and carried out. Work is fairly distributed among team members.
- *Shared leadership:* Although the team has a formal leader, leadership functions shift from time to time depending on the circumstances and the needs of the group and the skills of the members. The formal leader models the appropriate behavior and helps establish norms.
- *External relations:* The team spends time developing key outside relationships, mobilizing resources, and building credibility with important players in other parts of the organization.
- *Style diversity:* The team has a broad spectrum of team-player types, including members who emphasize attention to task, goal setting, focus on process, and questions about how the team is functioning.
- *Self-assessment:* Periodically, the team stops to examine how well it is functioning and what may be interfering with its effectiveness.

Why Not Teams? Existing Barriers to Teamwork in the Health Care Environment

Given what appears to be a universal and irrefutable organizational truism, why haven't teams become the predominant unit of performance in the delivery of health care at the sharp end? The answer to this question is complex and involves many interrelated factors:[27]

- Historical roles of women in society
- Traditional roles of physicians and nurses

- Institutional territory and politics
- Licensure and professional accountability
- Type and quantity of education
- Different styles of learning and information exchange
- Socialization of each group
- Methods and amounts of compensation
- Power of social and professional position
- Collaboration—an impediment because it assumes separation of groups
- Unresolved conflict, setting the stage for the expectation of future discord
- Inability to get common incentives
- Health care organizations operating under extreme stress and pressure

Some of these factors may be easily changed or overcome, whereas others represent challenges deeply embedded in the structure of our current health care system and therefore represent particularly difficult issues that stand in the way of effective team performance.

Historical Roles of Men and Women: The Gender Issue

Although women have made significant political, social, and economic progress in the last century, the historical role of women in society remains a factor in how nurses and physicians communicate, interact, and ultimately work together in the clinical setting. Ninety-five percent of nurses in the United States are women.[28] This ratio of male to female professionals in the health care workplace perpetuates the traditional male physician (dominant)–female nurse (submissive) model of interaction, rather than the equality needed for true team behavior.[29] How this form of interaction affects other potential team members remains to be elucidated.

Although the increasing numbers of female physicians might be expected to alter the historical way nurses and doctors relate to each other, current observations suggest that the current socialization of female physicians during medical education perpetuates the traditional male–female roles rather than creating behavior based more on female–female interaction.[30] The resulting interactional dichotomy between what might be expected based on gender and the reality created by professional training is confusing and disappointing to many nurses. For example, informal conversations between female physicians and nurses about common challenges faced by working women (e.g., childcare difficulties and long hours away from families) that could invite camaraderie and collaboration can be quickly followed by unilateral and authoritarian "physician orders" with no input invited or desired from the nurses providing direct care. What could have been the basis for establishing the trust required for effective team performance quickly disappears under the differential socialization of the involved professionals.

Understanding the powerful effect of socialization and how resulting roles influence behavior may be helpful in explaining how gender differences have an impact on nurse–physician relationships. Kearny and White examined behaviors associated with work and categorized people as "warriors" or "villagers" based on the way they interacted with each other and approached the tasks to be completed.[31] Warriors are aggressive, competitive, and distrustful of others, viewing life as a struggle or contest to be won on the battlefield of living.[32] Warriors are not inclined to ask other warriors for help, fearing that would imply weakness or incompetence. However, warriors make excellent leaders because they have a firm resolve to meet their objectives and their confident attitude inspires others to follow their directions.[33] Warriors make decisions on data they see as black or white, rarely letting emotion influence the decisions they make.

By contrast, villagers are cooperative and eager to please, even if that means giving in to the needs of others.[34] The goals of the village outweigh individual objectives or desires. Villagers reach decisions by consensus and are generous in giving praise to other team members, irrespective of whether those praised are pulling their own weight on the team.[35] Villagers excel at working together, recognizing the value of cooperation and fostering relationships. They are generally sensitive and caring and use these feelings to guide decision making over more objective data.[36]

Importantly, these behaviors are *not* determined by genetics, but rather are learned as an integral by-product of the socialization that defines the unique culture of each society. Historically (and stereotypically) in this society (the United States), men have been taught the characteristics and behaviors of warriors, whereas women have been assigned the villager role. Traditional training of both nurses and physicians has reinforced these generalized societal expectations. While the place and status of women in society and in health care has been altered toward more equality in recent years, the male–female/physician–nurse hierarchy and the personality types attracted to these roles remain a strong barrier to the establishment of effective service teams.

Traditional Roles of Physicians and Nurses: Who Is in Charge and How Do We Talk to Each Other?

Interaction and communication among physicians, nurses, and other professionals occurs in a hierarchical model (based on tradition and training) in which physicians give orders and nurses (and everyone else) are expected to follow those orders without question.[37] Communication of this type does not always create optimal patient care and is potentially dangerous. Examples include rapidly changing patient status, where the nurse at the bedside has more information than the physician at home or in the office; training situations, where the nurse has more experience than the physician in training; situations where the nurse has more up-to-date knowledge than the attending physician; or situations where the nurse has learned important information from the patient or family that the family has chosen not to communicate with the physician. In circumstances such as these, experienced nurses have developed strategies designed to overcome the fact that many physicians are not comfortable with nurses making overt diagnoses or clinical suggestions concerning how their patients should be cared for (i.e., violating the expected hierarchal model of communication).

Instead of mutually desirable direct communication leading to a plan of care developed through the wisdom and experience of two knowledgeable professionals, nurses are forced to revert to the "doctor–nurse" game to achieve what they believe is in the patient's best interest. Although this technique was first described in the literature over 30 years ago,[38] it was used for many years before Dr. Stein's classic article was published and is still alive and well today. Tips on how to play this game are given by experienced nurses to new graduates as part of socialization to the role of the professional registered nurse.[39] For example, one of the most common techniques taught is how to get physicians to think it was their idea to order an intervention, medication, or laboratory test rather than that of the nurse. The doctor–nurse game avoids open disagreement and conflict and allows the nurse to give recommendations and the physician to request recommendations without appearing to do so.[40] Nurses are expected to learn how to phrase suggestions (different for each physician) in such a way that the physician will reach the same clinical decision or course of management that the nurse thinks is correct.

This situation can be dangerous for patients and lead to adverse outcomes or decreased patient safety in multiple ways: first, when nurses are unable to find the right "story" or words that convey the emergent nature of an evolving clinical situation;[41] second, when the nurse is wrong in her assessment because of a clinical fact known to the physician but not the nurse; and finally, when the assessment is correct but the description misunderstood by the physician. In these as well as other easily imagined clinical scenarios, patient safety suffers because of delays and clinical miscues inherent in the dysfunctional communication adopted as part of the doctor–nurse game. A recent study described common strategies used by intrapartum nurses in dealing with obstetricians. These strategies included letting them feel in control; avoiding making them feel threatened; not lying for them, but not contradicting them; being tactful and subservient; and doing whatever would keep them happy.[42] Routinely using these strategies serves as a powerful barrier to real communication and collaboration. The doctor–nurse game is a real problem because it does not foster the open dialogue needed to provide safe patient care.[43]

By contrast, one hallmark of team behavior is clear language agreed to and understood by all members. Patient care would be much better if telephone communication with the physician were direct and to the point. For example, "Patient status is deteriorating quickly and I need you here now." Instead, many nurses find themselves searching for the "right words or story" designed primarily to not offend the attending physician while at the same time attempting to obtain the required clinical action. The result is indirect, inefficient, and often inaccurate communication.

Physicians may not understand the real sense of clinical urgency when nurses are reluctant to communicate directly. In cases resulting in medical accident or patient injury, physicians are often quoted as saying, "If she had only told me this was a real emergency, I would have come right in, but I didn't know things were that bad." This can be a valid concern and legitimate statement if the nurse did not communicate effectively. Urgent time is lost playing the doctor–nurse game, and miscommunications are common with this approach to physician–nurse interactions.

An important by-product of this dysfunctional communication is an underlying attempt to shift blame away from oneself and onto other professionals. Mutual accountability, the hallmark of successful teams, does not develop or is easily destroyed in the resulting "culture of blame."[44] Ultimately, an escalating cycle of mistrust between health care providers is created, accentuated, and perpetuated, with resulting deterioration in patient care.

This is more than a theoretical possibility. In a classic study of how the quality of nurse–physician interactions in an intensive care setting affects patient outcomes, Knaus and colleagues demonstrated that the most powerful determinant of severity-adjusted patient death rates was how well nurses and physicians worked together in the planning and subsequent delivery of patient care.[45] They concluded that a high degree of involvement and interaction between nurses and physicians directly influences patient outcomes. Another study found that for each severity level of medical condition studied, patients were at greater risk of dying or being readmitted when nurses and resident physicians failed to communicate and effectively work together.[46] The current system of nurse–physician and other team professional interaction could benefit from a significant reevaluation and fundamental change to minimize the chances of system error or medical accident.[47]

Institutional Politics and Organizational Structure

In addition to the factors previously discussed, institutional politics and organizational structure contribute to difficulties in physician–nurse interactions and, by implication, entire health care team interactions. Physicians traditionally have been viewed as customers who bring patients and revenue to the health care system or institution. As a result, physicians are treated with a level of organizational deference and respect not afforded the registered nurse or other professionals employed by the health care organization (who, after all, are a cost on the balance sheet). An institution can more easily replace a nurse or pharmacist than a revenue-generating physician. Historically and in the extreme, a physician could demand that a particular nurse be terminated (for good reasons or bad) and expect that the institution would cause it to happen. By contrast, physician behavior that is inappropriate and disruptive will often be tolerated by those same institutions.[48] Nurses or other professionals behaving similarly would be terminated. In addition to these behavioral and operational observations, the differential status of nurses and physicians may be seen in hospital organizational charts, where nursing services are placed on a lower level than that of the medical departments.

Methods and Amount of Compensation

Differences in methods and amount of compensation for physicians, nurses, and other team members further divide the professions. Nurses are compensated for hours worked, and unless they are in a managerial role, responsibility and accountability for patient care end when a nursing shift is completed. Physician compensation is commensurate with years of education and 24-hour ultimate responsibility for patients under their care. This results in physicians earning 5 to 10 times more than staff nurses who provide most of the direct hands-on care. The disparity in compensation creates not only a professional barrier but a social barrier as well. There are distinct differences in lifestyles between those who are middle class and those who are upper class, and these discrepancies carry over into professional attitudes and interaction as well.[49]

Wide Disparity in Level of Educational Preparation

The disparity in educational preparation between physicians and nurses affects professional working relationships in multiple ways. Differential levels of education influence clinical interactions, contribute to inequity in compensation and professional respect, and result in real or perceived differences in social status. One of the most serious challenges facing nurses today is the issue of educational criteria and entry level into professional practice. According to the latest data, 59% of registered professional nurses in the United States do not hold a four-year college degree.[50] This inequity in education when compared with other health care disciplines is not only a significant barrier for advancing the professional practice of nursing, but also a significant barrier to team work. Consider that laboratory and radiation technicians are required to hold a baccalaureate degree; social workers and speech, occupational, and physical therapists require a master's degree; and pharmacists require a doctorate in pharmacology. There is no other profession that nurses must collaborate with professionally that does not require at least a four-year college degree.

For reasons not entirely clear, nurses do not insist that they cease to be the poorest prepared of all health care professionals.[51] Because nurses are the least educated, they are also the lowest-earning and least respected of the health care professionals.[52] Given the wide disparity in education between nurses and other members of the health care team, clinical discussions that involve research, outcomes, and clinical judgment can be challenging at best. Without at least a baccalaureate education, nurses have a hard time evaluating evidence and deciding how to provide care that is based on science rather than tradition.[53] All members of the health care team need a solid background in science and the scientific method in order to effectively collaborate with the medical profession. Access to the latest scientific information and use of the most appropriate technology to gather information and provide care are critical.[54] This knowledge is critical for nurses when planning with physicians and other team members the pros and cons, risks and benefits, and expected outcomes based on what is known about interventions for specific clinical conditions.[55] An equal voice in clinical discussions must be the voice of one who has been educated in an institution of higher learning in a manner similar to the other members of the health care team. The discrepancy in educational preparation between physicians and nurses plays an important role in less than optimal professional communication and clinical interactions and thus ultimately adversely affects patient outcomes.

Interestingly, physicians have a paradoxical view regarding nurses increasing their level of education. When asked to list weaknesses of nurses in a recent survey, some physicians noted that nurses had too many credentials and spent too much time in the classroom, whereas others believed that nurses had low initiative and suffered from a failure to seek advanced education.[56] By contrast, in a July 1999 Harris poll, 76% of Americans indicated they expected nurses to have four or more years of education to be successful clinicians. Perhaps the time has come for the nursing profession to stop arguing about the entry level into practice issue and set a date by which nurses would be required to hold a baccalaureate degree in nursing. Movement toward higher and more uniform educational requirements could significantly increase the potential of the nursing profession as well as teamwork in the clinical arena.

Licensure and Professional Accountability

Licensure and professional accountability are generally not thought of when factors that inhibit collaboration and teamwork between physicians, nurses, and other professionals are considered. However, their effect may be as powerful as any of the previously mentioned factors. Physician licensure gives the physician authority and demands accountability for admission, discharge, treatment (including all procedures and medications), and general oversight of all patient care. In short, physicians have the ultimate responsibility for patient care. Nurses, by contrast, provide the majority of direct patient care ordered by physicians, with other professionals contributing on a more fragmented or limited basis. However, nurses and other professionals have an independent responsibility for ensuring that orders received and followed are reasonable and appropriate. This differential responsibility is highlighted when litigation ensues as a result of patient injury. For example, nurses are responsible for their own clinical judgments and interventions. It is unacceptable to "delegate up" (a process whereby nurses avoid responsibility for their decisions for implementing care by invoking the authority of physicians as the basis for their decision making) when there is a question about appropriateness of orders.[57] However, it is not uncommon for some nurses to claim in retrospect that "the doctor made me do it," even when they were aware that the ordered course of treatment was not in the best interests of the patient. If patient well-being is at risk, nurses or other professionals have the moral responsibility to refuse to carry out that order and should be given institutional protection from potential physician-initiated repercussions.[58] This clearly defined principle of high-reliability organizations ("anyone can stop it") is not widely known or adhered to in contemporary health care organizations.

From the regulatory and legal perspective, a nurse is expected to know which orders given by a physician (who has many more years of education, training, and experience) are unreasonable or inappropriate, that is, which should be questioned either directly with the physician or, alternatively, result in a request for additional assistance (going up the chain of command) in the event of physician nonresponsiveness to a question asked by a nurse. This nursing accountability specified by licensure is in conflict with the hierarchical roles of physicians giving orders and nurses following those orders without question; in addition, it reinforces the factors previously cited that led to the historical role definition in the first place. Licensing requirements place a nurse in the difficult theoretical position of needing to know more than the physician giving the order. Nurses are compelled to take steps to directly go against physician orders, with serious institutional and professional ramifications if they are found to be wrong in retrospect. Clinical conflicts not able to be resolved by direct communication that result in chain-of-command initiatives not only inhibit physician–nurse trust and collaboration but also are a strong indicator that teamwork is nonexistent in the first place.

Health Care Under Pressure: Resulting Stress Makes Teamwork Difficult

Teamwork, although logical and intuitive, is not the organizational norm found in health care today. In large part, this is because of the antiteam forces previously discussed, but in addition and importantly, it is because of the extreme challenges produced by the rapid, constant change facing all health care organizations. Under stress, the natural reaction of any professional is to revert to previous individual history, socialization, and teaching, all of which conflict with the fundamental operational descriptors and characteristics of teamwork.[59]

Effective teams operate in an informal, comfortable, and relaxed atmosphere,[60] the very antithesis of the professional climate found in health care today. Cost pressure, staff reductions, legal and regulatory concerns, and marketplace competition all combine to create time pressure, nonaligned incentives, and potential mistrust among the professionals who must cooperate for a team to succeed. In addition, these same environmental forces serve to confuse teams in selecting and maintaining effective necessary partnerships. Cooperating and competing simultaneously with stakeholders who, at the same time, may likewise be competing and cooperating with each other can occupy inordinate amounts of energy that could otherwise be devoted to productive team activity. Finally, the characteristics of participation, listening, civilized disagreement, consensus decisions, open communication, and shared leadership are often difficult to achieve because of the socialization and psychology of physician participants.[61]

Highly individualistic, trained to be self-reliant, competitively aggressive under stress, and imbedded with a historical mistrust of hospital administration, physicians do not easily adapt to team dynamics and participation. In fact, the key ingredient necessary for effective clinical team development is physician leadership that understands the importance and operating principle of the team as the functional unit of production. Absent physician leadership, nurses and other professionals are forced to develop secondary, much less effective, often dysfunctional coping mechanisms for the delivery of clinical care.[62]

Within the clinical team, physicians have ultimate legal and regulatory responsibility and accountability for patient assessment and diagnosis, as well as for ordering treatments, interventions, surgeries, and medications. However, these responsibilities can be, and in fact are, best met through the coordinated and supportive efforts of the entire clinical team. Some believe that the historical paradigm of the physician as the "captain of the ship" precludes true teamwork because in a real team all members are mutually accountable as they work toward a common goal. Even some leaders in the nursing profession have contributed to this perception by describing nursing as an "inherently subservient role." To defeat these traditional but outdated views, physicians must learn to appreciate, value, and invite each member of the health care team to contribute the diverse opinions and perspectives that create superior decision making and performance. Although every team requires a leader, and in health care this role typically is assumed by a physician, it is necessary for physicians to remember that different roles or contributions do not necessarily mean unequal or no value.

Fortunately, nurse and physician perceptions of each other have improved significantly over the last few years. A 1998 study of physician–nurse relationships revealed that in general, nurses and physicians have positive perceptions about each other.[63] Nurses and physicians were asked to describe the role of the other's profession and to list respective strengths and weaknesses. In this study, nurses described physicians as leaders and the most important member of the health care team, collaborative, involved, and caring.[64] Physicians described nurses as patient and physician advocates, emotionally supportive and comforting to patients, the ones who provide minute-to-minute care, and as partners with physicians.[65] Thus, mutual respect and admiration between professionals appears to be increasing and needs to be nurtured so that teamwork becomes the model for delivering clinical care.

It should be noted however, that the social and organizational reality previously described is powerful and not easily ignored or dismissed. Therefore, it should be apparent that transforming these disparate professional groups into a team-based model of clinical care will not be accomplished easily. Nor will the transformation occur quickly or without a significant commitment of organizational resources. Nonetheless, it is our belief that if the commitment is understood, planned, and budgeted appropriately, the result will be well worth the dollars and effort expended. After all, despite many historical, professional, and cultural differences, nurses, physicians, and other members of the health care team share a powerful common goal around which effective teamwork can be developed: the safest care possible for patients who have placed their trust in us.

Aligning Operations to Build Team-Based High-Reliability Organizations: Where to Start and How to Succeed

The Blunt End: Organizational Leadership Shapes the Clinical Environment

The Role of Organizational Leaders

Although all health care professionals have the potential to substantially contribute to the development of effective team development, two participants hold significant enabling influence: physicians (see the previous discussion) and health care administrators. Health care administrators have the basic responsibility for ensuring that adequate financial, personnel, and other organizational resources (i.e., training and equipment) are available to provide safe and effective care. Without continued commitment of these resources, the clinical team faces significant and at times insurmountable challenges and frustration.

In addition, all clinical teams reflect explicit organizational culture and values; thus, an assessment of executive organizational group process and work environment is the first step in evaluating the potential for successful clinical teamwork. Unfortunately, in many health care organizations, senior management currently use group processes that resemble ineffective or nonfunctioning teams[66] and therefore create conditions under which clinical teamwork cannot emerge or flourish.

Safety is a fundamental patient right. Establishing an organizational culture that can deliver on that promise falls squarely on the shoulders of senior leadership. Moving to establish an organizational culture that creates teamwork and maximizes patient safety requires that four principles be focused on and visibly displayed at all times:

1. Commit and accept responsibility for safety.
2. Invite communication and dialogue.
3. Encourage risk taking and thinking and reward behaving courageously.
4. Foster creative thinking and seek innovative solutions and systems.

Leadership's Commitment to and Acceptance of Responsibility for Safety

The importance of patient safety relative to production is a fundamental clue to all employees and medical staff of how serious the organizational commitment is. When production and safety come into conflict, it is important that the choices made are explicit and the consequences clear to everyone throughout the organization.[67,68]

Without executive leadership continuously championing patient safety, the fundamental shifts necessary in an organization's behavior, in the work, in the systems, and in the relationships necessary for high reliability will be minimal. Becoming informed and knowledgeable about the principles of safety science is fundamental. A commitment to educate staff in these principles must follow. Using the language of safety in day-to-day conversation is a must; a demonstration to staff that leadership understands the basic concepts of "sharp end/blunt end," "Swiss cheese" thinking, and the pitfalls of "hindsight bias" (to use Reason's terminology) is paramount. With a grounded perspective in the principles of safety science, adopting a nonpunitive policy in reporting accidents becomes second nature. Essentially, these principles must be on public display at all times (especially in those difficult times following the accidents that inevitably will occur).

Armed with the language and informed of safety science literature, the next step is to "walk the talk" and lead by example. Strategies to demonstrate leadership commitment to patient safety include the following:

- Establish patient safety goals in department and unit work plans.
- Integrate patient safety into management and staff incentive programs.
- Acknowledge patient safety and medical accident reduction as a foundation for quality.
- Conduct walking rounds and eliminate weak links in the systems as they become known.
- Make sure that zero tolerance for procedural violations through intent or negligence is fundamental to organizational operations.
- Celebrate increased reporting of hazard identification and unnecessary system complexities and weaknesses. Eliminate those discovered.
- Create blameless reporting loops so all can stay informed about patient safety issues.
- Foster ongoing real-time dialogue about patient safety and the lessons learned from medical accidents.

Inviting Communication and Dialogue

The second leadership principle necessary in advancing a patient safety agenda is to consistently model inviting communication and dialogue. By listening more and using "inviting" questions, leaders can gain greater understanding of the culture and more in-depth analysis of the patient safety issues. Using simple and standard language and "inviting" communication techniques sets the stage for blameless reporting. Senior leadership must constantly model the approach. Examples of inviting questions include the following:

- What happened? (rather than, Who did it?)
- What is getting in the way of your ability to do your job effectively?
- Tell me about a significant accident waiting to happen.

Leadership must create opportunities for staff to develop communication skills, to understand the principles of effective communication, and to practice discussing bad outcomes with colleagues. Intentionally improving all communication processes is a significant patient safety success strategy. The message of safety is contained in the series of stories waiting to be told and retold throughout every organization.

Risk Taking and Thinking and Behaving Courageously

The third principle essential for advancing a patient safety agenda is to encourage risk taking and reward acting courageously. The traditional hierarchical culture of health care and silence will not easily be eliminated. Without effective teamwork, reporting lines continue to be rigidly defined and are not often crossed, even in the name of safety. Nurses often report using extreme caution in approaching certain physicians or not mentioning a concern at all because of the risk of a punitive or even abusive response. This fearful, blame-ridden, individual-driven hierarchy is detrimental to patient safety. Instead, leaders should demand a culture driven by respectful professional, patient, and family partnerships. Everyone must hear the message from those in leadership positions that it's a necessity and a fundamental responsibility to speak up, identify risks, avert risks, and always act thoughtfully to ensure patient safety. A leader can readily interview key personnel, posing the question, "Have you ever held back and hesitated to intervene or speak up when a patient's safety was in jeopardy?" The "inviting" interview needs to ensure the ground rules of honesty and nonpunitive reporting. The resulting leadership strategy is to further encourage risk taking and courageous behavior and not reward risk aversion. Leaders must deliver the following key message: The voice of safety belongs to us all, and all of us have a duty to speak directly and clearly.

Creative Thinking and Innovative Solutions and Systems

The fourth principle of leadership essential in solidifying a culture of patient safety is fostering creative thinking and seeking innovative solutions and systems. Simultaneous production and safety goals cannot be met by continuing to work in the manner to which we have currently become accustomed. Changes in the way our highly complex system works are necessary. Rigorous, increasing demands on the systems, the staff, and the infrastructure are created by 24-7-365 needs. Additionally, much has changed over the last decade, with a spiraling evolution of technology, excessive drug manufacturing, shrinking workforce, and dwindling reimbursement dollars. Yet the care delivery systems and the work of the patient care team remain essentially unchanged. Attempts to simplify and reduce the inherent complexity in the systems and the infrastructure have been largely unsuccessful. Health care providers have been placed in reactionary positions to all the forces of change coming to confluence at the sharp end. Leaders, by being open to ideas and thinking more creatively, can encourage an infusion of lessons from highly reliable industries. The work of leadership is to design and operate systems. Increased patient safety is an outcome of reliable systems based on teamwork. Leaders must dispel the myths of traditional thinking and infuse energy, enthusiasm, and innovative approaches to the work, systems, and relationships currently existing in the organizations they lead.

The Sharp End: A Reflection of Blunt-End Organizational Priorities

Self-Assessment

After reviewing the operational principles and characteristics of successful teams, it should be possible to decide if a given clinical unit is functioning as an effective highly reliable team with safety as its primary mission. For example, it should be evident whether patient safety is a clearly stated organizational goal. From that starting point, it should then be possible using the following tools to determine whether the behaviors of the clinical professionals working together exhibit any or all of the attributes of a well-functioning team.

The Teamwork Continuum

Based on established work patterns and observed professional communication, a point along the continuum of teamwork (Figure 25-1) can

Hostile (Open or Covert) Parallel ⟶ Peaceful Coexistence ⟶
Collaboration ⟶ Teamwork and Competing Forces

FIGURE 25-1   The continuum of teamwork

be assigned to any clinical work group. Most clinical units fall midway between peaceful coexistence and collaboration. Much has been written about moving clinical professionals toward teamwork, and many suggestions for creating fully operational teams have been offered. However, for any of these techniques to be effective, it is first up to the sharp-end clinicians to decide that teamwork is a desirable goal. Simply put, they *must agree to agree.* This is much easier said than done because of long-standing barriers (previously discussed) as well as current cynicism rooted in the beliefs of many that true teamwork is an impossible goal in the current health care environment.

Hostile Competing Forces   This is the most dysfunctional and potentially dangerous work environment for both patients and health care workers. When health care professionals are openly abusive or distrustful of each other and in effect are working against each other, it is self-evident that patient care will suffer. Absent effective clinical leadership and mutually agreed-upon goals to achieve patient well-being, health care professionals tend to compete for resources, favor, and rewards from both administrators and patients. If this natural form of competition is not held in check (or worse, is openly encouraged) by senior management or decision-making processes, open hostility at the sharp end will be the result. Decisions are then made on the basis of power, politics, or the squeaky wheel rather than data or common sense based on what is in the patient's best interest. Fortunately, this extreme of the continuum is rare in the current health care environment, but where it exists, it is often driven by long-standing personal and professional animosity and often requires expert outside consultation to eliminate it.

Peaceful Coexistence   In this predominately unit practice structure, physicians, nurses, and other allied health care workers meet separately to discuss clinical issues or processes that have implications or consequences for all team members and patients. Goals defined by each professional group remain part of the agenda in attempting to set and achieve larger work group objectives. Representatives from each group typically meet to "let each other know" what their group has decided. These parallel committee processes and resulting need to check back create inefficient duplication and excessive use of time and energy. Because no clinical issue or process definition can be decided or implemented without simultaneous input from all representatives of the health care team, peaceful coexistence is ultimately not sustainable. Eventually, more and more meetings must be scheduled to reach consensus among representatives of each discipline to determine plans for implementing anything, with the process ultimately sinking under its own weight. However, an interesting paradox exists in peaceful coexistence because the absence of overt hostility leads clinicians to believe they are truly functioning as a team rather than at the low end of the teamwork continuum. While seeing themselves as cooperating and doing their best in trying to improve existing clinical processes or patient care outcomes, clinicians often become frustrated by the lack of observable progress that is part and parcel of peaceful coexistence. A peaceful retreat of all parties to the "land of nothing getting done" ultimately occurs.

Collaboration   Collaboration implies members of at least two different professional groups agreeing to simultaneously work together toward defined clinical unit goals. Often, goals are brought forward or are championed from one member group rather than being first agreed on collectively. Working simultaneously together, with collaborative decisions taking precedence over those of member interests (in theory, if not often in practice), distinguishes this organizational form from peaceful coexistence. Importantly however, collaboration differs from true teamwork in that different interests or priorities of collaborating groups are *not subsumed* to those of the larger group. Patient care goals can be achieved only if the interests of each participating group represented in the collaborative process are also achieved (which does not occur very often). Often, the result is a compromise that is not entirely satisfactory to anyone. Although collaboration is preferable to peaceful coexistence because some operational and clinical decisions actually occur, collaboration is an inefficient and fragile means of working together.

Teamwork   A team implies professionals working collectively and in nonhierarchical fashion toward mutually agreed-upon common goals, with each member contributing and being valued for his or her unique talents, education, experience, background, and perspective. Individual member contributions are evaluated based on merit without regard for that member's status in the traditional health care hierarchy. For example, the ideas of a staff nurse have as much value as those of an attending physician, and the input from a resident physician is just as important as that of an advanced practice nurse. The value of contributions is defined by existing data or merit rather than presumed organizational position. Further, the needs of individual members are subsumed to those of the group. Importantly, team members hold each other mutually accountable for achieving the agreed-upon goals. Team members may offer views of the implications of operational and clinical initiatives on their respective disciplines, but they are not acting as "representatives" of these disciplines. The focus of any potential change in practice remains on patient outcomes rather than provider convenience. Forming, maintaining, and effectively working as a clinical team is very hard personal work and requires immense organizational support; thus, it does not occur very often in contemporary health care.

How close to teamwork is any clinical group operating? The position on the teamwork continuum may be defined by observing the following behaviors and characteristics.

Characteristics of Clinical Groups Operating Without Teamwork or High Reliability (Those at High Risk for Medical Accidents)

- The mission, vision, or goals of the clinical team are not uniformly agreed to or able to be described by all participants. Several subagendas, often in conflict with each other, are readily apparent.
- Safety is not explicitly stated as a primary and important goal or value.
- Reporting of accidents and near misses is not done or valued.
- Errors are blamed on people rather than prompting an evaluation of system processes and unit operations.
- Accidents are often attributed to an "act of God" or "circumstances beyond our control."
- Meetings are formal, tense, and uncomfortable when multidisciplinary professionals are present.
- Trust among members is low or nonexistent.
- Hierarchical professional relationships are emphasized.
- Physician–nurse conflict is ongoing (may be open or underlying).
- Dysfunctional or disruptive team members are not held accountable for their behavior or lack of action.
- Conflict is downplayed or avoided rather than used as an opportunity for learning.
- Professional communication often requires deception (i.e., the "doctor–nurse" game) in a misguided attempt at patient advocacy.
- A formal chain of command is frequently used instead of informal group norms to regulate behavior.
- The ratio of output to discussion in meetings is low. Similar agenda items appear over and over again.

- Little accountability for work assignments or follow-up exists.
- Disagreements and discussion continue outside of team meetings.
- Parallel group processes are in place, duplicating work efforts and creating boundaries, ownership of issues, and lack of effective coordination.
- Decisions are made unilaterally after "input" was sought, rather than by consensus.
- There are wide variations in clinical practice for which clear national standards and guidelines exist.
- Practices are based on what is most convenient for providers rather than what is best for patients.
- Practices are based on "the way we've always done it" instead of evidence and standards.
- Consistent external or internal assessment of teams as a discrete unit of production is not done.

Strategies for Implementing Effective Teamwork at the Sharp End

Successful clinical services in which teamwork is an operational reality are found selectively throughout health care. In our experience, there are key characteristics and strategies that set them apart from units functioning at the opposite end of the teamwork continuum. A review of these behavioral and organizational characteristics and how clinical teams can implement them may be helpful in further evaluating the status of teamwork in any clinical setting as well as in moving forward on the teamwork continuum.

At the outset, it should be noted that high-reliability clinical environments that support teamwork and patient safety do not occur randomly or by luck. They are the result of strong interdisciplinary leadership that instills and frequently communicates safety as its main value and operational principle. Teamwork requires more time and more professional energy than traditional models of care and traditional methods of communication and workplace behavior. It is possible, however, for an organization to learn and refocus on the principles of high reliability, teamwork, and the clinical practices that are needed to ensure patient safety. In our experience, effective teamwork within a high-reliability organization will result in fewer preventable adverse events as well as a more pleasant and energized work environment.

Characteristics of and Strategies to Create High-Reliability Clinical Units and Teamwork

- Safety is the hallmark of the organizational clinical culture and individual behavior, actions, and decision making.

Safety is understood to be the shared responsibility and individual duty of every team member. It is explicitly stated repeatedly that "we will not knowingly compromise safety." Patient safety is the number one consideration when care practices that may cost more, generate controversy among team members, or are deemed inconvenient to providers are under consideration. When the philosophy of safe care is challenged, it is up to all team members to keep everyone focused on the ultimate goal. For example, if controversial clinical practices or new technologies are being considered for introduction to a clinical unit, care providers promoting the new practice will sometimes insist that professionals who are opposed produce rigorous data to prove the practice is unsafe (and therefore should not be used or introduced). However, the elementary principle underlying consideration of risks and benefits of all clinical interventions is "first do no harm." Clearly, it would be much better for our patients if the alternative argument were needed (i.e., "prove" the practice is safe) before a specific clinical practice was implemented.

Because many patient injuries and adverse outcomes are not reported in the literature, it is difficult to quantify the risks of questionable practices with any degree of certainty. In the absence of a mature and robust reporting system, patient injuries are many times discovered only as a result of accident or litigation. Although all health care providers have been educated to rely on the best evidence from rigorously designed research studies to guide clinical practice, prospective randomized controlled trials do not exist to provide definitive "proof" that a questionable practice is unsafe. These types of trials cannot be done because it is difficult to prove a negative, plus there are medicolegal implications and ethical issues regarding what is commonly known (but not formally reported in the literature) about the adverse risks of certain practices. Lack of data to prove it's *not* safe does not mean it *is* safe. Redefining risk based on what has not happened as opposed to what may occur will not create safety. This lesson in safety was learned (unfortunately too late) by the members of the team at NASA who made the decision to launch the *Challenger* space shuttle.[69] Sometimes anecdotal data, common sense, and a gut feeling about doing the right thing will be the best and only guides to determining the best approach to handling controversy about questionable clinical or organizational (e.g., staffing) practices. An open, interdisciplinary approach to reaching consensus in the face of clinical or administrative controversy based on "safety first" creates an optimal process for managing organizational risk. Erring on the side of patient safety is always preferable to using a technique that could potentially cause patient injuries.

- Operation of the system is considered to be a team rather than individual function.

In a high-reliability organization, whatever hierarchical organizational relationships otherwise exist, at the point of service or care they are replaced with teamwork and cohesiveness. Because this is a concept generally foreign to health care, introduction of this important concept usually requires education and training based on simulation or example taken from other high-risk industries. Following a systematic validation of individual credentials, training, and skill sets, all team members are considered competent and therefore have an obligation to speak up ("call it off") if a question of safety arises. Leadership backing and congratulations to those who "stop the line" is absolutely essential. Teams, rather than individuals, are defined as the unit of production and safety creation. This concept needs to be introduced at employee orientation and periodically reinforced. Systems are designed to prevent, detect, and minimize the likelihood of a medical accident, rather than attributing blame or error to individuals. The process of effective teamwork is subject to ongoing examination and improvement. Individuals are evaluated and are provided incentives through their contribution to team performance.

- Communication is highly valued and rewarded.

All professionals use open and extensive communication to orient, plan, update, adjust to the unexpected, test assumptions, and debrief regarding unusual or unexpected events. Introducing debriefings in the normal course of doing business instead of just when things go wrong is a good way to create team communication and organizational learning. It is understood that when professionals fail to engage in respectful interactions, effective communication is hindered and patient safety is threatened. To avoid preventable adverse outcomes, an environment where health care professionals respect each other and value input into clinical decision making is developed and nurtured. Different perspectives are valued and contribute to successful outcomes. Each team member has the opportunity, indeed the obligation, to add a viewpoint that others may have overlooked or not previously considered. In many instances, the otherwise overlooked information may prove to be the essential missing component necessary to make a good decision. Simulations based on role playing are useful practice in this regard.

- Clinical standards and unit practices are developed by an interdisciplinary committee.

Important aspects of creating effective teamwork and a safe environment for patients and health care workers include creating a unified picture of what needs to be accomplished (shared vision) as well as agreed-upon operational goals, standards, and tactics of each clinical unit. Fostering teamwork through the creation and adoption of "the way we do business" is best accomplished within the structure of an interdisciplinary unit practice committee.

An interdisciplinary practice committee has two purposes: first, to establish the basis for and to define current clinical practice; second, to redefine practice accordingly as knowledge, professional guidelines, or regulatory requirements change.[70] Clinical teamwork within a practice committee enhances the quality of the decision-making processes for practice issues. There should be frequent and established meetings, with the expectation that all team members will make every attempt to attend. The committee should be empowered to make decisions about practice changes based on review of appropriate literature and standards.

A systematic team process for evaluating clinical practice, products, and services in terms of their respective contribution to patient outcomes has been described.[71] Through the use of quantitative data, evidence from the "safety scientists," and a measure of common sense, practices without an apparent or adverse effect on patient safety can be reevaluated, while practices thought to be beneficial can be enhanced and supported. It is possible to offset some of the costs of the additional resources necessary to provide safe care by eliminating routine practices not proven clinically effective or valued by patients.

Joint nurse–physician leadership of the clinical practice committee is essential for success.[72] Selection of these leaders should be based on peer respect, clinical expertise, and ability to influence and manage change. This latter attribute may need formal development or training for the individuals involved. Skilled clinicians are not necessarily skilled at effective group processes. In some cases, the leaders may be the physician chairperson of the clinical department and the nurse manager. However, today many of those in administrative roles are not clinical experts. In this situation, a clinical nurse specialist, nurse educator, charge nurse, or nurse expert in an informal leadership position and a designated expert physician may be better choices. The key requirements for co-chairmanship of the practice committee are recognized clinical expertise, peer respect and support, and enough influence to implement committee decisions (simple positional power will not succeed).

Committee membership should include physicians from specialties represented by the unit patient population, advanced practice nurses, and staff nurses. Members should be selected based on their ability to be articulate and assertive and their willingness to share their perspectives with professional colleagues. A physician or nurse researcher with experience in critiquing evidence would be a valuable member of the committee. Providers from other disciplines and departments such as pharmacy, social services, occupational and physical therapy, grief support, and risk management are also important committee members and should be encouraged to attend and participate.

Based on our experience working with institutions that have implemented this type of committee successfully, the following ground rules work well:

1. Professionals requesting practice or product/technical change are responsible for developing a proposal that includes a review of appropriate standards and guidelines for care (if available); review of available literature; the potential impact on the unit resources, such as staffing or clinical operations; cost data; and potential benefits to patients, as well as any foreseeable safety issues or concerns.
2. The proposal should be distributed well in advance of the committee meeting when it will be discussed so members have the opportunity to gather additional data if desired.
3. There should be an agreement that no practice change will be approved that is inconsistent with available research or established standards and guidelines from professional organizations. Likewise, no change will occur until all potential patient safety concerns have been addressed.

After team consensus is obtained, these best practices can be outlined in the form of protocols or routine order sets and presented to the entire group of health care providers. Administrative support and influential committee members are key factors in implementing practice changes using this type of process.

Commitment to practice based on evidence, standards, and concern for patient safety is an ongoing process and may require substantial changes from the usual methods of implementing and evaluating changes in patient care. Discussions about clinical practice that are based on evidence and standards of care rather than hierarchical relationships, personal preferences, and old routines can be helpful in setting the stage for real teamwork.

For some, the process of agreeing to establish this type of committee and select committee members may require months of negotiation. It may be foreign to some unit cultures for nurses to have an equal voice in clinical practice development and to be viewed as credible members of an interdisciplinary clinical practice committee. The "way we've always done it" may include physicians telling nurses about the latest research and standards of care and nurses "complying" without discussion or reviewing these data themselves. Ability to critically review literature and evaluate published standards as the basis for clinical practice changes is not inherently dependent on professional group membership. It is a skill that can be learned by both nurses and physicians who are committed to the process and open to changes that can enhance patient care.

Significant changes in unit culture will not occur overnight. Professional relationships between nurses and physicians that include trust and mutual respect evolve progressively and are based on many interactions. Developing and nurturing an environment that supports real teamwork may take years. It may be helpful for the committee members to participate in team-building exercises to enhance the likelihood of success. Initial success may be measured in small steps and implementation of simple practice changes that do not involve controversy or conflict. Once members are more comfortable with the process and with working together, more complex clinical practice issues can be addressed.

Based on our experiences, it is not unusual for there to be periods of time when it seems that nothing can be accomplished and that group consensus is impossible or—even more frustrating—when members revert to the old ways of interacting and decision making. A firm resolve to focus on the mutual goal of providing the safest possible patient care can help get through these periods. Addition of new members or rotation of membership may help energize the committee. One key to success is to expect these frustrations at times and acknowledge that the process is ongoing and dynamic. Although a team approach to clinical decision making may not evolve as quickly as desired and may involve significant professional energy, the initial investment of time to get oriented to this process is worth the effort. The main advantages of care based on the latest evidence, standards, and guidelines from professional associations and regulatory agencies are as follows: care practices that can be defended as internal budgets become more restricted (almost guaranteed to happen); establishment of true teamwork between nurse and physician colleagues that will have a positive spillover effect on clinical operations and therefore patient safety; and the assurance to the public and purchasers that practices are clinically sound, consistent with scientific data and existing professional standards of care.

- Professionals learn through interdisciplinary education.

Physicians, nurses, and other health care professionals work together to provide patient care; thus, education about patient care practices should occur in sessions with all members in attendance. Everyone can learn the same lessons, and there is opportunity to discuss methods of implementation and communication about clinical practices. Issues with the potential to cause controversy in the middle of the night can be openly discussed in the light of day, and strategies to avoid clinical disagreements that can adversely affect patient care can be developed.

- Professional competence is a necessity.

Health care providers who are responsible for patient care must be competent in both clinical assessment skills and intervention strategies. Various methods to validate competence have been used over the years, and there are pros and cons to each of these methods. One method that avoids the inherent observer bias of skills checklists and the limitations of written examinations is periodic evaluation of clinical practice via medical record audits. Audit tools can be developed using guidelines and standards from professional associations and regulatory agencies. Consistency with published guidelines and standards can help to avoid preventable adverse outcomes and decrease liability should the institution be involved in litigation related to patient care.

- Technology and interventions are used appropriately and only when indicated.

Use of technology and interventions should be appropriate for the clinical situation, rather than based on provider convenience and cost issues. Overuse of technology and unnecessary interventions can result in iatrogenic patient injuries as well as drain financial and human resources that could be better used in more effective methods of providing patient care.

- Emergencies are rehearsed and the unexpected practiced.

In each practice specialty, clinical situations occur with the potential to result in great harm, or even death, to a patient. These clinical situations should be identified and emergency procedures developed and rehearsed. For example, every team member should be competent in cardiopulmonary resuscitation, know how to make preparations for emergency surgery, and know what to do when there are adverse reactions to blood products and medications. Rehearsing the unexpected but possible clinical emergency promotes patient safety. Clinical appropriateness and timeliness during rehearsed emergencies can be evaluated by the interdisciplinary team retrospectively in a systematic manner. Opportunities for improvement can be identified and incorporated into future emergent clinical situations.

- Successful operations are viewed as potentially dangerous.

Routine, repetitive, successful operations naturally lead to process shortcuts and simplification, or what Vaughan in her analysis of the *Challenger* space shuttle disaster termed "normalization of deviance."[73] She concluded that all work groups continuously redefine risk in the context of accidents that do not occur. Unknowingly, professional, technical, and behavioral standards degrade as time goes on. Incrementally, all group cultures become unsafe over time because "they get away with it." Because accidents are rare, there are no immediate or apparent consequences for not strictly adhering to defenses created to prevent their occurrence. When the inevitable disaster occurs (and it always does), the negative impact is magnified because risk is then redefined in terms of impact on the individual(s), rather than the number of times the accident did not previously happen.

At times operational systems and clinical practices that are known to be risky may continue because the unit is short-staffed or because some team members feel powerless to challenge other team members. Ongoing limited financial and human resources contribute to a stressful, error-prone clinical environment. Physicians react to the pressures of demands for efficiency by third-party payers and hospital administrators. For example, they are sometimes tempted to speed things up and may override clinical protocols in the interest of time. Nurses may initially go along unwillingly but develop mistrust and hostility toward physicians in the process. Physicians in turn, often play "I told you so," thereby perpetuating the developing deviance until disaster strikes. As an alternative, nurses may use deceptive countermeasures in a misguided attempt to advocate for their patients; however, at times, lacking knowledge of the complete clinical situation, these techniques may actually result in patient harm.

To combat this natural tendency toward normalizing deviance, high-reliability clinical units actively and continuously question assumptions. They promote orderly challenge of operating systems and practices so that the successful lessons of the past do not become routine to the point of safety degradation. The "outside" view is actively solicited or created through interdisciplinary review of the routine and debriefing of the unusual. Clinical units are especially vulnerable to normalizing deviance. Because an outcome is "good" (no harm, no foul in legal terms), near misses are frequently not viewed as opportunities to learn about or improve system behaviors. Once the concepts are understood, however, it is very easy for a clinical unit to identify specific deviances it has normalized over time. Professionals new to a unit are frequently amazed at potentially unsafe conditions or clinical practices attributed to "the way we've always done it." Six months later these same professionals are just as amazed by newcomers questioning the same practices with which they themselves have now grown comfortable. Newcomers present an ideal opportunity for an "outsider view" of clinical practices. Their perspectives and suggestions for improvement should be given serious consideration.

- Clear language is routinely used to describe clinical conditions and patient well-being in all professional communication and medical record documentation.

Members of the unit team should establish clear language to describe common clinical situations and deviations, and that language should be used in all professional communication and medical record documentation.[74] A common language enhances communication and avoids misconceptions about patient status. This is especially important when communicating over the telephone. Much of the communication about patient conditions occurs over the telephone between the nurse at the bedside and the physician at home or in the office. Each team member must be able to accurately convey the patient's clinical status and clearly understand the substance, implications, and urgency of what is being communicated.

- Clearly defined policies and practices exist that everyone knows and agrees to follow.

Policies and practices promulgated by the unit practice committee should be clearly written and widely disseminated. There should be a process in place to ensure that every team member is made aware of practice changes and updates. An expectation that all professionals agree to follow established unit policies and practices is critical to safe care. A system of accountability and zero tolerance for violations (or repeated violations) of these policies and practices should be developed and followed.

- Organizational resources and systems are in place to support clinically timely interventions in the event of unexpected patient deterioration.

Sufficient nurse-to-patient ratios are critical to identifying deterioration in a patient's condition in a timely manner. There is ample evidence to support the idea that patient outcomes improve and adverse events are less frequent as the number of nurses per patient is increased.[75–81] A higher number of registered nurses per patient is consistently related to lower adverse outcome rates, shorter lengths of stay, and lower patient morbidity. The nurse manager can use these data to argue that any plans for downsizing, reengineering, or restructuring of the clinical workforce should be evaluated in the context of the potential impact on patient safety. Although decreasing the number of registered nurses may appear to be a cost-saving measure initially, over time patient morbidity and adverse incidents will increase and patient and nursing satisfaction decrease. Thus, there may be significant unplanned negative financial implications in addition to lower-quality care.

Accurate identification of deteriorating or significant changes in patient condition should be followed with clinically timely interventions. Twenty-four-hour availability of a medical emergency or surgical team (including an anesthesia provider, scrub nurse, circulating nurse, surgical first assistant, and surgeon) is essential. Institutional financial constraints that do not permit intensive care, anesthesia, or surgical standby for potential emergencies or for calling the surgical team in before the attending physician has arrived when there is clear evidence of patient deterioration are inconsistent with safe care.

- Interdisciplinary debriefings are held for near misses and medical accidents.

When clinical situations result in an adverse outcome, an interdisciplinary process that allows all parties to review the events in a blame-free environment works well as a strategy to potentially prevent future occurrences. The key issue is to focus on the process and systems that contributed to the adverse outcome rather than assigning fault to individual professionals.

When a Preventable Adverse Outcome Occurs in a High-Reliability Clinical Unit

It is important to realize that medical accidents, mistakes, and patient injuries cannot be avoided with absolute certainty.[82] The best clinical teams on occasion experience adverse patient outcomes. When these unfortunate incidents do occur, a lawsuit is not inevitable, and therefore organizational response should not use the medicolegal system as the primary basis for determining communication policy for providers and patients. Data suggest that six patient injuries occur for every one that results in legal action.[83] The key variable that separates these outcomes is effective patient communication.[84] The ability to communicate effectively in times of crisis is a skill that can be learned and must be practiced.[85] Clinical units with few lawsuits are succeeding at setting realistic patient expectations as well as communicating effectively when those expectations are not met. Self-appraisal and the practice of an effective communication style are taken seriously by every team member involved.

In addition to communicating with patients and families following adverse outcomes, health care professionals on effective clinical units communicate with and support each other. Besides debriefing following patient injuries in an effort to learn and improve system performance, there is recognition that an adverse event has high potential for personal and professional costs as well. Most professionals are perfectionists, and failure creates extreme vulnerability that can result in personal disruption and suboptimal future performance, and therefore the potential for further errors.[86,87] The ultimate success of a high-reliability clinical unit is its ability to avoid casting personal blame while creating an environment that is mutually supportive at the time of high stress secondary to catastrophic outcome. A supportive environment that maintains psychological well-being protects future individual performance and diminishes the chances of recurrent patient injury.

Conclusion

Ultimately, the creation and maintenance of teamwork, high reliability, and an environment safe for both patients and health care providers come down to a series of decisions. Organizations are composed of professionals who have the ability to decide what the conditions of where they work and how they work will be. Safety is an active choice that can be embraced or rejected. Although the principles and benefits of teamwork are easily summarized, the choice to move forward has proved to be more difficult. The answer to this paradox is as important as any question facing health care today. The work required in "first doing no harm" will only occur when people make up their minds to embrace it seriously.

References

1. Simpson, K. R., and Knox, G. E. (2001). Perinatal teamwork: Turning rhetoric into reality. In K. R. Simpson and P. A. Creehan (Eds.). *AWHONN's Perinatal Nursing* (2nd ed., pp. 53–67). Philadelphia: Lippincott.
2. Knox, G. E., Kelley, M., Simpson, K. R., Carrier, L., and Berry, D. (1999). Downsizing, reengineering and patient safety: Numbers, newness and resultant risk. *Journal of Healthcare Risk Management, 19*(4), 18–25.
3. Pavlovich-Davis, S., Forman, H., and Simek, P. F. (1998). The nurse-physician relationship: Can it be saved? *Journal of Nursing Administration, 28*(7), 17–20.
4. Harvard Risk Management Foundation, personal communication (2000).
5. Katzenbach, J. R., and Smith, D. K. (1993). *The Wisdom of Teams.* Boston: Harvard Business School Press.
6. Morey, J. C., Simon, R., Jay, G. D., Wears, R. L., Salisbury, M., Dukes, K. A., and Berns, S. D. (2002). Error reduction and performance improvement in the emergency department through formal teamwork training: Evaluation results of the Med-Teams project. *Health Services Research, 37*(6), 1553–1581.
7. Gaba, D. M., Howard, S. K., Flanagan, B., Smith, B. E., Fish, K. J., and Botney, R. (1998). Assessment of clinical performance during simulated crises using both technical and behavioral ratings. *Anesthesiology, 89,* 8–18.
8. Knox, G. E., Simpson, K. R., and Garite, T. J. (1999). High reliability perinatal units: An approach to the prevention of patient injury and medical malpractice claims. *Journal of Healthcare Risk Management, 19*(2), 27–35.
9. Roberts, K. H. (1990). Some characteristics of high reliability organizations. *Organization Science, 1*(2), 160–177.
10. Ibid.
11. Knox et al. (1999). Downsizing, reengineering and patient safety.
12. Ibid.

13. Ibid.
14. Roberts (1990). Some characteristics of high reliability organizations.
15. Simpson, K. R. (2000). Creating a culture of safety: A shared responsibility. *MCN American Journal of Maternal Child Nursing, 25*(2), 61.
16. Katzenbach and Smith (1993). *The Wisdom of Teams.*
17. Briscoe, G., and Authur, G. (1998). CQI teamwork: Reevaluate, restructure, renew. *Nursing Management, 29*(10), 73–80.
18. Klein, G. (1998). *Sources of Power: How People Make Decisions.* Cambridge, MA: MIT Press.
19. Roberts (1990). Some characteristics of high reliability organizations.
20. Mannarelli, T., Roberts, K. H., and Bea, R. G. (1996). Learning how organizations mitigate risk. *Journal of Contingencies and Crisis Management, 4*, 83–92.
21. Smith, P. G., and Reinhart, D. G. (1991). *Developing Products in Half the Time.* New York: Van Nostrand Reinhold.
22. Katzenbach and Smith (1993). *The Wisdom of Teams.*
23. Ibid.
24. Knox et al. (1999). Downsizing, reengineering and patient safety.
25. Simpson and Knox (2001). Perinatal teamwork.
26. Parker, G. A. (1996). *Team Players and Teamwork: The New Competitive Business Strategy.* San Francisco: Jossey-Bass.
27. Simpson and Knox (2001). Perinatal teamwork.
28. Department of Health and Human Services (2001). Sample survey of registered nurses. Washington, DC: Author.
29. Bickel, J. (1997). Gender stereotypes and misconceptions: Unresolved issues in physician's professional development. *Journal of the American Medical Association, 277*(17), 1405–1407.
30. Pasko, T., and Seidman, B. (1999). *Physician Characteristics and Distribution in the Workplace.* Chicago: American Medical Association.
31. Kearny, K. G., and White, T. I. (Eds.). (1994). *Men and Women at Work: Warriors and Villagers on the Job.* Hawthorne, NJ: Cancer Press.
32. Ibid.
33. Ibid.
34. Ibid.
35. Ibid.
36. Ibid.
37. Keenan, G. M., Cooke, R., and Hillis, S. L. (1998). Norms and nurse management of conflicts: Keys to understanding nurse-physician collaboration. *Research in Nursing and Health, 21*, 59–72.
38. Stein, L. I. (1967). The doctor-nurse game. *Archives in General Psychiatry, 16*, 699–703.
39. Willis, E., and Parish, K. (1997). Managing the doctor-nurse game: A nursing and social science analysis. *Contemporary Nurse, 6*(3), 136–144.
40. Peter, E. (2000). Ethical conflicts or political problems in intrapartum nursing care. *Birth: Issues in Perinatal Care, 27*(1), 46–48.
41. Knaus, W. A., Draper, E. A., and Wagner, D. P. (1986). An evaluation of outcome from intensive care units in major medical centers. *Annals of Internal Medicine, 104*, 410–418.

42. Sleutel, M. R. (2000). Intrapartum nursing care: A case study of supportive interventions and ethical conflicts. *Birth: Issues in Perinatal Care, 27*(1), 38–45.

43. Peter (2000). Ethical conflicts or political problems.

44. Leape, L. L. (1994). Error in medicine. *Journal of the American Medical Association, 272,* 1851–1857.

45. Knaus, Draper, and Wagner (1986). An evaluation of outcome.

46. Baggs, J. G., Ryan, S. A., and Phelps, C. E. (1992). The association between interdisciplinary collaboration and patient outcomes in a medical intensive care unit. *Heart and Lung, 21,* 18–24.

47. Katzman, E. M., and Roberts, J. I. (1988). Nurse-physician conflicts as barriers to enactment of nursing roles. *Western Journal of Nursing Research, 10,* 576–590.

48. Knox, G. E. (1999). Doctors behaving badly and the people who let them. *Trustees, 52*(4), 18–19.

49. Roberts, S. J. (1983). Oppressed group behavior: Implications for nurses. *Advances in Nursing Science, 5*(4), 21–30.

50. Department of Health and Human Services (2001). Sample survey of registered nurses. Washington, DC: Author.

51. Christman, L. (1998). Who is a nurse? *Image: The Journal of Nursing Scholarship, 30,* 211–214.

52. Gennaro, S., and Lewis, J. (2000). Is the goal of a BSN as the criteria for entry into professional nursing practice still worthwhile and realistic? *MCN American Journal of Maternal Child Nursing, 25*(2), 62–63.

53. Ibid.

54. Ibid.

55. Simpson, K. R., and Knox, G. E. (1999). Strategies for developing an evidence-based approach to perinatal care. *MCN American Journal of Maternal Child Nursing, 24*(3), 122–132.

56. Pavlovich-Davis, Forman, and Simek (1998). The nurse-physician relationship.

57. Rubin, J. (1996). Impediments to the development of clinical knowledge and ethical judgment in critical care nursing. In P. Benner, C. A. Tanner, and C. Chelsa (Eds.). *Expertise in Nursing Practice: Caring Clinical Judgment and Ethics* (pp. 170–192). New York: Springer Publishing.

58. Peter (2000). Ethical conflicts or political problems.

59. Simpson and Knox (2001). Perinatal teamwork.

60. Parker (1996). *Team Players and Teamwork.*

61. Kassebaum, D., and Culter, E. (1998). On the culture of student abuse in medical school. *Academic Medicine, 73*(11), 1149–1158.

62. Simpson and Knox (2001). Perinatal teamwork.

63. Pavlovich-Davis, Forman, and Simek (1998). The nurse-physician relationship.

64. Ibid.

65. Ibid.

66. Parker (1996). *Team Players and Teamwork.*

67. Reason, J. T. (1997). *Managing the Risks of Organizational Accidents.* Aldershot, UK: Ashgate Publishing.

68. Reason, J. T. (2001). Understanding adverse events: The human factor. In C. Vincent (Ed.). *Clinical Risk Management* (2nd ed.). London: BMJ Books.

69. Vaughn, D. (1996). *The Challenger Launch Decision: Risky Technology, Culture and Deviance at NASA.* Chicago: University of Chicago Press.

70. Simpson and Knox (1999). Strategies for developing an evidence-based approach to perinatal care.

71. Ibid.

72. Ibid.

73. Vaughn (1996). *Challenger launch decision.*

74. Simpson, K. R., and Knox, G. E. (2003). Communication of fetal heart monitoring information. In N. Feinstein, K. L. Torgersen, and J. Atterbury (Eds.). *Fetal Heart Monitoring Principles and Practices.* Washington, DC: Association of Women's Health, Obstetric and Neonatal Nurses.

75. Aiken, L. H., Clarke, S. P., Sloane, D. M., Sochalski, J., and Siber, J. H. (2002). Hospital nurse staffing and patient mortality, nurse burnout, and job satisfaction. *Journal of the American Medical Association, 288*(16), 1987–1993.

76. Blegen, M. A., Goode, C. J., and Reed, L. (1998). Nurse staffing and patient outcomes. *Nursing Research, 47*(1), 43–50.

77. Bond, C. A., Raehl, C. L., Pitterle, M. E., and Franke, T. (1999). Health care professional staffing, hospital characteristics, and hospital mortality rates. *Pharmacotherapy, 19*(2), 130–138.

78. Callaghan, L. A., Cartwright, D. W., O'Rourke, P., and Davies, M. W. (2003). Infant to staff ratios and risk of mortality in very low birthweight infants. *Archives of Disease in Childhood: Fetal and Neonatal Edition, 88*(2), F94–F97.

79. Kovner, C., and Gergen, P. J. (1998). Nurse staffing levels and adverse events following surgery in U. S. hospitals. *Image: Journal of Nursing Scholarship, 30*(4), 315–321.

80. Lichtig, L. K., Knauf, R. A., and Milholland, D. K. (1999). Some impacts of nursing on acute care hospital outcomes. *Journal of Nursing Administration, 29*(2), 25–33.

81. Needleman, J., Buerhaus, P., Mattke, S., Stewart, M., and Zelevinsky, K. (2002). Nurse-staffing levels and the quality of care in hospitals. *New England Journal of Medicine, 346*(22), 1715–1722.

82. Kohn, L. T., Corrigan, J., and Donaldson, M. S. (Eds.). (1999). *To Err Is Human: Building a Safe Health System.* Washington, DC: National Academy of Sciences Press.

83. Localio, A. R., Lawthers, A. G., Brennan, T. A., Laird, N. M., Hebert, L. E., Peterson, L. M., Newhouse, J. P., Weiler, P. C., and Hiatt, H. H. (1991). Relation between malpractice claims and adverse events due to negligence: Results of the Harvard Medical Practice Study III. *New England Journal of Medicine, 325*(4), 245–251.

84. Hickson, G. B., Clayton, E. W., Githens, P. B., and Sloan, F. A. (1992). Factors that prompted families to file malpractice claims following perinatal injury. *Journal of the American Medical Association, 287*(10), 1359–1363.

85. Markakis, K. M., Beckman, H. B., Suchman, A. L., and Frankel, R. M. (2000). The path to professionalism: Cultivating humanistic values and attitudes in residency training. *Academic Medicine, 75*(2), 141–150.

86. Charles, S. C. (1986). Malpractice litigation and its impact on physicians. *Current Psychiatric Therapies, 23,* 173–180.

87. Charles, S. C. (1991). The psychological trauma of a medical malpractice suit: A practical guide. *Bulletin of the American College of Surgeons, 76*(11), 22–26.

CHAPTER TWENTY-SIX

MOVING BEYOND BLAME TO CREATE AN ENVIRONMENT THAT REWARDS REPORTING

Doni Hass

The story related in this chapter describes the coordination of one hospital's response to a sentinel event that ultimately took the life of 7-year-old Ben Kolb. Woven throughout the story of Ben's fatal journey are the actions of many on the hospital staff that supported risk management efforts in the coordination of the response to and investigation of an unusual event.

The control of risk and promotion of patient safety had always been at the forefront of Martin Memorial's corporate objectives. Every employee was evaluated annually on specific risk and safety measurements. Each manager had specific goals, and the bar was always rising. Because of the emphasis on and support for risk management, unfortunate events were approached by a team seeking solutions, not micromanagers seeking to place blame. The following story is not about people making mistakes, it is about a failed system that allowed humans to err. The case also illustrates how Ben's family responded when the event, its investigation, and the disclosure were handled with diligence, integrity, and compassion. It is a story of tragedy and of trust. This is Ben's story.

December 15, 1995, was the first day of Christmas vacation. It was a good day for Ben Kolb to have some routine ear surgery in plenty of time to be able to enjoy the Christmas holidays with his 12-year-old sister Margaret and their parents. Ben was scared, but he had known his surgeon since he was a baby. They were "buddies." Mom and the nurses joked with him to ease his fear. Like many Moms before and since, she gave her only son a kiss and he was wheeled off to the operating room.

Twenty minutes into the operation, the surgeon injected the local anesthetic into the four quadrants surrounding Ben's ear. The scrub technician felt the child's chest "pounding" through the surgical drapes as the Certified Registered Nurse Anesthetist (CRNA) saw precipitous changes in the blood pressure and pulse. The supervising anesthesiologist was summoned to lead the management of the hypertension and tachycardia. The child responded immediately to the treatment and stabilized within minutes. The anesthesiologist, recognizing the timing of the event, instructed the scrub technician to save the syringes, intending to follow up on the cause of this unusual reaction to lidocaine 1% with epinephrine 1:100,000.

Nine minutes later, the child experienced a cardiac arrest. The chaplain was summoned for family support and the risk manager for coordinating the response to and investigation of an unusual event. It was weeks later that the error that caused the reaction was identified.

When Ben left the operating room 2 hours later, he was in a profound coma and on a ventilator. A pacemaker had been inserted during the resuscitative efforts. Meanwhile, in the surgical waiting room, Tammy Kolb had been anxiously wondering what was taking so long when the volunteer quietly told a visitor, "I'm sorry sir, they have asked me to hold all visitors to intensive care. They are getting ready for a critical child from OR." Tammy rose to her feet.

The surgeon and anesthesiologist, after meeting briefly with the risk manager, came to tell Tammy Kolb. In a private room, they gently gave a thorough explanation of how Ben's heart had stopped and how difficult it was to restart. The chaplain joined them to support Tammy, who insisted "I know he'll get better, I've seen this on TV." Again, the physicians tried to help her begin to cope with the seriousness of his condition. "Ben is in a deep coma, he may not be able to wake up . . . we'll do everything we can."

Usually, operating rooms (ORs) are cleaned and readied for the next operation rapidly. This room was left undisturbed as the director of surgical services met with the risk manager to review details of the event with the staff. The risk manager focused on the timing of the event and selected the syringes of lidocaine with epinephrine, the original vial, and the bottle of topical adrenalin. The vials had been discarded in the "red box." There was one other vial of each in the box. The two syringes and four vials were handed directly to the risk manager.

Thinking she was dealing with a product problem, the risk manager took the items directly to the pharmacist, who initiated the product recall procedure, removing all solutions with the same lot numbers. An alert was faxed to the U.S. Pharmacopoeia. A portion of the contents of one syringe was drawn into a third syringe and prepared for shipment with a vial of adrenalin and lidocaine with epinephrine to a lab capable of analysis. The pharmacist searched for the lab. The risk manager went to the intensive care unit and met with Ben's mom, who was holding her son's limp hand and calling softly to awaken him. Tammy wanted to know what happened. The risk manager replied, "We honestly do not know, but it is my job to try to find out what happened. I will exhaust my resources to find you an answer. I will let you know as soon as I find out." She then met with the CEO and marketing director, outlining the event and her plan for response. Returning to the pharmacy, she and the pharmacist selected the lab at the University of Georgia. The items were sent by overnight mail.

Ben died the following day, after being transferred to a tertiary care center. The risk manager called the defense counsel and insurer to alert them to the event, review the planned response, and obtain advice on the proposed investigation. The board and senior management were called in to a special meeting. The coroner was contacted and told of the analysis under way in Georgia.

Individual meetings were held with every person who entered the OR suite during the procedure. Each one made drawings detailing the location of all equipment and people. The anesthesia team had been positioned at the child's feet to allow room for the microscope to be wheeled into position over Ben's head. Each person's role was outlined, step by step, on poster paper. Everyone seemed to know the proper procedure and appeared to be very competent. After each interview, the risk manager taped the drawings and procedural detail to the walls in an empty office. Procedurally, the only variation was a failure to label the syringes of lidocaine. A pharmacist was relieved of her usual duties by the CEO and assigned to the investigation. She and the risk manager pored over the posters, the procedure, and Ben's previous medical records. Both investigators, to learn how others handled medications in the operating room, called colleagues across the country. They searched the literature for similar cases. One was identified in London. The article described a cardiac arrest in a small boy during ear surgery. The child did not respond to treatment. Efforts to identify the site failed.

The lab notified them that two substances had been isolated in the product test. Further tests were under way to match the substances with the vial contents.

During this time, the risk manager called the Kolb family to express sympathy and renew her pledge to seek an answer. "Please, don't let this happen to another child. Please don't stop, don't ever, ever stop.

Please find an answer," was Ben's mother's plea. The anesthesiologist attended the funeral home viewing. The surgeon attended the funeral.

During a routine sentinel event meeting, the details of the event were described by the CRNA, anesthesiologist, and surgeon. The chief of anesthesia, chief of surgery, vice president of medical affairs, physician chair of the quality committee, the president of the medical staff, and the risk manager brainstormed a root cause. At this meeting, the chief of anesthesia said, "I'll bet I know what happened; we saw the same thing in Miami years ago. Someone had mixed up the two medicines. The child died from receiving an injection of the concentrated adrenalin." Everyone agreed that scenario would explain the resultant symptoms. The risk manager focused the discussion on the medical management because she was getting the product analyzed. "If that happened, we will know it," she reminded the group of concerned physicians.

After the meeting, the risk manager met with the director of surgical services to question her on the possibility of a drug mix-up. "That's impossible," insisted the nurse. "We followed procedure. It simply cannot happen—we used the same procedure everyone else does. It simply cannot happen, period." In a later meeting with the medical center administrator, a group of circulating nurses and scrub techs in the OR were assigned to a process improvement task force to examine the procedures used in the OR when handling medications.

On December 19, the University of Georgia called to say they were unable to identify the contents. They would continue to try if an additional sample was available. That afternoon, the coroner called to see if the lab results were in. He said he was ruling the death an idiosyncratic reaction to lidocaine with epinephrine. The story could have ended here with a resultant lawsuit and no answers, no truth for Ben's parents.

An additional sample was sent. January 2 brought a chilling call from Georgia. The sample did not match the control of lidocaine with epinephrine. They were running tests for the topical adrenalin properties.

During this time, the director of surgical services, working closely with risk management and the task force, identified an unnecessary step in the commonly accepted process for transferring medications to the sterile operating room environment. This step was also identified as an opportunity for error that could be eliminated. That step was the use of intermediate containers. Using sterile technique, pharmaceuticals were transferred to small plastic and stainless containers on the operating room table by pouring or by use of a syringe. The circulating nurse and scrub technician would verify visually and audibly the contents and expiration dates. The intermediate containers had been labeled by the scrub tech during set-up. The scrub tech would then finish the preparation by withdrawing the injectable pharmaceutical into a syringe. The syringe should have been labeled. The investigation found that it was not uncommon for this step to be skipped when only one injectable was used. The topical solution was poured on cotton pellets to dab on bleeders during the procedure. As the tech finished, the circulating nurse would finish the room set-up and bring the patient to the OR. The task force recommended the use of a filter straw or spike for the scrub tech to attach a labeled syringe to. Intermediate containers were eliminated.

The risk manager, pharmacist, vice president of medical affairs, and the president decided to engage a crisis management firm and locate a second lab with different testing methods in order to confirm the findings.

A quarter of a cubic centimeter of the substance remained in the syringe that had actually been used on Ben. All of the pharmaceuticals had been sealed in wax on December 15 to protect their integrity. That syringe was hand-carried along with control vials to National Medical Services in Willow Grove, Pennsylvania. The pharmacist accompanied the specimen throughout the testing processes. The following day, she called to tell the risk manager the findings, which confirmed what had been learned at the University of Georgia. The syringes of lidocaine 1:100,000 actually contained topical adrenalin. There had indeed been a tragic, fatal error.

As soon as the written reports were received, the risk manager called the Kolb family. Arrangements were made to meet them the following day at their attorney's office. The surgeon and anesthesiologist were notified. A copy of the lab reports was taken to the coroner. He informed the hospital that he would have to change his ruling, but agreed not to do so until after the family was informed.

The following day, the risk manager, accompanied by the anesthesiologist, went to the Kolbs' attorney's office. There, in the presence of many attorneys, the Kolb family, and a court reporter, the risk manager sat near the Kolbs and focused directly on them. They were told how and why the two medicines were used in the surgery, how the risk manager had saved the pharmaceuticals and sent them for testing, and what the tests found. She told them on behalf of the hospital that Martin Memorial accepted full responsibility. This was their error, and it was no one else's. The staff somehow had made a mistake in the transfer process. They are working diligently to make the process safer so that this event never occurred again. She told them sincerely that they were very, very sorry. The attorney escorted them out to another office. It was a very emotional time for everyone. The attorney said he did not know how to respond: The law firm had never had this happen, but they had an obligation to their client. The risk manager, having worked closely with her defense counsel and the insurer, was prepared to respond: "Our defense counsel and insurer are fully informed and are willing to meet with the Kolb family today or as soon as you specify, to try to bring this part of the tragedy to closure. We feel a settlement would be in their best interest."

That evening the Kolb family, their attorney, the risk manager, and the hospital attorney reached a confidential settlement and approved a mutually acceptable press release. The story again could have ended here. Martin Memorial, using the new procedure, would have eliminated one system problem that placed caring, competent professionals in an environment where error occurred. They could try to put this event, their darkest hour, behind them. They could hope as time passed that the OR staff members, manager, and physicians would no longer awaken in the night, no longer doubt their competence, no longer feel that others did not trust them.

"Please don't let this happen to another family. Don't stop, don't ever stop!" These were the words that haunted the risk manager. The picture of Ben's smiling face, bright eyes, and blond hair was a constant reminder that this was not about Martin Memorial, this was about health care as an international industry. This industry had accepted the use of intermediate containers; untold numbers of patients were at risk. Any surgical staff member, given the right circumstances, could make the same error. The risk manager therefore wrote an article for an OR management journal, describing the error and the procedural changes that were developed to keep this type of error from occurring. Copies of the new procedure were offered. Many requests were received.

During 1996, in the months following the error, the American Medical Association was planning what eventually became the first Annenberg Conference on Medical Error, where the National Patient Safety Foundation was officially announced. The insurer of Martin Memorial was on the committee planning the conference. When the committee needed a case study, Ben's story was considered.

In October 1996, Ben's story was told to a hushed audience of 300-plus researchers, clinicians, and concerned citizens. Several other journal articles followed. Lectures were given 12 times a year. Ben's story began a journey of many years as the face of health care and the mystique of medical error went through radical changes.

The calls began. Five calls were received in which risk managers, insurers, and attorneys who had heard about Ben were inquiring to see if their cases, all children having ear surgery, were similar to Ben's experience. Four were. They were from all over the country, the children ranging from 4 to 7 years of age. They did not survive. The fifth call was about a young girl having ear surgery. Her pulse and blood pressure rose. Her nurses called the risk manager, who called Martin Memorial's risk manager for guidance. She was reminded what the investigation had found. In real time, the team was told and was able to realize it had made the same mistake. Now they knew the treatment had to be different. The child lived.

Ben's family supported continued reference to their tragedy. In return they have witnessed a sea change in operating room procedures and patient safety. They are grateful that other families have been spared their loss. That is Ben's story.

Ben's legacy will serve as an inspiring example of the value of system analysis and the futility of a culture that places blame. Safety is being redefined for patients. The environment of health care delivery is in the international spotlight. Error is no longer the other person's problem or the other institution's problem: Error is everywhere. The discovery, reporting, and proper management of error have great value. All must learn to embrace error and hold it up for the world to see. Hold it up, and the world will change.

CHAPTER TWENTY-SEVEN

ADDRESSING CLINICIAN PERFORMANCE PROBLEMS AS A SYSTEMS ISSUE

John A. Fromson, MD

Systems issues can contribute to addressing clinical performance problems. Suboptimal clinical performance can be related to knowledge and skill deficits or the result of health-related issues. Barring an underlying organic etiology to the problem, such as dementia, various knowledge and skill deficits can usually be addressed with educational or remediation activities. Yet, like the general population, practitioners are also susceptible to psychoactive substance use disorders, mental health issues, and physical illness and disability. Left untreated, these conditions can interfere with professional performance. Knowledge and skill deficits, as well as a clinician's illness, can be mediated or influenced by the context or system in which they take place.

Practice setting systems, from major academic teaching centers to private office venues, are sometimes unable to respond to suboptimal performance in a proactive, timely, and decisive way. The reasons for this are multifold. The practitioner's problem may be difficult to detect at an early stage when the ability to practice is not affected. In addition, the institution may have organizational, supervisory, and economic issues that serve as barriers to an effective administrative response to the problem. This chapter looks at how addressing substandard performance can be influenced by systems issues.

In institutional settings, deficits in knowledge or in specific skills are usually identified by clinical supervisors or by risk managers utilizing quality improvement thresholds. When administrative procedural thresholds, such as timely dictation, or clinical thresholds, such as mortality, have not been met, the data can be deidentified and shared in a group setting, or outliers can be given feedback on an individual basis. Because of the difficulty of giving constructive feedback to a colleague, this process is one of the more administratively challenging tasks that a chief of service or a department head faces. However, a factor that helps facilitate the process is that there is usually a staff person at the institution whose responsibility is to monitor these indices. It is also required by the Joint Commission on Accreditation of Healthcare Organizations (JCAHO) and other certifying organizations, so that the institutionalization of this process has been going on for decades.

Constructive feedback is usually enough to engage the practitioner to take corrective action. If a specific clinical procedure or outcome measure such as infection rate persists, the institution can recommend specific educational programs with the hopes that outcomes will improve. If these fail, the institution then has the option of engaging assessment and remediation programs.[1] Using psychometric testing, chart reviews, observed clinical examinations of standardized patients, and fund-of-knowledge testing, the assessments are designed to ascertain the etiology of the problem. If it is due to knowledge or skill deficits, a remediation plan is devised. If the problem is found to be secondary to an illness, appropriate treatment or counseling the clinician out of the field may take place. When a physician does not comply with recommendations for performance enhancement, administrative sanctions such as restriction or suspension of clinical privileges may be necessary.

Currently, the Federation of State Medical Boards and the National Board of Medical Examiners have instituted a testing protocol, the Special Purpose Examination (SPEX). If the physician in question fails the exam, he or she is referred to the Colorado Personalized Education Program (CPEP) at the Institute for Physician Evaluation for a comprehensive assessment. Physicians can also go to the CPEP program without taking this test or having respective state medical board involvement. If deficits are detected, an educational remediation program can then be recommended.

A much more complex and difficult situation arises when a practitioner, such as a physician, is not falling short of quality improvement thresholds, but manifests aberrant behavior that has the *potential* to place patients and other staff at risk for harm. While most medical staff bylaws are written in such a way as to give wide latitude towards interpreting the seriousness of these kinds of behaviors, the lack of clear thresholds makes it much more difficult for an administrative response to be initiated. Thus, it may be easier for a system to respond to a health care professional who clearly crosses thresholds of performance based on knowledge or skill, than it is to respond to one who has subtle manifestations of a substance use disorder, mental or physical illness, or behavioral problem.

Psychoactive substance use disorders occur generally at the same rate in health care professionals as they do in the general population.[2] Interestingly enough, for physicians, problems associated with alcohol use actually increase with age, as opposed to the general population, where they decrease.[3] Why this is so is not clear. Yet, throughout a physician's active professional life, a significant amount of time and energy is directed toward developing clinical competence, savvy, and acumen. This can come at the exclusion of cultivating and nurturing interpersonal relationships. If one enters middle and late adulthood and begins to limit the number of hours practicing medicine, it can be hypothesized that there is more time for intimacy, especially with a significant other. The very short-term disinhibiting effect of alcohol may be used to facilitate closeness with a loved one. Conversely, the longer term sedating effects may contribute to avoiding intimacy altogether. Perhaps this contributes to the age-related increase in alcohol-related problems among physicians.

In active clinical practice, stress, isolation, accessibility, family history, and chronic medical conditions such as ongoing pain, contribute to drug and alcohol use.[4] As one becomes more addicted and physiologically dependent on psychoactive substances, relationships and activities begin to become impaired. First, spousal or significant other relationships deteriorate, followed in turn by nuclear family member relationships, extended family member relationships, friends, extracurricular-type activities, community and religious involvement, and the last area to be affected is professional practice. The drug of choice may determine the timeframe for identification. For example, a short-acting synthetic narcotic analgesic such as sufentanil may take weeks to months before impairing the ability to practice. At the other end of the spectrum, detection in the workplace of alcohol use could take years.

In the practice setting, avoidance in confronting or reporting a colleague can also be secondary to denial of observing colleagues or to over-identification with the physician who has a problem. In the latter case, peers are reluctant to intervene as they are all too familiar with the rigors associated with achieving professional credentials and subsequent success and feel they do not want to "punish" their flailing colleague. They also feel doing it would be too emotionally painful for them, at once mindful that inactivity in the face of the risk of harm to patients is inexcusable.

Illustrating this point is a 42-year-old cardiologist[5] found to have alcohol on her breath while engaging in an office-based practice. While her practice partner acknowledged the problem after it was brought to his attention by office staff, it took two more episodes and an inquiry by a patient before she was referred to the state's physician health program. During the referral process, the practice partner acknowledged that he was fearful to do anything, even as he was mindful of the risk to patients, because he had had trouble successfully hiring for his partner's position. He also depended on the practice partner for coverage and handling the large caseload of referred patients with cardiac problems. He was given positive reinforcement for trying to get help for his colleague. However, he had a difficult time appreciating that loss of revenue and the added stress of not having full coverage paled in comparison to a bad outcome with harm to a patient due to his ambivalence in referring the physician for help.

The changes that take place with drug or alcohol use over time are subtle. There seems to be a very thin line that is crossed between being a productive practitioner and one that is beginning to go down the slippery slope of addiction. It takes an astute observer to pick out these subtle changes in their early stages. Finally, when the point is reached where there are overt manifestations of impairment in terms of the ability to practice medicine, interventions are usually made. These manifestations can occur on many levels:

- *Personal:* Deteriorating hygiene, accidents, inappropriate behavior, excessive prescriptions for self and family members, and escalating emotional crises
- *In home and family:* Behavior excused by family and friends, drinking activities given priority, arguments, violent outbursts, sexual problems, withdrawal from family, fragmentation, neglect of children, financial crises, separation or divorce, unexplained absences at home
- *With friends and community:* Personal isolation, embarrassing behavior, drunk driving arrests, legal problems, neglect of social commitments, inappropriate spending
- *In the office:* Workaholic behavior (which may be seen as role modeling by colleagues), disorganized scheduling, unreasonable behavior with patients and staff, frequent absences, excessive prescriptions for drugs, excessive ordering of drug supplies, frequent complaints, prolonged breaks, and alcohol on the breath[6]

It is only when these later signs are manifested and patients are placed at risk that colleagues are mobilized into action to intervene.

Psychiatric and physical illness may present in a similar fashion and engender the same reluctance on the part of colleagues to intervene. Often the only early signs are mental status and physical changes that slowly manifest and progressively worsen over time, as illustrated by the following case.

A 54-year-old surgeon began making negativistic and inappropriate comments to the hospital staff. At the same time, he initiated "midnight rounds," claiming, "I'm not tired, so we should see the patients now and I can get started early with surgery." Inability to fall asleep, agitation, negativistic behavior, and later lewd and problematic comments to patients were the early signs of a manic phase of bipolar illness. Despite the knowledge by the chief of his department of these overt stigmata of a mood disorder, there was no attempt to confront this physician until he was pulled over for speeding and arrested after assaulting a police officer. After inpatient hospitalization, outpatient treatment is now monitored by the state physician health program. When questioned, the department chief commented that at his community hospital he had taken on the administrative role of chief on a voluntary, unpaid, rotating basis. He felt he had no real supervisory authority over this physician since the physician was not an employee of the hospital but "just" had attending privileges there. He also commented that he and others were willing to give the physician in question the "benefit of the doubt" because the revenue the affected physician generated for the hospital was crucial during a particularly trying financial time the institution was experiencing.

Also difficult to stop or prevent in its early stages are repetitive verbalizations, deeds, or actions that are not the result of what one would usually refer to as easily recognizable mental illness, but have the potential to be a detriment to patient care. These physicians are often referred to as "disruptive" and manifest inappropriate anger, blaming, threatening, uncooperative, and unprofessional behavior. They often have an underlying personality disorder and see themselves as always "right" and the rest of the world as "wrong."

An example is a 72-year-old obstetrician-gynecologist with a large and lucrative practice who would use profanity when under stress during routine or difficult hospital procedures. When told that his words were negatively affecting the work environment, he responded by saying that the lack of staff support was responsible for the undue stress he was experiencing and that he had to say what he did to get the operating team to respond to critical situations. In essence, he felt he behaved the way he did in the interest of patient care. Only when nurse retention was at stake did the administration take action and require him to attend a physician health program–sponsored anger management course. He also voluntarily entered into psychotherapy.

Whether clinical performance problems arise from knowledge or skill deficits, health concerns such as psychoactive substance use disorders, mental or physical illness, or be a behavioral issue, early intervention that can result in treatment and recovery are difficult to initiate because of the subtle signs and symptoms of the underlying problem and by system barriers. The latter can range from administrative inactivity due to denial and over-identification with the affected professional, to over-reliance on formal professional relationships such as partnership and the need to provide patients with coverage. Administrative barriers at this level may also include an open staff model where there is a paucity of direct supervision and accountability. This can be seen when there is a voluntary, rotating, supervisory administrative position such as a chief of a department, who may be dependent on the physician in crisis. Economic dependency may also contribute to inactivity.

A model for identifying the source of professional performance problems and the strategy to correct them is similar to the various proposed confidential near miss reporting systems used for medical errors. However, instead of looking at a specific error or harmful event, the focus can be placed on the health care professional such as a physician. There are physician health programs in all 50 states. There are also similar programs for nurses and other health care professionals as well. Most physician programs are designed to help identify, refer to treatment, guide, and monitor physicians with psychoactive substance use disorders. Most also deal with physicians who have mental or physical illness, or behavior issues. Where there has been no risk of harm to patients, many state licensing boards of registration in medicine allow physicians to be referred to these peer review protected (and hence confidential) programs in lieu of a board administrative response. In essence, this is very similar to a voluntary near miss medical error reporting system, where medical errors that do no harm are reported to a confidential data repository. Where there is patient harm, those reports are made to a governmental regulatory agency. The difference here is that instead of reporting a specific error or harmful event, it is a physician who is the entity being referred. Not only is the physician referred to appropriate treatment and monitored so he or she can return to practice, but de-identified data are compiled and shared among physician health programs for educational and preventative purposes.[7]

Effective January 1, 2001, JCAHO has required that hospital organizations have their medical staff implement a process to identify and manage matters of individual physician health, which is separate from the medical and staff disciplinary function. The intent of the JCAHO requirement (Physician Health MS.2.6) is consistent in many aspects to the mission of most physician health programs, which is to assist physicians with health concerns and therefore provide protections to patients. In this regard, JCAHO requires medical staff and organization leaders to design a process that provides education about physician health, addresses prevention of physical, psychiatric, or emotional illness, and facilitates confidential diagnosis, treatment, and rehabilitation of physicians from a potentially impairing condition.

As JCAHO provides, the purpose of the process is assistance and rehabilitation, rather than discipline, to aid a physician in retaining or regaining optimal professional functioning, consistent with protection of patients. If at any time during the diagnosis, treatment, or rehabilitation phase of the process it is determined that a physician is unable to safely perform the privileges he or she has been granted, the matter is forwarded to medical staff leadership for appropriate corrective action, which includes strict adherence to any state or federally mandated reporting requirements.

The process design should include:

- Education of the medical staff and other organization staff about illness and impairment recognition issues specific to physicians;
- Self-referral by a physician and referral by other organization staff;
- Referral of the affected physician to the appropriate professional internal or external resources for diagnosis and treatment of the condition or concern;
- Maintenance of the confidentiality of the physician seeking referral or referred for assistance, except as limited by law, ethical obligation, or when the safety of a patient is threatened;
- Evaluation of the credibility of a complaint, allegation, or concern;
- Monitoring of the affected physician and the safety of patients until the rehabilitation or any disciplinary process is complete;
- Reporting to the medical staff leadership instances in which a physician is providing unsafe treatment.[8]

Physicians' performance problems can be the result of knowledge and skill deficits, psychoactive substance use disorders, mental and physical illness, or behavioral problems. Barriers to taking early and decisive intervention leading to referral for remediation or assessment, treatment, and monitoring can be related to systems issues. These include practice setting, supervisory and collegial relationships, and economic associations. Assessment and physician health programs can assist both the individual physician and systems experiencing these difficulties.

Notes

1. Physician Prescribed Educational Program (PPEP) Syracuse, NY (315) 464-6997.

Colorado Personalized Education for Physicians (CPEP), Denver, CO (303) 750-7150.

2. Flaherty, J.A., Richman, J.A. 1993. Substance use and addiction among medical students, residents and physicians. *Psychiatric Clinics of North America.* *16*(1): 189–97.

3. Ibid.

4. Farley, W.J. 1992. Addiction and the anaesthesia resident. *Can Journal Anaesth. 39*(5) R11.

5. Cases have been de-identified to protect confidentiality.

6. Physicians Recovery Network—Alabama Physicians Health Program.

7. To access more information about state physician health programs, contact the Federation of State Physician Health Programs at www.ama-assn.org.

8. Physician Health Services, Inc., a Massachusetts Medical Society subsidiary, at www.physicianhealth.org.

CHAPTER TWENTY-EIGHT

ADVANCING PATIENT AND HEALTH CARE WORKER SAFETY BY PREVENTING INFECTIONS

Tammy Lundstrom, MD, Judene Bartley, MS, MPH, CIC and Gina Pugliese, RN, MS

With the publication of the landmark 1999 Institute of Medicine (IOM) report *To Err Is Human: Building a Safer Health System,*[1] much attention has been drawn to the subject of medical errors. The report shocked the public by estimating that medical errors are the eighth leading cause of death in the United States, higher than motor vehicle accidents or breast cancer. Numerous studies of medical errors were reviewed in the IOM report. Overall, errors related to medications constituted approximately 20% of all errors, while infections accounted for approximately 15% of errors. Much attention has been focused on medication errors; less has been focused on the already broad body of research regarding improving patient safety through infection control practices outlined in the literature. Given that infections are a major cause of breaches in patient safety, this chapter focuses on the relationship between infection control initiatives and patient and worker safety. Three aspects of infection control and safety interactions are explored:

- Handwashing, one of the most important means to prevent infections in patients, is discussed as an example of an intervention that requires alteration of human behavior to improve compliance.
- The link between staffing and patient safety, perhaps best evidenced in the infection control literature, is reviewed.

- An examination of the experience with implementation of needleless intravenous delivery systems highlights the importance of attending to health care worker and patient outcomes following interventions affecting both populations. An apparent improvement in health care worker safety may or may not result in safer patient outcomes.

Handwashing

The association between the hand hygiene of health care workers and patient safety has been recognized for over 150 years. In 1847, Semmelweis noted that patients delivering babies outside the hospital were less likely to die of puerpural sepsis than mothers who delivered babies inside the Vienna Lying-in Hospital. As a result, he theorized that infectious agents were being spread to patients via health care workers' hands. Once a program of handwashing with chlorinated lime was instituted, cases of puerperal sepsis declined dramatically.[2]

From a historical perspective, between 1879 through 1986, an additional 423 articles relating specifically to handwashing were published.[3] It is known that handwashing causes a significant reduction in the carriage of potential pathogens on the hands.[4] It is better accepted that handwashing can result in reductions in nosocomial (hospital-acquired) infections[5,6] as well as infections in other settings, such as day care, schools, and the community.[4,7,8]

Handwashing Compliance Rates

It is widely accepted that practicing good hand hygiene is the single most important means to prevent the spread of infection.[8,9] Despite this evidence, readily acknowledged by most health care professionals, rates of compliance with hand hygiene programs in hospitals remain low (e.g., 25% to 50%) and vary with the setting.[10-14] Reasons often given for lack of compliance include lack of time, skin irritation, doubt regarding effectiveness, and the perception that peers are not compliant.[3,15] Compliance has also been shown to vary with job title. In one study, overall compliance was 48%; however, rates varied from a high of 52% among nurses to a low of 30% among physicians.[16]

Handwashing and Staffing

An observational study in a teaching hospital in Switzerland associated understaffing with poor handwashing compliance.[16] Compliance was seen in nearly half of the directly observed opportunities for handwashing. Compliance rates were higher for nurses compared with physicians, as has been demonstrated in many other handwashing studies. In addition, compliance was higher during weekdays versus weekends and on general medicine wards versus intensive care units (ICUs), but decreased when the activity index increased, suggesting that understaffing may play a role in decreasing hand hygiene compliance.

Human Factors Engineering and Interventions

Sustained compliance with improved hand hygiene is difficult to achieve. Human factors engineering, or the study of interrelationships between humans, the tools they use, and the environments in which they live and work, is applicable to the study of handwashing behavior. New products, such as waterless hand hygiene agents, can save time;[17] however, even with conveniently located dispensers, compliance has been inconsistent.[18,19] In one study, increased handwashing compliance with the use of a waterless agent resulted in a decrease in overall nosocomial infection rates—evidence that improved handwashing can improve patient safety.[20]

Multiple Interventions

Approaches to improve handwashing with a single intervention such as staff education, feedback of rates, and increasing the availability of automated sinks have proven largely unsuccessful by themselves.[21] Several studies suggest that a multifaceted approach that includes new technologies or products, administrative support, and the use of role models and feedback is necessary to a successful and sustained improvement.[21-24]

One creative approach for improving handwashing compliance parallels recommendations for improving medication safety. Those recommendations involve education of the patient regarding his or her role in medication safety, including questioning of health care providers regarding prescribed and dispensed medications to reduce the risk of error. A similar approach was used to create a patient awareness program that encouraged patients to remind their caregivers about handwashing and was found to increase handwashing compliance.[25] In the outpatient arena, a program educating seniors to wash their hands, which also provided convenient belt packs with waterless hand rubs, decreased the respiratory infection rate among attendees at a senior day care center.[26]

Multiple interventions are usually needed to improve and sustain handwashing compliance. Larson and colleagues compared two organizations for sustained improvements in hand hygiene behavior by involving top-level management in multiple interventions that emphasized creating a culture in which handwashing was a clear expectation. They concluded that an organization's leadership and a safety culture of handwashing behavior were essential for effective and sustained improvements in compliance. The same study demonstrated a statistically significant reduction in the rates of infection with a drug-resistant organism (vancomycin-resistant enterococci) with sustained improvements in handwashing compliance.[27]

Clearly, the evidence linking improved handwashing and reduction in nosocomial infection risk exists. The challenge remains to further improve patient safety by identifying the most effective strategies that increase and sustain hand hygiene compliance rates.

Staffing

Evidence is accumulating regarding the links between patient care staffing ratios and staffing mix and patient safety. Of approximately 21 studies on staffing published since 1981, 50% are reported in the infection control literature. The Joint Commission on Accreditation of Healthcare Organizations (JCAHO) has examined this issue with regard to the setting of minimum staffing standards for nursing as well as ancillary personnel.[28] The association between staffing ratios and the acquisition of nosocomial infections has been reported in a number of studies. Most of these studies are retrospective in nature and were initiated as a result of noting an increase in infection rates in an intensive care unit setting. Although infection risk is often hard to ascribe to a single factor, and staffing issues pose additional complexities, it is clear that an association between staffing and infection risk does exist.

Infection Risk and Staffing

Neonatal Unit

Some of the earliest studies on the association between staffing and patient safety were prompted by outbreaks of nosocomial infection in neonatal nurseries that led to the deaths of several neonates from staphylococcal infections.[29] Patients in these units are highly susceptible to infection and at risk from cross-contamination from inadequate infection control measures; lack of handwashing was cited as a risk factor in many of these outbreaks.

In an investigation of a neonatal outbreak, four risk factors were identified in a preliminary analysis: bathing with chlorhexidine, admission during summer months, overcrowding, and understaffing. The nurse workload was defined as the number of infants at daily census divided by the number of nurses working the night shift. There were a total of 299 cases of *Staphylococcus aureus* infection, 41% of which occurred prior to discharge. Understaffing was the most powerful factor associated with nosocomial *S. aureus* infection. The infection rates during the outbreak period were 16 times higher after periods of understaffing than during other periods. The rate of clustered infections after periods of overcrowding was 7 times higher than during other periods. This landmark study did not attempt to correlate the infection risk with staffing experience or skill mix.[29]

Neonatal Intensive Care Units

A second study by the same investigator published in 1995 found that even colonization rates (not infection) by methicillin-resistant *S. aureus* (MRSA) were increased during periods of understaffing and overcrowding in a neonatal intensive care unit.[30] This study was unique in that it was a prospective surveillance study for nosocomial colonization. Again, no efforts were made to quantify skill mix or training.

In another neonatal ICU investigation of an outbreak of eight cases of *Enterobacter cloacae* infection, the infection rate in the pre-outbreak period was 0.86 infections per 1,000 patient-days versus 5.73 infections during the outbreak period.[31] The rate of compliance with handwashing was roughly equivalent during the outbreak and nonoutbreak periods. The maximum bed number recommended for the unit was 15, but occupancy was exceeded by 50% during the outbreak period. A Project Research in Nursing (a Canadian information system for managing nurse staffing) system calculated staffing needs at 35, but only 20 staff were present during the outbreak period. Not only was the relative risk for *E. cloacae* higher during all periods of overcrowding and understaffing, but the risk for bloodstream infections from all organisms was also increased during these periods. As with most outbreaks, multiple interventions were implemented simultaneously. In this case, termination of the outbreak was associated with enforcement of universal precautions, use of single-dose vials, and a decreased census.

Pediatric Cardiac Care

An outbreak of *Serratia marcescens* infection was investigated in a pediatric cardiac intensive care unit (CICU).[32] A retrospective study was then initiated to assess fluctuations in staffing and their correlation with nosocomial infection rates, utilizing Centers for Disease Control and Prevention (CDC) definitions for bloodstream infections. Data on total numbers of hours worked by CICU nurses each month stratified by level of training were collected, including extra hours worked during longer shifts and overtime. The central venous catheter–associated bloodstream infection (CVC-BSI) rate was 6.5 infections per 1,000 catheter-days. The median monthly nursing hours to patient-day ratio was 15.2:1. The increased patient density and decreased ratio of nursing hours to patient days were associated with nosocomial infection risk. Although the investigators considered nursing skill level, there was no correlation between level of experience and nosocomial infection risk.

Burn Unit

An increase in MRSA colonization and infection among burn patients prompted an investigation to determine the cause.[33] It was found that the cases of MRSA were clustered during peak occupancy. There were 2.5 cases of infection or colonization per 100 patient-days during peak occupancy periods, compared with 0.83 cases per 100 patient-days for other periods. The investigators found that the risk for colonization with MRSA paralleled nurse overtime and the use of temporary staff.

An earlier study of *E. cloacae* infection in a burn unit found dramatic differences in infection and colonization rates in the pre-outbreak and outbreak periods—27.4% versus 50%, respectively.[34] In the pre-outbreak period, the hours of nursing care per patient per shift were 20% above the optimum level as previously defined by the nursing service. However, during the outbreak period, staffing rates fell to 30% to 34% below normal, meeting their definition of a staffing shortage. The outbreak was terminated when the number of nurses was increased.

Adult Intensive Care Units

Fridkin and colleagues utilized several study designs during an investigation of CVC-BSI in a surgical intensive care unit (SICU).[35] First, a case-control study was carried out on all patients who developed a CVC-BSI during the study period to identify risk factors specific to the development of bloodstream infections. Next, a cohort study was conducted on all SICU patients during the study period. Nursing hours worked and patient census were used to calculate monthly patient-to-nurse ratios during the cohort study. These calculations only considered registered nurses, because the ratios for licensed practical nurses and medical assistants were constant throughout the study. The rate of SICU CVC-BSIs correlated with patient-to-nurse ratios. An increased patient-to-nurse ratio of 1.40 during the study period was observed, compared with 1.18 during the pre-outbreak period. Evaluation by logistic regression analysis confirmed the association between CVC-BSI and higher patient-to-nurse ratios.

Another intensive care unit study in a tertiary care hospital found that the incidence of new cases of MRSA correlated with peaks of nursing staff workload and times of reduced nurse-to-patient ratios within the unit.[36]

Robert and coworkers reported the results of surveillance for primary bloodstream infections in a 20-bed SICU in a large inner-city university-affiliated teaching hospital. This was a landmark study because of its prospective design.[37] During the study period, all nurses providing care were registered nurses. Nurse-to-patient ratios were calculated for both the regular nurses and the pool (agency or temporary) nurses. Researchers found that the BSI rate per 1,000 patient-days was 2.8 in a period with a higher regular nurse-to-patient ratio and lower pool (agency or temporary nurses) nurse-to-patient ratio, compared with a BSI rate of 7.6 with a lower regular nurse-to-patient ratio and a higher pool nurse-to-patient ratio. There were no other significant differences between the cases and controls. The regular nurse-to-patient ratio was 8.8 for cases and 9.9 for controls (highly statistically significant at a p value of less than .001). This study suggests that an increased use of pool nurses may increase the risk of BSI in patients in critical care units.

The use of temporary ICU nurse staffing and the risk of BSI has been studied in more detail by the CDC in an ongoing research project as part of its National Nosocomial Infection Surveillance (NNIS) System. Data from this project, the Detailed Intensive Care Unit Surveillance Component (DISC) of NNIS, have shown that a critical factor is the time a nurse spends in a given unit; that is, BSI rates increased when more temporary staff were utilized (unpublished data, presented at Enhancing Working Conditions and Patient Safety: Best Practices conference, Pittsburgh, October 2000).

Nursing Homes

A study in a nursing home in New York state examined outbreaks of patient illness reported to the state health department.[38] During 1992, there were 424 outbreak reports from 692 nursing homes, primarily respiratory or gastrointestinal infections. Although there were no differences between staffing levels of case (those with more than two outbreaks) and control nursing homes, the mean bed capacity for case nursing homes was higher, and each 100-bed increase in size increased the risk for an outbreak 1.7-fold. In addition, there was an increased risk for nursing homes with single patient units (all patients housed in a single location) and for homes with multiple nursing units that shared the same staff. Interestingly, a decreased risk for an outbreak was identified in nursing homes that provided paid sick leave to health care workers, suggesting that removing workers who are ill, often with transmissible illnesses such as gastrointestinal and respiratory infections, will reduce infection risks among patients. This study suggests that both staffing issues and health care worker conditions may affect patient safety.

Summary

Despite the stated limitations of these studies, one can conclude that decreased nurse staffing ratios adversely affect patient safety. Although most of the current retrospective studies were initiated because of an observed increase in infections, several prospective studies support the same association. More prospective, randomized, controlled studies of the effects of staffing are needed, as well as clear definitions of nurse-staffing ratios. Studies variably describe nurse-to-patient ratios, patient-to-nurse ratios, and formula calculations of nurse hours per patient per day. Standardized definitions are necessary to compare results of disparate studies. Furthermore, more recent studies suggest that it is not sufficient to study nurse-to-patient ratios alone without consideration of skill mix, educational level, and time or experience on a specific unit. The optimal staffing ratios as well as staffing mixes are yet to be determined. Finally, unpaid sick leave may actually encourage ill employees to continue working, further endangering patients.

Sharps with Engineered Safety Protection

Interventions that initially improve the safety of either a patient or health care worker population may have unintended outcomes. The implementation of the needleless intravenous (IV) devices used to access IV delivery systems highlights the importance of examining the consequences to both populations when making any change to improve the outcome of one population.

Background

Much attention has been focused on the prevention of blood and body fluid exposures in health care personnel. The use of devices to reduce or eliminate needlestick injuries has been recommended as one of the primary approaches to reduce risk. Recent regulatory and legislative actions have mandated the use of devices with engineered safety features to prevent needlestick injuries.[39,40]

One of the most widely implemented approaches to engineered safety protection is the use of a needleless device to access the IV delivery system (e.g., to administer IV medications or add a second IV line). Currently, some form of needleless system is used in 70% of U.S. hospitals in order to improve health care worker safety; these systems use a variety of designs, including blunt cannula and valve-type devices.[41] Prior to the introduction of these systems, needles used on intravenous tubing were the number one cause of sharps injuries to health care workers.[42,43] Multiple studies have demonstrated the efficacy of these needleless IV access devices in preventing health care worker injuries.[44-55]

Although successful in reducing the risk of needlestick injuries, there have been several reports of an increase in BSIs in patients associated with the use of these devices. One of the first reports by Danzig described an increased number of bloodstream infections in patients receiving intravenous therapy in the home setting for nutritional support. This was found to be the result of changing the needleless device end cap every 7 days instead of every 3 days.[56] Similarly, Do reported an increase in BSIs associated with extending changes of a needleless system from 3 to 7 days. That study also showed that patients who showered without covering their needleless access site were at higher risk for infection.[57] A number of reports described an increased risk of BSI associated with needleless devices due to poor IV site care, lapses in aseptic technique for catheter flushing and intermittent access, and contamination of multiuse saline solution bags used to fill syringes for IV flushes.[58-60]

These studies suggest that lapses in infection control technique, and not the devices per se, contribute to the increased risk of BSI. A number of studies have demonstrated that needleless IV access devices do not increase the risk of infection in patients when properly maintained with aseptic technique for all manipulations.[61,62]

These studies illustrate that patient and employee safety cannot be considered in isolation. Consideration of techniques to improve safety in one arena may lead to increased risks elsewhere in the system; all variables must be considered when measuring patient as well as health care worker outcomes.

Conclusions

This chapter highlights just a few of the areas where infection control investigations have illuminated the relationship between patient and worker outcomes. However, much research is still needed even in this area. Infection control investigators need to partner with experts in human behavior and human factors engineering to identify factors that will improve compliance with handwashing. New technologies that improve hand hygiene, such as waterless products, need to be studied within the context of a safety culture, organizational leadership, and human factors engineering to determine the most effective ways to sustain measurable improvements.

The research on the effects of staffing in relationship to patient safety is in its infancy. Variables needing further study include some of the following: the most accurate and accepted definitions for staffing assessment; evaluation of staffing skill mix, education, and competency; the impact of physician staffing; the impact of trainee programs; and the impact of staffing levels on aspects of patient safety other than infection control. It is hoped that continued research will ultimately assist organizations in determining the optimum staffing ratios that lead to the best patient outcomes.

Employee and patient safety are interrelated, as noted in the effects on workers and patients of implementing a sharps safety system. Efforts to improve safety in one dimension cannot afford to ignore the impact on other aspects of safe care delivery.

Finally, much of the data reported in the studies summarized in this chapter were obtained from ongoing surveillance of infections in hospitals that use the standardized definitions and methodology that are part of the CDC and its Nosocomial Infections Surveillance System.[63] The NNIS surveillance system for hospital-acquired infectious adverse outcomes is the recognized standard throughout the world for data collection, analysis, and interhospital comparisons. It has demonstrated its usefulness in the ability to track decreases in nosocomial infection rates following adoption of evidence-based practices.[64] This surveillance system, established over 25 years ago, is anonymous, nonpunitive, voluntary, and credible and serves as a model upon which patient safety data collection and reporting should be based.

References

1. Kohn, L. et al., eds., *To Err Is Human: Building a Safer Health System* (Washington, DC: Institute of Medicine, National Academy Press, 1999), 1–223.
2. Semmelweis, I. F. "The Etiology, the Concept, and the Prophylaxis of Childbed Fever." In: *Hartleben's Verlag-Expedition, 1861*, ed. C. A. Pest (translated by F. P. Murphy; republished. Birmingham: Classics of Medicine Library, 1981).
3. Larson, E. "A Causal Link Between Handwashing and Risk of Infection? Examination of the Evidence," *Infect Control Hosp Epidemiol* 9, no. 1 (1988):28–36.
4. Larson, E. "Skin Hygiene and Infection Prevention: More of the Same or Different Approaches?" *Clin Infect Dis* 29 (1999):1287–94.
5. Webster, J. et al., "Elimination of *Staphylococcus aureus* from a Neonatal Intensive Care Unit After Handwashing with Triclosan," *J Paediatr Child Health* 30 (1999):59–64.
6. Zafar, A. B. et al., "Use of 0.3% Triclosan (Bactistat) to Eradicate an Outbreak of *Staphylococcus aureus* in a Neonatal Nursery," *Am J Infect Control* 23 (1999):200–8.
7. Hugonnet, S. et al., "Hand Hygiene Revisited: Lessons from the Past and Present," *Current Infectious Disease Reports* 2 (2000):484–9.

8. Larson, E. "APIC Guideline for Handwashing and Hand Antisepsis in Healthcare Settings (Review)," *Am J Infect Control* 23 (1995):251–69.

9. Bauer, T. M. et al., "An Epidemiologic Study Assessing the Relative Importance of Airborne and Direct Contact Transmission of Microorganisms in a Medical Intensive Care Unit," *J Hosp Infect* 15 (1990):301–9.

10. Albert, R. K., and Condie, F. "Handwashing Patterns in Medical Intensive Care Units," *N Engl J Med* 304 (1981):1465.

11. Jarvis, W. R. "Handwashing—the Semmelweis Lesson Forgotten?" *Lancet* 1344 (1994):1311–12.

12. Khatib, M. et al., "Hand Washing and Use of Gloves While Managing Patient Receiving Mechanical Ventilation in the ICU," *Chest* 116 (1999):172–5.

13. Thompson, B. L. et al., "Handwashing and Glove Use in a Long Term Care Facility," *Infect Control Hosp Epidemiol* 18 (1997):97–103.

14. Sproat, L. J., and Inglis, T. J. "A Multicenter Survey of Hand Hygiene Practice in Intensive Care Units," *J Hosp Infect* 26 (1994):137–48.

15. Weeks, A. "Why I Don't Wash My Hands Between Each Patient Contact," *BMJ* 319 (1999):518.

16. Pittet, D. et al., "Compliance with Handwashing in a Teaching Hospital," *Ann Intern Med* 130, no. 2 (1999):126–30.

17. Voss, A. et al., "No Time for Handwashing? Handwashing Versus Alcohol Rub: Can We Afford 100% Compliance?" *Infect Control Hosp Epidemiol* 18 (1997):205–8.

18. Muto, C. A. et al., " Hand Hygiene Rates Unaffected by Installation of Dispensers of a Rapidly Acting Hand Antiseptic," *Am J Infect Control* 28 (2000):273–6.

19. Bischoff, W. E. et al., "Handwashing Compliance by Healthcare Workers: The Impact of Introducing an Accessible, Alcohol-Based Hand Antiseptic," *Arch Intern Med* 160 (2000):1017–21.

20. Pittet, D. et al., "Effectiveness of a Hospital-Wide Programme to Improve Compliance with Hand Hygiene," *Lancet* 356 (2000):1307–12.

21. Dubbert, P. M. et al., "Increasing ICU Staff Handwashing: Effects of Education and Group Feedback," *Infect Control Hosp Epidemiol* 11 (1990):191–3.

22. Gruendemann, B. J., and Larson, E. L. "Antisepsis in Current Practice." In: *Disinfection, Sterilization, and Antisepsis in Health Care,* ed. W. A. Rutala (Washington, DC: Association for Professionals in Infection Control and Epidemiology, and Champlain, NY: Polyscience Publications, 1988), chap 17. Proceedings of the International Symposium on Disinfection, Sterilization and Antisepsis in Health Care, New Orleans, LA, June 12–13, 1997.

23. Graham, M. "Frequency and Duration of Hand Washing in an Intensive Care Unit," *Am J Infect Control* 18 (1990):77–81.

24. Tibballs, J. "Teaching Hospital Medical Staff to Handwash," *Med J Aust* 164 (1996):395–8.

25. McGuckin, M. et al., "Patient Education Model for Increasing Handwashing Compliance," *Am J Infect Control* 27 (1999):309–14.

26. Falsey, A. R. et al., "Evaluation of a Handwashing Intervention to Reduce Respiratory Illness Rates in Senior Day-Care Centers," *Infect Control Hosp Epidemiol* 20 (1999):200–2.
27. Larson, E. et al., "An Organizational Climate Intervention Associated with Increased Handwashing and Decreased Nosocomial Infections," *Behavioral Medicine* 26 (2000):14–22.
28. Joint Commission on Accreditation of Healthcare Organizations, *Comprehensive Accreditation Manual for Hospitals: The Official Handbook* (Oakbrook Terrace, IL: JCAHO Press, 2000).
29. Haley, R. W., and Bergman, D. A. "The Role of Understaffing and Overcrowding in Recurrent Outbreaks of Staphylococcal Infection in a Neonatal Special-Care Unit," *J Infect Dis* 145, no. 6 (1982):875–85.
30. Haley, R. W. et al., "Eradication of Endemic Methicillin-Resistant *Staphylococcus Aureus* Infections from a Neonatal Intensive Care Unit," *J Infect Dis* 17, no. 3 (1995):614–23.
31. Harbarth, S. et al., "Outbreak of *Enterobacter cloacae* Related to Understaffing, Overcrowding, and Poor Hygiene Practices," *Infect Control Hosp Epidemiol* 20 (1999):598–603.
32. Archibald, L. K. et al., "Patient Density, Nurse-to-Patient Ratio, and Nosocomial Infection Risk in a Pediatric Cardiac Intensive Care Unit," *Pediatr Infect Dis J* 16, no. 11 (1997):1045–8.
33. Arnow, P. M. et al., "Control of Methicillin-Resistant *Staphylococcus aureus* in a Burn Unit: Role of Nurse Staffing," *Journal of Trauma* 22, no. 11 (1982):954–9.
34. Mayhall, C. G. et al., "*Enterobacter cloacae* in a Burn Center: Epidemiology and Control of an Outbreak," *J Infect Dis* 1139, no. 2 (1979):166–71.
35. Fridkin, S. K. et al., "The Role of Understaffing in Central Venous Catheter-Associated Bloodstream Infections," *Infect Control Hosp Epidemiol* 17 (1996):150–8.
36. Vicca, A. F. "Nursing Staff Workload as a Determinant of Methicillin-Resistant *Staphylococcus aureus* Spread in an Adult Intensive Therapy Unit," *J Hosp Infect* 43 (2000):78–80.
37. Robert, J. et al., "The Influence of the Nursing Staff on Primary Bloodstream Infection Rates in a Surgical Intensive Care Unit," *Infect Control Hosp Epidemiol* 21 (2000):12–7.
38. Li, J. et al., "The Impact of Institution Size, Staffing Patterns, and Infection Control Practices on Communicable Disease Outbreaks in New York State Nursing Homes," *Am J Epidemiol* 143 (1996):1042–49.
39. Occupational Safety and Health Administration, Department of Labor, "Occupational Exposure to Bloodborne Pathogens; Final Rule," 29 CFR § 1910.1030. 56 *Fed Reg* 64004–182 (1991).
40. Pub Law No. 106-430, Needlestick Safety and Prevention Act (HR 5178), November 6, 2000.
41. Pugliese, G. et al., "Selecting Sharps Injury Prevention Products." In: *Medical Device Manufacturing and Technology,* ed. E. Cooper (London: World Markets Research Centre, 2000), 57–64.
42. Jagger, J. et al., "Rates of Needlestick Injury Caused by Various Devices in a University Hospital," *New Engl J Med* 319 (1988):284–8.

43. Jagger, J. "Estimated Incremental Costs of Safety Features by Device Type and Percentage of Market Using Safety Devices," *Adv Exp Prev* 3 (1998):55.

44. Gartner, K. "Impact of a Needleless Intravenous System in a University Hospital," *Am J Infect Control* 20 (1992):75–9.

45. L'Ecuyer, P. B. et al., "Randomized Prospective Study of the Impact of Three Needleless Intravenous Systems on Needlestick Injury Rates," *Infect Control Hosp Epidemiol* 17 (1996):803–8.

46. Yassi, A. et al., "Efficacy and Cost Effectiveness of a Needleless Intravenous Access System," *Am J Infect Control* 23 (1995):57–64.

47. Lawrence, L. W. et al., "The Effectiveness of a Needleless Intravenous Connection System: An Assessment by Injury Rate and User Satisfaction," *Infect Control Hosp Epidemiol* 18 (1997):175–182.

48. Ippolito, G. et al., "Device-Specific Risk of Needlestick Injury in Italian Healthcare Workers," *JAMA* 272 (1994):607–10.

49. Beason, R. et al., "Evaluation of a Needle-Free Intravenous Access System," *J Intraven Nursing* 15 (1992):11–6.

50. Skolnick, R. et al., "Evaluation and Implementation of a Needleless Intravenous System: Making Needlesticks a Needleless Problem." *Am J Infect Control* 21 (1993):39–41.

51. Rutkowski, J., and Peterson, S. I. "A Needleless Intravenous System: An Effective Risk Management Strategy [Reader's Forum]," *Infect Control Hosp Epidemiol* 14 (1993):226–7.

52. Wolfrum, J. "A Follow-up Evaluation to a Needle-Free IV System," *Nursing Management* 125 (1994):33–5.

53. Orenstein, R. "The Benefits and Limitations of Needle Protectors and Needleless Intravenous Systems," *J Intraven Nurs* 22 (1999):122–8.

54. Orenstein, R. et al., "Do Protective Devices Prevent Needlestick Injuries Among Healthcare Workers?" *Am J Infect Control* 23 (1995):3344–51.

55. Mendelson, M. H. et al., "Study of a Needleless Intermittent Intravenous-Access System for Peripheral Infusions: Analysis of Staff, Patient, and Institutional Outcomes," *Infect Control Hosp Epidemiol* 19 (1998):401–6.

56. Danzig, L. E. et al., "Bloodstream Infections Associated with a Needleless Intravenous Infusion System in Patient Receiving Home Infusion Therapy," *JAMA* 273 (1995):1862–4.

57. Do, A. et al., "Evaluation of the Role of Needleless Devices in Blood Stream Infections," paper presented at the annual meeting of the Society for Microbiology, 36th Interscience Conference on Antimicrobial Chemotherapy, New Orleans LA, September 1996, Abstract J61.

58. Kellerman, S. et al., "Bloodstream Infections in Home Infusion Patients, the Influence of Race and Needleless Intravascular Access Devices," *J Pediatr* 129 (1996):711–7.

59. McDonald, L. C. et al., "Line-Associated Bloodstream Infections in Pediatric Intensive Care Unit Patients Associated with a Needleless Device and Intermittent Intravenous Therapy," *Infect Control Hosp Epidemiol* 19 (1998):772–7.

60. Chodoff, A. et al., "Polymicrobial Gram-Negative Bacteremia Associated with Saline Solution Flush Used with a Needleless Intravenous System," *Am J Infect Control* 23 (1997):357–63.

61. Adams, K. S. et al., "Comparison of a Needleless System with Conventional Heparin Locks," *Am J Infect Control* 21 (1993):263–9.

62. Rossingol, J. "Interlink Needleless IV Access System—Hospital Conversion to a Needleless IV Access System Achieved Through Valuable Industry Linkages," *Can Intravenous Nurses Assoc J* 9 (1993):12–15.

63. Centers for Disease Control and Prevention, "Monitoring Hospital-Acquired Infections to Promote Patient Safety—United States, 1990–1999," *MMWR Morb Mortal Wkly Rep* 49, no. 8 (2000):149–53.

64. Centers for Disease Control and Prevention, "National Nosocomial Infections Surveillance (NNIS) System Report, Data Summary from January 1992–April 2000, Issued June 2000," *Am J Infect Control* 28, no. 6 (2000):429–448.

CHAPTER TWENTY-NINE

THE BALDRIGE APPROACH TO PATIENT SAFETY

Diane R. Weber, RN, BSN, MHA

Error Reduction in a Quality Improvement Framework

Since the 1999 Institute of Medicine (IOM) report on medical errors, health care organizations have been under intense scrutiny by accreditation agencies, regulatory bodies, opinion leaders, advocacy groups, media representatives, and communities served by health care organizations. To regain public confidence, health care organizations must build patient safeguards into the health care delivery system and convince consumers that such mechanisms are fail-safe. Building a safe environment requires health care leaders to challenge their assumptions about their mission, core competencies, market, competitors, technology, and structures in which they currently operate.

Even if errors aren't occurring at the alarming rates put forth in the 1999 Institute of Medicine report (McDonald, Weiner, and Hui, 2000), the public believes that they are endangered, a concern reinforced by media reports. Appropriately, health care providers are scrambling to allay societal fears.

Quality Improvement Revisited

Quality improvement covers many dimensions of patient care, including the availability, appropriateness, and effectiveness of care. Another critical dimension of quality is the safety of the patient, specifically defined as "the degree to which the risk of an intervention and the risk in the care environment are reduced for the patient and others, including the health care provider" (Joint Commission on Accreditation of Healthcare Organizations [JCAHO], 1993, p. 52). During a 1998 conference sponsored by the National Patient Safety Foundation, Don Berwick explained how the campaign to reduce errors and improve safety "stands somehow aside from or even in competition with the rising tide of will in this country and abroad to improve the quality of health care" (p. 4). Instead of instituting a new set of improvement processes for patient safety, health care providers should capitalize on quality improvement as an appropriate framework for problem resolution.

Considering the approaches offered by Crosby (1979), Deming (1988), Palmer, Donabedian, and Povar (1991), and Juran (1988), an organization that effectively practices continuous quality improvement or total quality management is one that

- Is proactive, designing for quality up front
- Focuses more on improving processes and systems than disciplining people
- Is customer driven (including both internal and external customers)
- Utilizes knowledgeable, multidisciplinary, cross-functional teams
- Compares performance with that of organizations providing "best practices"
- Measures, assesses, and improves the systems of care
- Uncovers root causes of variation
- Learns and changes
- Holds gains
- Involves the organization in the quality culture

Whether these concepts have been achieved in health care is in question. Even though health care organizations are required by regulatory and accreditation agencies to embed a systematic improvement approach into their organizational systems and processes, it is likely that quality improvement is alive and well only in segments of an organization as opposed to organization-wide. Yet unless all members of an organization demonstrate a commitment to and involvement in a systematic quality improvement process linked to strategic priorities (what Baldrige criteria refer to as *deployment*), the effectiveness and value of the process are limited.

Over time, quality rhetoric has changed to "performance improvement" to reflect the breadth of quality improvement practices and emphasis on results. Systems to improve organizational performance in health care organizations across the United States must comply with standards and regulations set forth by the Health Care Finance Administration, the Joint Commission on Accreditation of Healthcare Organizations, and state regulatory agencies. Such requirements generate compliant behavior as opposed to the pursuit of excellence.

A promising approach to performance excellence in recent years is the Malcolm Baldrige National Quality Award (MBNQA). This chapter focuses on how the MBNQA criteria and application process can test the quality of an organization's systems and processes of care in an effort to identify strengths and opportunities for error reduction.

Systems Contributing to Errors

What do health care organizations believe are the root causes of error? In 2000, the University HealthSystem Consortium in Oak Brook, Illinois, surveyed 42 academic medical centers across the United States about their opinion of factors that contribute to health care error. Targeted respondents were health care clinicians, leaders, and professionals involved in improving care. The most common factors identified appear in Table 29-1.

These factors convey the need to improve the processes and systems of care, such as communication, education, and medication handling. Almost as interesting as what made the list is what did not—poor,

TABLE 29-1 Factors Contributing to Errors

Communication
Education
Medication procedures
Policies/procedures not followed
Environment
Order entry
Patient identification
Resident supervision
Human error and lack of fail-safes
Information/data lacking
Knowledge
Systems issues
Complex systems
Pharmacy issues
Standardization of processes lacking
Decision making
Documentation

Source: University HealthSystem Consortium, *Performance Improvement Benchmarking Survey Results* (Oak Brook, IL: Author, 2000). Used with permission.

unsafe, or unskilled performers—which conflicts dramatically with the media portrayal of health care error, as indicated by the following examples:

"Replacement Nurses Fired After Care-Related Mistakes" (Opus
    Communications, 2000)
"Nursing Mistakes Kill, Injure Thousands" (Berens, 2000)
"Following 'Dr. Death,' Britain Sets Up Intervention Agency" (Reuters,
    Associated Press, and Universal Press, 2001)

Certainly, a safe organization relies on well-trained, experienced, competent teams. If care providers are not trained or are inexperienced in the safe use of medications and equipment, errors are more likely. Assessment of competence through observance and peer input helps to validate that training was effective, in particular for students, residents, and other trainees.

However, as the complexity of the care delivery environment increases, so seems the number of people who come in contact with the patient, requiring more coordination, communication, and understanding of accountability. Safe patient care relies on effective communication of patient information across service providers, among staff, between clinicians, and with patients. In the complex environment of health care delivery, there is great potential for breakdown, delays, and errors in communication.

Much can be said about the complex environment of health care organizations. Caregivers often perform multiple tasks simultaneously in a hectic environment, at times circumventing established fail-safe mechanisms. Today's health service environment operates in a culture of "do more with less." Expense reduction is commonplace as organizations strive to regain financial viability in their respective markets. When these reductions involve the workforce, organizations expose themselves to error risk associated with staff morale and inadequate staff to perform care delivery in a safe manner.

Evaluation of Systems and Processes Supporting Safety

To address the systems and processes of care that influence the safety of care requires a close, honest examination of the current state of performance. Since the release of the IOM report, many health care organizations have revisited their procedures to uncover gaps that may present opportunity for error. Such a "gap analysis" can be executed using checklists and evaluative tools comparing current performance to preexisting standards, guidelines, or proven practices for error reduction.

Organizations can use a variety of resources to examine specific processes pertaining to patient safety. For example, to identify recommended procedures to avoid a particular error type, they can examine the literature. Organizations such as the Institute for Safe Medication Practices (ISMP, 2000) have constructed specific tools that can be used to examine specific processes (e.g., medication safety). Another example is the JCAHO's *Sentinel Event Alert,* which provides lessons learned from sentinel event experiences such as infant abduction, wrong-side surgery, and fatal patient falls (JCAHO, 2000). These tools can be used to compare current performance with generally accepted or evidence-based practices in one or more areas pertaining to patient safety.

However, for a comprehensive analysis of the systems and processes to support patient care, health care organizations are turning to the criteria for the MBNQA (or versions of the criteria for regional or state quality awards). Several characteristics make Baldrige criteria attractive to health care organizations:

- The criteria are generally accepted in all industries.
- The evaluation process is comprehensive and organization-wide.
- There is a strong focus on results.
- It reflects performance in all areas, including leadership.
- Support systems are integrated.
- The focus is on excellence, not what is required by regulatory or accreditation agents.

Even before health care criteria were available from MBNQA, other entities had developed awards mirroring the Baldrige criteria. Today, over 40 states have a quality award program, many of which are Baldrige based (*Quality Digest,* 1999).

When external objective expertise is desired, health care organizations often enlist the services of a consultant. Consultants help leaders in strategic planning, cost reduction, and standards compliance. The latter are often referred to as "mock" surveys, designed to mimic the inspection and advice one might expect from an accreditation or regulatory surveyor. However, the use of consultants often comes with a high price tag.

Background of the Malcolm Baldrige Award

This section discusses the history of the Baldrige Award, the criteria, and the values and concepts embedded in the criteria, and reflects on how health care organizations have used the criteria to improve their systems.

Purpose of the Baldrige Award

In 1987, Congress created the Malcolm Baldrige National Quality Award out of concern for the declining competitive position of U.S.

businesses. At the time, Japan's powerful position in the economy was apparent. Japan was credited for adopting and applying the quality-focused teachings of Juran and Deming, which were previously ignored by other countries.

The award was created by Public Law 100–107 and was designed to promote, award, and publicly recognize achievements in quality and performance. Among other findings, Public Law 100–107 stated that "strategic planning for quality and quality improvement programs, through a commitment to excellence . . . are becoming more and more essential to the well-being of our Nation's economy and our ability to compete effectively in the global marketplace" (Findings and Purposes section, no. 8, 1987). The award was named in honor of Malcolm Baldrige, a strong proponent of quality management who was secretary of commerce from 1981 to his death in 1987.

The U.S. Commerce Department manages the award through the National Institute of Standards and Technology (NIST). The private sector also plays a role in the management of the award—for example, organizations receiving the award serve as quality advocates. In addition, more than 300 industry experts serve as examiners (NIST, 2000a).

The award first applied only to three types of businesses: manufacturing, service, and small businesses. Early in the 1990s, the NIST began pilot-testing criteria for two new categories—education and health care. The new criteria were formally established in 1999. It is helpful to understand how the Baldrige health care criteria set differs from its predecessor, the business criteria. For a closer examination, see Table 29-2.

Characteristics of Award Applicants and Recipients

Since 1988, 41 organizations have received a Baldrige Award (Table 29-3). Although health care organizations have applied, until recently none has won the award. In fact, very few have made it far enough in the application process to be visited by award examiners. SSM Health Care (SSMHC) in St. Louis became the first health care system in the United States to be awarded the Malcolm Baldrige Quality Award in May of 2003. The reason it originally applied for the award "was not to win recognition, but to undergo a thorough self assessment . . . organizations that participate in the [MBNQA] process find they are better able to align their effort toward enhanced customer satisfaction, performance and quality" (SSM Health Care, 2001).

It is clear that the organizations that have won the award are well positioned in their markets. An index of 24 publicly traded Baldrige award recipients (known as the "Baldrige Index") as a group outperformed the

TABLE 29-2　Contrasting Baldrige Health Care Criteria with the Business Criteria

It is helpful to understand how the Baldrige health care criteria differ from their predecessors, the business criteria. Consistent with the business criteria, the health care criteria support a systems perspective — health care organizations must maintain organization-wide alignment of goals. The primary emphasis of the health care criteria, however, is on the improvement of health care performance, which stretches beyond business results (2001 Health Care Criteria, p. 8).

Other special considerations for health care organizations are evident in the Baldrige criteria. In the examination of an organization's results according to mission, it is understood that the mission will vary depending on type of health care organization and services offered. For example, if the mission includes a research or teaching component, the performance results of these areas will be captured.

The Baldrige criteria place a high value on customer-driven excellence; however, the term *customer* is replaced by *patient* in some areas of the health care criteria. Criteria pertaining to customer relationships are flexibly applied to accommodate the important stakeholders in a health care organization. For example, because of the responsibility to the public inherent in health care, the criteria also target a health care organization's community as a customer. The community as a customer is emphasized in the core value of the Baldrige health care criteria entitled "responsibility of community health" (referred to as "public responsibility and citizenship" in the business criteria).

In the Baldrige criteria for business, staff are specifically identified as *employees.* The term *staff* appears in the health care criteria, which more appropriately addresses the various practitioners and professionals involved in health care delivery. As key providers of services for a health care organization, staff include administrative, support, and clinical staff (including physicians) regardless of whether they are on the payroll of the organization.

Standard and Poor's 500 by nearly 3.8 to 1 in 1999 (NIST, 1999, p. 2). The National Institute of Standards and Technology found that "incorporating the Baldrige performance excellence concepts pays off in increased productivity, satisfied employees and customers, and improved profitability—both for the companies and investors" (1998, p. 8).

An example of the benefits reaped from superior performance and reflected by Baldrige recipients is customer loyalty. The Ritz-Carlton Hotel Company (1992 and 1999 Baldrige recipient) reports that "75% of its customers would not use a competitor regardless of the offer" (NIST, 1999, p. 3). Other award recipients demonstrate reductions in cycle time and increased new product sales, employee involvement, customer satisfaction, product reliability, revenue per employee, and profit growth (NIST, 1999).

Core Values and Criteria Categories

The Baldrige health care criteria are built on a result-oriented framework. At the foundation of the health care criteria is a set of core values

TABLE 29-3   Past Recipients of the Malcolm Baldrige National Quality Award, Organized by Award Category

Year	Manufacturing	Service/Other	Small Business
2002	Motorola Inc. Commercial, Government and Industrial Solutions Sector	SSM Health Care (Health care)	Branch-Smith Printing Division
2001	Clarke American Checks, Incorporated	Chugach School District (Education)	Pal's Sudden Service
2001	—	Pearl River School District (Education)	—
2001	—	University of Wisconsin-Stout (Education)	—
2000	Dana Corporation-Spicer Driveshaft Division	Operations Management International, Inc.	Los Alamos National Bank
2000	KARLEE Company, Inc., Garland, Texas	—	—
1999	STMicroelectronics, Inc., Region Americas	BI	Sunny Fresh Foods
1999	—	The Ritz-Carlton Hotel Company, L.L.C.	—
1998	Boeing Airlift and Tanker Programs	—	Texas Nameplate Company, Inc.
1998	Solar Turbines Incorporated	—	—
1997	3M Dental Products Division	Merrill Lynch Credit Corporation	—
1997	Solectron Corporation	Xerox Business Services	—
1996	ADAC Laboratories	Dana Commercial Credit Corporation	Custom Research, Inc.
1996	—	—	Trident Precision Manufacturing, Inc.
1995	Armstrong World Industries, Inc., Building Products Operations	—	—
1995	Corning Incorporated, Telecommunications Products Division	—	—
1994	—	AT&T Consumer Communications Services (now the Consumer Markets Division of AT&T)	Wainwright Industries, Inc.
1994	—	GTE Directories Corporation	—

Table 29-3   (Continued)

Year	Manufacturing	Service/Other	Small Business
1993	Eastman Chemical Company	—	Ames Rubber Corporation
1992	AT&T Network Systems Group Transmission Systems Business Unit (now Lucent Technologies, Inc., Optical Networking Group)	AT&T Universal Card Services (now part of Citigroup)	Granite Rock Company
1992	Texas Instruments Incorporated Defense Systems & Electronics Group (now part of Raytheon Systems Company)	The Ritz-Carlton Hotel Company (now part of Marriott International)	—
1991	Solectron Corporation	—	Marlow Industries, Inc.
1991	Zytec Corporation (now part of Artesyn Technologies)	—	—
1990	Cadillac Motor Car Company	Federal Express Corporation	Wallace Co., Inc.
1990	IBM Rochester	—	—
1989	Milliken & Company	—	—
1989	Xerox Corporation, Business Products & Systems	—	—

For more detailed information, visit the National Institute of Standards and Technology website at www.quality.nist.gov/.

and concepts that serves to integrate all of the specific requirements. The core values and concepts are as follows (NIST, 2001, pp. 5–7):

- Visionary leadership
- Patient-focused excellence
- Organizational and personal learning
- Valuing staff and partners
- Agility
- Focus on the future
- Managing for innovation
- Management by fact
- Public responsibility and community health
- Focus on results and creating value
- Systems perspective

There are seven categories of criteria, each containing specific items and associated point values. The criteria are scored according to how they are approached, or deployed, within an organization, and by the results. The seven categories are as follows (NIST, 2001, pp. 5–7):

1. *Leadership:* Targeted toward examining how the senior leaders of the organization guide operations and how they fulfill their responsibility to the public
2. *Strategic Planning:* Focuses on how strategic decisions are made and how actions are determined
3. *Focus on Patients, Other Customers, and Markets:* Examines the methods by which the organization assesses the market requirements and expectations of patients and other health care partners
4. *Information and Analysis:* Investigates how data are effectively analyzed, how information is managed, and how it is used to support health care processes and manage performance
5. *Staff Focus:* Examines the organization's ability to use staff to their full potential, while maintaining alignment with organizational goals
6. *Process Management:* Examines how the processes involved in the design and delivery of health care services are effectively managed and improved
7. *Organizational Performance Results:* Results of performance in key areas are examined, including patient- and other customer-focused results, financial and market results, and staff and work system results

Apparent in all criteria sets—be it health care, business, or education—is a tremendous emphasis on results. Organizational performance point values represent nearly half of the total attainable points (see Table 29-4 for point values). The areas of organizational performance results addressed in the Baldrige health care criteria include the following (NIST, 2001, pp. 5–7):

- Patient- and other customer-focused results
- Health care results
- Financial and market results
- Staff and work system results
- Supplier and partner results
- Organizational effectiveness results, including operational and supplier performance
- Public responsibility and community health results

Examples of organizational performance results submitted for a Baldrige-based state award application appear in Table 29-5. It's

TABLE 29-4   Criteria and Point Values

Criteria Categories and Items	Point Values

Leadership
   Organizational leadership
   Public responsibility and citizenship
	120

Strategic Planning Strategy development and deployment	85

Focus on Patients, Other Customers, and Markets
   Knowledge of the health care market
   Relationships and satisfaction
	85

Information and Analysis
   Measurement and analysis of organizational performance
   Information management
	90

Staff Focus
   Work systems
   Staff education, training, and development
   Staff well-being and satisfaction
	85

Process Management
   Health care service processes
   Business and support processes
	85

Organizational Performance Results
   Patient- and other customer-focused results
   Financial and market results
   Staff and work system results
   Organizational effectiveness results
	450

Source: National Institute of Standards and Technology, Baldrige National Quality Program (2001). *Health Care Criteria for Performance Excellence 2001.* Gaithersburg, MD: Author, 5–7. Used by permission.

important to understand that the Baldrige criteria are clearly linked across categories, results, and core values. This has been done intentionally to emphasize cause–effect thinking and process orientation.

Examining the Baldrige Criteria in the Context of Patient Safety

The assessment of structure, processes, and outcomes pertaining to patient safety is embedded throughout the criteria. Examples pertaining to patient safety are presented.

One of the core values and concepts in the health care criteria is patient-focused excellence. The value of health care services to patients or other customers depends on quality and performance. Many attributes of the system of care delivery, including those that are not clinically oriented, factor into customers' value judgments.

The core value of public responsibility and community health calls for effective organizational planning, including basic practices for

TABLE 29-5   Examples of Organizational Performance Results Submitted for Baldrige-Based Quality Award in New Mexico

The Malcom Baldrige Health Care Criteria for Performance Excellence are utilized by the New Mexico Quality Awards. In their application for the 1999 award, University of New Mexico Health Sciences Center reported the following results.

Patient/Customer Satisfaction

1. Satisfaction results for ER, diagnostic services, inpatient, outpatient
2. Measures related to "patient dissatisfaction"
3. Community perception
4. Referring physician satisfaction
5. Percentage of billings from referrals
6. Internal satisfaction survey progress

Financial and Market Results

1. Income statement (expenses and revenue), 1992–1999
2. Current ratio (total current assets divided by total current liabilities)
3. Days cash on hand at University Hospital (UH)
4. Days revenue in patient accounts receivable at UH
5. Cost per all patient discharged
6. Market share % (Albuquerque market) for medical/surgical, obstetric, pediatric, newborn, acute care, emergency care, outpatient office visits, outpatient surgeries

Health Care Results

1. Appointment lag times for primary and specialty care
2. Overall primary care physician availability
3. ED average length of stay prior to admission
4. Hours on divert for the medical intensive care unit (this has also remained high)
5. Number of calls to telephone triage
6. Telephone transaction completion rate
7. Pharmacy, lab, and radiology cost per adjusted discharge (CMI adjusted)
8. Mislabeled lab specimens
9. Mortality of patients with simple pneumonia and pleurisy (DRG 89)
10. Pediatric patients with bronchitis or asthma readmitted <31 days

Source: Kathryn Karnaze, Interim Director for Quality Assurance, University Hospital, University of New Mexico Health Sciences Center, Albuquerque, NM. Used with permission.

protecting public health and safety. Among other priorities, effective planning addresses problem prevention and resolution. The criteria also call for health care organizations to provide support systems and information needed to maintain public confidence. Public responsibility and citizenship, part of the leadership category, speak to the societal obligation to address risks associated with health care services and any public concerns.

Health care services have design and delivery processes. The Baldrige criteria examine how these processes are managed (criteria category 6). Related to patient safety is the expectation that processes are tested to reduce errors, inspections and audits are conducted to minimize errors, and prevention-based processes are in place. To manage processes, the criteria call for key performance measurements, customer interactions, and observations to be made and shared with appropriate staff. Contained within the criteria for health care service processes, "specific reference is made to regulatory and payor requirements, key . . . measurements/assessments and patient interactions, and how results are made available in a timely manner to all appropriate staff" (NIST, 2001, p. 45). The criteria expect organizations to respond appropriately to performance information, and convey the importance of a root cause approach:

> When deviations occur, corrective action is required. Depending on the nature of the process, the corrective action could involve technical and/or human considerations. Proper corrective action involves changes at the source (root cause) of the deviation. Such corrective action should minimize the likelihood of this type of variation occurring again or elsewhere in your organization. (NIST, 2001, p. 45)

Another core value conveys the importance of organizational and personal learning, and calls for learning to become part of everyday work and of how the organization operates. Organizational learning, according to the criteria, supports problem solving at the source or "root cause." This can enhance value in many ways, among them "reducing errors, defects, waste, and related costs" (NIST, 2001, p. 2). Staff who are supported by a learning organization will be more adaptive, responsive, satisfied, and innovative. On a similar note, the staff focus category of the criteria speaks to how the organization fully utilizes staff in alignment with the organization's plans. The criteria seek out work systems that support how the organization enables staff to achieve high performance. One motivator and enabler of performance is the use of problem-solving teams.

The core values provide a *systems perspective* for organizational management. The system perspective value calls for strategic planning that reflects alignment across the criteria categories, focuses on customers, and manages performance according to results. A systems perspective is critical to the provision of a safe environment, effective analysis of root causes to errors, and innovation required to prevent errors. Antithetical to the systems perspective is the traditional punitive approach to error, which does little to prevent another error, and creates defensiveness. According to Bryan-Brown and Dracup (2001), "an adversarial situation between the operator and the system is a recipe for counter-production" (p. 2).

Applying the Baldrige Criteria for an Organization-wide Evaluation

Completing an Award Application

If a health care organization chooses to complete a Baldrige (or Baldrige-like) award application, it need not send in the application. Often, the Baldrige application can be used as a valuable tool to identify weaknesses, strengths, and opportunities to improve. The process of using the Baldrige tool as a self-assessment is discussed further in the next section.

Organizations that send in an application do so for one of two reasons: to seek external opinion and consultation or to compete for award status and recognition for high performance. Regardless of the motivation, an organized approach is needed to complete a well-written application, because the process is time consuming and difficult. The best strategy is to take a team approach similar to that described in the self-assessment section.

In addition, examiners have suggested some general tips for submitting an application (B. Ohm, presentation, August 7, 1998):

- Pay particular attention to the performance results section because it is highly weighted in scoring. Specific suggestions are to
  - Include only data relevant to the organization's strategic priorities
  - Provide data points for a long enough period of time to demonstrate improvements
  - Demonstrate that measurement procedures offer a comprehensive view of service and product lines (for example, patient satisfaction measurement should be present for more than just a few service lines)
- Establish linkages across the major criteria topics; for example, leadership functions should be closely linked to customer service.
- Ensure that the application is well written and grammatically correct.

Other Baldrige-based award applicants and examiners have offered additional suggestions for the content of the application. The "methods used to proactively assess and mitigate risk" was among the areas not given enough attention by applicants for the Baldrige-based VHA Quality Achievement Grant, demonstrating the need to better incorporate risk management and patient safety methods (Weeks et al., 2000, p. 381). Participants also suggested that to streamline the application process, an organization should understand its core competencies and customers, tested by answering the following questions (Weeks et al., 2000, p. 386):

- What do we make?
- Who do we make it for?
- What do our customers want?
- What are our processes to meet those wants?
- What is the end-process metric?
- How do we improve what we make?

The examiner's review of an organization's award application can uncover critical opportunities that are unknown to the organization. These judgments are often sought from consultants at a much higher price than an award application fee. All applicants for the Baldrige Award undergo a rigorous examination process, using an independent board of examiners, that takes from 300 to 1,000 hours.

Applications submitted for the Malcolm Baldrige National Quality Award receive a feedback report, written by a team of expert examiners, that outlines the organization's strengths, opportunities, and results. The feedback report includes a summary of the most significant findings, a summary of findings and scores for each criteria category, actionable items for the purposes of strategic planning, and data on how the organization's scores compare with other applicants.

Site visits, granted to a few organizations under consideration for the award, offer a more in-depth review of performance and provide the opportunity for face-to-face dialogue with examiners. Organizations visited through the Baldrige-based VHA Quality Achievement Grant gained a comprehensive and more clearly articulated perspective on the health care delivery process, improvement efforts, and strategies (Weeks et al., 2000).

Using Baldrige as a Self-Assessment Tool

Even if an organization has no interest in applying for a quality award, the criteria can be used as a valuable internal assessment tool. The primary benefit of a self-assessment, explains Ohm (2000a, p. 12), is to "identify strengths and opportunities for improvement for the organization's performance improvement system and to assess overall organizational effectiveness." Self-assessments help to establish baseline information that can be tracked over time. Areas needing further investigation or improvement are identified, leading to well-informed deliberations on planning and prioritization for change. In addition, organizational performance self-assessments demonstrate to important constituents that your organization is taking a proactive approach to improving performance, for patient safety reasons or otherwise. Finally, when done as part of a larger collaboration, self-assessment provides an understanding of performance as it compares with similar organizations.

To simplify the criteria and application, various survey instruments, tools, and checklists have been developed, for example, those developed by Jennings and Westfall (1994), Brown (1992), and Ohm (2000b). To assess critical safety functions, VHA (2000) developed a Baldrige-based tool designed to "evaluate current processes and systems and measure ongoing progress in establishing a safer organization" (p. 1). Using the Baldrige criteria as a foundational framework, VHA developed a comprehensive checklist of evaluation questions organized around key aspects of safety and strategies that would demonstrate a comprehensive approach to safety.

Regardless of the tool selected, the self-assessment process requires commitment and involvement of leaders as well as front-line employees, caregivers, suppliers, and patients. Organizational leaders responsible for quality, safety, and performance improvement should initiate and provide ongoing leadership support for the assessment process. An appropriate group might be the clinical leadership team, patient safety committee, or quality council. As the project oversight group, these leaders should allocate sufficient resources to the project, facilitate commitment across the organization, and ensure a coordinated approach.

Although it is possible for an individual or single department to conduct the assessment, the involvement of a multidisciplinary, cross-functional team is preferred. This is because the assessment process will afford opportunity to collaborate, communicate, and learn about organizational systems and processes, providing all participants with a rich educational experience. It would be beneficial to involve participants from different units who have different roles and different functional responsibilities. The assessment process should also incorporate the perspectives of patients and other customers. As with any team exercise, it is important to keep the team at a manageable size (6 to 10 individuals), set expectations early on, and facilitate participation by all.

The team leader should ensure that the team understands the purpose, content, and structure of the assessment tool. Agreement should be reached on the areas of focus and how to integrate the various organizational systems, processes, and results into the assessment. When necessary, time should be spent ensuring that team members understand organizational systems and processes.

Other individuals should be involved as the assessment process ensues. For example, representatives of human resources, medical staff, and information services units will need to be involved as appropriate. The idea is to gather the most comprehensive view of the organization's performance across the criteria categories.

An organization can apply all seven categories of criteria simultaneously or focus on a single category before moving on to the next. The Baldrige National Quality Program (NIST, 2000b) offers a 10-step approach to the self-assessment process at www.quality.nist.gov.

Summary

To gain recognition and strive for excellence in providing high-quality products and services, many health care organizations are now competing with other industries for prestigious awards. One such award is the Malcolm Baldrige National Health Care Quality Award. Because the award offers a comprehensive evaluation of the performance of structures, processes, and systems, completing an award application can be a beneficial exercise to understand the systems that support patient safety.

References

Berens, M. J. (2000). Nursing mistakes kill, injure thousands. *Chicago Tribune,* September 10, 2000. Retrieved November 1, 2001, from the World Wide Web: http://chicagotribune.com/.

Berwick, D. M. (1998). Taking action to improve safety: How to increase the odds of success. *Conference Proceedings from the National Patient Safety Foundation Conference Enhancing Patient Safety and Reducing Errors in Health Care,* November 8, 1998. Rancho Mirage, CA: Annenberg Center for Health Sciences.

Brown, M. G. (1992). Measuring your company against the Baldrige criteria. *Journal for Quality and Participation,* June, 82–87.

Bryan-Brown, C., and Dracup, K. (2001). An essay on criticism. *American Journal of Critical Care,* 10(1), 2.

Crosby, P. (1979). *Quality Is Free: The Art of Making Quality Certain.* New York: McGraw-Hill.

Deming, W. (1988). *Out of Crises.* Cambridge, MA: MIT Center for Advanced Engineering Study.

Institute for Safe Medication Practices. (2000). Retrieved November 1, 2000, from the World Wide Web: http://www.ismp.org/ISMP/start.html.

Jennings, K., and Westfall, F. (1994). A survey-based benchmarking approach for health care using the Baldrige quality criteria. *Joint Commission Journal on Quality Improvement,* 20(9), 500–509.

Joint Commission on Accreditation of Healthcare Organizations. (1993). *1994 Accreditation Manual for Hospitals. Volume 1, Standards.* Oakbrook Terrace, IL: Author.

Joint Commission on Accreditation of Healthcare Organizations. (2000). *Sentinel Event Alert.* Oakbrook Terrace, IL: Author. Retrieved February 23, 2001, from the World Wide Web: http://www.jcaho.org/patient_safety_mpfrm.html.

Juran, J. M. (1988). *Juran on Planning for Quality.* New York: Free Press.

McDonald, C., Weiner, M., and Hui, S. (2000). Deaths due to medical errors are exaggerated in Institute of Medicine report [Letter]. *Journal of the American Medical Association,* 284, 93–95.

National Institute of Standards and Technology. (1998). *Baldrige National Quality Program: Ten Years of Business Excellence for America.* Gaithersburg, MD: Author, November 1998, 8.

National Institute of Standards and Technology. (1999). *Baldrige National Quality Program: Why Apply.* Gaithersburg, MD: Author, 2–10.

National Institute of Standards and Technology. (2000a). *Baldrige National Quality Program: Fact Sheet.* Gaithersburg, MD: Author. Retrieved December 4, 2000, from the World Wide Web: http://www.nist.gov/public_affairs/factsheet/baldfaqs.htm.

National Institute of Standards and Technology. (2000b). *Baldrige National Quality Program: Getting Started.* Gaithersburg, MD: Author. Retrieved December 1, 2000, from the World Wide Web: http://www.quality.nist.gov.

National Institute of Standards and Technology. (2001). *Baldrige National Quality Program: Health Care Criteria for Performance Excellence 2001.* Publication Number T1107. Gaithersburg, MD: Author, 2, 5–7, 45.

Ohm, B. (2000a). Evaluating your performance improvement system using a Baldrige-based self-assessment. *QRC Advisor,* 16(7), 11–12.

Ohm, B. (2000b). 2000 Baldrige performance criteria for healthcare–assessment survey. *QRC Advisor,* 16(8),10–12.

Opus Communications. (2000). Replacement nurses fired after care-related mistakes. *Patient Safety Monitor* [Electronic Newsletter]. Opus Communications, a Division of HCPro, received April 3, 2000.

Palmer, R., Donabedian, A., and Povar, G. (1991). *Striving for Quality in Health Care: An Inquiry into Policy and Practice.* Ann Arbor, MI: Health Administration Press.

Public Law 100-107. (1987). Findings and Purposes section, no. 8.

Quality Digest. (1999). 1999 state quality awards directory. *Quality Digest,* January 1999, 59–64.

Reuters, Associated Press, and Universal Press Syndicate. (2001). Following 'Dr. Death,' Britain sets up intervention agency. *Chicago Tribune.* Retrieved January 10, 2001, from the World Wide Web: http://chicagotribune.com/.

SSM Health Care. (2001). Our quality initiatives. St. Louis, MO: Author. Retrieved January 21, 2001, from the World Wide Web: http://www.ssmhc.com/internet/home/ssmcorp.nsf.

VHA, Inc. (2000). *The Patient Safety Organizational Assessment.* Irving, TX: Author, 1–15.

Weeks, W. B., Hamby, L., Stein, A., and Batalden, P. (2000). Using the Baldrige management system framework in health care: The Veterans Health Administration experience. *Journal on Quality Improvement,* 26(7), 379–387.

CHAPTER THIRTY

OUTLINING THE BUSINESS CASE FOR PATIENT SAFETY

James E. Vance, MD, MBA and Nancy Wilson, MD, MPH

Although few would argue that patient safety isn't a worthwhile goal to pursue, the business case for safety has not yet been defined.[1] Intuitively it makes sense that improving patient safety can add significant costs to the operation of a health care enterprise, but data demonstrating financial returns are still limited. This is largely due to the underreporting of adverse events and errors in patient care. Furthermore, there are virtually no funds available from either government programs or private insurance to support these initiatives, nor are there financial incentives to make patient safety a priority.

It is the purpose of this chapter to explore approaches and methodologies to analyze and link the impact of patient safety improvement initiatives to quality *and* financial outcomes. In today's environment, the basic principles of economics are applicable to health care just as they are to other sectors of the economy. The national attention given to the publication of the Institute of Medicine (IOM) report *To Err is Human: Building a Safer Health System*[2] should motivate clinical leaders to rise to the challenge of critically evaluating health care systems and seeking opportunities for improving patient safety.

This chapter is divided into four sections:

1. A review of pertinent literature
2. Experience from other industries
3. Impact on health care organizations
4. Implications for consumers

Literature Review

A number of studies have attempted to estimate the cost impact of medication errors and adverse drug events (ADEs). One such report, from the General Accounting Office (see appendix), noted that the lack of overall incidence data for ADEs in the United States impedes attempts to reliably estimate nationwide costs of adverse drug events, although a number of studies have reported similar costs for treating patients with ADEs in hospitals.[3]

Researchers have followed different approaches to generate information about the direct costs of treating adverse drug events, but only one study attempted to calculate indirect costs such as lost income. Most of the published studies either focus on one or two individual institutions, use expert panels, or extrapolate from random chart samples to estimate costs of ADEs.[3] The IOM report, extrapolating from a number of published studies, estimated the total national costs, including lost income, lost household production, disability, and health care costs, due to preventable ADEs to be $17 billion to $29 billion. Health care costs constitute over one half of this estimate.[2] A number of organizations, such as the Joint Commission on Accreditation of Healthcare Organizations and the Midwest Business Group on Health, are gathering data that patient safety advocates believe will help fill in the research gaps and further demonstrate the financial benefits of error prevention.

Unfortunately, the reluctance to document error in the official medical record, largely because of legal liability issues, is one of the major limitations of all previous studies of the incidence of adverse events. Published studies on medication errors, surgical complications (such as infection rates), and many current "quality improvement" initiatives continue to depend largely on self-reporting through incident reports or similar retrospective analyses of hospital records. Universal underreporting, in turn, limits the ability to measure error accurately. Therefore, the precise prevalence and magnitude of medical error is unknown, but it is probably enormous.[4] One study reported that medical adverse event underreporting is estimated to range from 50% to 96% annually.[5]

Deming suggested that data collection should be ongoing rather than retrospective and should be done in a nonpunitive manner. Aggressive case finding may identify injuries and errors that are not documented in a patient's chart.[4] Studies have demonstrated that it is feasible to collect ongoing data regarding the surgical care of patients and that the incidence of error was found to be far greater than other studies when data are obtained in a nonjudgmental context.[6,7] The studies prospectively analyzed adverse event rates in 1,047 patients admitted to three surgical units. One or more adverse events or errors occurred in 480 patients, or 45.8%.

There is a long tradition in medicine of examining past practice through conferences on morbidity and mortality, grand rounds, and peer review, to understand how things might have been done differently.[5] However, these traditional methods all currently share the same shortcomings:

- Lack of human factors analysis and thinking about systems
- A narrow focus on individual performance to the exclusion of contributory team and larger social issues
- Hindsight bias
- A tendency to search for errors as opposed to the myriad causes of error induction
- A lack of multidisciplinary integration into an organization-wide safety culture

New and innovative initiatives to reduce mishaps in medical management are essential requirements for future efforts to improve quality and lower costs in health care. Many stakeholders in health care are working together to achieve the goal of developing an environment that fosters the rich reporting culture that must be created to capture accurate and detailed data about nuances of care. Only with consistent, accurate reporting can we hope to more accurately quantify the business case for safety.

Lessons from Other Industries

What can we learn from other industries? Systems for reporting near misses, close calls, or sentinel (warning) events have been institutionalized in aviation, nuclear power technology, petrochemical processing, steel production, military operations, and air transportation.[5] In health care, efforts are now being made to create incident reporting systems for medical near misses to supplement the limited data available from mandatory reporting systems focused on preventable deaths and serious injuries. In the nuclear power industry, the intensified approach to process improvement accomplished through focusing on safety resulted in financial gains through more efficient power production, as measured by fewer outages, shutdowns, and reduction of capacity.

The Impact on Health Care Organizations

Many health care organizations are still far behind in adapting to the expanding world of information technology.[8] Even though they have seen technology—such as CAT scans and MRIs—revolutionize medicine,

many hospitals have not yet put computers to use to increase productivity, streamline administrative functions, enhance research, and
improve quality and patient safety. Although new information technologies are becoming more widely used in hospitals, relatively little
data are available regarding their impact on the safety of the process
of medication administration.[9]

Exceptions include computerized physician order entry and computerized physician decision support systems, which have been found
to improve drug safety. Other innovations, including using robots for
filling prescriptions, bar coding, automation of dispensing devices, and
computerization of the medication administration record, though less
studied, should all eventually reduce error rates.

Even scarcer is information on the return on investment in technology for improving patient safety. Though error reduction strategies
may pay off in the long term, they aren't cheap, requiring significant
investments in time, personnel, and equipment. Computerized medication and medical records systems, for example, can easily cost $1 million
or more.[1] The Brigham and Women's Hospital developed a computerized order entry system in 1993 at a cost of approximately $1.4 mil-
lion; thereafter, maintenance has cost about $500,000 a year.[8] The
system has saved the hospital between $5 and $10 million a year. Other
payoffs have included a reduction in serious medication errors by 55%
over the past few years, and saving doctors and nurses time as well as
making them feel more professional, efficient, and confident. It is the
direct benefit to patients—namely, reduced errors—that will likely com-
pel other hospitals to follow suit.

Senior executives in most community-owned health care organizations do not track the financial return on their investment in performance improvement initiatives.[10] For the near future, information
required to better understand the business case for safety will depend
heavily on documentation from individual health care organizations as
they prospectively track, measure, and report the clinical and financial
impact of their patient safety improvement initiatives. So far, only a
few studies have attempted to quantify the actual or potential savings
resulting from patient safety programs.

- In a 1997 study conducted at Brigham and Women's Hospital in
  Boston and published in the *Journal of the American Medical
  Association,* researchers concluded that preventable medication
  errors increased the cost of patient care by nearly $4,700 per case.[11]
- In another 1997 study published in the *Journal of the American
  Medical Association,* researchers at LDS Hospital in Salt Lake City
  concluded that patients with ADEs incurred an additional $2,013
  in cost per case.[12]

Using the range of added costs reported in these two studies, health care organizations could run a rough estimate of the cost of ADEs in their institutions by using the following formula:

Assumptions

15,000 admissions/year
Bates ADE rate = 6.5%
Classen ADE rate = 2.4%

Example (Bates, *JAMA* 1995)

- 15,000 admits × 0.065 × $4,685 = $4,567,875
- If 33% are preventable = $1,507,398

Example (Classen, *JAMA* 1997)

- 15,000 admits × 0.024 × $2,262 = $814,320
- If 33% are preventable = $271,168

These estimates are conservative because they do not include the costs of injuries to patients or malpractice costs. A recent study reported that improved teamwork in the emergency department could improve patient safety and influence the outcome (prevent or mitigate the error) in 43% of the closed cases studied. The resulting projected savings were $345,460 per 100,000 emergency department visits, or $3.50 for every patient seen.[13]

Impact on Consumers

Patients or consumers, for the most part, have believed that they are safe and protected from harm when they enter the health care system. The IOM report serves as a reminder that although not every medication error will result in harm to the patient, many will, and clearly enough data exist to suggest a serious concern for patient safety.[14] The intent of the IOM report was to stress that inaction or "silence" regarding finding solutions to the serious problem of patient safety will no longer be tolerable, and that expert, expedient attention is required.[2] A VHA research study reported that consumers would be influenced in their choice of provider knowing that a hospital or doctor uses evidence-based treatment plans, and that poor or below-average clinical quality reports would persuade them to choose a different hospital or doctor.[15]

To date there have only been estimates of the impact of adverse events on patient functional status, quality of life, and time lost from employment. A recent study compared the litigation rate for patients with adverse events with that for surgical patients without ADEs.[7]

Consumer momentum appears to be building, however. The Leapfrog Group (www.leapfrog.org), a coalition of 60 of the nation's largest employers, with a total of 20 million workers, announced plans to use its members' purchasing clout to steer patients to hospitals that implement a variety of patient safety initiatives, including computerized medication systems and the use of specialist physicians to supervise care in intensive care units. The impact of these initiatives on the cost of care will certainly be of interest to this powerful group.

Conclusion

The business case for patient safety is beginning to evolve but has a long way to go. There is an enormous opportunity and responsibility for clinical, financial, and administrative leaders in health care organizations to gather and report the clinical and financial impact of their patient safety initiatives. The results of these efforts will have a sweeping effect on future health care policy, regulation, and payment methodologies, as well as the safety and restored credibility of the U.S. health care system. Most important of all the benefits of the business case, however, is safety for each and every patient.

Appendix: Costs of Adverse Drug Events

1. Most studies of ADE costs (Table 30-1) focused on one or two individual institutions.[3]
   a. Three of the four studies that specifically analyzed the average excess hospital costs resulting from ADEs reported estimates ranging from $1,939 to $2,595.[11,12,22] An outlier study reported average ADE costs of only $783.[26]
   b. Two of the studies also extrapolated their findings on ADE incidence and costs to all hospital patients in the United States, producing estimates of $1.56 billion and $4 billion in additional hospital costs per year nationwide from ADEs.[13,15]
   c. While these estimates may help indicate the general scope of ADE costs, because each is based on just one or two hospitals, their precision for estimating costs on a national level is limited.
2. Three other studies used expert panels to generate ADE cost estimates.[14,19,20] Results included an estimate for the costs of drug-related morbidity and mortality in the ambulatory setting of $76.6 billion annually, primarily because of the resulting projected admissions to hospitals, costing $47.4 billion, and long-term-care facilities, costing $14.4 billion. Because the cost

TABLE 30-1 Summary of Studies Estimating Adverse Drug Event Costs in the United States

Study (Ref.)	Site	Eligible Patients	Method	Cost Estimate
Bates et al., 1997 (11)	Brigham and Women's Hospital and Massachusetts General Hospital, Boston	4,108 patients admitted to a random sample of med/surgical units, intensive and nonintensive care units; excluded obstetric units	Compared comparable patients with ADEs to those without	Hospital cost increased $2,595/ADE and $4,685 per preventable ADE; $5.6 M/year in additional costs, with $2.8 M attributable to preventable ADEs
Bootman, Harrison, Cox, 1997 (16)	Nursing facilities (no specific sites studied)	No patients studied	Expert panel estimated ADE rates and needed treatments	$7.6 B costs to payer from drug-related morbidity and mortality in nursing homes
Classen et al., 1997 (12)	LDS Hospital, Salt Lake City	All 91,574 hospital admissions	Compared comparable patients with ADEs to those without	Hospital cost $2,013/ADE; 4-year cost $4,482,951 (excl. costs of liability and the injury to patients)
Col et al., 1990 (17)	Unspecified community teaching hospital	315 consecutively admitted elderly patients	Assessed ADEs in patients who experienced them; no comparison group	Hospital cost $2,147 per patient admitted with ADE related to noncompliance ($77,289 for 3 mo); $4,237 per patient admitted with ADE ($224,542 for 3 mo)
Cooper, 1987 (18)	Unspecified nursing home	All residents; sample of 6 cases of ADEs to generate cost estimate	Assessed ADEs in patients who experienced them; no comparison group	$3,749/episode that resulted in hospitalization; up to $340,942 in costs potentially avoided over a 2-year period

(Continued)

469

TABLE 30-1 (Continued)

Study (Ref.)	Site	Eligible Patients	Method	Cost Estimate
Cullen et al., 1997 (19)	Brigham and Women's Hospital and Massachusetts General Hospital, Boston	All 4,031 patients admitted to sample of intensive care and general care units	Comparisons between patients who had first ADE in the ICU and the remaining ICU patients and between medical and surgical patients with an ADE	Costs after ADE of $9,192/ADE in surgical unit, $17,437 in medical unit, $17,577 in medical ICU, $20,959 in surgical ICU; total cost $1,366,840 over 6 months
Dennehy et al., 1996 (20)	University of California	1,260 (68%) of emergency department patients	Assessed ADEs in patients who experienced them; no comparison group	Hospital costs $283/ADE not hospitalized, $2,815 if admitted; $308 per preventable ADEs not hospitalized, $2,752 if admitted; annual cost $602,597, $391,342 from avoidable ADEs
Evans et al., 1993 (21)	LDS Hospital, Salt Lake City	All hospitalized patients	Compared patients with ADEs to those without	Average cost, patients with ADEs, allergic or idiosyncratic reactions $30,617; known toxicities $23,256; average cost without ADEs $6,320
Evans et al., 1994 (22)	LDS Hospital, Salt Lake City	60,836 hospitalized patients	Compared comparable patients with ADEs to those without	$1,939 higher cost for patients with an ADE than without; annual cost $1,103,291
Johnson et al., 1995 (23)	Unspecified ambulatory settings	No patients studied	Expert panel estimated ADE rates and needed treatments	$76.6 B annual costs to payers associated with management of drug-related mortality and morbidity

Study	Setting	No. patients studied	Method	Results
Johnson et al., 1997 (24)	Unspecified ambulatory settings	No patients studied	Expert panel estimated ADE rates and needed treatments	$45.6 B savings for payers if pharmaceutical care was instituted nationwide, a 59.6% reduction from $76.6 billion
Prince et al., 1992 (25)	Mercy Hospital, Pittsburgh	10,184 emergency room visits	Assessed patients with ADEs; no comparison group	Average hospital charge/ADE $8,888; total annual cost of $631,048
Schneider et al., 1995 (26)	Ohio State University Medical Center, Columbus	Reviewed 109 patient charts; selection criteria not stated	Assessed patients with ADEs; no comparison group	Average cost $783/ADE; total annual cost of $1,497,148
Stoukides, D'Agostino, and Kaufman, 1993 (27)	Roger Williams Medical Center, Brown University, Providence, RI	13,703 emergency room visits	Assessed patients with ADEs; no comparison group	Average cost $333.81 per ED visit; total cost $39,389.58 for 6 mo
Sullivan, Kreling, and Hazlet, 1990 (28)	Unspecified hospitals (based on other studies)	2,942 admissions; seven studies reviewed	Meta-analysis	$8.5 B 1986 hospitalizations for noncompliance
Thomas et al., 1999 (29)	28 hospitals in Colorado and Utah	14,732 randomly selected hospital discharges	Physicians and malpractice claims adjusters estimated extent of disability and future health care use from data from medical records of patients with ADEs	$5.2 B hospital costs for ADEs nationwide; $12.2 B, including outpatient care, lost wages, and lost household production

Source: Modified from United States General Accounting Office, *Adverse Drug Events: The Magnitude of Health Risk Is Uncertain Because of Limited Incidence Data*, GAO Report GAO/HEHS-00-21 (Washington, DC: General Accounting Office, 2000).

estimates are based on these estimated incidence rates, the cost estimates are also open to question.

3. A 1999 study conducted in Colorado and Utah studied 14,732 randomly sampled discharges from hospitals in two states and included indirect as well as direct treatment costs for ADEs.[29]

   a. Using data extracted from the patients' medical records, physicians and malpractice claims adjusters estimated the patient's degree of disability and likely use of health care in the future. Projected inpatient and outpatient health care costs, lost wages, and lost household production were then estimated, and the total was reported as an aggregate national figure.

   b. The estimated $5.2 billion for hospital costs alone exceeded the two earlier study estimates from individual institutions.

   c. Total direct and indirect costs were estimated at $12.2 billion in 1996 dollars by adding in the estimated cost of outpatient care, lost income, and lost household production.

   d. In a subsequent publication,[30] the authors reanalyzed data from the Utah and Colorado medical practice study in order to describe the incidence and types of preventable adverse events in elderly patients and the morbidity and mortality caused by these events in elderly compared with nonelderly patients.

References

1. "Does Safety Pay? [Editorial]," *HealthcareBusiness*, January–February, 2001.

2. Kohn, L. T. et al., eds., *To Err Is Human: Building a Safer Health System* (Washington, DC: National Academy Press, 1999).

3. United States General Accounting Office, *Adverse Drug Events: The Magnitude of Health Risk Is Uncertain Because of Limited Incidence Data*, GAO Report GAO/HEHS-00-21 (Washington, DC: General Accounting Office, January 2000).

4. Weingart, S. N. et al., "Epidemiology of Medical Error," *BMJ* 340 (2000): 774–777.

5. Barach, P., and Small, D. "Reporting and Preventing Medical Mishaps: Lessons from Non-medical Near Miss Reporting Systems," *BMJ* 320 (2000):759–763.

6. Andrews, L. B. et al., "An Alternative Strategy for Studying Adverse Events in Medical Care," *Lancet* 349, no. 9048 (1997):309–313.

7. Krizek, T. J. "Surgical Error–Ethical Issues of Adverse Events," *Arch Surg* 135 (2000):1359–1366.

8. Findlay, S. ed. *Reducing Medical Errors and Improving Patient Safety: Success Stories from the Front Lines of Medicine* (Washington, DC:

National Coalition on Healthcare and the Institute of Healthcare Organizations, 2000).

9. Bates, D. W. "Using Information Technology to Reduce Rates of Medication Errors in Hospitals," *BMJ* 320 (2000):788–791.

10. *The Business Case for Quality,* VHA Research Series 1 (Irving, TX: VHA, 2000), 21–22.

11. Bates, D. W. et al., "The Costs of Adverse Drug Events in Hospitalized Patients," *JAMA* 227 (1997):307–311.

12. Classen, D. C. et al., "Adverse Drug Events in Hospitalized Patients: Excess Length of Stay, Extra Costs, and Attributable Mortality," *JAMA* 277 (1997):301–306.

13. Risser, D. T. et al., "Improved Teamwork Reduces Medical Errors in the Emergency Department," *Annals of Emergency Medicine* 34, no. 3 (1999):373–383.

14. Briceland, L. L. "Medication Errors: An Exposé of the Problem," *Medscape Pharmacists* 1, no. 3 (2000). Available: http://www.medscape. com/Medscape/pharmacists/journal/2000/v01.n03/mph0530.bric/ mph0530bric01.html.

15. *Consumer Demand for Clinical Quality: The Giant Awakens,* VHA Research Series 3 (Irving, TX: VHA, 2000), 27–29.

16. Bootman, J. L. et al., "The Health Care Cost of Drug-Related Morbidity and Mortality in Nursing Facilities," *Archives of Internal Medicine* 157 (1997):2089–2096.

17. Col, N. et al., "The Role of Medication Noncompliance and Adverse Drug Reactions in Hospitalizations of the Elderly," *Archives of Internal Medicine* 150 (1990):841–845.

18. Cooper, J. W. "Adverse Drug Reactions and Interactions in a Nursing Home," *Nursing Homes and Senior Citizen Care* 36 (1987):7–11.

19. Cullen, D. J. et al., "Preventable Adverse Drug Events in Hospitalized Patients: A Comparative Study of Intensive Care and General Care Units," *Critical Care Medicine* 25 (1997):1289–1297.

20. Dennehy, C. E. et al., "Drug-Related Illness in Emergency Department Patients," *American Journal of Health-System Pharmacy* 53 (1996): 1422–1426.

21. Evans, R. S. et al., "Prevention of Adverse Drug Events Through Computerized Surveillance," in *Sixteenth Annual Symposium on Computer Applications in Medical Care* (New York: McGraw-Hill, 1993), 437–441.

22. Evans, R. S. et al., "Using a Hospital Information System to Assess the Effects of Adverse Drug Events," in *Seventeenth Annual Symposium on Computer Applications in Medical Care* (New York: McGraw-Hill, 1994), 161–165.

23. Johnson, J. A. et al., "Drug-Related Morbidity and Mortality: A Cost-of-Illness Model," *Archives of Internal Medicine* 155 (1995):1949–1956.

24. Johnson, J. A. et al., "Drug-Related Morbidity and Mortality and the Economic Impact of Pharmaceutical Care," *American Journal of Health-System Pharmacy* 54 (1997):554–558.

25. Prince, B. S. et al., "Drug-Related Emergency Department Visits and Hospital Admissions," *American Journal of Hospital Pharmacy* 42 (1992):1696–1700.
26. Schneider, P. J. et al., "Cost of Medication-Related Problems at a University Hospital," *American Journal of Health-System Pharmacy* 52 (1995):2415–2418.
27. Stoukides, C. A. et al., "Adverse Drug Reaction Surveillance in an Emergency Room," *American Society of Hospital Pharmacy* 50 (1993):712–714.
28. Sullivan, S. D. et al., "Noncompliance with Medication Regimens and Subsequent Hospitalizations: A Literature Analysis and Cost of Hospitalization Estimate," *Journal of Research in Pharmaceutical Economics* 2 (1990):19–33.
29. Thomas, E. J. et al., "Costs of Medical Injuries in Utah and Colorado," *Inquiry* 36 (1999):255–264.
30. Thomas, E. J., and Brennan, T. A. "Incidence and Types of Preventable Adverse Events in Elderly Patients: Population Based Review of Medical Record," *BMJ* 320 (2000):741–744.

CHAPTER THIRTY-ONE

THE ECONOMICS OF PATIENT SAFETY

Pamela K. Gavin and Peter L. Saltonstall

Is there a strong economic basis for a health care organization to develop an enterprise-wide medical error reduction program? Based on early research findings and the experience of other high-risk industries, the answer is an overwhelming yes. The most effective way to proceed with such an error reduction program is through the auspice of a corporate patient safety initiative. The potential for return on investment in a corporate patient safety initiative is significant. Its power lies in the unique ability of a patient safety program to align an organization's financial, clinical, and cultural initiatives and bridge the gap between everyday care and optimal "safe care." Some of the benefits will be tangible, such as the reduction of repeated or unnecessary services, improved employee retention, enhanced contracting abilities, and improved quality of care, whereas other benefits will be intangible, such as improved morale and community trust. Nevertheless, taken together these benefits can have a tremendous impact on a health care organization's performance and reputation in the long run.

The fundamental principle behind the economic basis for health care safety, including the safety of patients, employees, and visitors, is that a safer health system is overall a more productive one. Patient safety plays a role in improving not only the quality of care delivered but also in improving an organization's overall performance through enhanced operational efficiencies. Dollars spent on having to repeat lab tests, treat the consequences of prescribing the wrong medication, or treat a hospital-acquired infection are unavailable for other purposes. In fact, Andrews and colleagues found in their observational study of 1,047 patients admitted to three surgical units of a large, tertiary care, urban teaching hospital that the likelihood of experiencing an adverse event increased about 6% for each additional day a patient stayed in the hospital.[1] In addition to measurable cost savings, a demonstrated reduction in medical errors can lead to contract opportunities with managed care organizations and employers such as members of the Business Round Table's program called the Leapfrog Group. The Leapfrog Group is leveraging its health care purchasing power by basing its purchase of services on principles that encourage more stringent patient safety measures. The group has identified three initial hospital safety measures that will be the focus of provider performance comparisons and hospital recognition and reward.

In addition, the psychological cost of medical errors to an organization should not be overlooked. Although more difficult to quantify than the cost of five extra days in the intensive care unit (ICU), errors lead to frustration, loss of trust, decreased employee morale, and guilt among professionals, who are often held responsible despite estimates suggesting that almost 70% of adverse events are preventable.[2] W. Edwards Deming documented that most errors in industry occurred as a result of a breakdown in the system rather than individual negligence. Reports have highlighted the significance of system failures in the occurrence of preventable adverse events, such as in the case of a Florida man who had the wrong leg amputated.[3] Such psychological effects not only fuel a destructive culture and unfriendly work environment but also affect an organization's productivity. A no-fear, no-fault safety reporting program enhances an organization's ability to collapse the learning curve necessary to implement solutions that eliminate the potential for future harm and its associated costs. An organizational commitment to safe work practices offers significant advantages not only in employee retention but also in employee recruitment. A health care organization will only realize an adequate return on investment in employee orientation and training when the employee stays with an organization for the long term.

The Time Is Now

Given the financial struggles health care organizations continue to face, with high occupancy rates and shrinking margins, we believe that a focus on health care safety is one of the last remaining opportunities to eliminate waste and excessive costs while simultaneously improving quality, corporate culture, and marketplace image.

If the opportunity for improvement through the reduction of medical errors is so prevalent, then why has it taken so long to address it? Wagner and colleagues point out that there are at least four competing values involved in any business decision—institutional interests, employee interests, employee rights, and the community good—and at any time a decision may favor one value over another.[4] Historical experience indicates that in the case of patient safety, the institutions' and employees' financial and legal interests were the key values at work. However, with the changes in financial reimbursement brought about by the current payment systems, including managed care, hospitals will have to absorb the cost of extended stays brought on by medical errors, leaving a clear financial incentive to address the problem. In addition to reimbursement, the blame aspect of error reporting and the fear of being fired or sued have made it impossible for health care organizations to establish a realistic assessment of the effectiveness of the care delivery process relative to patient harm. Cultural barriers reinforced for generations have played a significant role in where the industry is today. Fortunately, the environment is changing. With the assistance of rising health care costs and the increase in medical information available through the Internet, the power is now shifting toward the consumer and toward an environment of accountability. Health care administrators are not only accountable for the financial position of their organizations, but also for the quality of care and the safety of the organization's patients and employees.

An anonymous, or de-identifying, safety reporting and management system helps to create the paradigm shift necessary to focus on the "what" instead of the "who" involved in analyzing near misses and adverse events. Only then can we begin to establish accurate benchmarks for the economic opportunity available through the reduction of medical errors. Unlike other industries such as manufacturing, hospital cost accounting programs presumed defect-free care when budgeting for the following year's services and resource requirements. Furthermore, the cost accounting process historically addressed the budgeting of services by discrete departments despite the fact that patients flow from one department to the next. Although many medical errors occur within a given department or service, still others occur as a result of ineffective transitions. Without an educational process and system to track errors that occur in the coordination of services, those events fall into a big black hole and their underlying causes continue to lurk in the darkness of the unknown, awaiting the next victim. As a result, we cannot effectively manage what we do not measure.

Safety as a Business Strategy

The recent focus on evidence-based standards in medicine is a promising step toward sustainable improvements because it takes a more comprehensive approach to identifying the economic agents involved in establishing standards, both moral and financial. Economic assessment in the absence of qualitative measures of outcomes underestimates the true scope of the opportunity for improvement. Historical experience shows that a cost–benefit analysis (the ratio between economic gain and loss) may not always result in the right choice with regard to evidence-based standards or, in the case of our topic of discussion, reducing harm to the patient. As an example, for many years cost–benefit analysis performed on nosocomial infections supported extended hospital stays until changes in fee-for-service reimbursement came about. In contrast, a cost-effectiveness analysis takes a more comprehensive view of the opportunity for improvement. The ratio between economic gain and loss is valued as a means to achieving such noneconomic interests as health and loss prevention.[5] Therefore, cost-effectiveness analysis is a more accurate method for establishing patient safety standards as well as a comprehensive business strategy to support those standards.

To succeed in the future, health care organizations must realize the overarching value of patient safety and position it as a key driver of their business strategy. Ritter and colleagues developed a comprehensive multifaceted model of the business case for patient safety.[6] Its components and their interrelationships are illustrated in Figure 31-1. Although this model was initially designed for an academic health system, its applicability across the spectrum of health care provider organizations in existence today is quite clear.

Ritter eloquently summarizes the model as follows:

> To realize the full impact of safety as a business strategy, the organization must continue its commitment to employee education and skill development, continually refine its complex processes with patient and employee safety in mind, openly espouse a blame-free "Culture of Safety," and implement a no fear/no fault error reporting system. In turn, through continuous improvement and risk management activities, using information generated through analysis of adverse event reports, and implementing "best practice" systems, the health care organization will be able to demonstrate its value as a provider of highest quality healthcare services and as a safety-conscious employer in the healthcare market. The top line is the impact on the bottom line. In addition to the cost savings generated by reduction of errors and their consequences, less employee turnover, and improved productivity of better-designed processes, opportunities for new revenue will develop. All of which mean greater organization value to the communities it serves.

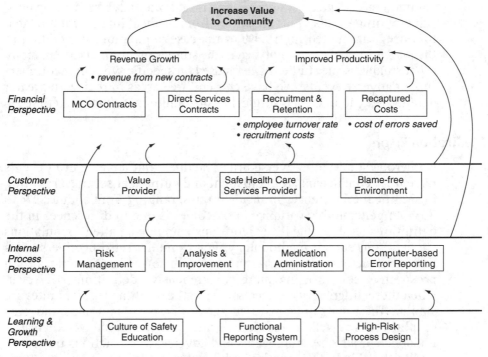

FIGURE 31-1   The business case and safety reporting system strategy map

What Do the Numbers Say? Data from Research Findings and the Private Sector

The national estimates on the deaths of inpatients resulting from medical errors published in the Institute of Medicine (IOM) report stem predominately from two major studies: the Harvard Medical Practice Study and a study of the costs of medical injuries in Utah and Colorado.[2,7,13] Much public attention has been placed on the estimated number of deaths due to medical errors, with extrapolated figures ranging from 44,000 to 98,000 lives per year.

The methodologies of both studies were similar, using a retrospective review of about 45,000 medical records for patients hospitalized in three states. The results of both studies reflect similar adverse event rates. The Utah and Colorado study estimated the total cost of preventable adverse events to be $308 million in discounted 1996 dollars, with 46% or $141.7 million attributable to health care costs. Given the results of their study, Thomas and coworkers estimated that the cost of preventable errors at a national level is a staggering $17 billion.[7]

Of the 1,133 hospitalized patients in the Harvard Medical Practice Study who experienced clinically important adverse events, the most common nonsurgical adverse event found was adverse drug events. Adverse drug events, injury resulting from medical intervention related to a drug, accounted for 19.4% of the case population. In addition to the large group of cases analyzed in the studies mentioned earlier, many other smaller-scale studies have focused on specific types of medical errors or adverse events. We have chosen three areas to review in greater detail: medication errors, surgical errors, and nosocomial infections.

Medication Errors

Numerous studies on adverse drug reactions and adverse drug events have been conducted across inpatient and outpatient settings, resulting in significant differences in incident rates, ranging from about 2.9% to 35%. In general, this variance in outcomes is due to differences in the definitions used, probability algorithms employed, patient populations studied, and survey methodology. For example, retrospective studies and strict definitions were associated with lower incident rates than prospective studies using more comprehensive definitions. However, when these differences are accounted for, the resulting incident rates are similar. The results are consistent across diverse populations and geographic areas as well. In addition, results consistently showed increased incidence of adverse drug events and adverse drug reactions in women and in the elderly.[5] Studies by both Bates and Classen sought to quantify the cost of adverse drug events and their impact on hospitalization. The results are briefly summarized here.

Bates and colleagues have broadened the definition of adverse drug event beyond that proposed by the World Health Organization and Food and Drug Administration to include "an injury resulting from medical intervention relating to a drug."[8] This definition is not only more comprehensive but favored by many because of its clinical relevance. Using this definition, Bates and colleagues conducted a case control study over 6 months for patients hospitalized at a 700-bed hospital. Over the course of the study, 190 adverse drug events were identified, with about one third being preventable. The baseline adverse drug event rate was 2.0 per 100 admissions. Patients who experienced an adverse drug event had longer hospital stays, and the costs of those cases exceeded the control group by more than $5,000. When the results of the study were annualized, the cost of preventable adverse drug events totaled $2.8 million for the 700-bed hospital.

In a matched case control study, Classen and coworkers evaluated mortality, length of hospitalization, and costs attributable to adverse drug events in a 520-bed hospital over a 4-year period.[9] The study consisted of 20,000 control patients, with adverse drug events voluntarily reported in 1,580 case patients. A baseline adverse drug event rate of

2.43 events per 100 admissions was computed. The average length of stay for patients experiencing adverse drug events increased to 7.69 days versus 4.46 days for the control group. In addition, hospitalization costs for patients experiencing adverse drug events increased, with an average cost of $10,010 per patient versus $5,355 for the control group. The cost attributed to one adverse drug event exceeded $2,000 among the case patients.

Surgical Errors

Andrews and colleagues developed a prospective, observational study of the care of all patients admitted to three surgical units of a large urban teaching hospital over the course of 9 months.[1] Patient and provider responses to events that occurred during the observational period of the study were tracked for another 2 years, and data about the outcome of claims were obtained 6 years after the study period. Of the 1,047 patients in the study, one or more adverse events or errors occurred in 45.8% of the patients. The results indicated that 17.7% of patients had a least one serious adverse event, ranging from temporary physical disability to death, whereas 18.2% had events whose seriousness was not discussed. One third of the patients were admitted more than once, resulting in a total of 1,716 admissions. Ethnicity, gender, age, and payer class of patients experiencing a serious initial adverse event were similar to those patients without adverse events. The mean length of stay was 8.8 days for patients without adverse events, and 23.8 days for those with adverse events. For patients with a serious illness adverse event, the mean length of stay was 22.2 days, compared with 15.3 days for all other patients. Their findings indicated that patients who had a serious adverse event were 74% less likely to be discharged from the hospital on any given day after the event than were patients who did not have a serious event. Also, their findings showed a greater rate of adverse events for sicker patients (those in the ICU) and for those with longer hospital stays.

Nosocomial Infections

Data from the comprehensive multisite Study on the Efficacy of Nosocomial Infection Control (SENIC) are commonly referenced in discussions on the cost benefit of reducing the occurrence of nosocomial infections in the hospital setting within the United States. The study estimates that approximately 3 million people a year are affected by nosocomial infections, which cause 60,000 deaths and contribute to $4 billion in direct health care costs. Despite these astronomical numbers, SENIC found that a hospital could reduce its infection rates by one third by implementing organized surveillance and control protocols. Such infection control programs cost on average about $60,000 a year for a 250-bed hospital to maintain.[5]

In a study on the socioeconomic impact of nosocomial infections, Jarvis summarizes selected studies on the prolongation of hospitalization and the costs associated with various categories of infection.[10] Urinary tract infections prolonged hospital stays by an estimated 1 to 4 days and added an estimated average cost of $558 to $593. Surgical site infections prolonged hospital stays by about 7 to 8.2 days and added $2,734 in additional costs per infection. Bloodstream infections prolonged hospitalization by an estimated 7 to 21 days and contributed additional costs of about $3,061 to $40,000 per infection. Finally, pneumonia, one of the most common infections in ICU patients, was found to prolong hospitalization by an estimated 6.8 to 30 days and added about $4,947 in costs per infection.

Data from the Private Sector

Some of the most extensive data on the economic benefits of patient safety and the reduction of medical errors have been generated by a private, for-profit company called Safety-Centered Solutions (SCS). Over the last 5 years SCS has collected data on occurrence rates of adverse events from various hospitals, including community and tertiary facilities with private, not-for-profit, and publicly owned governance structures. Their findings reflect a database containing over 90,000 adverse events of varying types, which have resulted in 158,474 additional days of care and have added approximately $137 million to the annual operating costs of the participating hospitals.[11] A consistent finding over this 5-year period is that 25% to 35% of the patients admitted to a general acute facility will most likely be subjected to at least one adverse event prior to discharge. These statistics include near misses that were caught prior to reaching the patient. The costs of these events add, on average, 10% to 15% to the hospital's annual operating costs. For a typical 200-bed hospital, these additional costs may easily be $10 to $12 million a year.

SCS provides its participating organizations with a safety reporting and management information system that calculates the variances in length of stay and additional costs for those cases where a near miss or adverse event was recorded. A significant benefit is the system's ability to calculate the approximate additional days and costs for a vast number of cases without having to review a medical record, making it a practical management tool. Such directional costs can be included in the analysis necessary to determine where limited performance improvement or process redesign resources may be spent.

TABLE 31-1   Safety-Centered Solutions' Findings on Costs of Medical Errors

Category	Additional Length of Stay (days)	Additional Costs ($)
Patient falls	2.22	1,146
Nosocomial infections		
Urinary tract	3.3	2,220
Surgical site	2.2	2,109
Bloodstream	2.2	4,661
Pneumonia	3.1	4,386
Adverse drug events	1.9	1,032*
Decubit	2.9	1,681[†]

*Includes near misses.

[†]Includes stages I to IV.

Source: Safety-Centered Solutions. *The Impact of Medical Errors on Hospital Costs and Productivity.* Tampa, FL: SafeCare Systems, LLC. 2001. Used with permission.

As with other referenced studies (such as Andrews et al.), there is still underreporting of adverse events in the facilities where SCS is working; therefore, the resulting costs stated previously are conservative at best. More important, however, is SCS's experience that the reporting of adverse events increases 50% to 100% when disincentives are removed and effective efforts to reduce occurrences are rewarded.

Table 31-1 summarizes SCS's findings in some of the more common categories of adverse events, listing both the additional days and costs by category. In most cases where the cost estimates differ substantially from independent research organizations, SCS's findings are lower, which is primarily because of the differences in definition or severity of adverse events being reported. As previously mentioned, SCS's participating hospitals capture the reporting of near misses as well as adverse events.

The Cost of Medical Malpractice

Up to this point in our discussion we have excluded the medical malpractice costs associated with medical errors. Although the percentage of claims settled or won over $1 million continues to steadily climb each year as our environment becomes more litigious, the number of adverse events that evolve into a claim or lawsuit remains relatively low. In Andrews and coworkers' study, for example, 17.7% of the patients experienced serious events, yet only 1.2% of the patients in the study made claims for compensation.[1] From a volume perspective, medical malpractice claims and suits are the tip of the iceberg. Another reason for omitting malpractice costs from our discussion is the number of factors that affect the outcome of a case. For example, not all claims and suits are a result of a medical error or adverse event. State laws such as those that support various forms of charitable immunity can also affect a case's outcome. Furthermore, philosophical approaches to defense strategy may favor one economic tactic over another, resulting in a different outcome as well.

Other Costs

For the purposes of our discussion, we have focused on the costs of preventable medical errors to health care organizations providing patient care, with the intent of shining a spotlight on the extensive opportunities for improvement at the operational level. There are, however, numerous other costs associated with preventable adverse events, such as the costs of lost earnings, lost household production, dependent care, and the human costs of pain and suffering.[12]

Moving Forward

Practically speaking, an exact measure of the scope of the medical error problem to date is not necessary in order to justify an investment in information systems that assist in the identification and elimination of medical errors. Rather than debate over the finite costs attributable to a surgical complication or adverse drug error, efforts are better spent in establishing a methodology and plan and then in operationalizing the plan to meet the goal recommended by the IOM.[13]

A comprehensive, integrated approach to patient safety includes at a minimum three key elements: education, data, and performance improvement activities (Figure 31-2). This methodology establishes a foundation for health care organizations to realize the overarching value of patient safety and position it as a key driver of their business strategy. First, educational programs must support and assist administrators in changing the culture and promoting safety reporting. The health care organization's staff, including administrators, clinicians, and support personnel, should understand the impact that safety practices have on an organization's productivity, its culture, its patient outcomes, and its reputation for quality within the community. They should also be able to report what they experience without fear of reprisal.

Second, a data-driven approach is essential for establishing trust and ultimately leading to evidence-based decision making. A safety reporting and management system provides a vehicle for aggregating

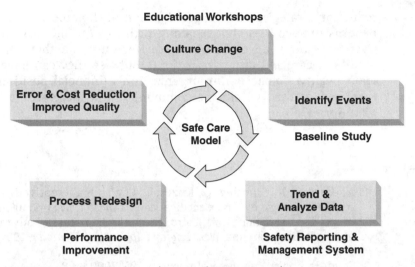

FIGURE 31-2   An integrated approach to patient safety

and analyzing event data for trends, pattern identification, and systemic causes as well as for measuring the impact of performance improvement initiatives to reduce medical errors. The information must include as much as is known about medical errors, including patient demographics, clinical and financial data, and specific information regarding the event. The system should be made available to members of a multidisciplinary care team, because each member brings unique expertise and perspective to the patient's experience. In support of Deming's fundamental belief, the system serves as a tool for employees to manage their own areas of responsibility, because those closest to the errors are often the most likely to have the solutions necessary to eliminate the causes and subsequent recurrence. Financial information is extremely valuable because it helps to make the economic case for administrators interested in monitoring their return on investment in their organization's safety initiatives. It is also important for employees responsible for line operations to not only understand the economic impact of safe care but also to be able to monitor and affect their own areas of responsibility moving forward.

The third element of an approach to patient safety is the performance improvement (PI) and process redesign activities that assist in either eliminating the causes of errors or in positioning permanent controls to catch the possible recurrence of errors. This is a critical stage in quality improvement because it ensures that we close the feedback loop. The PI process serves as a tool to assist clinicians and management in maintaining their focus and energy on patient safety. The process allows for continuous evaluation of the effectiveness of error reduction strategies and the proliferation of a blame-free culture. The benefits of such PI activities, along with tools to monitor their effectiveness, cannot be underestimated. Not only can they improve the quality of care and safety for patients, but also they can have a significant positive impact on an organization's financial position, its culture, and its trust within the community, and therefore on its future viability.

References

1. Andrews, L. B., Stocking, C., Krizek, T., et al. An alternative strategy for studying adverse events in medical care. *Lancet* 1997;349:309–313.
2. Leape, L. L., Brennan, T. A., Laird, N., et al. The nature of adverse events in hospitalized patients. *New England Journal of Medicine* 1991;324:377–384.
3. Scott, D. Preventing medical mistakes. *RN* 2000;63:8.
4. Wagner, J. T., Meier, C., and Higdon, T. A perspective from clinical and business ethics on adverse events in hospitalized patients. *J Florida MA* 1997;84:8.
5. Sharpe, V. A., and Faden, A. I. *Medical Harm: Historical, Conceptual, and Ethical Dimensions of Iatrogenic Illness*. Cambridge, UK: Cambridge University Press, 1998.
6. Ritter, G. E. et al. *Safety as a Business Strategy*. Unpublished report by the Division of Healthcare Quality, Baystate Health System, 2001.
7. Thomas, E. J., Studdert, D. M., Newhouse, J. P., et al. Costs of medical injuries in Utah and Colorado. *Inquiry* 1999;36(3):255–264.
8. Bates, D. W., Spell, N., Cullen, D. J., et al. The costs of adverse drug events in hospitalized patients. *JAMA* 1997;277:307–311.
9. Classen, D. C., Pestotnik, S. L., Evans, R. S., et al. Adverse drug events in hospitalized patients: excess length of stay, extra costs, and attributable mortality. *JAMA* 1997;277:301–308.
10. Jarvis, W. R. Selected aspects of the socioeconomic impact of nosocomial infections: morbidity, mortality, cost and prevention. *Infection Control and Hospital Epidemiology* 1996;17:8.
11. Safety-Centered Solutions. *The Impact of Medical Errors on Hospital Costs and Productivity*. Tampa, FL: Safety-Centered Solutions, 2001.
12. Bogner, M. S. *Human Error in Medicine*. Hillsdale, NJ: Lawrence Erlbaum Associates, 1994.
13. Kohn, L. T., Corrigan, J. M., Donaldson, M. S., eds. *To Err Is Human: Building a Safer Health System*. Washington, DC: National Academy Press, 1999.

CHAPTER THIRTY-TWO

THE ROLE OF ETHICS AND ETHICS SERVICES IN PATIENT SAFETY

Erin A. Egan, MD, JD

Clinical medical ethics has existed since the time of Hippocrates and Aristotle.[1] Currently many hospitals offer clinical ethical services, and the Joint Commission on Accreditation of Healthcare Organizations now mandates that hospitals have a process in place for dealing with ethical issues.[2] Clinical ethics services are important tools in patient protection and in development of an institutional ethic that emphasizes patient safety. Hospitals and other institutional providers of health care must foster an atmosphere that values patient safety in order to improve patient safety. Offering competent and clinically relevant ethics services is a key element of this atmosphere.

Medical ethics is grounded in traditional Western philosophy and has always been a fundamental aspect of health care provision. The oath taken by physicians as they become doctors, the Hippocratic oath, and similar oaths taken by many health care providers, provide a framework for professionalism and ethical provision of care. These philosophical underpinnings reflect the inherent moral obligations assumed by health care providers. The moral obligations create a series of duties incumbent on providers. Central among these duties is the responsibility to guard the safety of the patient. Medical ethics is therefore fundamentally tied to patient safety.

Several well-respected medical ethicists have considered patient safety as a fundamental aspect of clinical medical ethics. Patients are in a position of particular vulnerability and need as a result of their illness, and medical ethics places the patient's specific vulnerabilities and needs at the center of the ethical analysis.[3] This is particularly important as the health care environment becomes increasingly subject to a variety of economic and administrative interests that are not inherently patient oriented. Ethics consultation services, whether provided by an individual, a team, or a committee, should be guided by the following goals:

- To maximize benefit and minimize harm to patients, families, healthcare professionals, and institutions by fostering a fair and inclusive decision-making process that honors patients'/proxy preferences and individual and cultural value differences among all parties to the consultation.
- To facilitate resolution of conflicts in a respectful atmosphere with attention to the interests, rights, and responsibilities of those involved.
- To inform institutional efforts at policy development, quality improvement, and appropriate utilization of resources by identifying the causes of ethical problems and promoting practices consistent with ethical norms and standards.
- To assist individuals in handling current and future ethical problems by providing education in healthcare ethics.[4]

Any ethics committee that makes an effort to live by these goals can play a vital role in patient safety initiatives.

Principles of Clinical Medical Ethics: Beneficence, Paternalism, Nonmalificence, Justice, and Fiduciary Duties

Clinical medical ethics is a field grounded in the practical application of the duties physicians and other health care providers have to patients. These duties serve as starting points for analyses of ethical behavior. All these duties involve an understanding of the patient's experience and the patient's needs in obtaining care. These principles, when adhered to for the patient's best interest, promote a focus on patient safety. The basic foundation of these duties is the legal and moral obligation of providers to act in their patients' best interest. The ethical implication of these duties can be applied to solve problems, make policy decisions, and guide behavior on issues of patient safety.

Beneficence is the principle of acting for the benefit of others and contributing to their welfare. Rules of beneficence, as articulated by Beauchamp and Childress, include protecting the rights of others, preventing harm, rectifying conditions that may cause harm, and aiding those in need of rescue. Adherence to principles of beneficence lays an excellent foundation for a safety-oriented environment. Practical application of this principle seeks a course of action, policy, or solution that is of maximal benefit and most likely to prevent or reduce harm. In analyzing patient safety problems and issues, identifying beneficent principles can help reach a plan that emphasizes benefit and patient welfare.[5]

Paternalism is a subtype of beneficence where someone with more knowledge, experience, or authority determines what actions would be in another's best interest. The intent in paternalism is beneficent, but it generally involves the imposition of one set of values on another. The typical, healthy manifestation of this type of beneficence is, as the name suggests, parenting. Parents use their superior judgment and experience to make decisions for their children, at times against the child's wishes, until the child has the maturity to assume responsibility for his or her own best interest. Health care often involves a similar paternalism, which can facilitate a healthy doctor–patient relationship and promote safety or can act to undermine those things. A patient seeks out health care to utilize the knowledge, experience, and skills of health care professionals. Trust in the provider allows the patient to rely on the beneficence of the caregiver and accept some level of paternalism in the interest of preventing or treating diseases. Paternalism is a fundamental part of the relationship because the patient must rely on the knowledge, judgment, and skill of the provider to do what is best for the patient. However, paternalism has a limited role in health care, and the failure of providers to curb their own paternalism can compromise patient safety. The balancing principle, respect for the patient's autonomy, is discussed next. A proper balance between paternalism and respect for patient autonomy is the cornerstone of quality health care and safe health care.

Autonomy is respect for the patient's ability and right to determine what happens to his or her own body. The Greek roots of the word mean "self-governance."[6] Autonomy in health care requires that certain conditions be met. The patient must be competent—capable of understanding and making health care decisions. The decision itself and the process of making the decision must be voluntary. Respect for a patient's autonomy requires full disclosure, with adequate explanation to facilitate decision making.[7] Autonomy is the interest that balances paternalism. To respect patients' autonomy and to facilitate their autonomous decision making, the provider or providers must limit their own paternalism. Some patients may demand that the health care team limit its feelings of paternalism by insisting on autonomy. Other patients may not do so, but are entitled to a similar limitation, self-imposed by the provider. Respect for a patient's autonomy is still important outside the decision-making context. Disclosure of mistakes respects patients' right to know the truth about their care and their body. There may not be any decisions, or at least health care decisions, that need to be made or are affected by a mistake, but the patient has the right to know about errors as an autonomous entity. Less than full disclosure may be premised on the belief that it will only hurt the patient or family more to know the truth, but this belief is an expression of paternalism and ignores the patient's or the family's autonomous rights.

The principle of *nonmalificence* is embodied by the phrase "first, do no harm." Patient safety concerns are firmly rooted in this principle. Before a provider or institution undertakes the effort to improve a patient's health, each should be very sure that the patient wouldn't be injured and in worse condition as a result of the care received. Patient safety is not a movement aimed at creating new and better cures or treatments. It is aimed at ensuring that no preventable harm is done to patients. It is important to note that patient safety is not completely devoted to nonmalificence. Patient safety focuses on eliminating preventable harm, but not eliminating all harm. Some genuinely indicated and competently performed health care services cause harm. The nonmalificence embraced in the patient safety movement is not that no risks are justified for better health, because the decision of what is acceptable risk lies with the competent patient. Nonmalificence does not always override autonomy. Our respect for patients' abilities and right to make their own decisions means that we will allow them to experience risk. Patient safety emphasizes eliminating preventable, unnecessary injury. The role of nonmalificence in patient safety is immense but requires proper limitation in its application.

Justice is a principle based on rights and fairness. Something is unjust if it denies rights or distributes benefits and burdens unfairly.[8] Typically, the rights of individuals and what is fair or unfair distribution are concepts defined by a society. Some are common to most societies, such as the injustice of killing. Others vary widely, such as the injustice of modes of access to health care. In medical ethics, justice can be a troubling consideration. Societal considerations of fairness and scarcity issues may have a very limited role in bedside decision making. In the area of patient safety, however, justice is usually a proper consideration. Justice enters into issues of disclosure, as well as issues of policy and institutional ethics. Allocation of resources is important in patient safety, both as a cause of medical error and as a solution. How an institution distributes its efforts to improve patient safety will have implications for what is accomplished and how successfully. Throughout this discussion, justice is an underlying concern, even if it is not expressly mentioned.

Fiduciary duties are legal duties, which, in health care, consider the relative vulnerability of the patient relative to the provider. The legal concept of a fiduciary responsibility attempts to enforce some professional ethical principles by creating legal consequences for violating them. A *fiduciary* is a person who voluntarily agrees to act primarily for the benefit of another.[9] Generally, a fiduciary relationship involves "good faith, trust, special confidence, and candor."[10] Breaching a fiduciary duty has legal and professional consequences. Physicians, and often other health care providers, have a fiduciary duty to patients and are required to act in the best interest of the patient. This duty is somewhat paternalistic, but it recognizes that patients seek health care for knowledge that they don't have and to receive services they can't perform. Sometimes the patient must rely on the health care provider's perception of what is good for him or her under the circumstances. However, fiduciary duties include candor and trust. Therefore, disclosure is a fiduciary, as well as a moral and ethical, duty. Similarly, ensuring the safety of the patient, especially in a hospital setting where the individual has little control over his or her own environment, is a fiduciary duty because it is undertaken in the patient's best interest. In many ways the fiduciary relationship between a patient and a health care provider is merely a formal, legal recognition of the ethical obligations the provider has to the patient.

Ethics Committees and Consultation Services

Although medical ethics began thousands of years ago, ethics committees and ethics services are relatively new concepts. Ethics committees, ethics consultation teams, and individual ethics consultants allow ethics to be an active clinical service. Ethical analysis is useful to proactively prevent problems through education and formation of policies, and is important for retrospective review to learn from mistakes and identify weak areas. The strength of providing ethics consultation services is that ethical considerations need to guide decision-making processes and pervade clinical care. Clinical medical ethics focuses on the role of ethics in the active clinical environment. The American Medical Association *Code of Medical Ethics* recommends that ethics committees or services be educational and advisory, and that they be available to health care professionals, families, and patients to provide information and assistance when asked.[11] Ethics committees typically espouse three primary goals: case consultation, education, and policy development.

The idea of hospitals providing ethical assistance in active cases through ethics services was the result of a suggestion by the judge charged with deciding the case of Karen Ann Quinlan.[12] *Quinlan* was one of the first cases to look at the possibility of discontinuing a ventilator in a patient who was in a persistent vegetative state but with no immediately terminal conditions.[13] The court in *Quinlan* suggested that situations such as the one faced by the Quinlan family would be best addressed by medical personnel with some training and ability to deal with complicated and emotionally charged dilemmas and disagreements.[14]

Ethics committees are often composed of members with diverse backgrounds, including physicians, nurses, attorneys, patient advocates, and religious leaders. Ethics committees can consider active cases by allowing medical personnel to attend the meeting and present a case, or by offering consultation services and later discussing the case with the committee. The consultant is able to respond quickly to a request, gather information, and talk to providers and families. The consultant is more experienced in ethical consultation than a typical medical team and is therefore able to collect information quickly and sort out relevant information. If the medical team needs to make an immediate clinical decision, the consultant is available for an immediate recommendation. However, whenever possible, the consultant will meet with the full ethics committee and present the case prior to making a recommendation. If there is not time to present the case prior to offering a recommendation, a recommendation is made to the team, and the committee reviews the case and gives feedback at the next meeting. This mixed committee/consultant structure allows for immediate clinical ethics involvement in active cases, providing the capability of responding to the pace of clinical medicine, while maintaining the benefit of a group process and the input of people with varied backgrounds whenever possible.[15] This interaction between a consultant and the larger committee has been analogized to the interaction between a trial court and a court of appeals.[16]

There are many variations in the way ethics services are offered by hospitals or other institutions. Services may be limited to an ethics committee without consultation services, or may involve a consultation service without an ethics committee. Many institutions have a single person, often with formal or informal training in ethics, available for ethics consultation. Whichever structure an institution uses, it is important that the ethics consultant or committee make a distinct effort to provide education and policy assistance in addition to clinical case consultation.

The role of clinical ethics consultants or committees in patient safety involves all three facets of clinical ethical services. Any active case where there is any type of patient safety concern warrants an ethics consultation. The role of the ethicist in specific situations is discussed in depth later in this chapter. However, the ethicist can provide a framework for determining which obligations are most important to meet the patient's needs and improve the outcome. An ethics committee can provide an opportunity for discussion of the issues and the conflicts involved in a nonthreatening, patient-focused environment. It is important that the ethics committee be a forum for discussion and not a penalty tribunal.

The educational and policy roles of ethics are important in developing a safe patient environment. The ethicist can assist in making ethical, patient-oriented, outcome-improving policies that help prevent problems and conflict. Developing an ethically sound institutional policy on issues of provider incompetence, medical mistakes, and informed consent helps ensure patient safety as a preventive measure and facilitates rapid action in the face of problems. Educating all members of the health care team on their duties and responsibilities to patients as a result of their moral, ethical, and legal obligations assists team members in understanding their role in patient safety and emphasizes the importance of a patient safety commitment. Educational interventions should be provided both case by case, educating the team members as consults arise, and in broader efforts that target groups, including lectures, journal clubs, case conferences, and lunch seminars.

Ethics consultation services are frequently consulted on issues of withdrawing or withholding therapy, more than any other single issue and constituting 49% to 65% of consultations in one study.[17] An additional 37% of consultations in the same study involved end-of-life decision making and how to approach resuscitation.[18] Making sure these decisions are made competently and ethically, with maximum participation by the patient and family, is both a quality of care issue and a patient safety issue. Other ethical issues of particular importance for patient safety are medical mistakes and disclosure, impaired or incompetent providers, issues of informed consent, and disagreements between professionals or between patients, families, and providers. Finally, the ethical atmosphere of the institution, the way the institution values ethical and safe health care provision, and emphasis on candid and critical discussions about patient safety and quality improvement are all within the scope of ethics services and are the basis for long-term improvement in patient safety.

Patient Safety as an Ethical Issue

The previous section focused on ethical principles and the nature of clinical ethics services. This section discusses patient safety as a clinical medical ethical issue. The principles discussed earlier provide the philosophical framework for analyzing patient safety issues in a clinical ethical context. The next section focuses on application of ethical principles in specific types of patient safety–related problems. Medical ethics, to be relevant, must move beyond the philosophical roots of ethics and become clinically relevant. Clinical relevance requires a meaningful contribution to the process of providing care to patients and improving the outcomes for individual patients. Ethics in this context becomes a dynamic application of principles to improve care and assist the health care team in resolving the issues they face daily.

The common ground of ethics, health care, and the patient safety movement is that all emphasize improving outcomes. This common ground is all that is necessary for these fields to interact synergistically for the benefit of the patient. All three areas begin with nonmalificence, the desire to do no harm, and strive for maximal beneficence, the opportunity to do the most possible good. Providers seek these goals through their technical knowledge and the healing quality of their interactions with patients. Ethicists seek these goals through "improving the process and outcomes of patients' care by helping identify, analyze, and resolve ethical problems."[19] Patient safety becomes involved because the patient's well-being is the goal of health care, and safety is essential to well-being. Patient safety concerns are in a realm where the philosophical, technical, and personal aspects of medicine overlap.

A further basis for patient safety issues as an ethical concern is that the focus on patient safety needs to be pervasive and requires a paradigm shift in the way professionals deal with mistakes and problems. Creating a paradigm shift in a field such as health care requires constant vigilance to ethical principles in order to avoid creating a system that is ethically flawed.[20] This paradigm shift requires the development of an institutional ethic, a pervasive policy of commitment to ethical principles that is reflected in how the institution as a whole prevents and responds to patient safety concerns. The institutional ethic should be something that goes far beyond a policy governing certain situations to be a general atmosphere of commitment to patient safety that is as apparent in unpredictable occurrences as in established policies. An institutional ethic that focuses on complete internal consistency in protecting the patient's interest will inherently promote patient safety, because safety is clearly in the patient's best interest. The institution must accept and enhance the fiduciary duties of providers to protect the patient's interest. The principles of beneficence, nonmalificence, and fiduciary responsibility must be apparent in every policy and action endorsed by the institution.

As a result of framing patient safety concerns as ethical issues, additional benefits arise from the central involvement of the ethicist or committee in patient safety promotion. Ethics services frequently assist teams and patients when the primary problem is one of disagreement. As many as 24% to 45% of an ethics service's consultations involve dispute resolution.[21] Formal clinical medical ethics training usually includes some dispute resolution training.[22] Dealing with the aftermath of a medical mistake can foster hostility and disagreement, and because ethicists are experienced in dispute resolution, they can provide valuable guidance.

Finally, ethical concerns and ethical services can play an important role in quality improvement efforts. Improving patient safety is inherently quality improvement, and these fields can go hand in hand. Especially when quality improvement and utilization review are closely linked in the hospital's administrative structure, ethical principles and quality improvement initiatives help create boundaries to the effort to control costs so that patient safety is not compromised by cost control. Ethics and quality improvement are similar in that they promote a goal of ideal behavior and policy, which although never perfectly achieved should always be sought.[23]

Specific Applications of Ethics in Particular Situations

Medical Mistakes

The first and foremost issue in patient safety is medical mistakes. Since the publication of the Institute of Medicine's report indicating that medical error is a severe problem in U.S. health care, this issue has properly received a lot of attention both from patients and providers.[24] Medical error, and the aftermath of errors, has always been an area of focus for clinical medical ethics. Most legal, professional, and ethical guidelines agree that disclosure and the duty to report are fundamental issues.

Disclosure is often the hardest aspect of mistakes for health care professionals. Disclosure refers to being honest with the patient or the family or both about the mistake and the consequences of the mistake. Despite the difficulty providers have with disclosure, it is the cornerstone of the relationship between patients and providers. Disclosure is a fundamental manifestation of respect for autonomy. The American Medical Association's Principles of Medical Ethics require a physician to "deal honestly with patients."[25] The legal fiduciary duty requires trust and candor, and candor requires honest disclosure. In 1999 the *British Medical Journal* published the Tavistock Group's statement of "shared ethical principles for everybody in health care."[26] These principles include cooperation and leadership by health care professionals, and an approach of personal responsibility for errors.[27] Ethics education and prioritization of ethical behaviors facilitate this personal responsibility. In addition to being traditionally considered the ethical response, disclosure may decrease the likelihood of litigation.[28] Providers and institutions must realize that disclosure and honesty are important parts of the health care process. Understanding autonomy and its implications facilitates this realization.

Another issue, one that precedes the issue of disclosure, is the duty to report. Medical errors may go unreported 50% to 96% of the time.[29] For obvious reasons, there can be little improvement without accurate information about the nature and frequency of medical mistakes. Ethics education can provide the basis for each provider believing that the importance of reporting outweighs the possible negative effects to the provider who is the reporter. Justice and respect for autonomy demand reporting. Conversely, the immediate unpleasant consequences, real or imagined, of reporting the errors of colleagues or one's self can create a compulsion to keep things quiet. However, if providers and those around them are constantly encouraged to place the patient's interests above all others, and are rewarded for doing so, reporting mistakes will be easier for providers to undertake.

Provider Impairment and Incompetence

All health care providers are aware of the potential and actual danger of incompetent and impaired providers. However, this is an area where health care professionals have extreme difficulty. In contrast to medical mistakes, which are a fact of being human, incompetence or impairment is limited to a group of providers and is not a common experience. The one element of commonality, which influences providers to be forgiving and supportive, is that most providers have had to practice in an impaired condition from lack of sleep. However, persistent impairment from drugs or other problems, or persistent incompetence, is an intolerable danger in health care. No one wants to be the snitch. Providers may feel that reporting will do little good and make their own lives intolerable. Every provider accepts the principle that he or she has a duty to report problems with colleagues, but often the practical barriers to doing so seem insurmountable.

This is an area where ethics education and an institutional ethic are crucial. Every provider must feel a personal responsibility to ensure the safety of every patient. Every provider must be willing to take all possible steps to prevent unnecessary harm. If providers value their ethical and legal duties, they are more likely to act on those principles in spite of barriers. Reminding providers of the moral underpinning of their responsibilities will cause providers to reflect on these duties and prioritize adherence to them. The institution must create an environment that encourages reporting. Whistle blowers should be given genuine protection. If the whistle blower requests, he or she should be transferred to avoid retribution. However, immediate intervention with all members of a department or area where there has been a report to review and emphasize the obligatory nature of reporting may help other providers realize the value of reporting. Because this is a particularly threatening area for providers, change will be slow and institutions and ethics services must commit to long-term education and support.

Informed Consent

Informed consent is one of the areas most traditionally considered "ethical." Informed consent issues can be complicated, and ethics services are well positioned to assist in complex cases. More important, ethics services can emphasize the importance of proper informed consent in every routine instance. Proper informed consent can prevent a variety of problems and misunderstandings. The institution must insist that providers make a concerted effort to have a detailed personal conversation with each patient on issues of consent. Obtaining consent for a procedure may fall to the lowest person on the totem pole and may be viewed as one more paperwork requirement. Institutions need to require the provider performing the procedure to obtain the consent. Providers need to be reminded of the importance of the consent process, including preventing misunderstandings or disappointment after a procedure. Providers should be trained in giving consent, and quality management or utilization review should ensure that the consent form was signed by a provider who was appropriate to obtain the consent. The principles of informed consent and the reasons for it are topics of education. Enforcing proper informed consent procedures is administrative.

Conclusion

This overview of ethical principles and applications has attempted to integrate clinical medical ethics services into a coordinated patient safety initiative. Acting alone, ethics service providers may have little material impact on improving patient safety. Ethics education and clinical ethical consultations will have an effect on improving patient safety, but require an organized effort for maximal effectiveness. As institutions evaluate mechanisms to improve patient safety, diverse groups should be involved. Ethicists and ethics committees have a unique role, and their potential contribution to patient safety is critical. Even without a designated ethicist or ethics service, these principles can and should be incorporated into any patient safety initiative. In institutions that have the advantage of having designated ethicists or ethics committees, those people should be given a central role in developing a comprehensive patient safety agenda.

Notes

1. Aristotle, *The Nichomachean Ethics,* and the writings of Hippocrates in general.
2. Joint Commission on Accreditation of Healthcare Organizations, *1995 Comprehensive Accreditation Manual for Hospitals* (Oakbrook Terrace, IL: JCAHO, 1994).
3. Edmund Pellegrino, "Allocation of Resources at the Bedside: The Intersection of Economics, Law and Ethics," *Kennedy Institute of Ethics Journal,* vol. 4 (1994), 309.
4. John C. Fletcher and Mark Siegler, "What Are the Goals of Ethics Consultation? A Consensus Statement," *J Clin Ethics,* vol. 122 (Summer 1996), 125.
5. Tom L. Beauchamp, and James F. Childress, *Principles of Biomedical Ethics* (New York: Oxford University Press, 1994), 277–318.
6. Ibid., 120.
7. Ibid., 146.
8. Kathleen Mitchell et al., "The Synergistic Relationship Between Ethics and Quality Improvement: Thriving in Managed Care," *J Nursing Care Quality,* vol. 1 (Oct. 1996), 9.
9. *Black's Law Dictionary,* abridged 6th ed. (St. Paul, MN: West Publishing, 1991), 431.
10. Ibid.
11. American Medical Association, *Code of Medical Ethics* (Chicago: AMA, 1997), 151. Although this citation is to an older edition of the code, the substance of this reference has not changed in later editions.
12. *In re Quinlan,* 70 N.J. 10, 355 A.2d 647 (1976).
13. Ibid.
14. Ibid.
15. Peter A. Singer, Edmund D. Pellegrino, and Mark Siegler, "Ethics Committees and Consultants," *J Clin Ethics,* vol. 1 (Winter 1990), 263.
16. Mark Siegler, Edmund D. Pellegrino, and Peter A. Singer, "Clinical Medical Ethics," *J Clin Ethics,* vol. 1 (Spring 1990), 5.
17. John LaPuma et al., "An Ethics Consultation Service in a Teaching Hospital: Utilization and Evaluation," *JAMA,* vol. 260 (Aug. 12, 1988), 808.
18. Ibid.
19. Fletcher and Siegler, "What Are the Goals of Ethics Consultation?" 124.
20. Cheryl A. Anderson, "Ethics Committees and Quality Improvement: A Necessary Link," *J Nursing Care Quality,* vol. 11 (Oct. 1996), 17–25.
21. LaPuma et al., "Ethics Consultation Service," 809.
22. For example, the postdoctoral fellowship in clinical medical ethics offered through the MacLean Center for Clinical Medical Ethics at the University of Chicago Hospitals includes formal and informal training in dispute resolution.
23. Anderson, "Ethics Committees and Quality Improvement."
24. Institute of Medicine, *To Err Is Human: Building a Safer Health System* (Washington, DC: National Academy Press, 1999), 1.

25. American Medical Association, *Code of Medical Ethics*, xvii.

26. R. Smith et al., "Shared Ethical Principles for Everybody in Health Care: A Working Draft of the Tavistock Group," *BMJ*, vol. 318 (1999), 248.

27. Peter A. Singer, "Medical Ethics: Clinical Review," *BMJ*, vol. 321 (July 29, 2000), 282.

28. Robert L. Lowes, "Made a Bonehead Mistake? Apologize," *Med Econ*, vol. 74 (May 12, 1997), 94.

29. Paul Barach and Stephen D. Small, "Reporting and Preventing Medical Mishaps: Lessons from Non-medical Near Miss Reporting Systems," *BMJ*, vol. 320 (March 18, 2000), 759.

CHAPTER THIRTY-THREE

HOW WE STARTED PATIENT SAFETY IN ISRAEL: WITHOUT A BUDGET BUT WITH ENTHUSIASM

Yoel Donchin, MD

It was a time before the dawn of the human error period in health care, before the topic became so popular. It all started one day when in the operating room. We used to have small bottles on our anesthesia cart, like phenol, eye drops, and nasal drops. Mr. Barmatz, a practicing physician, poured a few drops of phenol into a child's nose and immediately cried (and I shall never forget it in my life), "What have I done! I killed him!" He did not, and an immediate flush with water dissolved the toxic agent. I took the three bottles from the operating room to a well-illuminated place and, with my old camera, immortalized them. The picture and the incident report went to the head of pharmacy, a pedantic old-fashioned scholar. He loves his product, and was sure that the kind of labeling used on the bottle was the best there is. "You should read the label," he used to say, "even if it is printed in small letters! This is your responsibility." I did not share his enthusiasm.

It took another year for me to discover the world of human factors engineering. A fortuitous meeting with Professor Gopher, head of industrial engineering at the Technion, the Israeli institute of technology, changed everything. "What is your specialty?" I asked him after being introduced. He explained to me that he looks at human performance at work: why workers are tired early in the morning, as well as looking at failures or mishaps in the working place.

"I have a nice picture to show you," I told him. I brought the three-bottle photograph, told him the story behind it, and invited him to tour our operating room and the intensive care unit (ICU). A few weeks later we hosted at Hadassah Medical Center, in Jerusalem, a group of six faculty members from the Technion. They all changed into scrubbing suits and started the tour. They observed how we prepare our drugs, arrange them on the anesthesia table, record the data, calculate the proper doses, and look after our critically ill patients in the nearby intensive care unit. At the end of this tour the group was shocked. "This is the first time we have toured a 'plant,' and the solutions to your problems are so obvious. We do not understand how it is possible to work under such circumstances. All you have to do is . . . ." What followed was a list of steps to improve hospital safety that could be done by paying attention to details and creating moderate change without the need for huge investment.

The changes took place immediately: labeling the syringes, changing the location of the various items and devices in the anesthesia trolley, writing protocols, and above all getting people to start thinking about their working place.

A few months later in the ICU, during the morning hour, we discovered that there were a lot of calculating errors made by the nurses. The fluid balance looked very strange, for example. One patient got 7 liters of clear fluids during the last day and his total urine output was 2 liters, even though at noontime he had already given 3.500 mL. Checking the calculation showed a constant error in the adding process (recent volume + total). No wonder that at 04:00 everybody was so tired from correctly performing simple adding, especially since in our chart, addition is done horizontally rather than vertically, as normal people add numbers. Adding a calculator improved the situation. However, handwriting was not always clear, and the numbers punched into the electronic device were wrong. . . . At that point we called our friends from the Technion and asked for help. The problem was that we were discovering too many errors on a daily basis.

Calculation was not the main problem. Drugs were being administered to the wrong patient, dosages were being given that exceeded the therapeutic level, and there were devices that happened to deliver 100 mg dopamine in 5 minutes (rather than 12 hours). We had a real problem! The literature was scant. There were few papers, most of them retrospective studies.

The department of industrial engineering at the Technion took the challenge. This was the first time a request had come from a medical department that was opening its gate to "aliens" from a nonmedical field! The hospital director general was positive from the first minute and gave us full support and backup. He was aware of the fact that we were going to investigate the causes of human error in the hospital and knew what the legal department thought of it, but he told us, "If you can reduce errors by this, let's try it." The first step was to acquire full cooperation with the nursing team and have their confidence and trust, in order to get reliable reporting of errors. The planning meetings took place at my home, with every member of the medical as well as the nursing team. The atmosphere was relaxed, and together we designed a special form for reporting, the study, and the way to cooperate with the investigators from the Technion.

From the moment the nursing team became a full partner in the planning of research methods, the nurses' cooperation was without reservation. This manifested in a willingness to report mistakes, albeit on anonymous forms, and evolved into a race to report as many mistakes as possible.

Forms for recording of mistakes were placed in a special box located in the ICU. Each form was intended to report on a single mistake. The severity of the patient's condition was not graded according to one of the accepted severity rating scales (e.g., the APACHI, which takes into account physiological measures such as blood pressure and respiration on admission), but rather according to the number of cables and pieces of equipment to which the patient was attached. The greater the number of pieces of equipment to which the patient was connected, the higher the severity rating, because the greater the risk for mistakes to be made.

To verify the nurses' reports, researchers trained in human factors analysis, who were specially trained to observe in the ICU, carried out observations. They accompanied the medical team for uninterrupted 24-hour periods, during which time the researchers would conduct their observations and write systematic reports on mistakes they had witnessed. Comparison of the observers' reports with those of the independent participants revealed a good correlation, demonstrating that the staff was reporting accurately.

It was important not just to look at the error rates and analyze the causes, but also to describe the ICU profile—what kind of activities are carried out in the unit—and to look at the ratio between activities and errors. An *activity* is defined as "any interaction involving the patient and his or her immediate bedside surroundings." Activities around the patient's bed during the 24-hour observation periods were recorded.

Examples of recorded activities included replacing intravenous fluids, calibrating a transducer, and administering a drug. Family talking with the patient or an x-ray technician working near the bed were also regarded as activity. Every interaction, regardless of the time required, was counted as a single activity. Activities were recorded on a special form prepared for the study, which detailed the time, type, and nature of the activity, as well as the member of the team who performed the activity. These observations provided a baseline profile of daily activity in the ICU and a reference point for estimating the rate of error making. They also served as an independent measure of the accuracy and completeness of the medical and nursing staff records of human error.

During the 4 months of data collection, the research observers recorded 554 human errors. Doctors and nurses recorded 476 errors. The severity rating demonstrated that 147 (29%) were errors that might have caused significant deterioration in the patient's status or even death. Of the total number of errors reported by the ICU medical staff, 206 (46%) were made by physicians, and 240 (54%) by nurses. That distribution was found to be consistent whether the reporters were doctors or nurses. On average, more errors per hour occurred during the day than at night. The major findings were published in 1995. The main reason for errors was not the physical setup of the unit or fatigue after a long night shift, but rather the lack of communication between teams.

We presented the preliminary results at a medical conference in Jerusalem. To clearly demonstrate the results, we stated that we have a 1.4% fatal error rate per patient per 24 hours (if error was not discovered on time). The local tabloid came out the next day with the headline "Two Patients Killed Each Day in the Hospital." The hospital response was immediate and very supportive. "Only a strong and healthy organization is able to conduct such a study," it responded. "Care is much safer at Hadassah, as we took measures to eliminate errors by taking responsibility and not resorting to the usual tactics of denial. The public confidence in our medical center remains intact."

Based on the findings in the first study, lack of communication is the main reason for mistakes, as the data gathered indicate that effective communication between physicians and nurses depends more on the information quality than the information quantity. A second study to look into the way physicians and nurses communicate was carried out in a simulation that portrayed the process of patient reception at the shift change. During the simulation the subjects (nurses and physicians at various levels of expertise) were requested to "think aloud" and describe how they were going to act and whether they needed more information. Actually, they were describing to us how they build their own "mental model" of the patient's clinical state that leads to operational activities. The verbal protocols produced in this way were processed by the SHAPA program developed by James and Sanderson.

The results enabled us to diagram the formal structure of the thinking processes both of physicians and nurses in the ICU and showed that physicians think differently from nurses. Physicians tend to filter information according to their perception of the situation, whereas nurses gather information from the patient, that is, from the monitoring devices and pure clinical assessment. Because the physician takes more steps on the way to reach a diagnosis—his or her data processing is longer than that of the nurse—the physician is more prone to "produce" error. Analysis of the text demonstrates that in addition, we have in the unit two groups that have different "mental models" of the clinical situation and that are talking two different languages!

These two studies were simple to conduct, and we were able to do it on a very low budget that we received from the ministry of work and welfare. As a by-product of the research, we developed a new chart for the ICU as well as forms for doctors' orders. This is the only form in the hospital with the logos of the Technion and Hadassah. It was later recommended by the ministry of health as the standard form for Israeli hospitals.

The ground was ready now for preaching and spreading the notion of the benefits to be had from cooperation between the medical world in Israel and the department of human factors engineering in the Technion. It was perfect timing because our leading newspaper, *Haaretz,* ran almost every week in its health section a new "case" of negligence—of a patient who had died in the operating room, of the wrong unit of blood administered, and so on. The stories were aggressive ("They murdered my child," "How many more must die until . . ."). Doctors were attacked in the emergency room, and lawyers specializing in malpractice started to prosper. At this time I wrote to the editor of *Haaretz* and asked to respond to the articles regarding errors in medicine. I told him that the "right of the public to know" included the information as to why we err and what measures Hadassah is taking. The editor opened the gate and I changed my career and supplied the paper with articles explaining that prevention is important, that we need to dedicate more money to research, and that the right way to investigate an event is not by a reporter but by an expert. When conducting an investigation, these experts will conduct root cause analysis and will find the reason for an accident and not who to blame. The call was for the creation of a nonpunitive atmosphere.

Gradually, first nurses and later hospital administrators "discovered" that they can benefit from cooperation. They learned that it is a good investment to call us as early as possible in the process of the design of a new ICU, that in case of an accident we can carry out the inquiry immediately after the event, and that we are not looking for someone to blame but to try to avoid the next unfortunate case. Lectures and presentations were requested by almost all medical associations in Israel. "How to reduce errors in the ICU" and "How to avoid mistakes in CPR" were common topics. All of these activities were done at no charge.

Finally, the time arrived to start the Israeli National Patient Safety Organization. At this point the ministry as well as the Israeli medical organization were reluctant to give a hand. The medical insurance companies thought that a thorough investigation and root cause analysis would damage their income, and that they wouldn't be able to protect in court physicians who talked freely to the independent investigator. In spite of this attitude, the director general of Hadassah Medical Center in Jerusalem supported and convened a 3-day workshop. Its topic: Avoiding Medical Errors in the Hospital: Mission Possible? Guests from the United States (Richard Cook, Paul Barash, and Emanuel Donchin) came to Jerusalem and addressed the 80 selected participants on the major topics of error prevention. Moreover, the hospital opened its department to the participants and the media in a walkthrough of sensitive, "error-prone" locations. The participants, guided by human factors engineers, looked at the process of receiving pathology samples in the laboratory, followed nurses at their stations, and looked at drug administration. The forum discussed their findings immediately, and feedback was requested from the different hospital units. This was the first time journalists had participated in the process of error prevention, and they were able to realize that we are not criminals, and how complicated the system is. The results came later in their writing. The participants are now part of an unofficial patient safety group.

Activities spread over the 32 hospitals in Israel, as well as in the clinics and the pharmaceutical world. They even penetrated to the health ministry. I have to admit that a lot of moral help and support came after then President Clinton announced the importance of error prevention (more people listened to him than to those who read *To Err Is Human*).

The story is just at its beginning. We are trying to work without a budget, against the medical establishment, but with a lot of support from those who work on the sharp end. The road is long, but I do believe that the path is paved already.

CHAPTER THIRTY-FOUR

PUBLIC LEGISLATION AND PROFESSIONAL SELF-REGULATION: QUALITY AND SAFETY EFFORTS IN NORWEGIAN HEALTH CARE

Geir Sverre Braut, MD, DPH

This chapter gives an overview of the quality and safety efforts in a health care system designed according to the Scandinavian welfare state model. Norway is used as an example. The Norwegian system is described and briefly compared with current efforts in some other countries. The text concentrates on the elements that are particular to the Norwegian way of approaching health care. A lot of the quality improvement process work in health care in Norway does not differ from what is taught and practiced in other countries, but these similarities need not be mentioned in this chapter.

The Parliamentary Basis

The Norwegian health care system, as developed during the last half century, is based on the institutional welfare state model. Thus, it is considered a public obligation to ensure that every citizen gets medical and nursing services when necessary. As a matter of principle, the quality of comparable services should be the same wherever and whenever the patient meets the system.

The government is responsible for providing the necessary resources for universal coverage, which are made available through public taxation. The government therefore becomes responsible for superior prioritizing at the system level, and must gain support for its decisions in the Parliament (Stortinget). The main means by which the government and the Parliament rule and make their priorities are legislation and the yearly budgeting process.

Especially in the budgets, it is quite common for the Parliament to decide upon specific details related to the level of quality in health services. The Parliament, for example, has decided that every patient in nursing homes should be entitled to have his or her own single-bed room. In fact, the Norwegian Parliament has decided upon matters that in many other countries would be regarded as medical administrative decisions, such as the extent of screening programs for breast cancer and the total number of radiation therapy units at Norwegian hospitals.

Legislation distributes public responsibilities and tasks for the provision of health care to different subordinate levels of administration, in addition to specifying the basic norms to which health services and professionals should adhere. There is nothing in Norwegian legislation that prohibits private enterprises from carrying out health care; in addition, nothing precludes private enterprises from working on contracts for public health care. However, the extent to which this is done in practice is very small. It is almost always general practitioners (family doctors) and some physiotherapists who work on contract for public health care. The number of purely private health care institutions is negligible. Most hospitals, nursing homes, and home nursing services are publicly owned and run. It is important, however, to realize that legislation related to the quality and safety of health care is the same for both private and public services and institutions.

Care facilities and services for alcohol and drug addiction and social security are not part of the health care system. They have their own legislative basis and a structure deviating from the description given here. The influence of private enterprises is also stronger in this sector than in ordinary health care.

The Current Structures of Health Care

The Municipal Health Care Act (1982) states that the local elected authorities (municipalities) are responsible for all kinds of primary health care. Municipal primary health care is, for example, supposed to provide service by general practitioners, physiotherapists, home-based nursing services, nursing homes, and different types of preventive health care. Primary health care is financed by transferring resources from the government to the municipalities according to the amount and structure of the population.

The Specialist Health Care Act (1999) originally stated that the regional elected authorities (counties) were responsible for specialized health care such as hospitals, ambulances, clinical laboratories, and specialized outpatient services. In 2002 these responsibilities were transferred to five state-owned regional health enterprises. The counties still are responsible for public dental services. Specialized health care is financed partly by transferring resources from the government according to population, and partly by DRG-based fee-for-service payment. In 2003 the financing system of specialized health care came under consideration. The aim is to get a closer relation between economic incentives and planned effects, not just to focus clinical activity. The population of the five regions was from 500,000 to 1,500,000 inhabitants in 2003.

Public participation in the planning and development of health care is usually regarded as occurring because health care is operating in the public field, governed by democratically elected bodies. But it may be claimed that these boards, although democratically elected, are responsible for the services but are not really representative of the consumers' view. There are no legal requirements for population or consumer participation in the planning and delivery of health care. The Patients' Rights Act (1999) requires participation from the patient and relatives only in connection with treatment of the individual patient.

In 2000 a board of professionals and lay people was established to advise the Ministry of Health on prioritizing public health services. This board concentrates on health care programs and methods, not on needs in individual cases. This board is one method Norway has chosen for prioritizing work, instead of making extensive lists of core services.

The Legislative Basis of Health Care Standards

The legislative basis of health care standards in Norway consists of a set of acts laid down by the Parliament and supplemented by regulations given by the government and the Ministry of Health. The amount of local legislation in Norway is generally small, and in the health sector it is negligible. The Norwegian judicial system is based on statutory law as opposed to common law, as it is known in the Anglo-American tradition. Thus, written laws formally published by the state have a central function in health care. Health professionals are supposed to know in detail the laws concerning their area of work. In this way laws gain a position even as important as professional and ethical standards. The Norwegian tradition of written laws regulating the work of medical practitioners goes back to 1672.

The purpose of the Health Personnel Act (HPA, 1999) is to contribute to the safety of patients and the quality of health care, as well as confidence in health personnel and health care. The act relates to all kind of health personnel, medical practitioners and nurses included. In addition, it contains detailed requirements regarding the duties and rights of personnel, confidentiality, information to patients (in some cases even to the authorities), documentation of clinical work, and abstention from use of alcohol and addictive medicines at work.

The system whereby health personnel are authorized is also described in the HPA. Through the European Evaluation Society agreement, Norway is obliged to comply with the European Union directives on requirements for health personnel. The authorization of health personnel is a state duty, but the task of approving professional and clinical specialists is delegated to the professional associations. The Norwegian Medical Association thus approves medical specialists on behalf of the state, according to the requirements set down in the Health Personnel Act.

Perhaps the most important section of this act is related to the requirement of maintaining sound professional standards. It is stated that every health professional should work for the best interest of the patient according to his or her qualifications, the requirements of the actual task, and the context of the situation. If a situation requires that health personnel should seek advice from, cooperate with, or hand patients over to other health professionals, they are by law obliged to do so. This section formulates a legal standard that leaves room for the variables related to any given situation. To live up to this standard, it is important for the practitioner to know what sound professional practice is and entails. It is difficult to see how this can be achieved without practitioners having lasting relations with a professional community. The Health Personnel Act also requires health personnel to inform supervisory authorities about situations and conditions that constitute a safety risk for patients.

The current legislation is quite new. It is based partly on a governmental committee report from 1997 called *The Patient First*. This report dealt mainly with the organization and management of hospitals. Ten statements on the basic principles of health care were formulated: *accessibility* of services, *attention* from personnel, *professionality, reasonability, accountability, punctuality, transparency, holism, friendliness,* and *dependence* among the personnel. These principles are obviously inspired by English developments in the late 1990s. But the main principles on rights and duties for health personnel are derived from the former Medical Practitioners' Act (1980) and the Dentists' Act. What is different in the HPA is that the requirements now relate to all kinds of health personnel, not only doctors and dentists. Before 1980 it was thought unnecessary to legally specify the obligation to practice according to sound professional standards because this norm could be derived from common principles in medical ethics (beneficence and nonmaleficence).

The Specialist Health Care Act and the Municipal Health Care Act both assume that the service provided is based on the principle of sound professional practice. During the 1990s regulations were written to help hospital doctors prioritize patients according to national standards. These regulations were abolished at the end of 2000. The general impression among clinicians was that the regulations did not work as intended. Now hospitals are required to keep systematic waiting lists to ensure that patients with a legal right to necessary health care get it in reasonable time.

In the Patients' Rights Act (1999), the obligations of health services and health professionals may be traced as rights for patients. The aim of this law is to ensure equity and quality of health care and to maintain respect for human life, individual integrity, and dignity. The act's detailed requirements concern the limits of individual choice in health care, and the various elements of cooperation between patients and their relatives and the health service and personnel. The act also contains detailed descriptions on how to put forward complaints regarding health care and health personnel.

A special set of requirements related to compulsory treatment of persons with serious mental disorders is laid down in the Act on Health Care for Mentally Ill Persons (1999). The legal requirements here are more specific and detailed than in other areas in health care. There are detailed regulations relating to housing and staffing as well as how to carry out compulsory treatment in practice. A special control board connected to every institution was established, in addition to the ordinary supervisory system described in the next section.

Governmental Supervision

The Health Care Supervisory Act (1984) states that there shall be a national supervisory body, the Norwegian Board of Health, NBH (Statens helsetilsyn). There shall also be a chief county medical officer (*fylkeslege*) in every county of Norway. This is a governmental representative who is responsible for running the regional branches of NBH. The supervisory activities of NBH are aimed at both public and privately owned and run services. NBH employs different kinds of professionals at both the central office and the regional branches. Medical practitioners, legal officers, and nurses constitute the core personnel. The supervisory system was reorganized in 2002 and 2003 in an attempt to combine the supervision system for health care with the supervision of social services. The main principles of supervision are described next and apply both to health and social care, as well as to public and private providers of care.

The main tasks of the supervisory systems are to inform health services and health personnel about current legal requirements and to carry out control activities related to these entities. The results of the control activities at the regional offices are reported to the central body of NBH, which can apply formal measures when necessary to compensate for failure of care. Examples of such formal measures are withdrawal of authorization of health personnel, reporting cases (both related to failure of systems and failure of individuals) to police investigation, closing down care providers, and fining care providers when they do not correct failures that are regarded as a safety risk for patients. The reports made by NBH are published (e.g., on the Internet, at www.helsetilsynet.no), as far as this can be done without violating legal requirements of confidentiality related to individuals.

The control activities may be divided into three groups:

- An overview of data on the health, quality, and quantity of health care
- Systematic audits related to the provision of services
- An evaluation of complaints and reports of deviations

Making overviews based on available data is more or less an epidemiologic activity. NBH cooperates both nationally and regionally with other organizations that generate and evaluate data on health and health services. As stated in law, the aim of this activity is to gain an overview of the health situation and to ensure fulfillment of the population's health care needs. The main products from this activity are annual medical reports on the health situation and health care provision in the counties and in the nation as a whole. These reports commonly generate vivid debates among the democratically elected representatives as well as in the press when published.

Audits of Systems for Health Care Provision

The systematic audits of health care provisions are relatively new activities in the way they now are performed. Formerly the county medical offices made inspections at health care institutions just to check out that requirements set forth in legislation were adopted at the time of the inspection. Since about 1994 this kind of simple inspection has been replaced by a systematic approach that is more concerned with the system's ability to live up to its legal requirements at any time. The method chosen so far in Norway is based on the ISO 10011 standard for audits of quality systems.

This method was adopted in 1994 partly because it was the chosen method of other supervising authorities, for example, in petroleum activities and in the control of health and safety at work. It was also chosen because the Health Care Supervisory Act states that every provider of health care shall establish a system for internal control so that services are planned, provided, and maintained according to commonly accepted professional standards and requirements in acts and regulations. This compulsory system may easily be audited by the method chosen by the supervising authorities. This method may also be used by the enterprises themselves when they are controlling their own system.

The potential of, and experiences with, this method in health care still have not been scientifically evaluated. The method seems to be a useful tool when the task is to uncover deviations from legal and other specified requirements. Many will claim that it is not so good if the task is to build a platform for further quality development. Thus, it might be a powerful tool for the authorities in their controls, even if the enterprises themselves choose other methods for monitoring and stimulating quality development. The county medical offices have a general impression that deviations discovered by this kind of supervisory activity are commonly accepted and readily dealt with by the service provider.

The requirement for a system for internal control was put into law in 1992. Since 1984 there has been a more general requirement stating that every provider of health care should control its own performance to avoid failure of its services. This requirement was based on the assumption that the legislation of sound professional standards in the Medical Practitioners' Act of 1980 was in fact an imperative for professional self-regulation. The formulation of the legal requirement regarding internal control systems was inspired by the safety regulations of the petroleum industry. After the *Bravo* blowout in the North Sea in 1977, legislation on safety in the petroleum sector in Norway put forward the importance of each participant guaranteeing safety by its own, systematic activities, and not relying only on correcting conditions found by the authorities' inspectors.

Because systematic audits seem to be a powerful tool for supervisory authorities, they should be used with care. An authority should use systematic audits on important matters, not only on service elements where the requirements are so constructed that they are easily approached by this method. The audited provider will pay attention to the deviations described by the authorities and adjust its own prioritizing accordingly. Thus, there is a risk that attention will be drawn from important matters simply because they aren't audited by the authorities, and diverted to the described deviations even if they are not as important. This risk is enhanced by the fact that results from most reports on systematic audits are published in the local press. The Hawthorne effect seems to be valid even with supervisory work.

Dealing with Complaints and Deviations

Evaluation of complaints and reports of deviations (nonconformities) is regarded as a task for the supervisory authorities. The right of a patient to pose a complaint on the quality of health care is laid down in the Patients' Rights Act. The Health Personnel Act states that supervisory authorities should be informed about situations and conditions that constitute a safety risk to patients. The Specialist Health Care Act states that the county medical office should be notified as soon as possible if health care has led to serious damage to patients or if there has been any situation that had the potential to inflict serious damage. It should also be noted that medical practitioners are obliged to report to the police deaths that are due to, or should be suspected as due to, medical failure. In such cases the police are obliged to notify the county medical office when starting investigations.

Thus, the supervisory authorities are engaged in many cases of suspected failure or deviations in health care. The common procedure in these cases is to get hold of as much documentation as possible (e.g., patient files, x-rays) as well as comments from the personnel and institutions responsible for the provision of service. If necessary, they are evaluated by external specialists. Thereafter the cases are evaluated against legal requirements and professional standards. If the county medical office finds that any of these may have been violated, the law states that the case should be handed over to the Norwegian Board of Health, which should then decide on formal actions against the enterprise or individual health personnel. Any formal actions from the board against individual personnel can be appealed further to a special committee. Health personnel may also be tried in court.

The yearly number of formal complaint cases related to the quality of health care and competence of health personnel handled by the supervisory authorities is about 1,500. That is approximately 3.5/10,000 inhabitants per year. Still, this may be regarded as a low number. It is expected to rise in coming years, based on the effect of the new legislation focusing on patients' rights to complain and because of the general evolving consumerism in health care.

Many of the judgments made by authorities are based on evaluations in relation to current professional standards. In this way the supervisory authorities act more or less as an administrative tribunal for health care systems and health personnel. The activity performed by the supervisory authorities has some similarities with the judging process according to the common-law principle of Anglo-American courts, because both written law and former practice (from courts and the supervisory authorities themselves) as well as views on good practice are taken into account.

It may be claimed that this great supervisory interest in failures and deviations may draw attention away from important quality improvement processes at an institutional level. It is hard to say if this claim is true, as no data have been gathered and analyzed to support or refute such a hypothesis.

The Patients' Rights Act created the position of a public paid patients' ombudsman in every county. This officer helps patients with problems related to the provision of specialist health care. Ombudsmen do not have a supervisory function, and are obliged to inform the supervisory authorities on matters that require formal attention.

Quality Projects at the Institutional Level

The Specialist Health Care Act states that every hospital shall have a quality commission as part of its mandated system of internal control. A comparable requirement is not defined for primary health care. The function of this commission varies from hospital to hospital. In addition, some institutions have quality subcommittees for each department. Commonly, this kind of commission initiates and promotes quality work at the hospital. The commissions are not responsible for the quality themselves. The sole responsibility for quality rests with the line organization, from the doctor and nurse meeting the patient through the chief of a department up to the director of the hospital. The Specialist Health Care Act states that there shall only be one responsible leader at every level of the organization. It is not required that this be a medical practitioner or a nurse. This change, enacted in 2001, represented a fundamental departure from the past. By tradition, Norwegian hospitals have had a dual leadership at the department level. The overall responsibility has been divided between the medical head of the department and the chief nursing officer.

Since 1995 the Ministry of Health and Social Affairs and the Norwegian Board of Health have taken some initiatives to stimulate quality work in hospitals and primary health care. In addition, some professional health care organizations, especially the Norwegian Medical Association, have run projects relating to quality improvement.

The Norwegian strategy of quality improvement is based on the goal relating to the development of quality assurance systems in the European version of the Health For All by 2000 strategy of the World Health Organization. Its aim is to gain results with the least risk for patients and through efficient use of available resources. The goal was for all enterprises in Norwegian health care to have effective quality systems by 2000. It is commonly agreed that this goal was not achieved, even if there has been an immense improvement in the building of quality systems in health care during the period from 1995 to 2000. A new strategy on quality in health care and social services was scheduled to be launched by 2003. It presumably will focus more on quality improvement processes than on establishing quality systems alone.

The former strategy of health care improvement had focused on building systems based on the internal control principle. Many practitioners claim that this has led to a lot of paperwork, without comparable real improvement in the quality of patient-related services. Every county medical office has had a person dedicated to stimulating quality work in the municipalities, and many hospitals have appointed persons among their personnel to be front-line figures in quality work. Running courses on quality improvement processes has been a core activity for these persons. This has led to a greater knowledge of different models of quality work among leaders in the health sector.

One of the main activities of the Norwegian Medical Association has been to establish trials of different models for quality improvement at some hospitals; among these is the model for total quality management. In evaluating these trials it has been ascertained that much has been accomplished, but not as much as initially intended. The quality language seems to be too difficult when presented to health care professionals. In addition, the leaders do not seem really to grasp the system approach.

Education as a Quality Assurance Mechanism

Observing that the new way of thinking in quality work has not been as successful as expected, attention should be paid to the traditional quality-assuring mechanisms in health care. One may comfortably assert that the most important quality assurance mechanism in health care in Norway, at least up to the late 1980s, has been the structure of basic education and following specialization.

Basic education for medical practitioners, dentists, and psychologists has been the responsibility of the universities. There have been no national, formal, defined standards on the curricula for these studies, but the standards defined by the universities themselves on the basis of their self-governing traditions have guaranteed an adequate level of education. The basic education of other groups, for example, nurses, is based on standards laid down by the Ministry of Church, Education and Research, as are the standards for specialization in these groups.

For the specialization of medical practitioners, the standards are, in practice, defined by the Norwegian Medical Association and the profession itself. Up until 1980 there had been no legislation regulating the specialization of medical practitioners. Since 1980 this has formally been a public responsibility, but the task of approving individual specialists is still delegated to the association. It is the state's obligation to decide on the criteria for approving practitioners as specialists. The decision is based on recommendations from the National Board for the Education of Specialists and the Distribution of Medical Practitioners and the Norwegian Medical Association. The Norwegian Medical Association organizes a set of committees, one for each group of specialists, which give advice in this process. Many medical practitioners are engaged in this work, ensuring that the advice given is based on practical experiences and also that the medical community feels education of specialists is a part of ordinary work. What is taught to the candidates may be regarded as sound professional standards.

In addition to the traditional hospital-based specialists, it is possible to become a specialist in community medicine, general practice (family medicine), and occupational medicine. Approval as a specialist lasts in principle until the age of 75, except in general practice, where it must be renewed through practical work and attendance of courses every fifth year. Even for the "life-lasting" specialists, it is regarded as sound performance to attend a certain amount of courses. These courses are to a large extent financed by the medical association on the basis of grants transferred from the government after negotiations. This system covers only medical practitioners. Probably this system has kept the amount of industry-sponsored courses in Norwegian medicine low. Because the grants are diminishing nowadays, the situation may soon change.

Providers of health care are by law obliged to ensure sufficient postgraduate education for all kinds of health personnel. Experience tells us that the extent of this obligation is, in practice, far less than what is ensured for doctors based on the system described previously.

Public Initiatives on Clinical Standardization

Many state institutions publish guidelines on different aspects of clinical practice, not only pharmaceutical treatment. The directorate of health and social affairs (Sosial og helsedirektoratet), the Norwegian Board of Health (Statens hlesetilsyn), the National Institute of Public Health (Nasjonalt folkehelseinstitutt), the Norwegian Medicines Agency (Statens legemiddelverk), and the Norwegian Center for Health Technology Assessment (Senter for medisinsk metodevurdering) are the most important institutions defining standards related to quality in Norwegian health care. To some extent these institutions are cooperating, but not in an explicit and systematic way.

The directorate of health and social affairs has published a guideline on making guidelines, based on a proposal from the Norwegian Board of Health. This document is inspired by evidence-based medicine. The Norwegian experience, though, is that such a standard is not used much as a basis for planning and developing new guidelines.

Comparison with Some Other Countries

The Swedish system is fairly comparable to that of Norway. The provision of health care is based on strong legislation that emphasizes the role of professional self-regulation and sound professional standards. There is a national supervisory board (Socialstyrelsen) with regional offices that set standards and perform systematic audits of health care. But Sweden has organized a separate system for dealing with complaints and making formal decisions, such as on the withdrawal of professional authorizations (Hälsooch sjukvårdens ansvarsnämnd). It has also organized committees at the local level to deal with minor complaints (Patientnämnder). A peculiar detail is that in Sweden since the 1930s, there has been a legal obligation to notify the authorities of medical failures. This legislation was made because of some deaths due to medical failure that got great public interest.

In Denmark there is a national supervisory board (Sundhedsstyrelsen) and county medical officers (*embedslæger*), similar to the situation in Norway. However, they have not, up to now, focused as much on systematic audits as in Norway.

In Finland there are no inspecting or supervising units. There is a centralized board for dealing with serious accusations of malpractice (Rättsskyddsinstitutet). The responsibility for developing and maintaining quality is placed solely on the regional and local bodies responsible for providing health care to the public.

Holland has a system quite similar to that of Norway in regard to the use and function of systematic audits, organized with a central unit (Inspectie voor de Gezundheitssorg) and regional offices. Holland's complaint-handling system relies more on activities at the local level than seems to be the situation in Sweden and Norway. Both the Swedish and the Dutch supervisory authorities use audits according to the model described for Norway. To a greater extent than in Norway, they also use other models for evaluating the performance of health care, such as surveys of provision and output of health care systems.

Norway and all the countries mentioned here have organized separate systems for economic compensation after medical failures. They aim to keep these cases out of court. Still, they do not hinder cases that eventually do go to court. The Norwegian failure compensation system (Norsk pasientskadeerstatning) only covers activities performed by public health care. To gain compensation it is enough to show that a loss measurable in economic terms is due to a medical failure. It is not necessary to show any negligence on the part of health personnel.

In all the mentioned countries, the quality evaluation of pharmaceutical products and the supervision of systems for the provision of pharmaceuticals are organized separately. Comparable institutions in all these countries take care of the development of national guidelines and technology assessment. Sweden especially has a long tradition in this area. All the countries discussed here seem to have problems not with the development of strategies and guidelines, but with their practical implementation in the health care system.

Conclusion

Quality and safety efforts in Norwegian health care are based on strong legislation with very detailed requirements for professionals. At the core of the legislation, however, is the principle of self-regulation. Thus, it is up to the professional communities and associations to decide what is regarded as good and conducive to a strong health care environment and what is not. If this situation is to continue, it requires that the professional communities actively work for the development of professional standards and communicate them to the professionals. Legislation should be regarded as a framework for these activities, not as a net used by the authorities to catch professionals. In addition, legislation can secure basic patients' rights that should have priority before or at the level of professional standards.

Bibliography

Molven, O. ed., *Health Legislation in Norway* (Oslo: University of Oslo, Centre for Medical Studies, Moscow, 2002).

Molven, O. ed., *The Norwegian Health Care System* (Oslo: University of Oslo, Centre for Medical Studies, Moscow, 1999).

Nordlund, Y. G., and Edgren, L. "Patient Complaint Systems in Health Care: A Comparative Study Between the Netherlands and Sweden," *European Journal of Health Law* (1999): 133–154.

Øvretveit, J. *Integrated Quality Development in Public Healthcare: A Comparison of Six Hospitals' Quality Programmes and a Practical Theory for Quality Development* (Oslo: Norwegian Medical Association, 1999).

Øvretveit, J., and Aslaksen, A. *The Quality Journeys of Six Norwegian Hospitals: An Action Evaluation* (Oslo: Norwegian Medical Association, 1999).

Sørensen, Ø., and Stråth, B. eds., *The Cultural Construction of Norden* (Oslo: Scandinavian University Press, 1997).

Internet

Norwegian Strategy for Quality Improvement in Health Care. (Oslo: Norwegian Board of Health, 1999). http://www.helsetilsynet.no/trykksak/ik-2564/ik-2564.pdf.

General information in English on health care in Norway from the directorate of health and social affairs is available at http://www.shdir.no.

General information in English on health care in Norway from the Norwegian Board of Health is available at http://www.helsetilsynet.no.

General information in English on health care in Norway from the Ministry of Health and Social Affairs is available at http://www.dep.no/hd/engelsk.

General information in English on health care in Sweden from the Swedish National Board of Health and Welfare is available at http://www.sos.se/sosmenye.htm.

CHAPTER THIRTY-FIVE

THE HANDLING OF A CATASTROPHIC MEDICAL ERROR EVENT: A CASE STUDY IN THE USE OF A SYSTEMIC MINDFUL APPROACH TO ERROR REDUCTION

Victoria L. Rich, PhD, RN

The handling of any catastrophic event, from both the personal and organizational perspective is emotional and very stressful. Throughout the last 20 years, the media have heightened our global awareness of catastrophic organizational errors with detailed, eyewitness accounts of the events. Three well-known examples are Union Carbide's crisis in Bhopal, NASA's handling of the explosion of the *Challenger,* and the Johnson & Johnson Tylenol crisis in 1982. The handling of each of these crises has been scrutinized and criticized by the public, regulatory bodies, and the media. Johnson & Johnson is considered the poster child of how to correctly handle a catastrophic event. The keystone to the effective management of the Tylenol crisis was the Johnson & Johnson credo. This credo, established by Robert Wood Johnson over 40 years ago, created a culture that lives by a basic message: Johnson & Johnson employees have four responsibilities, which are, listed in priority, (1) to the consumer, (2) to the employees, (3) to the communities they serve, and (4) to the stockholders (Hollingsworth, 1999). Hence, as the Tylenol crisis escalated, Johnson & Johnson's credo guided its public announcement: "We believe our first responsibility is to the doctors,

This chapter is dedicated to Norm Stein, Chief Executive Officer of University Community Hospital. Mr. Stein is the visionary leader who persevered through the events of 1995 and has presided over the rise of the phoenix.

nurses, and patients, to mothers and all others who use our products and services" (Fink, 1986, p. 217).

The handling of catastrophic events in the health care industry, however, has not been as well defined. This lack of definition stemmed from physicians' and administrators' traditional strong beliefs that medical errors were isolated occurrences and that studies were based on poor data that were unrepresentative of the actual events (Millenson, 1999). The perfectibility model assumed that if doctors and nurses were properly educated and trained, then mistakes would not be made. The approach to obtaining this perfection was thus better training and punishment for personal carelessness (Leape, 1994). Hence, the belief system that remains to this day in medicine is that if a medical error occurs and the patient suffers deleterious effects or death, the health care professional directly responsible for the error needs to be reeducated, remotivated, and, most important, punished. This reasoning culminates in perceptions held by hospital boards, administrators, the media, the public, health care professionals, and regulatory bodies that retraining and punishment address the crisis of a catastrophic event.

This health care "head in the sand" approach sufficed for the most part until media coverage of three particular medical accidents in the years 1994 and 1995. Interestingly, many of these cases have achieved such a level of prominence in the collective public psyche that one can elicit a collection of images simply by mentioning the "Florida wrong leg" or "Willie King case," the "Betsy Lehman case," or the "Libby Zion case." All of these cases evoke our empathy for some tragic loss (Cook et al., 1998, p. 7). Suddenly, it seemed CEOs, boards of trustees, and the medical profession had to assure their publics that crisis measures were being implemented immediately to make their hospitals safe to continue providing care.

The handling of the wrong-leg surgery (the Willie King case) at University Community Hospital (UCH) in Tampa is used in a case study format here to exemplify how the mishandling of a catastrophic event can culminate in repercussions so severe that University Community Hospital still deals with negative patient comments and unfriendly media coverage. It is a gauntlet that UCH still traverses today.

The wrong-site surgery event resulted in an organizational crisis best portrayed by the *Rashomon* effect. The *Rashomon* effect derives its meaning and name from Akira Kurosawa's 1951 Japanese film classic *Rashomon,* in which several witnesses see the same tragic event differently. The *Rashomon* effect is a metaphor for the relative and partial nature of truth and memory. The result is a Tower of Babel, where many different perspectives and discipline voices speak in different languages about the causes, consequences, cautions, or concerns of the event. This *Rashomon* effect is even further complicated by each individual's personal coping style (Shrivastava, 1993).

The effective solution to recognizing, respecting, and integrating the *Rashomon* effect is in creating a systemic mindful crisis management plan prior to an actual adverse catastrophic event. This systemic mindful approach interweaves the psychological, sociopolitical, and technological-structural issues (Pearson & Clair, 1998) of all the disciplinary voices into a "pattern of system-wide mindful attention that forestalls the escalating of error" (Sutcliffe & Weick, 1998, p. 147).

The systemic mindful approach derives from social psychology. *Mindfulness* as defined by Ellen J. Langer (1989) is a process orientation. It is a mechanism in which one is aware of every outcome that is preceded by a process. Mindful choices are expected to result in benefit (Langer, 1989). *Systemic mindfulness* (Sutcliffe & Weick, 1998), therefore, is a process orientation to every step in a system. Assuming that each step is correct and safe, one can proceed to the next step.

A systemic mindful approach to crisis evolved at UCH after the Willie King event. It was an approach learned, adopted, and maintained by the board, management, and health care professionals. The remainder of this chapter depicts UCH's journey to a culture of systemic mindfulness and the effective handling of adverse catastrophic medical events.

Reaction to Medical Errors at University Community Hospital

In February 1995, Willie King's wrong leg was amputated. Going into detail about the circumstances surrounding this wrong-sided surgery and its root cause is not the intent of this chapter; rather, the intent is to elaborate subsequent happenings and the behaviors and decisions of the stakeholders (disciplinary voices) at that particular time.

Subsequent to the UCH administration's discovery of the wrong-site surgery that was performed on Willie King, an "A-Team" was established. This A-Team consisted of key administrators, board members, medical staff, public relations personnel, and legal counsel. Legal counsel strongly advised the UCH A-Team not to talk to the media or answer any questions until further discoveries could be made about what exactly happened in the surgery. In 1995, the concept of self-disclosure was thought by most to be a disastrous path that would only lead to increased public scrutiny and misinformation.

The vitriolic reaction by the media to UCH's silence was unexpected and found the A-Team at odds with each other on how to proceed. The *Rashomon* effect was operating. Each of the stakeholders blamed one another, and each had an opinion on who should be punished. The patient and family were also included in the blame game.

The media continued to add to the crisis, and just when the A-Team felt the crisis was de-escalating, another story, regulatory agency

TABLE 35-1   A Three-Month Summary of Local Newspaper, Local Television, and National Coverage of the UCH Wrong-Sided Surgery Event

Local Newspaper Coverage

- 125 newspaper stories in the *Tampa Tribune* and *St. Petersburg Times,* filling 18.5 full newspaper pages.
- The cost of buying that space would have been at least $167,000.

Local Television Coverage

- 447 local television newscasts.
- 13.5 hours of newscast coverage.
- $1,529,200 of commercial time.
- In the news 50 of 58 days.
- On April 13, 1995, alone, 22 news stories were aired regarding UCH.

National Coverage

- *Time, Newsweek,* the *New York Times,* the *LA Times,* the *Miami Herald,* and the *Orlando Sentinel,* among others, ran the story.
- CBS, NBC Nightly News, CNN, *Inside Edition,* and *Prime Time* reported the events.
- Jokes were made on the Jay Leno, David Letterman, and Howard Stern shows.
- The Associated Press printed 678 articles in less than 3 months.

investigation, or complaint would arise. The magnitude of the media coverage within a 3-month span is depicted in Table 35-1.

A malpractice flurry also occurred, in which requests for medical records by attorneys, patients, and families tripled from March 1994 to March 1995.

Following the Willie King incident in February 1995, the A-Team at UCH found itself dealing with two more catastrophic events in March 1995. These two incidents involved a 70-year-old man who was inappropriately removed from his ventilator and died and a female patient who received arthroscopic surgery on the wrong knee. As Millenson (1995) states in his book *Demanding Medical Excellence,* tragic though the individual episodes were, they revealed much about the state of modern American medicine (p. 53).

April 1995 proved more deleterious to UCH when the state of Florida ordered a moratorium on elective surgery and the Joint Commission on Accreditation of Healthcare Organizations (JCAHO) rescinded the hospital's accreditation.

As the A-Team worked endless hours to correct patient care systems, the media bombarded the hospital's premises and employees' privacy. It was reported that employees would watch the news to find out what was happening in their own institution. The A-Team had forgotten to communicate effectively even to themselves and to their employees.

By July 1995, UCH and its A-Team had effectively corrected patient care systems from the numerous regulatory bodies' points of view and were granted full accreditation from the Joint Commission, the Health Care Financing Administration and the state of Florida. Dr. Robert McAfee, president of the American Medical Association, toured UCH on his own behalf in May 1995 and reported in a news conference that UCH is "one of the safest, if not the safest, hospital in the country" (personal communication, Dr. Scott Bronleewe, January 2001).

The lessons learned from these numerous crises and events are multifaceted and symbolized best by the myth of the phoenix rising from its own ashes. The phoenix, according to Egyptian legend, was a beautiful bird, that, when it became 500 years old, burned itself on a pyre and, from its own ashes, became reborn, renewed to start life fresh again.

It is this rebirth at University Community Hospital in Tampa that is shared in how best to handle a catastrophic medical error event. After the 1995 event, the A-Team reflected on what occurred and designed not only patient safety systems but also procedures to manage crises proactively. This proactive management of medical error crises has created the error reduction culture of systemic mindfulness at UCH (Sutcliffe & Weick, 1999).

Systemic Mindfulness

The Systemic mindful process orientation has six basic tenets:

1. Critical issue management plan
2. Investigation
3. Truth telling
4. Nonpunitive approach
5. Root cause analysis
6. Clinical compliance

Critical Issues Management Plan

The management plan is a written plan contained in a notebook entitled "Critical Issue Management" that is available to the administrators of the hospital. If a critical event occurs and emotions begin to run high, the plan is already prepared, delineated, and ready for use. This plan contains the following items:

1. The definition of a critical issue. This definition should be germane to each institution, with consideration of local, state, federal, and JCAHO requirements.
2. The names and phone numbers of those responsible for convening the critical issues team. This is the UCH A-Team. Team

members may include outside counsel and, as needed, experts. Alternate A-Team members are also identified.

3. The meeting sites and headquarters.
4. The agendas for the meetings, the facilities, and the equipment needed.
5. A prepared list of critical issue responses and means to track and follow up on responses.
6. Communication to important publics. It is prudent to provide pertinent factual information to publics other than the internal groups. These important publics include medical executive staff, medical staff, and office staff; Foundation Board and staff; managed care companies; state and federal regulatory bodies and JCAHO representatives; city, county, and state elected officials; state and national groups; and political linkages. The plan designates specific spokespersons to contact important publics and communicate an appropriate written statement that is adapted to each unique public. The A-Team is the approval body. Name, address, contact person, and phone number identify each of the important publics.
7. The final component is a plan for getting the message out and telling the story. Questions to answer include the following:

- When do we release information to the media? (Not *if* !)
- What communication tools (e.g., press releases, faxes, phone calls) will best provide information to the varied publics?
- Who is best to be the spokesperson? This answer is dependent on the event and the message intended. Each member of the A-Team is trained by a public relations firm on how to effectively be a spokesperson to the media.
- What will be the two to three strong messages we want the press to communicate? A press release is always prepared proactively.

Update the critical issue management plan as needed, but do so at least annually. To quote M. P. Follet as cited in Langer (1989), "A system built around a purpose is dead before it is born. Purpose unfolds and reflects the means."

Investigation

There exists a formalized approach to thoroughly investigating a reported sentinel event or adverse medical error, which is to say anything that would result in serious harm or death to a patient. This formalized approach is organized as a top priority by the risk management department. Members of the formalized A-Team include the vice president of performance improvement, the risk manager, the chief of medical staff, the vice president of patient care, the CEO or COO, legal counsel, and the clinical compliance officer. The chairperson of the board of trustees is an ad hoc member.

All facts are gathered by the risk management department in conjunction with pertinent others and presented to the A-Team. Each member of the A-Team is now aware of varying perspectives and the *Rashomon* effect. The common integrated goal for all disciplinary voices is to be focused on the investigation, the patient or family outcomes, and the system's failures. The culture of the A-Team is now such that the critical issue management plan is inherent and automatic.

Truth Telling

Truth telling is the hallmark of the systemic mindful approach to handling catastrophic events. Naturally then, the question "What should be disclosed to the patient and family about the suspected or alleged catastrophic event?" must arise. First of all, as soon as possible, speak with the patient or family or both about what has happened. The choice of spokesperson(s) is dependent on circumstances and relationships. At least one spokesperson is a member of the A-Team. Commonly used spokespersons are the physician involved (with prior coaching), the risk manager, and the vice president of patient care.

Second, the spokesperson apologizes for the medical mishap. Third, a proposed plan of action to improve the involved patient care system for future patients is discussed. Future improvement plans are many times communicated to the patient or family at a later date. Patient and family ideas are also considered and followed up.

The truth-telling tenet is an interactive process and truly is "a matter of the heart." Legal concerns as always are ever present but are demonstratively secondary to truth telling.

Nonpunitive Culture

Developing a nonpunitive culture involves many approaches, starting with leadership. The board and the CEO must demonstrate that patient safety is the utmost priority. This safety priority must then have a vehicle of communication to spread the message to all health care professionals at the sharp end of care that speaking out when something goes wrong or when near misses occur is rewarded, not punished. The performance improvement plan at UCH is designed to address this communication to all health care providers. A nonpunitive culture is best fostered at UCH by story telling. That is, UCH shares stories of errors and near misses and the risk reduction strategies used to combat them in collaboration with key stakeholders. This improves systems without the need for punishment.

Root Cause Analysis

The root cause analysis approach has become the cornerstone for any near miss or error at UCH. This process is used not only to go through the inductive and deductive reasoning process of identifying systems failures, but also to give the participants the experience of being in the process. That is, every practitioner or stakeholder who attends a root cause discernment meeting slowly begins to see that patient care is a complicated, complex system and that focusing only on the special cause (i.e., the patient and the caregiver who made the error) means looking at only a very small part of what failed or a very small part of what could have failed.

If a root cause analysis is effective, the involved participants change their beliefs regarding medical errors and hence should change their behaviors to be more aware of safe practices and error identification. The change in mind-set and in awareness of error and error reduction is really how a culture of systemic mindfulness begins, then slowly rises and begins to disseminate throughout the organization.

Clinical Compliance Program

University Community Hospital has two Clinical Compliance registered nurses who provide direction and continuity to the culture of systemic mindfulness. The Clinical Compliance nurse functions to assure board, administration, and medical staff leadership that the risk reduction strategies created through the root cause process, the corrective action plans for regulatory bodies, and performance improvement processes are maintained and that all gains achieved are held. The Clinical Compliance personnel meet periodically with the A-Team to update progress on initiatives and report on a scheduled basis to the board Performance Improvement Committee. This approach is especially important in providing continuity and institutional memory for the rapid changes in personnel in the health care arena, and is an excellent mechanism for celebrating successes and positive outcomes.

UCH and the Surgical Safety Program

The catastrophic events in 1995 prompted UCH to examine safety, as this chapter has clearly discussed. The most important systemic mindful error reduction initiative that resulted from 1995 was and is the Surgical Safety Program. The procedures that were developed in 1995 have continued to be strictly followed. UCH is a national model for surgical safety. Many hospitals visit UCH to view this process.

The Surgical Safety Program is a thorough and continuous process. Much like a pilot's actions before takeoff, the safety check at UCH includes all persons who encounter the patient or enter information related to the patient. This Surgical Safety Program applies to *all* patients scheduled for operative or invasive procedures. The process begins before the patient is admitted to UCH, that is, when the patient is scheduled by a physician's office for surgery. The patient's records from all of the various sources are examined and coordinated to be sure entries refer to the same procedure and area to be operated on. The safety check by professionals continues in the preoperative phase, where another check is completed by a different team of professionals.

When the patient arrives in the operating room, the scheduling board is reviewed. Before the procedure begins, everyone involved in the procedure, including the physician, all the health care providers, and the patient, gather together to go through a final checklist before the patient is anesthetized. If the patient is able, he or she is asked to be an active participant in his or her care. For example, if the patient is going to have site surgery and her left knee is going to be operated on, she will be asked to put an "X" on her unaffected knee. If the patient is unable to do that, it is done by the health care professional, and a signature is placed in the chart on the checklist. Each individual in the review also verifies that the patient is the correct patient, that the procedure is the correct one, that the correct area will be operated on, and that all the processes are being followed. If at any time in the chain of events a practitioner from any of the professions feels that something is wrong or that a step has been taken prematurely, he or she is empowered to say, "We are going to stop and check further."

This Surgical Safety Program has had the endorsement of the entire medical staff, the entire board of trustees, the CEO, the administration, and all the employees. UCH has created a culture that truly believes that safety is the utmost priority and takes great pride in tracking the near misses of the Surgical Safety Program.

Professional Words of Wisdom from the Phoenix

As the story has been told, the journey certainly has taught UCH many nuggets of wisdom. As mentioned earlier in this chapter, the rising of the phoenix from its ashes certainly symbolizes the journey that UCH has taken over the last few years. From the 1995 event to the dawn of the 21st century, UCH can feel proud of learning from its mistakes and of learning to hold the gain that has taken place in performance improvement. However, the most important gain in how to handle catastrophic events centers on "matters of the heart" and truth telling. The morals and ethics of self-disclosure and truth telling not only are the right things to do but also are the best things to do. Truth telling and self-disclosure liberate the entire health care team to feel that it's right to tell the truth, that one is supported for telling the truth, and that one need not be afraid to say "I'm sorry." To speak out is a key component of UCH's nonpunitive culture. Bearing false witness to a variety of events that health care professionals experience on a daily basis becomes draining, and "matters of the heart" do affect all health care professionals. The pearl of wisdom that is the most valuable in how to handle catastrophic events is to tell the truth and believe that the consequences of that truth telling are secondary to the potential risk of losing the systemic mindful culture in error reduction.

References

Cook, R. I. et al. (1998). *A Tale of Two Stories: Contrasting Views of Patient Safety* (Chicago, IL: National Patient Safety Foundation at the AMA).

Fink, S. (1986). *Crisis Management: Planning for the Inevitable* (New York: AMACOM).

Hollingsworth, P. (1999). "Crisis Management: Planning for the Unthinkable," *Food Technology* 28, no. 1, 53.

Keys, C. (1997). "Responding to an Adverse Event," *Forum-Risk Management Foundation of the Harvard Medical Institutions, Inc.* 18, no. 1, 81–83.

Langer, E. J. (1989). *Mindfulness* (Cambridge, MA: Perseus Books).

Leape, L. L. (1994). "Error in Medicine," *Journal of the American Medical Association* 272, 1851–1857.

Millenson, M. L. (1999). *Demanding Medical Excellence: Doctors and Accountability in the Information Age* (London: University of Chicago Press).

Pearson, C. M., and Clair, J. A. (1998). "Reframing Crisis Management," *Academy of Management Review* 23, 59–76.

Shrivastava, P. (1993). "Crisis Theory/Practice: Towards a Sustainable Future," *Industrial and Environmental Crisis Quarterly* 7, 23–42.

Sutcliffe, K. M., and Weick, K. E. eds. (1998). "A Reduction of Medical Error Through Systemic Mindfulness," *Proceedings of Enhancing Patient Safety and Reducing Errors in Healthcare: Conference held at Annenberg Center for Health Sciences at Eisenhower,* 147–150.

Witman, A., and Hardin, S. (1997). "Patients' Responses to Physicians' Mistakes," *Forum-Risk Management Foundation of the Harvard Medical Institutions, Inc.* 18, no. 1, 4–5.

Wu, A. W. (1999). "Handling Hospital Errors: Is Disclosure the Best Defense?" *Annals of Internal Medicine* 131, no. 12, 970–972.

CHAPTER THIRTY-SIX

WHY, WHAT, AND HOW OUGHT HARMED PARTIES BE TOLD? THE ART, MECHANICS, AND AMBIGUITIES OF ERROR DISCLOSURE

John D. Banja, PhD

Although the law bases the patient–health provider relationship on the latter's "reasonable and prudent" behavior, ethics understands that relationship as grounded in beneficence, wherein the professional subordinates his or her self-serving interests to furthering and advancing the welfare of his or her patients.[1-3] Virtually all ethical codes of physician behavior require that health providers elevate their patients' welfare above their own, and state licensing laws and regulations generally begin by noting that their primary purpose is to protect the interests of citizens and consumers of the professional service.[3-5]

Using the language of ethics, then, we might translate the question of "What ought persons who have been harmed from medical error be told?" into the following questions:

- What does ethics say persons are "owed" by way of informational disclosure when they have experienced adverse consequences from medical error?
- Assuming the existence of a moral obligation requiring disclosure of harm-causing medical error to affected parties, what ought the content and scope of that disclosure be?
- How ought the persons involved in the error understand and communicate it—in a purely factual way, as a breach of trust, as sorrow and regret, or as legally owing a compensation?

- How ought health care training programs and institutional attitudes be configured according to the ways these questions are answered?

This chapter addresses these questions and offers a series of suggestions as to how to conduct what is not only a bad-news conversation, but one wherein the error operators expose themselves to the possibility of adverse litigation as a consequence of their disclosure. Also, a number of ambiguities surrounding certain facets of the disclosure process that require further discussion and even research will be identified as the chapter proceeds. As a prelude to all of this, however, I will offer a fundamental ethical argument as to why the disclosure of serious harm-causing medical error *must* occur because without such a conceptual foundation, harm-causing error operators might not admit a need to learn and implement the mechanics of an error disclosure conversation.

Why Error Disclosure Is a Moral Imperative

A considerable amount of literature appeared during the 1990s attesting to the utility of error disclosure. Commentators noted that the policy and practice of error disclosure can result in a diminished incidence of malpractice litigation or its associated costs, improve quality of care and diminish future risk of error, alleviate guilt and relieve stress among error operators, heighten the public trust, improve health professional–patient relationships, and abolish counterproductive myths (e.g., physician omniscience and perfectionism) that are slow to leave institutional cultures.[6–8]

Besides the benefits that derive from disclosure, however, we ought to note a substantive moral reason for disclosure whose merit and persuasiveness does not derive from its positive or materially useful consequences. This reason has been alluded to earlier by way of the primacy of the patient's welfare. A fundamental concentration on the patient's good not only derives from our traditional and historical understanding of the health provider's obligation to patients and the ideal formation of his or her character, but from the very meaning of normative ethics itself. That is, to be ethical or act ethically *means* to be other-regarding. The ethical act is ordinarily understood to be the one that furthers the interest of the other for his or her own sake, not for the sake of the moral agent's.[9] Whether one adopts a Kantian ethic of duty or a utilitarian ethic of realizing the greatest good for the greatest number, both moral theories are unequivocal in requiring the decision maker to be other-regarding.[10] It is simply counterintuitive—indeed, it runs contrary to the way we talk about and understand professional ethical behavior—to call an act ethical that primarily promotes the actor's self-interest.

The unassailability of this simple observation—that professional ethics is grounded in other-regarding sensibilities—explains why the discovery of an intentional act of concealment of harm-causing error is so shocking, embarrassing, and shameful. The guilty parties have no argument that is morally acceptable with which to justify their concealment because no publicly acceptable justification for their behavior exists.[6] Rather, their motivation for concealment is as obvious as their guilt: Their refusal to disclose derives from placing their own interests (in the form of averting harm to themselves, usually in the form of malpractice litigation) over those of the very party whose welfare they had promised to protect. Not only did they fail the patient once by delivering care that fell below a professional standard, they failed a second time by placing their own interests above the patient's, thereby depriving him or her of some recourse based in justice.

The idea of a "recourse based in justice" deserves some elaboration. Simply put, when a patient places his or her welfare into the hands of a health provider, not only does that patient have the right not to be maltreated, he or she has a fundamental right to know how his or her welfare is being affected by the ministrations of the health provider.[1,6] The contractual as well as fiduciary dimensions of the professional–patient relationship obligate the professional to inform the patient about how his or her care program is faring, given the fact that the health professional is morally responsible for whatever outcomes are reasonably connected with or result from that care. Consequently, whether the care program is succeeding or failing, the patient has a categorical right to know "What is causing this?" when that information is reasonably available because of the trust and honesty that must prevail in their relationship. (In the alternative, how many patients would enter into such a relationship if the understanding was that the physician will only tell you why you are feeling better, not why you are feeling worse?)

Now, this does not imply that patients have the right to be free from harm when they enter into a health care relationship, since a patient's condition might deteriorate despite the most technically sophisticated and skillfully delivered care. Patients do have the right, however, to understand how their health is a function of the care they are receiving, as well as to be free from behavior that fails to accommodate how a reasonable and prudent health provider ought to act.[2] A patient who experiences a harm-causing error, then, not only has a right to know about it, but also has a justice-based right to determine whether and how his or her harm (or loss) should be managed or remedied.

Section 8.12 of the American Medical Association's *Current Opinions on the Code of Medical Ethics* nicely underlines the trust and honesty that are at the basis of this "right to know," especially in the event of error:

> It is a fundamental ethical requirement that a physician should at all times deal honestly and openly with patients. Patients have a right to know their past and present medical status and to be free of any mistaken beliefs concerning their conditions. Situations occasionally occur in which a patient suffers significant medical complications that may have resulted from the physician's mistake or judgment. In these situations, the physician is ethically required to inform the patient of all the facts necessary to ensure understanding of what has occurred. Only through full disclosure is a patient able to make informed decisions regarding future medical care. . . . Concern regarding legal liability that might result following truthful disclosure should not affect the physician's honesty with a patient.[4, pp. 141–142]

Dispatching that duty, of course, might require enormous courage. Besides the way an individual's interest in professional self-preservation can be threatened by error disclosure, error operators might feel so wretched that exposing themselves to scrutiny via disclosure would be intolerably painful. Indeed, perhaps an emphasis on the way moral argument requires disclosure entirely misses certain broader and more powerful psychological forces that militate against it. Enormous fear of professional and public censure coupled with shame, guilt, and humiliation can easily persuade the professional whose error caused harm to numb himself or herself to recollections of the event, to "misremember" certain details or forget the incident altogether, to blame but then excuse someone else, or to reinterpret the error or its gravity (e.g., "the patient was desperately ill anyway," "these things happen—we can't always be perfect," "perhaps the error wasn't the harm-causing event after all").[7,11–13]

To the extent these factors play an influential role in error concealment, this chapter ends with some comments on how health care institutions, practicing professionals, and programs of medical education must commit themselves to changing the *character* of health care delivery and education in responding to medical error. Otherwise, it is unlikely that the following recommendations and strategies on how best to communicate harm-causing error will be taken seriously.

How to Communicate Harm-Causing Error

The following suggestions are inspired by and frequently taken directly from Robert Buchman's and Yvonne Kason's classic treatise *How to Break Bad News*.[14] For any number of reasons—but perhaps most important, because professional training programs often do not sufficiently teach and maintain the skills associated with bad-news conversations—this book ought to be required reading for health professionals. Because the disclosure of medical error is a species of bad-news conversation, this text's numerous suggestions and insights are immensely valuable in conducting error disclosure conversations.

Assuming, then, that risk management and whatever other parties involved in error analysis have determined that a harm-causing error has indeed occurred and that the requisite professional courage has been secured to disclose it, the following considerations are offered with the hope that their implementation will reduce the occurrence of additional harm resulting from a poorly or ineptly conducted error disclosure conversation.

Consideration 1: The Initial Contact

If the harmed individual is of legal age and able to tolerate and engage in an error disclosure conversation, then he or she ought to be the first individual contacted. Because he or she sustained the harm, the institution's first obligation is to respect his or her right not only to know what happened but to determine what redress, if any, should be considered. If the harmed individual is not able to engage in the conversation, then his or her legally authorized surrogate, proxy, guardian, or nearest next of kin ought to be contacted and told.

If the individual who has suffered the harm-causing error is no longer receiving care at the facility—which may often be the case—then the patient or the patient's legally authorized representative or both will need to be contacted, probably telephonically, which raises the issue of framing that conversation. I shall assume in most of what follows that the harm-causing error was at least moderately serious and that, in all likelihood, the harmed party or his or her representatives will desire to schedule a face-to-face meeting after an initial telephonic contact. Whether the harm was serious or not, however—which, after all, is for the harmed party to decide—I suggest the telephone caller should be prepared at the outset to clarify the reason for the contact. Although some professionals might prefer that the caller say, "Mr. Jones, we'd like to discuss some issues with you that came up while your father was receiving care here some weeks ago. What date and time might fit your schedule for a meeting here at the hospital?" and then hedge or obfuscate if Mr. Jones asks for details, a better strategy, I believe, is for the caller to say, "Mr. Jones, the reason I'm calling is to discuss with you or whomever you'd like something we've learned that transpired with X's care while he was here. Would you like me to go into any details right now, or would you prefer to wait until we can set up a face-to-face meeting here at the hospital?" If Mr. Jones asks for details, then he should receive them—as discussed later—since they might assist him in deciding whether a face-to-face meeting is warranted and, if so, who else he might want to invite, such as an attorney. Also, if Mr. Jones does opt for a formal meeting, it might be wise to suggest to him that he might regard the information to be discussed at that meeting as confidential and so should choose his invitees according to their sensitivity toward maintaining confidentiality.

The identity of the telephonic caller is a significant issue for consideration and, perhaps, debate. One report in the literature has the initial contact to the harmed party made by the hospital's chief of staff.[8] Another strong candidate would be the harmed party's attending physician. Yet another might be someone from risk management or administration. Still another might be the health provider with whom the patient had the most favorable rapport, which might be a night nurse. In any case, the telephonic caller should anticipate that many if not most persons will want some detail about X's care, and that if the caller admits that an error was committed, many if not most persons will request considerable detail. Proceeding with such detail, however, will not only require a deep familiarity with the harm-causing error but might well cause considerable psychological pain to the listener. Indeed, the situation is not unlike a telephonic death disclosure to a family member.

Buckman and Kason's suggestions for handling that situation seem relevant to the error disclosure conversation as well. That is, if the caller is asked to go into some detail about the harm scenario, he or she might preface his or her remarks by saying something like, "Mr. Jones, what I'm going to say might be difficult for you to hear. Is there someone with you right now in the event you might want or need some company? [pause and wait for answer] Would you like me to contact someone to be with you? [pause and wait for answer] Do you believe you'll be all right until we can arrange a meeting?"

Although many health professionals will object to my suggestion that the telephonic caller be prepared to discuss the harm-causing error because they believe it would be too traumatic for the listener, the ability of persons to withstand the disclosure of painful news is usually much better than health care providers have traditionally supposed. Decades of experience with providing risk disclosure information in informed consent scenarios—which was once repudiated as unnecessarily upsetting for the "average" patient—show that most persons can handle bad news at least tolerably well.[15,16] Indeed, the health care provider who argues that it would be cruel for patients or family members to learn telephonically about harm-causing error may well be transferring his or her own anxiety about disclosing the information to the listener. Nevertheless, a very small number of persons likely exist for whom such telephonic disclosure would have devastating and perhaps even disabling impact. Further research and commentary is needed to provide confident procedures for discerning who this population might be and determining how best to proceed.

Should a face-to-face meeting be requested, which is likely, its scheduling should obviously respect the harmed parties' schedules because it is for their benefit. Indeed, consideration should be given to holding the meeting at the harmed party's dwelling. The purpose of the meeting, after all, is for the harmed party's sake so that the institution can fulfill its ethical duty to provide whatever benefits might culminate from disclosure. Consequently, as soon as a facility confirms that a harm-causing error has occurred, it should notify the involved parties and prepare for the meeting. The more time that elapses between the error discovery and the error disclosure, the more the harmed parties might feel they have been ignored or deprived of their right to know and of whatever time is necessary to heal from the event.

Consideration 2: The Meeting Setting

Buckman and Kason point out that bad news is frequently communicated in noisy, public environments (hospital hallways, waiting rooms, in front of elevators, at the bedside within earshot of strangers, etc.) that disrespect and can even heighten the emotional discomfort the news might precipitate. Consequently, a first order of business is to schedule the conversation in a private and quiet space that is free from background disturbances (e.g., conversations among other staff, phones or faxes ringing) and that promotes a calm atmosphere.

Communicators ought further to eliminate any artifacts that suggest institutional superiority or power. Buckman and Kason urge that when bad news is about to be communicated, not only ought the communicator(s) sit down, but that there be no desk between the conversants because a desk creates a geographical space that demarcates one zone of power—that is, where the doctor or administrator sits—from another, considerably disempowered one. The psychological context of an error disclosure conversation ought to be one wherein institutional authorities refrain from striking a politically superior position to the harmed parties.

Individuals disclosing the bad news must recognize that their communicational style ought to convey concern and profound regret. Once the harmed parties realize what has happened, they might feel enormously angry and betrayed and convey their emotions to the staff. Thus, communicators who are used to managing angry patients or family members by getting angry back or by assuming a bodily posture such as a stiffened spine, an icy or disapproving stare, a jutting, defiant chin, or an aloof communicational style (e.g., haughty, sermonizing, condescending, authoritative) should realize that these behaviors will be interpreted as arrogant and will probably arouse the anger of the patient or the family all the more.

Consequently, not only should the physical environment convey respect for the emotional gravity of the occasion, but extreme consideration should be paid to the tone of one's voice and even one's bodily posture. Buckman and Kason even suggest that bad-news communicators consider sitting lower in their chairs, because it is psychologically more difficult to have sadistic feelings toward someone positioned beneath your eye level than someone at or above it. Casual body language such as sitting back with one's legs crossed should be forgone in favor, perhaps, of a slightly forward-leaning sitting posture that communicates concern. The communicator's voice should be soft and gentle, and words should be expressed slowly. The communicator should speak in plain English, not medicalese. As will be noted later, the communicator should pause frequently so as to give the listeners an opportunity to ask questions. A box of tissues should be available if someone begins to cry.

Consideration 3: Who Should Be Present?

Root cause analysis overwhelmingly suggests that errors more often occur from systemic breakdowns than from a single individual making a terrible blunder with no one to blame but himself or herself. Indeed, analysis shows that in most cases, the error operator's mistake may simply have been the last in a mistake event chain that enables or facilitates the harm's occurrence.[17,18] If most harm-causing errors are the result of a systemic breakdown, then one might argue that key representatives of that systemic breakdown ought to be present.

I believe that the professional members attending a disclosure meeting should minimally include the patient's attending physician, a representative from hospital administration, and probably a representative from hospital risk management. It might also be a good idea to invite someone with experience in managing emotionally painful or traumatic conversations, such as a psychiatrist, psychologist, or social worker. Kraman and Hamm note that when such meetings occurred at their facility, the institutional representatives included "the chief of staff, the facility attorney, the quality manager, the quality management nurse, and sometimes the facility director."[8]

Additional commentary and study seem warranted here on how to achieve the best chemistry among and representation of institutional staff so as to enable an artful conveyance of harm-causing error. For example, should the facility's legal counsel be present, especially if the harmed party has announced that he or she will be accompanied and represented by counsel? Can the facility's legal counsel be expected to foster the objectives of a truthful and "healing" disclosure of information, or would his or her advocacy role for the facility cause a situation that might result in the attorney's guiding the conversation toward something less than a comprehensive disclosure of information?

Another area where serious disagreement might occur is over whether any of the error operators should be present. There are a number of reasons suggesting they should be. Consider that the error operator was an eyewitness to the error, might best know what happened (assuming his or her psychological stability and veracity), and represents the physical embodiment of the institution's intention to deal truthfully, directly, and honestly with the situation. Consider, too, how this individual might use the meeting to gain some sense of guilt relief over what has happened.[12] Also consider how the absence of the error perpetrator from the discussion (e.g., "Please forgive Dr. or Nurse X for not being here; he or she was simply too shaken to attend our meeting.") might aggravate a patient's or family's desire for revenge. After all, the harmed parties are present and are experiencing the anguish of the disclosure. Why should the error operators be spared? A patient or family who has been harmed and is feeling terribly angry is unlikely at first blush to pity the error operator or, for that matter, pity anyone directly involved in the error's commission. Sadly but understandably, during the early moments of error disclosure, certain harmed parties might experience intense feelings of hatred or sadism. This invites yet a third suggestion on impaneling the meeting participants. That is, so as not to make it appear that the error operator is being offered up as a sacrificial lamb to the harmed party, the facility might consider inviting as many staff involved in the error as possible. The psychological effect of inviting a large number of professionals is not only to show in a most dramatic fashion how each person might admit a role in the error's occurrence, but to redirect the patient's or family's anger from one or a few persons to many persons, who might more effectively absorb that anger.

Many aggrieved parties might be impressed by such a generous admission and demonstration of concern, culpability, and regret, but certain harmed parties might feel suffocated by a large number of institutional representatives, not to mention how such a large group would need to be prepared in advance for comporting themselves during what might be an emotionally wrenching discussion. (Indeed, suppose the principal error operator is a particularly inept communicator or is psychologically fragile. What, when, and how much ought he or she be prepared to discuss?) Moreover, regardless of how many or how few persons represent the institution at the disclosure conference, care must be taken to ensure that they substantially agree on what happened.

Again, it seems that more research and reflection is needed. How to determine the best mix and number of institutional persons is an important issue that deserves future study and insight.

Consideration 4: Framing the Disclosure

Buckman and Kason suggest that the following considerations guide the form and content of a bad-news conversation:

- Be guided by the patient's or family's agenda (i.e., their questions, considerations, concerns, speculations, accusations, and anxieties).
- Speak slowly, pause often, and refrain from medical jargon.
- Deliver the bad news gently but truthfully and straightforwardly.
- Don't assume how the bad news will be received.
- Use empathic listening skills (e.g., "This must be awful [dreadful, astonishing] for you to hear").
- Respect and use the therapeutic power of silence.

In bad-news conversations such as delivering a dreadful diagnosis, Buckman and Kason strongly recommend finding out how much the patient or family already knows about the situation, which can be elicited by asking, "Mr. Jones, what is your understanding of what has happened to you thus far?" Or, "Mr. Jones, tell me what your doctors have told you thus far." The point of these questions is to determine the extent and accuracy of Mr. Jones's information as well as to gauge the level of informational complexity the patient or family can handle.

Error disclosure is a different case, however, wherein these questions seem inappropriate because the harmed party's knowledge of what has occurred up to that point will largely be irrelevant to the actual purpose of the meeting. Therefore, after introducing the persons attending the meeting, it would be best for the principal communicator—who might well be either the attending physician or chief of staff—to begin by saying, "Mr. Jones, the reason for having this meeting today is to discuss with you a very serious situation that we have learned occurred with X's care. This is very difficult for me to tell you, but an error occurred that probably contributed to or outright caused Y to happen. [pause] Now, the individuals gathered in this room are prepared to talk about this with you and answer any of your questions. So, I'd like for you to tell me how to proceed. Would you like me to go into considerable detail, or would you like to know just in general what occurred? Or if you'd prefer for me to discuss this information at length with someone else whom you'd appoint, I'd be perfectly willing to do that." At this point, the communicator should stop and allow Mr. Jones to speak.

Consideration 5: How to Talk

One of the most challenging aspects of the conversation for the communicator, especially if he or she is a physician, will be to *remain silent and listen* to the harmed party or his or her representative while they speak or display emotions. Medical curricula generally pay insufficient attention to teaching empathic listening skills, and many physicians complain they don't have time to listen to patients. Furthermore, the institutional representative who communicates the error disclosure may feel frightened or anxious and be unable to resist his or her own psychological defenses insinuating themselves into the conversation. Thus, the communicator might be tempted to downplay the gravity of the harm committed, use humor inappropriately, anxiously and continually interrupt the harmed individual, or even, as has been reported on at least one occasion, lecture the harmed party at length on the theological merits and value of forgiveness.[19] The point of the conversation, however, is not for the communicator to protect his or her feelings but to inform the harmed party in a compassionate way about the error and allow that individual to express his or her feelings. The artful communicator, then, will know how to manage his or her feelings, not only in the midst of what might be a very emotionally charged discussion, but in a way that enables the harmed party to discharge his or her feelings in a nonharmful manner. In effect, once the communicator discloses the error, he or she ought to be led by the questions, concerns, and expressions of feeling of the harmed party, not the feelings and concerns of the institution (even though they will be powerfully present and always wanting to intrude).

Furthermore, communicators ought not to sugar-coat the bad news. For example, physicians sometimes communicate a diagnosis of cancer obscurely with words like *irregularity* or *shadow,* but this language primarily serves to lessen the discomfort of the communicator, not the patient. (And often the patient finds out anyway and becomes angry at the physician's reluctance to be more truthful.) While it is as simple to say as it is difficult to do, the best delivery of bad news ought to be done straightforwardly, concisely, truthfully and, of course, respectfully: "Mr. Jones, just before your father's surgery, he received twice the dosage of a drug that was ordered. This probably caused his heart to stop during the operation and contributed to his eventual death [pause, wait for response]." The communicator should look at the harmed party while saying this, not down at the floor or away. If direct eye contact is too painful for the communicator, he or she should pick out a spot on the harmed party's forehead and direct his or her gaze there.

Although arguments may occur over the precise content of the error disclosure, institutions might give serious consideration to including the following in an error disclosure conversation: an apology; a description of the nature of the harm-causing error and the time, place, and circumstances of the harm occurrence; the likely consequences of the harm-causing error for the patient; actions taken to treat or diminish the harmful consequences of the error on the patient; institutional measures taken to prevent recurrence of the accident; names of persons who will manage ongoing care of the patient; a description of the error analysis so far; names and phone numbers of persons who will manage ongoing communication with the patient or family; information on obtaining support and counseling regarding the error; and that charges and expenses directly related to the harm-causing error will be removed from the patient's account.[20]

Interestingly and importantly, Buckman and Kason urge that the communicator anticipate nothing as to how the news will be received. The intent of this rule is not to denigrate the psychological astuteness or insight of the communicator, but rather to encourage him or her to adopt a mind-set that enables an honest and straightforward informational disclosure. The communicator who, during the disclosure of error, cannot get his or her mind off imagining some dreadful scene erupting just moments away risks delivering a distracted, fragmented, fitful, and incoherent account of what occurred. By not anticipating how the news will be received, the communicator is in a better psychological position to articulate the error disclosure articulately and efficiently.

Consideration 6: Empathizing

Although a common definition of empathy is "feeling what another feels," a more correct characterization of empathy is understanding or imagining what the other is feeling and then exploring the roots of that feeling.[19] An empathic communicator not only does not dismiss or ignore a person's displaying his or her emotions, but realizes that they represent that person's being at that moment. How I *feel* is a manifest expression of what, at that moment, I *am*. Consequently, the communicator's saying, "Mr. Jones, I realize this is difficult but please try to get control of yourself" is in effect saying, "Mr. Jones, I'm uncomfortable with the 'Mr. Jones' I'm observing right now, so please present me with a different 'Mr. Jones' whose behavior I find more acceptable." If Mr. Jones is beside himself with anger or grief, what he really wants is an indication that his emotional pain is recognized and respected. The best response to Mr. Jones is either to be silent—because silence communicates respect—or to say, "This must be unimaginably difficult for you to bear."

A guiding consideration for the communicator is that he or she should mightily resist his or her own defensive behaviors. Whereas the purpose of activating our psychological defenses is so they protect us, the purpose of the error disclosure conversation is to inform and support the harmed party. The communicator, therefore, must be prepared to feel vulnerable and even to absorb the harmed party's rage, grief, bewilderment, and so on. The more the communicator expresses respect for and permission to the harmed party to say or express his or her feelings, the better. These facilitations best occur through empathic techniques such as reframing the other's statements or questions, for example, "What I hear you saying, Mr. Jones, is . . ." Or "Let me see if I understand your question, Mr. Jones. You're asking me whether. . . ." The communicator might also simply reflect back the harmed party's feelings: "I realize you're feeling awful, Mr. Jones. This is utterly dreadful."

Many harmed parties might try, without realizing it, to provoke the communicator's rage by projecting their own rage onto the communicator. Thus, the harmed party might cry out, "How can you sit there and tell me this? I don't believe this. Is this some kind of joke? Are you sitting there telling me you killed my father? My God, then you're the ones who should be dead, not him." The most unproductive thing for the communicator to do at this moment would be to get angry or testy because doing so would only aggravate the harmed party's pain. Nor would it be particularly prudent for the communicator to argue or try to convince the harmed party how sorry everyone on the staff is: "But Mr. Jones, don't you see how sorry we are? Look at all we went through to set up this meeting and the courage it takes to sit down and tell you this. We could have kept the error a secret, you know, but we chose not to. Surely, you must give us credit for that." Although this might seem a perfectly logical response, an emotionally traumatized person might not be thinking logically or might not be inclined to sympathize with how rotten the error operators are feeling. An enraged harmed party might rather focus exclusively on his or her own grief, anger, or sense of betrayal. Consequently, the best response to the harmed party's provocations will be either to say nothing or say, "I am so sorry."

All of this will likely be extremely difficult for individuals not trained in empathic skills. Health care providers are accustomed to talking a lot, which is understandable. After all, persons come to them requesting their expertise and clinical knowledge. Consequently, when health providers feel uncomfortable in a professional situation, it is natural for them to preserve their self-esteem by calling upon what they know best and are most comfortable with: namely, reaching into their knowledge banks and talking. But in a bad-news situation such as error disclosure, elaborate explanations or justifications may be nontherapeutic unless the patient or harmed party requests them. Again, the rule is to be guided by the harmed party—who might indeed request lengthy and repeated descriptions of what went wrong or, instead, express a desire to terminate the present meeting and schedule another one. Consequently, delivering bad news requires the health professional to tolerate what will occasionally be deafening and heart-wrenchingly uncomfortable periods of questions, accusations, threats, and silence.

Consideration 7: Follow-up

When an individual hears emotionally devastating news, a common reaction is for that person to feel terribly isolated and alone.[21] One of the objectives of a bad-news conversation, therefore, is to convey to the patient or family that he or she will not be abandoned in the days, weeks, and months ahead. Thus, in a typical bad-news communication, Buckman and Kason suggest the communicator say something like, "Mr. Jones, I wonder if you might want to consider the following [treatments, self-help groups, other professionals, information, etc.]." In the context of an error disclosure conversation, a variant might be: "Mr. Jones, please know that despite what has happened, we're here to answer any questions or schedule any future meetings with you that you'd like. Although you may not desire it, please know we sincerely want to support you in any way we can. We'll give you contact information for certain members of our staff whom you can call anytime, day or night. And should you wish to secure an attorney, please know that our staff will accommodate his or her questions or requests." Although an interest in a continuing relationship might sound odd in an error disclosure conversation, it implies the possibility of a nonhostile, supportive, and continuing relationship that can be extremely therapeutic (not unlike airline staff who assist family members whose loved ones died or were injured in airplane disasters with shopping, laundry, housecleaning, and so forth).

Error disclosure communicators must realize that many individuals who have been harmed by medical error can come to admire an institution's effort to disclose. If done artfully, disclosure will impress many harmed parties that their welfare remains a significant concern among the error operators and institutional representatives. Consider, in the alternative, how the relationship between the harmed and harming parties might transpire if institutional representatives intentionally engage in a conspiracy of error concealment and the harmed parties find out.

Error communicators ought to develop a list of suggestions or considerations for the harmed parties. Institutional authorities ought to suggest their availability for future meetings to work with harmed parties and their representatives to bring emotional closure. Harmed parties might especially want precise and elaborate information as to how the error-causing chain of events played out. A need to know in great detail everything that happened helps certain types of persons by providing a sense of calm, as it not only takes the individual's mind off of his or her pain by focusing it on the facts associated with the harm-causing event, but also allows a harmed party to feel a vicarious sense of empowerment (i.e., "Well, even though I couldn't prevent what happened, at least I know what happened"). Indeed, institutions might want to include broaching the issue of a financial settlement early on in conversations with the harmed party. This might prove very wise in instances where the resultant harm has reached significant proportions because a settlement, if skillfully negotiated, might turn out to be considerably less than what an elaborate malpractice trial culminating in a jury verdict would cost.[8]

What Is Required for a Patient-Centered Policy on Error Disclosure?

Carrying out these steps of error disclosure calls for organizational, psychological, communicational, and ethical sensibilities and skills that are missing in many, if not most, of today's health care institutions. I believe that if something like the steps in error disclosure discussed here become commonplace in America's health care facilities, it will primarily be due to profound changes in the training, attitudinal formation, and core beliefs of health care providers and institutional representatives that incorporate some of the following suggestions.

First, unnecessarily oppressive elements of medical training need to be eliminated in undergraduate and graduate medical education programs. These include not only the common practice of having students and residents go for long periods without food or sleep, but also the elimination of various unethical practices that trainees not only frequently observe but in which they are asked to participate. Considerable literature on third-year medical students' experiences, for example, describes how they are privy to conversations wherein certain patients are called derogatory names ("dirtball" or "stool"), are asked to secure consents from patients for procedures with which the medical student is thoroughly unfamiliar, are expected to conspire in subterfuge or outright lying to patients and even to attending physicians, forge interns' signatures at their request, and knowingly expose patients to nonsterile procedures.[22-24] If we wonder how it comes about that health care providers can subordinate the ethic of patient-centered care to protecting their own self-interests by concealing harm-causing error, the ubiquity of unethical practices occurring in training programs might provide part of the explanation. Because actual behaviors and practices usually win out over moral rhetoric or exhortation, it is extremely tempting to believe that exposure to unethical practices early on—such as in the third year of undergraduate medical training—lays the groundwork for concealing harm-causing error. As such, training programs must operationally insist that disrespecting the rights and dignity of patients in any form is absolutely forbidden.

Second, institutions must recognize that health care providers who are brutally intolerant of performance that is less than perfect and who teach or instruct by embarrassment or humiliation are probably troubled souls in need of lengthy counseling or psychotherapy. Also, these persons might respond maladaptively when error occurs because their reaction will likely issue from painful, probably childhood, experiences that derive from problematic rather than caring relationships.[25] Consequently, hospitals should not only routinely maintain counseling programs for their staff but should also recognize that those services might be especially valuable for error operators who are terribly disturbed over the harm their error has caused.

Third, institutions need to operationalize an understanding of what root cause analysis has shown for some time, namely, that health care institutions are complex systems, that complex systems are hazardous, and that where hazard and complexity exist, error is inevitable.[26] Risk management strategy, therefore, ought to reject the myth of error-free care, but should design clinical systems with a keen eye to the probability of their malfunctioning. In other words, at every step of system design, the architect should ask himself or herself, "How might this system, as it incorporates elements A, B, C, and so forth, break down?" and then build in appropriate fail-safe elements.[18] Accordingly, error disclosure will be facilitated as more and more institutions become convinced of what errorologists such as James Reason have been observing for over a decade: that serious errors are more often the result of system flaws such as poor monitoring or supervision, faulty technological design, or unreasonably high levels of psychological stress than they are the result of a single individual doing something inexplicably inept.[27]

Last but hardly least, more research is needed on the economic value of error disclosure. At first blush, the idea that comprehensive error disclosure does not increase but might actually decrease the associated cost of malpractice litigation seems counterintuitive, although some early data seem to indicate precisely that.[8] However, if this counterintuition is consistently supported by data and the data are widely and conspicuously disseminated, such efforts should ultimately have a positive effect on encouraging error disclosure.

A Final Point

There is some literature that suggests that individuals choose health care as a career because of deep, unconscious insecurities about the threat of sickness and their own mortality.[28] On this account, their vocational choice of health care turns out to be an unconscious defense mechanism or derives from a psychological formation that mollifies their deepest worries and insecurities. Interestingly and fortunately, these unconscious insecurities become consciously expressed by a disposition toward altruism, wherein health providers feel good by advancing the welfare of others. Perhaps, though, these psychodynamic phenomena offer another explanation as to why error disclosure is as difficult as it is infrequent: Error disclosure powerfully threatens the deepest and most profound insecurities of health care providers. As James Reason has pointed out, an error operator may often manifest "a desire to escape from the evidence of one's own inadequacy."[27, p. 93] Thus, those health care providers and their institutional representatives who have decided to disclose error truthfully and comprehensively, as painful as it might have been, have successfully managed their insecurities with a sense of right and a sense of self that is, I believe, punctuated by a healthy regard for their own dignity, self-respect, and, indeed, self-love. That is, the individual who has a healthy regard for himself or herself—a healthy narcissism—will be better poised to care for patients and do the right thing when error occurs than those who may be supremely technically skilled but whose singular concentration on the development of those skills occurred at the expense of dismissing the patient who is presumably the beneficiary of those skills. It has been said that, "Great physicians are great human beings first, and great clinicians second." To the extent that health care training programs and institutions can operationalize that idea and concentrate on developing narcissistically healthy human beings who are also skillful clinicians, the practice of truthful and comprehensive error disclosure should witness substantial improvement.[25]

References

1. Beauchamp, T., and Childress, J. F. *Principles of Biomedical Ethics*, 4th ed. New York: Oxford University Press, 1994, pp. 259–325.
2. King, J. H. *The Law of Medical Malpractice in a Nutshell*, 2nd ed. St. Paul, MN: West Publishing Company, 1986, pp. 9–82.
3. Rodwin, M. A. *Medicine, Money & Morals*. New York: Oxford University Press, 1993.
4. Council on Ethical and Judicial Affairs, American Medical Association. *Code of Medical Ethics, Current Opinions with Annotations, 1998–1999 Edition*. Chicago, IL: American Medical Association, 1999.
5. Gorlin, R. A. (ed.). *Codes of Professional Responsibility*, 2nd ed. Washington, DC: The Bureau of National Affairs, 1991.
6. Smith, M. L., and Forster, H. P. Morally managing medical mistakes. *Cambridge Quarterly of Healthcare Ethics* 2000;9:38–53.
7. Joint Commission on Accreditation of Healthcare Organizations. *What Every Hospital Should Know About Sentinel Events*. Oakbrook Terrace, IL: Author, 2000, pp. 89–106.

8. Kraman, S. S., and Hamm, G. Risk management: Extreme honesty may be the best policy. *Annals of Internal Medicine* 1999;131:963–967.

9. Bayles, M. *Professional Ethics*. Belmont, CA: Wadsworth Publishing, 1989.

10. Munson, R. (ed). *Intervention and Reflection: Basic Issues in Medical Ethics,* 4th ed. Belmont, CA: Wadsworth Publishing, 1992, pp. 1–45.

11. Christensen, J. F., Levinson, W., and Dunn, P. M. The heart of darkness: The impact of perceived mistakes on physicians. *Journal of General Internal Medicine* 1992;7(July/August):424–431.

12. Wu, A. W., Folkman, S., McPhee, S. J., and Lo, B. How house officers cope with their mistakes. *Western Journal of Medicine* 1993; 159:565–569.

13. Wu, A. W., Folkman, S., McPhee, S. J., and Lo, B. Do house officers learn from their mistakes? *JAMA* 1991;265:2089–2094.

14. Buckman, R., and Kason, Y. *How to Break Bad News*. Baltimore, MD: Johns Hopkins University Press, 1992.

15. Gillick, M. Talking with patients about risk. *J Gen Intern Med* 1988;3(Mar–Apr):166–170.

16. Meisel, A., and Kuczewski, M. Legal and ethical myths about informed consent. *Arch Intern Med* 1996;156:2521–2526.

17. Leape, L. L. Error in medicine. *JAMA* 1994;272:1851–1857.

18. Joint Commission on Accreditation of Healthcare Organizations. *Root Cause Analysis in Health Care: Tools and Techniques*. Oakbrook Terrace, IL: Author, 2000.

19. Platt, F. W., and Gordon, G. H. *Field Guide to the Difficult Patient Interview*. Philadelphia: Lippincott Williams & Wilkins, 1999, p. 81.

20. Adapted from the Disclosure of Patient Safety Events policy of Licking Memorial Health Systems. Available from Legal Services, Licking Memorial Health Systems, 1320 West Main Street, Newark, Ohio 43055.

21. Gunther, M. Countertransference issues in staff caregivers who work to rehabilitate catastrophic-injury survivors. *Am J Psychother* 1994;48:208–220.

22. Feudtner, C., Christakis, D. A., and Christakis, N. A. Do clinical clerks suffer ethical erosion? Students' perceptions of their ethical environment and personal development. *Academic Med* 1994;69:670–679.

23. Novack, D. H., Epstein, R. M., and Paulsen, R. H. Toward creating physician-healers: Fostering medical students' self-awareness, personal growth, and well-being. *Academic Med* 1999;74:516–520.

24. Branch, W. T. Supporting the moral development of medical students. *J Gen Intern Med* 2000;15:503–508.

25. Miller, A. *The Drama of the Gifted Child,* 3rd ed. Translated by Ruth Ward. New York: Basic Books, 1997.

26. Cook, R. I., Render, M., and Woods, D. D. Gaps in the continuity of care and progress on patient safety. *BMJ* 2000;320:791–794.

27. Reason, J. *Human Error*. Cambridge, UK: Cambridge University Press, 1990.

28. Graber, G. The role of compulsiveness in the normal physician. *JAMA* 1985;254:2926–2929.

CHAPTER THIRTY-SEVEN

DISCLOSURE OF MEDICAL ERROR: LIABILITY, INSURANCE, AND RISK MANAGEMENT IMPLICATIONS

Grena G. Porto

Since the release of the Institute of Medicine's (IOM) report in 1999,[1] medical error has been a topic of much thought and debate throughout the health care provider community. Although the challenge of reducing the frequency of medical error is a daunting one, an even greater concern is that of finding ways to talk to patients about medical error in a litigious and blame-oriented society.

A variety of arguments can be made in favor of disclosure of medical error to patients.[2-9] Disclosure can be beneficial to both patients and providers, as well as to the system, by permitting learning from past mistakes. Disclosure of error can also restore patients' trust in a system they have begun to question, and it can help smooth the way for resolution of conflicts that result from error-related injury.

Despite the many arguments in favor of disclosing errors to patients, the prospect of speaking openly and candidly about one's error to a patient is frightening to most practitioners and is not routinely done.[10-13] Physicians cite a number of reasons for not wanting to disclose medical errors to patients, including concern that the disclosure could harm the patient or the relationship.[14] They also cite concerns related to their own well-being, such as loss of the respect of their peers and professional isolation and embarrassment. But perhaps the greatest fear associated with the disclosure of medical error is the risk of a lawsuit.[15-18]

But does disclosure of medical error increase the likelihood of a lawsuit? Does disclosure increase the potential value of a claim? Does disclosure jeopardize the practitioner's liability insurance coverage? These questions have been considered by many researchers as well as by the courts. This chapter presents research, writings, and court findings about these issues as well as the consensus that is emerging regarding the liability, insurance, and risk management implications of disclosing medical errors to patients.

Is There a Duty to Disclose Medical Mistakes?

There are currently no federal or state statutes requiring practitioners to disclose mistakes to patients.[19] However, courts have held that the provider–patient relationship is fiduciary in nature,[20-23] based on trust, and thus creates a duty that the provider act in the best interests of the patient. Because of this, courts have found that providers have a duty to disclose medical mistakes, and this duty has been applied not only to physicians but to nurses and others as well.[24,25] Health care organizations have been found to have an independent duty to disclose errors to patients.[26] Thus, even in the absence of statutory requirements, courts have clearly established the duty to disclose medical error to patients.

Professional societies have also articulated a duty to disclose error to patients, based on ethical principles. The American Medical Association has identified an ethical obligation on the part of physicians to disclose mistakes to patients:

> Situations occur in which a patient suffers significant medical complications that may have resulted from the physician's mistake or judgment. In these situations, the physician is ethically required to inform the patient of all the facts necessary to ensure understanding of what has occurred. . . . Concern regarding legal liability which might result following truthful disclosure should not affect the physician's honesty with the patient.[27]

The American College of Physicians, in its *Ethics Manual,* states:

> In addition, physicians should disclose to patients information about procedural or judgment errors made in the course of care if such information is material to the patient's well-being. Errors do not necessarily constitute improper, negligent or unethical behavior, but failure to disclose them may.[28]

The American Nurses' Association and the American College of Healthcare Executives have codes of ethics[29,30] that require professionals to respect human dignity and conduct professional activities with honesty. The American Society for Healthcare Risk Management's Code of Professional Responsibility[31] calls for practicing the profession with honesty and integrity while avoiding unjust harm to others.

In November 2000, the board of directors of the National Patient Safety Foundation, composed of representatives from health care providers, consumer organizations, insurers, the legal profession, academia, and regulators, adopted a statement of principle calling for providers to disclose medical injury to patients.[32]

Practicing physicians and researchers also believe that there is an ethical duty to disclose medical error to patients.[33-44] Although some view this as primarily a physician responsibility,[45] it is clear from court cases and professional journals that other professionals and the organization itself also have a duty to disclose errors to patients, independent of the duty of physicians. Some researchers have gone further, stating that physicians must disclose errors to patients regardless of the personal cost to themselves;[46-49] both the American Medical Association and the American College of Physicians agree with this viewpoint.

Most recently, the Joint Commission on Accreditation of Healthcare Organizations (JCAHO) implemented standards requiring that accredited organizations disclose to patients "unanticipated outcomes," including errors.[50]

Barriers to Disclosure: Provider Attitudes, Expectations, and Fears

A significant barrier to disclosure is physicians' reluctance to admit mistakes, even to themselves. This is due in part to the blame-oriented culture that permeates the medical community, which is not conducive to openly admitting mistakes. A common perception among physicians is that good doctors don't make mistakes.[51-53] Because of this, physicians learn to keep mistakes to themselves rather than risk the judgment of their peers.[54] In one study, only 54% of house officers disclosed an error to the attending physician, and less than 25% told the patient.[55] In fact, the pressure to be perfect is so great that doctors admit they would lie to colleagues or patients to cover up a mistake.[56-58]

Another barrier to disclosure of medical error is lack of training. The communication skills required are not routinely taught to physicians.[59,60] In one study, 50% of physicians said they had never received any training on the handling of medical mistakes.[61] In other studies, although physicians agreed that disclosure was required, they questioned their ability to do so.[62,63]

Physicians also believe that the health care delivery system does not support such honesty. They receive conflicting advice and are discouraged by insurers, attorneys, and risk managers from disclosing mistakes.[64-66] The primary reasons for this are fear of litigation and possible compromise of insurance coverage. Yet, according to a recent survey, health care risk managers overwhelmingly favor disclosure and often believe that their organizations are not as forthcoming with patients as they, the risk managers, would like.[67] Again, liability and fear of litigation were often cited as the reasons that the organization would be reluctant to disclose. Clearly, litigation-related concerns appear to be driving decisions in this area, although there appears to be consensus that disclosure is the right thing to do.

The Relationship Between Disclosure of Medical Error and Litigation

Although litigation-related concerns plague health care providers, particularly physicians, and play a prominent role in decisions to disclose, a cause-and-effect relationship between disclosure of medical error and malpractice litigation remains speculative at best. In fact, there is mounting evidence that disclosure does *not* increase litigation, and that in fact it is the *failure* to disclose that actually triggers lawsuits.

Being involved in an error evokes emotions such as shame, humiliation, fear, panic, guilt, anger, and self-doubt in physicians.[68,69] In response to this stress, physicians employ several coping mechanisms, including denial and distancing.[70,71] This is compounded by fear of litigation, which causes physicians to feel guarded in their dealings with patients following an error.[72] Patients interpret this withdrawal as rejection, and they feel angry and betrayed. It is this anger and betrayal, coupled with a sense that the physician is not being honest, that prompts patients to file claims.[73-75] Thus, the physician's fear of litigation becomes a self-fulfilling prophecy, reinforcing the physician's fear of disclosure, and a repetitive cycle develops (Figure 37-1).

However, there is evidence to suggest that disclosure does not lead to litigation and may in fact curb liability and expense payments. A study by the Veterans Affairs Medical Center in Lexington, Kentucky, found that disclosure of medical error did not adversely affect claims experience.[76] The hospital adopted a policy of full disclosure in 1987, following two high-verdict cases, as part of an aggressive program of risk management that also included earlier identification of liability cases, prompt determination of relevant facts, and early resolution of problem cases. The hospital found that claims frequency and severity did not increase after the policy of full disclosure was adopted, and that severity may have in fact decreased. Lexington's claims experience during that time was comparable to that of similar hospitals in the VA system. The hospital identified only five claims in a 7-year period that would probably not have been filed had the full disclosure policy

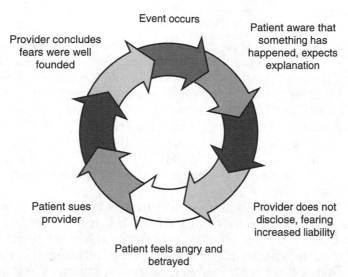

FIGURE 37-1   The nondisclosure/liability cycle (Copyright G. Porto, VHA, 2001)

not been in place. In addition, the hospital was able to secure lower settlements because claimants' attorneys were more amenable to early and amicable settlement following full disclosure, thereby reducing not only indemnity but expense payments in those cases.

Several studies go further to suggest that failure to disclose leads patients to file claims. Hickson found that 24% of patients surveyed filed claims because they believed that the physician was not being totally honest with them or was covering up important information.[77] Vincent found that 39% would not have filed claims if they had received an explanation and an apology.[78] Witman found that patients were significantly more likely to sue if they learned of a physician's error from some other source.[79]

In general, physicians' concerns about litigation appear to be exaggerated. Studies have shown that physicians significantly overestimate the risk of being sued.[80] Far fewer patients than are injured through negligence actually sue, and only a small percentage of those are compensated.[81,82] Most injured patients do not file claims, finding other ways of venting their dissatisfaction with their care.[83]

Thus, providers' fears about disclosure and litigation are not well founded. Rather than leading to litigation, disclosure may well prevent it. In addition, the propensity of patients to sue is overestimated by providers. Further, of injured patients who do file claims, only a small percentage ever receive compensation. Finally, disclosure has been shown to have a moderating effect on liability and expense payments.

Fraud and Fraudulent Concealment

Failure to disclose can cause other legal problems for providers as well. Several courts have found that failure to disclose an error can void the statute of limitations, allowing a patient to file a claim when an error is discovered even if the statute has expired.[84] Other courts have applied the doctrine of equitable estoppel to permit the filing of a claim after expiration of the statute of limitations when the failure to file the claim within the statute occurred because the provider concealed the error from the patient.[85] Thus, by failing to disclose an error to a patient, the provider grants the patient an unlimited extension of time within which to file a claim.

In addition, failure to disclose an error has been found to be fraud or fraudulent concealment by the courts.[86] This is true even if no false statements are made, but all of the relevant facts are not revealed.[87] In fact, mere silence is enough to sustain a claim of fraudulent concealment.[88] Thus, failure to respond to a patient's questions about an error can be enough to sustain a claim of fraudulent concealment.

Claims of fraudulent concealment present many legal problems for defendants. First, fraud and fraudulent concealment are intentional torts and are thus not covered by insurance. Therefore, any part of a malpractice judgment that is attributable to claims of fraud or fraudulent concealment would represent out-of-pocket payments for the defendant. Second, fraud and fraudulent concealment claims are very likely to result in punitive damages. In many states, punitive damages cannot be covered by insurance as a matter of public policy, again leaving the defendant with an out-of-pocket exposure. Finally, allegations of fraud are highly inflammatory, and the prospect of a large verdict by a jury would likely make such a case extremely difficult to settle for a reasonable amount. Thus, not only would indemnity payments be higher in such cases, but expense payments would be likely to increase as well.

The problems and potential consequences associated with claims of fraud and fraudulent concealment provide powerful motivation for providers to avoid such claims. Disclosure of medical error is an effective risk management strategy that accomplishes this while respecting the rights of patients.

The Role of Apology in Disclosure of Medical Error

Disclosure by itself may not be enough to satisfy patients' need for information; several studies suggest that an apology is also necessary to completely restore trust in the physician and repair damage to the relationship.[89-91] Cohen describes the function of apology as "subtracting insult from injury."[92] Apologies benefit both the victim and the wrongdoer: The victim feels acknowledged, and the wrongdoer feels forgiven. In addition, the role of forgiveness in the physiological as well as psychological well-being of patients is gaining acceptance in the medical community.[93]

Although there are no legal requirements or ethical standards that mandate apologies, some attorneys recommend apology as a means to facilitate resolution of disputes, including medical malpractice cases.[94,95] However, apologies are not without risk—such statements can be considered admissions of wrongdoing and thus could be submitted to a jury as evidence in a malpractice case.[96,97] In spite of this, apologies are gaining acceptance as a means to ameliorate a patient's dissatisfaction over an error. California, Massachusetts, and Texas have enacted laws protecting apologies, and cases in Georgia and Vermont have also held that they are protected from admissibility in court cases. There are no known cases in which a physician's coverage was voided as a result of an apology.[98]

By subtracting insult from injury, as Cohen suggests, apologies can play an important role in preventing a lawsuit. An injured patient who was not already contemplating a claim is unlikely to be persuaded to do so merely by receiving an apology. In fact, such a patient may be sufficiently mollified by an apology to abandon plans to file a claim, or to pursue an alternative method of gaining redress for a perceived wrong. However, even if an apology fails to prevent the lawsuit, it may sufficiently reduce hostility to allow a reasonable settlement earlier in the claim, thereby reducing not only indemnity but expense payments as well.[99,100] Further, if a claim were filed and the apology was ultimately presented to a jury, this does not signal disaster for the defendant provider. The apology itself is not an admission of liability, and the jury will be asked to weigh that statement along with all other evidence in the case.[101] It is also possible that an apology would cause a jury to look more kindly on the defendant—research shows that people who admit their mistakes are perceived as more honest and are more liked.[102]

Implementing a Policy of Full Disclosure

Health care organizations are starting to realize that a policy of full disclosure benefits both patients and providers, and have begun implementing such policies. Children's Hospitals and Clinics in Minneapolis and St. Paul adopted its policy of full disclosure in 1999 as part of a comprehensive patient safety initiative.[103] Although the impact of this policy on Children's claims experience cannot yet be measured, the hospital is confident it is already reaping other benefits from this approach. Patients and families report that this approach has increased their confidence in Children's and its physicians. Staff members are supportive of the policy because it enables them to talk openly and learn from their mistakes. Additionally, this approach of informing patients about errors has the hidden benefit of involving patients and families more in their care, and their vigilance can serve as an additional safety net in avoiding errors.

Of course, a policy of full disclosure of errors to patients and families cannot succeed in an organization that is blame oriented. For such a program to succeed, the organization must eliminate guilt, fear, and reprisal by promoting a nonpunitive system of reporting, analyzing, and responding to errors. This can only be done through the concerted efforts of all layers of the organization, beginning with top layers of management.

Also, extensive educational training for practitioners is needed prior to implementation of such a policy. As noted earlier, half of physicians surveyed reported they had received no training in handling medical errors.[104] It has been shown that poor communication skills in the face of bad outcomes cause patients distress[105] and can lead to malpractice litigation.[106] Continuing medical education programs are effective in teaching communication skills to physicians.[107,108]

Organizations that adopt a policy of full disclosure should also develop mechanisms for supporting the decision-making process. Availability of consultations for second opinions and access to an ethics committee for discussion and debate about whether disclosure should take place have been suggested as ways of accomplishing this.[109] Risk managers also play a critical role in helping providers frame comments for the disclosure discussion, providing support for the providers involved in the process and dealing with lingering patient concerns related to poor outcomes.

Insurance Implications

Increasingly, insurers are moving toward advising their insureds to be more candid with patients when mistakes occur.[110] They recognize the benefits of disclosure for patients and providers as well as the advantages of such an approach in managing any claim that may result. However, this does not mean that an insurer will support an insured's policy without reservation. Health care providers need to determine their insurer's approach to disclosure and apology prospectively rather than at the time a serious mistake occurs. This determination should be part of the due diligence process and may become a selection criterion for a provider who is contemplating a policy of full disclosure.

Providers also need to bear in mind that although a carrier may support disclosure, it may still have concerns about the wording of the disclosure. Therefore, health care providers should consult their insurers when disclosing a serious error resulting in patient injury.

Additionally, insurers can bring resources to the disclosure process, such as access to peers who can lend emotional support, that the insured might not otherwise have. Furthermore, for disclosure and apology to work successfully as a loss control measure in the case of serious injury caused by error, the provider must be prepared to offer compensation as appropriate, rather than forcing the patient to seek legal counsel or file a claim. An insured cannot offer such compensation without consent of the insurer; thus, collaboration with the carrier in these circumstances is essential.

Conclusion

Disclosure of medical mistakes to patients is a moral, ethical, and legal duty of both individual practitioners and health care organizations. It confers emotional and physical benefits on patients, and allows providers to recover from the great emotional turmoil of being involved in an error. In addition, disclosure of error provides intangible benefits to providers, such as restored trust, esteem, and confidence of patients; reduced animosity from injured patients; and increased ability to dispose of valid claims in a timely and cost-effective manner. Disclosure of medical error does not appear to lead to increased claims frequency and may lead to decreased claims severity.

Disclosing a mistake to a patient is difficult and frightening for providers. Providers' fears are compounded by lack of training, lack of peer support, and a blame-oriented culture that seeks to punish those who make mistakes. Health care organizations must create cultures that support disclosure of medical error, including training and support for providers.

Apologies are gaining acceptance as a means of restoring a patient's trust in a provider following a medical error. Like disclosure, apologies confer benefits on both patients and providers and play an important role in reducing hostility so that disputes regarding medical error can be more amicably, reasonably, and quickly resolved. Although they are not without legal risk, the benefits of apologies appear to outweigh the risk.

Insurance companies are increasingly supporting disclosure of error and even apology as a means to restore trust between patients and providers and reduce animosity if a claim is subsequently filed. Insurers have an important role to play in the disclosure process. Health care providers should seek carriers whose philosophy about disclosure is similar to their own and who can provide the necessary support for disclosure in the event of a serious patient injury.

Notes

1. Kohn, L. T., Corrigan, J. M., and Donaldson, M. (eds). *To Err Is Human: Building a Safer Health System.* Washington, DC: National Academy Press, 2000.
2. Wu, A. W., Cavanaugh, T. A., McPhee, S. J., et al. To tell the truth. Ethical and practical issues in disclosing medical mistakes to patients. *Journal of General Internal Medicine,* 1997;12:770–75.
3. Applegate, W. B. Physician management of patients with adverse outcomes. *Archives of Internal Medicine,* 1986;146:2249–52.
4. Rosner, F., Berger, J. T., Kark, P., et al. Disclosure and prevention of medical errors. *Archives of Internal Medicine,* 2000;160:2089–92.
5. Wu, A. W., Folkman, S., McPhee, S. J., and Lo, B. How house officers cope with their mistakes. *Western Journal of Medicine,* 1993;565–69.
6. Hilfiker, D. Facing our mistakes. *New England Journal of Medicine,* 1984;310:118–22.
7. Wu, A. W., Folkman, S., McPhee, S. J., and Lo, B. Do house officers learn from their mistakes? *JAMA,* 1991;265:2089–94.
8. Quill, T. E., and Williamson, P. R. Healthy approaches to physician stress. *Archives of Internal Medicine,* 1990;150:1857–61.
9. Christensen, J. F., Levinson, W., and Dunn, D. M. The heart of darkness: the impact of perceived mistakes on physicians. *Journal of General Internal Medicine,* 1992;7:424–31.
10. Wu, 1991.
11. Gray, J. Should you tell the patient when you mess up? *Medical Economics,* July 23, 1990.
12. Hingorani, M., Wong, T., and Vafidis, G. Attitudes after unintended injury during treatment: a survey of doctors and patients. *Western Journal of Medicine,* 1999;171:81–83.
13. Sweet, M. P., and Bernat, J. L. A study of the ethical duty of physicians to disclose errors. *Journal of Clinical Ethics,* 1997;8(4):341–48.
14. Sweet, 1997.
15. Wu, 1997.
16. Orenstein, A. Apology excepted: incorporating a feminist analysis into evidence policy where you would least expect to find it. *Southwestern University Law Review,* 1999;28:221–79.
17. Brazeau, C. Disclosing the truth about a medical error. *American Family Physician,* 1999;60(3):1013–14.
18. Maithel, S. Iatrogenic error and truth-telling. A comparison of the United States and India. *Issues in Medical Ethics,* 1998; VI(4). Available at www.healthlibrary.com/reading/ethics/oct98/index.htm.

19. Vogel, J., and Delgado, R. To tell the truth: physicians' duty to disclose medical mistakes. *UCLA Law Review,* 1980;28:52–94.
20. Robin, M. R., Brian, D. D., and Rumsey, T. J. Truth-telling, apology and medical mistakes. *The Medical Journal of Allina,* 1998;7(3):10–13.
21. LeBlang, T. R., and Kink, J. L. Tort liability for nondisclosure: the physician's legal obligation to disclose patient injury and illness. *Dickinson Law Review,* 1984;89:1–52.
22. Shapiro, R. S., Simpson, D. E., Lawrence, S. L., et al. A survey of sued and nonsued physicians and suing patients. *Archives of Internal Medicine,* 1989;149:2190–96.
23. Greely, H. T. Do physicians have a duty to disclose mistakes? *Western Journal of Medicine,* 1999;171:82–83.
24. Nowicki, M., and Chaku, M. Do healthcare managers have an ethical duty to admit mistakes? *Healthcare Financial Management,* 1998;52:62–64.
25. Regan, W. A. When your silence is tantamount to fraud. *RN,* October 1980.
26. *Nutty v. Jewish Hospital,* 571 F. Supp. 1050; *Wohglemuth v. Meyer,* 293 P; *Esener v. Kinsey,* 240 Ga. App. 21 1999.2d 816; *Borderion v. Peck,* 661 S.W.2d 967.
27. American Medical Association's Council on Ethical and Judicial Affairs, Southern Illinois University School of Law. *Code of Medical Ethics: Annotated Current Opinions.* Chicago: American Medical Association, 1994.
28. American College of Physicians. *Ethics Manual,* 4th ed. Reprinted in *Annals of Internal Medicine,* 1998;128:576–94.
29. American Nurses Association. *Code of Ethics for Nurses with Interpretive Statements.* Washington, DC: ANA Publishing, 1985.
30. American College of Healthcare Executives. *Code of Ethics,* rev. 2000. Available at http://www.ache.org/abt_ache/code.cfm.
31. American Society for Healthcare Risk Management. *Code of Professional Responsibility,* rev. 1996.
32. National Patient Safety Foundation Statement of Principle, 2000. Reprinted in *Focus on Patient Safety,* 2001;4(1):3.
33. Wu, A. W. Handling hospital errors: is disclosure the best defense? *Annals of Internal Medicine,* 1999;131(12):970–72.
34. Finkelstein, D., Wu, A. W., Holtzman, N. A., et al. When a physician harms a patient by medical error: ethical, legal and risk management considerations. *Journal of Clinical Ethics,* 1997;8(4):330–35.
35. O'Connell, D., and Keller, V. F. Communication: a risk management tool. *Journal of Clinical Outcomes Management,* 1999;6(1):35–38.
36. Applegate, 1986.
37. Ritchie, J. H., and Davies, S. C. Professional negligence: a duty of candid disclosure? *British Medical Journal,* 1995;310:888–89.
38. Greely, 1999.
39. Strunin, L. Professional negligence: disclosure is right. *British Medical Journal,* 1995;310:1671.
40. Sweet, 1997.
41. Smith, M. L., and Forster, H. P. Morally managing medical mistakes. *Cambridge Quarterly of Healthcare Ethics,* 2000;9:38–53.

42. Rosner, 2000.

43. Brazeau, 1999.

44. Hilfiker, 1984.

45. Wu, 1999.

46. Rosner, 2000.

47. Smith, 2000.

48. Wu, 1997.

49. Strunin, 1995.

50. Available at http://www.jcaho.org.

51. Robin, 1998.

52. Green, M. J., Farber, N. J., and Ubel, P. A. Lying to each other. *Archives of Internal Medicine,* 2000;160:2317–23.

53. Mizrahi, T. Managing medical mistakes: ideology, insularity and accountability among internists-in-training. *Social Science & Medicine,* 1984;19(2):135–46.

54. Newman, M. C. The emotional impact of mistakes on family physicians. *Archives of Family Medicine,* 1996;5(2):71–75.

55. Wu, 1991.

56. Green, 2000.

57. Novack, D. H., Detering, B. J., Arnold, R., et al. Physicians' attitudes toward using deception to resolve difficult ethical problems. *JAMA,* 1989;261(20):2980–85.

58. Gray, 1990.

59. Wu, 1993.

60. Pichert, J. W., Hickson, G. B., and Trotter, T. S. Malpractice and communication skills for difficult situations. *Ambulatory Child Health,* 1998;4:213–21.

61. Maithel, 1998.

62. Sweet, 1997.

63. Gray, 1990.

64. Lowes, R. L. Made a bonehead mistake? Apologize. *Medical Economics,* 1997;74:94, 97, 101–3.

65. O'Connell, 1999.

66. Finkelstein, 1997.

67. Ruroede, K., and Porto, G. Healthcare risk managers' attitudes about disclosure of medical error. (Unpublished study.)

68. Wu, 1991.

69. Hilfiker, 1984.

70. Mizrahi, 1984.

71. Wu, 1993.

72. Robin, 1998.

73. Hickson, G. B., Clayton, E. W., Githens, P. B., et al. Factors that prompted families to file medical malpractice claims following perinatal injuries. *JAMA,* 1992;267:1359-63.

74. Witman, A. B., Park, D. M., and Hardin, S. B. How do patients want physicians to handle mistakes? A survey of internal medicine patients in an academic setting. *Archives of Internal Medicine,* 1996;156(22):2565-69.

75. Hingorani, 1999.

76. Kraman, S. S., and Hamm, G. Risk management: honesty may be the best policy. *Annals of Internal Medicine,* 1999;131(12):963–67.

77. Hickson, 1992.

78. Vincent, C., Young, M., and Phillips, A. Why do people sue doctors? A study of patients and relatives taking legal action. *Lancet,* 1994;343:1609–13.

79. Witman, 1996.

80. Lawthers, A. G., Localio, A. R., Laird, N. M., et al. Physicians' perception of the risk of being sued. *Journal of Health Politics, Policy and Law,* 1992;17(3):463–82.

81. Brennan, T. A., Sox, C. M., and Burstin, H. R. Relation between negligent adverse events and the outcomes of medical malpractice litigation. *New England Journal of Medicine,* 1996;335(26):1963–67.

82. Andrews, L. B., Stocking, C., Krizek, T., et al. An alternative strategy for studying adverse events in medical care. *Lancet,* 1997;349:309–13.

83. Meyers, A. R. "Lumping it:" the hidden denominator of the medical malpractice crisis. *American Journal of Public Health,* 1987;77(12):1544–48.

84. *Kreugar v. St. Joseph's Hospital,* 305 N.W.2d 18; *Koppes v. Pearson,* 384 N.W.2d 381, 386 (Iowa 1986); *MacMillen v. A. H. Robins Co.,* 348 N.W.2d 869, 871 (Neb. 1984); *Carrow v. Streeter,* 410 N.E.2d 1369, 1373–74 (Ind. Ct. App. 1980); *Midland-Ross Corp. v. Adamson Co. Inc.,* 6 Va. Cir. 512, 513 (Va. Cir. 1977).

85. *Esener v. Kinsey,* 240 Ga. App.21 1999; *Robinson v. Shah,* 936 P.2d 784 (Kan. App. 1997); *Bryant v. Adams,* 448 S.E.2d 832 (N.C. App. 1994).

86. *Stafford v. Shultz,* 42 Cal.2d.

87. *Kreugar v. St. Joseph's Hospital,* 305 N.W.2d 18.

88. *Garcia v. Presbyterian Hospital Center,* 593 P.2d 487.

89. Witman, 1996.

90. Wu, 1997.

91. Vincent, 1994.

92. Cohen, J. R. Advising clients to apologize. *Southern California Law Review,* May 1999;72:1009.

93. Lattin, D. Forgiveness as a salve for sin. *San Francisco Chronicle,* 24 March 2000, p. A1.

94. Cohen, 1999.

95. Orenstein, 1999.

96. Slovenko, R. Saying you're sorry in a litigious society. *Medical Law,* 1992;11:669–71.

97. Berlin, L. Malpractice issues in radiology. Admitting mistakes. *American Journal of Roentgenology,* 1999;172:879–84.

98. Cohen, 1999.

99. Cohen, 1999.

100. Lowes, 1997.

101. Orenstein, 1999.

102. Nazareth, A. M., and Kanekar, S. Effects of denying or admitting a mistake. *Journal of Social Psychology,* 1986;126(4):531–37.

103. *News and World Report,* 1999;129(3):50–66.

104. Maithel, 1998.

105. Vincent, C. A., Pincus, T., and Scurr, J. H. Patients' experience of surgical accidents. *Quality in Health Care,* 1993;2:77–82.

106. Levinson, W., and Roter, D. L. The effects of two continuing medical education programs on communication skills of practicing primary care physicians. *Journal of General Internal Medicine,* 1993;8:318–24.

107. Roter, D. L., and Hall, J. Improving physicians' interviewing skills and reducing patients' emotional distress: a randomized clinical trial. *Archives of Internal Medicine,* 1995;155:1877–84.

108. Levinson, 1993.

109. Wu, 1997.

110. Lowes, 1997.

CHAPTER THIRTY-EIGHT

MEDICAL ERROR AND PATIENT SAFETY: COMMUNICATING WITH THE MEDIA

Stephen E. Littlejohn

The 1999 Institute of Medicine (IOM) patient safety report, *To Err Is Human,* is often cited as putting the prevention of medical error on the nation's media agenda. Fact is, "medical mistakes" have been on the media's list of favorite stories for quite some time. What's different is how coverage of the story has evolved over time.

The term *medical mistake* began appearing in the Nexis database in 1978, just a year before Charles Bosk's book, *Forgive and Remember: Managing Medical Failure.* Both the book and early news articles typically concentrated on individual failure, often by physicians and usually accompanied by references to medical malpractice.

More than 20 years later, the complexity of medical error is far better understood, especially its roots in systems failures that can extend far beyond single individuals. The IOM report validated the systems approach for the media, providing credibility for what would have been viewed as an excuse—rather than an explanation—just a few years ago.

Playing a major role in this change of perspective were several key media events, beginning with the first Annenberg conference on patient safety in 1996, covered extensively by *USA Today* and other media.

Also contributing were a pivotal *New York Times Magazine* article by medical writer Lisa Belkin in 1997 and coverage of the launch of the National Patient Safety Foundation, which appeared on all the major television networks.

In 1998, the *Journal of the American Medical Association* called for more systems-based patient safety research, CBS and *USA Today* both focused on systems and error prevention, and a second Annenberg conference showcased patient safety research gains.

Although it is fair to say that the patient safety movement has achieved considerable progress in shaping media coverage of medical error and its prevention, media coverage conversely has exerted a substantial impact on the movement itself. In fact, the media were present at the beginning.

In 1982, an ABC *20/20* segment on anesthesia accidents spurred the formation of the Anesthesia Patient Safety Foundation (APSF). Two years later, the APSF completed work on anesthesiology practice standards that many credit with ultimately helping transform the specialty, making it one of the safest instead of one of the most dangerous for patients.

There is no evidence that medical error increased significantly in 1995, but news coverage certainly escalated. Perhaps it was more than a coincidence that attempts at securing federal medical malpractice reform reached their high-water mark that year following the Republican takeover of the U.S. House of Representatives. Reform opponents responded by regularly faxing medical mistake stories to the media.

The political contest created the perfect environment for explosive national coverage, which came with stories about errors at institutions such as University Community Hospital in Tampa, Florida, and Boston's respected Dana Farber Institute. Meanwhile, also in 1995, Lucian Leape and colleagues, writing in the *Journal of the American Medical Association,* reported statistical evidence of significant error rates.

The stark contrast between horror stories and noble aspirations once again—as it had in the case of anesthesiology—triggered action, this time spreading across all of health care. Immediate results were the first Annenberg conference and the establishment of the National Patient Safety Foundation.

Notably, the theme of the third Annenberg conference, held in 2001, was communications: "Let's Talk—Communicating Risk and Safety in Health Care." The attention given by the patient safety movement to the importance of effective communications reflects a natural and logical outcome of finding causes and seeking solutions in systems.

If the systems approach has any hope of producing greater patient safety, greater openness is required—to find out how many and what kind of errors are occurring, to create a safe, blame-free environment for providers, and to secure and keep the confidence of patients and the public while solutions are found and implemented.

In fact, the Joint Commission on Accreditation of Healthcare Organizations (JCAHO) implemented a new standard designed to facilitate prompt and informative communication with patients and families regarding errors that may have affected them. Putting more information on error out in the open should prove to be a plus. However, in the meantime, it will surely create further challenges for providers, especially in dealing with the media.

Much is at stake. Most important, how you communicate publicly through the media creates a climate that either enhances safety or doesn't. Are you quick to blame someone when asked by a reporter who was responsible? Or too fast in jumping to conclusions about what actually happened when pressed to explain how it could have happened? Do you see the incident as an opportunity to promote greater awareness and understanding that may prevent errors?

Professionally, an organization's accreditation—not to mention the status of its Medicare contract with the federal government—is at stake. News coverage is part of the JCAHO sentinel event accreditation watch criteria. Also under the spotlight are your reputation for good management, quality, and safety; your relationships with your local community, other professionals, and institutions; and, especially, your credibility.

Unfortunately, how well or poorly you communicate can also have legal consequences. Will the patient or his or her family find it necessary to file a lawsuit? If there is a lawsuit, will there be a settlement and, if so, at what amount? Will adverse publicity attract lawyers and lawsuits on other issues?

With so much at stake, every organization and health care professional who communicates with the media in connection with a clinical crisis should keep the following objectives uppermost as a guide for action: (1) safety, (2) integrity, (3) relationships, and (4) reputation.

In making choices, decide first for safety. Respond and act in ways that enhance and advance safety. Always maintain your integrity by telling the truth and sticking to the facts. Relationships matter, especially with fellow professionals, patients, the community, and many others. Be respectful of those relationships. Reputation, which may cause the most concern in difficult times, comes last on the list. Act in ways that reinforce safety, maintain integrity, and foster relationships, and reputation will take care of itself.

You will need these other objectives and other guides because there is no simple, follow-the-dots cookbook for communicating with the media during a clinical crisis. The usual crisis communications rule of "tell all, tell fast" does not easily apply to the health care setting. More often than not, you don't know what "all" is yet. You can't "tell it fast" either because it takes time to do a root cause analysis.

For example, you may immediately know that a patient died, that a heart attack preceded death, and that certain medications were administered prior to the heart attack. Determining whether and to what extent these events—and others still unknown—are linked usually is not rapidly accomplished.

In fact, beware of premature certainty. Often, when an error occurs, the "corridor wisdom" will immediately pinpoint a cause. People need a reason—some explanation—for tragedy, and hospital staff members are no different. That explanation, although having the potential of ultimately being correct, can just as easily be the result of preconceptions about the people involved or previously felt concerns about "an accident waiting to happen."

For those directly involved, the emotion of the moment may drive some to distribute or even embrace blame: "They did it" or "I did it." Others may retreat into the formality of saying "it was included in the list of possible explanations," or the futility of concluding that "it couldn't be helped."

Most especially, you don't control "all." You cannot unilaterally remove Tylenol from supermarket shelves, as Johnson & Johnson's chief executive officer did when it became clear that someone had tampered with some bottles of the pain reliever.

In any given hospital operating theater, any number of "independent" entities may be present, such as the hospital's nurses, the surgeon, the anesthesiologist or anesthetist, possibly the patient's internist, and the patient. Although all may have worked together seamlessly as a medical team, typically none can immediately speak or act for the other afterward, particularly if an error has occurred.

So, instead of starting with "tell all, tell fast" as your crisis communications rule, start with knowing your audiences. Recognize, first, that you have many audiences. Here is a short list: the patient, other patients, families, the community, physicians, nurses, other health professionals, employees, unions, insurers, the media, government, accreditors, industry, payers, employers, boards, lawyers, activists, and many others.

Then, acknowledge that your first and most important audience is not the media but the patient, the patient's family, and the patient's friends. Be sure to open lines of communication. Be factual and sincerely concerned. And, wherever possible, ease their situation by addressing logistical and other needs.

It is the rare patient and family who desire a maelstrom of media attention. So work with the patient and the patient's family on their and your preference to avoid a media circus. Ensure that they do not feel the need to use the media to get your attention. Tell them that the media may call you, but you will respect their privacy. At all times, keep them apprised of media interest and what you have told the media. What you have to say, they should hear first directly—not through the media.

Your second audience includes your employees and associated professionals—nurses, hospital staff, physicians, and so forth. To the extent an incident is known and talked about in the corridors, consider holding meetings to brief employees and associates on the situation's status. As statements are given to the media, simultaneously share them with employees and associates. Once again, what you have to say, they should hear first directly—not through the media.

Should employees be "allowed" to talk to the media? Ideally, to ensure accuracy, information provided to the media should come from a designated, official source, and media should be referred to that source. However, media contact should not be explicitly forbidden, for example, by posting a notice to that effect throughout your facility. That alone will create a story, usually a story that suggests you have something to hide. Instead, seek to persuade employees and associates that it makes the most sense for them and their colleagues to refer media calls to the designated spokesperson.

What about the general public? They also have a deep interest in medical error. They could be, or about to be, your patient. They may have received care in your hospital or from you. The same could be said about their family members. Or, they could be your neighbors when you go home, your suppliers, the people who ultimately pay the bills, and so on. More generally, it is a public that is quick to go on the Internet to find out the latest news and information about their health. More profoundly, it is a public where a major cohort—the baby boomers—are entering into their older years when health care needs increase, even as they care for their parents on the one hand and children on the other.

Accordingly, and depending on how visible an error might have become, it is advisable to be prepared to acknowledge public interest as legitimate, to answer questions when that is possible, and to provide other information when it is verified and available. Consider who on your team interacts with the public on a regular basis—your admissions staff or receptionist, your business office, the emergency department, and so forth—and provide them with responses or somewhere to which they can direct a questioner for an answer.

The media, at their best, aspire to be the public's surrogate, its servant, asking questions on behalf of their readers, viewers, listeners, and, increasingly, Internet surfers. However, the best journalist's best intentions exist within a business framework, one that depends on attracting ears and eyes for the advertising and subscription fees that pay the bills. Serving and attracting can differ dramatically. It is not unusual for a journalist to have a good story his or her editor is unwilling to publish because it lacks an attractive, eye-catching lead.

On the other hand, stories of medical error often write their own leads and even their own text. There's no need to hire expensive Hollywood scriptwriters—just air more news and magazine shows using real life as a source of stories. Human interest, particularly tragedy, makes for riveting stories. Moreover, as Congress and state legislatures debate health issues, the public wants to know the implications. In addition, the highly competitive news businesses at all levels need more stories to fill more hours and boost circulation.

As if the media needed further encouragement to cover medical error stories, sometimes there are people, typically engaged in disputes of one kind or another with health providers, who have an interest in pushing stories of medical error into the media. They do so to prove a point or seize advantage. Whether it is the right thing for them to do is another question. Valid arguments can be made on either side. The point for this discussion is that it happens and you have to be prepared for it.

Ironically, health care providers and facilities outside major urban areas typically receive more media attention than those in big cities. Often, the spotlight is brightest about an hour's drive away from a big city, in municipalities large enough to support a daily paper with a strong local circulation. For those papers, health care and the local hospital usually are the best day-to-day source of stories. The hospital may even be the largest employer. In fact, little of significance occurring within its walls fails to reach reporters, sometimes more quickly than important information moves between departments.

All of that said, it often is still an open question whether the media will call for information following the occurrence of a medical error. However, a number of factors can increase the likelihood of such a call and thus the need for and advisability of advance preparation.

First, assess recent news coverage. Is there a routine focus on health care or a reporter assigned to the health care beat? If so, if the journalist is doing his or her job, he or she will be constantly looking for new stories and will have developed a network of sources quick to provide alerts regarding new events, such as the occurrence of an error.

Also, are there any ongoing controversies, such as ongoing medical malpractice cases, labor issues, or layoffs or other incidents, that, although factually unrelated, can be construed by some as being linked in some fashion? It is common in the news business to group similar but unrelated stories together. For example, when a plane crashes with large loss of life somewhere in the world, the media will insert into the news flow other adverse aviation incidents, regardless of scale and significance. These are stories that would otherwise not garner much notice.

Looking inward, you should also assess the type of incident. If it involves the unexpected death of a mother or child, expect a media call, if only because everyone can relate to the case. We all have mothers, we've all been children, we have children, we are mothers, and so on. Emergency departments are spaces where the outside world and the inner clinical world overlap dramatically—hence the popularity of television shows like *ER*. Thus, if an incident occurs in an emergency department, expect a call.

The likelihood of an immediate media call diminishes to the extent an error is complicated or ambiguous. Journalists on deadline typically refrain from attempting to write difficult-to-explain stories. The exception occurs when a story, although complicated, is brought to and put into an understandable context for a reporter, and the reporter takes the time to report the story. However, reporters are more likely to cover "simpler" stories, for example, a death or serious injury, a symmetry error, or a medication error. Why? Because the general public would ask incredulously: "How could they cut off the wrong leg or give the wrong medicine? Even I can get that right!"

Another factor in whether the media will call is the circle of knowledge. Who knows? How far will it spread? Are the police involved, such that everyone with a police radio scanner can listen in? Are there official reporting requirements? From the family and patient standpoint, how are they responding? Have they hired a lawyer? Are there relatives nearby and involved to the extent that they might take matters in their own hands and go to the media with the story?

Once again, there is absolutely nothing wrong about people spreading news of an incident, and it's not something you can or should try to prevent. In particular, whatever the family and patient may do with information about an error affecting them is fully their prerogative. In fact, they alone can say whatever they want, to whomever they want, whenever they want, whereas others may have the duty to protect privacy or be certain of the facts.

The point of assessing whether the media will call is to prioritize properly whether and how extensively and promptly to prepare for a media call amid everything else that must take place following an incident. These actions include but are not limited to steps such as preserving the scene, initiating a root cause analysis, reaching out to the patient and family, working with employees and professional associations, and undertaking all official notifications. The checklist is long and detailed.

Whether or not you need to move quickly in preparing for a possible media call based on the assessment, undertaking such preparation can be clarifying and calming, even if a media inquiry does not materialize. It can reduce the level of uncertainty and, most important, remove the complications and diversion of effort that occur when media inquiries arrive unanticipated. In those cases, responding to the media inquiry too often takes on disproportionate importance, moving to the top of the priority list and dominating the attention of people who have other, more significant duties.

The first step in the preparation process is to draft a statement for use if a reporter calls even before you are fully ready. Begin by getting the facts and determining what you can say and when. Keep all audiences in mind and recognize that audiences cross-communicate. Above all, the initial statement should express concern for the patient and his or her family without implying cause or responsibility beyond what is known. Stay within the facts, recognizing that early knowledge or conclusions (i.e., the corridor wisdom) is more likely to be wrong than right. Note that you are in the process of learning all the facts as quickly as possible.

Sometimes, you may know more than you can say, particularly about the patient and his or her medical condition. "Following confidentiality rules" and "meeting your duty to protect patient privacy" are equivalent phrases. However, the former sounds self-serving, whereas the latter reflects a stance everyone expects you to take with his or her own information. You should use the latter as the more accurate and effective statement.

There are situations in which preparing such a statement is sufficient. However, other circumstances may require ongoing attention and more thorough preparation because of scale, significance, or a high level of continuing media interest. In these circumstances, it is useful to set forth a range of possible scenarios that may unfold and to prepare responses and answers to likely reporters' questions in advance.

For example, an error may trigger an investigation by your state's department of health, on behalf of the Health Care Financing Administration (HCFA). Or, it may result in your facility being put on accreditation watch by the Joint Commission. In either event, other issues unrelated to the error incident may arise that require responses. At one extreme, your facility may have its HCFA Medicare contract suspended during the course of official surveys and investigations.

Once you have agreed on what you can say and how to say it, you need to decide who will say it for you. If the incident is particularly serious, particularly if it involves an unexpected death, the hospital chief executive officer is best for this job. In other cases, it is advisable and preferable to designate as your spokesperson someone who knows the issues, can speak authoritatively about clinical matters, was not directly involved in the incident, can knowledgeably add supplemental information that is helpful but not directly related to the case, and can project accurately and sincerely your organization's empathy for patient and family.

In terms of skill, you need as your spokesperson someone who can think quickly on his or her feet and see the point of questions and where they are heading well before their completion, thereby providing precious seconds to decide how to answer based on prior preparation. Even for the most experienced spokesperson, practice sessions where reporters' questions are simulated and answered are advisable.

The posture you, your organization, and your spokesperson adopt in responding to reporter's inquiries can be as important as the words you say. First, remember that although your organization may not have been at its best when the error occurred, you must commit to being the best you can be at handling the posterror situation—communicating forthrightly and effectively, but also dedicating yourself to and being seen as making the changes that will improve safety going forward. Commit to learning as much as possible about the error and how it occurred, with a view toward sharing your knowledge with others in health care and thereby improving safety for many beyond your own setting. Although tragic, errors also provide vital opportunities for advancing safety.

The second posture guideline is to separate the principle of responsiveness from how much you are able to say. In other words, don't question the questions. Respect the questions and the questioners. Answer when you can and respond "I wish I could" for the rest. Always stick to the facts and provide general background information whenever possible. If the media visit, be cordial and professional. If there is a large number or they remain on site, provide space for them to work, assist with logistical needs, and provide ample supplies of coffee, donuts, pizza, and soda. In other words, welcome reporters' questions as well as their presence.

In communicating with the media, it's advisable to follow these do's and don'ts:

- Do give only the facts and avoid speculation.
- Do be as informative as possible.
- Do appear open and responsive.
- Do be controlled.
- Do empathize.
- Do stick to your message.
- Do stop talking when you're finished.
- Don't accept "what if" questions.
- Don't speak for another party.
- Don't use jargon.
- Don't go off the record.
- Don't accept an untrue or inaccurate premise.
- Don't be afraid to say you don't have an answer.
- Don't be argumentative.

For people in health care, perhaps the most important "do" is to stop talking when you're finished. Being helpers by nature, health providers often will keep talking until a reporter indicates that he or she is satisfied with an answer. You may have answered the question, but a reporter will let you continue talking simply to see what you might say. Too often, what you say might not be accurate or you may wish you had said it differently once it appears in print.

A corollary of this rule is to stick with what you have prepared to say. In other words, stay on message—that is, say what you and your team have agreed is appropriate to say at the time. Then, stop. More is not necessarily better. More could easily hinder communication by muddling rather than clarifying understanding. A related rule is never to speak for another party. Bound what you say by what you and your organization are in a position to know. This is particularly important in health care settings, where many different parties with different expertise and knowledge bases may be involved in a given situation.

Above all, remember that your exchange with a reporter may feel like a conversation. Both you and the reporter have a stake in appearing to be relaxed. However, never for a moment fail to remember that your exchange is a professional interaction, not a personal one. It always helps to have a personal relationship with reporters—outside of doing your respective jobs. Even the best of friends must respect each other's professional responsibilities, however.

After the media call or visit, always be sure to follow up with any promised information. Or, if you later discover that you cannot provide the information, be sure to close the loop by letting the reporter know. It is also appropriate to call a reporter back to ask, politely, if he or she has any further questions, particularly regarding any technical information you may have supplied. It often helps to provide background information to reporters following an interview.

At the same time, you should not attempt to change a reporter's story or ask for an advance copy. Journalists jealously guard their prerogatives to write freely—that is, under the watchful and sometimes demanding eye of their editors. In fact, if you receive follow-up calls from reporters asking for more information, there's a chance the reporter is tracking down information in response to questions posed by an editor about the story. Speaking of editors, it is never appropriate to go over the reporter's head in an attempt to stop a story.

In my years of assisting health care professionals and organizations to respond to the media in the midst of a clinical crisis, I have yet to encounter two errors, let alone two media relations situations, that are identical. Each situation is different, as yours will be when it confronts you. Thus, there can be no rote response—only guidelines and useful rules to follow.

I've outlined some of the more useful rules and guidelines in this chapter. But don't rely on them alone. Seek help. Include your public relations team and other professional communicators on the team, not to mention your legal counsel. Better yet, form your team now, to be ready. Meet and talk through how you can work together in communicating with the media should you have to do so in the future. Even better, begin to acquaint the media that cover you regularly with your ongoing efforts to enhance patient safety.

Above all, and at all times, stick to the facts. Be open with the media, but say only what you can say when you can say it. Don't forget your first two audiences or your first two objectives. At each point along the way, set your course in terms of what is best for the patient and the patient's family, as well as for your employees and professional associates. And, with high integrity, aim always for greater safety and a culture that fosters safety.

CHAPTER THIRTY-NINE

USING BEST PRACTICES TO IMPROVE MEDICATION SAFETY

Ken Farbstein

Rueful patients have long joked about errors caused by doctors' handwriting, and an astonishing number of people can tell stories about adverse drug events that afflicted friends or family members. The Institute of Medicine (IOM) reports[1] and their attendant publicity have crystallized this in stark statistical terms to clinicians as well as the broader public. The shocking finding in the first IOM study that 44,000 to 98,000 deaths yearly befall hospitalized patients has become mantralike in its repetition, though having opposite physiologic effects.

This chapter discusses ways to improve medication safety through adopting and spreading best practices in medication ordering, dispensing, administering, and reporting. It excludes other forms of medical and surgical error, though much of the analysis is readily applicable to the broader topic of medical error. Looking beneath the prima facie appeal of this strategy, this chapter discusses the value and shortcomings of the adoption of best practices as a strategy, and describes ways to accelerate their spread throughout a hospital. Examples are taken primarily from the author's consultation with six hospitals.

The first section discusses reasons for using best practices; next is a discussion of where to start. The spread of best practices throughout a hospital or other health care organization, which follows pilot-testing, is described in the next section. Success factors and problems and limitations are listed after that. Ways to measure the extent of use of the best practices that have presumably been implemented are discussed next. The chapter closes with a description of the values and premises underlying the strategy of promoting best practices.

Why Adopt Best Practices?

Best practices prevent errors that may injure patients. Table 39-1, for example, lists safety improvements that resulted from an aggressive drive to use best practices at one hospital system. Additional successes have been achieved as spin-offs from the strategy of promoting best practices. For example, an improvement in the use of coumadin occurred through independent work at a community hospital; it might not have been recognized publicly, or used to rally enthusiasm and subsequent participation by the team, without the parallel work in best practices. Although significant changes had made the use of patient-controlled analgesia safer at one hospital, it was only upon measurement by the

TABLE 39-1   Tangible Improvements in Medication Safety from Best Practices at One Hospital System

Ordering Medications

Reduced the time to reach therapeutic range of blood anticoagulation at a midsized hospital—the fraction of patients who achieved a therapeutic level within the first 3 days of heparin use more than doubled, from 44% to 93%.

Reduced heparin incidents more than threefold at a community hospital, coinciding with the use of a weight-based heparin protocol.

Reduced to zero the need for intubation and intensive care for patients in acute ethyl alcohol withdrawal.

Dispensing Medications

Reduced certain look-alike/sound-alike incidents to zero at a midsized hospital.

Reduced by more than 50% the number of incidents caused by omitted medications at a community hospital. The rate has fallen from 1 every 6,000 doses (every 3 days) to 1 every 13,000 doses (every 6.5 days).

Reduced by 46% the number of doses not available for medication administration at a midsized hospital.

Reduced expired medications in the automated medication dispensing machines by 67%.

Administering Medications

Reduced adverse events concerning patient-controlled analgesia by 77% at a teaching hospital.

Coinciding with the use of patient-allergy wristbands, more than 500 days have elapsed without an allergy event.

Reduced epidural incidents by more than 50% at a teaching hospital.

author that the magnitude of the 77% improvement was appreciated and publicized widely.

The same team that was responsible for spreading best practices at a community hospital also used the Plan-Do-Study-Act method to halve both omitted medications and the time needed to process the morning dispensing backlog in the pharmacy, as listed in Table 39-1. These successes are a natural by-product of the aggressive effort to adopt best practices.

We are trying to spread the belief that systems set up the errors that individuals commit, and we have met with some success in this attitudinal change. In addition to reducing errors, this effort has raised clinicians' willingness to report error. We view as a positive development the sustained increase in the self-reporting of incidents throughout the six hospitals.

Just as we use best practices because they prevent injury and death, so we use them because that is who we are. Although the many cynics in this cynical era will scoff, the plain fact is that many of us are in health care because healing is our calling. It is the right thing to do.

In the Beginning

After Moses lumbered down Mt. Sinai with the Ten Commandments, his colleagues were distracted with their merrymaking, and greeted him coolly. Indeed, they enraged him so much that he threw down the stone tablets in a fit. After this rocky start, the children of Israel eventually accepted these rules, and by and large complied with them. Later, in a continuing frenzy of scholarship and rule making, scholars over the ages pored over the first five books of Moses and compiled a list of 613 rules in the Talmud. Compliance with this much larger set of rules is more spotty.

In today's world, our secular leaders have set forth various lists of best practices—for example, those from the Institute for Healthcare Improvement and the Massachusetts Coalition on the Prevention of Medical Error and, more recently, 194 best practices by the Institute for Safe Medication Practices (ISMP), the National Patient Safety Foundation (NPSF), the Joint Commission on Accreditation of Healthcare Organizations (JCAHO), the United States Pharmacopeia (USP), and others.[2] Your clinical colleagues may not eagerly welcome living by 194 new commandments. Even you, dear reader, who have reached Chapter 39 of this book, may not relish the prospect of diving into all 194. How to make this manageable? How to improve medication safety while preserving your own sanity and what's left of your *joie de vivre*? That is the subject of this chapter.

Leadership is tough, and inaction is easy. In much of the United States, hospital pharmacists are burdened by changes: Dispensing machines and computer systems are being enhanced, new medications are proliferating, and hospital staff are leaving for more highly paid retail pharmacy jobs. As pharmaceutical costs rise, so does the financial pressure to constrain cost increases. Nurses are facing more assertive patients and, in many hospitals, are experiencing cutbacks, often spreading the same workload over fewer nurses. In the absence of a clear mandate for improvement, crises du jour often drive out the time to select, plan, make, and review changes. Doctors, like highly trained airplane pilots, are difficult to lead at the best of times. Financial pressures may complicate an already difficult task. Many community hospitals have only modest financial levers over physicians.

First, assess your standing, your sanity, and your stage of readiness for change.[3] Determine the standing of the hospital. Use an inventory like the list of 16 best practices used by the CareGroup hospital system or the much longer ISMP/JCAHO assessment instrument to ascertain where your hospital might benefit from best practices.

Identify, in the light of your own standing in the hospital (i.e., your role) which practices are within your control to bring about. Appropriate best practices for clinicians of various roles are discussed in turn later in this section. Many of the best practices require collaboration across professional disciplines. Developing a weight-based heparin protocol, for example, requires nurses and doctors to work together. Sequestration and labeling of high-risk medications, on the other hand, probably requires the authorization of a single person—the pharmacy director.

In assessing your sanity, ask a friend how to find the wherewithal for this effort. Last, consider your stage of readiness to make this change, as outlined in Table 39-2.

TABLE 39-2   Assessing Your Readiness to Adopt a Best Practice

If you have not previously considered participating in the adoption of a best practice:
  First, learn more about the consequences of medication error, before jumping into action.

If you have previously considered participating, but chose not to:
  First, learn about the sometimes tragic consequences of medication error, by viewing the videotape *Beyond Blame* or reading newspaper stories about individual tragedies.

If you have been planning to adopt a best practice, but not have not yet adopted one:
  Find a partner to help you act on your plan.

If you have already adopted a best practice and want to do so again:
  Just do it! Git! Put down this book!

Staff Nurses

Take something manageably small and do it. Think back to the last medication error that occurred that you are familiar with, and the chain of causes that produced it. Among the factors that contributed to the error, identify one under your control. Scan the list of best practices to find one that would have prevented that error. Try it among your patients for a week.

Build support by discussing the results with a colleague and asking him or her to try it for a week, and then reviewing the effects with you. In short, do something specific, and do something to build support for doing more in the future.

Nurse Managers and Pharmacy Directors

Learn what investment of time and money is required, and then commit to it, setting parameters. A nurse manager can authorize patient information and patient partnering work among nurse reports. A pharmacy director can unilaterally authorize a pharmacist to highlight or capitalize distinctive syllables on the labels of high-risk look-alike/ sound-alike medications like DOPAmine and DoBUTamine.

Doctors

Protocols for ordering cardiac, narcotic, and other high-risk medications and laboratory tests improve safety by replacing often-illegible handwriting with much less ambiguous check marks. Help develop such a protocol. Or test a Palm Pilot for entering orders that are printed and faxed to the pharmacy. These orders will avoid the need for nurses and pharmacists to guess at scribbled words and numbers. Chief residents can routinely ask about and briefly discuss specific safety issues such as medication errors with junior house officers.[4]

House Officers

Print all your orders. Get some sleep.

CEO and Quality Improvement Directors

Leadership is crucial for this effort, so the following section discusses the selection of improvement strategies, stretch goals, and best practices in detail.

Selection of Strategy

Broadly, four strategies are available to widely improve medication safety. Chances are that self-initiated, scattered improvements are already under way or accomplished at the reader's hospital. As a first strategy, of course, the hospital can continue, and seek to broaden, these preexisting efforts. Although such voluteerism is important, it is unlikely to suffice for the breadth of improvement needed in complex medication processes. Second, in a high-tech approach, hospital leaders can choose to rely on the acquisition or development of an electronic order entry system, bedside bar coding, pharmacy computer system, dispensing machines, and so forth. This strategy is likely to be expensive and to require drastic revision of existing medication processes. Third, leaders can choose a Pareto approach, addressing problem areas in the order of descending frequency and severity. This approach, while commendable, assumes that accurate, unbiased measures are available. Moreover, for best results, the identification and categorization of root causes are required. This is laborious and potentially fruitless, for medication errors typically do not cluster into "vital few" categories.[5] Fourth, leaders can opt to spread attitudinal changes of a "culture of safety."[6,7] Internal news media are available to readily communicate the requisite pleas to enhance the culture of safety, and leaders may be quite willing to speak on this topic. This chapter focuses on a fifth approach—the installation and adaptation of best practices. Table 39-3 compares these strategies.

This final approach has prima facie legitimacy from the label itself and the prestige of the expert and regulatory bodies that proposed the best practices. The methodical nature of this effort will appeal to those nursing and pharmacy staff who are orderly and meticulous by nature.

TABLE 39-3 Comparison of Strategies for Improving Medication Safety

Strategy	Breadth of ADEs Prevented	Cost	Allure to Clinicians
Self-initiation	Narrow	Low	High
High-tech systems	Broad	High	Variable
Pareto analyses	Broad	Moderate	Variable
Culture of safety	Variable	Low	Mom and apple pie
Best practices	Variable	Low	High

ADE, adverse drug event.

Stretch Goals

Executives should set medication safety improvement as a clear and formal priority, should state this often, and should check and celebrate progress. Dr. James Reinertsen's goal that CareGroup should become the world standard in medication safety offers an excellent example of setting and sticking with such a stretch goal.

Selection of Specific Best Practices

At least four sets of best practices exist. The Institute of Healthcare Improvement (IHI) and the Massachusetts Coalition for the Prevention of Medical Error identified 20 best practices in late 1998.[8] More recently the ISMP, together with the JCAHO, U.S. Pharmacopeia, Voluntary Hospital Association (VHA), Premier, and others identified 194 best practices. The Advisory Board has listed and described 22 best practices.[9] Judith Miller, an independent consultant, has identified a set of well over 100 practices.[10] The sets of practices span the processes of medication ordering, dispensing, administering, and reporting.

There are three ways to select a manageably small number of best practices. First is to select the entire set from the IHI, as CareGroup did initially. One-page operational definitions of each of these practices are available for free download.[11] An alternative is to have team members rate the best practices in the ISMP set—for example, in terms of their clinical significance. This would subsequently build commitment to implement the practices. CareGroup has performed such a culling, selecting six of the ISMP set for its second round. Definitions of these should be available for download. A third alternative is to select the subset of best practices in the domain of the single professional group that is most enthusiastic about such an effort. For example, if nurses are most eager to begin improvement, the hospital leaders might begin with the one-year IHI nursing practices—patient partnering, colored allergy wristbands, and so on.

Make sure that the ones who sow will also reap. Early on in the spread of best practices, choose those best practices whose benefits should accrue to the type of clinicians who invest the time in adopting that best practice. A nursing flow sheet for heparin requires development by nurses, and nurses benefit when they are able to clearly read and interpret the notations of a nurse on the earlier work shift. On the other hand, standardized prescribing requires extra work by doctors. Nurses and pharmacists benefit because they have to do less rework. Doctors, however, benefit only slightly in incurring fewer interrupting pages to clarify ambiguous orders.

Spreading Best Practices Throughout the Hospital

Assume staff have put a best practice into routine use throughout the hospital and would next like to implement others. Or perhaps staff have pilot-tested a best practice on a small scale—perhaps on one patient floor, or for one class of medications—and have decided it is worth spreading to other units or throughout the hospital. In either case, spreading these changes will require a series of steps, that is, a spreading process. This section describes and recommends a way to spread best practices once they have been partially implemented. First, a well-known but rarely used formal process is described; then, ways to capitalize on informal communication patterns are described.

Top-Down Strategies

Jeanette Clough, the CEO of Mt. Auburn Hospital, has described a large set of actions that hospital CEOs can take to promote best practices. CEOs should set the climate for change and model the changes in their own actions, by making rounds on patient floors with the medical director or chief nursing officer, setting goals with deadlines, talking frequently about error, learning at conferences, and so on.[12] This is critical because staff will make time for true priorities, and they will set their priorities in light of the CEO's actions.

Pharmacy Leadership

The first two of the 16 best practices to be adopted throughout the six CareGroup hospitals were the sequestration of potassium chloride in the pharmacy and unit dosing. Both practices reside within the pharmacy. Moreover, hospital teams led by pharmacists spread the best practices faster than teams led by nurses. Why? Pharmacists have unique and primary responsibility for medication safety, whereas for nurses, medication safety can be one of many priorities. So although CareGroup's nursing leaders have been excellent, it is recommended that other hospitals designate the pharmacy director to lead the day-to-day operation of the adoption of best practices, at least for the first year.

Identify and Tap Natural Communication Patterns

An ex-CEO spoke of the "initiative overload" afflicting his staff. How can already overburdened clinicians be persuaded to take on more work? While the easy way out is for managers to tell staff to "just do it," this approach is unlikely to succeed. Staff are likely to already have full plates. Instead, managers should tap the psychology that motivates clinicians, and use several approaches that take into account their characteristic frames of reference.

In deciding which changes to adopt, pharmacists generally listen to other pharmacists. Nurses heed other nurses. Doctors learn from other doctors.

In the Pharmacy

Consider a best practice based in the pharmacy, like the dispensing of medication in unit doses. Assume that on the authorization of the pharmacy director, staff have already pilot-tested a small-scale change such as dispensing antibiotics in unit-dose form for one patient floor for a week, and that staff favorably critiqued the results. To spread such a change to all non-IV medications, for example, the authorization of the pharmacy director is necessary, and with training of staff and subsequent spot-checking, will probably be sufficient to put this practice into routine use.

In improving the capture of accurate information on patients' allergies at Mt. Auburn Hospital, the acting pharmacy director first gathered data on the presence of information about specific allergies and the "no known drug allergy" (NKDA) status, and the team flowcharted the documentation process. After training pharmacists in the proper classification and entry of allergy information, the director mandated the routine use of this practice. He then tracked the data entry of allergies for 3 months, calculating the fraction of patients with coded allergy information that had been correctly coded into the pharmacy computer in 13 data points. He needed the support of his staff; support of outsiders was much less important. The entry of allergy information rose by 78%.

In short, best practices based in the pharmacy are likely to have substantial prima facie support among pharmacists because of their awareness of the potential and frequency of error, and because medication safety is innately their primary focus. The process for spreading changes within the pharmacy is primarily about the exercise of authority by the pharmacy director.

Among Nurses

Nurses, however, are more numerous and more dispersed throughout the hospital than pharmacists, and their jobs are more diverse. They interact with patients in private, in patients' rooms. As a result, their compliance with certain best practices may be more difficult to measure. The spreading process is somewhat different and more elaborate for changes that primarily affect nursing practices.

A case in point is the spread of a successfully pilot-tested nursing flow sheet for documenting changes in the heparin infusion rate and prothrombin time lab tests showing the degree of a patient's blood anti-coagulation. The nurse manager of a patient floor showed her staff nurses data on the completeness of documentation, showed them mock patient data on a revised flow sheet, and asked them to consider using the revised flow sheet. They agreed to perform the pilot test, which they later evaluated enthusiastically. Their favorable comments encouraged nurses in other floors to use the form, which was rapidly adopted throughout the hospital. The subsequent inspection of small samples of charts has verified the routine use of the flow sheet and the complete-ness and clarity of its documentation, throughout the hospital. As with the pharmacy best practice described earlier, the use of data both be-fore and after the change was a success factor. By contrast with the pharmacy change, this more ambitious change succeeded because the relevant committees approved the change and because a pilot test built support initially and then encouraged word of mouth that "sold" the change elsewhere in the hospital. This spreading process tapped informal communication channels that the pharmacy change had not required. It also made use of formal authorization, through the committees.

Reaching Physicians

Like nurses, doctors are numerous and are dispersed throughout, and indeed beyond, the hospital. Their jobs are diverse. Moreover, in com-munity hospitals, they act more as partners to the hospital than as em-ployees. The process for spreading a change that all doctors will use routinely is therefore even more multifaceted than that for nursing changes.

For example, consider Mt. Auburn Hospital's experience with the spread of a best practice of standardized nomenclature for physicians' orders (no trailing zeros, spelling of *units* instead of the abbreviation *U,* etc.). To build support for the change, incomplete orders were tabu-lated and the counts were presented to the medication safety team, the Pharmacy and Therapeutics Committee, and other committees, as were specific examples of incomplete orders. The CEO and other clinical leaders repeatedly described the policy and gave it a catchy name, call-ing it the "Never Guess Again" policy. Specific near misses and errors were discussed with numerous committees. A *Newsday* article that described the deaths and injuries of several patients due to illegible orders was made available to clinical leaders.[13] The policy was announced by electronic mail and by newsletter in a broad educational campaign. In short, every available formal communication channel was used repeatedly to spread the change.

Overall, it is important to appropriately use both formal and informal communication channels:

1. Create the conditions that will encourage informal word of mouth among the professional peer group you most need to influence.
2. Then formally approve and mandate the change through relevant policies and committees.

Set Up a Contest

Clinicians have far more work than they can handle, so the logical solution is to make work into play. People love to compete if the game matters to them and if they have a fair chance to win if they play hard. The competition must be managed.

We use a best practice scorecard to track the status of each of the 16 best practices across the hospital network. We also track progress among the six CareGroup hospitals on a scorecard of tangible, measured improvements in patient safety (Table 39-4) and track the overall number of best practices that have been adopted into routine use on a run chart (Figure 39-1). The number of best practice adoptions has grown more than 10-fold since the spring of 1999, from 6 to more than 60. Indeed, the CareGroup system is nearly two thirds of the way to completion of an ambitious goal of fully spreading all 16 of the first round of best practices throughout all six hospitals. These scorecards are presented to CEOs and their boards, stimulating the CEOs to ask teams about their progress.

Seek Best Practices with Natural Supporters

Pick something that will naturally gather the support of nurses and doctors. Pick a best practice with a measurable outcome, and do that first. Publicize the measured improvement widely among doctors and ask for a volunteer to pilot-test another one. Repeat. Or pick one that will get people talking about error. This might be particularly effective for rallying nurses' support. For example, pick patient partnering, which is close to nurses' hearts.

Find Outside Partners

As Barbara Sher says, "Isolation is the dream-killer."[14] Get yourselves a support group. Correspond with colleagues via the listserv, or electronic bulletin board, maintained by the National Patient Safety Foundation.[15] Talk to colleagues at conferences. Participate in a collaborative offered by the IHI, Premier, VHA, or Melior.

TABLE 39-4 Scorecard as of 9 March, 2001

Hospital A	Hospital B	Hospital C	Hospital D	Hospital E	Hospital F
77% fewer PCA incidents	Reduced missed doses of coumadin; no recurrences	Doubled number of patients in therapeutic range for anticoagulation with heparin	Reduced time to therapeutic range for anticoagulation with heparin by 70%	Reduced heparin incidents threefold	Reduced time to process backlog of morning pharmacy orders by 50%
Color-coding of syringes for 15 OR meds	Reduced to 0 the need for intubation and ICU for patients in acute alcohol withdrawal	Reduced expired meds in Pyxis by 67%	Reduced omitted meds by 46%	501 days without allergy event	Increased number of days between missing meds by 117%
Reduced epidural incidents by at least 52%		Improved pharmacy information and alerts for patients with allergies (78%) and with no known drug allergies (79%)			

PCA, patient-controlled analgesia; ICU, intensive care unit.

Date	Target	Black	Red	Piloting	White	Check sum
May 99	96	6	67	2	20	95 exclu NEBH ER
Jun	96	12	63	4	17	96
Jul	96	18	57	9	17	101 5 red & piloting
Aug	96	21	55	10	17	103 7 red & piloting
Sep	96	22	56	15	13	106 10 red & piloting
Oct	96	21	57	15	13	106 10 red & piloting
Nov	96	22	56	15	13	106 10 red & piloting
Dec 99	96	26	53	14	13	106 9 red & piloting
Jan 00	96					
Feb	96					
Mar	96	35				
Apr	96	36				
May	96	40				
Jun	96	52				
Jul	96	55				
Aug	96	56				
Sep	96	55				
Oct	96	58				
Nov	96	59				
Dec 00	96	60				
Jan 01	96	61				
Feb	96	62				

Excludes (the more ambitious) nonpunitive error reporting.

Counts only the markings made electronically as of the last date each month for which a scorecard had been printed.

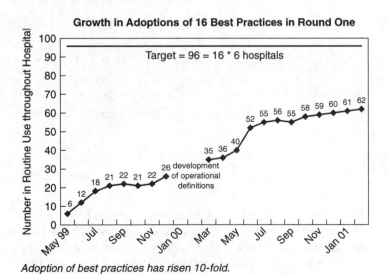

Growth in Adoptions of 16 Best Practices in Round One

Adoption of best practices has risen 10-fold.

FIGURE 39-1   Progress at spreading first 16 best practices according to scorecard

At this rate we'll get to 96, all black, in Jan 2002 (2.7 more black cells/month)

x		y	Predicted	
1	5/15/1999	6	9	2.734084 slope
2	Jun-99	12	12	6.065945 Y-intercept
3		18	14	
4		21	17	
5		22	20	
6		21	22	
7		22	25	
8		26	28	
9	Jan-00	29.001	31	
10		32.001	33	
11		35	36	
12		36	39	
13		40	42	3.538462
14		52	44	
15			47	
16			50	
17			53	
18			55	
19			58	
20	Dec-00		61	
21	Jan-01		63	
22			66	
23			69	
24			72	
25			74	
26			77	
27			80	
28			83	
29			85	
30			88	
31			91	
32	Dec-01		94	
33	Jan-02		96	

FIGURE 39-1   (Continued)

Problems and Barriers

Is It Worth It?

Some best practices add complexity and work and prevent few adverse drug events (ADEs), for example, added checks. A double check of a pump setting may be important, but it is a chore. It is appropriate to consider whether the time that clinicians spend in planning, implementing, and using the best practice would be better spent in direct patient care. Currently, in only 4 to 5 days, on average, staff of acute hospitals are able to treat and resolve the health crisis that led the patient into the hospital. Every action they take is designed to promptly treat and resolve the patient's acute condition. That's the real work of hospitals, and we have to carefully protect and focus staff's time for that. We have to weigh the hours spent on a quality improvement team and in committee meetings, planning, training, forms design, legwork, and so on in light of the marginal number of adverse drug events that can be prevented by a particular best practice. Because data on ADEs are so inadequate, no calculation of the time costs vis-à-vis the safety benefits can be made. We must apply a more intuitive judgment in considering the value of individual best practices.

Allow the Use of Functionally Equivalent Alternatives

Although it is important to safeguard against wrong-drug errors of giving medications to a patient with a drug allergy, the data on the best safeguard are ambiguous. One hospital has reported that more than 500 days have elapsed without an allergy event since it began using wristbands. At other hospitals, apparently no nurses have reported any cases where the wristband prevented an error. In this case, improving the documentation of allergy information in the pharmacy computer, which triggers automatic alerts when needed, is functionally equivalent. At CareGroup, teams are permitted to substitute another best practice if it is functionally equivalent.

Protocols

With some key exceptions, guidelines and protocols, which require more physician leadership, have been more slowly adopted at CareGroup than have other best practices. Most of the discontinued pilot tests of best practices had tried to change physicians' behavior—for example, having them write the reason why a drug was ordered to aid in the pharmacist's decision of which of two similarly named drugs was meant by an ambiguously written order. The education of physicians about specific serious adverse drug events before any pilot test that seeks to change physicians' behavior is strongly recommended. Many doctors are apparently not yet readily persuaded that such a change is warranted. Given the early stage of readiness for change of these doctors, educational strategies may be the most effective in ultimately building new habits.[16]

When Best Is Too Good for the Real World

Teaching hospitals use house officers who work very long hours. Consider the best practice of requiring 10 hours of rest between shifts, or a maximum of 12-hour shifts, for clinicians. Practically speaking, it is nearly impossible for a teaching hospital to meet this best practice. The dilemma appears rigid, and the entrapment of the CEO complete. As an old Yiddish proverb suggests, When life gives you only two options, you should always take the third. Stepwise implementation and innovation may provide the answer. A hospital can begin by rigorously limiting the shifts of nurses and pharmacists.

Making Sure

It is important to know whether best practices are truly in routine universal use in the hospital. Knowing that certain policies about best practices have been developed, leaders and staff may wrongly assume that best practices are in routine use. They may even report to the JCAHO, Department of Public Health, and so on, that best practices are in place, only to be shocked when an adverse event occurs.

Measurement for verification should be easy and routine and should be performed by the risk manager or someone else with formal authority, perhaps as part of the maintenance of records for the next JCAHO visit. To verify that the best practice about the ordering of heparin by doctors is in use, for example, have the medication safety team take 10 minutes of a meeting, once a quarter, to review 10 charts of heparinized patients. During the 3 years of a JCAHO review cycle, the team will have reviewed 120 charts for their inclusion of the heparin protocol, and can show a run chart of compliance by quarter with 12 data points.

The pharmacy director should run computer reports over time to verify that the best practices located in the pharmacy are in routine use. For best practices in medication administration by nurses, spot checking of the medication administration record (MAR), reports from the automated dispensing machine, and observation can be used. Best practices in reporting should be graphed as run charts over time.

Premises and Underlying Logic

Three natural laws, in Steve Covey's terms,[17] underlie the strategy of best practices. First, lofty goals, chosen freely, inspire hard work, perhaps because people seek meaning for their work in superordinate goals.[18] Second, competition within a set of rules evokes intense effort. Third, clinicians who want to change their habits (e.g., regarding the daily ordering, dispensing, and administering of medication) will proceed faster with a helper.[19]

Best practices help when they make a hard job easier. They remove undesired variation and thereby make certain errors impossible or at least highly unlikely. A doctor doesn't need to remember which of several concentrations to use (and thereby risk that he or she remembers wrong and that this wrong recollection will be transcribed, dispensed, and administered as the doctor presumably intended)—he or she just checks a box on an order sheet. Best practices reduce the reliance on memory; they substitute for memory.

Keep the Faith

Best practices are worth sweating for. It is no crime to make an error; everyone does. We need to set up medication systems to be so robust that they will keep our patients safe in the face of normal human frailties, as Donald Berwick notes.[20] In an era when role models are few and authority figures are distrusted, patients still, for the most part, trust clinicians. Earn their trust.

Notes

1. Institute of Medicine, *Crossing the Quality Chasm: A New Health System for the 21st Century.* William Richardson, ed. Washington, DC: National Academy Press, 2001. Institute of Medicine, *To Err Is Human: Building a Safer Health System.* Linda Kohn, Janet Corrigan, and Molla Donaldson, eds. Washington, DC: National Academy Press, 2000.
2. Michael Cohen, *ISMP Medication Safety Self-Assessment.* Huntingdon Valley, PA: Institute for Safe Medication Practices, 2000.
3. Our discussion draws on James Prochaska et al., *Changing for Good.* New York: William Morrow, 1994.
4. Saul Weingart et al., "Confidential Clinician-Reported Surveillance of Adverse Events Among Medical Inpatients." *J Gen Intern Med* 15:470–477, 2000.
5. Bartley Moore, J. *Prescription for Change: Toward a Higher Standard in Medication Management.* Washington, DC: The Advisory Board Co. Presented in a seminar in Atlanta, July 26–27, 1999.
6. Laura Adams, "A Culture of Safety: Reducing Errors in Healthcare." Presentation, Massachusetts PRO, Waltham, MA, April 27, 1999.
7. *Proceedings of Enhancing Patient Safety and Reducing Errors in Health Care.* Rancho Mirage, CA, November 8–10, 1998.
8. Leslie Kirle et al., Massachusetts Coalition for the Prevention of Medical Errors, "Best Practice Recommendations for Medication Administration Processes and Procedures," 1998.
9. Moore, *Prescription for Change.*
10. Private communication at Mt. Auburn Hospital in Cambridge, MA, June 23, 2000.
11. Free downloads are available at www.meliorconsulting.com.

12. "It Starts at the Top," IHI National Forum presentation with the author, December 2000, San Francisco. These slides are available for free download at www.meliorconsulting.com.

13. Delthia Ricks, "Poison in Prescription: Illegible Writing Can Lead to Dangerous Medication Errors," *Newsday,* March 19/20, 2001.

14. Barbara Sher, seminar at Emerson College, Boston, MA, spring 1995. See also Barbara Sher, *Teamworks.* New York: Warner Books, 1989.

15. See www.npsf.org.

16. Prochaska, *Changing for Good.*

17. Stephen Covey, et al., *First Things First.* New York: Simon & Schuster, 1994.

18. Rollo May, *The Cry for Myth.* New York: Bantam Doubleday Dell, 1991.

19. Prochaska, *Changing for Good.*

20. Quoted in Jennifer Steinhauer, "So, the Tumor's in the Left Brain, Right?" *New York Times,* April 1, 2001, p. A-23.

CHAPTER FORTY

IMPROVING THE SAFETY OF THE MEDICATION USE PROCESS

David A. Ehlert, PharmD and Steven S. Rough, MS

Although there is a substantial body of literature describing medication errors and preventable adverse drug events, historically, medication safety has not been a topic that generated much attention. Medication errors were often thought to be a result of human lapses, rather than system failures. Efforts to improve the reporting of medication errors were often met with resistance by hospital administrators and risk management departments. However, the release of the Institute of Medicine's (IOM) report *To Err Is Human: Building a Better Health System* in November 1999 has helped to foster the development of a national agenda for reducing errors and improving patient safety.[1] With estimates of 44,000 to 98,000 deaths annually due to medical errors, and more than 7,000 deaths per year due to medication errors alone, this IOM report has heightened awareness and has stimulated many health care organizations to develop strategies to address the situation. In March 2001, the Institute of Medicine released *Crossing the Quality Chasm: A New Health System for the 21st Century.*[2] This was the second and final report of the Committee on the Quality of Health Care in America. Whereas the first IOM report focuses largely on patient safety, the second report has a broader focus and provides strategic direction for redesigning the health care delivery system for the 21st century.

Rather than waiting for health care institutions to address the issue of medication safety on their own, many health care purchasers and payers are demanding that hospitals and health systems implement specific safeguards to maximize the safety of the medication use process. For instance, the Business Roundtable, an association of chief executive officers of leading corporations, recently unveiled its Leapfrog Group initiative.[3] This consortium of more than 135 employers and other major health care purchasers collectively provides health benefits to more than 33 million Americans. The Leapfrog Group is attempting to leverage this purchasing power to ensure that hospitals and health systems appropriately address the medical and medication error problems. The Leapfrog Group proposed three initial hospital safety measures that will facilitate comparisons that can be used to help determine which hospitals and facilities the companies contract with for their employees. The group estimates that their initial three improvements—computerized prescriber order entry (CPOE), staffing intensive care units with board-certified intensivists, and evidence-based hospital referral—could save up to 58,000 lives per year and prevent 522,000 medication errors if implemented by all nonrural hospitals in the United States.

Groups other than health care purchasers are beginning to mandate that health care facilities focus on improving medication safety. Since July 2001, the Joint Commission on Accreditation of Healthcare Organizations (JCAHO) has had standards focused on improving patient safety and reducing medical and medication errors.[4] These initial standards require hospitals to foster a conducive, nonpunitive environment that encourages error identification and reporting. Hospitals also are required to inform patients and their families about the results of care, including unanticipated outcomes, and to aggregate patient safety-related data to identify risk to patients. In January 2003, the first six JCAHO national patient safety goals became effective. For instance, goal 2 is to improve the effectiveness of communication among caregivers. Included in that goal is the implementation of a process for taking verbal or telephone orders that requires a verification "read-back" of the complete order by the person receiving the order. Also included in goal 2 is the development of a list of unacceptable abbreviations, symbols, and order-writing conventions.

The general public's interest in and awareness of the risk of medication errors and adverse drug events is also increasing. A survey conducted by the Kaiser Family Foundation and the Agency for Healthcare Research and Quality indicated that quality of care is the biggest concern in choosing a health plan.[5] Although few Americans use comparative quality information to help them make their health care choice (because of a lack of quality information and the fact that approximately 40% of Americans have no choice in health plans), most Americans believe that information about medical errors would tell them a lot about the quality of physicians. The general public is more concerned about serious errors or mistakes happening when they receive health care than when they fly on airlines. Furthermore, 73% of those surveyed reported that the government should require health care providers to report all serious medical errors to make sure this information is publicly available.

The purpose of this chapter is to provide some background on the medication safety problem, to provide very practical examples of how a health system is responding to this problem, and to identify best practices for maximizing medication safety.

Background

Terminology

Medication misadventures, medication errors, adverse drug events (ADEs), and *adverse drug reactions* (ADRs) are terms that are frequently used to describe medication-related occurrences. However, these terms cannot be used interchangeably. According to a consensus definition reached by the National Coordinating Council for Medication Error Reporting and Prevention (NCCMERP), a medication error is "any preventable event that may cause or lead to inappropriate medication use or patient harm while the medication is in the control of the health care professional, patient, or consumer. Such events may be related to professional practice, health care products, procedures and systems including: prescribing; order communication; product-labeling; packaging and nomenclature; compounding; dispensing; administration; education; monitoring; and use."[6] Analysis of the literature reveals that there is considerable variability in how medication error occurrences are defined. For instance, the first IOM report defined an error as the failure of a planned action to be completed as intended or the use of a wrong plan to achieve an aim.[1] The key components of these definitions are that medication errors are preventable, they do not always cause patient harm, and they can be caused by errors in planning (e.g., prescribing), not just errors in execution (e.g., administering the drug to the wrong patient).

The majority of medication errors are not adverse drug events. An ADE is defined as an injury from a medicine (or lack of intended medicine). In a study by Bates and coworkers, only 0.9% of medication errors resulted in ADEs.[7] The death of an infant from a 10-fold overdose of morphine (because the morphine order did not include a leading zero) is an example of a medication error that resulted in an adverse drug event (preventable adverse drug event). Adverse drug reactions

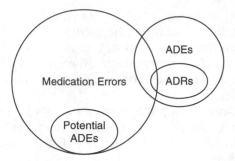

FIGURE 40-1. The relationships among the different types of medication misadventures[6,30]

are a subset of ADEs. The World Health Organization (WHO) defines an adverse drug reaction as "any response that is noxious, unintended, or undesired, which occurs at doses normally used in humans for prophylaxis, diagnosis, therapy of disease or modification of physiological function."[8] The majority of adverse drug reactions are not preventable; however, preventable adverse drug reactions do occasionally occur. For instance, red man syndrome from rapid administration of vancomycin could be considered a preventable adverse drug reaction (i.e., a medication error and an adverse drug reaction). Figure 40-1 illustrates the relationships among the different types of medication misadventures.

The Incidence of Medication Misadventures

The exact incidence of medication errors and adverse drug events is unknown and varies from one study and from one institution to another. Medication error rates depend on the methodology and intensity of surveillance used to detect them. Because many medication errors do not cause patient harm, many errors go undetected. Furthermore, spontaneous reporting, one of the most common methods for detecting medication errors, fails to identify the majority of medication-related occurrences. Therefore, it is nearly impossible to ascertain the true incidence of medication errors. Nevertheless, a variety of different methodologies have been used within the medical literature in an attempt to quantify and estimate the true incidence of medication errors and adverse drug events.

The Harvard Medical Practice Study, in which over 30,000 records were randomly selected from 51 New York hospitals, indicated that drug complications were the most common type of adverse event.[9,10] Nearly 20% of the injuries that prolonged hospitalization or produced patient disability were due to the use of medications. Of these drug-induced adverse events, 20% were judged to be due to negligent care.

In a different study that used an intensive, multidisciplinary surveillance process of self-reporting and extensive chart review, Bates and colleagues found that an average of 1.4 medication errors occurred for every admission at Brigham and Women's Hospital.[7] Stated differently, they found that there were 311 medication errors for every 1,000 patient-days (or 530 medication errors per 10,070 orders). Of the 530 medication errors identified during the study, only 0.9% actually caused patient harm and resulted in an ADE.

Other methodologies for detecting medication errors and adverse drug events have been used with success. For instance, integration of computerized detection programs into hospital information systems has been shown to be of utility. The reported ADE rates (per 1,000 patient-days) in four different publications, each using different error reporting and detection methods, ranged from 0.2% using a voluntary self-reporting system to 21% when a system of chart review and computerized screening was used.[11-14] The computerized detection programs screen for signs of potential ADEs such as abrupt medication discontinuation orders, antidote ordering (e.g., naloxone, flumazenil, diphenhydramine), and certain abnormal laboratory values.

Financial Impact

Medication misadventures result in significant consumption of resources in the form of increased lengths of stay, increased cost of care, rework time, patient costs (e.g., patient suffering, lost productivity), and malpractice claims. Using a decision analysis model, Johnson and Bootman estimated that the annual cost of drug-related morbidity and mortality in the ambulatory setting was $76.6 billion.[15,16] These authors estimated that almost 60% of the costs attributable to drug-related morbidity and mortality were preventable.

Other studies have focused more on the inpatient setting and have utilized prospective, case-control designs to estimate the additional resource consumption resulting from ADEs. For instance, Classen and coworkers found that each ADE increased the mean length of stay (LOS) by 3.23 days and the mean cost of hospitalization by $4,655.[17] In a different study, Bates and colleagues used a nested case-control design and found that each preventable ADE resulted in an additional LOS of 4.6 days and a $5,857 increase in hospitalization costs.[18]

Although the results of the aforementioned studies are impressive, the studies were not designed to take into consideration the amount of rework time and other costs (e.g., malpractice costs, costs to the patient) associated with ADEs, potential ADEs, and medication errors. For instance, although most medication errors do not result in patient harm, they frequently result in a significant amount of rework time (e.g., telephone calls for order clarification, tracking down missing doses).

The Medication Use Process

The medication use process encompasses all areas of medication use and is a highly complex, multidisciplinary process. In its simplest form, the medication use process consists of five domains: purchasing/inventory management; prescribing/medication determination; medication preparation, dispensing, and counseling; medication administration; and patient monitoring/assessment. Some medication use process models ignore the purchasing/inventory management phase. However, there are countless examples of medication errors and adverse drug events that could have been prevented by better purchasing/ inventory management practices. Removing dangerous products (e.g., concentrated potassium chloride, hypertonic saline) from patient care areas is an example of an inventory management function that because of some highly publicized cases has only recently become standard practice.

Thinking of medication use in terms of a multistep process or system is critical to being able to understand and develop strategies to improve medication safety (Tables 40-1 and 40-2). It is also essential to have an understanding of which phases of the medication use process are associated with the most medication errors and ADEs. Bates and coworkers used a four-phase medication use model to categorize the potential and preventable ADEs that were detected using an intensive surveillance process.[13] These four phases were ordering, transcription, dispensing, and administration. In this study, the majority of preventable

TABLE 40-1   Common Sources of Medication Error

Ambiguous orders	Incorrect drug selected
Drug device use	Incorrect patient
Environmental stress	Insufficient drug information
Errors in communication/ miscommunication of drug orders	Insufficient information about other drugs patient is on (therapeutic duplication)
Error-prone abbreviation	Insufficient laboratory information
Illegible handwriting	Known allergy
Improper dose	Limited patient education
Incomplete orders	Limited staff education
Incomplete/insufficient monitoring	Look-alike or sound-alike drugs
Incomplete patient information/patient information unavailable	Poor communication

TABLE 40-2   Common Strategies for Preventing Errors in Each Phase of the Medication Use Process

---

Purchasing/Inventory Management

Purchase products from different manufacturers (if possible) for products with similar packaging.

Streamline order procurement process; use bar code restocking.

Routine expiration date checking system is in place.

Dangerous products such as concentrated solutions (e.g., potassium chloride, hypertonic saline) are not stored in patient care areas.

Ordering/Prescribing

Implement computerized prescriber order entry.

Computer system is utilized for documentation of drug allergies and screening profiles for allergies or cross-sensitivities.

Allergy information is clearly documented in the chart and is readily retrievable (e.g., including allergy information on top of all inpatient medication ordering forms).

Forcing functions are printed on inpatient order forms or on prescription pads.

Maximize use of preprinted order sets for frequently prescribed orders.

Preprinted forms undergo multidisciplinary development and review.

A list of prohibited dangerous abbreviations is incorporated into employee training programs and order forms.

Orders such as "resume pre-op medications" or "resume home medications" are prohibited.

Verbal or telephone orders from prescribers who are on-site in the hospital are used only in true emergencies or during sterile procedures when ungloving and ungowning are impractical.

Pharmacist obtains complete drug history, including all prescription, OTC, and herbal/alternative therapies, illicit drug use, and immunization status.

Incorporate a pharmacist on the patient care units.

Ensure sufficient access to current drug information resources.

Circulate physician-directed newsletters.

Implement electronic medical records.

Laboratory results are available at time of prescribing.

Verbal orders for chemotherapy are never used.

Doses are adjusted for specific populations (e.g., pediatrics, elderly, patients with renal and/or hepatic impairment).

Dispensing

Automatic counting machines are used when filling prescriptions.

Entering information into the allergy field is a required function that cannot be bypassed before entering the order.

Pharmacy computer system screens medication profile against known allergies for potential problems or cross-sensitivities.

Bar-coded medication selection exists.

Dose-range checking is a feature of the pharmacy computer system.

Alerts are built into the computer software regarding look-alike/sound-alike drugs.

Products with look-alike drug packaging or look-alike drug names are stored separately, not alphabetically.

Alternatively, look-alike and sound-alike drugs are flagged on the shelf.

Pharmacy order entry shall occur prior to nursing staff access in automated dispensing systems.

(Continued)

TABLE 40-2   (Continued)

Administration

High-risk medication policies and procedures are in place.

All inpatient drug orders are reviewed by a pharmacist before being administered. If unable to be verified by a pharmacist, an independent double-check system is utilized.

Medication administration records are available at the bedside.

Medications should not be removed from their containers in advance of the time they are to be administered.

Limit the variety of devices and equipment. Eliminate free-flow infusion pumps.

Point-of-care technology that features bar coding is used to verify patient identity.

Patient wristband is verified before each medication is administered.

Monitoring

Provide educational brochure with tips patients can use to prevent errors in the inpatient and ambulatory setting.

Educate patients about new drug therapy prior to administration of the first dose.

Incorporate monitoring parameters into preprinted orders.

Miscellaneous

Improve training on the medication use process/system and how and when to report medication errors (incorporate into new employee orientation; incorporate into competency programs). Make sure training is consistent across all disciplines.

Communicate to staff about known medication errors from outside organizations.

Educate staff about strategies to prevent medication errors.

Improve interdisciplinary communication.

Embrace a nonpunitive culture.

Ensure an adequate work environment (e.g., sufficient light).

Develop computerized event monitoring that screens for signals that an error may have occurred.

Provide psychological support and counseling to professionals involved in an error.

New products should be screened for their error potential before being added to the formulary.

When drugs with heightened error potential are identified during the formulary review process, standardized order forms, prescribing guidelines, and/or some other limitations on use are instituted before initial use.

For recently approved formulary drugs that have been on the market less than 6 months, the literature is scanned to identify published errors or adverse drug reactions that may have been reported.

---

and potential ADEs occurred in the ordering and administration phases (49% and 26%, respectively). The dispensing and transcription phases were associated with 14% and 11% of the preventable and potential ADEs, respectively. When only medication errors that caused patient harm were considered (i.e., preventable ADEs), 56% occurred during the ordering phase, 34% during administration, 6% during transcription, and 4% during dispensing. These data suggest that system changes aimed at improving the ordering and administration phases of the medication use process are likely to have the greatest impact on reducing medication errors and preventable ADEs. The high incidence of preventable ADEs in the ordering phase is one of the major reasons why a well-designed CPOE system is touted as being so critical to improving the safety of the medication use process.

The study by Bates and colleagues also confirmed that errors were more likely to be intercepted if they occurred early in the process.[13] If errors occurred later in the medication use process, they were far less likely to be detected, as evidenced by the fact that no administration errors were intercepted in this study. This finding, coupled with the fact that the administration phase had the second highest incidence of preventable ADEs, reinforces the need for appropriate double checks in the administration process and, if possible, the use of point-of-care bar code scanning technology to build another layer of protection into the medication use system.

Although a macro-level view of the medication use process has been presented thus far, more complicated models of the process do exist. The medication use system in hospitals is inherently complex, often containing more than 100 steps with multiple handoffs. Flowcharting the existing medication use process lays the foundation for a systems approach to medication errors and preventable adverse drug events. Flowcharting the process also helps to illustrate weaknesses and unnecessary steps in the existing system and can help identify the multiple points in the system where breakdowns could occur and cause errors.

Systems Approach

Historically, medical and medication errors have been viewed as individual human failure. Punishing individuals for their mistakes was, and in some cases still is, common. Consequently, many health care practitioners are reluctant to report their mistakes or the errors of coworkers. However, a medication error is rarely the result of just one individual. It usually is the end result of a chain reaction of events that is fueled by faulty system design. Poor systems not only contribute to and make errors more likely, but can also make errors more difficult to detect and correct.

In developing a systems approach to reducing medication errors and preventable ADEs, it is important to understand the concepts of active and latent error. Active errors are usually visible because they occur on the "sharp end" (i.e., on the front lines of practice). Consequently, active errors generally garner the most attention and are the ones that tend to result in punishment and reprimand of health care professionals. However, even more important than active errors are latent errors. Latent errors are far more insidious than active errors and can include faulty design, bad management decisions, and poorly structured systems. Latent errors tend to occur on the "blunt end" and are difficult to associate with individual practitioners because their effects are not immediately felt. Often, latent error is inadvertently introduced into the system as a consequence of other decisions or changes in the system.

Latent errors are a real threat to organizations and their medication safety campaigns because they are difficult to detect and because they can result in several types of active errors. Therefore, to have a meaningful impact on the safety of the medication use system, latent error and failure need to be aggressively sought out and eliminated.

Because human beings are a key component of the medication use process, it is inevitable that mistakes will occur. One way to maximize the safety of the medication use system is to make it difficult for individuals to commit errors by building in double checks and other redundancies to ensure that any errors that do occur are detected and corrected before they reach the patient. It may be helpful to think of medication errors using an analogy of Swiss cheese. This analogy has been described elsewhere.[19] Each layer of safeguards and double checks in the medication use process can be thought of as a slice of Swiss cheese. Ideally, these layers of defense would be impenetrable; however, in actual practice, the defenses are usually flawed and contain one or more holes.

Even though safer systems tend to have more safeguards and layers of defense (i.e., slices of cheese), errors can still occur when a series of failures align to produce disaster. The *Challenger* disaster is an example of a situation in which several faults aligned to produce tragic results. By themselves, the unexpected cold weather or the brittle O-ring seals would not have caused the accident; however, the combination of these occurrences along with the presence of other contributing factors resulted in tragedy.

Another way to improve the safety of the medication use process is to incorporate human factors principles whenever possible. Human factors research in the health care setting has only recently begun to develop. Other industries, such as the nuclear power industry and the airline industry, have done an excellent job of examining why humans make mistakes and developing strategies to prevent them. Some of the core concepts and principles that have resulted from research in preventing errors in other industries include simplifying and standardizing processes; reducing reliance on memory; using constraints and forcing functions; improving information access; decreasing reliance on vigilance; increasing feedback; reducing handoffs; and sensibly using protocols. One way to think of human factors is to consider a statement eloquently articulated by James Reason: "We can't change the human condition, but we can change the condition under which humans work."

Medication Error Reporting

Obtaining accurate data on where medication errors and preventable ADEs occur in the system and ascertaining what system factors contributed to the error are critical to being able to develop strategies to minimize and prevent similar occurrences in the future. All too often, the reported medication error rate is only a small fraction of the actual medication error rate within an institution. The invisible, or unreported, errors tend to reflect the near misses and other potential ADEs that do not cause patient harm either because of chance or because they are detected before they reach the patient. These unreported or underreported errors are some of the most critical errors because understanding why they occurred and developing strategies for preventing similar occurrences in the future can lead to substantial improvements in the safety of the medication use process.

There are a number of reasons why health care professionals are reluctant to report actual and potential medication errors. The most common reason cited for not reporting incidents was that it was unnecessary—either the circumstances of the case did not warrant reporting or else the health care professional did not feel that incident reporting ultimately improves the quality of patient care.[20] Other common reasons given for not reporting errors include lack of time to complete a report when an incident is discovered, fear of discipline or other repercussions, the perception that only severe incidents require reporting (i.e., there is no need to report near misses), and a lack of familiarity with the reporting process.

Although a large portion of this chapter focuses on a health system's approach to improving medication safety, the literature has demonstrated that errors occur in all practice settings (e.g., hospitals, physician offices, emergency departments, nursing homes). Many of the error prevention strategies discussed in this chapter apply to nearly every practice setting.

Technology

The term *technology* refers to anything that is used to replace routine or repetitive tasks previously performed by people, or which extends the capability of people. The term *automation* refers to any technology, machine, or device linked to or controlled by a computer and used to do work. Automation can be designed to streamline and improve the accuracy and efficiency of the medication use process. All automation is technology, but the inverse is not necessarily true.

Although information technologies and automated medication systems are widely used in health systems and are integral components of the first IOM report and the Leapfrog Group recommendations, very little data are available regarding their impact on patient safety. The only exception to this is computerized prescriber order entry (CPOE) with computerized clinical decision support. Other technologies, such as using robotic technology to fill medication doses, bar coding of medications, automated dispensing devices, and computerized medication administration records, are much more widely implemented than CPOE systems, yet their reported impact on reducing medication errors and preventable ADEs is variable at best. Implementing new technology can create major infrastructure changes that introduce new sources of error, and some vendors market their products without sufficient testing or without being able to fully implement the technology as advertised. Nevertheless, all of these systems intuitively show promise in their potential to reduce medication error. If properly integrated, all of these systems should ultimately improve patient safety and will likely be incorporated into most medication use systems of the future.

Technology has the potential to reduce medication errors by reducing complexity, simplifying and standardizing processes, avoiding over-reliance on memory, and improving efficiency. However, technology by itself will rarely prevent medication errors. Rather, it must be effectively integrated into the existing medication use system and appropriately managed for it to positively affect patient safety. In fact, if technology is not used properly, it can prolong a system of errors and introduce dangerous new ones. Implementing technology within a previously suboptimal manual system will most often yield a suboptimal automated system. Without a comprehensive system to ensure that patients are getting their drugs and dosages correctly and on time, errors will continue to occur. In anticipation of the implementation of new technology, policies and procedures must be modified to ensure that a safe and proper infrastructure continues to exist for medication purchasing, ordering, preparation, dispensing, administering, and monitoring. After all, technology does not preclude the need for safety checks and verification for appropriateness.

Health systems are often unrealistic in what they expect from technology. Technology can instill a false sense of security, leading to carelessness by health care professionals. For instance, health care professionals often neglect to exercise sound double- and triple-check procedures with medications obtained from automated dispensing devices because of an over-reliance on the technology. To avoid such problems, it is critical that all personnel be adequately educated so that they understand that technology cannot completely substitute for human safety checks. Additionally, managers must make certain that staff levels are not overly reduced in response to system automation and that staff are not forced to work at a pace that precludes the ability to deliver safe and effective health care. With all technology, it is absolutely critical that appropriate quality control systems exist to ensure its accurate and safe use.

This section briefly describes the advantages, disadvantages, and issues surrounding the use of several existing technologies that (if appropriately deployed) can help improve the safety of the medication use process. This section describes only those technologies thought to have the greatest potential impact on patient safety, and is not designed to be inclusive. More extensive reviews of automated technologies and their impact on the medication use process exist elsewhere.[21]

Desired Features for Reducing Errors

There is little doubt that the innovative and appropriate use of technology within the medication use process can significantly improve patient safety. Furthermore, it is reasonable to draw four conclusions about information technology and automation as they apply to preventing medication errors.

1. The use of bar-coded medications should be maximized throughout the medication use process, including the administration and documentation phase of the process.
2. Information technologies can be used to analyze and prevent medication errors. For instance, sophisticated pharmacy or CPOE systems may be integrated with patient-specific laboratory and nursing clinical documentation systems to identify adverse drug events and medication errors when they occur. Analyzing data from such integrated systems will provide better data for trends analysis than existing manual medication error reporting systems, thus enabling the development of systems for measuring and managing adverse drug events and the clinical and economic implications thereof. Additionally, potential errors identified by electronic prescribing and point-of-care scanning devices could be analyzed for common problems to facilitate minimization and elimination of recurring root causes of potential errors within organizations.
3. Automated dispensing systems, especially those incorporating the use of bar code technology, have the potential to improve medication dispensing accuracy and patient safety.
4. Aggressive implementation of CPOE will improve patient safety, as long as the system incorporates appropriate computerized decision support and is properly designed, implemented, and maintained.

Decentralized Automated Dispensing Devices

Decentralized automated dispensing systems, sometimes referred to as unit-based dispensing cabinets, are secure storage cabinets capable of handling most unit-dose and some bulk (multiple-dose) medications.* These devices are typically connected via a real-time interface to the hospital's pharmacy computer system in an attempt to maintain control over drug dispensing. Automated dispensing devices were originally installed in hospitals in the late 1980s and early 1990s to provide increased control over controlled substances and floor stock medications in patient care areas. In addition to their traditional uses, many hospitals now use these devices for storing and dispensing nearly all medication doses, thereby eliminating the manual medication cart-fill and delivery process.

The primary focus of these automated dispensing systems is to provide prompt, real-time availability of medications for nurses and patients. They can also help to improve controlled substance accountability, increase productivity, improve charge capture and documentation accuracy, and reduce pharmacy and nursing labor costs. However, the impact of these decentralized automated dispensing systems on medication errors is less clear. Decentralized dispensing devices are increasingly incorporating bar code labeling and scanning into the replenishment process, thus improving restocking accuracy and potentially improving medication safety. Also, the use of automated dispensing systems can result in pharmacists not having to check manually filled medication carts and first doses and can result in the redeployment of pharmacists to patient care units to engage in clinical activities that optimize the safety and efficacy of medication use.

As with any technology, there is the potential for increased errors associated with the use of automated dispensing systems. For instance, purchasing an insufficient number of cabinets may preclude an institution's ability to maintain a truly efficient system, resulting in a higher potential for product selection and administration errors. Despite increasing pressure from the JCAHO and other interested parties, most organizations have yet to link their pharmacy computer systems to cabinets in such a way that restricts nurses from obtaining medications that are not ordered for patients. Other medication administration safety concerns with automated dispensing devices include the following:

- Nurses may retrieve an incorrect medication because of open access to all drugs in a drawer.
- Carelessness or lack of verification of drug labels may occur because of a belief that the system is computerized and therefore

---

*Examples of automated dispensing systems currently on the market include Pyxis, AcuDose, OmniCell, and Sure-Med.

not susceptible to errors (or the belief that the pharmacy placed the drug there and the pharmacy does not make mistakes).

- Changing the location of the drug in the cabinet may cause errors because the health care professional may choose drugs from particular locations by habit rather than verifying each drug's identity.
- Drugs may be stocked in the wrong pocket either because one or more doses inadvertently fell into the wrong slot or because of a pharmacy restocking error.

Conflicting reports exist in the literature on the impact of automated dispensing devices on medication error rates.[22-24] Unfortunately, significant capital investments have been made in these systems without full evaluation of the operational changes needed to ensure that efficiency goals were met without compromising patient safety. Regardless of whether state regulations exist to ensure safe use of automated dispensing systems, it is extremely important that every organization develop, enforce, and continuously improve multidisciplinary policies and procedures to ensure patient safety, accuracy, security, and confidentiality. Table 40-3 provides an extensive list of guidelines and considerations for the safe use of decentralized automated dispensing systems.

Centralized Robotics for Dispensing Medications

Centrally located automated dispensing devices are designed to automate the entire process of medication dispensing, including medication storage, dispensing, restocking, and crediting of unit-dose medications.* An interface must be created with the pharmacy information system to provide the centralized dispensing device with access to each patient's medication profile. Bar coding of medication doses allows dispensing accuracy to approach 100% with centralized robotics technology. Thus, as long as a patient-specific computerized medication profile is maintained in an accurate and timely manner, pharmacists may be freed from medication-checking duties.

The centralized robotic system was traditionally used exclusively to dispense unit-dose bar-coded medications for scheduled medication cart filling; however, several organizations have recently expanded the use of this technology to include automation of first-dose dispensing. Another recent expanded use of this technology is its ability to pick medication doses to be restocked in decentralized automated dispensing cabinets. This has the potential to reduce medication administration errors by improving restocking accuracy.

---

*The two most prevalent systems on the market are Robot-Rx (McKesson) and the ATC-212 and ATC-Profile (Automed Technologies, Inc.). Other centralized automated dispensing systems exist, but currently are in the alpha- and beta-testing stages.

TABLE 40-3   Guidelines for Safe Use of Decentralized Automated Dispensing Systems

Agree with the vendor on a documented preventive maintenance schedule that does not
    disrupt workflow.
Any high-risk medications stocked in devices should be accompanied by an alert
    system for nurses (such as a maximum-dose prompt).
Carefully select stored drugs based on the needs of the patient care unit, patient age,
    diagnosis, and staff expertise.
Conduct monthly expiration date checks, concomitantly verifying inventory accuracy.
Configure devices to provide single-dose (or single-drug) access whenever possible,
    focusing such control on high-risk medications and controlled substances.
Develop an ongoing competency assessment program for all personnel who use or
    affect the system, including direct observation and random restocking accuracy
    audits, as well as observation of dispensing accuracy as part of the assessment.
Develop a system to remove all recalled medications.
Develop clear, multidisciplinary system downtime procedures that are included in an
    ongoing competency program.
Develop strict safety criteria for selecting medications that are (and are not) appropriate
    for storing in devices.
Develop systems to account for narcotic waste, and routinely audit controlled substance
    dispenses versus patient orders and medication administration records.
Do not stock look-alike and sound-alike drugs in the same open-access drawer.
Have strict security procedures to limit unauthorized access.
Place allergy reminders for specific drugs such as antibiotics, opiates, and NSAIDs on
    appropriate drug storage pockets, or have them automatically appear on the
    dispensing screen.
Require all personnel to attend formal training and demonstrate competency prior to
    assigning them access to the system.
Require nurses to return medications to a return bin, never back to the original storage
    pocket or location.
Require pharmacist medication order review and approval before administration of the
    first dose of medication (profile dispensing), and limit medications in which profile
    dispensing may be overridden.
Use open-access drawers only for stocking drugs with low potential for causing patient
    harm if administered in error.
Whenever possible, use bar coding capabilities for restocking medications and for
    retrieval.
With few exceptions, maximize use of unit-dose medications in ready-to-administer
    form.

Potential advantages of robotics include reducing pharmacy labor
costs; eliminating certain technical tasks of pharmacists, allowing for
their redeployment to perform clinical activities; and improving medication dispensing accuracy. No published data are available on these
advantages, but in one unpublished study a robot decreased the dispensing error rate from 2.9% to 0.6%.[25] However, this improved dispensing accuracy has never been proved to result in improved patient
safety since nurses still have open access to all robot-dispensed medications after they are distributed to patient care areas.

Perhaps the greatest advantage of implementing robotic technology is that all doses dispensed by the robot are bar coded, thus facilitating the implementation of point-of-care drug administration and documentation scanning systems. However, the necessity for bar codes on all medications dispensed by the robot has the potential to introduce new error into the medication use system. Although some manufacturers provide bar-coded medications, most unit-dose medications must be accurately repackaged and bar coded by the pharmacy department.

In addition to the automated dispensing devices that exist for hospitals, dispensing systems for ambulatory and retail pharmacies that automate the filling of individual patient prescriptions exist.[*] Adoption of these technologies in community pharmacies has been limited by their high cost and space requirements. Nevertheless, the advantage of these automated dispensing devices for ambulatory pharmacies is that medication dispensing errors are reduced by automating manual tasks such as counting, pouring, and filling. Furthermore, most of these technologies offer visual imaging systems that help the pharmacist verify the appropriateness of the medication being dispensed.

Point-of-Care Bedside Medication Charting Systems and Bar Coding

Point-of-care technology enables caregivers to enter and retrieve patient-specific data in an electronic format at the bedside. Advanced portable medication scanners are used by nurses at the point of care to electronically verify and document medication administration.[†] Some of the devices utilize wireless handheld personal digital assistant (PDA) technology to increase their portability. The point-of-care technology receives real-time patient information and medication profiles from the pharmacy computer system, usually by way of a radio frequency network. When a medication order is initiated, modified, or discontinued in the pharmacy computer system, the order information is updated into the point-of-care system. For all scheduled doses, the device alerts the nurse when it is time to administer the medication.

To ensure accurate medication administration and documentation, these point-of-care systems require the scanning of three items prior to medication administration: the bar code on the medication dose, the caregiver's unique bar code (often on the nurse's name badge), and the patient's unique bar code identifier (often a wristband). These

---

[*]Some of the systems on the market are Baker Cells (McKesson), QuickScript (Automed Technologies), Optifill II (Automed Technologies), and Pharmacy 2000 (McKesson).

[†]Some of the systems on the market are AcuScan-Rx, Autros, Bridge Medical Medication Management System, BD-Rx, and PYXISVERI5.

point-of-care systems ensure the "five R's" of medication administration: right patient, right drug, right dose, right time, and right route. When the nurse scans the medication he or she is planning to administer, that medication is electronically compared to the patient's medication profile. These point-of-care systems can identify incorrect and omitted medications and alert the nurse in real time if a physician has cancelled or changed a patient's medication order. This technology offers the potential to dramatically reduce the risk of drug administration errors. Organizations that have implemented this technology report that between 5% and 10% of all doses scanned result in one of the following discrepancies: wrong patient, wrong drug, wrong dose, wrong route, or wrong time.

Although improvements are being made in point-of-care patient information systems and electronic medication administration records (MARs), effectively implementing these systems can be costly and complicated. Major limitations to implementing point-of-care technology include the following:

- The cost of the devices is high.
- All medications must be bar coded to achieve the optimal safety benefit (usually requiring labor-intensive and potentially error-prone repackaging in the pharmacy).
- Commercial products are still at a very early stage of development.
- Nursing workflow redesign issues exist.
- Elaborate interfaces between information systems are necessary to ensure accurate patient records on the point-of-care system.
- Installation of a dedicated radio frequency network within the hospital may be incompatible with certain patient monitoring devices in the hospital.

These stated limitations and incompatibilities have limited the use of point-of-care technologies in many health care settings.

Because one of the major limitations of point-of-care technology is bar coding all medications, a cursory understanding of the information contained in a bar code is necessary. A bar code is simply a method of encoding numbers and letters by using a combination of bars and spaces with varying widths stacked side by side in such a way that the scanner interprets the rows as data. Each bar code has specific identification encoded in it, and those data are used by a computer/scanner to look up all specific information associated with the code. Bar codes on medications contain specific information about that drug, including but not limited to the product name, dose, dosage, form, route of administration, expiration date, and lot number. A critical component of a bar code system is the scanner's ability to quickly and accurately interpret the bar code data, which depends on two criteria: the quality of the bar code print on the product and the symbology of the bar code. The space available on most unit-dose packages is limited, yet some manufacturers have been able to successfully bar code these products.

Bar coding of drugs would seem to be useful for reducing errors because it can help to rapidly ensure that the drug at hand is actually the intended one. The major barrier to implementing bar codes on all medications is the lack of consensus among pharmaceutical manufacturers on the appropriate approach for adding bar coding to unit-dose product labels. Currently, no universal standard bar code symbology has been adopted for medications. However, in August 2000, the National Coordinating Council for Medication Error Reporting and Prevention (NCCMERP) organized a meeting of pharmacy organizations, information technology vendors, pharmaceutical manufacturers, and other interested parties to facilitate a dialogue for developing a standardized bar code symbology. The NCCMERP later disseminated a white paper entitled *Promoting and Standardizing Bar Coding on Medication Packaging: Reducing Errors and Improving Patient Care.* In 2002, the Food and Drug Administration worked to further develop a proposal that would require a bar code on the label of all drug and biological products for human use. Then, in early 2003, Pfizer announced that it would place bar codes on each of its unit-of-use packaged products. However, until standards exist for bar coding, the ability of many scanning devices to accurately scan all products may be severely limited. Symbology standardization within health care is essential in order for bar code technology to be applied successfully throughout the medication use process.

Computerized Prescriber Order Entry

CPOE is a system in which prescribers enter medication and other orders (e.g., laboratory and radiology) for patients via an electronic software application. CPOE probably has the greatest potential of any technology for reducing medication errors. However, for a CPOE system to prevent errors other than those due to illegible handwriting, the system must have the following critical characteristics:

- Relevant patient-specific information (e.g., demographic data, laboratory and diagnostic test results) must be readily available at the time of prescribing or order entry.
- Drug–drug interaction, drug-allergy, drug-laboratory, drug contraindication, and maximum/minimum dosing alerts for potentially serious mistakes must be provided. These alerts must be carefully established so that they are not easily overridden.

Furthermore, the sensitivity of these alerts must be set such that clinically insignificant alerts are minimized. Otherwise, if prescribers are frequently alerted with nonsignificant warnings, they may become desensitized to all alerts and may then miss the clinically significant warnings.

- The selection of standard order sets (medication use algorithms and guidelines for high-risk patient populations) should be automated at the point of prescribing.
- The system must be efficient and easy to use. If the system is too complex and it takes too long to learn all the nuances and intricacies, physician compliance with implementing and maximizing the use of the CPOE system will suffer.

Although ideal, systems that fulfill these criteria are uncommon. One published study[26] demonstrated that serious medication errors fell 55% following implementation of a CPOE system, while the rate of all errors fell 83% in another study.[27] Most inpatient physician order entry systems currently on the market provide the benefit of improved prescription legibility and medication turnaround time, but they are inefficient in that they often require a high level of pharmacist intervention, including reentering of medication orders. Although such systems may result in the reduction of some errors by simply computerizing the process, they do not provide the physician with the necessary clinical information and decision support at the point of decision making that would result in the greatest impact on error reduction. Literature documenting the "efficient" use of computerized prescriber medication order entry systems is limited. Most successful systems have been home-grown and have not achieved the theoretical safety benefits of an integrated system that incorporates pharmacy, laboratory, and other patient-specific clinical information into one database. Some commercially available pharmacist computer order entry systems exist that provide some of the ideal capabilities listed earlier, but commercially available integrated systems for physicians are in the very early stages of development.

A few guidelines for maximizing the likelihood of successful implementation of an inpatient physician order entry system include the following:

- Use a unique prescriber order entry system, *not* a modified pharmacist order entry system. Physicians generally do not think like pharmacists, nor will they have the time to pay attention to the high level of detail required in most pharmacy order entry systems.
- Identify physician project champions at a very high level in the organization and involve them in the decision-making and planning process from the very beginning.

- Set realistic time frame expectations and make sure the implementation team is multidisciplinary.
- Pay close attention to the process and the flow of information in the proposed CPOE system.
- Plan on 5 or more years of system development and enhancement after the product is initially piloted.
- Do not be discouraged by initial dissatisfaction among physicians, and do not interpret initial negative reactions as failure. Physician transition may be easier in a teaching hospital versus a private or nonteaching hospital. More experienced physicians are sometimes less eager to embrace the change unless they can enter orders from their office during the course of the day as test results become available for their inpatients. In teaching hospitals, resident physicians are generally more adaptable and can usually be required to make the change.

Over the past few years, great strides have been taken to improve ambulatory CPOE technologies. Many physicians are using PDA-based prescribing devices to directly link themselves with dispensing pharmacies at the time the prescription is written. These systems essentially replace the traditional paper prescription pad. The capabilities of these systems include fast prescription processing with few keystrokes, online claim submission within 20 seconds, provision of generic alternatives, dosing and allergy alerts, prescribing histories, and plan-specific formulary recommendations and therapeutic alternatives (many systems contain formulary information from nearly 800 plans).

Medication Use Process Strategic Plan Within a Health System

Historically, automation had to result in proven cost reduction, quality improvement, improved service, and increased efficiency to be deemed successful. Although expense continues to be one of the major barriers to implementing new technologies, the 1999 IOM report and other news media have persuaded many organizations to invest heavily in new technologies that improve patient safety. For example, Allina Health System in Minneapolis, Minnesota, has committed $25 million to the development and implementation of an integrated CPOE and bar-coded medication administration system over the next 5 years. Integrated health systems should not view automation and technology as a means to an end, but rather as a series of sophisticated tools to help them optimize the medication use process. The value achieved by implementing new technology within organizations depends primarily on three factors: the efficiency of the system being replaced, the level of detail applied to managing and making the most of the system following implementation, and cooperation between departments to ensure the success of the system.

Within most hospitals, there is consensus that the inpatient medication use process should be automated, but there are many questions and much debate as to the best way to automate the process. There is no right or wrong answer, and any of the previously discussed approaches can succeed or fail, depending on how well they are managed. Suggested characteristics of an ideal system will likely include patient care and safety benefits, responsiveness to customer needs, cost-effectiveness, and ability to leverage the purchase of other existing and pending technologies. It is very important that decision makers evaluate the clinical, cost, and safety advantages and disadvantages of competing technologies, as well as safety claims made by the manufacturer, before reaching a final purchase decision. Table 40-4 lists ideal features to ensure patient safety throughout the medication use process, regardless of which automated technologies are employed.

TABLE 40-4   Desired Safety Features for Incorporating Technology into the Medication Use Process

All actions and usage on a system must be reportable in an easily reviewed format, including identification of the user, the medication, the patient for whom the drug was dispensed, and the time of the transaction.

At medication administration, one system must be able to identify and document the medication, person administering the medication, and patient by utilizing bar code technology.

Hospital admit/discharge/transfer and medication order entry computer systems should be interfaced with automation devices to provide caregivers with warnings about allergies, interactions, duplications, and inappropriate doses at the point of dispensing and/or administration.

Information necessary to properly manage patient care must be accurate, accessible, and timely.

Pertinent patient- and medication-specific information and instructions entered into pharmacy and/or hospital information systems should be available electronically at the point of care (administration), and the system should prompt the nurse to record pertinent information before administration may be documented.

Real-time systems integration should exist from the point of prescribing (order entry) through dispensing and through documentation of medication administration.

The system must accommodate bar-coded unit-dose medications and utilize the bar code capability for drug restocking, retrieval, and administering medications.

The system should force users to confirm their intention whenever medications are accessed or administration is attempted outside of the scheduled administration time or dosage range. Such events should be signaled visibly or audibly for the user, and all such events should be electronically documented and reported daily for follow-up.

The interface with the pharmacy computer system should allow the nurse to view and access only those medications that have been ordered for the specific patient.

The nurse should be electronically reminded when a medication dose is due (and by a different mechanism when it is past due).

User access should be restricted to a unique user identification code and password, or a unique bar code.

Maximizing Medication Use Safety Within an Integrated Health System: The University of Wisconsin Hospital and Clinics Model

The University of Wisconsin Hospital and Clinics (UWHC) is an integrated health system that consists of UW Hospital, UW Children's Hospital, UW Comprehensive Cancer Center, University Community Clinics, University Physicians and Physicians Plus, Unity Health Plans, and Chartwell Wisconsin. The hospital is a 471-bed academic tertiary medical center. UW Hospital consistently ranks among the finest academic medical centers in the country, with centers of excellence in organ transplant, hematology/oncology, ophthalmology, HIV, and critical care. There were nearly 130,000 patient-days in fiscal year 2002, with an average daily census of about 390 patients (not including observation patients).

Approximately 214 full-time equivalents work within the Department of Pharmacy at the University of Wisconsin Hospital and Clinics. Comprehensive pharmacy services are provided at UWHC 24 hours a day. On weekdays, there are eight decentralized pharmacy teams, with 14 pharmacists covering these teams on the first shift and 9 pharmacists covering on the second shift. Weekend and holiday staffing features fewer teams and fewer pharmacists to offset the decreased patient volume. The night shift features one central pharmacist and one decentralized pharmacist who covers the ICUs and all hospital codes.

Decentralized pharmacy services are provided to every patient. The highest priority of decentralized pharmacists is to ensure safe and appropriate medication use. In addition, pharmacists assist in education and research and assist with quality improvement and cost-containment initiatives. Pharmacists perform a number of valuable clinical services on a daily basis, including medication admission histories, participation in daily work rounds with the different medical teams, therapeutic drug monitoring (e.g., renal dosing, pharmacokinetics, IV-to-oral conversion, antibiotic streamlining), and patient discharge counseling.

Through the years, the Department of Pharmacy at UWHC has taken great pride in being at the forefront of technological innovation and novel improvements in the medication use process. The hospital was one of the first in the country to fully implement a unit-of-use system in the late 1960s. In 1993, UWHC was the second hospital in the United States to implement a robotic cart-fill system that automated, streamlined, and improved the accuracy of the cart-fill process. In the current dispensing and distribution process, medications not filled by the robot are prepared in unit-of-use doses in the central pharmacy or in the sterile products area located within the central pharmacy. Narcotics as well as all floor stock and as-needed (PRN) medications are stored and dispensed from automated dispensing systems located in the patient care units.

The provision of safe, rational, and cost-effective therapy was a component of the pharmacy department's mission well before the first IOM report was released. With the release of that report and subsequent reports offering best-practice recommendations (e.g., the Advisory Board's *Prescription for Change* series), members of the pharmacy department have given multiple presentations to senior hospital administrators comparing the hospital's existing medication use system with best-practices recommendations found in the literature. The UWHC pharmacy department has found these presentations to be an excellent way to improve awareness of senior management and secure the necessary buy-in to make medication safety a hospital-wide initiative and priority. Benchmarking an organization's medication use processes with best practices described in the literature is also extremely valuable in that it helps identify areas for improvement.

There are several unique elements of the UWHC medication use process and hospital information system that are believed to make them extremely safe. These elements were in place well before the Institute of Medicine released its 1999 report and include the following:

- Pharmacist-conducted admission histories and discharge counseling for every patient.
- Unit doses of virtually all medications, including individual patient-specific doses of oral and injectable products, are prepared by the pharmacy.
- Pharmacy-maintained medication administration record (MAR) using computer-generated labels (except for one-time or nonrecurring medications, there is no hand transcription onto the MAR).
- Expanded roles for pharmacy technicians. The pharmacy technical support staff perform many functions performed by pharmacists in other institutions (e.g., order entry). This gives the pharmacists more time to complete clinical activities.
- Advanced clinical reference information readily available on the hospital intranet (e.g., Micromedex, Stat-Ref, full-text electronic journals).
- Advanced electronic repository with a substantial amount of patient information that is readily available on personal computers throughout the health system. (It should be emphasized that UWHC does not have a complete electronic medical record.)

Lucian Leape and colleagues identified drug knowledge dissemination and patient information availability as two of the most common system failures that lead to medication errors and preventable ADEs.[27] The last two items on this list address these areas.

Although the UWHC health system already has many key safety components incorporated into the medication use system, it is recognized that there still is significant room for improvement for UWHC to strive to achieve a zero-defect rate in its medication use process. To further enhance medication safety at UWHC, the pharmacy department has developed six guiding principles:

1. Improve organizational awareness about medication safety by providing education to health care professionals and hospital administrators.
2. Improve medication error reporting and root cause analysis.
3. Foster and promote a nonpunitive culture regarding medication errors within the organization.
4. Maximize the appropriate use of new technologies by standardizing systems and incorporating best demonstrated practices for safety.
5. Enhance collaboration across all disciplines.
6. Continue to leverage and maximize the use of decentralized clinical pharmacists.

Medication Safety Committee

The Medication Safety Committee is a multidisciplinary subcommittee of the Pharmacy and Therapeutics (P&T) Committee. Initially called the Medication Error Committee, the committee's name was changed and its membership expanded shortly after the release of the 1999 IOM report. The membership expansion and the name change were intended to reflect an expanded systems approach to medication safety. In August 2000, an afternoon-long retreat was organized to provide sufficient time to develop a strategic plan and mission statement that would help define the expanded scope and focus of the committee. The committee accomplished three objectives during its retreat:

1. A summary of key medication use safety principles, literature, and national recommendations was presented to the group.
2. A mission statement was developed (Table 40-5).
3. An extensive list of potential system improvements that could maximize patient safety was identified.

The final objective, to identify medication safety initiatives that could be the focus of the committee during the subsequent year, was identified after the retreat. Each committee member ranked the possible system improvements identified during the retreat according to

TABLE 40-5   Mission Statement of the UWHC Medication Safety Committee

Medication Safety

- Oversee and maximize the safety of the medication use process throughout the UWHC continuum of care by incorporating fail-safe procedures and safety surveillance systems.
- Ensure systems are in place to conduct and review root cause analysis and trends for reported medication errors and preventable adverse drug events. Facilitate implementation and monitoring of system changes to help prevent similar events in the future.

Medication Error Reporting

- Maintain simple, consistent reporting procedures for both actual and potential medication errors in all UWHC care areas.
- Ensure that a nonpunitive system exists so that fear of retribution is not a barrier to medication error reporting.

Awareness

- Increase health care practitioner and administrator awareness about medication safety.
- Ensure that employees know how the medication error reporting process works at UWHC.
- Increase consumer/patient awareness about medication safety.

their potential impact and feasibility (i.e., time and resources necessary). The four highest-impact system improvements were (1) developing safety criteria for an ideal ambulatory and inpatient CPOE system to help guide the selection and implementation of this technology, (2) improving the medication error and ADE reporting form, (3) developing an electronic MAR using point-of-care technology, and (4) developing computerized maximum dosing alerts for high-alert drugs. The four most feasible system improvements were (1) having a clinical pharmacist in the emergency department (ED), (2) including a space on the medication error and ADE reporting form for employees to provide ideas for improving medication safety, (3) working with public affairs to promote medication safety initiatives to patients and the public, and (4) improving the dissemination of information included in the bi-weekly *Institute of Safe Medication Practices (ISMP) Medication Safety Alerts.*

These eight system improvements served as the focus of the committee for the subsequent year. The Medication Safety Committee now holds an annual afternoon-long retreat to review new published best practices, review occurrence trends, and develop annual committee goals based on impact and feasibility.

UWHC Medication Error Reporting Process Task Force

Improving the medication error and ADE reporting process was one of the high-impact initiatives identified during the Medication Safety Committee retreat. A multidisciplinary task force was formed with volunteers from the Medication Safety Committee to improve the medication error reporting process by redesigning the reporting form; developing a new hospital-wide, nonpunitive medication error/preventable ADE policy and procedure; and improving the tracking, trending, and analysis of medication error data.

The group began by redesigning the form used to report medication errors and other medication-related occurrences. The previous process for reporting medication-related incidents involved the use of a general Occurrence Screen form that was also used to report a variety of non-drug-related incidents such as slips and falls, equipment malfunction, and incorrect blood administration. Some of the problems that were identified with the previous form included the following:

- The form lacked space for health care professionals to suggest ways to improve the medication use system.
- No mechanism was provided to distinguish actual from potential errors.
- Too much narrative and time were needed to complete the form.
- The form was not scannable.
- Very few reports were generated in the emergency department, operating room/recovery room, and ambulatory clinics.
- Attributable and root cause assessments were not incorporated into the form.

The process for following up on error reports was also not standardized, and the path for routing the form to the appropriate disciplines often was very convoluted. Consequently, follow-up on medication errors and report processing were often severely delayed.

The redesigned Medication Occurrence (Error) Report is now used for reporting actual and potential medication occurrences. A section has been incorporated into the form for suggesting system changes that could improve medication safety. A check box format exists throughout the form to minimize the time necessary to complete the form. The form prompts health care professionals to report the following characteristics of the occurrence: whether it is an actual or potential occurrence; the location; the practitioner(s)/staff involved; the timing; the suspected type of occurrence (e.g., incorrect dose, incorrect drug); the name, dose, and route of medication ordered compared to that given; the age of the patient; the source of the medication (e.g., automated dispensing device, patient's medication drawer); and the name and discipline of the person completing the report.

The revised reporting process also consists of a follow-up form that is completed by pharmacy managers. The sections on this form include assessment of the attributable system factors that contributed to the occurrence, assessment of the patient outcome (utilizing the NCCMERP scale), an assessment of any additional costs incurred, the category of medication(s) involved in the occurrence, and a section to record the follow-up actions taken. The follow-up section also utilizes a check box format and is completed for all reported occurrences and near misses.

The revised UWHC medication error occurrence policy and procedure incorporates many of the points already described. In addition, the policy also emphasizes that "the focus of the program is quality improvement, not punishment. UWHC assumes that practitioners are doing their very best and that occurrences are not the result of incompetence or misconduct." These statements reflect the organization's evolving nonpunitive systems approach to reporting errors. In the past, there have been instances in which medication errors had been used in the performance review of employees. However, using medication errors in employee performance reviews undermines efforts to encourage reporting. The task force realized that creating a nonpunitive organizational culture is an ongoing process that is not as simple as adding a statement to a policy. Unfortunately, all of the hard work invested to create the culture change can be undone by one instance in which an employee is disciplined or terminated for committing an error. Even one instance is enough to change employees' perceptions about the policy and suggests that the organization is not as committed to a nonpunitive culture as the policy implies.

Development of a database to facilitate the trending and analysis of medication occurrences is ongoing. UWHC participated as an alpha site with University HealthSystem Consortium to develop and test an anonymous online occurrence-reporting program. The goal of using the database to run queries and generate reports is to easily identify areas for potential system improvements and to communicate meaningful feedback to health care professionals. Preliminary experience with the system indicates that it makes reporting more convenient and efficient for staff, electronically prompts managers via an email message that follow-up is needed, prevents the need for data entry into a trending database, and automates the generation of useful trending reports. This program is now being utilized by 15 other academic medical centers who actively share data and learning about errors and error reduction.

Medication Ordering Performance Improvement Project

A multidisciplinary team was commissioned to develop and implement a standardized system for medication order initiation and implementation for all patient care areas at UWHC.* The original impetus for the project was to improve efficiency and minimize the time from when medication orders are written to the time that medication orders are entered into the pharmacy computer system.

The team approached the problem by flowcharting the existing ordering systems, in which orders could be stored, initiated, and implemented in one of three ways. Having three nonstandardized systems was one of over 30 problems identified with the UWHC medication ordering system. As the group began to explore strategies for improving the efficiency of the system, it quickly became clear that many of the system changes that would improve efficiency would also improve medication safety. For instance, standardizing systems, eliminating handoffs and unnecessary steps, improving training about the system, and improving interdisciplinary communication are all efficiency enhancers that are also best practices for improving medication safety.

One of the most valuable components of the new medication ordering system has been the requirement that all health care professionals attend a 30-minute training presentation and complete a competency examination on the new system before it is implemented on a given unit. The training describes the specifics of the new program and includes 10 minutes on safe order-writing practices (Table 40-6 lists some of the safe order-writing practices covered in the training program). The classes, especially the component of the class describing safe order-writing practices, have been very well received. A training video has also been developed to facilitate participation by health care professionals who primarily work on the third shift. The system was implemented housewide over a 12-month period. A Web-based medication ordering system training course and safe order-writing training course and accompanying competency test will be incorporated into new employee orientation for all clinical disciplines via the hospital's intranet.

High-Alert Medication Policy

High-alert drugs are broadly defined as those drugs that have a heightened potential for causing patient harm when misused. The UWHC P&T Committee has approved a policy and procedure identifying specific medications that will be considered high risk (e.g., neuromuscular blocking agents, dobutamine, dopamine, heparin, and insulin). The safety procedures incorporated into the high-alert policy and procedure

---

*Please note that the new medication ordering system is not a CPOE system. It is a manual system with improved processes for flagging and processing orders.

TABLE 40-6   Safe Order-Writing Practices

All orders are handwritten in ballpoint pen. Orders are never written in felt tip pen or
    pencil.
All the required elements of an order are included: patient name (or addressograph),
    generic name of medication, drug strength, dosage form, amount to be dispensed,
    complete directions for use, and signature/title. An optimal order would also include
    indication, duration of therapy (when applicable), and the prescriber's pager number.
Appropriate policies and procedures exist for verbal orders.
    Numbers should be communicated by pronouncing each numerical digit separately
        (e.g., "one three" instead of "thirteen").
    The health care professional (HCP) receiving the order should confirm the indication
        with the prescriber to verify that the medication makes sense for the patient.
    The HCP receiving the order should repeat the order back to the prescriber for
        verification.
    The HCP should record the order directly onto an order sheet in the patient's chart
        immediately.
    The HCP should time, date, and sign the orders per institution policy.
    The physician countersigns all verbal orders in a timely manner per institution policy.
    The use of verbal orders is minimized by limiting verbal orders to situations when the
        prescriber is with another patient and cannot leave (e.g., surgery) or when the pre-
        scriber is not in the hospital and direct physical assessment of the patient is not necessary.
    Unfamiliar drug names should be verified by spelling out the name.
    Verbal orders for chemotherapy are never accepted.
For institutions that utilize a duplicate or triplicate order form, orders must never be
    written on order forms when the duplicate and/or triplicate order form has already
    been pulled.
Indications are provided.
Leading zeros are used for any decimal expression of dosage less than 1 (e.g., 0.3 mg
    not .3 mg).
Medication orders are complete and contain no ambiguity. Examples of ambiguous
    orders include "continue previous medications," "take as directed," or "resume all
    pre-op medications."
Potentially dangerous abbreviations and medication abbreviations are prohibited.
Specify infusion rate when ordering IV solutions (TKO is not acceptable).
Specify the exact dosage strength rather than the dosage form unit when writing
    medication orders. (Do not use terms such as *one vial, one ampule, one tablet,* or
    one bottle. Many drugs have multiple strengths.)
Specify the salt when ordering electrolytes (e.g., calcium chloride vs. calcium gluconate).
Terminal zeros are never used when expressing doses (e.g., write 2 mg *not* 2.0 mg).
Weights, volumes, and units are expressed with the metric system. The apothecary
    system is not used.

are designed to minimize the potential for patient harm. These safety
procedures include the following:

- Double-checking with another licensed professional occurs when
  the medication is being prepared from a multidose vial.
- Nurses complete a competency examination for appropriate
  high-alert medication administration procedures. The competency
  program is incorporated into new nurse orientation.

- Nurses complete an annual competency examination for administering high-alert medications.
- At the end of each shift, on admission and transfer, the off-going and oncoming nurses check intravenous infusions of high-alert medications to ensure appropriateness (e.g., right medication, right patient, right infusion rate, and right medication concentration). The amount infused is also reset each shift.
- Infusion pumps are labeled with the name of the medication being infused by placing a label or piece of tape across the door of the pump.
- High-alert medications are specially labeled when they are dispensed from the pharmacy.
- The pockets of the automated dispensing cabinet that contain high-alert medications and the MAR for each high-alert medication are specially labeled to call attention to their high-alert status.

Chemotherapy medications are one group of high-alert medications. Within UWHC, a multidisciplinary chemotherapy quality improvement team standardized the chemotherapy administration process among all settings and populations (e.g., inpatients, outpatients, adults, pediatrics). This team also revised all UWHC chemotherapy policies, developed a new process for annual review of preprinted orders and order sets for investigational protocols, and developed a new chemotherapy order function that incorporated fields to help stimulate the provider to include all the required elements of a chemotherapy order.

Recheck Campaign

In response to several high-profile reports of health care professionals overrelying on automated dispensing systems, a campaign was designed to provide health care professionals with simple strategies to maximize medication administration accuracy and patient safety. Because of the multiple-check system required to ensure safe medication administration, the initiative is called the "Re-✓" campaign (Figure 40-2). The campaign was launched in the summer of 2001 as part of a hospital-wide medication safety awareness program. Laminated stop signs with the "Stop and Re-✓" phrase have been placed throughout the hospital in certain strategic areas (e.g., on the automated dispensing cabinet and other conspicuous locations in patient care areas). A Web-based training program is currently under development for all clinical disciplines to complete during new employee orientation via the hospital's intranet.

Check and re-check
Practice the "3-time check." First compare the medication label with the original order or patient kardex, second when preparing the medication for administration, and third just before giving the patient the medication. Keep drugs in their labeled packages until you are ready to administer them at the patient's bedside. Read all labels very carefully. Realize that two completely different medications may have very similar packages and even similar sounding names. Always check back with the physician or pharmacist if you cannot clearly read the order.

Engage the patient
Remind patients about the importance of proper identification before drug administration, and suggest that they actively participate by stating their name and holding out their name bracelet. Always verify patient identity via the patient's wristband (inpatient setting) and/or verbally by verifying the patient's name (ambulatory setting) before administering a medication. Additionally, one should verbally verify the drug name and purpose with the patient before administering the medication. Take the patient's concerns seriously. If a patient says a pill looks different than what he or she usually takes, double-check the medication identity and/or indication for that drug prior to administration. Additionally, perform all necessary monitoring before administering select medications (e.g., heart rate and blood pressure for beta blockers, blood sugar for antidiabetics, etc.).

Do not take automation for granted
Do not assume that the medication in the AcuDose™ cabinet is exactly the medication that has been ordered for the patient. Incorrect medications may be placed in the wrong location within the AcuDose™ cabinets or they may become dislodged from their correct storage pockets. Additionally, matrix drawer configurations allow for the wrong medication to be retrieved and dispensed if one is not careful. Except in emergency situations, first doses of medications stored in AcuDose™ cabinets should not be administered to patients until the pharmacist has reviewed and signed off on the medication order.

First do no harm
It is easy to be tempted to take shortcuts when one is busy. For instance, one may be tempted to not be as rigorous in performing the 3-check process. However, being busy is never an excuse for taking shortcuts that may jeopardize patient safety. Additionally, never administer a medication with which you are unfamiliar.

You are part of a team
Every person working in the medication use process provides an opportunity to assure that the appropriate medication is administered to the patient. Asking co-workers to verify one's work when handling complex or powerful medications, or whenever there is ambiguity, is a best practice. It also is best practice to perform this double check when drawing a dose from a multiple-dose vial. This means double-checking the order, the label on the medication, as well as the dose that is drawn up. Remember, too, that there are several double checks provided by pharmacists on the inpatient units. One of the checks provided by pharmacists is verification of all the medications that are sent to the floor. Because pharmacists provide this double check, medications should never be removed from the pharmacy delivery bins by anyone other than a pharmacist. While it is important to start drug therapy as soon as possible, often the clinical need for quick administration does not outweigh the safety of having the pharmacist review the order first.

Write all verbal orders immediately after they are received
Verbal orders are one of the most common causes of medication errors. Best practice is to completely eliminate such orders. However, this may not always be feasible. Strategies to make the verbal order process more safe include immediately repeating the order back to the prescriber to ensure that you clearly understood the order, as well as documenting the order in writing and having it reviewed by another health care professional prior to administering the first dose of medication. In the inpatient setting, if urgency necessitates administration of a scheduled medication before it is reviewed by a pharmacist, the nurse should check the medication label against the original order to verify accuracy prior to administration of the medication. Medications may only be administered pursuant to an order from an authorized prescriber.

Forgive yourself, report all errors, and make suggestions to improve the system
No one is perfect. Most health care professionals have had at least one experience with an error. If you are involved with an error, immediately report the facts to your supervisor and fill out a medication variance reporting form. It is only through insightful information from those who have made errors that we learn about their system-based causes and remedies.

FIGURE 40-2 A portion of the recheck campaign

Abbreviations

One of the recommendations made by the Institute of Medicine was to "standardize prescription writing and prescribing rules." Minimizing the use of problem-prone abbreviations is one way to standardize prescription writing. As part of a citywide patient safety collaborative (please see the section "Citywide and Statewide Approach," later in this chapter), UWHC and the other hospitals in Madison are targeting the elimination of error-prone abbreviations (Table 40-7). UWHC collected baseline data and found the use of problem-prone abbreviations to be very prevalent.

To educate health care professionals about problem-prone abbreviations, an interactive educational session was developed for all UWHC health care professionals to complete on the hospital intranet. The training program is now mandatory and is included in the new nurse orientation, new pharmacist training, and the orientation for new house staff. Incorporating a safe prescription-writing course into the medical school curriculum is also being explored. In addition to the training programs, educational pocket cards were distributed to all clinicians to highlight the problem-prone abbreviations. Pharmacists provide timely feedback on actual error-prone abbreviation use directly to prescribers via an audit form. A duplicate of these forms is maintained in the quality improvement office for trending purposes. Follow-up data on the use of problem-prone abbreviations are being collected at periodic intervals to assess the impact of the program after the educational sessions are complete.

Medication Safety Week

To help improve organizational awareness about medication safety, a dedicated UWHC Medication Safety Week is held. UWHC hosted several nationally renowned speakers who provided Grand Rounds lectures for all interested Madison-area health care professionals. Other presentations and posters were offered that week to launch new safety programs (e.g., the "Re-✓" campaign and the new reporting process) and to present existing UWHC initiatives that maximize medication safety.

UWHC Technology Model

The vision at the University of Wisconsin Hospital and Clinics is to develop an integrated information system that follows medication orders and medications from the physician's electronic prescription pad to the pharmacy and then to the patient. It is believed that such a system, when integrated with appropriate automation, will maximize patient

TABLE 40-7   Problem-Prone Abbreviations

Abbreviation	Intended Meaning	Error	Recommendation
U	Units	Misread as 0, 4, or cc (e.g., an order for 10 U of insulin can be misread as 100)	Write out "units."
BIW, TIW	Two times a week, three times a week	Misread as two or three times a day	Specifically write out "two" or "three times a week," or write out specific days medication is to be administered (e.g., q Mon, Wed, Sat).
µg	mcg	Misread as mg, or µ misread as 0 and units read as grams	Use "mcg" instead.
AU, AS, AD	Both ears, left ear, right ear	Misread as OU, OS, OD	Specifically write out intended route of administration.
OU, OS, OD	Both eyes, left eye, right eye	Misread as AU, AS, AD	Specifically write out intended route of administration.
cc	Cubic centimeters (milliliters)	Misread as "U" (units)	Use "mL" instead.
QD, QID, and QOD	Every day, four times daily, and every other day	Each can be mistaken for one of the others	Write "daily," q am or q pm; write "four times daily" or "4x daily"; write "every other day."
Trailing zero (e.g., 1.0 mg)	1 mg	Misread as 10 mg	*Do not use* trailing zeros after a decimal point.
No leading zero (e.g., .1 mg)	0.1 mg	Misread as 1 mg or 11 mg	Always use a zero before a decimal point.
X3d	For three days	Misread as for three doses	Write out "for 3 days."
Apothecary symbols (e.g., 10 gr)	10 grains	Misread as 10 grams	*Do not use* apothecary symbols.
IU	International units	Misread as intravenous	In most cases, eliminating the word "international" and fully writing "units" will suffice.

TABLE 40-7 (Continued)

Abbreviation	Intended Meaning	Error	Recommendation
Medication Abbreviations*			
Nitro	Nitroglycerin or nitroprusside	Misread as the unintended agent	
PIT	Pitocin (oxytocin) or Pitressin (vasopressin)	Misread as the unintended agent	Never abbreviate medication names. Always use the full generic name of drugs.
Levo	Levofloxacin, levothyroxine, levodopa, others	Misread as the unintended agent	
MSO_4	Morphine sulfate	Magnesium sulfate	
$MgSO_4$	Magnesium sulfate	Morphine sulfate	
ARA-A	Vidarabine	ARA-C (Cytarabine)	

*These are just a few of the many medication abbreviations that exist. Because of their error potential, *all* medication abbreviations should be avoided.

safety and the efficiency of the medication use process. Figure 40-3 illustrates the UW Hospital vision for the acute care medication use process, whereby a CPOE system is coupled with heavy use of automated dispensing systems that rely on the use of bar codes. Every drug product is bar coded at each phase of the medication use process, from the point of purchasing through documentation of medication administration to the patient.

The department currently uses a single integrated pharmacy computer system for processing all inpatient and ambulatory medication orders and prescriptions at all sites. To maximize patient safety and minimize costs, a hybrid approach to medication distribution has been implemented throughout the organization using centralized robotics. Decentralized automated dispensing cabinets are used to dispense controlled substances and as-needed medications. Matrix drawers are used only to store drugs with low potential for harm, abuse, or misuse. A handheld wireless point-of-care system for verifying and documenting medication administration is currently implemented on a 27-bed inpatient hematology/oncology unit. The system is used by all nurses on the unit and employs bar code technology to provide a three-way link between the patient, medication, and nurse to help ensure accuracy. All drugs as well as patients' and health care professionals' name badges are bar coded. This system receives real-time patient information and medication profiles from the pharmacy computer system.

Integration of Technology Throughout the UWHC Medication Use Process

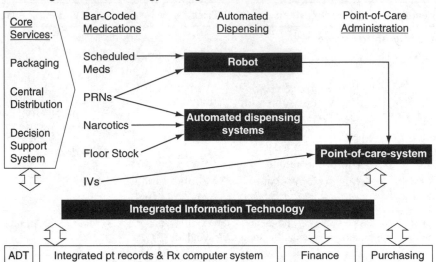

FIGURE 40-3 Vision of the UWHC medication use process

A multidisciplinary team is in the early stages of planning the use of an inpatient CPOE system. UWHC has developed extensive safety criteria for an ideal CPOE system to help guide the implementation of this technology from a patient safety perspective. An implementation team has recently been created, and a physician champion has been identified. The resources and technological infrastructure are being developed to meet a target CPOE implementation date of 2003. A centralized pharmacy data repository has been established that ties together data from all pharmacy, billing, and admit/discharge/transfer (ADT) information systems, as well as automated dispensing technologies. Responsibility for developing an integrated patient medical record rests with the hospital's information systems department, but the organization's goal is to provide caregivers rapid access to patient information and electronic documentation of care by integrating all hospital information systems, including pharmacy, laboratory, billing, ADT, and nursing.

Citywide and Statewide Approach

UWHC has taken an active role in several Madison-area and Wisconsin-wide medication and patient safety initiatives. The Madison Patient Safety Collaborative is a group of Madison-area hospitals that have been meeting since the middle of 2000 to help design strategies to minimize medical errors. The first strategies being worked on by the group include the elimination of error-prone abbreviations, initiatives to reduce falls, and the distribution of consistent consumer information on how to avoid medication errors throughout the community.

UWHC has also been involved at a state level to improve medication safety. In May 2000, representatives from a diverse group of Wisconsin organizations (e.g., health care purchasers, state professional societies, health care organizations, consumer groups) assembled to discuss ways to improve patient safety and reduce medical errors in the state of Wisconsin. The group endorsed the concept that patient safety must be a priority in every health care setting. A subgroup of that original panel developed 10 recommendations designed to improve medication safety, which were ultimately presented at the Patient Safety Forum in November 2000 (Table 40-8).

TABLE 40-8   Medication Safety Recommendations for Wisconsin Health Providers

1. Hospitals, extended care facilities, nursing homes, and other health care facilities need to provide 24-hour pharmacy coverage either on-site or on-call (by telephone access to a staff pharmacist or contracted through a community pharmacist).
2. Hospitals, community pharmacies, ambulatory clinics, and other health care facilities that dispense medication should utilize available computer software to provide clinical screening to maximize patient safety in the dispensing of all prescription medications.
3. Hospitals and other appropriate health care facilities should conduct an evaluation of an integrated computerized prescriber order entry (CPOE) system with clinical decision support for medications and other ordered services by January 1, 2002, with implementation by January 1, 2004.
4. Hospitals, extended care facilities, nursing homes, and other appropriate health care facilities responsible for the administration of medications to patients should implement an oral and inhalant unit-dose distribution system for all non-emergency medications administered within the facility by January 1, 2002.
5. Hospitals and ambulatory health care centers should utilize a pharmacy-based and pharmacist-managed process for the preparation of intravenous admixture solutions.
6. Pharmacies and physicians should include the generic name on the label of prescription medications dispensed to patients.
7. Hospitals and other appropriate health care facilities should investigate and evaluate the use of bar-coding systems for packing and administration of medications by January 1, 2002.
8. Hospitals and other appropriate health care facilities should prepare and maintain written policies and procedures for the use of select high-risk medications within the facility.
9. Prescribers should institute actions to eliminate the use of symbols and phrases that are commonly misinterpreted by pharmacists and other health care providers.
10. Prescribers and pharmacists should include the intended use on all prescription orders and prescription drug labels and packages for consumers.

Developed by the Wisconsin Patient Safety Institute

These 10 recommendations were the first steps that the group made toward improving patient safety in Wisconsin. The group has since been incorporated into a funded nonprofit entity called the Wisconsin Patient Safety Institute (WPSI). The mission of the WPSI is to enhance and promote patient safety by advocating the adoption of safe practices in health care organizations throughout Wisconsin. The Institute encourages research leading to improvements in patient safety, the improvement of public and professional awareness of patient safety issues, implementation of effective safety initiatives, and partnerships among health care providers, consumers, purchasers, educators, researchers, and leaders in government. Future efforts of the group will also involve developing practices to assist health care purchasers and patients; ensuring appropriate medication administration procedures, including the use of infusion devices; and expanding the scope of the group beyond medication errors to include fall prevention, blood transfusion errors, wrong-site surgeries, and other medical errors.

The authors of this chapter have been involved at a state level with the Pharmacy Society of Wisconsin (PSW). They have helped to develop the *PSW Medication Use Practice Standards to Maximize Patient Safety*. This resource has been distributed to health care professionals and other interested parties (e.g., health care purchasers, legislators, media, and patients) within the state of Wisconsin as well as nationally. It is available for free on the PSW website (www.pswi.org). The document is an effort by PSW to identify minimum practice standards and best demonstrated practices that maximize consumer safety and safe medication use; provide consumers with practical strategies to make safe use of their medications and protect themselves from errors inside and outside the hospital; and recommend criteria that health care purchasers should consider when selecting a health care organization, health system, or pharmacy to care for their members. This resource was later reviewed and revised by a multidisciplinary team. WPSI has subsequently published *Maximizing Patient Safety in the Medication Use Process: Practice Guidelines and Best Demonstrated Practices*.

General Considerations for Health Systems

Given the complexity and the multitude of steps in the medication use process, designing safe systems that prevent and eliminate medication errors can seem like a daunting task. However, it is critical that institutions begin to address the problem. For some organizations that are struggling to find their way, it may be best to pick the low-hanging fruit by choosing projects that are the most feasible. This strategy of considering both the impact and the feasibility of potential projects has worked well at UWHC. After all, it does not make sense for an organization to begin with a project that is not very feasible and has low potential for making a significant difference in improving medication use safety.

The following 10 items are key principles that organizations can use to help guide them as they strive to improve the safety of the medication use process.

1. Collaboration is essential. Various departments need to interact. Avoid the "silo approach" that historically has been prevalent in many hospitals and health care institutions. Improving medication safety should be a multidisciplinary process because the processes that create medication errors span many disciplines.
2. Secure buy-in from key leadership. Support and leadership from upper administration is essential to accomplishing meaningful change.
3. Learn from other organizations. In other words, interhospital collaboration is needed in addition to intrahospital collaboration.
4. Seek to have better reporting of actual *and* potential errors. System improvements can only be made if there is a good understanding of existing problems.
5. Embrace a nonpunitive culture for medication errors by adopting a systems approach. Punishing health care professionals for mistakes does little to fix the underlying problem and will hamper reporting efforts and identification of system problems. Medication errors often result from a complex interplay of multiple factors and are rarely caused by the carelessness or misconduct of single individuals.
6. Technology is helpful, but it is not a cure-all. Existing systems need to be sound before technology is implemented. Remedy process problems within the existing system before implementing technology. Do not place sole emphasis, resources, or reliance on automation at the expense of sacrificing other safety initiatives.
7. Understand the existing system (consider flowcharting it). Conduct prospective analyses to understand where errors can occur in the process. (This is a process known as failure mode effects analysis. More information has been published elsewhere.[28,29]) Seek to simplify the existing system by standardizing, reducing the number of steps and handoffs (e.g., transfer of orders from one person to another), using forcing functions and constraints, avoiding reliance on memory, using protocols and checklists, and improving access to information.
8. Include front-line personnel in efforts designed to improve medication safety. Health care professionals who are on the sharp end of active failures possess unique insight into the importance and feasibility of any initiative designed to improve the safe use of medications.

9. Leverage clinical pharmacists. Pharmacists are critical to the safety of the medication use process. Make sure that pharmacists are deployed in patient care areas and are able to provide clinical services and are not just relegated to a strictly dispensing role.

10. Perform a safety self-assessment. Organizations should compare their medication use system with the best practices advocated in the Institute of Medicine report and other literature on safe medication use processes (e.g., the Advisory Board's *Prescription for Change I* and the Medication Safety Self Assessment from the Institute of Safe Medication Practices).

Conclusion

Health care organizations should strive for a zero defect rate in the medication use process. Although many of the examples described in this chapter are from an academic medical center, many of the concepts and strategies can be applied across a variety of practice settings. It is hoped that this chapter has helped to further stimulate ideas for improving the safety of the medication use process. Creativity and ingenuity will be necessary to achieve a zero defect rate because as Albert Einstein once said, "We should not try to solve problems with the same ideas that created them in the first place."

Acknowledgments

The authors would like to acknowledge the following members of the UWHC Medication Safety Committee for their contributions to many of the projects described in this chapter:

Bonnie Albaugh, RN
Sarah Bland, RPh
Jan Brassington
Myra Enloe, RN
Robert Judd, MD
Jim Klauck, RPh
Sue Lehnherr, RN
Diana Renken, PharmD
Ian Robins, MD
Mark Schroeder, MD
Carl Selbo
Kathy Speck, RN
Deb Tinker, RN

References

1. Kohn, L. T., Corrigan, J. M., Donaldson, M. S., ed. *To err is human: building a safer health system.* Washington DC: National Academy Press, 1999.
2. Committee on Quality of Health Care in America. *Crossing the quality chasm: a new health system for the 21st century.* Washington DC: National Academy Press, 2001.
3. Business Roundtable. Press release: The Business Roundtable launches effort to help reduce medical errors through purchasing clout. Available at: http://www.brtable.org/press.cfm/464. Accessed November 16, 2000.
4. Joint Commission on Accreditation of Healthcare Organizations. Revisions to Joint Commission standards in support of patient safety and medical/health care error reduction. Available at: http://www.jcaho.org/standard/fr_ptsafety.html. Accessed January 21, 2001.
5. Kaiser Family Foundation and the Agency for Healthcare Research and Quality. *Americans as health care consumers: an update on the role of quality information.* Available at: http://www.ahrq.gov/qual/kffhigh00.htm. Accessed December 12, 2000.
6. National Coordinating Council for Medication Error Reporting and Prevention. http://www.nccmerp.org. Accessed August 1, 2000.
7. Bates, D. W., Boyle, D. L., Vander Vliet, M. B., Schneider, J., and Leape, L. Relationship between medication errors and adverse drug events. *J Gen Intern Med* 1995;10:199–205.
8. World Health Organization Technical Report, Series 425, 1969.
9. Brennan, T. A., Leape, L. L., Laird, N. M., Hebert, L., Localio, A. R., Lawthers, A. G., et al. Incidence of adverse events and negligence in hospitalized patients: results of the Harvard Medical Practice Study I. *N Engl J Med* 1991;324:370–6.
10. Leape, L. L., Brennan, T. A., Laird, N., Lawthers, A. G., Localio, A. R., Barnes, B. A., et al. The nature of adverse events in hospitalized patients: results of the Harvard Medical Practice Study II. *N Engl J Med* 1991;324:377–84.
11. Cullen, D. J., Bates, D. W., Small, S. D., Cooper, J. B., Nemeskal, A. R., and Leape, L. L. The incident reporting system does not detect adverse drug events: a problem for quality improvement. *Jt Comm J Qual Improv* 1995;10:541–8.
12. Classen, D. C., Pestotnik, S. L., Evans, R. S., and Burke, J. P. Computerized surveillance of adverse drug events in hospitalized patients. *JAMA* 1991;366:2847–51.
13. Bates, D. W., Cullen, D. J., Laird, N., Petersen, L. A., Small, S. D., Servi, D., et al. Incidence of adverse drug events and potential adverse drug events. *JAMA* 1995;274:29–34.
14. Jha, A. K., Kuperman, G. J., Teich, J. M., Leape, L., Shea, B., Rittenberg, E., et al. Identifying adverse drug events: development of a computer-based monitor and comparison with chart review and stimulated voluntary report. *J Am Med Informatics Assoc* 1998;5:305–14.
15. Johnson, J. A., and Bootman, J. L. Drug-related morbidity and mortality: a cost-of-illness model. *Arch Intern Med* 1995;155:1949–56.

16. Johnson, J. A., and Bootman, J. L. Drug-related morbidity and mortality and the economic impact of pharmaceutical care. *Am J Health-Syst Pharm* 1997;54:554–8.

17. Classen, D. C., Pestotnik, S. L., Evans, R. S., Lloyd, J. F., and Burke, J. P. Adverse drug events in hospitalized patients: excess length of stay, extra costs, and attributable mortality. *JAMA* 1997;277:301–6.

18. Bates, D. W., Spell, N., Cullen, D. J., Burdick, E., Laird, N., and Petersen, L. A. The costs of adverse drug events in hospitalized patients. *JAMA* 1997;277:307–11.

19. Reason, J. Human error: models and management. *BMJ* 2000;320:768–70.

20. Vincent, C., Stanhope, N., and Murphy, M. C. Reasons for not reporting adverse incidents: an empirical study. *J Eval Clin Prac* 1999;5:13–21.

21. Rough, S. The pharmacist-technology interface: current and future implications for the practice of pharmacy. In: Mueller, B., Bertch, K., Dunsworth, T., et al., eds. *The pharmacotherapy self-assessment program,* 4th ed. Kansas City, MO: ACCP, 2001.

22. Sutter, T. L., Wellman, G. S., Mott, D. A., Schommer, J. C., and Sherrin, T. P. Discrepancies with automated drug storage and distribution cabinets. *Am J Health-Syst Pharm* 1998;55:1924–6.

23. Barker, K. N. Ensuring safety in the use of automated medication dispensing systems. *Am J Health-Syst Pharm* 1995;52:2445–7.

24. Borel, J. M., and Rascati, K. L. Effect of an automated, nursing unit-based drug-dispensing device on medication errors. *Am J Health-Syst Pharm* 1995;52:1875–9.

25. Weaver, P. E., Perini, V. J., and Pierce, D. Random sampling process for quality assurance of the $R_x$obot dispensing system. *ASHP Midyear Clinical Meeting* 1998;33:289E.

26. Bates, D. W., Leape, L. L., Cullen, D. J., Laird, N., Petersen, L. A., Teich, J. M., et al. Effect of computerized physician order entry and a team intervention on prevention of serious medication errors. *JAMA* 1998;280:1311–6.

27. Bates, D. W., Teich, J. M., Lee, J., Seger, D., Kuperman, G. J., Ma'Luf, N., et al. The impact of computerized prescriber order entry on medication error prevention. *J Am Med Informatics Assoc* 1999;6:313–21.

28. Leape, L. L., Bates, D. W., Cullen, D. J., Cooper, J., Demonaco, H. J., Gallivan, T., et al. Systems analysis of adverse drug events. *JAMA* 1995;274:35–43.

29. Cohen, M. R., Senders, J., and Davis, N. M. Failure mode and effects analysis: a novel approach to avoiding dangerous medication errors and accidents. *Hosp Pharm* 1994;29:319–30.

30. American Society of Health-System Pharmacists. Suggested definitions and relationships among medication misadventures, medication errors, and adverse drug reactions. http://www.ashp.org/public/proad/mederror/draftdefin.html. Accessed August 31, 2000.

CHAPTER FORTY-ONE

DESIGNING A SAFER SYSTEM FOR MEDICATIONS: A CASE STUDY

Lynne S. Nemeth, MS, RN, Pamela F. Cipriano, PhD, FAAN and Paul W. Bush, PharmD, MBA

The 1999 Institute of Medicine report, *To Err Is Human*,[1] focused national attention on the need for prevention of medical errors. Although errors represent only one aspect of a quality agenda in health care and cannot be studied in isolation from other issues, it is important to note the significance of adverse drug events (ADEs). The unintended and harmful effects of medications represent one of the most serious, unremitting problems in health care. The annual direct cost of the impact of ADEs is estimated at over $4 billion. One in 300 patients experiencing an ADE will die as a result, and it remains the most frequent complication as well as the most frequent trigger to a malpractice suit.[2]

Redesign of Core Processes: Medical University of South Carolina Case Study

Large-scale system redesign of the inpatient drug distribution system at the Medical University of South Carolina (MUSC) was implemented in November 1997 to improve turnaround time and introduce the use of automation for streamlined routine operations. With this redesign process a "batch pharmacy" and "first-dose" pharmacy replaced the medical center's separate adult and pediatric pharmacies. The batch pharmacy primarily provided automated cart fill and routine or scheduled IV preparations to the inpatient units. The first-dose pharmacy provided all first doses and all stat and after-hours medication orders. Although the concept and configuration of such a system had been successfully implemented elsewhere, the result at MUSC was the unmasking of numerous individualized adaptations to a medication system that had evolved over many years, and an unstable medication management system. Over time, staff pharmacists had altered their practices to accommodate physician- or service-specific preferences, without written protocols or policies, and with only informal knowledge passed from one worker to another. The rapid implementation of the new system, and in particular the move away from a dedicated pediatric pharmacy, led a number of experienced staff to seek employment elsewhere, thus taking the institutional memory of these practices with them.

Approximately 6 months following the new system implementation, the number of reported potential errors began to increase, as well as complaints about delays in delivery of medications to inpatient units. A great deal of energy was placed into ensuring the accuracy of dose-checking templates, and assuring that standardized practices were being taught and used in everyday practice by the pharmacists and pharmacy technicians. At the same time, a new medication error reporting form was developed and implemented to enable better analysis and trending of medication errors. Although there was good appreciation of the potential improvements that could be gained from the implementation of a computerized physician order entry system, the reality of such a system remained too far off in the future to help resolve some of the problems being identified at that time.

MUSC's actions were consistent with many of the American Society of Health-System Pharmacists' (ASHP) top-priority actions for preventing adverse drug events in hospitals.[3] These included steps such as review and revision of policies set forth by the Pharmacy and Therapeutics Committee; remedial training; new supervision and evaluation of staff involved in medication ordering, preparation, dispensing, and administration; patient education; hiring of staff to fill vacancies; and reestablishment of standard medication administration times. A Medication Cycle Improvement Group (MCIG) had been appointed, composed of pharmacy and nursing staff, to assist in determining root causes of and solutions to the potential errors. Other activities to identify physical plant changes, hire new supervisory personnel, and augment services to the clinical areas were also under way.

In addition, every occurrence that was reported was thoroughly investigated by the coordinator of pharmacy systems, and corrective measures were implemented. Once again, these were primarily potential errors. The definition used for potential error is that of the ASHP, "a mistake in prescribing, dispensing, or planned medication administration that is detected and corrected through intervention (by another health care provider or patient) before actual medication administration."[4]

Despite these efforts, the numbers of potential errors remained unabated. A high degree of frustration and mistrust developed between the nursing and pharmacy staffs. Medical faculty also expressed dissatisfaction and concerns regarding medication safety as they became aware of the issues. Collaboration became more difficult, with each discipline responding somewhat defensively about their practices.

The organization's response to investigation of error-prone situations had matured to one of looking for systems issues; however, not all staff trusted the culture to be "safe" relative to reporting errors or problems with systems. Reporting of errors and potential errors was up, but there were divergent views on the rationale. Many believed it was because of the redesigned medication distribution system; others attributed it to the newly developed reporting form. The risk manager was intimately involved in working together with nursing and pharmacy leadership to come to consensus on reporting and categorization of data so the problems could be examined in more detail.

Organizational Learning: Next Steps

Because of the sustained trend of increased medication-related occurrences over an 18-month period after the implementation of the new pharmacy system, it was determined that an external review of systems would be valuable in evaluating the medication use process from a global perspective. The first such review was a brief visit in June 1999 by two professionals (nurse and pharmacist) who had led the Institute for Health Care Improvement's (IHI) collaborative on reducing adverse drug events. The visit was arranged collaboratively with the chair of the Department of Pharmacy Practice at the College of Pharmacy at MUSC. Because the college and medical center share some staff, there was a shared commitment to improving medication safety in the hospital. The review confirmed much of what was known and underscored the need for more in-depth work to systematize the medication use process. In order to do a comprehensive evaluation, a consultation was arranged with the Institute for Safe Medication Practices (ISMP), which is well known in the area of safety, quality improvement, and medication error prevention. The invitation of the ISMP was shared with MUSC's Quality Council, which endorsed the plan without question.

The leadership embraced the visit of ISMP professionals as a means to more quickly put in place a plan to address gaps at any point in the system and broaden the focus from primarily the dispensing pharmacist to the entire medication use process. The pharmacy and nursing staff had varying expectations of the outcome of the review and were aware that the interdisciplinary conflict was contributing to some of the ongoing difficulty. The ISMP consultants arranged for a systematic assessment of our practices in most of the known high-risk areas during a 3-day visit to MUSC in August 1999.

Following thorough fact finding, touring, and interviewing, the ISMP consultants presented a comprehensive list of recommendations to strengthen weaknesses in the medication use process and improve medication safety beyond its current level. In addition, initial priority items were excerpted for quick action. The major areas with priority recommendations were patient information; drug information; communication of drug information; drug storage, stock, standardization, and distribution; environment, workflow, and staffing patterns; staff competency and education; and quality processes and risk management. Throughout the engagement, all pharmacy, nursing, and medical staff were invited to participate. Likewise, the summary findings were presented with significant detail to a large interdisciplinary group on the last day of the consultation visit.

A new director of pharmacy services joined the organization soon after receipt of the ISMP's report. Within 1 month of receiving the report, and on the second day of the new director's employment, administration of a 10-fold dose of a medication, prepared in error, resulted in the death of a patient. The unthinkable had happened. The situation we were working diligently to prevent had slipped from our grip. The stopgaps had failed. Even though the computerized pharmacist order entry for this drug was set for dose-range checking, the dose was not recalculated and was not caught by the nurse, and two doses of the medication were given within 8 hours.

As expected, this sentinel event had a devastating effect on all involved and became a catalyst for immediate action. The Medication Safety Task Force, a group designed on paper but not yet formed, was brought together to prioritize the plan for improvement that would ensure safer medication systems throughout the hospital, paying special attention to the root causes of the fatal medication error.

Prioritizing Actions for Improvement

The Medication Safety Task Force (MSTF) met within 2 weeks of the sentinel event. The task force was co-chaired by the director of pharmacy services and the chief operating officer/nurse executive. Task force members represented adult and pediatric nurses and pharmacists, as well as pharmacy and nursing performance improvement leaders. Medical staff input was obtained through the medical director and a representative of the house staff. The charge to the task force was to expeditiously evaluate the two consultant reports and the current medication system and to implement process improvements.

Copies of the consultant reports were distributed at the first meeting, and members were asked to review the documents and identify those recommendations, which, if implemented, would have the greatest potential to reduce medication errors. Recommendations were prioritized and three teams were formed. Team 1 focused on issues related to human resources (people) and the role of the pharmacist, team 2 focused on the distribution plan and distribution locations (places), and team 3 focused on development of systems to support a safer practice setting for medication administration (performance). There was a lot to be done, and the need for an effective organizational structure for change was recognized. Table 41-1 outlines the goals and priorities assigned to each team.

TABLE 41-1　Goals of the Medication Safety Task Force

Team 1: People

- Attract and retain qualified pharmacy staff
- Improve orientation and training
- Revise and improve staffing patterns and increase second-shift pharmacist staffing
- Decentralize the pharmacists and enhance coordination with clinical specialists
- Increase direct communication between pharmacists and prescribers for order clarification
- Reduce nonformulary medication usage

Team 2: Places

- Revise the drug distribution plan
- Reestablish the adult inpatient pharmacy and pediatric satellite
- Deliver medications directly to patient medication bins

Team 3: Performance

- Implement a double check at order entry for high-alert drugs
- Assure all dispensed doses are checked before delivery
- Increase the consistency of the nurse check of medication administration records and reporting of discrepancies to pharmacists
- Require an independent calculation of high-alert drug dosages by pharmacists and nurses
- Require an independent double check for high-alert medication administration at the bedside
- Reduce the use of fax machines to improve order clarity (use only for stat orders)
- Evaluate pharmacy computer system allergy and dose-check alert utilization

---

Focus on the Pharmacy

Teams met on a regular basis to develop detailed plans to accomplish assigned objectives. Team 1 was composed of the pharmacy director, newly recruited pharmacy managers, and staff. They focused on recruitment, retention, orientation, and training. The team surveyed the situation and learned that an unusually high turnover of both pharmacists and technicians had resulted in a shortage of well-trained staff. Because of the shortage, pharmacists who were decentralized to patient care units had been centralized to the first-dose pharmacy. Prior experience at MUSC had shown that pharmacists preferred the decentralized pharmacist practice model because it improved communication with the medical and nursing staff and facilitated order clarification and problem resolution. It was also apparent that the complexity of drug therapy in the academic medical center necessitated an adequate complement of very well-trained pharmacists.

Components of the plan included defining and projecting a clear vision for pharmacy practice, improving the work environment, and proposing implementation of an improved compensation program. The plan was developed, reviewed with pharmacy leadership and staff, and implemented within 60 days. Within 6 months the complement of pharmacists had improved enough to decentralize the pharmacist staff on the first shift. This markedly improved service, decreased medication occurrences, and enhanced staff morale. A pharmacy technician training course was developed to improve the number of well-trained pharmacy technicians employed at MUSC. The course was offered to hospital and retail pharmacy technicians in the Charleston area three times during the year. This program was designed to assist technicians improve their knowledge and skills and prepare for the national Pharmacy Certified Technician Exam.

The second team focused on evaluation of the pharmacy dispensing locations. This group was asked to make a determination whether the first-dose pharmacy and batch pharmacy implemented in 1998 should be discontinued in lieu of the prior plan of a pharmacy dedicated to adults located in the main hospital with a pediatric satellite located in the Children's Hospital. Pharmacy staff had suggested that the prior configuration was more appropriate because of the acuity of neonatal and pediatric care provided at MUSC. Nursing and medical staff confirmed this. Team members evaluated the adequacy of the physical space, need for renovation, and equipment requirements and developed a timeline for reorganizing services to the prior configuration.

The pharmacy teams also expanded the number of dose-checking templates available in the pharmacy computer system and required that the pharmacists document the reason for overriding a dose-check alert.

As an additional safety precaution, a list of high-alert medications was developed that required a second pharmacist to double-check the order as entered in the pharmacy computer system. For these medications, the second pharmacist would review the order and computer entry for appropriateness and document his or her involvement in the computer system. These additional safety measures were implemented shortly after the sentinel event and monitored on an ongoing basis with feedback to the managers and staff until pharmacists were consistently compliant.

Focus on Nursing

The policies and performance improvement team followed up on some specific recommendations that were made in the ISMP report. There were issues identified that were not sufficiently addressed within the medical centers' policies for administration of medications. Although there were numerous policies pertaining to the administration of medications and intravenous infusions within the clinical services policy manual, they were scattered throughout the manual and not organized as an effective resource to staff. Development of a comprehensive medication and intravenous infusion administration policy for staff became an overarching goal. It was obvious that establishing new policies would take a coordinated educational effort, followed by an intensive program of monitoring and feedback to the staff implementing changes. The changes in the medication administration system were made in response to a sentinel event that should not recur, and a significant effort was needed to manage this more successfully.

The comprehensive policy that was developed consolidated and clarified the many complex issues inherent in the process of medication administration. It listed qualifications of personnel administering medications and clarified handling of investigational drugs and non-FDA-approved uses of medications. The policy specified how orders for medications were to be handled, including written orders, verbal orders, pediatric dosing requirements, and transcription and transmission of orders to the pharmacy, as well as routine, stat, and missing dose communication. The policy stated how medications were to be administered and documented, and identified a new class of medications known as "high alert medications."[5] A new section on the use of herbal supplements was added to clarify to staff how to address the use of complementary approaches that have become popular within the past few years. The policy reinforced the standard medication administration times that were adopted, and identified a consistent approach to documentation of medication that had been administered or held.

Specific procedures for handling the medication administration record (MAR) discrepancy resolution process and reconciling differences between pharmacy and nursing records were outlined. The policy addressed the handling of narcotics and controlled substances, occurrences and adverse drug reactions, medication distribution and storage on the units, intravenous infusions (both lipids and nonlipids), intravenous sites, use of filters, handling of chemotherapy, intravenous push medications, intravenous lock insertion and maintenance, patient education and discharge instructions, and medication reference materials to be used within this medical center.

The policy included appendices that serve as reference materials to staff. These references include adult and pediatric IV push guidelines that outline where within the medical center specified medications could be given via the IV push route, a list of high-alert medications requiring an independent double check, herb–drug interactions, standard medication administration times, expiration dating for opened medications, continuous infusion administration guidelines, pediatric dosing guidelines, and filtration methods and medications.

Safety enhancements to the policy focused on a few key areas: the development of an independent double check for high-alert medications, consistent documentation process on the MAR, and implementation of a reliable system for communicating discrepancies on the MAR to the pharmacy. Within these three areas, specific monitoring processes were implemented to assist in measuring progress toward the goal of a safer system. Progress in these areas continues after 6 months of implementation of the changes, and there is greater awareness of how to better engage staff to achieve full compliance of the safeguards that have been designed.

The high-alert medications independent double check has been the most challenging new aspect of the medication safety plan, yet one that has the potential to yield the most positive effects. The first step toward developing this process related to learning the root cause involved in the sentinel event. Because of the devastating consequences of an inadvertent calculation error, there needed to be a forcing function to ensure safe practice. An independent double check was defined in our policies directly from the ISMP report to MUSC as "verification of the drug, dose concentration, dose rate settings, patient and any line connections, by two licensed practitioners authorized to administer medications."[6] A big challenge arose when the policy drafts were presented to the nursing management team, because there was good recognition of how difficult this policy's adoption would be for current nursing practice. The list of high-alert medications that had been developed jointly by the ISMP and IHI was used as the policy was crafted and a list developed, and modifications were made accordingly for our medical

What is an Independent Double Check?

Definition: An independent double check is verification of the drug, dose concentration, dose rate settings, patient and any line connections, by two licensed practitioners authorized to administer medications.

- Any intravenous controlled substance
- PCA and epidural medications (see PCA and epidural policies)
- Titrated IV infusions: see (drip cards)
- Chemotherapy (see Chemotherapy policies)
- Insulin IV & SC
- Bolus doses of electrolytes
- Thrombolytics (except for catheter clearance)
- Heparin and Lepirudin Drips
- Digoxin (IV in peds and adults and PO in peds)
- Neuromuscular blockers
- Irrigation solutions
- Continuous venovenous hemodiafiltration

Step 1. Nurse member prepares high-alert medication according to orders, insuring that dose, time, method of administration, patient identity all are accurate.

Step 2. All IV equipment is prepared and readied at bedside. When setup is completed and before administration process begins, nurse solicits another licensed professional to check all preparations that have been made to administer the prescribed medication.

Step 3. Second staff member reads MAR or orders, verifies drug, dose, administration method and time, and identity of patient.

Step 4. Medication should be administered ONLY after BOTH professionals verify all aspects of medication, dose, timing, method, and patient identity, and distal line connections for IV tubing are secure.

Step 5. Both Licensed Professionals sign MAR.

FIGURE 41-1 Poster for nurse education regarding the independent double-check process for medications

center. Nursing education included the dissemination of a poster (Figure 41-1) outlining the key steps in the independent double-check process, so all staff could be clear about the intent of this change.

Focus on Physicians

Concurrent to the work being done in the initial stages of the MSTF, the Children's Hospital Medical Executive Committee identified that reducing variation in medication order-writing practices had the potential to significantly improve patient safety and medication process efficiency. Guidelines were developed and approved for order writing that specified the required elements of a medication order, outlined the proper

Number	Essential Element	Specifications for PEDIATRICS (≤ 17 years of age (except for obstetrics))
	APPROVED ABBREVIATIONS must be used on ALL orders. Drug names must be spelled out EXCEPT for chemical symbols (e.g., CaCl)	
1	**DATE AND TIME** must be written on ALL orders.	
2	**WEIGHT** (in kg or gms)	**PEDIATRICS:** Need on **ALL pediatric patients.** **ADULTS:** Need **ONLY** for those drugs which are dosed based on patient weight (e.g., chemotherapy)
3	**DRUG NAME:** (generic, formulary) No abbreviations except for approved chemical symbols; specification of appropriate salts (e.g., potassium *chloride* or potassium *phosphate*) must be written on ALL orders.	
4	**DOSE**	
	a) Pediatric patients weighing LESS THAN 40 kg*	**PEDIATRICS:** a) Dose/kg/interval for all patients < 40 kg (e.g., mg/kg/dose q4h or mg/kg/day ÷ q4h). b) For medications given in combination, the dose/kg/interval should be given for one of the medications in the combination. NOTE: m^2 dosing is acceptable if either the body surface area in m^2 or the height in cm and the wt in kg are provided as part of the order.
	b) Oral electrolytes (e.g., ferrous sulfate, calcium carbonate)	**PEDIATRICS:** Elemental preparations (e.g., iron, zinc) should be ordered based on the desired dose of the element (not the salt).
	c) Proper use of Zeros: For ALL orders. —**Always** use a zero before the decimal point for a dose that is <1 (e.g., 0.15 mg). —**Never** use a zero after the decimal point for a whole number dose (e.g., 1 mg *not* 1.0 mg).	
5	**DOSAGE UNITS** in metric units (except in cases where a standard unit, e.g., insulin, is used. Spell out "unit")	
	a) **Metric units** only (except for standard "unit"-based dosing, e.g., insulins)	
	b) **Always specify a dose**, not the package unit (e.g., no "Amps" in ordering sodium bicarbonate)	
	c) If specify a volume as a dose, **specify the concentration** as well (e.g., mg/mL)	
	d) **Phosphate salts** ALWAYS ordered in **mMol** (representing the phosphate component).	
6	**DILUENT:** Specify if requiring diluents OTHER THAN the standards (D5W or 0.9% NaCl).	
7	**ROUTE OF ADMINISTRATION**	
8	**FREQUENCY or INTERVAL:** All orders for PRN (as needed) medications MUST include an interval and an indication.	
9	**LEGIBLE SIGNATURE** (including credentials) and **PAGER NUMBER**	
	IF APPLICABLE, include the following items: SITE OF ADMINISTRATION, TIME(s) OF ADMINISTRATION, DURATION of the order (# doses or # of hours), VOLUME (e.g., intrathecals)	

*EXCEPTIONS to the DOSE PER KG PER INTERVAL rule:

1) Topical creams or ointments, powders, eye and ear drops, inhalers or nebulizers, IV fluids, tapered doses (e.g., steroids after the first order).

2) All medications must be rewritten postoperatively. Medications that the patient was receiving in-house preoperatively and for which the dose, route, or interval is NOT CHANGED may be resumed as follows: Resume ampicillin 500 mg IV q6h (no dose per weight designations needed).

3) *Orders for conscious sedation/pain medications parameters of dose by weight apply with a titrating dose written before beginning the procedure. Documentation of the exact amount subsequently given is documented on the MAR.*

4) Medications added to parenteral nutrition solutions (e.g., ranitidine, famotidine, L-carnitine) will require all the elements above. Additives other than medications (e.g., zinc, L-cysteine, vitamin K, multivitamins) do not require these elements as the appropriate dosage is listed on the back of the form.

FIGURE 41-2 Required elements for inpatient medication orders

use of zeros, and limited the use of abbreviations. The guidelines specified that the medication order must include the dosage expressed per patient weight (dosage/kg/interval) for patients weighing less than 40 kilograms. Rapid implementation and full compliance with the policy were of the highest priority. An extensive educational process was developed and implemented for all staff, and a measurement process was implemented to evaluate compliance with this new policy. Additional work by the Children's Hospital Medical Executive Committee focused on developing a short list of approved abbreviations for medication orders. Nursing and pharmacy staff members collaborate to ensure that medication orders are written correctly and have been providing feedback to physicians. Efforts are currently under way to implement a hospital-wide policy that outlines the essential elements of a medication order (Figure 41-2).

Conclusions

Integrating physician, nursing, and pharmacy practice related to medications is a large, systemwide process. The ongoing challenge is achieving a culture of safety in which medication errors are fully reported and can be analyzed for system causes that can be addressed. The medical center has a 24-hour hotline for the reporting of adverse drug reactions, and a specific medication error reporting form. Because the data flow either to the pharmacy or to the risk management department, it is important to develop ways to integrate these data consistently.

Implementing improvements in medication systems requires a strong organizational commitment to expanding information system capacity and moving toward direct physician order entry. The reality is that the organization is limited in taking the most effective actions. The development of a MAR discrepancy database that nurses and pharmacists will use to communicate discrepancies, rather than relying on fax and paper transmission from the nursing station to the pharmacist, is the most current project under way. This database will track information that is not consistent between both disciplines and identify reasons for discrepancies so the causes of this inaccurate data can be better understood.

At the present time, views related to understanding medication errors are expanding and are moving toward a fuller definition of *medication error*, such as the definition published by the National Coordinating Council for Medication Error Reporting and Prevention:

> A medication error is any preventable event that may cause or lead to inappropriate medication use or patient harm while the medication is in the control of the health care professional, patient or consumer. Such events may be related to professional practice, health care

products, procedures and systems, including prescribing; order communication; product labeling, packaging, and nomenclature; compounding; dispensing; distribution; administration; education; monitoring; and use.[7]

Much work lies ahead. Learning and enhancements will make safer systems for medication processes within this medical center. Through a coordinated effort between nurses, pharmacists, and physicians and the increased awareness of the public on the issue of medication safety, a difference can be made in the future.

References

1. Kohn, L. T., Corrigan, J. M., and Donaldson, M. S. *To Err Is Human: Building a Safer Health System.* Washington, DC: Institute of Medicine, National Academy Press, 1999, 2000.

2. Rashke, R. "Collateral Damage: Adverse Drug Events." *Cerner Report* 2000;1(January):12–14.

3. American Society of Hospital Pharmacists. "ASHP Guidelines on Preventing Medication Errors in Hospitals." *Am J Hosp Pharm* 1993;50:305–314.

4. American Society of Health-System Pharmacists. "Top-Priority Actions for Preventing Adverse Drug Events in Hospitals." *Am J Health-Syst Pharm* 1996;53:747–751.

5. Cohen, M. R., and Kilo, C. M. "High-Alert Medications: Safeguarding Against Errors," in Cohen M. R., ed. *Medication Errors.* Washington, DC: American Pharmaceutical Association, 1999.

6. Institute for Safe Medication Practices report presented to Medical University of South Carolina. Huntingdon Valley, PA: ISMP, October 1999.

7. National Coordinating Council for Medication Error Reporting and Prevention 1998–1999. http://www.nccmerp.org/aboutmederrors.htm, accessed 9 May 2000.

CHAPTER FORTY-TWO

ONE ORGANIZATION'S ADVOCACY EFFORT FOR ERROR PREVENTION: THE INSTITUTE FOR SAFE MEDICATION PRACTICES

Michael R. Cohen, RPh, MS, DSc and
Judy L. Smetzer, RN, BSN

Prescription drugs are a blessing when they reduce suffering, promote healing, and improve health. Yet the number of drug products available in the United States has grown drastically and the technology used for drug delivery has become much more complex, thereby increasing not only the benefits involved but also the risks. Concurrently, older and sicker patients are increasing among the population and require ever more potent and complex drug therapy. Thus, the combinations in which drugs are prescribed and used over the counter have increased dramatically, as have the ways we use them in health systems, helping to make the risk of medication errors a frightening reality. The results are too often tragic and costly in both human and economic terms, for patients, health professionals, and health care organizations alike.

National Efforts to Address the Problem

U.S. Collaborative Efforts

Recently, the escalating situation regarding medication errors has spurred sharp growth in the number and variety of prevention activities and products throughout the nation. For instance, error reporting to the United States Pharmacopoeia's (USP) Medication Errors Reporting Program (MERP), operated in cooperation with the nonprofit Institute for Safe Medication Practices (ISMP) and for which ISMP provides independent analysis and comment, has increased dramatically in recent years. As a voluntary reporting program, MERP is a front-line defense against errors. Through MERP, health care professionals can complete a preaddressed mailer, enter a report on the USP (www.usp.org) or ISMP (www.ismp.org) website, or dial a toll-free number (800-23-ERROR) to report with complete confidentiality (or anonymity if desired) any medication error. Examples of errors and near errors reported through MERP include administering the wrong drug, strength, or dose; confusion over look-alike and sound-alike drugs; incorrect routes of administration; miscalculations; misuse of medical devices; and errors in prescribing and transcription.

To expand the benefit of such collected information, ISMP and USP, as FDA MedWatch partners, automatically share all MERP information and prevention ideas with the U.S. Food and Drug Administration (FDA). In return, FDA forwards MedWatch reports that are coded as user errors. Indeed, collection and analysis of error information, from MERP and many other sources around the globe, are the foundation upon which ISMP's educational efforts are based. If errors go unreported, no one benefits. Conversely, if everyone in the health care picture, including patients, learns more about the nature and causes of medication errors, there is a much stronger possibility of preventing them.

In recent years, many national groups have begun working to make error prevention a multidisciplinary effort and to develop and disseminate further error prevention information. ISMP has actively collaborated with these groups, including the American Medical Association (AMA), American Nurses Association (ANA), American Pharmaceutical Association (APhA), American Society of Health-System Pharmacists (ASHP), American Society of Consultant Pharmacists (ASCP), and the Joint Commission on Accreditation of Healthcare Organizations (JCAHO). Because of such joint efforts with health care groups and the FDA, health professionals today can learn much more about drug errors and solutions than at any time in the past. Collaborative efforts have led to many successes in improving medication safety recently. For instance, a reduction in accidents related to potassium chloride concentrate for injection is rooted in an ISMP campaign begun in the 1980s that focused on changing dangerous drug-storage situations and encouraged regulatory authorities, standards organizations, and manufacturers to use special labeling, including black caps, closures, and warning statements, to differentiate it from other pharmaceuticals.

International Commonality and Collaboration

ISMP is also working actively with health care professionals in nations around the globe to help them develop their own national medication error reporting programs and to further ISMP's ultimate vision of an international medication error reporting program. Toward those ends, ISMP is working with health care professionals, governmental representatives, and others in Australia, Canada, Hong Kong, Ireland, Israel, Spain, Sweden, and the United Kingdom. ISMP has active affiliates in Canada (www.ismp-canada.org), Spain (www.usal.es/ismp/principa.htm), and much of the remainder of Europe (www.efahp.com).

This work benefits medication error prevention in the United States and around the world because over the past 25 years since ISMP was founded, it has been demonstrated that many medication errors are common to more than one country. Thus, international sharing of error information and greater coordination of trade names around the world could have a significant impact on medication safety everywhere. This was most obvious when ISMP participated in a medication error symposium at the International Pharmaceutical Federation's international pharmacy forum in Jerusalem, Israel, in September 1996. Participants worldwide spoke of the types of errors occurring in their countries. The lack of a formal mechanism for information sharing was obvious and distressing.

Losec (omeprazole) and Lasix (furosemide) provide an excellent example. In the United States, many mixups and at least one death have been attributed to look-alike/sound-alike confusion in the similarity of names and conflicting dosing schedules between these two. To address this dangerous situation, ISMP conducted a concerted campaign to resolve the confusing name situation, at least in the United States. As a result, the trade name for omeprazole in the United States was changed from Losec to Prilosec. In this dramatic success story here at home, no medication errors between the two products have been reported since the name change. Yet despite this lifesaving success at home, confusion between the two drugs continues in other nations because the trade name Losec was not changed elsewhere. Unfortunately, deaths and injuries continue to be reported outside the United States.

An important new body of information and information sharing about errors, nationally and internationally, is growing. As a result, a variety of new services are increasingly available to health professionals, regulatory agencies, and pharmaceutical manufacturers who are serious about preventing errors. But information and services alone are not enough to prevent errors. Health professionals must learn about information and services, but they must also follow up by incorporating the expanding body of information and services into carefully designed systems that can help prevent errors.

ISMP: Addressing the Problem with 25 Years' Experience

ISMP, an entirely nonprofit organization, was formally established in 1994, but its program is among the earliest and most aggressive in the battle to prevent medication errors. ISMP itself is rooted in the ongoing work of its founder, Michael R. Cohen, RPh, MS, DSc, who began publishing error prevention information through an ongoing feature in the journal *Hospital Pharmacy* in 1975.

From its office in Huntingdon Valley, Pennsylvania, in the United States, ISMP has become well known throughout the nation and around the globe as an educational resource for drug use system errors. Working with practitioners, regulatory agencies, health care institutions, professional organizations, and the pharmaceutical industry, ISMP provides timely and accurate medication safety information, including safety alerts, throughout the United States. It also encourages safe use of medications by working toward improvements in drug distribution, naming, packaging, labeling, and delivery system design.

As a nonprofit entity, ISMP takes no advertising and is funded entirely through publishing efforts, educational programs, on-site safety reviews, donations, and grants. Although pharmaceutical companies have solicited ISMP to provide expertise in product packaging, labeling, and nomenclature issues, the organization typically receives no payment for its proactive work with various companies to address product problems related to reported errors. However, product testing and other confidential, proprietary work is undertaken through a separate, wholly owned for-profit division of ISMP (www.med-errs.com) known as Med-ERRS (Medical Error Recognition and Revision Strategies), which is separately staffed.

Communication and Education

To help practitioners learn and benefit from its storehouse of information and analysis about medication error prevention, ISMP widely publishes case studies, continuing columns, articles, a biweekly fax alert system called *ISMP Medication Safety Alert!* and emergency warnings that reach millions of health professionals around the world in pharmacy, nursing, and medicine. The Institute also uses electronic communication channels, regularly reaching thousands of health care professionals and others with vital information via its own website (www.ismp.org). In both electronic locations, ISMP posts safety information from *Medication Safety Alert!* as well as prevention strategies and basic information about the organization.

Another way ISMP gets information to the people who need it most is through ongoing educational efforts. Widely known for its expertise in medication error prevention, the organization plans and produces its own educational seminars on medication errors for a variety of health professional audiences. Similarly, ISMP personnel are regular guest speakers at hospitals and at state, national, and international meetings. Insurance companies often ask ISMP to speak on the subject as well. The organization welcomes all opportunities to spread the word about medication error prevention.

Self-Assessment Tools

The ISMP Medication Safety Self Assessment is an example of a useful ISMP-designed tool that was made available for use by all U.S. acute care hospitals. This comprehensive tool identifies 184 characteristics of a safe medication delivery system for hospitals and allows hospital teams to collaboratively rate and score themselves for each characteristic. It helps them to evaluate the safety of medication practices at their facility, identify opportunities for improvement, and compare their experience with the aggregate experience of demographically similar hospitals. Most of the characteristics included in the self-assessment represent system improvements that ISMP has recommended in response to medication errors reported to the USP–ISMP Medication Errors Reporting Program or problems identified during ISMP on-site hospital consultations. Several major health care organizations and group purchasing organizations endorsed the project, and numerous state hospital associations and purchasers worked closely with ISMP to enhance the value of this project for their constituents. The tool allows hospitals to receive weighted, numerical scores for each of the self-assessment characteristics, with data confidentially submitted to ISMP.

The benefits of collecting aggregate data on a national level for both health care providers and consumers are immense. First, the self-assessment tool provides hospitals with important baseline information that can be tracked over time. Such data are useful to managers who seek to identify areas of weakness, in comparison to the national experience, so that leadership support can be sought for improvements in critical areas. The data also provide ISMP and others with the ability to identify common system weaknesses and offer practical system enhancements with the highest leverage for overall error reduction activities. ISMP and others are able to focus education efforts and design useful programs to help hospitals implement strategies that can positively affect patient safety. The project is also designed to help regain consumer confidence in health care. Recent surveys and consumer advocates have expressed the belief that U.S. hospitals are "hiding" information from the public. This project is designed to help reduce this perception, as the public will be able to see (in the aggregate sense) that hospitals are being proactive in identifying safety issues. Follow-up data can be used to track progress over time. The project was funded under a grant from the Commonwealth Fund. More recently, a similar project for the nation's community pharmacies was funded under a grant from the American Pharmaceutical Association Foundation. That project is a cooperative effort of the APhA and the National Association of Chain Drug Stores (NACDS).

Preparing the Next Generation for Prevention

ISMP's collaboration, communication, and education efforts are effectively reaching today's health care practitioners. However, it is equally important to prepare tomorrow's practitioners. Thus, ISMP focuses a great deal of time and energy on its annual Safe Medication Management Fellowship Program.

The fellowship is designed to train post-PharmD pharmacists in adverse drug event prevention methods and administration. Working out of the ISMP office, ISMP fellows each year make site visits to the USP, the FDA, hospitals, professional organizations, and pharmaceutical companies. In addition, they network extensively throughout the nation's pharmaceutical, health care, and legislative and regulatory communities. Because of ISMP's international effort to prevent adverse drug events, the fellowship also includes broad exposure to program development outside the United States.

Fellows spend time on specific medication error-related projects and initiatives. Communication about preventable adverse drug reactions is a primary responsibility. As such, fellows contribute to journal publications, including the monthly columns in *Hospital Pharmacy, Pharmacy Today* (APhA), *Physician Assistant, Nurse Practitioner,* and *Oncology Times*.

The program is a 1-year fellowship. It includes vacation and health care benefits and extensive travel. Applicants must be graduates or expect to graduate from an accredited PharmD program by the start date of the fellowship. Strong consideration is given to applicants with practice or residency experience or both.

Graduates of this fellowship program have and will go on to positions in health systems, the pharmaceutical industry, health care professional associations, and governmental and regulatory agencies.

Understanding Medication Errors

Prevention requires a thorough understanding of the nature of medication errors. Until recently, many studies defined errors differently, making it difficult to use the information effectively. Fortunately, the

National Coordinating Council for Medication Error Reporting and Prevention (NCCMERP), a group composed of 19 health care organizations, reached a consensus in defining a medication error as

> Any preventable event that may cause or lead to inappropriate medication use or patient harm, while the medication is in the control of the health care professional, patient, or consumer. Such events may be related to professional practice, health care products, procedures and systems including: prescribing; order communication; product labeling, packaging and nomenclature; compounding; dispensing; distribution; administration; education; monitoring; and use.[1]

System Solutions for System Problems

Learning from Other Industries

Perhaps the most regrettable aspect of medication errors is that most of them truly are preventable, but not typically by a single individual. To undertake medication error prevention, it is important to acknowledge and plan for the fact that human beings make errors. However, assessment of blame is not a productive approach to solving the problem; it is better to search for more complex factors that may have led to the error.

Within the health care community, ISMP has pioneered the use of a technique called failure mode and effects analysis (FMEA).[2] FMEA has long been used by the space, airline, and auto industries to develop error prevention strategies.

Using FMEA strategy, pharmacists must examine medication therapy as a *process* to identify where within that process people and systems are most likely to fail. Then, possible effects of such failures can be analyzed before they happen. Using this kind of analysis, appropriate safeguards can be developed and put in place to prevent and catch errors before they can reach a patient or cause harm. FMEA is so effective at preventing errors that the FDA is currently considering making it a requirement in the pharmaceutical industry's review process for all naming, packaging, and labeling decisions.

Hospital Consulting

To help pharmacists begin this process, ISMP uses FMEA strategies to conduct medication safety reviews at community, teaching, and pediatric hospitals; cancer centers; outpatient clinics; and other ambulatory care sites. The analysis reviews the key elements of the medication system that are outlined in Table 42-1. Cooperating with pharmacy departments, risk managers, and quality assurance programs, ISMP capitalizes on its knowledge base to carefully analyze medication delivery processes. A complete, written report of safety recommendations

TABLE 42-1   Frequent Problems with Medication Systems Noted During ISMP Hospital Evaluations

ISMP is often asked to assist health care organizations by performing a systems analysis of the medication administration process. So often we see evidence of enthusiastic and creative efforts that effectively prevent many errors. Nevertheless, we also see weaknesses in medication systems that are common to many institutions. Some examples of the most frequently occurring problems and our recommendations for improvement are listed here.

Patient Information

Critical patient information (diagnoses, lab values, allergies, etc.) is often unavailable to pharmacy and nursing staff prior to dispensing or administering drugs for new admissions. More than 25% of prescribing errors alone are directly associated with inadequate patient information, most notably renal and hepatic function, allergies, and pregnancy status.* When drugs are dispensed or administered without adequate patient information, a critical system of double checks is bypassed. Thus, errors in prescribing may not be detected. Health care professionals must identify effective ways to obtain and communicate pertinent clinical information and never rely on admission office staff or unit clerks to supply this data. Do not dispense any drugs unless specific clinical information is included in order screening.

Drug Information

Pharmacists often are not readily available face-to-face on patient care units. Because errors occur most often during the prescribing and administration stages, accessible drug information must always be readily available and close at hand for all staff who prescribe and administer drugs. In addition to computerized drug information, an effective way to accomplish this is by moving the pharmacist, an expert on drugs, into patient care areas. In this way, pharmacists can establish close working relationships with patients and staff, follow the patient's clinical course, and regularly consult with staff about drug selection, dosing, and administration. A growing body of research shows that when such moves are made, patient outcomes are improved and both errors and drug costs are significantly reduced while improving patient outcomes. Begin by having pharmacy personnel make daily rounds on units or enter orders directly at terminals on patient care units. Then, progress to a stronger clinical presence in high-priority areas, such as critical care, pediatrics, oncology units, operating rooms, and the emergency department.

Communication of Drug Information

Policies for handling medication use conflicts between practitioners are often ineffective or absent. Flawed communication, often precipitated by intimidation, contributes to about 10% of the serious errors that occur during drug administration.* In fact, ISMP receives many reports of lethal errors in which orders were questioned but not changed. Institutions should develop a process that clearly specifies the steps practitioners should take to resolve drug therapy conflicts. All staff should feel the process is workable and effective. Establish maximum doses for high-alert drugs so that orders that exceed these doses automatically trigger the policy.

Labeling, Packaging, and Drug Nomenclature

Although most drugs are dispensed through a unit-dose system, drug administration procedures do not ensure that medications remain labeled until they reach the patient's bedside. Often, staff members prepare drugs at a central location by removing

TABLE 42-1   (Continued)

pharmacy or manufacturer drug packaging and labeling and placing the open medications in cups for administration. Thus, the chance for errors, including most often the administration of a drug to the wrong patient, is greatly increased. Institutions should therefore require labeling throughout the drug use process, up to the actual point of administration. Focus groups of pertinent staff members should be used to explore and remedy any obstacles to following these policies, or they will not become practice.

Drug Storage, Stocking, and Standardization

Lack of safety procedures for use of automated dispensing technology often contributes to problems. Inadequate check systems may result in drug storage errors. Further, product safety may not be considered when determining which items will be stocked and their location. Also, the usual pharmacist–nurse check systems are often bypassed, especially with first doses. Thus, specific procedures are needed to ensure that items are properly stored. Problematic and dangerous drugs should be dispensed only from the pharmacy. In addition, medications should not be routinely available for administration to patients without appropriate order screening by pharmacists.

Drug Device Acquisition, Use, and Monitoring

There frequently is no independent check system for verifying dose and rate settings on patient-controlled analgesia (PCA) pumps. The second most frequent cause of serious errors during drug administration is the misuse of infusion pumps and other parenteral device systems. The settings on PCA pumps often default to a standard concentration, requiring the operator to change the setting if a nonstandard concentration is used. Even with expertise in the proper use of drug delivery devices, serious dosing errors are often associated with improper flow rate settings. PCA pump settings should be set by one individual, independently checked by another before administration, and then documented.

Environmental Stressors

Staff transcribing orders are consistently exposed to noise, interruptions, and nonstop unit activity. The process of transcribing orders is particularly vulnerable to distractions in the environment, because unit secretaries or pharmacy personnel are frequently answering telephones and other requests for information while performing order transcription or computer order entry. A study confirms that simple slips due to distractions are responsible for almost three quarters of all such errors.[†] Minimize these distractions creatively (overlapping coverage during peak times, dividing job responsibilities, encouraging fax or email instead of calls to pharmacy, etc.) to help staff remain focused on order transcription.

Competency and Staff Education

Many practitioners have limited awareness of well-known error-prone situations reported within their own organization or published in professional literature. Without this information, staff are likely to make similar errors; with this information, staff can assist the organization in identifying ways to prevent similar errors from occurring or recurring. Upon hire (or joining the medical staff) and regularly thereafter, provide staff with updated information about errors that have occurred both within the organization as well as those occurring elsewhere. Develop a test that includes questions addressing problem-prone areas such as morphine and insulin dosing or cross-allergenic medications such as Toradol and aspirin. Require a score of 100% (any incorrect answers should be discussed with staff until it is assured that they understand the correct answer).

(Continued)

TABLE 42-1   (Continued)

Patient Education

Pharmacy staff are not routinely involved in direct patient education. Medication use is a multidisciplinary process that includes patient education. Each discipline adds a specific focus to this education process, reinforcing the information necessary for patients to prevent an error while hospitalized and to safely self-administer medications at home. Begin by implementing automatic educational consultations with pharmacists when patients are receiving certain classes of medications or being discharged on more than five medications. Increased clinical presence of pharmacists on patient care units will allow the necessary time to provide this valuable service.

Quality Processes and Risk Management

Many organizations attempt to compare their error rates with other organizations for the perceived purpose of benchmarking. These rates are usually based solely on spontaneous voluntary reporting programs that are influenced by how the organization handles employees who make and report errors. Thus, there is much variability between the methods used to detect and report errors in different organizations. Consequently, there is no accurate "national error rate," and arbitrarily determining an "acceptable error rate" leads to complacency, with a dramatic slowdown in prevention efforts. In addition, the term *benchmarking* is erroneously used when organizations attempt to compare error rates. In reality, benchmarking is a process of identifying the best practices through a consistent and accurate method of measuring outcomes while determining the practices that lead to these outcomes. Comparing error rates without an understanding of the processes and systems behind the numbers serves no useful purpose. Spend time more constructively by focusing error prevention efforts on the use of high-alert drugs that have the capacity to seriously harm patients if misused.

*T. S. Lesar et al., "Factors Related to Errors in Medication Prescribing," *JAMA* 277 (1997): 312–317.

†L. L. Leape et al., "Systems Analysis of Adverse Drug Events," *JAMA* 274 (1995):35–43.

that can become a blueprint for change in an institution results from this careful review. ISMP also provides consultations to guide hospitals in the selection of computerized prescriber order entry systems and automated dispensing equipment. Its partner in this activity, ECRI, is an internationally respected nonprofit medical device safety organization that for many years has provided assistance to organizations wishing to enhance the safety of medical devices and hospital safety systems.

In short, the premise of FMEA is that no matter how careful people are, errors will still occur in any human process, including medication therapy or piloting an airplane full of passengers. The commonality is, there is no room for error in either of these activities. That's why it is so important to create systems that have a series of fail-safe and redundant checks at every stage of the process to effectively balance the scale against human error.

Teamwork Is Fundamental

Medication errors most often occur because of breakdowns in systems for handling and processing drugs—from prescribing and ordering to distribution and administration. Such systems cross all professional and responsibility boundaries within the health care environment. Therefore, in hospitals and other health systems, collaboration among pharmacists, nurses, physicians, risk managers, hospital executives, patients, and others is a fundamental key in making medication error prevention systems work effectively.

Yet hospitals, like individuals, are unique. Each has a variety of circumstances with which to contend that may be more or less particular to that institution. Thus, no single book chapter could hope to cover the many strategies the variety of health care professionals at many kinds of institutions could or should employ to prevent errors. However, four general recommendations introduce the steps managers must begin taking to get a handle on the potential for medication errors in their institutions and put in place prevention programs that can effectively reduce risk and manage errors. They are as follows:

1. Development and implementation of a formal review process
2. Broad, interdisciplinary representation and participation in the review process and all institutional error prevention activities
3. Careful exploration and thorough understanding of all internal medication error incidents and the factors that led to them
4. Thorough exploration and understanding of medication errors reported outside the institution, such as those reported in ISMP publications, other anecdotal reports, newspaper accounts, and more

Where to Focus First

Among medication error-related deaths reported in journal articles, newsletters, and educational materials published by ISMP, a few drugs seem to be most frequently associated with serious medication errors. They include the following:

Anticoagulants
Cancer chemotherapy
Parenteral narcotics
Insulin
Lidocaine for cardiac use
Magnesium sulfate
Neuromuscular blockers
Potassium chloride injection concentrate
Thrombolytic agents
Vasoactive substances

Managers must, at the very least, assure themselves that these substances are being handled as safely as possible. Remove or relocate certain drugs to eliminate confusion. Limit access through special storage. Use reminders and warnings as effective tools to increase awareness.

Focus on Oncology

ISMP has worked recently with oncology specialists to develop specific guidelines and safety recommendations on the handling of oncology products, including verification of doses, establishment of chemotherapy dose limits, and standardization of prescribing vocabulary. These safety guidelines have been published in the *American Journal of Health-System Pharmacy*.[3]

ISMP has also sponsored programs at national meetings to help practitioners become more aware of problems in cancer chemotherapy. Among the successful results of such efforts are the following:

- Inclusion of a maximum-dose statement on cisplatin vial caps and seals to increase recognition of dose limits
- Special hazard warnings and label practices for vincristine injection, to help health professionals prevent repeated problems with accidental intrathecal injection
- Elimination of lidocaine 1 and 2 g concentrate injection packaged in prefilled syringes that were meant for dilution in IV bags but were given in error by direct IV push

What's Already Working

On the positive side, the best overall error prevention efforts seem to have in common excellent systems in six general areas of activity.

- *Communication of drug orders:* A trustworthy system to communicate drug orders is essential. It avoids verbal orders that can be misheard or mistranscribed, and handwritten orders that can be misread. Ambiguous orders are not tolerated, and abbreviations are avoided because of the potential for misunderstanding. Computerized systems are an especially valuable tool.
- *Patient information:* Systems that provide adequate and readily available information about patients to physicians, pharmacists, and nurses at the time of prescribing, order screening, dispensing, and drug administration are also imperative.
- *Patient education:* A sound system to educate patients about their medication therapy is a powerful force in preventing medication errors. Informed patients can be a final valuable protection,

especially if patients have been taught to challenge anything that seems amiss about their treatment, outcomes, or drug therapy.

- *Naming, packaging, labeling:* A good system must be in place to deal with labeling, packaging, and drug nomenclature issues. Unit-dose packaging is a front-line protection against medication errors.
- *Drug preparation and distribution:* A system built on checks and balances at every stage can minimize the potential for error in drug preparation and compounding as well as distribution.
- *Quality assurance:* Procedures that key on the quality and integrity of every aspect of patient care and that encourage free exchange of thoughts and information about patient safety are invaluable in guarding against errors.

Pharmacy's Role in Error Prevention

Although pharmacists have long focused on the distribution aspects of their profession, today's pharmacists must turn to a broader and more clinical role to prevent errors effectively. In general, the pharmacist, as the expert in medication therapy, must assume a leadership role in the following:

- Serving as a multidisciplinary information source for hospital staffers and others regarding drugs and drug therapy
- Identifying and addressing potential problems with the prescription, dispensation, and administration of drugs, wherever and however they occur in the drug delivery process
- Providing multidisciplinary and patient-centered education that can help everyone on the patient care team, including the patient, be more effective in preventing errors

The documented results when pharmacists assume such aggressive roles are nothing short of cost saving and lifesaving.

References

1. New York State Department of Health, Bureau of Hospital Services. Hospital Incident Reporting Program annual reports (Albany, NY: 1989–93).
2. Cohen, M. R. et al., "Failure Mode and Effects Analysis: A Novel Approach to Avoiding Dangerous Medication Errors and Accidents," *Hosp Pharm* 29 (1994):319–24, 326–28, 330.
3. Cohen, M. R. et al., "Preventing Medication Errors in Cancer Chemotherapy," *Am J Health-Syst Pharm* 53 (1996):737–46.
4. Scott, L. "Medication Managers Cut Drug Costs," *Modern Healthcare* (1996).

CHAPTER FORTY-THREE

THE ROLE OF THE LABORATORY IN PATIENT SAFETY

Lee H. Hilborne, MD, MPH

Recent interest in patient safety and error reduction has helped focus the spotlight on the clinical laboratory as a resource to reduce errors in medicine. To a great extent, "patient safety" represents a new way to examine the performance improvement and risk reduction efforts of risk management; however, the principles, processes, and expertise are nearly the same.

In the late 1990s, health care quality experts focused their attention on outcomes assessment and improvement. In the outcomes process, it is important to measure those things that matter most to patients— quality of life, satisfaction with care, improvement in functional status, reduced mortality and morbidity from disease, and the ability to perform activities of daily living (ADLs). There is no question that laboratory medicine profoundly affects these important patient expectations for care, but it has been difficult for laboratorians to define "laboratory outcomes" in the same context as clinical disciplines have done.

Almost all laboratory outcomes, by their very nature, are proximate outcomes because they represent inputs to subsequent processes of care. Although there are a few situations in which the laboratory product or result is the ultimate outcome (e.g., a negative Papanicolaou smear or the satisfaction of helping others through donating blood or blood products), the fact that the laboratory output is an input to subsequent care makes it challenging for laboratory medicine to take a seat at the same outcomes table with practitioners from disciplines with more direct patient care responsibilities.

The current focus on patient safety provides a genuine opportunity for the laboratory medicine professional to excel. Laboratory medicine professionals include pathologists, medical technologists, cytotechnologists, bioanalysts, and other professionals at the doctorate and other levels with expertise in anatomic and clinical pathology. Anatomic pathology conventionally includes the disciplines of surgical pathology (the review and assessment of tissues removed from patients), cytopathology (the examination of cells through exfoliative cytology or fine needle aspiration cytology), and autopsy pathology (including forensics). Clinical pathology encompasses clinical chemistry, laboratory hematology, medical microbiology, and transfusion medicine. Newer techniques that include molecular diagnostics and genetic studies bridge the gap between anatomic and clinical pathology. Because of the laboratory's central role in the care of almost all patients, in both inpatient and ambulatory care settings, the opportunity for laboratorians to evaluate and improve patient safety is great.

A discussion of the laboratory's roles and responsibilities related to patient safety naturally centers around two distinct spheres. First are those contributions laboratorians can make to improve their own processes to reduce errors. Second are the activities that laboratories and laboratorians participate in to help prevent colleagues from other disciplines from making or perpetuating errors to the point of actual patient harm.

Intralaboratory Activities to Reduce Medical Errors

The laboratory has long been committed to analysis of its performance using process-based controls. In 1922 the American Society of Clinical Pathologists was formed to, among other objectives, "establish uniform standards for the performance of various laboratory examinations" and to encourage closer cooperation between pathologists and clinical personnel.[1] One of the early initiatives of the newly formed organization was the development of a proficiency testing program under the guidance of Dr. William Sunderman, Jr.[2] The voluntary program distributed unknown samples to participating laboratories and provided feedback to the laboratories on their performance relative to their peers. Laboratories with performance outside statistical control limits would then evaluate their operations and initiate corrective action.

In late 1946, the College of American Pathologists (CAP) evolved from the American Society of Clinical Pathologists, and the College assumed responsibility for the proficiency testing program. Proficiency testing evolved from its early stages as a voluntary program to a requirement for almost all laboratories. Specific requirements for participation are currently delineated by the Clinical Laboratory Improvement Amendments of 1988 and subsequent regulations. Laboratory proficiency testing has reduced variation in testing results, ensuring patients that when they receive services from any licensed or accredited laboratory, they will receive an accurate and precise laboratory result.

Proficiency testing programs measure laboratory processes and provide the laboratory director and staff with an external benchmark for their performance. In addition to external benchmarking, laboratories are required to internally benchmark their performance at regular intervals (commonly once a day or once per shift). Ensuring process integrity through proficiency testing and quality control reduces the risk of error, increasing the likelihood of a desirable patient outcome.

To assess whether laboratories had the appropriate structure to produce reliable and valid results, the CAP established a peer-based laboratory inspection and accreditation program in 1962. Laboratories accredited by CAP, the Joint Commission on the Accreditation of Healthcare Organizations (JCAHO), or other accrediting bodies must follow specific standards of laboratory practice in terms of physical plant, staffing, and operations. Although the identification of error and the conduct of thorough and credible root cause analyses have been implicit in laboratory and organizational accreditation standards from the beginning, explicit standards are now being developed to ensure that all laboratories are familiar with and conduct an appropriate investigation in response to any adverse events or mishaps.

In the mid-1980s the Centers for Disease Control and Prevention (CDC) promulgated the concept of the "total testing process." The process begins with the clinician's conceptualization of the need for a laboratory test and concludes when the result is received, interpreted, and acted upon. Because error is inherent throughout the total testing process, a laboratory result that is unexpected and inconsistent with the patient's clinical presentation should be repeated before a clinical intervention is undertaken.

Beyond the standard structure and process measures that the laboratory has in place to reduce internal errors, each facility establishes additional safeguards to reduce the likelihood of adverse consequences inherent in any complex, error-prone laboratory operation. Some of the common safeguards that laboratories employ are detailed in the following sections.

Delta Checks

Most laboratory information systems now have the capacity to check patient results and compare them with previous analyses on the same analytes.[3] The laboratory selects common analytes that, under normal conditions, are expected to be stable over short periods of time (e.g., creatinine). Then, when subsequent results on the same patient deviate significantly from previous results (the significance level is determined by the laboratory director), the technologist responsible for results reporting is prompted to reassess the specimen integrity, specimen identification, and instrument operations. In addition to providing a quality check on the intralaboratory processes, a patient identification error may also be the source of nonagreement. A delta check error, if it persists with retesting, should prompt the laboratory technologist to review the findings with the clinical laboratory and the requesting physician to ensure that the difference is appropriate given the patient's clinical condition.

Specimen Correlation

The laboratory often receives different types of specimens from the same patient, either at the same time or over a period of time. This provides the opportunity to correlate the findings from previous specimens with the ones most recently received. This practice is most common among the anatomic pathology disciplines. For example, a patient who receives a Papanicolaou smear that shows evidence of cancer will likely undergo a subsequent surgical procedure to treat the disease. This subsequent procedure will result, most often, in a surgical pathology specimen. The surgical pathologist will review the previous cytology findings as the new specimen is reviewed. Discrepancies are noted and explanations sought as part of what most laboratories consider their quality assessment procedures. When cervical biopsy findings were correlated with previous cytology specimens, researchers observed a sensitivity of 89.4%, specificity of 64.8%, and predictive value of a positive cytology of 88.9%.[4] Most of the discrepancies were attributed to cytology sampling error; however, the study points out the limitations of diagnostic tests and highlights the importance of persistent investigation when the clinical circumstances so dictate.

Although correlation activities may be part of a quality assessment or performance improvement program, they serve to identify problems in the diagnostic process so that systematic errors or individual practitioner limitations may be identified. Furthermore, these correlation activities provide an additional layer of patient safety by rechecking previous diagnoses and prompting a more detailed search for the abnormality found on the original specimen if it appears initially to be absent on the subsequent resection. Lastly, if specimens are inadvertently mixed up, as rarely occurs in operating suites, clinics, and pathology laboratories, a check on the specific histology of the lesion will help to highlight the error.

Rescreening of Cytology Specimens

Routine cervicovaginal cytology specimens are screened by cytotechnologists, and any abnormal findings are referred to the cytopathologist for confirmation and diagnosis. A sample of the routine specimens considered to be within normal limits by the cytotechnologist must be rescreened to ensure that diagnoses rendered are correct. This process is designed to catch systematic errors in diagnosis and to highlight situations in which an individual may need additional training to assure competence. Any abnormality that appears to have been over- or underdiagnosed during the specimen correlation process should also be rescreened and sources of error identified. Studies show that when cytology specimens that were initially interpreted as benign are rescreened to assess error following a subsequent low- to intermediate-grade squamous intraepithelial lesion being found, 3.5% were reclassified as carcinoma, 5.9% as squamous cells of uncertain significance (i.e., equivocal) and 0.5% as unsatisfactory.[5] When patients presenting with high-grade intraepithelial lesions or frank carcinoma had their recent (within 5 years) negative Papanicolaou smears rescreened, false-negative rates varied from 10.1% to 19.7%, depending on the definition applied.[6]

Screening cytology slides for malignancy is a methodical process that requires intense concentration, and with that concentration comes the fatigue that can result in error. The federal government has therefore limited the number of slides a technologist screens to 100 per day. New computerized techniques to prescreen or rescreen cytology slides offer the hope of increased sensitivity by reducing the time professional cytotechnologists must screen benign fields for the occasional malignancy.[7]

Language Standardization for Textual Reports

Although many clinical laboratory results are quantitative (e.g., serum sodium level, hematocrit, bacterial colony count) or semiquantitative (e.g., urine dipstick results, selected serologies), other reports from both anatomic and clinical laboratory disciplines are interpretive and produce a textual report. Different language may be used, depending on the pathologist, to describe similar situations. Although synonyms may be familiar to pathologists and other laboratory personnel, they may cause confusion for the report recipient. Because the ultimate goal of a report is to convey information succinctly and accurately to the requesting practitioner, all laboratory personnel who produce textual reports should use the same terms to describe the same findings. To improve standardization of high-volume, high-risk situations, the laboratory community, in conjunction with clinical colleagues, has standardized the recommended language for key clinical situations. The most familiar examples are the Bethesda classification for routine cytology[8] and the standardized classifications for hematologic malignancies.[9,10]

To help laboratory personnel standardize textual diagnoses, some facilities have adopted standardized reports that employ coded comments for common situations. Although some have resisted using a more structured report format because, they argue, this represents a form of "cookbook medicine," most now agree that patients are best served by consistent reporting.[11] As with all areas of medicine, laboratory medicine leaders must work, and are working, to create the culture change necessary within the profession to accept standardization.

Education and Training of Testing Personnel

Health care has undergone tremendous changes over the last few decades, and the laboratory has not been insulated from those changes. One area of considerable change is the extent of automation in the clinical laboratory. Tests that were previously performed individually using manual or at most semiautomated technologies are now performed on complex, multichannel automated instruments capable of performing many different analyses on hundreds of specimens simultaneously.

With increased automation, laboratories have altered their staffing plans and expertise levels, reducing the number of licensed or certified medical technologists. Studies by the Centers for Disease Control and Prevention and by the state of California provide some insight into differences in laboratory performance based on laboratory and testing personnel characteristics.[12,13] These studies evaluated proficiency testing performance for regular licensed clinical laboratories (e.g., hospital and reference laboratories) and compared them with physicians' office laboratories. Successful performance was 99% for regular laboratories and 96% for physicians' office laboratories. The California study went one step further and determined the type of testing personnel involved in the physicians' office laboratories. Those that used trained laboratory personnel either as consultants or employees in some phase of the testing process had a 98% success rate, compared with 96% for those physicians' laboratories not using trained laboratory personnel. The authors suggested that, irrespective of the testing venue, those performing tests must have sufficient education, training, and expertise to produce the highest-quality product. This conclusion, of course, is no different from studies performed for various clinical procedures that demonstrate that high-volume facilities have the best clinical outcomes.

Notwithstanding the conclusions regarding performance on proficiency testing as a surrogate for laboratory quality, many have argued that the advantages of rapid turnaround time and the ability of the clinician to immediately interpret the findings in the context of the patient's condition outweigh the benefit of a more analytically precise test. There is no question that timely results are advantageous; the studies only demonstrate the importance of education and training for production of a quality product, irrespective of the testing venue.

The Role of the Laboratory and Laboratorian as Members of the Health Care Team

In addition to the roles laboratory professionals have in ensuring the integrity of their laboratory operations in maintaining a safe environment, there are very important roles the laboratory and laboratorian must assume as part of an integrated health care team. These responsibilities fall into two major areas: assurance of the integrity of the total testing process, and serving as a resource to detect potential concerns in the process of care.

With respect to the integrity of the total testing process, one can divide the total testing process into three phases: the preanalytic, analytic, and postanalytic phases. The preanalytic phase involves the steps a specimen goes through before reaching the laboratory. The analytic phase refers to the intralaboratory processes that were discussed earlier. The postanalytic phase refers to the steps following the time when the result leaves the laboratory.

With respect to ensuring patient safety, all three phases of care are important. Whereas the laboratory alone can control the processes related to the analytic phase, the laboratory and laboratorian must work together as a member of the health care team to assure an error-free process in the pre- and postanalytic phases.

The preanalytic phase begins when the patient's care provider conceives of the need for a particular test. Providers may be unfamiliar with the spectrum of laboratory offerings or may not be precise in the way that they specify their requests. For example, a clinician may be looking to exclude a diagnosis of multiple sclerosis[14] and will submit a cerebrospinal fluid (CSF) specimen for analysis. Detection of oligoclonal bands requires a specific high-sensitivity electrophoretic process. A request for routine electrophoresis on the CSF specimen would not provide the desired information, yet it may consume the entire specimen collected, precluding the laboratory from performing the desired procedure without subjecting the patient to a second invasive collection of additional spinal fluid. Providing the laboratory with the differential diagnosis can clue the technologist and pathologist to question the appropriateness of a laboratory request if the clinical circumstances seem inconsistent with the tests ordered. Similarly, knowing the differential diagnosis on a surgical pathology specimen guides the surgical pathologist to select the appropriate diagnostic tests (e.g., molecular diagnostics, special stains, electron microscopy) to avoid missing the desired result. With respect to the impact of missing information on surgical pathology specimens, the College of American Pathologists found that 0.73% of specimens required additional information for diagnosis; of these, there was a substantial change in the diagnosis in 6% of cases.[15]

After the need for a test is determined, a specimen must be collected properly. In terms of errors in medicine related to laboratory practice, this is a very frequent source of error. In a busy hospital or clinic practice, specimens may be collected without attention to collection and labeling protocols. Although this inattention to protocol rarely results in actual patient harm, either because the identification process reaches the correct conclusion or because an error occurs but does not result in patient harm, the potential for error is real.

In hospital inpatient settings and outpatient clinics, the importance of proper patient identification cannot be overstressed. Many errors related to laboratory and other services result because patients are not properly identified despite the fact that procedures exist to ensure proper patient identification. In no area is the risk for patient harm greater than in the blood bank. Many blood banks will refuse to give anything but type O blood without first performing a type check. This means that the transfusion medicine service will search its records for a record of the patient's blood type. If one does not exist, the blood bank may request a second draw to ensure that the specimen collected and analyzed actually reflects the patient's blood type. Although the risk of patient misidentification is probably no greater with a transfusion medicine sample than with other samples, the consequences of transfusing the wrong blood type can be devastating. Therefore, the type-check process creates an additional safeguard in the transfusion process that does not exist for other laboratory medicine services.

Recognizing the importance of patient identification in the inpatient setting, many health care facilities have instituted programs to ensure that patients have identification bands and that they are correct. The laboratory, provided it runs the phlebotomy service, may be directly involved in the assessment of compliance. Phlebotomists, following patient identification protocols, can identify and trend information regarding either missing or incorrect identification bands. These data can be used to identify sources of error and provide guidance regarding where resources must be invested to reduce the identification errors. A 1993 study found patient wristband errors in 2.2% of patients.[16] The most frequent problem was a wristband that was missing

(50%). The wrong patient identified on the wristband accounted for 0.5% of the errors. Although participation in a successful patient identification program will reduce the number of laboratory errors caused by misidentification, it will also have much broader implications for reducing clinical errors related to misidentification that may be less frequent but more serious (e.g., wrong surgery, wrong x-ray, wrong medication).

An increasing number of health care systems and laboratories are capitalizing on the power of laboratory information systems and clinical information systems to reduce specimen misidentification errors. Specifically, many are beginning to employ bar coding as a means to positively identify patients and specimens. Newer systems can integrate specimen and patient data to confirm that the specimen label is properly linked with the patient information and that the proper transfusion medicine specimen is selected for the patient. By scanning the specimen and patient identification bar codes at the patient bedside, an alert can sound when a mismatch is detected. Although this process reduces the number of errors related to human fallibility, it still does not guarantee a mistake-free environment. In most clinical settings, procedures and protocols already exist that, if followed, would nearly eliminate all errors. Bar code checking is only an additional protocol. If individuals become complacent and neglect to follow the bar code protocol as well, errors will persist.

Bar code technology is now routinely used within laboratories to identify specimens with information system–interfaced instruments. This reduces transcription and data entry errors by the instrument operator. Many facilities are now moving to direct physician order entry. Fully integrated systems will print a bar-coded label at the conclusion of the test selection process, precluding transcription errors by clerical staff either at the patient care location or in the laboratory. In addition to reducing transcription-type errors, integrated systems are just now beginning to evaluate laboratory requests in the context of other clinical information within the system. For example, systems can detect whether similar requests have been made for the same analytes at an interval that would generally be inappropriate for repeat testing. Treatment protocols and practice guidelines may be established and invoked when patients meeting clinical criteria are encountered. For some conditions that heavily depend on laboratory results to guide care (e.g., malignancy requiring chemotherapy, autoimmune disease, infection), information systems can ensure that certain laboratory parameters are checked before subsequent phases of care begin (e.g., blood counts are checked before a dose of chemotherapy is administered).

On the postanalytic side of laboratory testing, there are again a number of steps where the laboratory and laboratorian must work closely with the clinical team to ensure that patient safety is maximized. Timely result reporting was mentioned earlier in the context of advantages related to physicians' office laboratory testing. Laboratories that serve physicians and institutions must be very cognizant of their turnaround times. They must also be sensitive to the fact that turnaround time, from the clinician's standpoint, begins when the specimen is requested and ends when the result is received. Although laboratories frequently measure intralaboratory turnaround time as a performance measure, the laboratory team must also understand obstacles their clinical colleagues face in result retrieval.[17-28]

With respect to result retrieval, consider the two general situations of urgent results and routine results. Results may be urgent either because they were requested "stat" by the clinician[29] or because, following analysis, the results are such that, irrespective of how the specimen was requested, the requester should be notified immediately to prevent patient harm (i.e., the results show a critical or panic value). To reduce medical errors that may result from inappropriate interventions or non-interventions, laboratorians must be sensitive to the clinical needs of their colleagues. For critical values, the laboratory and clinicians must agree on what constitutes criteria for emergent notification. Then, when the ordering clinician is contacted by the laboratory, irrespective of the time of that call, the clinician must understand that the laboratory is following through on its agreement to provide immediate notification. Trained laboratory personnel must always review results before they are reported, and if findings suggest a worrisome picture when interpreted in the context of the clinical history available, the clinician should be called even if the finding is not explicitly listed on the "critical value" notification protocol.

Laboratories and their clients must also work together to establish guidelines for the use of stat requests and parameters for routine turnaround times. An urgent request to the laboratory invariably slows down the entire testing process, increasing turnaround time for routine specimens. At times, stat requests are made for either patient or physician convenience. Although patient and physician satisfaction with the laboratory service is an important marker of quality, often clients are unaware that the routine turnaround times are within acceptable parameters, such that there is no need for a stat request.[30] Minimizing unnecessary use of stat requests improves laboratory turnaround time for all patients, improving quality and reducing the risk of error that could result from not having a result.

Physicians also have the responsibility to review all laboratory results that are requested for their patients. It is incumbent on the physician to develop a practice whereby all results are reviewed in a systematic fashion. The process, over the last decade, has become more complex given the pressures of managed care. Now many clinicians must use different laboratories depending on their patients' specific insurance plans. In addition to receiving reports in different formats and at different times, the physician must review quantitative results in the context of reported reference intervals because different laboratories may report results using different testing methodologies, units (i.e., English vs. SI units), or reporting formats.

Perhaps the biggest opportunity for the laboratory and laboratorians to become champions for patient safety capitalizes on the central role of the laboratory in patient care, particularly in organized health care systems. Because the laboratory receives specimens and consultations from practitioners throughout the system, careful analysis of laboratory results, in conjunction with available clinical, radiographic, pharmacy, and other data, provides an opportunity for rapid detection of possible medical errors or modification of potentially inappropriate treatment. As laboratory information systems become increasingly integrated with hospital information systems, laboratories and laboratorians will be expected to be integrally involved in defining clinical–laboratory scenarios that should prompt timely intervention.

Evaluation of Drug Toxicity

One of the most apparent and commonly cited opportunities is the ability of the laboratory to identify and flag potential drug toxicity situations. Consider the two most common situations: drug levels approaching or at toxic levels and situations where drug toxicity may manifest as abnormalities in commonly measured laboratory tests.

Often the laboratory is the first to detect drug toxicity because therapeutic drug monitoring studies suggest a level in the toxic range. The laboratory in a health care system should develop parameters whereby the pharmacy is notified of the toxicity so that clinical pharmacists may intervene and reevaluate, with the ordering physician, drug dosing levels. As systems become more sophisticated, laboratory and pharmacy information systems will have the capacity to extrapolate serial therapeutic drug levels to evaluate whether patients are overdosed or underdosed. Although clinicians are expected to evaluate drug levels over time, with the volume of data that physicians must manage, it is easy to miss an important trend. In reality, evaluating large volumes of data is a task much better performed by a computer than by an individual.

The laboratory also has the capacity to establish presumptive diagnoses that warrant special attention when common drugs are prescribed. Certain laboratory tests can be used as surrogates for renal (e.g., urea nitrogen, creatinine) or hepatic (e.g., alanine aminotransferase, bilirubin) insufficiency. Because many drugs are either hepatically metabolized or renally excreted, identification of renal or hepatic insufficiency may suggest that a modified dosing schedule is warranted. For example, although maintenance and replacement fluids frequently contain potassium, including potassium in these fluids is usually contraindicated in patients with renal failure. If the laboratory detects elevated creatinine levels, according to a parameter agreed upon by the laboratory, pharmacy, and medical staff, a pharmacy information system flag may automatically be set to prompt a clinical pharmacy intervention before standard replacement fluids are dispensed. Similarly, an increasing serum creatinine level in the setting where a patient is receiving nephrotoxic aminoglycoside antibiotics should prompt a clinical pharmacist consultation.

Appropriateness of Chemotherapeutic Interventions

Most cancer chemotherapy protocols specify certain laboratory parameters to guide the timing and dosing of subsequent treatment cycles. Oncologists and oncology nurses are very cognizant of treatment protocols and record laboratory and chemotherapy data with each patient visit. Although this system is nearly perfect, dosing and timing errors do occur because of the large amounts of data that must be collected and recorded. Chemotherapeutic errors represent some of the most devastating iatrogenic medical complications. A laboratory information system directly interfaced with a clinical system that monitors chemotherapeutic protocols and a pharmacy system that dispenses chemotherapeutic agents can profoundly affect the rate with which patients receive excess or insufficient doses.

Response to Infectious Diseases

Antimicrobial therapy was recognized as one of the key advances in the 20th century responsible for reducing morbidity and mortality from acute infectious diseases. Recent concern has been raised regarding the emergence of increased microbial resistance; therefore, it is critical that the most advanced antibiotics be reserved for patients resistant to more common antibiotics. Furthermore, it is incumbent on the physician to ensure that patients receiving any antimicrobial therapy be treated with those agents to which the specific infectious agent is susceptible. Monitoring antibiotic therapy and emerging resistance patterns is an essential component of every health care facility, particularly for those individuals specializing in infectious diseases and hospital epidemiology. Proper interfaces between laboratory and pharmacy systems can ensure that patients are receiving appropriate, yet not excessive, antibiotic regimens. Links to clinical systems with patient allergy histories ensure that the pharmacy does not dispense an incompatible drug despite high sensitivity identified by the medical microbiology laboratory.

The Autopsy as a Tool to Evaluate Error Reduction Opportunities

The Institute of Medicine's report *To Err Is Human: Building a Safer Healthcare System* recognizes that the autopsy can be an important source of information regarding potentially missed diagnoses.[31] Despite advances in technology, studies show up to a 40% discrepancy between antemortem and postmortem diagnoses.[32,33] Clinicians are reluctant to request autopsies from their patients' families, and pathologists have not regularly promoted the autopsy for various reasons, not the least of which is limited reimbursement for providing autopsy services. Furthermore, autopsy reports are frequently not timely, decreasing the value of feedback to the treating physicians.[33] Nevertheless, autopsies have proved to be a valuable tool for identifying missed diagnoses and improving diagnostic accuracy for subsequent patients with similar clinical conditions.[34] Efforts are under way among laboratory medicine specialty societies to promote the value of the autopsy in patient safety.

Conclusions

This chapter touched on some of the key roles that the laboratory and the laboratorian have in ensuring patient safety. It is easier for laboratory medicine professionals to explicitly delineate and measure their contributions to patient safety compared with assessment of laboratory performance on ultimate patient outcomes.

Laboratory roles include activities that are primarily intralaboratory and those activities that involve the interface between the laboratory and the clinical team. Intralaboratory quality assessment and improvement have existed for nearly a century. Pathology and laboratory medicine specialists were the first medical discipline to employ statistical process control to ensure accurate and precise results. Techniques to reduce medical error within the confines of the laboratory continue to improve with faster, more sophisticated electronic interfaces and identification systems. Most larger laboratories have been able to capitalize on electronic interfaces and technology to reduce transcription and other patient identification errors.

Reducing errors in medicine provides laboratory professionals with a new reason to reach out from behind their microscopes and laboratory benches to partner with colleagues from all disciplines.

References

1. American Society for Clinical Pathology. A history of the ASCP. Available: http://www.ascp.org/general/about/history.
2. Belk, W. P., and Sunderman, F. W. A survey of the accuracy of chemical analyses in clinical laboratories. *American Journal of Clinical Pathology* 1947;17:853–61.
3. Tan, I. K., Jacob, E., and Lim, S. H. Use of computers in quality assurance of laboratory testing. *Annals of the Academy of Medicine, Singapore* 1990;19:724–30.
4. Jones, B. A., and Novis, D. A. Cervical biopsy-cytology correlation. A College of American Pathologists Q-Probes study of 22,439 correlations in 348 laboratories. *Archives of Pathology and Laboratory Medicine* 1996;120:523–31.
5. Jones, B. A. Rescreening in gynecologic cytology. Rescreening of 8096 previous cases for current low-grade and indeterminate-grade squamous intraepithelial lesion diagnoses—a College of American Pathologists Q-Probes study of 323 laboratories. *Archives of Pathology and Laboratory Medicine* 1996;120:519–22.
6. Jones, B. A. Rescreening in gynecologic cytology. Rescreening of 3762 previous cases for current high-grade squamous intraepithelial lesions and carcinoma—a College of American Pathologists Q-Probes study of 312 institutions. *Archives of Pathology and Laboratory Medicine* 1995;119:1097–103.
7. Kok, M. R., and Boon, M. E. Consequences of neural network technology for cervical screening: increase in diagnostic consistency and positive scores. *Cancer* 1996;78:112–7.
8. Greer, B. E. The gynecologist's perspective of liability and quality issues with the Papanicolaou smear. *Archives of Pathology and Laboratory Medicine* 1997;121:246–9.
9. Harris, N. L., Jaffe, E. S., Diebold, J., et al. The World Health Organization classification of hematological malignancies: report of the Clinical Advisory Committee Meeting, Airlie House, Virginia, November 1997. *Modern Pathology* 2000;13:193–207.
10. Harris, N. L., Jaffe, E. S., Diebold, J., Flandrin, G., Muller-Hermelink, H. K., and Vardiman, J. Lymphoma classification—from controversy to consensus: the R.E.A.L. and WHO classification of lymphoid neoplasms. *Annals of Oncology* 2000;11 Suppl 1:3–10.
11. Ramsay, A. D. Errors in histopathology reporting: detection and avoidance. *Histopathology* 1999;34:481–90.
12. Hurst, J., Nickel, K., and Hilborne, L. H. Are physicians' office laboratory results of comparable quality to those produced in other laboratory settings? *JAMA* 1998;279:468–71.
13. Stull, T. M., Hearn, T. L., Hancock, J. S., Handsfield, J. H., and Collins, C. L. Variation in proficiency testing performance by testing site. *JAMA* 1998;279:463–7.
14. Navikas, V., and Link, H. Review: cytokines and the pathogenesis of multiple sclerosis. *Journal of Neuroscience Research* 1996;45:322–33.

15. Nakhleh, R. E., Gephardt, G., and Zarbo, R. J. Necessity of clinical information in surgical pathology. *Archives of Pathology and Laboratory Medicine* 1999;123:615–9.
16. Renner, S. W., Howanitz, P. J., and Bachner, P. Wristband identification error reporting in 712 hospitals. A College of American Pathologists Q-Probes study of quality issues in transfusion practice. *Archives of Pathology and Laboratory Medicine* 1993;117:573–7.
17. Dale, J. C., Steindel, S. J., and Walsh, M. Early morning blood collections: a College of American Pathologists Q-Probes study of 657 institutions. *Archives of Pathology and Laboratory Medicine* 1998;122:865–70.
18. Steindel, S. J., and Novis, D. A. Using outlier events to monitor test turnaround time. *Archives of Pathology and Laboratory Medicine* 1999;123:607–14.
19. Steindel, S. J., and Howanitz, P. J. Changes in emergency department turnaround time performance from 1990 to 1993. A comparison of two College of American Pathologists Q-Probes studies. *Archives of Pathology and Laboratory Medicine* 1997;121:1031–41.
20. Steindel, S. J., Jones, B. A., and Howanitz, P. J. Timeliness of automated routine laboratory tests: a College of American Pathologists Q-Probes study of 653 institutions. *Clinica Chimica Acta* 1996;251:25–40.
21. Steindel, S. J. Timeliness of clinical laboratory tests. A discussion based on five College of American Pathologists Q-Probe studies. *Archives of Pathology and Laboratory Medicine* 1995;119:918–23.
22. Novis, D. A., Zarbo, R. J., and Saladino, A. J. Interinstitutional comparison of surgical biopsy diagnosis turnaround time: a College of American Pathologists Q-Probes study of 5384 surgical biopsies in 157 small hospitals. *Archives of Pathology and Laboratory Medicine* 1998;122:951–6.
23. Novis, D. A., and Zarbo, R. J. Interinstitutional comparison of frozen section turnaround time. A College of American Pathologists Q-Probes study of 32,868 frozen sections in 700 hospitals. *Archives of Pathology and Laboratory Medicine* 1997;121:559–67.
24. Jones, B. A., and Davey, D. D. Quality management in gynecologic cytology using interlaboratory comparison. *Archives of Pathology and Laboratory Medicine* 2000;124:672–81.
25. Jones, B. A., Valenstein, P. N., and Steindel, S. J. Gynecologic cytology turnaround time. A College of American Pathologists Q-Probes study of 371 laboratories. *Archives of Pathology and Laboratory Medicine* 1999;123:682–6.
26. Howanitz, P. J., Cembrowski, G. S., Steindel, S. J., and Long, T. A. Physician goals and laboratory test turnaround times. A College of American Pathologists Q-Probes study of 2763 clinicians and 722 institutions. *Archives of Pathology and Laboratory Medicine* 1993;117:22–8.
27. Howanitz, P. J., Steindel, S. J., Cembrowski, G. S., and Long, T. A. Emergency department stat test turnaround times. A College of American Pathologists Q-Probes study for potassium and hemoglobin. *Archives of Pathology and Laboratory Medicine* 1992;116:122–8.

28. Howanitz, P. J., and Steindel, S. J. Intralaboratory performance and laboratorians' expectations for stat turnaround times. A College of American Pathologists Q-Probes study of four cerebrospinal fluid determinations. *Archives of Pathology and Laboratory Medicine* 1991;115:977–83.

29. Hilborne, L., Lee, H., and Cathcart, P. STAT testing? A guideline for meeting clinician turnaround time requirements. Practice parameter. *American Journal of Clinical Pathology* 1996;105:671–5.

30. Hilborne, L. H., Oye, R. K., McArdle, J. E., Repinski, J. A., and Rodgerson, D. O. Use of specimen turnaround time as a component of laboratory quality. A comparison of clinician expectations with laboratory performance. *American Journal of Clinical Pathology* 1989;92:613–8.

31. Kohn, L. T., Corrigan, J., and Donaldson, M. S. *To Err Is Human: Building a Safer Health System.* Washington, DC: National Academy Press, 2000.

32. Zarbo, R. J., Baker, P. B., and Howanitz, P. J. The autopsy as a performance measurement tool—diagnostic discrepancies and unresolved clinical questions: a College of American Pathologists Q-Probes study of 2479 autopsies from 248 institutions. *Archives of Pathology and Laboratory Medicine* 1999;123:191–8.

33. Lundberg, G. D. Low-tech autopsies in the era of high-tech medicine: continued value for quality assurance and patient safety. *JAMA* 1998;280:1273–4.

34. Nakhleh, R. E., Baker, P. B., and Zarbo, R. J. Autopsy result utilization: a College of American Pathologists Q-Probes study of 256 laboratories. *Archives of Pathology and Laboratory Medicine* 1999;123:290–5.

CHAPTER FORTY-FOUR

PARTNERSHIP AND COLLABORATION ON PATIENT SAFETY WITH HEALTH CARE SUPPLIERS

Charles R. Denham, MD

The traditional relationship between health care providers and health care suppliers is undergoing a profound paradigm shift. New forces are creating an entirely new reality. Patient safety is now a critical issue on the agenda of American health care leaders. Providers need integrated performance solutions, not products. This is no more clear than in the area of patient safety. The new reality and performance focus have created a terrific opportunity for providers and suppliers to develop win–win partnerships.

Cross-functional teams composed of clinicians, nurses, key technologists, administrators, department managers, and purchasing agents increasingly make purchasing decisions. These teams need more from suppliers than the traditional "features and benefits" product pitch. Gone are the days when purchasing decisions were made solely by individual clinicians.

Historically, clinical performance, operational performance, and financial performance have each been studied separately. Recently the health care industry has recognized that the three are intrinsically interdependent and tightly coupled. As integrated clinical, operational, and financial performance becomes increasingly important, collaborative, performance-centered relationships between providers and suppliers are defined by a new paradigm—performance partnerships and win–win collaboration.

New Forces and a New Reality

The health care market's dynamics are changing. We are at a "tipping point," where there is a power shift from providers of care to the payers or purchasers of care. The very forces that have made the health care market almost impenetrable to innovation and change are now driving a reversal in market dynamics. In isolation, no one force would cause change. At this point, however, many of the forces are all coming to bear at once. The providers, including hospitals and physicians, have fiercely defended the status quo from changes that would adversely impact market share, referral channels, and revenue. Quality and safety, however, are now becoming critical issues to consumers, employers, and the federal government. These purchaser stakeholders who control payment are now demanding verifiable performance. They are beginning to award market share and compensation to providers who are making performance changes and are penalizing those who are not.

Institute of Medicine Reports

The Institute of Medicine (IOM) report *To Err Is Human,* published in November 1999, specifically addressed patient safety as the most critical issue in American health care.[1] The report recognized that as many as 44,000 to 98,000 preventable deaths occur in U.S. hospitals each year.

The second IOM report, entitled *Crossing the Quality Chasm,* was published in March 2001 and made the case that the observed problems in patient safety are just the tip of the iceberg of a major quality problem in health care.[2] The report cites the requirements for redesign of the health care system. It proposes that the system be based on three principles and six aims. The principles include the requirement that the redesign effort apply evidence-based medicine, be patient centered in focus, and take a systems approach. The report outlines six major aims for health care reform, the first of which is patient safety. The other five aims are effectiveness, patient centeredness, timeliness, efficiency, and equity. The report clearly indicates that the concept of "no outcome–no income" may be on the horizon for health care providers.

Building on the recommendations of the first two Institute of Medicine reports, *Envisioning the National Health Care Quality Report* provides a tool to evaluate quality improvement in health care at the national and regional level.[3] A collaboration between the Institute of Medicine and the Agency for Healthcare Research and Quality, the report emphasizes the need for proper quality measures—not just from the policy perspective, but also from the patient's perspective. These measures should reflect the changing needs of the patient/consumer and the impact of the health care system across four major areas: prevention, acute care, chronic care, and end-of-life care.

The report was commissioned to determine what measures of health care quality should be included in the *National Health Care Quality Report* in order to accurately gauge progress in improving the health care delivery system. The purpose of the upcoming report is to enhance awareness of quality, monitor the impact of policy initiatives and decisions, and assess progress in meeting national goals.[3] A four-step process was undertaken in which the conceptual framework for the report was built. Criteria were then defined for the selection of quality measures, data sources, and audience-centered reporting.

The authors of *Envisioning the National Health Care Quality Report* issued 10 specific recommendations for the *National Health Care Quality Report*. The conceptual framework must include components of health care quality from the perspectives of both the health care system and the consumer. Health care must be safe, effective, patient centered, and timely. Equity is an important consideration for the report and includes equity across gender, ethnicity, geography, socioeconomic status, and insurance coverage. The report recommends the selection of appropriate measures and ongoing advisory support. The report stresses that new measures and new data sources will be required to accurately assess improvements in health care quality. Ultimately, new uniform data standards and nationwide computerized clinical data systems will be incorporated into the care process. A complete list of recommendations can be found in the report.

The upcoming series of the *National Health Care Quality Report* will be used to brief the president and Congress on the nation's progress in improving health care. Several versions of the report will be generated, each tailored to a specific group of health care stakeholders, including providers, purchasers, researchers, policy makers, and patients/consumers. Providers and suppliers alike will be well served by being thoroughly familiar with the measures advanced in the forthcoming *National Health Care Quality Report*.

JCAHO's 2001 Patient Safety Requirements

Early in 2001, the Joint Commission on Accreditation of Healthcare Organizations (JCAHO) instituted a set of new and revised safety and error reductions to be implemented by July 2001.[4] Physicians now must inform patients and their families about the possibility of adverse events. This focus on patient safety reflects growing recognition and support of the themes delivered in the IOM reports. The opportunity is self-evident for suppliers and providers to collaborate on the safety performance of products in general and on the performance of specific safety products.

The JCAHO standards that specifically relate to patient safety are as follows:

RI.1.2.2: Patients and, when appropriate, their families are informed about the outcomes of care, including unanticipated outcomes.

LD.3.4.1: Leaders provide for mechanisms to measure, analyze, and manage variation in the performance of defined processes that affect patient safety.

LD.4.4.5: Leaders assess the adequacy of the allocation of human, information, physical, and financial resources in support of identified performance-improvement and safety-improvement priorities.

LD.5: Leaders ensure implementation of an integrated patient safety program through the organization.

LD.5.1: Leaders ensure that the process for identifying and managing sentinel events is defined and implemented (previously LD.4.3.4).

LD.5.2: Leaders ensure that an ongoing proactive program for identifying risks to patient safety and reducing medical/health care errors is defined and implemented.

LD.5.3: Leaders ensure that the patient safety issues are given a high priority and are addressed when processes, functions, or services are designed or redesigned (scored at PI.2).

These new standards reflect a specific and deep interest in patient safety. Additionally, eight other JCAHO standards have been revised to include provisions for patient safety. Five of these revised standards concern leadership's role in improving patient safety when allocating resources for measuring and assessing hospital performance and when assigning personnel and allocating time for participation in performance improvement activities. Leaders should also take into account patient safety when providing information systems and data management processes for ongoing performance improvement, as well as for staff training in best practices of performance improvement. Leaders should also be concerned about improving patient safety when measuring and assessing their own effectiveness as leaders. Other standards revised to include patient safety concern organizational changes that lead to improved performance, and ongoing training to support an interdisciplinary approach to patient care. Doubtless, this is only the beginning. Over time we can expect more detailed and specific requirements as the science of patient safety evolves.

It is prudent for providers and suppliers alike to pay careful attention to the JCAHO interest areas. Not only are the recommendations appropriate, but they also provide further support to safety champions who are competing for precious resources at the business-line level of an institution. Compliance with these standards is not about return on investment (ROI), it is about SIB—Stay In Business.

Leapfrog Group Initiatives

The Leapfrog Group is a coalition of more than 140 public and various private organizations that provide health care benefits to their employees. It was founded by the Business Roundtable (BRT), a national association of Fortune 500 CEOs. The Leapfrog Group encourages large employers to recognize and reward health plans and hospitals that make breakthrough improvements in patient safety and quality with preferential use and other market reinforcements. Through BRT members—large companies who provide health insurance to approximately 34 million Americans in 50 states spending $59 billion health care dollars annually—the Leapfrog initiative is intended to provide a giant leap forward in health care and aims to improve the caliber of care furnished to millions of employees and their families who are enrolled in company-sponsored health plans.[5] Hospitals are feeling pressured to achieve the initial three safety practices the Leapfrog Group has deemed necessary for a hospital to improve patient safety.[6] As a next leap, due out in the second quarter of 2004, the Leapfrog Group will use the *National Quality Forum 30 Safe Practices* to score hospitals on Patient Safety. As these safety practices become further ingrained in the hospital industry, those facilities that don't keep pace could find themselves excluded from insurance provider groups and place the hospital in a perceived position of lesser value to employer, federal, and consumer groups. This quality improvement initiative is being implemented in conjunction with the JCAHO and the Centers for Medicare & Medicaid Services (CMS) quality improvement initiatives.

Consumerism

Patients and consumers are becoming better informed and much more concerned about health care quality and patient safety. As a result of the Internet and the development of online support groups, communication and geographic barriers have been broken and information flows freely. Patients are often completely up-to-date on the latest medical advances and are not afraid to ask questions and challenge clinicians as to the reasons for not using a specific product, safety measure, or treatment approach. Patients' increasing involvement in their own care and safety is reflective of other industries where consumerism is driving business decisions.

Several surveys reinforce the view that the public is very aware of issues concerning health care quality and patient safety. A survey released in 2000 by the Kaiser Family Foundation and the Agency for

Healthcare Quality and Research found that quality of care was by far the biggest concern in choosing a health plan.[7] Nearly 71% of respondents cited a high incidence of medical errors as being indicative of a poor-quality health care provider. In addition, 47% reported being very concerned about mistakes and serious errors during hospitalization. Even more telling is the finding that nearly three quarters of respondents favor government regulation requiring providers to report all serious medical errors and to make that information publicly available, regardless of concerns of physician or patient privacy.

These findings are echoed in a survey from the National Patient Safety Foundation at the American Medical Association.[8] More than three quarters of respondents support banning health care providers with poor track records on safety and mistakes from providing care. Another survey from the American Society of Health-System Pharmacists found that 60% of respondents reported being very concerned about being given the wrong medication or being given multiple medications with dangerous interactions.[9]

For these well-informed consumers, patient safety and health care quality will become the differentiator between health care provider institutions. Hospitals with legitimate safety programs will be rewarded with the patronage of these consumers. Health care providers and suppliers can collaborate to use patient safety awareness directly as a powerful and compelling marketing and public relations tool.

Financial Pressures

In the past, financial risk in health care has been borne by insurance companies and the government. Indemnity insurance margins were tied to the cost of the previous year's coverage. Medicare reimbursement flowed unchecked. There was little pressure on health care providers and suppliers to control health care costs or to address patient safety. The managed care movement severely reduced revenue streams to health care providers, with little or no impact on quality management. The Balanced Budget Amendment further reduced compensation to providers, placing more stress on an already fragile system.

Health care providers are under mounting competitive pressures, yet they continue to focus on cost containment. Historically, supplier value propositions have been primarily a "features and benefits sell," with only an underlying presumption of quality. These traditional marketing messages become more and more irrelevant in an increasingly sophisticated health care market driven by the need for verifiable performance. Health care providers are increasingly seeking measurable proof of value offered by suppliers: quality improvement, patient safety, clinical and operational effectiveness, and financial impact from products. Consequently, providers' decision cycle times for selection and purchase of new products are lengthening, especially if the new products appear to add to current health care costs without clear evidence of improved clinical outcomes performance.

Health care providers must be confident that new product choices exert solid beneficial impact on clinical and operational outcomes at predictable unit and operational costs. In the future, the onus will be on providers to articulate their own value propositions to purchasers of health care services (employers and health plans). They will have to express value in terms of verifiable care-centered and evidence-based outcomes. In turn, providers will demand the same of their suppliers. Providers will now insist that suppliers provide products that deliver clear performance-based benefits in patient safety.

For the savvy health care supplier, the new forces and new reality present a tremendous opportunity. Suppliers that provide not just products but performance solutions are at a distinct advantage. Providers who recognize the importance of performance-based evidence and who optimize verifiable clinical and operational outcomes are uniquely poised to take advantage of the new reality.

Pay-for-Performance

American health care is rapidly moving toward a pay-for-performance structure, rather than the traditional fee-for-service to which we had become accustomed. Put simply, those institutions that do not meet certain performance criteria for quality and safety will suffer financial consequences. Conversely, those institutions that proactively implement quality improvement initiatives based on these criteria stand much to gain. In correlation to this process, those suppliers who develop solutions that enable providers to attain success in these performance measures will achieve significant market reward.

Already we are seeing incentive programs being offered by health care purchasers to providers. As of summer 2003 more than 120 initiatives are underway, with the most significant being the CMS and Premier, Inc. (a large national group purchasing organization) "Quality Incentive Demonstration Project" where hospitals can voluntarily have their data reviewed by CMS in five clinical areas. Based on their performance, participants will be rewarded with a reimbursement incentive and be publicly recognized for their efforts on the CMS web site.

With so many stakeholders participating in this movement to improve health care quality and safety, the landscape is complex and often confusing. Currently, there exists no one set of measures, standards, or practices by which health care institutions are to be judged; however, programs like the one sponsored by CMS and Premier are clearly an indication of things to come. As the stakeholders come together, share common concerns, and realize the substantial overlap among their proposed performance criteria, a converged, workable set of Measures-Standards-Practices (M-S-Ps) is expected in the very near future, which will be tied to a pay-for-performance reimbursement structure.

The Four A's of Safety Initiatives

Unfortunately, health care often suffers from a severe case of magical thinking when approaching patient safety and the adoption of new technology. Many believe that an instant fix to a systems problem can be bought. Adverse events experienced by patients and caregivers alike are merely symptoms of systems failure. Positive and sustained impact will only be achieved by using products, services, and technologies as enablers for systems-based solutions to systems-based problems. Successful safety initiatives hold certain critical success factors. We capture them in what we call the four A's of safety initiatives:

- *Awareness:* It is critical that providers, suppliers, and purchasers in health care be aware of the systemic nature, the magnitude, and the real consequences of deficits in patient safety. All must comprehend that a safe environment for patients is not merely another program, but the underlying cultural foundation for all activities occurring in the health care environment. Clinicians and administrators must become aware of the integrated interdependence of clinical and operational processes and the consequent impact on patient and caregiver safety.
- *Accountability:* Awareness of patient safety is only the beginning. Without focused personal accountability by senior administrative and medical leaders, as well as a firm commitment to make patient safety a major strategic imperative, little sustained improvement is possible. Currently, health care is complex and fragmented. Accountability is distributed across many stakeholders and thereby diluted across the system.
- *Action:* Patient safety initiatives are difficult to launch. Few off-the-shelf solutions exist. Even fewer technologies can be implemented without a comprehensive systems approach. Any safety innovation requires careful consideration of four specific areas: culture, process reengineering, human factors, and specific examination of the product, service, or technology solution.
- *Ability:* Individuals and groups may be aware of the magnitude and system-ness of the patient safety problem, and they may feel personally accountable and recognize the collective accountability of the institution; however, without the ability to

act, little can be accomplished. Ability can be defined as having the knowledge (concepts, tools, and information resources), skills, and capacity (available time and effort) to act. Without investment and careful planning it is difficult to assure that health care teams will have such critical capacity.

Any sustainable safety improvement effort must be grounded in the bedrock of cultural change. Virtually every opinion leader has recognized that it is time to pull our collective heads out of the sand, recognize our denial, use innovations as enablers of overall systems improvement, and make the necessary tectonic shift from our current culture of blame and shame to one of awareness and constant improvement.

Any improvement effort, be it specifically focused on safety outcomes or any other clinical area, must recognize that clinical and operational processes are intimately interdependent. The concept of the blunt end and the sharp end of the health care system, elegantly described by Woods and Cook, is well known to most students of patient safety.[10] Be it a product, service, technology, or change concept for clinical processes, any innovation must be studied within the context of integrated clinical and operational processes in order to deliver the optimal outcome. There is a defendable position for making change only when one has applied an evidence-based-medicine approach to innovation assessment. The days of innovation transfer through ad hoc, shoot-from-the-hip assessment based solely on anecdotal evidence and informal relationships between high-volume caregivers and supplier representatives are over.

After addressing issues concerning cultural and clinical and operational processes, providers must then examine the human factors aspect of the proposed innovation. Human factors science is concerned with the design of user interfaces in complex environments.[11] Human factors specialists design systems that optimize safety by making it difficult for errors to occur. Industries such as aviation, nuclear power, and other high-hazard, complex systems have been great teachers. Health care now must pay attention to these lessons and recognize that the successful implementation of safety products revolves around how the users interact with those products.

Finally, any product, service, or technology must be specifically examined as a potential solution to a systems challenge or problem. We must consider products as more than just out-of-the-box items. We must scrutinize products and services over the full spectrum of implementation and use. Patient safety innovations, whether currently on the market or still in development, must be evaluated not in isolation, but rather within the context of enabling solutions that deliver sustainable and measurable impact on patients' safety.

Full-Value Performance

There is more to the story of a product than can be captured in a description of features and benefits. A product solution consists of the core product *plus* a number of value-added elements that enhance the product offering by the supplier (Figure 44-1). Specific value-added features may include training and support in the use of the product, clinical guidelines that incorporate the product, care process design elements, system integration, patient education materials, and reimbursement strategies to aid providers in receiving payment from third-party payers.

Today's leading cross-functional provider purchasing teams require that product solutions address the key barriers to adoption of the product by health care institutions. They require solid evidence of beneficial product performance in clinical, operational, safety, and financial outcomes. Purchasing teams should

1. Assess the *full value* of the product along the entire health care continuum, including the value to consumers, provider institutions, payers, employers, and caregivers
2. Map the clinical and operational processes affected by the innovation
3. Apply an evidence-based-medicine assessment of the innovation tied to maps of clinical and operational processes
4. Document the business case for purchase and adoption of the product or service, as well as the institutional fit of the innovation
5. Communicate the impact of the product or service within the provider institution

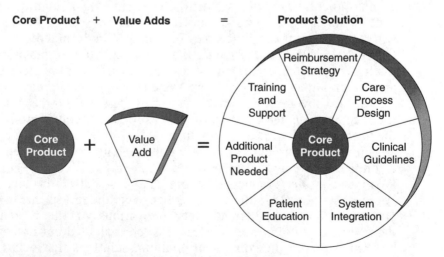

Core Product   +   Value Adds   =   Product Solution

FIGURE 44-1   The product solution (Copyright © 1999 HCC)

6. Identify any adoption methods required by the innovation
7. Develop an implementation strategy to overcome any barriers to adoption
8. Identify metrics and measures needed to track the true impact of the innovation for evaluation

Suppliers can create meaningful opportunities for collaboration and partnership with purchasing teams to generate win–win situations for both providers and suppliers to the extent that suppliers understand these responsibilities.

Common Performance Language Among Stakeholders

Rapid adoption of new innovations requires an integrated sell. Because diverse groups now select products using a committee process, suppliers must ensure success by developing a clear evidence-based value proposition for each stakeholder on the selection team.

The value proposition for each stakeholder must be communicated in the language of decision makers that emphasizes the benefits of the product of most interest to them. Additionally, value propositions for multiple stakeholders are increasingly required for more heterogeneous and fragmented alternate health care sites, such as outpatient clinics and physicians' offices. The advent of value-based health care purchasing by health care payers, such as the Leapfrog Group, creates a tremendous need for both providers and suppliers to effectively communicate the value impact of patient safety innovations along the entire supply chain.

Providers need to be sure that new product choices translate into a tangible positive impact on patient safety, clinical and operational outcomes, and financial performance at predictable unit and operational costs. Now that providers must articulate their own value proposition to health care purchasers in terms of patient safety, cost effectiveness, and care-centered and evidence-based outcomes, providers and suppliers must both communicate the value of new products in health care in the same terms. All health care stakeholders can benefit greatly by using a common language. We use the concept of full value as a common language of performance.

Quality, Cost, Value, and Full Value

Quality, cost, and *value* are the three key terms that are used in the context of performance. *Quality* has historically been communicated as improved clinical outcomes; however, consumer satisfaction is increasingly becoming a critical measure of quality.

The definition of *cost* has generally been restricted to the demand cost generated by health care providers; however, the full cost-of-care burden is far greater than this measure and includes costs incurred by consumers, payers, and employers.

Value is defined as quality delivered per unit cost. Although there are no standard approaches to defining quality and value that are applicable in all clinical situations, outcome measures for quality and value have evolved for most clinical areas. The true measure of value can be defined on a case-by-case basis using the best available knowledge. This is the essence of applying evidence-based medicine to individualized patient care. The unique and individual characteristics of each patient's situation can never be addressed by one definitive published paper or papers. The art of medicine entails studied interpretation of the best available evidence. This approach is particularly important for assessing the value of an individual innovation in patient safety. To quote the late Arthur Ashe, "You must start where you are, use what you have, and do what you can."

The concept of *full value* was developed to assess the full impact of an innovation across the entire health care continuum. Full value expands the traditional definitions of quality and cost. Quality is expanded to include both clinical outcome and consumer satisfaction of both patients and caregivers/providers. For example, the clinical outcome of a caregiver who experiences a needlestick injury is included in the concept of full value, as is the safety of all caregivers. Additionally, through full value, the definition of clinical outcome is further extended to include the impact of any potential adverse events experienced during an episode of care.

Under the concept of full value, the definition of cost is expanded to include the full cost impact to all stakeholders over the entire continuum of medical care (Figure 44-2). Similarly, direct care costs are incurred in caring for patients whether or not they contract a serious illness. Employers are subjected to costs due to lost work days (absenteeism) or presenteeism. *Presenteeism,* a term newly coined by the Leapfrog Group, is defined as the reduced productivity of an employee who remains at work but is affected by a health problem of his or her own or of a spouse or dependent. Under full value, the cost metric provides a more relevant estimate of the cost impact (full cost) of a patient safety innovation on all health care stakeholders.

Full cost is the total of four components:

1. *Medical care cost:* Includes all costs billed and generated by health care providers that are typically covered by Medicare, health care plans, and indemnity insurance. Medical care costs include those costs generated by adverse events.

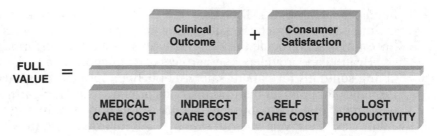

FIGURE 44-2   Full value equation (Copyright © 1999 HCC)

2. *Indirect care cost:* Includes nonmedical costs such as childcare, legal costs, and transportation expenses incurred by patients as they proceed through the process of care.
3. *Self-care cost:* Includes all costs paid by patients over and above direct billable medical costs and indirect costs. Self-care costs include outpatient medications and over-the-counter products.
4. *Lost productivity cost:* Employers sustain significant costs when employees are ill, because of absenteeism or presenteeism. Lost productivity includes lost work days as well as costs incurred in replacing employees who do not return to work. It includes retooling the workplace when an employee returns to work with a disability after illness, such as after back surgery, and it includes retasking other staff to cover the duties of an ill employee absent from work for an extended period.

By mapping the clinical and operational processes targeted by a patient safety innovation, providers and suppliers co-create the opportunity to clearly understand the practical impact of implementing an innovation. Such a process benefits both providers and suppliers.

From Products to Solutions

Integrated Performance

The clinical performance, operational performance, and financial performance of a patient safety innovation are intrinsically interlocked. As mentioned earlier, each of these elements can be measured and evaluated independently. The term *integrated performance* recognizes the interdependence of all three performance measures. According to research being published by Jack Cox, the leader of clinical performance at Premier, Inc. (a large national group purchasing organization), and Gene Nelson of Dartmouth University, there is a positive correlation between clinical performance and financial performance that is valid for hundreds of hospitals. Drs. Cox and Nelson found that institutions maintaining best practices consistently deliver optimal outcomes at the lowest cost and provide the best institutional financial performance.

Health care providers and partners can collaborate to seek out enabling solutions for patient safety that deliver optimal integrated performance for provider institutions. Such provider–supplier partnerships will prove vital in empowering suppliers and providers to align clinical process improvement with supply chain improvement, thus driving the best possible integrated performance for the provider.

Understanding Evidence-Based Medicine as Applied to Patient Safety Innovations

Enabling solutions are defined as products, technologies, services, or concepts related to the critical pathway of a process of care. In order for health care suppliers to collaborate with providers to deliver optimal integrated performance of patient safety innovations for provider institutions, it is incumbent on providers to thoroughly understand their own current processes, apply evidence-based assessment of both processes and potential innovations, and then examine how the current processes will be affected by the proposed innovation. Only by thoroughly comprehending their own care processes can providers ask suppliers to partner with them to provide full-value performance-based patient safety solutions. Whether building on existing internal product sourcing process or a new ground up redesign, providers should use a stepwise systematic application, as it is key to maintaining a consistent unbiased review of solutions. Furthermore, providers must understand how the recent convergence of new measures, standards, and practices is likely to affect their reimbursement as pay-for-performance programs emerge. They must request of suppliers solutions that will help them meet and exceed the pay-for-performance program requirements in order to receive maximum financial reward.

One project currently undertaken by the author that highlights the potential of provider–supplier partnership is the Adverse Drug Event Initiative. The project has engaged many suppliers of technologies designed to reduce the incidence of adverse drug events in the hospital setting. The project includes an extensive evidence-based review of the medical literature, a full economic analysis of potential enabling solutions, and a forum for 10 or more health care suppliers to present their Full Value propositions. The clinical and operational processes pertinent to a hospital medication management system are mapped and performance gaps identified. Innovations holding the potential to plug the performance gap, such as computerized physician order entry, are plugged into the existing process maps. The result will then be played back to all members of the project network. Suppliers complete a questionnaire similar to the framework for supplier collaboration presented later in this chapter. In this way, the full spectrum of technologies can be examined, prompting purchasers to receive solutions that deliver the best integrated performance and Full Value.

The Evidence-Based-Medicine Approach

It is widely believed by many clinical quality leaders that less than 25% of standard medical practice is substantiated by controlled studies published in peer-reviewed medical journals. This belief is corroborated by research published by the Congressional Office of Technology Assessment.[12]

Evidence-based medicine is increasingly driving clinical decisions for health provider institutions and for individual physicians. Evidence-based medicine involves taking into account the best available evidence regarding the effectiveness, risks, and cost of a medical procedure before implementing the procedure in clinical practice.[13] In *Crossing the Quality Chasm,* the second report on the crisis in health care quality issued by the Institute of Medicine, the Committee on Quality of Healthcare in America defines evidence-based medicine as the integration of best research evidence with clinical expertise and patient values.[2] This definition is adapted from David Sackett of the Centre for Evidence-based Medicine in Oxford, England. *Best research evidence* denotes the best clinically relevant research on the safety and efficacy of medical treatment and prevention strategies. *Clinical expertise* refers to the application of experience and clinical skills to quickly assess and treat each patient and acknowledge the patient's individual circumstances. *Patient values* signifies the personal concerns, expectations, and preferences that each patient brings to a clinical encounter.[2]

The field arose after observations of wide variability across and within institutions with respect to the frequency, usage, and outcomes of specific procedures. Dr. David Eddy of Duke University, a pioneer in evidence-based medicine, states that ideal clinical guideline policies must be designed with a commitment to the following goals:[13]

1. Policies must be based on clinical evidence, rather than group opinion, expert testimony, or consensus.
2. Any analysis should explicitly estimate the magnitude of treatment options on pertinent health and economic outcomes.
3. Any analysis must contain both guideline recommendations and estimated outcomes for the treatments of interest.

Quality of Evidence

A major challenge in applying evidence-based medicine to purchasing decisions for patient safety innovations is evaluating the quality of evidence in the medical literature. The *Journal of the American Medical Association* published a 25-part "Users' Guide to the Medical Literature" developed by the Evidence-based Medicine Working Group that details principles and parameters for evaluating published medical research.[14-16] Key issues in evidence-based medicine are the quality of randomized clinical trials, the quality of unbiased systematic reviews, the value of blinded research studies, the implementation of evidence-based practice guidelines at the level of the local hospital, and the determination of the best evidence for making clinical decisions.[17-19]

One way to determine the best evidence for specific patient safety innovations is to look at the hierarchy of medical evidence. Research studies can be graded on the basis of robustness and quality. Table 44-1 shows a common classification hierarchy adapted from the Centre for Evidence-Based Medicine.[20] A more comprehensive table of evidence grades can be found on the website for the Centre for Evidence-Based Medicine.[20]

Once the best-evidence clinical and operational care paths are defined and the gaps in the care path are identified, providers and suppliers can use the framework for collaboration provided in the next section to identify those products, services, and technologies most likely to enable patient safety improvement for provider institutions.

TABLE 44-1   Evidence Grades

Evidence Grade	Description
Grade A	Meta-analyses of randomized controlled trials Individual randomized controlled trials
Grade B	Systematic reviews of cohort studies Individual cohort studies Systematic reviews of case-control studies Individual case-control studies
Grade C	Case series Poor-quality cohort and case-control studies
Grade D	Expert opinion without explicit critical appraisal Evidence based on physiology, basic science research, or scientific principles

Source: Centre for Evidence-Based Medicine, University Department of Psychiatry, Warneford Hospital, Headington, Oxford. Copyright © 2002.

Tools for Evidence-Based Medicine

Although implementing evidence-based-medicine practices for purchasing patient safety innovations may seem daunting at first, several tools exist to support health care provider organizations. Several clearinghouses, resource centers, and libraries for evidence-based medicine are available on the Web. The U.S. government's Agency for Healthcare Research and Quality sponsors the National Guideline Clearinghouse, a public resource for evidence-based clinical practice guidelines and related documents, in partnership with the American Medical Association and the American Association of Healthplans (available at http://www.guidelines.gov/index.asp). The New York Academy of Medicine and the American College of Physicians–New York Chapter maintain the online Evidence-based Medicine Resource Center (available at http:// www.ebmny.org). The website of the prestigious Centre for Evidence-Based Medicine in Oxford, England, contains statistics, tutorials, and a host of other information (available at http://cebm.jr2.ox.ac.uk/). The Cochrane Library is a subscription-only resource that houses perhaps the most extensive collection of evidence-based-medicine reviews on a wide variety of clinical topics (available at http://www.cochrane.co.uk). Abstracts of Cochrane reviews are available for no charge on their website. Another recent trend is companies offering evidence-based consulting and forecasting services. These companies include Zynx Health Incorporated, Medical Matrix, and Praxis.md, among others.

From Products to Product Solutions

Providers can engage their suppliers in a practical and mutually productive way once they become less focused on individual products and more focused on enabling solutions, full value measures, and a process-centered evidence-based-medicine approach to innovation assessment. The reality of today's health care environment is that suppliers alone often do not have all the solutions; it is the responsibility of providers to build the optimal solution with their suppliers.

We developed the following framework to organize the appropriate information to assess and compare product and supplier performance. The framework was originally developed for leading group purchasing organizations to help them assess supplier offerings for potential contracting opportunities.

The framework consists of four parts: product description, product classification and regulatory issues, full-value breakthrough evidence, and supplier viability. The framework is provided to allow readers to develop their own institution-specific methods for knowledge management and assessment.

Product Description

Core Product Description

Ask the supplier to provide details pertaining to the core product (the product "out of the box" as delivered to the health care provider) and component elements. How is the product used? Where will it be used? What is the range of users?

Important Features and Benefits

Ask the supplier to provide specific details regarding the important features and benefits of its products, services, or technologies. The supplier may incorporate simple comparative tables or slides from marketing presentations.

Value Proposition

What is the value proposition of the supplier's offering? Ask the supplier to describe specific value propositions for each caregiver or consumer category, if appropriate. How does the supplier's offering compare to existing technologies? What is the available evidence to back up claims of value?

Product Solution Elements

Have the supplier describe the specific value-added elements of their offering in addition to the out-of-the-box core product. Value-added elements might include training components, support documents, clinical guidelines, implementation tools, and technical assistance. What is the scope and depth of the supplier's customer service capabilities? When the supplier is engaged in dialogue, the assessment team should address the major barriers for adoption of the innovation and map the "value adds" (i.e., the value-added features) to the barriers. Are they enough for successful adoption?

Product Classification and Regulatory Issues

Classification

Have the supplier provide any appropriate classification codes or UPN numbers that apply to its product.

Regulatory Status

What is the current regulatory status of the supplier's product? Have the supplier provide dates of pertinent approvals. What enhancements to the product are anticipated?

Intellectual Property Status

Have the supplier identify the intellectual property status of its product. Ask that the supplier reference any intellectual property infringement reviews.

Full-Value Breakthrough Evidence

It is important for health care providers to assess the full-value evidence for supplier products. Ask the supplier for specific and substantiated value evidence, understanding that some evidence may not (or not yet) be published in peer-reviewed articles. Some supplier companies have studies currently under way. Ask the supplier to supply data about any research in progress, if it feels comfortable with sharing that information with providers. Give the supplier a good opportunity to submit all evidence and to address all deliverables regarding quality and value to patients/consumers and caregivers/providers. Have the supplier specify the sources of any evidence.

Clinical Outcomes

Have the supplier describe how its product improves clinical care. Make sure it references all published, peer-reviewed studies, other pertinent published clinical studies, and other verifiable information pertaining to clinical outcomes. Ask the supplier for copies of the actual articles, if possible. Certain improvements in clinical outcome afforded by the product may be currently under study. Encourage the supplier to provide this information as well. Encourage the supplier to use whatever evidence-based grading method has been adopted by the provider institution.

Safety Profile

Have the supplier provide evidence to support the safety benefit profile of its product to patients, caregivers/providers, and the public at large.

Consumer Satisfaction

There are no standardized assessments for consumer satisfaction, though this area is becoming increasingly important in health care purchasing decisions. Have the supplier describe any published or known information regarding consumer satisfaction with its product or service.

Nonclinical Operational Profile

Have the supplier present evidence of any nonclinical process improvements (e.g., operational process improvements) and outcomes that the product may generate.

Direct Medical Care Cost Savings

What cost savings does the product provide relative to the delivery of care? This includes a provider institution's direct and indirect costs, physician charges, and any other cost absorbed by the provider or billed to the patient during an episode of direct care. Does the product eliminate other processes of care? What evidence is available to support these savings?

Indirect Care Cost Savings

Does the product or service reduce any nondirect, nonmedical costs to patients or providers beyond typical billing or demand care costs? Such costs may include legal, transportation, or childcare costs incurred during medical treatment. What evidence is available to support these cost savings?

Self-Care Cost Savings

Does the product reduce out-of-pocket costs for patients? Self-care costs include all costs paid by patients over and above direct billable medical costs and indirect costs, including outpatient and over-the-counter medications. Have the supplier provide evidence to support these cost savings.

Lost Productivity Cost Savings

Does the product reduce costs due to losses in employee productivity due to illness or medical treatment? Does the product or service decrease length of illness or number of lost workdays? Does the product or service save the patient's employer replacement or retraining costs? What evidence supports these claims?

Care Facility Operations Savings

What nonclinical operational savings does the product deliver to health care provider institutions? For example, does the product reduce expenditures on other products? What is the economic advantage of using the supplier's product? Have the supplier provide information to calculate the cost of conversion to its product from an existing product, as well as the cost of integration of the product into the provider's operation. What evidence supports these savings?

Clinical References

Have the supplier provide a list of current customers that the provider purchasing committee can contact regarding use of the product. Have the supplier include the contact name, title, facility name, address, phone number, and fax number. Ask the supplier to provide any case histories demonstrating successful use of the product.

Supplier Viability

Capacity

What is the approximate sales volume of the product over the last 3 years? How long has the product been in production? What is the supplier's capability for volume expansion? If the product is not in full production, what evidence can the supplier provide of potential capacity?

Quality Control

Have the provider furnish details of any quality control initiatives pertinent to its product.

Distribution and Field Support

How will the product be distributed within your health care institution? What relationships currently exist between the supplier, your institution, and affiliated networks? Have the supplier specify the size and strength of the distribution of its field support team.

Win–Win Supplier Partnering

The best approach to provider–supplier collaboration is to establish a dialogue based on principles advanced by Fisher and Ury in their timeless book *Getting to Yes*.[21] Suppliers and providers can concentrate on win–win relationships by focusing on meeting the interests of both parties, inventing options for mutual gain, using objective criteria, and refraining from engaging in positional tug-of-war interactions.

Fisher and Ury state that any negotiation should be based on three criteria:

1. The negotiation should produce a wise agreement (a wise agreement can be defined as one that meets the legitimate interests of each side to the extent possible, resolves the conflicting interests fairly, is durable, and takes the community interests into account).
2. The negotiation should be efficient.
3. The negotiation should improve, or at least not harm, the relationship between the parties.

It is recommended that suppliers and providers recognize the unique and important interests of each side, focus on developing full-value evidence, prioritize patient safety, and optimize the integrated performance of health care institutions.

Providers who craft the best supplier relationships recognize the importance of creating a "win" for the supplier. These providers refrain from driving unrealistic pricing or constantly requesting development funding support without in turn helping the supplier optimize its own value proposition. Nor do they unfairly play one supplier against another. To develop optimal provider–supplier relationships, providers need to be the best partner possible.

The same goes for suppliers. Suppliers who develop the best partnerships recognize the pressures on providers and make best efforts to live up to best pricing and optimal service and to support their obligations. They live up to their commitments, maintain an honest approach to delivering performance evidence, and respect the opportunity to develop broader market channels.

An additional advantage of partnering with providers may be reduced cost of sale to suppliers. Partnership will require a one-time sale of the product or service to a provider institution, rather than multiple sales calls to a host of individual clinicians. By bringing increased efficiency to the sales cycle, suppliers may experience reduced marketing costs due to a one-time institution-wide product deployment.

High-interest areas for providers are product pricing and support for research and development. In addition, the process of innovation adoption is subject to a number of critical success factors that must be included in the dialogue. Any collaboration should focus on helping develop the supplier's offering and enhancing the supplier's value proposition as an enabling solution to optimize performance.

A supplier–provider collaboration should recognize and address the critical success factors for providers to optimize innovation adoption. They include the following:

- *Solid economic argument:* As emphasized earlier, in this day of cost containment it is absolutely critical to have the strongest economic argument possible. Development of evidence of integrated performance that demonstrates the clinical, operational, and financial impact of an innovation is critical.
- *Active clinical champions:* The adoption of any patient safety innovation is critically dependent on active clinical champions who wholeheartedly believe in the value of the innovation. The role of clinical champions is vital in the current health care environment, where cost containment is often a major decision driver for provider institutions. Active clinical champions should be encouraged and empowered with the necessary tools for rapid and effective assessment of the patient safety innovation within their own institutions. Passive advocates may be positive about the product; however, they may not make a major effort to influence adoption. It is critical to have active champions in support of the cause of new innovations.
- *Key core competencies:* It is critical that there be an appropriate match of core competencies of caregivers at an institution and the competency requirements of an innovation. To successfully implement an innovation, it is crucial that the correct environment exists (clinically and culturally) to support adoption of the innovation. Otherwise, failure is almost guaranteed.
- *A rational adoption strategy:* Many great innovations fail at the adoption level because clinical and administrative players have not taken an organized approach to adoption.
- *Institutional fit:* Regardless of the terrific attributes an innovation possesses, in the end, a compelling case must be made for its adoption.
- *Full leadership support:* Senior leadership from both provider and supplier organizations must be fully committed to the patient safety initiative. That commitment must be felt throughout both organizations. Everyone must understand the importance of patient safety.
- *Strategic alignment of supplier and provider needs:* Suppliers must be cognizant of provider needs in today's safety-focused, evidence-based, patient-centered health care market. Suppliers that can articulate their products within the context of full value are at a distinct advantage. Also, providers must understand that suppliers still need to make money; there must be balance in the

supplier–provider relationship. On the other hand, suppliers cannot be held accountable for the success of a technology's implementation if there are significant factors beyond their control. Both parties must be held accountable.

- *Stakeholder incentives:* There are multiple stakeholders within the decision matrix of a hospital or health care institution. The more an individual institution is organizationally complex and clinically integrated, the greater the importance that all stakeholders grasp the clinical and economic value of patient safety innovations. Full value provides a framework within which provider institutions can gather pertinent evidence-based reference information, as well as meaningful tools for product assessment.
- *Systems approach:* Any patient safety product offering must be fully grounded in a systems approach that reengineers existing care processes using human factors principles for maximum effectiveness.
- *Focused approach:* Initially, it is advisable to take a narrow focus on provider–supplier collaborations, concentrating on those partnerships most likely to yield specific, concrete, and quantifiable improvements in patient safety.

To the greatest extent possible, any partnership with suppliers should generate evidence of the innovation's performance and of best methods for scalable adoption by other institutions. Partnerships should facilitate optimal and verifiable care in provider institutions. Peer-to-peer detailing is the most powerful arrow in the quiver of the marketer. A goal for suppliers will be the development of such reference sites.

Providers can assist suppliers in the following ways:

- *Core product, service, or technology development:* As in the past, suppliers will continue to need conventional product development. Delivering concrete evidence regarding the impact of their products on clinical and operational performance may be new to the product development dialogue of some suppliers. Suppliers will be well served to interact with providers regarding this topic.
- *Value-added development or solution:* The "value adds" that accompany a product, such as training, implementation methods, and a host of other elements, can help defeat adoption barriers. With the increased focus on performance and implementation, suppliers may need help in developing such elements.
- *Performance evidence:* Clearly, suppliers can gain the most by developing verifiable clinical, operational, and financial performance evidence for their innovations. All stakeholders will benefit from such collaboration.

- *Reference sites:* Reference sites, or centers of evidence where providers may examine the innovation's success in sites that they deem to be similar to their own, are as important as proper documentation of performance evidence. Successful peer-to-peer detailing is impossible without such sites.

Closing Remarks

In closing, we are pleased to report that supplier–provider win–win partnerships are indeed possible. Partnerships with such noteworthy companies as Fuji, Siemens, Roche Diagnostics, and Alaris Medical Systems have proved fruitful. All these companies exhibit demonstrated focus on Full-Value performance, invested more in broader enabling solutions than just products, and demonstrate verifiable performance in improved clinical, operational, and financial outcomes for suppliers. Clearly, these companies are marketplace leaders for these reasons.

From the provider side, there is real enthusiasm for improving patient safety from certain hospital boards, chief executive officers, and medical leaders. In the end, not only do these forward-thinking leaders believe that patient safety is the right and honorable strategy, but they also see it as a competitive advantage because many other providers are still in denial, resisting change. These reluctant players have differentiated themselves in the game by their passive approach to the problem of patient safety.

Patients and consumers are also becoming better informed and much more concerned about health care quality and patient safety. As a result of the Internet and the development of online support groups, communication and geographic barriers are broken and information flows freely. Patients are often completely up-to-date on the latest medical advances and are not afraid to ask questions and to challenge clinicians about the reasons for not using a specific product, safety measure, or treatment approach. Patients' increasing involvement in their own care and safety is reflective of other industries where consumerism is driving business decisions.

Patient safety is an exciting area of study. It truly is an emerging domain. Everyone has something to teach and everyone has something to learn. We challenge the reader to take to heart the words of Arthur Ashe: "Start where you are, use what you have, do what you can." Finally, for all concentrating on this area of study and impact, we need to be tireless in our pursuit of performance in patient safety. We know that the problem is probably larger in scope than described in the medical literature, will be harder to fix, and will require more effort than we expected to solve the problem. To those who have been given much, much is expected.

References

1. Committee on Quality of Healthcare in America, Institute of Medicine. *To Err Is Human: Building a Safer Health System.* (Washington, DC: National Academy Press, 1999).

2. Committee on Quality of Healthcare in America, Institute of Medicine. *Crossing the Quality Chasm: A New Health System for the 21st Century.* (Washington, DC: National Academy Press, 2001).

3. Committee on the National Quality Report on Health Care Delivery, Institute of Medicine. *Envisioning the National Health Care Quality Report.* (Washington, DC: National Academy Press, 2001).

4. Revisions to Joint Commission Standards in Support of Patient Safety and Medical/Health Care Error Reduction. January 12, 2001. Available at: http://www.jcaho.org.

5. The Leapfrog Group (http://www.leapfroggroup.org).

6. Birkmeyer, J. D. et al. "Leapfrog Patient Safety Standards: The Potential Benefit of Universal Adoption." A white paper for the Leapfrog Group, 2000. Available at: http://www.leapfroggroup.org/PressEvent/birkmeyer.pdf.

7. The Kaiser Family Foundation and Agency for Health Care Research and Quality. National Survey on Americans as Health Care Consumers: An Update on the Role of Quality Information. December 2000. Available at: http://www.ahrq.gov/qual/kffhigh00.htm.

8. National Patient Safety Foundation at the AMA and Louis Harris and Associates. Public Opinion of Patient Safety Issues: Research Findings. September 1997. Available at: http://www.ama-assn.org/med-sci/npsf/pressrel/finalrpt.pdf.

9. American Society of Health System Pharmacists and International Communications Research. Top Patient Concerns. 1999. Available at: http://www.ashp.org/public/public_relations/keyfindings.html.

10. Cook, R. I., and Woods, D. D. "Operating at the Sharp End: The Complexity of Human Error," in *Human Error in Medicine,* ed. M. S. Bogner (Hillsdale, NJ: Lawrence Erlbaum Associates, 1994).

11. Leape, L. L. "Error in Medicine." *JAMA* 272 (1994):1851–1857.

12. Office of Technology Assessment, U.S. Congress. *Report on Assessing Efficacy and Safety of Medical Technologies* (Washington, DC: Office of Technology Assessment, 1978).

13. Eddy, D. M., and Billings, J. "The Quality of Medical Evidence: Implications for Quality Care." *Health Affairs* (1988):19–32.

14. Guyatt, G. H. et al. "Users' Guide to the Medical Literature. II. How to Use an Article About Therapy or Prevention. A: Are the Results of the Study Valid? Evidence-Based Medicine Working Group." *JAMA* 270, no. 21 (1993):2598–2601.

15. Guyatt, G. H. et al. "Users' Guide to the Medical Literature. II. How to Use an Article About Therapy or Prevention. B. What Were the Results and Will They Help Me in Caring for My Patients? Evidence-Based Medicine Working Group." *JAMA* 271, no. 1 (1994):59–63.

16. Guyatt, G. H. et al. "Users' Guide to the Medical Literature. XXV. Evidence-Based Medicine Principles for Applying the Users' Guides to Patient Care. Evidence-Based Medicine Working Group." *JAMA* 284, no. 10 (2000):1290–1296.
17. Jadad, A. R. et al. "Assessing the Quality of Reports of Randomized Clinical Trials: Is Blinding Necessary?" *Control Clin Trials* 17, no. 1 (1996):1–12.
18. Khan, K. S. et al. "The Importance of Quality of Primary Studies in Producing Unbiased Systematic Reviews." *Arch Intern Med* 156, no. 6 (1996):661–666.
19. Greengold, N. L., and Weingarten, S. R. "Developing Evidence-Based Practice Guidelines and Pathways: The Experience at the Local Hospital Level." *Jt Comm J Qual Improv* 22, no. 6 (1996):391–402.
20. Centre for Evidence-Based Medicine. Oxford, England. November 1999. Available at: http://cebm.jr2.ox.ac.uk/docs/levels.html#notes.
21. Fisher, R., and Ury, W. (with B. Patton). *Getting to Yes: Negotiating Agreement Without Giving In* (New York: Penguin Books, 1991).

CHAPTER FORTY-FIVE

PATIENT SAFETY TRAINING AND NEW TECHNOLOGY

Carson Porter, JD

The patient safety era has dawned in the U.S. health care delivery system. Launched by the release in November 1999 of the Institute of Medicine (IOM) report *To Err Is Human,* we are witnessing a greatly increased emphasis on activities aimed at understanding medical error, improving systems to reduce error, regulating systems and people in order to make patient care safer, establishing reporting and analysis criteria, creating new governmental agencies to address the issue, and a host of other efforts all targeted at the worthwhile goal of improving the care provided. Time will tell which of these will prove to actually reduce the likelihood of medical error, but it is heartening to see the flurry of activity.

Americans have long believed that we enjoy the finest and most technologically advanced health care system in human recorded history. There is ample evidence to support that perception. However, there is also ample evidence to demonstrate that this complex system of care is far from safe.

People love to talk about quality health care, and many providers claim to deliver it. But we can never have true quality care if components of the delivery system are inherently unsafe. It is possible to have a safe system that still falls short of quality, yet we cannot claim to possess a quality health care system as long as segments of it remain unsafe.

Placing emphasis on enhancing the safety of our health care system is long overdue. The chilling evidence laid out in the IOM report compels action. A component of that course of action must be training. The question is: What type of training, and how can that training be delivered in the most effective manner?

What Training Should Be Provided and to Whom?

The subject matter of the training that will prove to be most effective will evolve from the outcomes of various research projects. As researchers begin to draw conclusions, potential training curricula will be developed to share that new information with health care professionals. While some of this training will likely be most appropriate for physicians and other highly technical personnel, there will also be a great deal of training regarding systems and procedures that all participants in the health care experience will need (including patients).

Quality health care organizations are learning organizations. They are constantly testing their assumptive knowledge and challenging old biases. They create a culture that rewards lifetime learning as a core value. In professional settings (like our highly complex health care delivery system), learning is a continuous process. In most organizations, increased resources are dedicated each year to conveying necessary information. According to Arie DeGeus of Royal Dutch Shell, "The ability to learn faster than your competitors may be the only sustainable competitive advantage."[1]

Developing a learning organization is essential in the information era. From a business competition perspective, DeGeus is on target. However, in this patient safety movement one must turn from DeGeus's hypothesis that one should keep that knowledge within one's own organization in order to have a business advantage. Patient safety transcends competition. This is where true collaboration must prevail. What one organization learns about better practices or systems to reduce the possibility of medical error must be shared so that all patients can benefit.

Health care providers who embrace ongoing learning participate in a variety of endeavors designed to continually enhance the quality of care they provide. Now, with the new emphasis placed on the safety of that care, we will see more programs designed to address where providers may lack appropriate systems to prevent medical error. Accreditation bodies or governmental entities will mandate some of these activities. Already the Joint Commission on Accreditation of Healthcare Organizations (JCAHO) has announced new standards aimed at reviewing certain patient safety issues within the organizations it accredits.

Self-Assessment Can Provide Valuable Insights

Wise providers will initiate self-assessment efforts to identify areas where their current systems may be lacking and could lead to potential medical errors. To provide the best result, these self-assessment reviews should include all members of the delivery team. The input of everyone involved in the care process can lead to valuable insights. Through the responses from a cross section of staff to a well-designed self-assessment process, management can learn where their efforts should be focused. The collective responses will identify areas of confusion or misunderstanding. The results will also provide the opportunity to focus on the issues that staff members deem most troublesome.

New technology can play an important role in the self-assessment process. The best self-assessment tools should be easy to use, interactive, and provide feedback in a meaningful manner. Well-designed computer-based tools can meet all of these goals while also collating the results across a cohort of respondents so that responsible parties can quickly and easily analyze the data and prioritize the follow-up plan of action. The technology is available to collect meaningful data in a cost-efficient manner. However, collecting data without a commitment to analyze that data in order to take appropriate action is counterproductive. It just becomes another exercise with no purpose—in short, a waste of precious time, which only creates cynicism among the participants.

An effective organizational self-assessment focusing on patient safety issues would do well to incorporate the issues identified in the IOM report as key areas for concern:

- Leadership and teams
- Communicating with patients
- Learning environment
- Systems for reporting and analyzing errors
- Medication safety practices
- Safety design concepts

A well-structured self-assessment instrument will collect responses from staff members that can lead to insights as to where systems are lacking or where systems may have been put in place but are not functioning as intended. The responses can also identify areas where more training may be required. Getting all staff members to participate and sharing the results in a positive manner leads to shared ownership of the patient safety initiatives throughout the entire organization. Furthermore, by using computer-based tools, detailed analysis can compare and contrast responses among different professional components of the staff as well as different work shifts within the facility.

These insights can be extremely valuable when attempting to pinpoint where problems may arise.

It is interesting that in all the legislation being advanced in Congress to address the problem of medical error, there has been much debate over how to best provide for systems to report errors *after* they occur (and this is quite important); however, none of the draft legislation addresses the necessity of providing incentives for an organization to engage in activities to analyze areas of potential weakness *prior* to an error occurring. Why do we place so much emphasis on preventive care for patients and ignore the same issue in dealing with potential medical error? What good does it do to try to prevent an episode of illness for a patient and then expose that same patient to death or injury from a systems failure when the patient requires care? We should be placing the same emphasis on the opportunity to identify potential system failures in advance as Congress is attempting to do after the error occurs. Comprehensive self-assessment tools are an effective component of an overall program aimed at identifying and correcting problems before they become tragic.

What Role Should New Technology Play in Patient Safety Training?

Once key issues have been identified, appropriate training can be initiated. The health care organization has a number of options for providing training to its staff members:

- *Traditional training methods:* On-site classes, off-site seminars, academic classes, and printed manuals (or other books or publications)
- *New technology methods:* Videoconferencing, computer-based training, and distance learning

Downsides of Traditional Training Modes

Workers in the heath care industry face a special challenge. Charged with the most important of roles—the care of human beings—physicians, nurses, technicians, and other allied personnel face significant challenges in keeping abreast of ongoing developments in their fields. But the health care work environment is not conducive to continuing education. Training courses are not offered when workers can attend, and the level of instruction (and information conveyed) can vary greatly from instructor to instructor.

Fortune magazine identified the limits of traditional classroom-delivered instruction:

> Classroom training is inefficient. Half the people in the room are secretly working on their real jobs; half are so relieved not to be doing their real jobs, they've turned their minds entirely off. Half already know half the stuff being taught and are playing Buzzword Bingo on their Palms; half will never need to know more than half of it.[2]

Some of the drawbacks of traditional training modes include the following:

- *Expense:* Traditional educational institutions are simply too expensive to serve as practical alternatives for corporations needing to educate hundreds, sometimes thousands, of employees. The high cost of courses is driven by the limited student volume they can serve at any given time, as well as the institution's need to support its physical plant. Furthermore, most health care organizations, in the throes of cost management initiatives, cannot afford to finance the expensive travel and lodging associated with off-site education.
- *Access:* Traditional educational institutions are difficult for the majority of interested participants to access. There is no guarantee that the institutions with the most relevant programs will be located in reasonable proximity to the participant's home or office.
- *Time:* Traditional educational modalities often require a significant time investment because students must commute to the class site. If the course if offered in another city, the cost includes travel time to and from the course as well as time away from work attending the course.
- *Lost productivity:* Opportunity costs of traditional modes of education are high. Requiring employees to take significant time off from work to travel to and attend off-site education programs has a meaningful negative impact on work productivity. Courses are given over days or even weeks, requiring employees to be absent from work for significant periods of time.

Substantial Benefits of New Technology Methods

Against this backdrop, education and training using modern technology (which includes videoconferencing and computer-based and distance learning delivered over the Internet or the organization's intranet, which we shall refer to collectively as *online education*) offers numerous advantages:

- *Flexibility:* Students taking courses online can learn at their own pace. They can replay material that they do not immediately understand, delay progression to subsequent topics until they digest the current material, or review material at a later date.
- *Accessibility:* Online education is immediately accessible— available at the student's home or office, or even on an airplane. The accessibility factor is especially important for workers in remote locations, such as caregivers in rural hospitals, who often find it difficult to access relevant courses in far-flung educational institutions.
- *Convenience:* Education is available "on call," 24 hours a day, 7 days a week. Students can choose when and where they want to learn, at a time and place convenient for them. For physicians, this may mean early mornings before hospital rounds; working mothers may choose to pursue course work at night.
- *Content quality:* Online course delivery provides a unique opportunity to utilize true experts who can present their material once and have it available to a wide audience whenever it is convenient for the student to access it. Online course providers incorporate various strategies to ensure the quality of course content. For example, course materials are carefully reviewed by a board of advisors to ensure quality and relevance before being offered to the public. Furthermore, content updates can be easily made to reflect state-of-the-art practices and are then instantly available to all users.
- *Faculty quality:* Online education providers attempt to enlist top-quality, often nationally renowned, faculty to develop and present course materials. At the same time, well-respected faculty find it easier to participate in online education efforts, given that the time requirement is small and the potential reach is enormous compared with traditional modes of education.
- *Targeted training:* Online training is targeted to meet the specific needs of specific individuals. Workers can get exactly as much training as they require, on the subjects of particular relevance to their professional needs. E-learning has been defined as providing the right information to the right person at the right time.
- *Higher retention of information:* Because online programs allow students to learn at their own pace, absorb content in small chunks, select only relevant material, and learn in a nonintimidating environment, these students are better able to

understand and retain information. Experts report that online training leads to a 60% faster learning curve compared with traditional instructor-led training, and that online training generates a 25% to 60% higher retention rate.[3] One study reported that online students performed 20% better on average than students who were taught in a classroom.[4]

- *Enhanced interaction:* Given that small instructor-led courses are relatively rare, online learning can, in fact, offer greater potential for student–instructor and student–student interaction. Interactive opportunities that can be offered by online courses include (but are not limited to) case studies, role playing, simulations, individualized coaching, chat rooms, and email. Good online course offerings create a community of learners. This becomes a low-cost ongoing opportunity to network with colleagues with similar needs and interests.
- *Consistent presentation of information:* By choosing online training programs for their employees, organizations can be sure that all workers will receive the same information presented in the same format. This ensures training consistency across employees, across departments, and across time.
- *Broad reach:* Online training makes it easy to quickly and conveniently share information with thousands of people.
- *Minimal negative impact on productivity:* Online courses can be taken in modules, so that employees are not absent for training for long periods of time.
- *Low cost:* Online education is, quite simply, much cheaper than traditional modes of education. Health care organizations (like other business entities) may enjoy savings of 50% to 70% when instructor-led training courses are replaced with online learning.[5]

Simply put, online training increases the productivity of training for both the individual learner and the health care entity that wants the staff member to receive the training.

Elements of Success

Experts note that several factors will affect the success of online education providers.[6] These include the following:

- *Ease of learning:* The best online course providers will ensure that course design, potential for interactivity, use of media, site design, site aesthetics, and ease of site navigation all contribute to ease of learning.
- *Evaluation and reporting:* Most, if not all, organizations seeking e-learning services will seek online learning programs that

evaluate user performance and then record and report results. Evaluative methods might include simulation results, section quizzes, or a "final exam." The course should provide for retention of outcomes by learners that can be collated and compared across a broad spectrum of participants. From this analysis the responsible parties within the health care organization can identify areas of potential concern and create plans of action to target improvement in those critical systems.

- *Provision of value-added services:* Many organizations will seek out online education providers who offer multiple services to meet clients' training needs. Such value-added services might include needs assessment, custom curriculum design, online mentoring, and reporting and tracking tools.

How Can Health Care Organizations Utilize New Training Technologies to Enhance Patient Safety?

Any strategy for reducing medical error and enhancing patient safety must employ a comprehensive approach. It is important to collect a variety of data to ascertain where the organization's systems may be lacking or functioning in an unsafe manner. Review of patient records, equipment maintenance review, and analysis of policies and procedures are all part of the process.

Gaining insights from staff as to what is really happening on a daily basis is also an invaluable source of intelligence. This can be accomplished in several ways: interviewing staff members, using suggestion boxes, and convening staff focus groups. However, each of these approaches lacks efficiency and may not yield the information that is really needed to improve the pertinent systems. For example, suggestion boxes rely on the staff member taking the initiative to raise the issue. Interviews and focus groups are preferable, but they both require a significant amount of time to organize and implement.

A more efficient approach to gaining valuable insights from staff is an interactive self-assessment survey instrument. In this fashion, the organization can get input from many participants and be able to collate that information so it can be analyzed for meaningful data. From that data input, the organization can develop and implement a focused plan of action that addresses the issues identified from information provided directly from staff.

In many instances the corrective action plan will require training. If the training needs to be delivered to a wide audience within the organization, some form of delivery method incorporating new technology capabilities is likely to be the lowest-cost and most efficient vehicle. Sharing information over a videoconferencing network provides the opportunity to disseminate information quickly throughout the organization.

In many instances the use of some type of Web-based delivery will prove to be even more effective. This is particularly true if the training requires the ability to determine whether the student is actually learning the new information. Because of the ability to test the student at key intervals throughout the learning experience (and to record the responses), it is easy to determine whether the student comprehends the information conveyed in the course.

Health care organizations may find it useful to employ a Web-based course aimed at introducing each staff member to the organization's commitment to patient safety as well as to educate staff on particular issues of concern. Safety policies and procedures pertinent to the individual organization can be presented to staff in an interactive training mode so as to make certain those policies are understood by the people responsible for following them. Also, updates or modifications can be easily and quickly provided to staff members whenever necessary.

By utilizing a combination of new technology methods, the health care entity can become a true learning organization. The benefits of interactive communication and ongoing learning for health care professionals cannot be understated. Our health care organizations are complex combinations of well-trained people and advanced technology. Most errors occur when systems designed to prevent error fail to perform as intended. Tragic consequences result. The cost in human misery and expense to the health care organization is staggering. Much of this could be avoided through careful and ongoing analysis of systems and training programs designed to provide pertinent information to the appropriate persons at the right time. Use of new technologies incorporating interactive self-assessment tools along with distance learning modalities can be a very effective component of an overall patient safety enhancement program for any health care organization.

References

1. Peter Senge, *The Fifth Discipline: The Art and Practice of the Learning Organization* (New York: Doubleday/Currency, 1990).
2. *Fortune,* April 2, 2001, p. 184.
3. Cornelia C. Weggen, and Trace A. Urdan, "Corporate E-Learning: Exploring a New Frontier," WR Hambrecht & Company, 2000.

4. Jerald G. Shutte, "Virtual Teaching in Higher Education: The New Intellectual Superhighway or Just Another Traffic Jam?" California State University, 1996.

5. *Training* magazine, as quoted in Weggen and Urdan, "Corporate E-Learning."

6. Weggen, and Urdan, "Corporate E-Learning"; Mary Gotschall, "E-Learning Strategies for Executive Education and Corporate Training," *Fortune,* May 15, 2000, p. S37.

CHAPTER FORTY-SIX

NO-FAULT COMPENSATION FOR MEDICAL INJURIES: THE PROSPECT FOR ERROR PREVENTION*

David M. Studdert, LLB, ScD, MPH and
Troyen A. Brennan, MD, JD, MPH

The Institute of Medicine's (IOM) 1999 report on error in medicine introduced a wide audience to the alarming extent of morbidity and mortality due to preventable adverse events in American hospitals.[1] The publicity that surrounded the report,[2-4] particularly attention given to iatrogenic death rates, has stirred interest among policy makers at both the state and federal levels. Legislative action appears imminent.

Leading proposals[5-9] promote two key strategies for enhancing patient safety: design and implementation of "systems approaches" to reducing errors, and improved tracking of incidents involving unintended harm. Scientific and regulatory goals are well aligned here. Experts generally agree that both systems-oriented interventions and data gathering are vitally important to any significant advances in patient safety.[10,11]

Unfortunately, because access to compensation for medical injury in our health care system hinges on blame and individual provider fault, the patient safety reforms spurred by the IOM report are on a collision course with the medical malpractice system. In the short term, that collision is likely to stymie much-needed attempts to make American hospitals safer. In the long term, it will substantially restrict the scope of public health gains that are achievable through error prevention efforts.

The challenge of addressing error in medicine demands a thorough reconsideration of the legal mechanisms currently used to deal with harms in health care. This chapter describes a no-fault alternative to litigation that does not predicate compensation on proof that providers' conduct failed to meet the standard expected in their practice community (i.e., negligence),[12] and argues that there is a pressing need to test its feasibility. We tackle traditional arguments against no-fault systems, specifically concerns about their cost and the presumption that eliminating liability will dilute incentives to deliver high-quality care. Recent empirical work suggests that a compensation model designed around avoidable or preventable injuries, as opposed to negligent ones, would not exceed the costs of current malpractice regimes in the United States.[13] Implementation of such a model promises to promote quality by harmonizing injury compensation with patient safety objectives, especially if it is linked to reforms that make institutions, rather than individuals, primarily answerable for injuries.

Systems Orientation and Data Collection

Medicine is a relative latecomer to the science of human mistakes, but previous work in other fields has firmly established their multifactorial nature.[14,15] Investigations of major disasters such as Three Mile Island, Chernobyl, and the *Challenger* explosion demonstrate that latent errors in the design of complex systems are an important predictor of accidents.[14,16,17] Active errors made by front-line operators often play a role, but these are typically of secondary importance in the chain of causation.[14]

Over the last decade, work has begun in translating this seminal insight into the health care domain.[1,18] Like in industrial settings, harmful accidents in health systems frequently involve human error, but their causes and consequences cannot be meaningfully understood by examining provider behavior alone.[19,20] Hence, the most promising patient safety initiatives seek to identify and correct latent errors, and to avoid what Reason has called the "blame trap."[18,21] For example, rather than emphasizing culpability, fault, or disciplinary action against physicians who read radiographs incorrectly, a sophisticated intervention might solicit candid input from staff and patients to isolate the source of problems, and then reengineer the reading process itself.[22]

It is increasingly recognized that a focus on individual provider judgment may not only limit the effectiveness of error-prevention efforts but actually exacerbate underlying causes of error.[11] One reason is that a punitive environment appears to chill providers' willingness to generate information about errors.[23-26] Rational redesign and evaluation of processes such as radiographic reading procedures,[27] drug ordering,[28] and shift changeovers[29] depend on sound data on how, when, and where mistakes occur. Data collection must be followed by careful epidemiological analysis and the dissemination of both anecdotal and statistical insights into prevention.

A pressing policy question in the wake of the IOM report is precisely how such data should be obtained from the field.[30] The various options for reporting systems are best classified by reference to two defining features: the degree of obligation placed upon prospective reporters, with the ends of this spectrum being voluntary and mandatory reporting, respectively; and the subsequent availability of reported data to third parties, ranging from strictly confidential to public information. Proposals considered in Congress to date mix combinations of these features.[5-9]

The Litigation Obstacle

System-oriented approaches to reform are fundamentally at odds with the medical malpractice system. At its core, malpractice law involves a set of adversarial proceedings, beginning with a patient's allegation of negligence against an individual provider. Processes of care are relevant only insofar as they may prove or disprove the defendant's negligence. Malpractice litigation induces silence and bitterness. Physicians do not believe it contributes to the quality of care,[31,32] except perhaps when targeted at institutions such as managed care organizations.[33] Hospital executives appear to share providers' skepticism, an outlook exemplified by the fact that many hospitals continue to conceive of risk management and quality improvement as substantively different enterprises.[34]

The tension between error reporting and the malpractice system is more complicated, and different models raise different questions. Organized medicine opposes mandatory reporting initiatives, arguing that a loss of confidentiality and an increase in the volume of malpractice litigation would follow.[35] A mandatory reporting system that made its contents available to patients or other interested parties would be likely to engender the distrust of those providers closest to errors and best positioned to report details of their occurrence. Physician and hospital leaders instead support a confidential, voluntary reporting system, an approach also recommended by the Institute of Medicine.[1]

There are doubts about whether confidentiality could really be guaranteed in voluntary or mandatory systems.[36-38] But more important, confidentiality and voluntary reporting, whether invoked jointly or separately, raise concerns of their own. Patient advocates fiercely oppose both.[39] Patients desire access to information about injuries they suffer, especially serious and preventable ones.[40-42] As well as facilitating consumer choice,[42] data on medical mistakes may alert patients to opportunities to seek compensation for their injuries.[43]

Each of the arguments just discussed has merit. Patients have compelling interests in knowing the facts and extent of injury they suffer. But the desired transparency will prove illusory if forced disclosure or publicity drives knowledge about errors underground.[23-25] Peer review statutes arguably prevent legal discovery of reported data,[36] but these laws vary widely across states and existing case law does not resolve their applicability to reported data.[44,45] To the extent that such information is accessible, plaintiffs' attorneys can be expected to take advantage of it to find new cases and to decrease their costs of discovery in existing cases. (Indeed, conscientious attorneys in pursuit of their clients' best interests should do no less.) Although some of the resulting suits may be perfectly appropriate, the taint of malpractice would immediately mark the reporting system that fueled them, prompting providers to avoid reports wherever possible.

In short, reporting systems are vital, yet no mix of mandatory/voluntary and public/confidential features can avoid trading off important interests of patients against those of providers. It is essential to recognize that this dilemma arises largely because reports must be made in the shadow of malpractice law. Thus, the need to collect error data in an environment where medical injury compensation calls for scrutiny of provider fault constitutes a troubling deadlock for the patient safety movement (Figure 46-1).

In addition, the fact that physicians, through their professionalization and training, conflate negligence with moral turpitude, cleaves malpractice litigation from the professional drive to provide better quality care. When mistakes are (or may be) the subject of litigation, physicians and institutions strive to cloak them in confidentiality, foregoing opportunities to learn from the problems that lawsuits can sometimes help to illuminate. These behavioral responses to malpractice law are so ingrained in medical practice that efforts to retrain physicians to better understand the opportunities that a negligence-based system provides for quality improvement are unlikely to provide the necessary breakthrough. Although some commentators continue to hold out hopes that the existing system may adapt,[46] it is increasingly clear that alternative approaches to patient compensation must be seriously considered.

Defining the Optimal System

An optimal system must address the need to prevent medical errors and efficiently compensate medical injuries once they occur. To achieve these broad goals, several system characteristics are essential. First, the program should encourage physicians and other health care providers

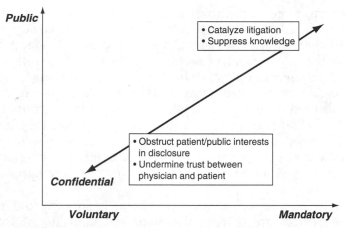

FIGURE 46-1 The reporting dilemma

to report errors, especially those that cause medical injury. These data would then be studied to understand key structural determinants of common errors, as well as the risky, persistent behavioral patterns that cause them.

Second, the program should strive to send strong quality improvement signals. Although most health care providers are committed to high-quality care as a matter of medical ethics, an effective program would buttress those impulses with financial incentives to reduce the number of errors and injuries. Third, in rare cases, patients are harmed by physicians who are incompetent, dangerous, or malevolent. Even a system of compensation that is not focused on fault must have mechanisms in place to deal with such practitioners, either directly or by triaging them to appropriate disciplinary bodies.[47]

Fourth, the compensation program should reinforce rather than undermine the honesty and openness of the doctor–patient relationship. Ideally, physicians would be able to inform their patients that an injury has occurred due to medical management and that there is a possibility that the injury may have been preventable. Fifth, wherever appropriate, patients should be compensated in a manner that is speedy, equitable, affordable, and predictable. A no-fault system of compensation based on enterprise liability would be well positioned to accomplish each of these five key goals.

The No-Fault Approach

Compensation programs that do not rely on negligence determinations are popularly referred to as *no-fault systems*.[48] In fault-based models, such as tort or the administrative system proposed by the American Medical Association in the late 1980s,[49] the claimant must prove four elements: duty, injury, causation, and negligence. No-fault systems eliminate the requirement of proving negligence. The workers' compensation schemes in operation in all states are a prominent example of the no-fault model. A number of states also have no-fault components embedded in their schemes for compensating automobile injury. Although claimants in these schemes must prove that they have suffered an *injury* that was *caused* by an accident in the workplace or on the road (where it is generally assumed that a third party has a *duty* of care to them), it is not necessary to show that the third party acted in a negligent fashion.

No-fault compensation systems are not completely unknown to medicine—several are in operation abroad.[13] Collectively, Denmark, Sweden, Finland, and New Zealand have accumulated nearly 80 years of experience in operating administrative schemes that replace medical malpractice litigation.[50-52] Aspects of the design of these systems can help to inform the kind of no-fault compensation model that might be implemented in the United States.

The health care systems in these countries differ significantly from the United States, with a heavier reliance on public payment and provision of services. Mechanisms for funding their compensation systems also differ from the physician premium that is characteristic of malpractice systems. For example, New Zealand's scheme draws from general taxation revenue, and Sweden's draws on premiums charged to regional councils and physicians. Nonetheless, core design features of these administrative schemes, such as compensation criteria, could be grafted onto existing arrangements between physicians, hospitals, and insurers in the United States. The simplest no-fault model would modify the distribution rules for compensation funds, without disrupting existing financing structures. However, elimination of negligence criteria would almost certainly signal a diminished role for attorneys in claims and pose a significant political obstacle to implementation.

Among the international models, the Swedish approach is perhaps the most attractive. Patients who believe they have been injured as a result of medical care in Sweden are encouraged to apply for compensation using forms available in all clinics and hospitals.[13] Physicians and other health care personnel are actively involved in approximately 60% to 80% of claims, alerting patients to the possibility that a medical injury has occurred, referring the patient to a social worker for assistance, and even helping patients to lodge claims[53]—the sort of assistance American physicians often provide to their workers' compensation patients. Physicians in Sweden tend to regard the facilitation of medical injury claims as a natural extension of their therapeutic responsibility to safeguard patients' best interests.[13]

Once a claim is made, the treating physician prepares and files a written report about the injury. An adjustor makes an initial determination of eligibility and then forwards the case for final determination to one or more specialists who are retained by the scheme to help judge compensability. The process is relatively fast, with the average claim taking 6 months from initiation to final determination.[53] Approximately 40% of claims receive compensation.[53] Patients who are dissatisfied with the outcome may pursue a two-step appeals process consisting of review of the determination by a claims panel followed by an arbitration procedure.

The key element of the compensation criteria in the Swedish model is the concept of avoidability. System designers recognized that compensating all injuries arising from medical care would be prohibitively expensive.[13] Thus, only a subset of medical injuries are eligible for compensation. We have described the test in detail elsewhere.[13] In essence, adjudicators ask whether (1) an injury resulted from treatment, (2) the treatment in question was medically justified, and (3) the outcome was unavoidable. If the answer to the first query is yes, and the answer to either the second or third queries is no, the claimant receives compensation.

Successful claims are paid in a uniform manner using a fixed benefits schedule, and include compensation for both economic and non-economic (pain and suffering) losses. But before a patient is eligible for compensation, he or she must have spent at least 10 days in the hospital or endured more than 30 sick days.[13] This "disability threshold" eliminates the minor claims that would not require significant compensation, but would, if processed, add considerably to administrative expenses.

Were such a scheme to be tested in the United States, its operation could be linked to vigorous efforts to analyze the claims data. Errors uncovered in the compensation inquiry—the number of which would likely dwarf those obtained under current fledgling reporting systems—could be subjected to root cause analysis, with primary responsibility for such analysis falling on the institution where the error occurred. Results would then be transmitted to a central agency, likely based at the state level, that would monitor the analytical work, categorize errors and causative factors, and then disseminate widely a redacted form of the data. Subject to strict confidentiality rules, a more detailed version of the database on avoidable errors and their causes would be available for both institution- and state-run prevention initiatives. Thus, the endpoint of the no-fault approach to data gathering, analysis, and publication closely resembles the one envisioned by the Institute of Medicine report under mandatory and voluntary reporting.[1]

The Fresh Case for No-Fault

In comparisons with medical malpractice, the capacity of no-fault systems to compensate injured patients is usually touted as their major strength.[54] Expectations about this capacity are not purely speculative: Recent studies of the two small schemes for no-fault compensation of birth-related neurological injuries currently in operation in the United States indicate fairly solid performance on compensation, as well as reductions in administrative costs.[55-57] The two chief criticisms traditionally leveled against no-fault systems are that the costs of achieving effective compensation are prohibitive,[49,58] and that removal of fault-based determinations will have a deleterious impact on deterrence goals.[48] Recent empirical findings and new patient safety imperatives debunk the rationale for both criticisms.

Affordability Through Flexibility

By combining data on the incidence and types of adverse events in Colorado and Utah in 1992 with estimates of the losses stemming from those adverse events, we have previously calculated the costs of three different compensation models: one that would compensate all medical injuries, one extending payment only to medical injuries attributable to negligence, and one that compensated injury according to Swedish avoidability criteria.[13,59] The calculations use a compensation package with standard components for each injury, including lost income, household production, health care costs, and compensation for pain and suffering associated with the medical injury. Our estimation methods are described in detail elsewhere.[13,59]

Table 46-1 summarizes our results. The upper half of the table shows that, relative to programs that would compensate all adverse events or negligent events respectively, a program that applied Swedish avoidability criteria to all claims (regardless of severity) and awarded a generous compensation package would be expected to occupy the intermediate ground both in terms of the number of compensable injuries and system costs. Such a program would make 67% more injuries eligible for compensation in Utah than the tort system, and 95% more in Colorado. However, the expenditures required to compensate this larger set of injuries would also increase costs by approximately 50% in both states.

Whatever promises a compensation program makes in terms of equity advances and error prevention, planners must be sensitive to the political reality of a cash-strapped health care system in designing an alternative compensation scheme. States cannot reasonably be expected to pilot no-fault schemes, much less adopt them, if their costs

TABLE 46-1   Number and Cost of Compensable Events Under Alternative Compensation Models, Utah and Colorado, 1992

Types of Events by State	Compensation Package	Compensable Injuries	Cost ($ Millions)
UT: All adverse events		5,614	227
Swedish compensable events	• No disability thresholds	2,940	91
Negligent events	• Full wage replacement	1,759	57
	• Lost household production		
CO: All adverse events	• Health care costs	11,578	418
Swedish compensable events	• Pain and suffering	5,919	129
Negligent events		3,032	84
UT: No-fault model based on Swedish compensable events	• 4-week disability threshold • 66% wage replacement • No household production • Health care costs • Pain and suffering up to $100,000	1,465	55
Medical malpractice system	Standard tort award	~126*	55–60†
CO: No-fault model based on Swedish compensable events	• 8-week disability threshold • Full wage replacement • No household production • Health care costs • Pain and suffering	973	82
Medical malpractice system	Standard tort award	~268*	100–110†

*The number of medical malpractice plaintiffs compensated annually has been calculated by dividing the estimated number of claims statewide (361 in Utah and 476 in Colorado for injuries suffered in 1992) by the number of paid claims. In Utah, the paid claim proportion (35%) was estimated using data gathered by the legislative auditor (Legislative Auditor General, State of Utah. A performance audit of the Medical Malpractice Prelitigation Panels. January, 1994. Report no. 93-07). In Colorado, the proportion of injury year 1992 claims paid at the state's largest insurer (56%) was used.

†Malpractice system costs were calculated by aggregating estimates of total premium dollars paid by physicians and hospitals to insurers in each state.

will significantly exceed those of the current malpractice system. The lower half of Table 46-1 addresses the question of affordability by comparing the cost of practical versions of a Swedish-style scheme in each state with the current malpractice systems. The versions of no-fault tested here are the ones that were actively considered by stakeholders in each state during the course of the Utah–Colorado Medical Practice

Study (1994–1998).[13] Our estimates show that many more injured patients may be compensated under no-fault than tort within budgets that are similar to or less than the costs of the current system.

Deterrence Reconsidered

The prevailing enthusiasm for error prevention may wane over time, and even the best regulatory oversight may fail to motivate providers everywhere to pursue error reduction strategies. Hence, external stimuli for improving quality generally, and preventing errors specifically, are valuable. But how can a system that jettisons individual blame for errors effectively provide such a stimulus?

Critics of no-fault have generally equated a shift to no-fault with abandonment of opportunities to use the compensation system to leverage positive influences on provider behavior. Setting aside the questionable role of deterrence in malpractice law,[48,60,61] there is ample evidence that no-fault systems can be structured to promote safety.[62,63] Indeed, new insights into the causes of medical injury suggest that they are actually far better placed to do so than negligence-based litigation.

Experience Rating and Enterprise Liability

In theory, a shift from tort to no-fault reduces incentives to take care. Several empirical studies of the introduction of no-fault automobile programs have detected modest increases in accident rates,[64–66] although some of these results are contested.[67,68] In any event, no-fault programs can be designed to guard against this outcome. The best example of deterrence in no-fault programs comes from the field of workers' compensation, where a variety of "experience rating" methods are used to create financial pressure on employers to pursue safety in the workplace.[69] Experience rating means that firms or individuals with higher rates of injury pay higher premiums. Viscusi and others have demonstrated the capacity for this kind of incentive structure to deter injuries.[62,66]

A number of academic hospital systems across the country, including the Harvard Medical Institutions in Boston and the Federation of Jewish Philanthropies in New York, already have "channeling" arrangements in place that mimic experience rating by covering the malpractice insurance costs of their physicians through a self-insurance mechanism. However, wide-scale application of experience rating in health care has not proven feasible because the typical form of malpractice coverage involves individualized commercial policies, and claims against any one physician are far too infrequent to allow calculation of premiums from year to year that accurately reflect risk.[70,71]

Linking a shift to no-fault with the adoption of enterprise liability would provide an opportunity to train the safety incentives of experience rating on the problem of medical injury. In its sharpest form, enterprise liability means that individuals do not directly bear the costs associated with an accident. Instead, the enterprise—whether it be a large group practice, a hospital with an integrated medical staff, or a health plan—would be "strictly liable" in both a legal and economic sense, by meeting the costs of liability premiums for all affiliated staff.[72,73] Premium levels could then be experience rated. For instance, a hospital would pay more in a given year if there was a rash of avoidable injuries and less if quality improvement initiatives curtailed the incidence of such events.

In addition to its deterrence promise, enterprise liability is thoroughly consistent with system-oriented quality improvement efforts.[1,73] If the aberrant behavior of individual providers is a relatively infrequent explanation for harm, as a growing body of empirical literature suggests,[1] then the greatest potential for patient safety advances must lie in institutional, not individual, accountability. Holding an individual pharmacist, physician, or nurse liable for an adverse drug event stemming from confusingly similar mixtures of potassium, for example, is unlikely to provide the institutional impetus necessary to bring about change in the packaging of the various potassium concentrations. Enterprise liability can effectively target financial incentives at institutions, and even at specific processes within institutions.[74] Those institutions with channeling programs in place report productive collaborations among physicians, hospitals, and the insurance entity regarding clinical guideline development and patient safety,[75] although the unique nature of these institutions makes it difficult to measure the extent to which such initiatives are actually spurred by the economic incentives at work.

An enterprise liability, no-fault system will not fit easily with every physician's practice. For example, for the solo practitioner who admits patients to several hospitals, the choice of a suitable enterprise to provide coverage may not be straightforward. More fundamentally, the workers' compensation experience indicates that it is not feasible for smaller firms to bear the full costs of injuries through self-insurance.[76] Year-to-year fluctuations in injury levels at small firms lead most of them to partially or fully pool their risks. The inability of some organizations to tolerate experience-rated premiums reignites concerns about reduced safety incentives in a shift from tort to no-fault.[63,77] However, two countervailing considerations—the general absence of experience rating in the malpractice system, and the paucity of evidence about the latter system's capacity to deter poor care—go some way toward mitigating these concerns; they also bolster our volume and cost estimates for a no-fault alternative (see Table 46-1).

With so little data available about the rates of avoidable medical injuries,[1] it is difficult to estimate the critical mass necessary for a health care institution to comfortably take on full experience rating in an enterprise liability model. However, the profile of self-insured organizations in workers' compensation suggests that reasonable candidates could emerge from among integrated delivery systems, hospitals, and even some medical groups.[73,78] Moreover, with ongoing consolidation in the health care industry and movement toward tighter integration of health care providers with institutions, the base for enterprise liability grows larger all the time.

An Incremental Approach to Reform

Most hospitals and physicians are not prepared for a rapid shift to a no-fault model, much less enterprise liability. There are likely to be many unanticipated outcomes of such a major transition, and these should be studied. In addition, a number of important design issues must be worked through, including the status of the compensation authority (private or public), the role of existing malpractice insurers, institutional oversight to guard against cover-ups of injuries, informed consent for patients cared for in a no-fault framework, the extent of attorney involvement (if any), appeal rights,[79] and the tensions that will inevitably emerge between no-fault and the coexisting tort regime.[56,57]

Rather than wholesale replacement of the tort systems with no-fault, we advocate enabling legislation at the state level that would allow selected organizations to experiment with no-fault, enterprise liability models. Such laws would no doubt face the sort of legal challenges that originally confronted workers' compensation regimes, no-fault auto insurance, and the mandatory arbitration processes that some health plans impose on their enrollees.[80,81] However, analysis of legal precedent in these areas suggests that, if it were carefully designed, a no-fault compensation system for medical injury would likely survive such challenges.[82] Thus, demonstration projects could proceed and allow the performance of no-fault models to be evaluated in three main areas: compensation, collection of data on errors, and advances in patient safety.

The political feasibility of demonstration projects may depend on permitting consumer choice. Patients should be permitted to opt into a no-fault model at the point of receiving care by choosing a participating physician or hospital. Patients who actively elected to receive care from such a provider would be committed to no-fault compensation avenues in the event of an injury; otherwise, patients would retain their usual rights to seek remedies in the malpractice system. Of course, special care would need to be taken to ensure that consumers were informed, had realistic choices at the opt-in point, and were not coerced into waiving rights to sue.

The benefits of a consumer choice model must be weighed against several efficiencies possible with a more encompassing, statewide scheme. The latter may eliminate conflict and administrative burden associated with gaining patients' informed consent to opt in at the point of care. It may also circumvent a "first mover" problem if institutions (initially) feared that transparency about iatrogenic injury would place them at a competitive disadvantage. However, issues such as due process and the appropriate firm size for enterprise liability would require much more careful scrutiny before such an expansive scheme could be launched.

The other advantage of the choice model is its potential to catalyze market-driven reform if the experiment is successful. We believe that institutions participating in a no-fault, enterprise liability program would quickly outstrip their competitors both in terms of their attractiveness to patients and their ability to bring about safety interventions. The no-fault option would offer patients the prospect of obtaining compensation for a substantially wider class of injuries, rapid and fair redress, and some rights of appeal. We also believe that physicians would be more satisfied with the process and outcomes. Perhaps most important, the combination of no-fault and enterprise liability would provide institutions with carrots to pursue error prevention efforts, in the form of a less punitive environment and instructive data, and sticks, in the form of experience-rated premiums. Our view is certainly optimistic. But it is a social experiment worth undertaking if we are to decrease significantly the number of injuries caused by medical errors.

References

1. Corrigan, J., Donaldson, M. (eds). *To Err Is Human: Building a Safer Health System*. Washington, DC: Institute of Medicine, 1999.
2. Pear, R. Group asking U.S. for new vigilance in patient safety. *New York Times,* November 30, 1999:A1.
3. David, B., and Appleby, J. Medical mistakes 8th top killer. *USA Today,* November 30, 1999:1A.
4. Goodman, E. In hospitals, to err is human, to fess up is necessary. *Boston Globe,* December 9, 1999:A23.

5. S.R. 2038. Medical Error Reduction Act of 2000 (Sen. Specter).

6. S.R. 2378. Stop All Frequent Errors (SAFE) in Medicare and Medicaid Act of 2000 (Sen. Grassley).

7. S.R. 2738. Patient Safety and Errors Reduction Act (Sen. Jeffords).

8. S.R. 2743. Voluntary Error Reduction and Improvement in Patient Safety Act (Sen. Kennedy).

9. H.R. 5405. Medicare Comprehensive Quality of Care and Safety Act of 2000 (Rep. Stark).

10. Leape, L. L. Error in medicine. *JAMA* 1994;272:1851–1857.

11. Berwick, D. M., and Leape, L. L. Reducing errors in medicine: it's time to take this more seriously. *British Med J* 1999;319:136–137.

12. Keeton, W. P., Dobbs, D. B., Keeton, R. E., and Owens, D. G. *Prosser & Keeton on the Law of Torts,* 5th ed. St. Paul, MN: West Publishing, 1984.

13. Studdert, D. M., Thomas, E. J., Zbar, B. I. W., Newhouse, J. P., Weiler, P. C., Bayuk, J., and Brennan, T. A. Can the United States afford a "no-fault" system of compensation for medical injury? *Law and Contemp Prob* 1997;60:1–34.

14. Reason, J. *Human Error.* New York: Cambridge University Press, 1990.

15. Maurino, D., Reason, J., and Lee, R. *Beyond Aviation Human Factors.* Aldershot, UK: Avery Press, 1995.

16. Perrow, C. *Normal Accidents: Living with High-Risk Technologies.* New York: Basic Books, 1984.

17. Reason, J. *Managing the Risks of Organizational Accidents.* Aldershot, UK: Ashgate, 1997.

18. Bogner, M. S. (ed). *Human Error in Medicine.* Hillsdale, NJ: Lawrence Erlbaum Associates, 1994.

19. Cooper, J. B., and Gaba, D. M. A strategy for preventing anesthesia accidents. *International Anesthesia Clinics* 1989;27(3):148–152.

20. Leape, L. L., Bates, D. W., Cullen, D. J., et al. Systems analysis of adverse drug events. *JAMA* 1995;274:35–43.

21. Reason, J. Human error: models and management. *Brit Med J* 2000;320:768–770.

22. Nightingale, P. G., Adu, D., Richards, N. T., and Peters, M. Implementation of rules based computerised bedside prescribing and administration: intervention study. *Brit Med J* 2000;320:750–753.

23. Scott, H. D., Thacher-Renshaw, A., Rosenbaum, S. E., et al. Physician reporting of adverse drug reactions: results of the Rhode Island Adverse Drug Reaction Reporting Project. *JAMA* 1990;263:1785–1788.

24. Rogers, A. S., Israel, E., Smith, C. R., et al. Physicians' knowledge, attitudes, and behavior related to adverse drug events. *Arch Intern Med* 1988;148:1596–1600.

25. Ross, L., Wallace, J., and Paton, J. Medication errors in a paediatric teaching hospital in the UK: five years operational experience. *Arch Disease Childhood* 2000;83:492–496.

26. Bosk, C. L. *Forgive and Remember: Managing Medical Failure.* Chicago: University of Chicago Press, 1979.

27. Leape, L. L. Why should we report adverse incidents? *J Eval Clin Practice* 1999;5(1):1–4.

28. Bates, D. W., Leape, L. L., Cullen, D. J., et al. Effect of computerized physician order entry and a team intervention on prevention of serious medication errors. *JAMA* 1998;280:1311–1316.

29. Petersen, L. A., Brennan, T. A., O'Neil, A. C., Cook, E. F., and Lee, T. H. Does housestaff discontinuity of care increase the risk for preventable adverse events? *Ann Intern Med* 1994;121:866–872.

30. Pretzer, M. Congress backs away from mandatory reporting of medical errors. *Med Econ* 2000;77(16):25.

31. Lawthers, A. G., Localio, A. R., Laird, N. M., Lipsitz, S., Hebert, L., and Brennan, T. A. Physicians' perceptions of the risk of being sued. *J Health Polit Pol Law* 1992;17(3):463–482.

32. Gostin, L. O. A public health approach to reducing error: medical malpractice as a barrier. *JAMA* 2000;283:1742–1743.

33. Studdert, D. M., Sage, W. M., Gresenz, C. R., and Hensler, D. R. Expanding managed care liability: what impact on employment-based health coverage? *Health Aff* 1999;18(6):7–27.

34. Brennan, T. A., and Berwick, D. M. *New Rules: Regulations, Markets, and the Quality of American Health Care.* San Francisco: Jossey-Bass, 1996.

35. Pear, R. Clinton to order steps to reduce medical mistakes. *New York Times,* February 22, 2000:A1.

36. Liang, B. A. Error in medicine: legal impediments to U.S. reform. *J Health Polit Pol Law* 1999;24(1):27–58.

37. Liang, B. A. Risks of reporting sentinel events. *Health Aff* 2000;19(5): 112–20.

38. Hallam, K. Next target: National Practitioner Data Bank. *Modern Healthcare,* September 4, 2000:32.

39. Gardner, J., and Hallam, K. It may be politics over policy in 2000. *Modern Healthcare* 2000;30:30–33.

40. Wu, A. W., Cavanaugh, T. A., McPhee, S. J., Lo, B., and Micco, G. P. To tell the truth—ethical and practical issues in disclosing medical mistakes to patients. *J Gen Intern Med* 1997;12:770–775.

41. Witman, A. B., Park, D. M., and Hardin, S. B. How do patients want physicians to handle mistakes: a survey of internal medicine patients in an academic setting. *Arch Intern Med* 1996;156:2565–2569.

42. Kaiser Family Foundation and Agency for Healthcare Research and Quality. National survey on Americans as health care consumers: an update on the role of quality information. December, 2000.

43. Peterson, L. M., and Brennan, T. Medical ethics and medical injuries: taking our duties seriously. *J Clin Ethics* 1990;1(3):207–211.

44. Scheutzow, S. O., and Gillis, S. L. Confidentiality and privilege of peer review information: more imagined than real. *J Law & Health* 1992/93;7:169.

45. *Carr v. Howard,* 689 N.E.2d 1304 (1998).

46. Palmer, L. I. Patient safety, risk reduction, and the law. *Houston Law Rev* 1999;36:1609–1661.

47. Gawande, A. When good doctors go bad. *The New Yorker,* August 7, 2000:60–69.

48. Bovbjerg, R. R., and Sloan, F. A. No-fault for medical injury: theory and evidence. *U Cinc Law Rev* 1998;67:53–123.

49. Johnson, K. B., Phillips, C. G., Orentlicher, D., and Hatlie, M. S. A fault-based administrative alternative for resolving medical malpractice claims. *Vanderbilt Law Rev* 1989;42:1365–1406.

50. Danzon, P. M. The Swedish patient compensation system: lessons for the United States. *J Leg Med* 1994;15:199–248.

51. Brahams, D. No fault compensation Finnish style. *Lancet* 1988;2(8613):733–736.

52. Miller, R. S. An analysis and critique of the 1992 changes to New Zealand's accident compensation scheme. *Maryland Law Rev* 1993;52:1070–1092.

53. Espersson, C. The Swedish patient insurance: a descriptive report. Paper presented at Balliol College, Oxford, England, 1992.

54. Weiler, P. C. The case for no-fault medical liability. *Maryland Law Rev* 1993;52:908–950.

55. Horwitz, J., and Brennan, T. A. No-fault compensation for medical injury: a case study. *Health Aff* 1995;14(4):164–179.

56. Sloan, F. A., Whetten-Goldstein, K., Entman, S. S., Kulas, E. D., and Stout, E. M. The road from medical injury to claims resolution—how no-fault and tort differ. *Law and Contemp Prob* 1997;60(2):35–70.

57. Studdert, D. M., Fritz, L., and Brennan, T. A. The jury is still in: Florida's Birth-Related Neurological Injury Compensation Association after a Decade. *J Health Polit Pol Law* 2000;25(3):499–526.

58. Saks, M. J. Medical malpractice: facing real problems and finding real solutions. *Will Mary Law Rev* 1994;35:693–726.

59. Thomas, E. J., Studdert, D. M., Newhouse, J. P., et al. Costs of medical injuries in Utah and Colorado. *Inquiry* 1999;36(3):255–64.

60. Schwartz, G. T. Reality in the economic analysis of tort law: does tort law really deter? *UCLA Law Rev* 1994;42:377–444.

61. Sloan, F. A., Entman, S. S., Reilly, B. A., Glass, C. A., Hickson, G. B., and Zhang, H. H. Tort liability and obstetricians' care levels. *Int Rev Law Econ* 1997;17(2):245–260.

62. Viscusi, W. K., and Moore, M. J. Promoting safety through workers' compensation: the efficacy and net wage costs of injury insurance. *Rand J Econ* 1989;20:499–515.

63. Worrall, J. D., and Butler, R. J. Experience rating matters. In: Borba, P. S., Appel, D. B. (eds). *Workers Compensation Insurance Pricing: Current Programs and Proposed Reforms*. Boston: Kluwer Academic Publishers, 1988.

64. Landes, E. M. Insurance, liability, and accidents: a theoretical and empirical investigation of the effects of no-fault accidents. *J Law & Econ* 1982;25:49–65.

65. Devlin, R. A. Liability v. no-fault automobile insurance regimes: an analysis of the experience in Quebec. In: Dionne, G. (ed). *Contributions to Insurance Economics*. Boston: Kluwer Academic Publishers, 1992.

66. Sloan, F. A., Reilly, B. A., and Schenzler, C. M. Tort liability versus other approaches for deterring careless driving. *Int Rev Law Econ* 1994;14:53–71.

67. Kochanowski, P. S., and Young, M. V. Deterrent aspects of no-fault automobile insurance: some empirical findings. *J Risk & Ins* 1985;52:269–288.

68. Zador, P., and Lund, A. Re-analyses of the effects of no-fault auto insurance on fatal crashes. *J Risk & Ins* 1986;52:226–241.

69. Spieler, E. Perpetuating risk? Workers compensation and the persistence of occupational injuries. *Houston Law Rev* 1994;31:119–264.

70. Sloan, F. A. Experience-rating: does it make sense for medical malpractice insurance? *Am Econ Rev* 1990;80:128–133.

71. Rolph, J. E., Kravitz, R. L., and McGuigan, K. Malpractice claims data as a quality improvement tool. II. Is targeting effective? *JAMA* 1991;266(15):2093–2097.

72. Abraham, K. S., and Weiler, P. C. Enterprise medical liability and the evolution of the American health care system. *Harvard Law Rev* 1994;108:381–436.

73. Sage, W. M., Hastings, K. E., and Berenson, R. A. Enterprise liability for medical malpractice and health care quality improvement. *Am J Law Med* 1994;10(1&2):1–28.

74. Kravitz, R. L., Rolph, J. E., and McGuigan, K. Malpractice claims data as a quality improvement tool. I. Epidemiology of error in four specialties. *JAMA* 1991;266(15):2087–2092.

75. http://www.rmf.harvard.edu/publications/forum/index.html. Accessed April 2, 2001.

76. Spieler, E. Perpetuating risk? Workers compensation and the persistence of occupational injuries. *Houston Law Rev* 1994;31:119–264.

77. Ruser, J. W. Workers' compensation and occupational injuries and illnesses. *J Lab Econ* 1991;9(4):325–350.

78. Abraham, K. S., and Weiler, P. C. Enterprise medical liability and the choice of the responsible enterprise. *Am J Law Med* 1994;10(1&2):29–36.

79. Patient Compensation Act of Colorado, 1997. In: Final report to the IMPACS Program of the Robert Wood Johnson Foundation, August 28, 1997.

80. *State Farm Mutual Automobile Insurance Company v. Brodnax,* 827 P.2d. 531 (1992).

81. *Madden vs. Kaiser Foundation Hospitals,* 552 P.2d. 1178 (1976).

82. Studdert, D. M., and Brennan, T. A. Toward a workable model of "no-fault" compensation for medical injury in the United States. *Am J Law Med* 2001;27(2&3):225–252.

CHAPTER FORTY-SEVEN

THE CRIMINALIZATION OF HEALTH CARE: WHEN IS MEDICAL MALPRACTICE A CRIME?

Karin J. Lindgren

Historically, a health care provider's error in judgment has been a civil matter, which, if proved, may result in monetary compensation for the allegedly injured patient. Since the early 1990s, a small but growing number of physicians and nurses have been the subject of criminal charges arising out of patient care and treatment, which, if proved, may result in the convicted provider being sent to prison (Figure 47-1).

These new criminal cases, which we will refer to as "clinical crimes," are clearly distinguishable from the more typical criminal charges of euthanasia, or "Angel of Death" cases, where the provider intentionally ended a patient's life. These new cases are also distinguishable from the case in which a New York surgeon carved his initials into the patient's abdomen after her cesarean section. Criminal charges are to be expected in those types of cases.

Instead, clinical crimes are cases in which a prosecutor steps into the medical decision-making process and accuses a provider of criminal intent, rather than an error in professional judgment or medical malpractice.

This chapter briefly reviews the fundamental differences between the civil and criminal justice systems, provides a history of physician criminal liability for negligent conduct, outlines several examples of charges brought against physicians and nurses for clinical crimes, and offers recommendations for risk managers and health care administrators for

731

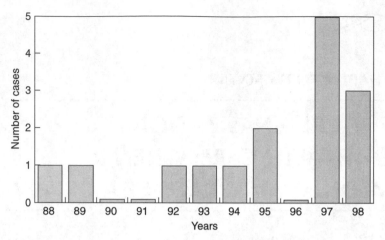

FIGURE 47-1 Trend in clinical criminal filings by prosecutors

handling a situation in which a charge of clinical crime is brought against a health care provider.

The Criminal System Versus the Civil System

The civil system of law provides a mechanism for patients to recover damages from their health care providers when a "therapeutic misadventure" allegedly occurs. This action is called a medical malpractice suit. Most malpractice claims are based on an allegation of negligence, which is the unintentional omission or commission of an act that a reasonably prudent person would or would not do under the same circumstances.

In a civil case against a health care provider, the plaintiff must prove, by a preponderance of the evidence, that the defendant is responsible for the plaintiff's alleged damages. A jury will thereafter render a verdict, and the defendant who is found liable may be ordered to compensate the plaintiff monetarily. In some states, additional punitive damages may also be awarded to the patient for pain and suffering.

On the other hand, in the criminal justice system, charges are brought against an individual by the state (or by the government if a federal crime is charged in a federal court). In any criminal court, the prosecutor has a significantly higher burden of proof than in the civil system. The prosecutor must establish the defendant's guilt beyond a reasonable doubt.

The courts are generally agreed that negligence exists where the physician or surgeon, or person assuming to act as such, exhibits gross lack of competency, or gross inattention, or criminal indifference to the patient's safety; and some courts hold that criminal negligence on the part of a physician or surgeon may arise through gross ignorance of the science of medicine or surgery and of the effect of the remedies employed, gross negligence in the application and selection of remedies and lack of proper skill in the use of instruments, or a failure to give proper instructions to the patient as to the use of the medicines. (50 AMJUR Homicide §93)

If the prosecution establishes guilt beyond a reasonable doubt, the jury will render a guilty verdict, and the convicted defendant may face prison time, a heavy fine, and years of probation. In addition, a felony conviction has lifelong consequences, such as depriving the provider of the right to hold elected political office.

A criminal conviction for a physician or other health care provider's mistake is one huge step beyond punitive damages. Most states have medical licensing rules that provide that criminal conviction of a felony is sufficient grounds to revoke a medical license and will also result in revocation of the physician's participating in Medicare. Therefore, a convicted physician can lose his or her liberty and livelihood in addition to paying a monetary fine.

When a criminal case is filed while a civil case arising from the same set of facts is already pending, the civil case is usually stayed until the criminal case is completed; therefore, a physician convicted of a felony can face a later civil trial with the potential for compensatory and punitive damages.

Another important issue that has significant consequences when a health care provider is criminally charged is the question of indemnity coverage for that physician. The general rule of insurability is that conduct causing expected or intended harm is generally not insurable on public policy grounds. Most policies have coverage limitations with specific exclusions for criminal acts. A medical malpractice carrier does not traditionally have a duty to defend a criminal prosecution.

It is clear that there are vast evidentiary, procedural, and punitive differences between the civil and the criminal justice systems in the United States (Table 47-1). Because of the prospect of prison time for a physician, in addition to the prospect of a later civil suit and potentially severe compensatory damages awards, a risk manager or hospital administrator must be particularly careful in handling a situation that gives rise to criminal charges against a health care provider.

TABLE 47-1   Comparison of Criminal and Civil Cases

	Clinical Crime Charged	Medical Malpractice Alleged
Timing	Urgent: Charges may be filed within hours of occurrence	Measured: Statutes of limitations allow up to 5 years to file suit (longer if a minor is involved)
Burden of proof	Beyond a reasonable doubt that defendant acted or failed to act as charged	Preponderance of evidence that the act or omission was not within the standard of care, as proven by expert testimony
Legal fees	Generally not covered by insurance	Covered by medical professional liability error and omissions policy
Evidence	Government controlled	Party controlled (by discovery process)
Remedy	Prison, monetary fine, and probation	Money damages
Rights to appeal	Defendant only	Any party

A History of the Prosecution of Clinical Crime

The idea of using criminal charges to punish negligent health care professionals is not a new phenomenon. However, in the past decade, there has been a marked growth in the number of prosecutions against providers whose negligence resulted in patient deaths.*

---

*See Alexander McCall Smith, "Criminal or Merely Human? The Prosecution of Negligent Doctors," *J Contemp Health Law & Policy* vol. 12, no. 131 (1995) (noting that the marked increase in the number of prosecutions against physicians for the death of patients has led to heightened concern among the medical community); "Doctors Concerned by Criminal Charges," *St. Petersburg Times,* April 2, 1991, 4B (noting that doctors in Florida are increasingly alarmed by the trend of charging doctors criminally for medical mistakes); Diane M. Gianelli, "MD Charged with Manslaughter After Nursing Home Patient Dies," *American Medical News,* April 22–29, 1991, 1, 2 (explaining that a state medical association raised money for a doctor's defense because it feared the case could have severe repercussions); Thomas Maier, "More Doctors Face Prosecution: Crimes Charged in Cases of Deadly Error," *Newsday,* April 18, 1995, A35 (reporting on the increased number of letters from concerned doctors to medical groups concerning the prosecution of physicians); "Malpractice or Homicide?" *Washington Post,* April 18, 1995, A16 (explaining that the medical community is concerned with the new approach of prosecuting health care professionals for medical errors that result in deaths).

One of the earliest cases concerning criminal culpability of a physician for the resulting death of a patient during treatment was *State v. Hardister and Brown,* 28 Ark. 605 (1882). In the *Hardister* case, the defendants were charged with manslaughter in failing to meet standards of care in providing medical assistance during childbirth. The defendant physicians allegedly treated the patient "without due caution and circumspection" by administering a large quantity of morphine and using forceps in a negligent manner to deliver a child, causing his death. The two physicians finished the delivery by pulling the child out by the head and then wrapping a string around its neck to pull it out completely. They left the mother unattended for three days. She died on the third day.

The court held that a physician is criminally liable for causing the death of a patient by virtue of gross ignorance in the selection or application of remedies; however, a physician could not be held criminally liable for misjudgment or mistake in the selection and application of those remedies. The *Hardister* court held that the actions of the defendants established a clear lack of concern for the welfare of the mother and the child. The force used by the defendants in the childbirth and the wantonness of their conduct toward the mother demonstrated the level of gross negligence the law requires to hold a defendant criminally negligent.

Another case, from 1905, establishes the rule of criminal negligence as being one of degree for a jury to decide. In *Hampton v. State,* 39 So. 421 (1905), the physician inserted into a female patient an unknown instrument that he forcefully pushed into the uterus and into her abdomen, causing a tear, after which he pulled out her intestines, causing her death.

Several years later, in *State v. Lester,* 149 N.W. 297 (1914), the defendant was charged with manslaughter for negligently operating an x-ray machine and causing mortal burns to the patient. The court stated:

> Culpable negligence exists where he exhibits gross lack of competency or inattention, or wanton indifference to the patient's safety, which may arise from his gross ignorance of the science or through gross negligence in either its application or lack of proper skill in the use of instruments.

These very early cases indicate that physicians will be held criminally liable for manslaughter when their conduct falls below reasonable standards and the degree of negligence is gross, wanton, or recklessly indifferent to human life. The level at which a physician or surgeon will be held criminally liable for negligent conduct will largely depend upon the degree of that negligence and the overall disregard that level of negligence demonstrates toward human life.

More recent cases establish clearly what types of activities and degrees of negligence courts are reviewing to determine whether a physician should be held criminally liable. In *State v. Weiner,* 194 A. 2d 467 (1963), the defendant was charged and convicted of 12 counts of involuntary manslaughter for the deaths of several patients from hepatitis after receiving intravenous injections. The issue was whether enough evidence was presented to establish a causal link between the intravenous injections and the death of the patients.

The court determined that the prosecution failed to demonstrate the causal relationship between the defendant's conduct and the hepatitis that caused the death of 12 patients. The court reiterated, "negligence, to be criminal, must be reckless and wanton and of such character as shows an utter disregard for the safety of others under circumstances likely to cause death."

In *People v. Klvana,* 11 Cal. App. 4th 1679 (1992), the defendant Milos Klvana was charged and convicted of nine counts of second-degree murder. Early in his medical career, the defendant, a physician, was found to exhibit deficient medical judgment, and he resigned from a residency program. He later applied for a medical license to practice in the state of California. During his tenure in California, he resigned from an anesthesiology residency when he was found to be incompetent. He later applied for residencies and staff privileges at various institutions. He purchased a medical clinic, where he was the attending physician for nine women whose babies died at childbirth or shortly thereafter.

Various scenarios presented in the *Klvana* case demonstrated the defendant's gross negligence in providing care to the women giving birth. The prosecution charged him with second-degree murder for his gross negligence in providing medical care and causing the deaths of these infants. The court outlined the distinction between a charge of involuntary manslaughter and second-degree murder as follows:

> Second degree murder based on implied malice is committed when the defendant does not intend to kill, but engages in conduct which endangers the life of another, and acts deliberately with conscious disregard for life. An essential distinction between second degree murder based on implied malice and involuntary manslaughter based on criminal negligence, is that in the former the defendant subjectively realized the risk to human life created by his conduct, whereas in the latter the defendant's conduct objectively endangered life, but he did not subjectively realize the risk.

The prosecutor decided to indict on a second-degree murder charge instead of involuntary manslaughter because the defendant's actions were so egregious that his malice was implied. The prosecution believed that, as a physician, the defendant had to subjectively recognize the threat his actions were posing to human life as he carried through with those actions. His actions were deemed to have gone beyond criminal negligence and to constitute implied malice. The defendant was convicted and sentenced to imprisonment for 45 years to life on three of the nine counts. The California Supreme Court affirmed Klvana's conviction.

Finally, in *State v. Warden,* 813 P.2d 1146 (Utah, 1991), the court further analyzed the concept of a clinical crime as it analyzed a case that involved a doctor treating a pregnant woman whose newborn infant was later born prematurely and died from respiratory distress syndrome. In this case, the defendant, Warden, allegedly failed to provide adequate care in the home delivery of his patient's baby. She went into labor on November 17, 1986. The defendant failed to show up until Mrs. Young was in the last stage of labor. The infant weighed 4 pounds, made grunting sounds while breathing, and had a purplish-blue complexion. The defendant allegedly placed the baby in a position to mask its breathing problems and told the Youngs that hospitalization was not necessary. Warden then left the patient's home and did not contact the patient until noon the following day, by which time the baby had died.

In analyzing this case, the court noted:

> A doctor may be held criminally liable only when the evidence establishes beyond a reasonable doubt that the doctor's treatment created a substantial and unjustifiable risk that the patient would die, that the doctor should have but failed to perceive this risk, and that the risk is of such a nature and degree that the failure to perceive it constitutes a gross deviation from the standard of care.

The court held that the defendant failed to determine if the infant was premature, failed to admit the baby to a hospital for needed care, and tried to hide the symptoms of the baby's condition from the family. Furthermore, the defendant physician failed to provide the ordinary reasonable care used by physicians in the delivery and care of infants. The court held that Warden knew or should have known that his actions would cause a substantial and unjustifiable risk to the patient and her newborn.

From these cases, one can begin to see a clearer picture of the degree of negligence required by courts and prosecutors in criminally prosecuting physicians for gross misconduct or clinical crimes. Distinctions between negligent civil liability and negligent criminal liability are measured by the degree of gross misconduct of the attending physician and the level of disregard for life that his or her actions demonstrate. As the *Warden* court said:

> Given the high showing required for negligent homicide, doctors' negligence in the treatment of patients will rarely precipitate criminal liability. It is also true, however, that if doctors act with criminal negligence, they should not escape criminal liability merely because the negligence occurred in a professional setting.

A Bad Clinician or a Criminal?

The following cases are more detailed examples of several physicians and nurses who were prosecuted for clinical crimes arising out of alleged acts of medical negligence, with varying degrees of success for the prosecution and the providers.

State v. Naramore: Pain Management or Euthanasia?

A Kansas physician, Stan Naramore, was convicted of both attempted murder and second-degree murder in connection with his treatment of two unrelated patients and was sentenced to 5 to 20 years in prison.

The first patient, a 78-year-old hospitalized terminal cancer patient, was in severe pain. The patient's son requested a higher dose of pain-killing medication. Naramore met with the family and explained that in sufficiently large doses, such medications often suppress the respiratory system and may actually accelerate the patient's death.

After the family consented, Naramore gave two injections and was preparing a third dose of morphine when the son (a paramedic) changed his mind. After the son said, "I would rather my mother lay there and suffer for 10 more days than you do anything to speed up her death," Naramore administered naloxone (Narcan) to reverse the effects of these painkillers and thereafter withdrew from the patient's care.

The patient was transferred to another hospital, where she was given additional morphine and died a few days later. In 1994, two years later, Dr. Naramore was indicted and later convicted of attempted murder of this 78-year-old woman.

The second case involved an 81-year-old diabetic with a pacemaker and a serious history of heart disease who refused to take his heart medication. He was found slumped over at a convenience store with an irregular heartbeat, difficulty breathing, and inability to speak.

The patient was taken by ambulance to the emergency room, where he was given vecuronium (Norcuron), a paralyzing agent, after which a mechanical ventilator was placed. After aggressively treating the patient for 3 hours in the emergency room, Naramore decided that further treatment was futile.

A second physician (a neurologist) agreed, after finding no pulse, respiration, or reflexes. The neurologist was not initially aware that Naramore had administered the Norcuron, but did not change his medical opinion when told of the drug. The ventilator was removed, and the patient died 8 minutes later.

Naramore was indicted and later convicted of second-degree murder of this patient. In July 1998, six years after these two patients' deaths, the Kansas Court of Appeals overturned both convictions. In its opinion, the court acknowledged the fine line between pain management and euthanasia and the difficulties facing medical practitioners in drawing that distinction. The court wrote, "there is nothing close to a medical consensus that Dr. Naramore's actions were homicidal. In fact, there was extremely strong testimony to the contrary."

State v. Turner: Agonal Breathing or Miraculous Recovery?

Eugene Turner, a 62-year-old pediatrician in Washington state, was charged with second-degree murder of a 3-day-old infant. In January 1998, an ambulance was called to the baby's home, where the emergency medical technicians (EMTs) found no respiration and no pulse. The EMTs' report described the baby as cold and blue, with pupils fixed and dilated; however, the police report agreed the baby had no pulse but described him as "warm, limp and pale."

In the emergency room, Turner tried to resuscitate the child for over 2 hours. The parents consented to a termination of these efforts. Thirty minutes later, an emergency room nurse saw the baby take four to eight "gasps" per minute and felt a heartbeat. She called a second nurse over, who documented a heartbeat of 160, improved color, and 10 respirations per minute.

Turner was then called into the room and tried to stimulate the baby by rubbing its back, but he said the baby would die "real soon." He went home but was called back after the baby became pinker and continued to take unassisted breaths. Turner made several unsuccessful attempts to put a tube in the baby's airway but continued to work on the baby.

Sometime later, two nurses assisting Turner saw him cover the child's mouth and pinch her nose closed, saying that the child was brain dead and that he "could not stand to watch this go on much longer." He claimed that he stopped only reflexive or "agonal" breathing, which he described as "an indicator of death, not an indicator of life."

Turner was recently charged with second-degree murder of the infant, and the case is pending.

State v. Steir: Murder or Complication of Second-Trimester Abortion?

In December 1996, Dr. Bruce Steir performed a second-trimester abortion on a 27-year-old patient in Riverside, California. During the procedure, Steir looked up at the ultrasound technician, who later testified that he said, "I think I pulled bowel." At trial, experts testified that the bowel cannot be reached without perforating the uterus, and Steir should have immediately rushed the patient to the hospital. After 1 hour in the clinic's recovery room, during which time she vomited blood, the patient's vital signs were recorded as normal and she was sent home.

Her mother drove the several-hour trip home to San Francisco. During the trip, they stopped at a fast food restaurant and then continued home. On arriving home, the patient could not be awakened and was rushed to the hospital, where she was pronounced dead. A uterine perforation and evidence of surface hemorrhaging was found on autopsy.

At the time of this abortion, Steir was on medical probation because of prior mistakes in abortions—including two uterine perforations. He was charged with second-degree murder. On April 5, 2000, Steir pled guilty to involuntary manslaughter.

State v. Schug: Wrongful Death or Delay in Transfer of Infant?

An 11-month-old infant was brought to a hospital emergency room in an isolated mountainous region in Northern California. Dr. Wolfgang Schug initially diagnosed an ear infection and prescribed an antibiotic. The next day, the child initially improved but then became "sicker," according to the parents. Schug saw the patient a second time in the emergency room and diagnosed a common gastrointestinal illness. He prescribed an electrolyte solution to prevent dehydration and sent the patient home a second time.

A few hours later, the child was rushed back to the hospital for a third time, after a serious deterioration in his condition. Schug spent 8 hours with the baby and was still unable to determine what caused his symptoms.

After consulting another pediatrician at a larger hospital, Schug recommended that the baby be transferred, by car, to the larger medical institution 55 miles away. He recommended that the patient be taken by private car due to "recent delays in the emergency transportation system" in that rural area. The baby died during the car ride. Schug prepared a four-page addendum to the medical record after his shift ended.

Schug was charged with second-degree murder. At trial, the prosecutor emphasized that the four-page addendum was evidence of both an attempt to "cover up" the doctor's actions and also implied knowledge of his reckless disregard for the patient's well-being.

The trial ended on February 20, 1998, when the judge dismissed the charges after the prosecution had presented its case. The judge ruled there were insufficient grounds to support a conviction. Schug is now facing a civil suit by the parents alleging wrongful death.

U.S. v. Wood: Murder by Potassium Chloride Injection or Heroic Emergency Effort?

In Tulsa, Oklahoma, Dr. Douglas Wood was treating an 86-year-old patient with a serious medical history, including tuberculosis, pneumonia, hypertension, and congestive heart failure. He was 5 days' postsurgery for a perforated ulcer when he was found to be suffering from significant hypokalemia, a low potassium level. Wood was called in to see the patient immediately.

Generally, potassium chloride is used to replenish potassium levels, but large doses of potassium chloride are also used to execute condemned inmates on death row. Although hospital policy dictated a slow drip of diluted potassium chloride over an hour or more, Wood felt that he had "maybe two minutes" to get potassium into the patient's system. Therefore, Wood administered a lethal dose of potassium chloride using a syringe. The patient promptly died.

Wood was convicted of involuntary manslaughter. Wood unsuccessfully defended the case by saying that desperate measures were warranted to try to save this man's life.

People v. Einaugler: Criminal Neglect or Delay in Hospital Admission?

On a Friday night, Dr. Einaugler admitted a new patient into a Brooklyn, New York, nursing home. Einaugler mistook the peritoneal dialysis catheter for a gastrostomy tube and ordered the nursing home personnel to begin feeding the blind, 78-year-old patient with end-stage renal disease through that catheter.

Two days later, a nurse discovered the error and called Einaugler at 6:00 on a Sunday morning. Einaugler then called the patient's nephrologist, who recommended that the patient be admitted to the hospital. There is a dispute as to how urgently she was to be admitted.

Instead of ordering an immediate admission, Einaugler proceeded to the nursing home, where he found that the feeding fluids had been drained from the patient's abdominal cavity and the patient was doing fine. He saw her again in the afternoon and decided to continue to manage her conservatively in the nursing home until Monday morning, when she would go to the hospital for dialysis and have the abdominal cavity washed out.

Later that afternoon, the patient became weaker. Einaugler met the patient in the hospital emergency room, where she was admitted. She died 4 days later of suspected chemical peritonitis, although no autopsy was done.

Einaugler was indicted for manslaughter and in 1993 was convicted at trial on two lesser included counts: reckless endangerment and criminal neglect. He was sentenced to 52 weekends in jail at New York's notorious Riker's Island.

Basically, Einaugler was convicted and sent to prison for choosing to hospitalize a patient in the afternoon instead of the morning. Interestingly, the New York State Board of Professional Conduct investigated the incident and declined to penalize Einaugler for any of his actions.

On appeal, Einaugler's conviction was upheld, and the court ruled that he was aware of, and consciously disregarded, a substantial risk of serious physical injury to the patient by delaying her transfer.

In June 1997, after Einaugler had served six weekends at Riker's Island, New York Governor Pataki freed him and commuted his sentence to 52 days of community service, consisting of treating patients at a homeless shelter.

State v. King, Golz, Fitchette: Medication Error or Manslaughter?

The recent proclivity of filing criminal actions is not just directed at physicians; it has also been directed at nurses. As an example, in 1997, criminal indictments were filed in Denver against three nurses for administering the wrong dosage of a medication via the wrong route. They were charged with involuntary manslaughter.

The case involved a healthy baby boy born at a Denver hospital to a mother who had a previous history of syphilis. The physician wrote an order for an intramuscular (IM) injection of penicillin G as a precaution. The pharmacist misinterpreted the dosage but did label the medication as IM only. Nurse King, the primary nurse, was concerned that the IM route of administration would mean that the infant would have to be stuck repeatedly. King consulted with two nursing supervisors, Nurse Golz and Nurse Fitchette. Golz, a pediatric nurse practitioner, changed the route of administration from intramuscular to intravenous (IV) without consulting with the pharmacy or the physician. The infant suffered a cardiac arrest within 3 hours of the IV injection.

An investigation following the death of the child led the Colorado Board of Nursing to suspend the licenses of the two supervisors for a year, followed by a 2-year probation. The primary nurse, King, was not disciplined by the board.

The Adams County district attorney determined that the conduct of all three nurses constituted "gross negligence." He pursued a felony charge of criminal negligent homicide, which is defined by Colorado law as a gross deviation from the standard of care that causes the death of another person. A guilty verdict would require a jail term of 1 to 3 years and a fine of up to $1 million.

Golz and Fitchette pled guilty to the charge of criminal negligent homicide. The judge in the case ordered a deferred judgment of 2 years. One of the conditions of the deferment required a public service component that included the education of nursing students regarding the facts of the case. After 2 years, the nurses would be able to withdraw their guilty pleas and the case against them would be dismissed. King, the primary nurse, chose to go to trial and was found not guilty of criminal negligent homicide.

Risk Management Suggestions for Handling Criminal Charges

Risk managers have been educating physicians and other health care professionals for many years on what to do when a malpractice claim is filed in the civil system. In light of prosecutors' recent efforts to criminalize malpractice, risk managers should become familiar with their responsibilities as they pertain to criminal law.

When a criminal charge is filed against a physician or other health care provider, the hospital is generally involved in the subsequent criminal investigation. Consideration should be given to the following recommendations, which are summarized in Table 47-2.

Education

Even before a criminal investigation is launched, risk managers should think about providing in-service education to hospital personnel and

TABLE 47-2   Criminal Charges: Checklist for Risk Managers

As soon as you have knowledge of a criminal investigation pending:

- Notify your corporate counsel and retain a criminal defense attorney.
- Notify public relations.
- Notify the board of trustees.
- Make sure all media statements go through your defense attorney.
- Sequester all original records, films, and specimens.
- Do not schedule press conferences without your attorney.
- Become familiar with the Fifth Amendment.
- Cooperate fully with law enforcement and investigators, with attorney approval.
- Provide a separate meeting room for use of investigators.
- Protect patient and physician confidentiality.
- Limit discussions within the organization on a need-to-know basis.
- Make sure the defense attorney reviews all information before submission to investigators.
- Be prepared for unannounced accreditation surveys.
- Make several copies of medical records.
- Follow sound risk management principles.

medical staff about these issues. It is critical to emphasize the importance of documentation concerns in a criminal investigation.

For example, any hospital personnel or provider who writes late entries in a patient's medical chart, especially if entries are written after the criminal investigation has started, or who attempts to add words of explanation to a lab report or chart note will raise the suspicions of a prosecutor. Thereafter, the prosecutor may consider new charges of fraud and cover-up against the provider or the hospital, and the hospital could face criminal liability exposure as an accessory after the fact or face civil liability for corporate negligence.

Notifications

As soon as you have knowledge of any criminal investigation, notify your corporate counsel or medical malpractice attorney immediately. They will identify an attorney who specializes in criminal law to work with you as a team to respond to the charges and protect the hospital's interests.

Cooperate fully with law enforcement and investigators, subject to your attorney's approval. Provide a meeting room for their use that is away from the main traffic of the hospital. Strongly consider a meeting room off campus, such as in an affiliated medical office; however, do not hand over any information unless your defense attorney first reviews those materials. Your attorney may appoint a contact person for the hospital to coordinate the process. The risk manager often takes this role.

Notify your public relations department and emphasize that they should work closely with your defense attorney: Remember that anything said could be used against the hospital and possibly against the accused provider as well. Make sure that all media statements go through your criminal defense attorney first. Ask the public relations department and hospital administration not to schedule any press conferences without having a discussion with that attorney. The criminal defense attorney should also be present during the press conference.

The board of trustees should be kept well informed regarding the issues. The medical staff and employees should also be informed on a need-to-know basis, but limit the discussion to facts.

Because many of these types of cases are media events, be prepared for regulatory agencies to make surprise visits. The Health Care Financing Administration (HCFA), the state Department of Health, and the Joint Commission on Accreditation of Healthcare Organizations (JCAHO) are but three agencies that may come in to conduct their own investigations. If appropriate, follow your hospital's sentinel event policies.

Sequester Medical Records

Immediately sequester all original medical records and any other material relating to the patient or incident, including original films, specimen samples, slides, or other evidence that may be relevant to the case that gave rise to the criminal investigation. Have copies of medical records and hospital policies and procedures prepared to give to your attorney, who will forward them to the prosecutors and other defense attorneys as appropriate.

During the investigation, patients and physicians still need to be protected from a confidentiality standpoint. Ask investigators for court orders if they request physician credentialing files or patient records that contain psychiatric, HIV, or substance abuse information.

Fifth Amendment Rights

Become familiar with the Fifth Amendment right against self-incrimination. Make sure that all clinical and nonclinical staff are advised of their Fifth Amendment rights before they are questioned by any investigator or law enforcement agent. Any hospital staff to be questioned must be represented by an attorney; because of potential conflicts of interest, they may be entitled to separate criminal counsel.

Conclusion

There are still relatively few criminal charges filed against health care providers. As such, there is little precedent on which to rely in determining whether a given "therapeutic misadventure" may result in criminal charges or remain in the civil courts as a medical malpractice case, as is more typical.

Until there is a sufficient body of criminal case law to establish such precedent, physicians and nurses should simply be advised of these potential criminal issues and continue to practice within the standards of good care. At this early stage in what may be a trend toward criminalizing medical malpractice, it is nearly impossible to predict whether a given situation will give rise to criminal charges.

The question is still being debated: Do criminal prosecutors have a legitimate role in medical decision making? Or should they allow state medical licensing boards, the civil justice system, and peer review committees to do the job of controlling the quality of care and weeding out health care providers who act below the accepted standard of care?

Acknowledgments

The author gratefully acknowledges the research assistance of G. Dirk Rozendale, an LLM candidate at Loyola University School of Law and an extern in the Legal Department at University HealthSystem Consortium.

Bibliography

"Case Against Doctor in a Death Is Dismissed," *New York Times,* section 1, p. 13:1 (Feb. 22, 1998).

Crane, Mark, "Practice Medicine, Land in Jail," *Wall Street Journal* (Feb. 1995).

"Doctor Convicted in Two Patient Deaths," *Denver Post,* sec. B, column B:2 (Jan. 27, 1996).

"Doctor Faces Second-Degree Murder Charge in Baby's Death," *American Medical News,* vol. 41, no. 35, p. 9 (Sept. 21, 1998).

"Doctor Predicts Reversal of Convictions in Patient Deaths," *American Medical News,* vol. 41, no. 10, p. 36 (Mar 9, 1998).

McCarthy, Kara M., "Doing Time for Clinical Crime: The Prosecution of Incompetent Physicians as an Additional Mechanism to Assure Quality Health Care," *Seton Hall Law Rev* vol. 28, no. 569 (1997).

Miniclier, Kit, "Family Doctor a Murderer?" *Denver Post,* section A, p. 1:3 (Jan. 21, 1996).

People v. Einaugler, 650 N.E.2d 1333, 627 NYS 2d 331 (1995), affirmed on appeal (U.S. Ct. of Appeals, 2d Cir. 1997).

Pozgar, George D., *Criminal Aspects of Health Care, Legal Aspects of Health Care Administration.* Gaithersburg, MD: Aspen Publications, 1996, 84–123.

Siegel, Barry, "Some Might Say Doctor's Only Crime Was His Compassion," *Los Angeles Times,* section A, p. 5:1 (Feb. 9, 1999).

Smith, Alexander M., "Criminal or Merely Human? The Prosecution of Negligent Doctors," *J Contemp Health Law and Policy* vol. 12, no. 131 (Fall 1995).

State v. Naramore, 25 Kan. App. 302, 965 P.2d 211 (1998).

Vanderbeken, Jaxon, "Abortion Doctor Says Politics Are Behind Murder Charge," *San Francisco Chronicle,* section A, p. 13:2 (Nov. 1, 1997).

Van Grunfven, Paul R., "Medical Malpractice or Criminal Mistake? An Analysis of Past and Current Prosecutions for Clinical Mistakes and Fatal Errors," *DePaul J Health Care Law* vol. 2, no. 1 (Fall 1997).

Waxman, Sharon, "After Infant's Death, Beloved Doctor Becomes Murder Defendant," *Washington Post,* section A, p. 3:1 (Jan. 31, 1999).

CHAPTER FORTY-EIGHT

WHAT DOES THE LEAPFROG GROUP PORTEND FOR HOSPITALS AND PHYSICIANS?

Arnold Milstein, MD, MPH

In market economies, seller survival depends on careful attention to evolving customer values. The Leapfrog Group, announced by the Business Roundtable's Fortune 500 CEO group in 2000 after a 3-year incubation, signals a new application to providers of long-standing values of large industrial purchasers. These values warrant the attention of hospitals and physicians beyond the importance of the more than 35 million consumers insured by a growing list of over 125 Leapfrog Group large employers. Employers sponsor the health insurance plans for a majority of Americans, and large private-sector employers influence health care purchasing trends for smaller employers and government health benefit programs such as the Center for Medicare and Medicaid Service (CMS). Both CMS and the Department of Defense, which sponsor health benefit programs for an additional 60 million Americans, are collaborating with the Leapfrog Group. CMS has linked its heavily trafficked Medicare beneficiary website to the Leapfrog Group's website, where hospitals are compared on their fulfillment of Leapfrog standards; in addition, it has encouraged quality improvement officers (QIOs) to support hospital efforts to fulfill the Leapfrog Group's three initial "leaps."

Portions of this chapter were included in two prior publications and have been incorporated with permission from JCAHO and *Seminars in Vascular Surgery*.

The Leapfrog Group is initially promoting three leaps aimed at improving patient safety in urban hospitals: computer physician order entry (CPOE); improved intensive care unit (ICU) physician staffing; and evidence-based hospital referral for seven complex, non-emergency treatments based on favorable risk-adjusted outcomes or higher annual volume.[1] Although attention has initially focused on the *content* of the Leapfrog Group's three initial safety leaps, understanding the associated *underlying values* of large industrial purchasers and the consumers whose health benefits they sponsor will prove equally important for physicians and other health care providers.

Eight principal values underpin the Leapfrog leaps and implementation approach.

- *Selecting specifications for improvement based on a preponderance of evidence.* Leapfrog purchasers operate on a different evidentiary basis than biological researchers. Preponderance of evidence, combined with expert judgment, is preferred to delaying selection of "leaps," until randomized control trials demonstrate statistically significant effects at the $p < .05$ level. Preponderance of evidence and expert opinion have anchored stunning progress in the safety of airlines, worksites, and general anesthesia over the past 75 years.
- *Setting stretch goals.* Leapfrog purchasers are focused on high-yield improvements that will be difficult for some hospitals to achieve. This reflects large purchasers' experience in their own businesses over the last 20 years, when more ambitious process reengineering goals usually generated much bigger yields than less ambitious goals. Former treasury secretary Paul O'Neill's setting a zero-error goal for Pittsburgh hospitals when he was Alcoa's CEO illustrates this value. A research team at Dartmouth has estimated conservatively that meeting the high Leapfrog safety leaps in nonrural American hospitals would annually prevent 60,000 deaths and over half a million serious medication errors.[2] More recent research on the benefits from Leapfrog's ICU leap suggests that adoption of the three leaps in all urban hospitals would prevent more than 170,000 deaths annually.[3]
- *Concentrating use in preferred suppliers.* Leapfrog purchasers encourage all urban hospitals to achieve the leaps. However, after an initial grace period, Leapfrog purchasers will use performance targets and/or incentives for their insurers, along with education and/or incentives for consumers, to reward with more market share hospitals that meet the standards.
- *Asking preferred suppliers to disclose their status.* In partnership with their health insurers, Leapfrog purchasers are asking their

high-use hospitals to disclose to purchasers on a Web survey their status on the first three safety leaps and, when available, their directly measured comparative performance. This reflects industrial purchaser expectations of other primary suppliers who are assessed via ISO (International Standards Organization) certification and direct, continuous supplier reporting of "critical-to-quality" measures determined or approved by the purchaser.

- *Migrating purchasing specifications to measured defect rates in the end product.* Industrial purchasers commonly base their specifications for preferred suppliers on low defect rates in the end product delivered to the customer. However, because the health care industry fails to capture electronically clinical data needed for valid outcomes or process comparisons, the Leapfrog Group's three initial standards default to measures of structural input. Leapfrog purchasers are dissatisfied with this equilibrium and are already partnering with the Joint Commission on the Accreditation of Healthcare Organizations (JCAHO), the National Committee for Quality Assurance (NCQA), the Agency for Healthcare Research and Quality (AHRQ), the National Quality Forum (NQF), and provider, plan, and consumer leaders to evolve national public performance reporting systems that would allow scientifically valid comparisons of hospital and physician defect rates. For example, in 2003, hospitals that participate in outcomes reporting programs operated by four state governments, the American College of Cardiology, and the Society for Thoracic Surgery will be credited for favorable outcomes in Leapfrog's publicly released algorithm for rating hospitals comparatively.

- *Soliciting supplier input on purchasing specifications.* The Leapfrog Group's development of new leaps and refinement of existing leaps systematically incorporates advice from a wide range of providers. Multiple provider organizations such as the American Medical Association, the American Hospital Association, the American College of Surgeons, and other provider or provider assessment organizations are invited to suggest new leaps and comment on proposed leaps and measures prior to adoption. To refine the initial three leaps for 2003, Leapfrog purchasers invited broad input via a public call for refinement ideas in the spring of 2002. They are also committed to considering the recommendations of national safety experts and additional stakeholders who anchor the National Quality Forum's safe practices endorsement process.

- *Broadly educating other customers.* Leapfrog purchasers understand that for hospitals to justify allocating their finite capital and management resources to meet high purchaser standards, hospitals need the widest possible market reinforcement. Accordingly, Leapfrog purchasers are committed to educating other purchasers, insurers, and consumers in the importance of patient safety improvements in general and the incremental value of the three Leapfrog leaps specifically.

- *Respecting consumer preferences.* For industrial purchasers, it is employees, retirees, and dependents who are the primary "customers" of employee health benefit programs. Accordingly, Leapfrog purchasers are committed to educating these customers on which hospitals meet or commit to rapidly meeting the three Leapfrog safety leaps and on the associated personal risk reduction, rather than blocking access to other hospitals. Though large industrial purchasers can influence hospital selection via education and economic incentives, consumers, guided by their physicians and the media, make the final decisions.

Increased consumer scrutiny of health care provider capability and performance is widely predicted.[4] Although the rate of spread of health consumerism is difficult to forecast, four market research findings suggest that Leapfrog safety leaps are likely to resonate well with consumers: (1) Multiple recent public surveys indicate that consumers attach a very high value to avoiding medical mistakes, (2) Stanford researchers Kahneman and Tversky have documented that consumers attach more importance to protection from tangible safety threats than to abstract improvement efforts such as continuous quality improvement,[5] (3) the Voluntary Hospital Association published findings in January 2000 that more than 80% of consumers are prepared to select a new physician or hospital based on credible comparative ratings,[6] and (4) the Foundation for Accountability documented strong consumer understanding of and support for the three initial Leapfrog safety leaps.[7]

The remarkable gains available through hospital and physician fulfillment of the leaps will require significant reprioritization of management effort and capital, and the support of physician leaders. In their response, hospitals and physicians must weigh multiple additional factors.

The Leapfrog Group will be broadening its leaps. During 2003, it plans to initiate a new leap that incorporates the wider array of safe practices endorsed by the National Quality Forum. It is also planning adoption, in partnership with CMS and AHRQ, of a leap in physician office electronic clinical decision support during 2004, and to move beyond safety and reward provider excellence on all six Institute of Medicine domains of quality.[8]

Although the content of the leaps warrants close attention by providers, the values that underlie these standards are more important predictors of private-sector purchasing priorities. Led by large industrial purchasers, the Leapfrog Group signals an era of more discerning consumers and purchasers. They will increasingly navigate toward physicians and hospitals ranking higher in quantified performance comparisons. Extrapolating from the experience of other industries, such as auto manufacturing, which faced rapid increases in public performance comparisons and customer safety consciousness, the market success for providers will increasingly pivot on their participation in valid, comparative, publicly reported performance measurement systems and on their success in comprehensive, rapid-cycle performance improvement, carefully targeted to the emerging values of their customers.

References

1. Milstein, A., Galvin, R. S., Delbanco, S. F., Salber, P., and Buck, C. R. Improving the Safety of Health Care: The Leapfrog Initiative. *Effective Clinical Practice* 2000;6:313–16.
2. Birkmeyer, J. D., Birkmeyer, C. M., Wennberg, D. E., and Young, M. *Leapfrog Safety Standards: The Potential Benefits of Universal Adoption.* Washington, DC: The Leapfrog Group, 2000.
3. Pronovost, P. et al. Physician Staffing Patterns and Clinical Outcomes in Critically Ill Patients: A Systematic Review. *JAMA* 2002;288:2151.
4. Robinson, J. C. The End of Managed Care. *JAMA* 2001;285:2622–28.
5. Tversky, A., and Kahneman, D. The Framing of Decisions and the Psychology of Choice. *Science* 1981;211:453–8.
6. *Consumer Demand for Clinical Quality: The Giant Awakens.* Vol. 3, 2000 Research Series. Irving, TX: Voluntary Hospital Association, 2000.
7. *Development of a Consumer Communications Toolkit: Report and Findings from the Leapfrog Group's 2001 Focus Groups.* Portland, OR: Foundation for Accountability, 2001.
8. Institute of Medicine. *Crossing the Quality Chasm.* Washington, DC: National Academy Press, 2001.

CHAPTER FORTY-NINE

THE FUTURE OF PATIENT SAFETY: REFLECTIONS ON HISTORY, THE DATA, AND WHAT IT WILL TAKE TO SUCCEED

Christopher Cassirer, ScD, PhD and Deborah Anderson

Increasing national attention continues to focus on the problem of patient safety in the medical workplace. According to the most recent population studies presented in the Institute of Medicine report (1999), on average 3.7% of hospitalized patients suffer an adverse event and approximately 1% of these events are due to negligence. Based on these rates, estimates are that as many as 44,000 to 98,000 patients are injured in U.S. hospitals every year.

Responses to the alarming data and statistics presented in the IOM report have appeared in both academic and professional literatures as well as the popular press. Renewed commitments to creating change and to doing no harm, to developing tools to address cultural and environmental challenges, and to improving systems of care that create opportunities for accidents and injuries to occur are continuing to grow. Although the business case has yet to be presented, many believe that enhancing patient safety is good for quality and for overall improvements in organizational performance.

Despite the wealth of commitment that is currently being generated to address the problem of patient safety, there is little to no evidence that current efforts will be more successful than in the past. Although many are willing to discuss patient safety, attend professional conferences on the topic, and debate the wisdom of emerging legislation and state regulation, among other topics, few are taking on some of the most significant barriers to creating sustainable change in behavior.

Although the past is not necessarily prologue for the future, it is important to remain mindful of some of the history of past efforts to address the problem of medical injury. This chapter presents information about the medical malpractice crises that occurred during the 1970s and 1980s, emphasizing some important insights for patient safety that can be gained from a closer examination of the history of risk management. It also discusses the evidence regarding state mandates to promote hospitals' efforts to better manage the risk of medical injury, suggesting that state mandates for risk management haven't worked. Next, this chapter talks about the new mind-set of patient safety and some key factors required to create sustainable change. It emphasizes the importance of making a fundamental commitment to address cultural barriers that stand in the way of developing effective patient safety interventions and suggests that collectively we must be willing to work across competitive boundaries and share information. These actions are imperative if patient safety is to succeed.

Medical Malpractice Crises of the 1970s and 1980s

During the 1970s and 1980s, periods of rapid to explosive growth occurred in the number (frequency) and size of payments (severity) for medical malpractice claims and lawsuits, causing many to declare a crisis in medical malpractice. Many insurers of professional liability risk began to withdraw from the market for medical malpractice insurance, leaving individual and institutional providers financially exposed to the risk of paying for malpractice claims. Many were also deeply concerned about accumulating data and evidence on the problem of adverse events and medical injury (Brennan et al., 1991).

In response, various interest groups, including insurance companies and members of the professional health care community, began to search for underlying causes and possible solutions to the problem. Few, however, could agree on a common definition of the problem or a potential solution. Some called for an evaluation of the laws governing professional liability and medical malpractice. Others argued for insurance market reforms and increased regulation of insurance company premiums and loss-reserving practices. Still others focused on introducing legislation to stimulate the incentive effects of the tort liability system to motivate changes in provider behavior. Many states, in turn, passed legislation designed to affect the malpractice claims litigation process as well as the frequency and severity of medical malpractice claims.

Despite the incredible amount of effort from various health and nonhealth industry segments, the data provide little evidence to suggest that most efforts to address the problem of medical injury through reform of the malpractice system have been effective (Danzon, 1985; Kinney, 1995). As the patient safety movement continues to unfold and explore issues related to adverse events, mistakes, and injury, it will be important to remain mindful of these past efforts.

An approach to categorizing the range of past proposed solutions to the problem of medical injury and malpractice is to divide them into first- and second-generation reforms (Bovjberg, 1989; Kinney, 1995).

Many first-generation reforms, for example, were implemented in response to both the 1970s and 1980s malpractice insurance crises. These included promoting insurance market reforms at the federal and state level as well as passing tort reform legislation in the states designed to control the frequency and severity of medical malpractice claims. Several insurance market reforms, for example, focused on providing alternatives for hospitals and other providers to finance professional liability risk. Instead of purchasing insurance from commercial liability insurance carriers, providers could self-insure for some or all of their professional liability risk (Sielnicki, 1983, 1989; Horn and Head, 1993).

Although definitions of self-insurance in health care vary, conceptually it can refer to the practice among hospitals and health systems of retaining a portion of the expected cost of financial loss associated with malpractice claims. In theory, retention of insurance through different self-insurance methods should create an incentive for providers to be more concerned about adverse events and medical injuries as well as associated malpractice claims and lawsuits. Neither history nor research has provided much evidence to suggest that first-generation reforms such as these have been effective in preventing and controlling injury or claims (Cassirer, 1997; Morlock, Cassirer, and Malitz, 1997).

Many second-generation reforms were also implemented in response to the medical malpractice crises of the past several decades. These second-generation reforms focused on improving the malpractice claims resolution process, promoting interventions designed to reduce the incidence of adverse events and patient injuries, and motivating providers to standardize clinical decision making and practice behavior (Kinney, 1995). An example of a second-generation reform that has close ties to patient safety and that has received increasing national support since the medical malpractice insurance crisis of the 1970s is the promotion of hospital risk management programs. In general, hospital risk management programs are defined as the systems designed to prevent and control patient injuries as well as losses associated with malpractice claims. In theory, these programs have the potential to control the problem of medical injury and malpractice by simultaneously addressing multiple dimensions of the problem. Based on their potential to prevent and control the problem of medical injury, increasing national support has been generated for risk management programs during the past 30 years.

Although the field of risk management has grown considerably since the medical malpractice crises of the 1970s and 1980s, its history should be of interest to those involved in the patient safety movement. Early forms of risk management programs in hospitals were often based in departments of safety and security. For the most part, these early programs were focused on ensuring access to a continued source of funds to pay for professional liability claims or ensuring compliance with occupational health and safety guidelines. Other programs, however, focused on addressing the problems of patient slips and falls as well as medication errors. Innovations that emerged from this period in the history of patient safety included placing guard rails on patient beds and providing patients with wristbands to indicate critical information regarding their personal statistics and health condition (Orlikoff and Vanagunas, 1988).

Critics of these early patient safety programs in hospitals argue, however, that the programs often focused only on patient slips and falls and medication error prevention. Few actually addressed the more severe incidents of injury in areas such as emergency services, obstetrics, and inpatient surgery (National Association of Insurance Commissioners [NAIC], 1980). The most recent publications on risk management and patient safety argue that there is a need to address the full range of adverse events and medical injury and to recognize the overlap between these two potential solutions to the problem (Vincent, 2001).

For example, according to Vincent and colleagues (2001), current conceptions of risk management view it as a tool for enhancing patient safety, arguing that harm to patients can no longer be viewed simply as the result of human error. Instead, an understanding must be created that uncertainty and risk are an inherent part of medical practice that must be managed by an overall examination of the systems underlying medical care. Much can be learned by examining the history and current works on risk management by those involved in the patient safety movement.

Legislative Mandates in the States

Another important lesson learned from the history of past efforts to address the problem of medical injury is that state mandates to reform provider behavior appear to have achieved only limited success. This is observed to be true even in states where there are financial incentives in place to motivate efforts to implement programs to prevent and control medical injury.

Currently, several states, such as California, have initiated the process of proposing legislative reforms to promote patient safety. It is important for California and other states to consider the history of risk management legislation, also designed to help prevent patient injury. In short, studies show wide variation exists in state definitions of risk management programs and institutional commitment to adopt such reforms during the past 20 years.

In response to the medical malpractice insurance crisis of the 1980s, 10 states passed mandates requiring hospitals to implement risk management programs (U.S. General Accounting Office [GAO], 1989). These 10 states were Arkansas, Florida, Rhode Island, Kansas, Washington, Massachusetts, North Carolina, Colorado, New York, and Maryland. Studies show that definitions of risk management, requirements for defined programs, and compliance with the mandates vary considerably.

For example, some states such as New York and Rhode Island refer to the risk management legislation as "quality assurance" (Harpster and Veach, 1989). Unlike the other eight states, both Florida and Kansas mandate reporting of specific incidents of patient injury in their legislation. Both Alaska and Rhode Island differ from the other states in that enabling regulations have never been passed. Thus, although there is a mandate in those states, there is nothing that helps to translate it into practical requirements that providers in the states must follow. According to Harpster and coworkers (1989), "incentives for implementing risk management programs are lacking in those states."

In Maryland, for example, hospital risk management programs are described as differing widely among hospitals in the state. The GAO (1989) reported that many hospitals in Maryland did not have all the required program elements in place, and many were considered out of compliance with the Maryland mandate. This finding is particularly striking because the Maryland risk management law has often been described as a model for the nation.

In a more recent study of hospital risk management programs in states with and without mandates, researchers from the Johns Hopkins and Harvard Universities examined variation in hospital risk management programs in Maryland, Colorado, and Utah (Cassirer, 2001). Both Maryland and Colorado have mandates; Utah does not. The Colorado and Utah hospitals examined are the same ones studied and reported on in the recent Institute of Medicine report on medical error (Kohn et al., 1999).

In this study, a modification of the hospital risk management program assessment survey developed by the American Society for

Healthcare Risk Management (ASHRM) was administered to risk managers in 77 acute care hospitals. The ASHRM survey identifies 134 structure, process, and outcomes measures that hospitals should have in place that are considered part of an effective program. In total, 13 hospitals in Utah, 15 hospitals in Colorado, and 49 hospitals in Maryland completed the ASHRM survey. Responding to the survey required hospital risk managers to indicate whether specific program activities were "in place" or "needed development." To estimate the level of hospital risk management program activity, total raw scores were computed for each hospital by counting the number of items of activity and dividing by 134.

The most striking finding from this research is that despite the mandates in both Maryland and Colorado, all three states had a similar level of risk management activity. On average, hospitals in all three states had approximately 65% of the recommended risk management programs and activities in place. The findings from this research and ongoing studies suggest that mandates and regulation may have only limited effects on providers' efforts to develop programs designed to prevent and control patient injury. Moreover, providers may be just as motivated to seek solutions to the problem of medical injury in the absence of state mandates or regulation. Any effort to promote mandates or legislation on patient safety should strongly consider the history and recent research on risk management program regulation in the states.

The New Mind-Set of Patient Safety

The history of the medical malpractice crises and interventions designed to prevent and control injury, such as risk management, provides important information for the patient safety movement. Although there are no direct correlations as yet, it is recognized that current efforts to develop patient safety concepts and tools have the potential to follow the path of initiatives like risk management.

To succeed, patient safety must appreciate history, particularly if it is to motivate a paradigm shift in conceptions of medical injury. Most important, this shift must occur for policy makers, managers, and providers at the blunt and sharp ends of medical care delivery.

Critical to the continued success of the patient safety movement will be a willingness on the part of both health care administrators and individual providers to accept that commitment to patient safety happens on an individual as well as a collective basis and that there is a great deal that can be learned from business and industry, in general, about approaches to designing safe systems.

As reported in the work of Reason (1990) and others, medicine is both a high-risk and a highly technical industry that needs to take into consideration the human and organizational factors that compose highly complex care delivery systems (Vincent, 2001). Although many argue that medicine is not like aviation or nuclear power and therefore these industries are limited in what they can offer for designing safe systems of medical care, these views are short sighted and self-limiting. Often, these views recognize the uniqueness of the human-to-human interaction that takes place in patient care delivery, but ignore the complex and dynamic work processes that shape the patient care experience.

At its core, overcoming resistance and a lack of commitment to adopting patient safety will require a resolution of this tension by each individual. For some, it is difficult to discuss the need to balance mission against margin considerations because of the assault on some of the basic values and commitments to "do no harm" and to always operate in ways that are in the best interest of patients. For others, the need to balance care decisions in light of costs is the unavoidable, current reality. If patient safety is to succeed, a new mind-set has to be adopted on faith that respects that the core business of medical care delivery is taking care of patients and that safety is both good patient care as well as a good business decision.

Need to Address Cultural Barriers to Treating Each Other Better at Work

Deep within the emerging language and conceptual frameworks for guiding patient safety initiatives is a need to operationalize and align a fundamental commitment to ensure respect, honesty, trust, and open communication in work relationships. In the absence of these values, patient safety as a paradigm cannot be sustained.

Working life in medicine, however, is continuing to become increasingly more complex and turbulent, bringing with it greater challenges to manage stress and change. At both the blunt and sharp ends, relationships are being affected. Although many institutional and individual providers believe that honesty, trust, and open communication are important values, the data provide evidence to suggest that on a day-to-day basis, we often behave in ways that are abusive rather than respectful. In short, our attitudes, beliefs, and systems for interpreting the changing nature of our environment and its impact on health care provider behavior are filled with the language and concepts of abuse.

Although there is a paucity of good empirical data on the topic of workplace abuse, it is basically defined as harm to another in professional relationships. In medicine, there is a growing body of information to suggest that blunt-end administrators and sharp-end clinicians are aware of and concerned about the experience of work-place abuse and its impact on patient safety as well as organizational performance (Cassirer et al., 2000).

Beginning in 1992, Respond2, Inc., a Minneapolis-based consult-ing company, began examining the issue of workplace abuse in medi-cine, believing that there are strong linkages between the experience of domestic violence and abuse in the home with the experience of abuse in the medical workplace. To date, Respond2 has accumulated 10 years of survey data from more than 13,500 health care workers. Based on a recent analysis of the data, abusive behavior appears to be a common experience that takes many forms in health care organizations. Of par-ticular note are the experiences of physicians who reported on what it was like to be a medical resident. Similar to findings in other published research, more than 50% of medical students reported experiencing some form of abuse during their training, including being yelled at, belittled, sleep deprived, and working in a state of overall impaired performance (Kassebaum and Cutler, 1998).

Other findings of note from the Respond2 analysis are that 95% of the surveyed staff in all organizations studied, including hospitals, clinics, and managed care organizations, reported experiencing or wit-nessing more abusive behavior in the workplace with each year and that abusive behavior is greater at work than at home. Moreover, another 62% to 96% of those surveyed reported experiencing or wit-nessing abusive behavior in the last year. Last, 3% to 25% reported ex-periencing or witnessing abusive behavior on a daily basis on the job.

Qualitative findings are also available from Respond2. Based on follow-up interviews with a sample of survey respondents, researchers identified specific examples of workplace abuse that appear to be com-mon to both clinical and administrative professionals. Further, these professionals shared their perceptions of how abuse affects perfor-mance. For example, the following quotations are drawn from qualita-tive interviews with respondents to the Respond2 survey:

- "Working for a manager who is very controlling, confrontational, and insensitive impacts on the staff. Many (nurses and other staff) are leaving because of how the managers treat people."
- "Co-workers [in our hospital] are not treating each other with respect—blaming, talking bad, angry voices/body language are the norm."
- "The Chief of one of our departments physically intimidates colleagues, jabs his finger into their chests, corners and yells at people during arguments."
- "Working for a supervisor that is demeaning, damaging, and non-supportive is abusive."

- "Patients aren't getting what they want and they start screaming and yelling in my face."
- "Arguments between two doctors are occurring in the clinic hallway. An M.D. could be overheard verbally berating a receptionist and a nurse."
- "A physician was criticizing another provider loudly to a group within earshot of patients."
- "Too much gossip by some people causes dissention in the group."

Understanding workplace abuse and its impact on patient safety is critical for a number of reasons. In its guidelines on the topic of workplace abuse in medicine, the AMA addresses workplace abuse and patient safety in medical care delivery, emphasizing the impact of unhealthy workplace behavior on the potential effectiveness of tools that are considered part of the emerging knowledge and resources for ensuring patient safety. Two approaches that are considered key to developing patient safety initiatives within health care organizations are effectively managing authority gradients and improving teamwork training and performance systems.

Teamwork training is considered critical for health care providers at the sharp end of medical care to ensure rapid response and coordinated delivery of care. An example might be activity in an operating room among a surgical team of clinicians. Their effectiveness often depends on communication and the ability to share information quickly with other members of the team. When abusive behavior by a member of the team is present, creating hostility, or lack of trust or disrespect is demonstrated, teams cannot perform. This is perhaps most critical during times of crisis, such as in trauma care or emergency surgery.

Authority gradients are the hierarchical relationships within organizational structures or team dynamics. Very often these types of relationships can be observed by examining an organization chart or other means of describing reporting relationships within dynamic systems. In clinical care, they operate in relationships between and among junior and senior physicians and nurses. They become barriers to ensuring safety when abusive behavior is present. Critical information that needs to be communicated up the hierarchy by those with lesser power or influence is stopped. Those down the hierarchy are prevented from speaking up or out because of fear of retaliation or punishment. From a performance standpoint, abusive behavior is inefficient. From a patient safety perspective, abusive behavior creates opportunity for communication and technical systems to fail, potentially causing harm to patients.

To overcome the problem of abusive behavior in the workplace, there are behaviors associated with operating in complex health care systems that can serve as modeling tools for providers. Additional data from Respond2 helps to identify examples of healthy workplace behaviors from the perspective of clinicians and administrators. The following are examples of healthy workplace behaviors as identified by health care workers:

- Trustworthy, honest, responsible, flexible, courteous, organized
- Professional, good attendance, dependable, team oriented, does fair share of work
- Respectful, friendly, calm when things get tough, helps out, supportive, thinks ahead
- Eager to learn and positive attitude, collaborates, forgives—no grudges
- Open communication, listens, inclusive, tolerance of imperfection, and a sense of humor

Addressing abusive behavior in the medical workplace is more than just a "nice thing to do"; it has serious implications for the potential effectiveness of patient safety–related initiatives operating within provider organizations.

Leadership from Every Level of Health Care Organizations

Leadership is a term widely used to describe the type of behavior that is required to continue to move forward patient safety initiatives and the development of tools to support them. Although there is no single definition of the term to which all can agree, in the context of the patient safety movement at this time in history there are leadership questions that providers must be prepared to answer if patient safety initiatives are to continue. There is a real tendency toward complacency and treating patient safety as yet another fad or topic. Both individual and organizational leadership is required.

The first question is: What do you believe is important about ensuring patient safety? Whether it is a personal commitment or an opportunity to engage in socially responsible action, leadership requires that each person must first identify a reason why patient safety is important to him or her and to recognize that it is fundamentally about acting on a commitment to "do no harm" to the patient.

Second, each person must decide who he or she will serve as part of the patient safety movement. The issues are complex, broad, and potentially diverse. Focus is required, and selecting key issues to work on is the type of leadership behavior that will help sustain patient safety.

The third question is: What are the core values? As noted, if patient safety initiatives are to succeed in organizations, a commitment has to be made to behaving honestly and openly, to trust, and to improve efforts to communicate. Absent the individual and organizational commitments to support and sustain these shared values, patient safety initiatives are at risk for remaining project oriented rather than organization-wide.

Willingness to Share Data and Information Across Competitive Boundaries

Practically, patient safety requires commitment from health care providers to gather, analyze, report, and share information about progress on patient safety initiatives. Together, policy makers, managers, providers, and consumers must recognize that the data that have been accumulated to date suggest one important theme: Unfortunately, there is no economy of opportunity when it comes to patient injury. Every day, patients suffer adverse events; injuries and mistakes are made in medical care. Only through collaborations, alliance formation, and a shared commitment to not compete will patient safety be made a reality.

References

Brennan, T. A., Leape, L. L., Laird, N. M., et al. (1991). Incidence of Adverse Events and Negligence in Hospitalized Patients: Results of the Harvard Medical Practice Study I. *New England Journal of Medicine*, 324, 370–6.

Bovjberg, R., Sloan, F., and Blumstein, J. (1989). Valuing Life and Limb in Tort: Scheduling Pain and Suffering. *Northwestern University Law Review*, 83, 4, 908–976.

Cassirer, C. (1997). Hospital Risk Management Programs in Maryland. Unpublished ScD dissertation, The Johns Hopkins University.

Cassirer, C., Anderson, D., Hanson, S., and Fraser, H. (2000). Abusive Behavior Is Barrier to High-Reliability Health Care Systems, Culture of Patient Safety. *QRC Advisor: Creating Value Through the Management of Quality, Risk, & Cost*, 17, 1, November.

Cassirer, C. (2001). Chapter 35: Risk Management Program Evaluation. In Carroll, R. ed. *Risk Management Handbook for Health Care Organizations, Third Edition*. San Francisco, CA: Jossey-Bass.

Danzon, P. M. (1985). *Medical Malpractice: Theory, Evidence, and Public Policy*. Cambridge, MA: Harvard University Press.

Harpster, L. M., and Veach, M. S. (eds.) (1989). *Risk Management Handbook for Health Care Facilities. American Society for Health Care Risk Management*. Chicago, IL: American Hospital Association.

Horn, G. L., and Head, S. H. (1993). *Essentials of Risk Management*. Malvern, PA: The Insurance Institute of America.

Kassebaum, D. G., and Cutler, E. R. (1998). On the Culture of Student Abuse in Medical School. *Academic Medicine, 73*, 11, 1149–58.

Kinney, E. D. (1995). Malpractice Reform in the 1990s: Past Disappointments, Future Success? *Journal of Health Politics, Policy, and Law, 20*, 1, Spring, 99–135.

Kohn, L. T, Corrigan, J. M., Donaldson, M. S., and Institute of Medicine. (1999). *To Err Is Human: Building a Safer Health System.* Washington, DC: National Academy Press.

Morlock, L. L., Cassirer, C., and Malitz, F. E. (1997). *Impact of Risk Management on Liability Claims Experience.* Final report submitted to the Agency for Healthcare Policy and Research.

National Association of Insurance Commissioners. (1980). *Malpractice Claims: Medical Malpractice Closed Claims, 1975–78.* California: National Association of Insurance Commissioners.

Orlikoff, J. E., and Vanagunas, A. M. (1988). *Malpractice Prevention and Liability Control for Hospitals,* 2nd ed. Chicago: American Hospital Association.

Pronovost, P., Morlock, L. L., and Cassirer, C. (2001). Chapter 20: Creating and Maintaining Safe Systems of Medical Care: The Role of Risk Management. In Vincent, C. (ed.), *Clinical Risk Management: Enhancing Patient Safety,* 2nd ed. London: BMJ Books.

Reason, J. (1990). *Human Error.* Cambridge, UK: Cambridge University Press.

Sielnicki, A. P. (1983). Risk Management Philosophy and Techniques: An Overview. *Topics in Health Care Financing, 9*, 4, Summer.

Sielnicki, A. P. (1989). Evolution of Risk Financing Techniques. *Topics in Health Care Financing, 9*, 3, Spring.

U.S. General Accounting Office. (1989). *Health Care Initiatives in Hospital Risk Management.* GAO/T-HRD-93-24. Washington, DC: U.S. Government Printing Office.

Vincent, C. (ed.) (2001). *Clinical Risk Management: Enhancing Patient Safety.* London: BMJ Books.

INDEX